Herodotus
THE HISTORIES

NEW TRANSLATION
SELECTIONS
BACKGROUNDS
COMMENTARIES

Norton Critical Editions in the History of Ideas

A NORTON CRITICAL EDITION

Herodotus

THE HISTORIES

Translated by Walter Blanco
NEW TRANSLATION
SELECTIONS
BACKGROUNDS
COMMENTARIES

Edited by

WALTER BLANCO

CITY UNIVERSITY OF NEW YORK

and

JENNIFER TOLBERT ROBERTS

SOUTHERN METHODIST UNIVERSITY

W · W · NORTON & COMPANY · *New York* · *London*

Printed in the United States of America
First Edition

The text of this book is composed in Electra
with the display set in Bernhard Modern
Manufacturing by the Maple-Vail Book Group
Book design by Antonina Krass

Library of Congress Cataloging-in-Publication Data
Herodotus.
    [History. English]
    Herodotus : the histories : new translation, selections,
    backgrounds, commentaries / translated
    Walter Blanco ; edited by Walter Blanco and Jennifer Tolbert
    Roberts.
        p.   cm. — (A Norton critical edition)
    Includes bibliographical references and index.
        1. History, Ancient.   2. Greece—History.   I. Blanco, Walter.
    II. Roberts, Jennifer Tolbert, 1947–   III. Title.
    D58.H4713   1992
    930.1—dc20   91-23729
ISBN 0-393-95946-5 (paper)

W. W. Norton & Company, Inc., 500 Fifth Avenue, New York, N.Y. 10110
W. W. Norton & Company Ltd., 10 Coptic Street, London WC1A 1PU

1 2 3 4 5 6 7 8 9 0

For Gabby and Chris

Contents

Preface

The preparation of an edition of Herodotus has been a labor of love; but it has also been a labor, and the authors would like to thank those who have encouraged, advised, and sustained them in their work. Thanks to Charles Fornara and Lowell Edmunds for early encouragement of the translation, and to Deborah Boedeker for a thoughtful, thorough reading of the finished product. Allen Ward's and Larry Tritle's notes and comments were also a great help. Donald Lateiner was an unfailing source of advice and information throughout the project, and Walter Dubler has been a colleague, a mentor, and a friend. Steve Forman is the compleat editor, and has led us through this project with patience and skill. Friends who cheered along the way have been Billy Collins, Earl Fendelman, Michael Juliar, Robert Lejeune, Luis Losada, Michael Paull, Victor Reed and Gary Schwartz. Valuable student perspectives were offered by Daniel Patanella and Diane Perera, and Otto Sonntag was indispensable in the final review of the manuscript. Special thanks are due, finally, to Ingrid Blanco, who made Herodotus—bag and baggage—a welcome guest in her home for several years.

W.B.
J.T.R.
November 1990

Introduction

Many consider ancient Greece to mean ancient Athens, because of the rich legacy Athens left us in literature, philosophy, and history. A corollary view is that ancient Greece was a homogeneous society. It was not. It was a conglomerate of fractious city-states, each with its own political system and customs. Although Greece was united by a common language, it was a language whose dialects differed markedly from one region to another, and the student of ancient Greek must learn to distinguish the dialectal differences among Homer, Pindar, Aeschylus, and Herodotus.

Herodotus lived on the eastern fringe of this varied Greek world, in the Ionian town of Halicarnassus, on the southwest coast of Asia Minor, or modern Turkey. He lived therefore on the edges of the great Eastern empires of Persia and Egypt, as well as the borders of Greece. This was a cultural and linguistic crossroads, a situation that helps explain Herodotus' intense interest in the history of both Greece and Persia. He loved and admired Athens, but he was no Athenian. He recognized the importance of Athens to Ionia, but rejected Ionian snobbery about ancestral Athenian hegemony over his native region. Herodotus also admired Egypt, which he considered the source of many Greek customs and accomplishments that Greeks claimed as their own. At times he seems to cite Egyptian precedence as a way of reminding Greeks that they did not invent culture and that they were, relatively speaking, historical newcomers. Herodotus also admired the power of Eastern kings like Cyrus and Darius to achieve great public works, but he perfectly understood the dangers of their ambitious and overreaching power.

He was, as he tells us, Herodotus of Halicarnassus, justly proud of an Ionian heritage of rationalism, of exploration, and of a literary tradition whose first great exemplar was Homer himself. He was born circa 480 B.C., the year of the Battle of Salamis, and it was said that he was the nephew of Panyassis, an epic poet. Whether this is true or not, the epic influence is strong in Herodotus, who, like his fellow Greeks, considered Homer and the other epic poets his historians. His own history embodies the epic intention of preserving from extinction the memory of people's great deeds and monuments. He traveled extensively throughout the ancient world: to Greece, Babylon, Egypt, Italy, Sicily, and elsewhere. It is not known why he traveled so widely, although some speculate that he was a shipping merchant and that this explains his interest in the depth and navigability of rivers. If he did travel for commercial reasons, he improved on this purpose to conduct historical research. And he undertook some of his excursions primarily for research. He tells us in book 2 of his *Histories*, for example, that he traveled to the Phoenician city of Tyre specifically to see a temple sacred to Heracles. In this sense, Herodotus was a historian, and not just a traveler who took an interest in the odd tales he heard from interpreters, priests, tour guides, and the person in the street.

Herodotus believed in the importance of seeing things for oneself. Whenever possible, he visited temples, battlefields, monuments, and cities, and conducted research into their history. When he could not see things for himself, he questioned the best sources available to him, and reported conflicting information given from different points of view. Although critics since antiquity have ridiculed Herodotus as a mere reteller of tales and fables, he was intensely concerned with what we can know with certainty. In his *Histories* he confidently offers descriptions and conclusions when he can draw on his own experience. In the absence of direct experience, though, when Herodotus considers anything possible, he lists almost every story he has ever heard about the subject of his inquiry—from a land in which the sky is filled with feathers, to a country of pygmies, from cattle with two sets of genitals to societies ruled by women. Herodotus' tales are delightful, and we are often amused by the naïveté of a historian capable of including so many absurdities in his universal history. Yet to Herodotus, who constantly hedges these descriptions with caveats like "people say, but I don't believe it," or "as the story goes," or "as legend would have it," such stories are plausible because he does not know for sure, has not seen for himself, and therefore must rely on hearsay. What seems most fabulous, most unbelievable in the *Histories* is there precisely because Herodotus was a careful, exhaustive historian who lived at a time when facts were deeply embedded in a matrix of mythology. Readers of this book will become familiar with the question of whether Herodotus was the father of history or the father of lies. He was certainly not the latter, and though we may justly think of him as the father of history, he would probably have preferred to be known as the father of research.

Herodotus' history is the first continuous prose narrative extant in Western literature. If the narrative sometimes seems confused, haphazard, digressive, and excessively garrulous, we must remember that Herodotus was inventing the form—inventing history itself—and feeling his way as he went along. He knows that whatever you have to say in a history, there is always something else you have to say first. Before he can relate the history of Croesus, for example, he must first tell the stories of Candaules, Gyges, and Alyattes, with digressions about Periander and Arion along the way. But though much in Herodotus seems miscellaneous, there is a central story, and that is the story of the clash between the Eastern empire of Persia and the Western association, led by Sparta and Athens, of the mutually hostile city-states we now call Greece. In spite of all his digressions, Herodotus purposefully moves to a description of that clash, which he sees as a conflict between a despotic monarchy ruled by a magnificent autocrat whose aim is the enslavement of the whole world, and a jury-rigged confederation of states determined to remain free.

From start to finish, Herodotus' history embodies a moral: those who overreach or attempt to vie with the gods are doomed. The gods are jealous and strike us down at the height of our glory, and no one can be considered happy until after his death. The history is filled with warning voices: Croesus warning Cyrus, Demaratus and Artemisia warning Xerxes, Tomyris warning Darius—all repeating in one way or another the central message that excessive ambition is a sure road to destruction.

It has been said that all history, no matter how remote the subject, is really contemporary history. In writing about the past, one also writes about one's own, deeply felt present. After the surprising victory of the Greeks—led by Sparta and Athens—over the Persians, Athens became the preeminent state in the Greek world. Sparta had no interest in participating in a counterattack against Persia and allowed Athens to assume the leadership of a new maritime confederacy—the Delian League— composed largely of coastal states located near Persian territory. Athens then became the leader of "the free world" of the fifth century B.C. and over time met increasing criticism for abuse of that leadership. Athens was beginning to exhibit disturbing signs of the same, bullying expansionism that Herodotus had seen in the reigns of Croesus, Darius, and Xerxes, and it is possible that Herodotus wrote his history as a warning to Athens against the arrogance that had led to disaster for Persia.

Quite apart from the historical importance of the narrative or the moral of the tale, Herodotus' history still speaks to us through the wonderful variety and appeal of its stories, the charm of its literary style, its author's open-mindedness and incessantly intelligent curiosity. These qualities make Herodotus' text what the ancients thought great literary works should be: sources of instruction and delight.

Walter Blanco

Chronology of Events

ca. 1185 B.C.?	Trojan War?
776?	traditional date of first Olympic Games, basis of Greek dating system
753?	traditional date of founding of Rome, basis of Roman dating system
ca. 680	Candaules murders and overthrows Gyges, becomes first known tyrant, establishes dynasty of Mermnadae in Lydia
ca. 650	Cypselus becomes tyrant of Corinth
ca. 625	Cypselus is succeeded by Periander
ca. 610	Thrasybulus is tyrant at Miletus
	Greeks settle Naucratis, in Nile Delta
594 or 592	reforms of Solon at Athens
ca. 561	Pisistratus becomes tyrant at Athens
ca. 560	Croesus becomes king of Lydia
546	Cyrus defeats Croesus, annexes Lydia
ca. 528	death of Pisistratus
525	Cambyses annexes Egypt
ca. 522	death of Polycrates of Samos
	Darius becomes king of Persia
514	assassination of Hipparchus by Harmodius and Aristogeiton
ca. 512	Darius' expedition against Scythia
510	Cleomenes of Sparta aids Athenians in expelling last ruling Pisistratid (Hippias)
507	reforms of Cleisthenes
499	Ionian revolt begins
ca. 498	burning of Sardis
ca. 494	Ionians are defeated at Battle of Lade
	Persians capture Miletus
	Phrynichus is fined at Athens for presenting tragedy on fall of Miletus
492	Persian fleet is shipwrecked off Mount Athos
490	Darius invades Greece
	Eretria is destroyed
September 490	Athenian victory over Persians at Marathon

ca. 430–425?	death of Herodotus
424	exile of Thucydides
404	Athens surrenders to Sparta
399	execution of Socrates at Athens
338	Philip II of Macedon defeats coalition of Greek cities at Battle of Chaeronea
336	Philip II dies and is succeeded by Alexander
323	death of Alexander the Great
	end of classical era in Greece
	beginning of Hellenistic era
146	Rome destroys Corinth and consolidates hold on Greece
49	Caesar becomes dictator at Rome
44	assassination of Caesar
27	Caesar's adopted son takes the name Augustus as sole ruler and first emperor of Rome

A Note on the Persian Wars

In 499 B.C. the Greek cities on what is now the west coast of Turkey joined in rebellion against the Persian empire, to which they had been subjected during the reign of Cyrus, in the last half of the sixth century. Ethnically united, these Ionian Greeks, as they were called, also had racial ties with several of the mainland Greek states, including Athens. The Ionians sought help in their enterprise from a variety of Greek governments, but many refused. The king of Sparta, which at that time enjoyed by far the highest military reputation among the Greek states, was particularly reluctant to undertake a campaign so far from home. Although the cities of Athens and Eretria sent help, the rebellion failed, and in the course of the hostilities the splendid Persian city of Sardis caught fire.

His anger at the burning of Sardis was probably one factor in the decision of King Darius of Persia to make war on Greece. But beyond that he had heard a great deal about Greece over the years and had probably been interested for some time in adding it to his domains. In 492 Darius sent out an expedition under the command of Mardonius, but it was shipwrecked rounding the Cape of Mount Athos, in northern Greece. A second expedition, commanded by Artaphernes and Datis, was more careful. This time, in 490, the Persians took Eretria, partly by treachery from within, and then encamped on the coastal plain of Marathon, about twenty miles north of Athens. The Athenians sought the aid of the Spartans in vain, and in the end it was a largely Athenian contingent that defeated the huge Persian force against enormous odds.

Darius at once began planning a third invasion, more massive than the second. In 486 he died, but his efforts against Greece were carried forward by his son and successor, Xerxes. In the meantime the Athenians had been persuaded by their dynamic leader, Themistocles, to build up their navy. The Greeks, whose strategy was largely directed by Themistocles, mounted an amphibious defense against Xerxes' troops. In the summer of 480 they met the Persian navy off the coast at Artemisium, north of Athens, and sought to hold the Persian army off at the mountain pass of Thermopylae for as long as possible. Aware of an oracle that his homeland could be saved by his death, King Leonidas of Sparta died fighting heroically alongside a fierce corps of three hundred Spartans after a traitor had revealed a hidden pass to the Persians. With their deaths, Leonidas and his fellow Spartans had bought Greece some time.

While the Persians descended on Athens and sacked it, the Greek navy gathered off the west coast of Attica (the territory of the Athenians). Badly demoralized, the Greek sailors contemplated scattering to their homes. But Themistocles resorted to a ruse to force a battle: a secret message sent to Xerxes persuaded the Persian king to attack. Themistocles' stratagem paid off. The battle that was fought off the island of Salamis in 480 B.C. turned the tide of the war in favor of the Greeks. The Athenian role in the victory led to a distinct shift in the balance of power within Greece, with Athens coming to rival Sparta as the leader of the Greek states. This rivalry in time led to the long Peloponnesian War (431–404), which had devastating consequences for the civilization of classical Greece.

After the Battle of Salamis, Xerxes returned to Persia, leaving Mardonius in command of the forces in Greece. Mardonius was defeated at the Battle of Plataea, near Athens, in 479, and around the same time— some say on the same day—the Greeks defeated the Persian navy off the Turkish coast at the Battle of Mycale. The Persians did not return to attack the Greeks after this, but the fear that they might do so played an important part in Greek politics throughout the first half of the fifth century.

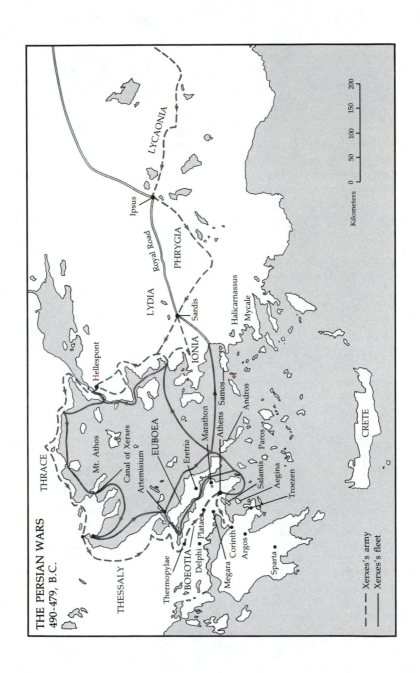

THE PERSIAN WARS
490–479, B.C.

THRACE

THESSALY

Mt. Athos

Canal of Xerxes

Artemisium

EUBOEA

Thermopylae

Delphi • Plataea

BOEOTIA

Eretria

Marathon

Megara

Corinth

Athens

Argos •

Sparta •

Salamis

Aegina

Troezen

Paros

Andros

Samos

CRETE

Hellespont

LYDIA

Royal Road

PHRYGIA

LYCAONIA

Ipsus

Sardis

IONIA

Halicarnassus

Mycale

Kilometers   0   50   100   150   200

- - - - Xerxes's army
——— Xerxes's fleet

THE HISTORIES

Book 1

Book 1 is an excellent introduction to Herodotus' methods and interests. His curiosity about the causes of the war between the Greeks and the Persians leads Herodotus to delve deeply into the history of the many peoples of the ancient world, as well as to focus on episodes in which irreconcilable interests led to conflict and violence. Women play a prominent part in the narrative both as resourceful, determined rulers and as objects of male dominance and concern. The wife of Candaules, who instigates her husband's murder, and Tomyris, the fierce queen of the Massagetae, are examples of the former; the latter is reflected in the story of the chain of woman snatchings that leads ultimately to the conflict between Greece and Persia. Herodotus' discussion of the Babylonians also reveals considerable interest in marriage customs and women's lives.

Herodotus was intrigued by the wide variety of cultural norms he encountered in his researches. Well aware that the average Greek reacted to alien ways with amusement, horror, or contempt, he plainly intended his work to undermine Hellenic ethnocentricity—to open the Greek mind to the rich diversity of the surrounding world and to make his fellow Hellenes aware that theirs was not the only way of viewing the world.

The long story of Croesus, king of Lydia, illustrates many of Herodotus' central concerns. Solon's stories of "happy" Greeks who endured no signal misfortunes while they lived and who died respected by their fellow citizens reflect the common Greek view about the importance of civic life. His caution not to pronounce people lucky until their lives have run their full course is also firmly grounded in Greek thinking.

Much can be learned about Herodotus' view of history from his account of Croesus' career. A fortunate man with well-being before him, Croesus nonetheless invites disaster by his refusal to think deeply and carefully. He sees what he wants to see in oracles, and he fails to consider the limits of materialism and the precariousness of human happiness. His encounter with Solon (not, alas, chronologically probable) suggests to readers the value of Greek wisdom generally and Athenian wisdom in particular. Though the gods are omnipresent, Herodotus throughout stresses the centrality of human psychology in determining the outcome of events. In his worldview, it is the choices people make—such as Gyges' choice to kill his master, Candaules—that determine the outcome of history.

This is the publication of the research of Herodotus of Halicarnassus,[1] so that the actions of people shall not fade with time, so that the great

---

1. A Greek city in southwestern Asia Minor.

and admirable monuments produced by both Greeks and barbarians shall not go unrenowned, and, among other things, to set forth the reasons why they waged war on each other.

Persian storytellers say that the Phoenicians[2] were the cause of the dispute, for they came from the so-called Red Sea[3] to our sea, inhabited the territory they now live in, and immediately set forth on long voyages. They shipped Egyptian and Assyrian merchandise to various places and they made a point of going to Argos. At that time, Argos was preeminent among the towns in the country which is now called Greece. Now, when the Phoenicians came to Argos, they laid out their cargo. On the fifth or sixth day after they arrived, when almost everything had been sold off, a large number of women—including the king's daughter— came down to the seashore. Her name (and the Greeks also agree in this) was Io, the daughter of Inachus. While the women stood at the stern of the boat, buying the goods that appealed to them, the Phoenicians urged each other on and rushed them. Most of the women ran away, but Io was captured, along with some others. The Phoenicians put them in the boat and sailed away, bound for Egypt.

Although the Greeks do not agree, that is how the Persians say Io came to Egypt; and this act was the beginning of the violations of law. After this, they say that some Greeks, whose names I am unable to give you, though they would probably have been from Crete, put into port at Phoenician Tyre and abducted Europa, the daughter of the king. This, though, was just a case of an eye for an eye, so the next crime, which the Greeks committed, was really the second in the series.

The Greeks sailed in a long warship to Colchian Aea,[4] on the river Phasis. After taking care of the business they had come about, they abducted Medea, the daughter of the king. The Colchian king sent a messenger to Greece asking for his daughter back and demanding damages for the kidnapping. The Greeks answered that since the Phoenicians had not given damages for the kidnapping of Io, the girl from Argos, they would not give anything, either.

They say that two generations after this event, Alexander, the son of Priam, heard about it and hankered to abduct a Greek woman for himself, fully persuaded that he would not have to pay any penalty. After all, no one else had. After he kidnapped Helen, it seemed to the Greeks that the first thing to do was to send messengers asking for Helen back and demanding damages for the kidnapping. In the face of these demands, the Trojans brought up the kidnapping of Medea: the Greeks had given neither damages nor the girl when they had been asked, and now they wanted damages to be given to them by others!

---

2. A Mediterranean sea-trading people primarily associated with the cities of Sidon and Tyre.
3. Herodotus means primarily the Indian Ocean and the Persian Gulf.

4. Colchis is the region south of the Caucasus Mountains at the extreme east of the Black Sea. The river Phasis is the modern Rion.

So far, say the Persians, they had merely been stealing women from each other, but after this the Greeks were most greatly to blame because they began to lead armies into Asia before the Asians began to lead them into Europe. The Persians believe that raping women is the work of evil men, but that making a great to-do about vengeance after women have been raped is the work of fools. Prudent men are not concerned about women who have been raped, since it is perfectly plain that they could not be raped if they didn't really want to be. The Persians say that they paid no attention to the abduction of their women from Asia, while the Greeks, for the sake of a Lacedaemonian[5] woman, assembled a huge army and then invaded Asia and destroyed the power of Priam. Because of this, the Persians have always considered the Greeks to be their enemies. You see, the Persians regard Asia and the barbarian people who live in it as their domain, while they think of Europe and the Greeks as separate.

That is how the Persians say it happened, and they trace the beginning of their hatred of the Greeks to the conquest of Troy. The Phoenicians, however, do not agree with the Persians about Io. They say that they did not have to resort to kidnapping to take her to Egypt, but that she had been having sex in Argos with the captain of the ship. When she found out that she was pregnant, she was so ashamed for the sake of her parents that she willingly sailed away with the Phoenicians to avoid discovery. That is what the Persians and the Phoenicians say.

I am not going to say that these events happened one way or the other. Rather, I will point out the man who I know for a fact began the wrongdoing against the Greeks, and then proceed with my story while giving detailed accounts of cities both great and small. Many that were great in the past have become small, and many that used to be small have become great in my lifetime, so I will mention both alike because I know very well that human prosperity never remains in the same place.

Croesus was a Lydian[6] by birth, the son of Alyattes, and the ruler of the people who live on this side of the Halys River,[7] which flows from the south between Syria and Paphlagonia[8] toward the north wind and into what is known as the Euxine Sea.[9] This Croesus was the first barbarian we know of to have subjected some Greeks to the payment of tribute and to have made friends with others. He conquered the Ionians, Aeolians, and Dorians in Asia, and befriended the Lacedaemonians. Before the reign of Croesus, all Greeks were free. (The Cimmerian[1] army which invaded Ionia before Croesus did not bring about the subjugation of the cities—it just engaged in hit-and-run raids.)

---

5. Helen's husband, Menelaus, was king of Sparta, or Lacedaemon.
6. Lydia was located in the center of western Asia Minor.
7. The present-day Kizil Irmak, which in Croesus' time separated the kingdom of Lydia from the Persian empire.

8. A territory in northern Asia Minor.
9. The Black Sea.
1. The Cimmerians were a people driven from what is now southern Russia by the Scythians, a fierce nomadic people who gave their name to the region.

The Lydian kingship, which was originally Heraclid,[2] devolved to the family of Croesus—known as the Mermnadae—in the following way. Candaules, whom the Greeks call Myrsilus, was the ruler of Sardis[3] and the descendant of Alcaeus, the son of Heracles. Agron the son of Ninus, the son of Belus, the son of Alcaeus, was the first Heraclid king of Sardis, and Candaules was the last. The men who ruled over this land before Agron were descendants of Lydus, the son of Atys, after whom this whole people are called Lydian. Formerly, they had been called Maeonians. The Lydians entrusted power to the Heraclids, who then held on to it because of an oracle. The Heraclids were descended from Heracles and a slave girl belonging to Iardanus, and they ruled for twenty-two generations, or five hundred and five years, passing the kingdom from father to son down to Candaules, the son of Myrsus.

Now, this Candaules actually fell in love with his own wife, and, being in love, he thought that she was the most beautiful of all women. Candaules had a favorite bodyguard, Gyges the son of Dascylus, whom he talked to about his most important affairs, and—since Candaules had this opinion of his wife—he kept carrying on to Gyges about his wife's good looks. Before much time went by (because Candaules was doomed to get into trouble), he said this to Gyges: "Gyges, since I don't think you believe me when I tell you about my wife's looks (after all, we trust our ears less than our eyes), I want you to work it so that you can look at her naked."

Gyges cried out and said, "Master, this is sick! Commanding me to look at my queen when she is naked! A woman takes off her modesty along with her underwear. They thought up some good advice for people long ago, and we ought to learn from it. Here's one piece of advice: let every man look to his own. I truly believe that your wife is the most beautiful woman in the world, and I beg you not to ask me to do something that is wrong."

So saying, he shied away from the proposal, fearing that something bad would come of it. But Candaules answered, "Don't worry, Gyges, and don't be afraid that I'm only saying this to test you or that some harm will come to you from my wife. In the first place, I'll fix things so that she won't even know that she is being seen by you. I'll stand you behind the open door of our bedroom. My wife will come in to bed after I enter. There is a chair near the entrance to the room. She lays her clothes on it one at a time as she takes them off, and you'll be able to look at her with ease. You'll be behind her back when she walks from the chair to the bed. Just make sure she doesn't see you as you go out the door."

Since he could not get out of it, then, Gyges got ready. When it was time for bed, Candaules led Gyges to the bedroom, and his wife came

2. Heraclid, because the founder of the family was Heracles, or Hercules.

3. Sardis, sometimes spelled Sardes, was the capital of Lydia.

in shortly afterward. Gyges watched her come in and take off her clothes. When she turned her back to go to bed, he slipped out from behind the door and left. But the woman saw him leave. She realized what her husband had done and neither cried out for shame nor let on that she knew—she intended to make Candaules pay for what he had done. You see, for the Lydians, as for practically all the other barbarians, it is a great shame for even a man to be seen naked.

So she held her peace and did not let on, and as soon as it was day she readied the servants she knew to be most faithful to her and called for Gyges. He came at her summons, having no idea that she knew what had happened. He had long been accustomed to come to the queen whenever she called. When Gyges arrived, the woman said, "I'm going to let you choose now, Gyges, between two paths. Go down whichever one you want. You can either kill Candaules and have me and the kingdom of Lydia, or you must yourself immediately die so that you will not in the future obey Candaules in everything and see what you ought not to see. In any case, either he who planned this must perish, or you, who saw my nakedness and violated our customs."

For a while, Gyges was astonished by what she had said, but then he begged her not to force him to make such a choice. He simply could not persuade her, though, and saw that he would really either have to kill his master or himself be killed by others. He chose to live. He asked, "Come then, since you force me to kill my master against my will, let me hear how we are going to attack him."

She answered, "The attack will come from the same place from which he showed off my nakedness. We will kill him in his sleep."

After they had made their plan and night fell, Gyges followed the woman into the bedroom, for he was not let off and there was no way out for him whatever—either he or Candaules must die. She gave him a dagger and hid him behind the very same door. Later, while Candaules was taking his rest, Gyges slipped out, killed him, and took over his wife and his kingdom. (Archilochus the Parian, who was a contemporary, mentions Gyges in some iambic trimeters.)

Gyges took over the kingdom, then, and consolidated his power through favorable oracles from Delphi. The Lydians, you see, were outraged over the death of Candaules and had taken up arms, but the supporters of Gyges made an agreement with them. If the oracle declared Gyges to be the king of Lydia, he would reign; if not, he would return the sovereignty to the Heraclids. The oracle answered in his favor, and Gyges became king. The Pythian priestess said, however, that the lineage of Gyges would extend only so far as the fifth generation, when vengeance would come for the Heraclids. The Lydians and their kings paid no attention to this prophecy, until, of course, it came to pass.

In this way, by robbing the Heraclids, the Mermnadae took power. During his reign, Gyges sent not a few votive offerings to Delphi. Indeed, of his silver offerings, most are in Delphi. Besides these, he offered a great deal of gold, of which the most deserving of mention are the six golden bowls he dedicated. These now stand in the Corinthian treasury and weigh about eighteen hundred pounds. Strictly speaking, though, the treasure does not belong to the people of Corinth, but to Cypselus, the son of Eetion. After Midas, the son of Gordias, and king of Phrygia, this Gyges was the first barbarian we know of to dedicate offerings to Delphi. Midas dedicated the royal throne from which he pronounced judgments while sitting in state, and it is well worth seeing. This throne is in the same place as Gyges' bowls. The Delphians nicknamed the gold and silver which Gyges dedicated "gygantic," after its donor.

After he became ruler, Gyges invaded Miletus and Smyrna and took the city of Colophon.[4] But since he didn't perform any other great deed during his reign of thirty-eight years, I will let it go at what has already been mentioned.

I will now speak of Ardys, who was Gyges' son and who ruled after him. He captured Priene and invaded Miletus.[5] During his reign in Sardis, though, the Cimmerians were driven out of their country by the Scythian nomads. They migrated to Asia and captured Sardis—except for the acropolis.

Ardys ruled for forty-nine years and was succeeded by his son, Sadyattes, who ruled for twelve years. Sadyattes, in turn, was succeeded by Alyattes, who made war on the Medes under Cyaxares, the descendant of Deioces. He also drove the Cimmerians out of Asia, took Smyrna, the colony of Colophon, and invaded Clazomenae,[6] which he didn't get out of as easily as he had expected, and suffered a great defeat instead.

These are the other great and noteworthy deeds Alyattes performed during his reign: he made war on the Milesians, a war he had inherited from his father. This is how he invaded and besieged Miletus: he brought his army as soon as the crop was ripe in the fields. They marched to shepherd's pipes and lutes, fifes and flutes. When he came to Miletus, he did not demolish or burn or even tear out the doors of any of the houses in the fields, but let them stand throughout the countryside. When he had completely destroyed the trees and crops in the fields, though, he would go back home. The Milesians controlled the sea, so there was no point in having the army set up a regular siege. The reason why the Lydian did not destroy the houses was so that the Milesians would be able to live in them while they went out to sow and work the fields, and so that he, after all their labor, would have something to destroy during his invasions.

He made war in this way for eleven years, during which the Milesians suffered two major defeats, one fighting on their own soil at Limeneium, and the other on the plain of the Maeander River. Actually, Sadyattes,

---

4. Miletus, Smyrna, and Colophon were all cities in Ionia, in western Asia Minor.
5. Like Miletus, Priene was an important city at

the mouth of the Maeander River, in Ionia.
6. A city in Ionia.

the son of Ardys, ruled Lydia for six of these eleven years, and it was he who led the invasions during that time. He was the one who started the war. His son, Alyattes, carried on the war for the next five years. As I said earlier, he inherited it from his father, and he gave it his fullest attention. Of the Ionians, only the Chians helped the Milesians to bear the burden on the war. The Chians helped in return for similar assistance the Milesians had given them earlier in carrying on their war with the Erythrians.

In the twelfth year, something happened, quite by accident, while the standing crops were being set afire by the army. As soon as the wheat caught fire, the flame, driven by the wind, set fire to the temple of Athena—Athena Assesia, by name—which burned completely to the ground. Nobody paid any attention to this at the time, but after the army returned to Sardis, Alyattes fell sick. Because the illness was protracted, he dispatched messengers to consult the oracle at Delphi—either acting on someone's advice or because he himself thought that he should send to the god to ask about the illness. When his envoys arrived in Delphi, though, the Pythian priestess told them that she would not give an oracle until they rebuilt the temple of Athena they had burned down at Assesus, in Miletus.

I know this is how it happened because I heard it form the Delphians myself. The Milesians add this to the story, though: Periander, the son of Cypselus, was a very close ally of Thrasybulus, who was then the king of Miletus. Periander found out about the answer which had been given to Alyattes and sent a messenger to tell Thrasybulus all about it so that, being forewarned, Thrasybulus could make plans to deal with the situation.

This is what the Milesians say happened next: when the Delphic message was given to Alyattes, he instantly sent an ambassador to Miletus with the intention of making a truce with Thrasybulus and the Milesians for as long as it would take to rebuild the temple. While the envoy was on his way to Miletus, Thrasybulus, who had reliable advance intelligence and who knew everything Alyattes intended to do, worked out the following scheme: he took all the food in the city—both state-owned and private—and collected it in the marketplace. Then he ordered the Milesians to start drinking and celebrating when he gave the signal.

Thrasybulus made these arrangements and gave this order so that when the envoy from Sardis saw the great heap of food piled up and the people having a good time, he would report it back to Alyattes. And that's just what happened, because the envoy returned to Sardis after he had seen these things and given the Lydian's message to Thrasybulus, and as far as I can tell there was no other reason for the peace. You see, Alyattes had expected that there would be a severe famine in Miletus and that the people would be worn down to utter misery, and then he heard a report from the envoy returning from Miletus which was just the opposite of what he had so firmly believed! After that, there was a peace whose terms were that they would be friends and allies with each other. Alyattes built two temples to Athena in Assesus instead of one, and he recovered from his illness.

That is the way it was as far as Alyattes' war on Thrasybulus and the Milesians is concerned.

Periander was the son of Cypselus, and it was he who disclosed the oracle to Thrasybulus. Periander ruled over Corinth.[7] Now, the Corinthians say (and the Lesbians agree with them) that an extraordinary event took place during his lifetime: Arion of Methymna—the greatest lyre player and singer of his time, and the first person we know of to write, title, and produce a dithyramb[8] in Corinth—was carried to Taenarum[9] on the back of a dolphin.

They say that this Arion had spent a lot of time at Periander's court and then had a desire to sail to Italy and Sicily. After earning a great deal of money there, though, he wanted to return to Cornith. He set sail from Tarentum,[1] but since he didn't trust anybody more than the Corinthians, he hired a Corinthian ship and crew. When they were at sea, though, the crew plotted to throw Arion overboard and keep his money. He pleaded with them when he realized this, offering to give them his money and begging them to spare his life. He just couldn't persuade them, though, and the crew ordered him either to kill himself, so that he could be buried on land, or to jump into the sea immediately. Seeing that their minds were made up, Arion begged them in this desperate situation to let him stand and sing on the quarterdeck in his full costume. He promised to do away with himself after he had finished singing. Since it occurred to them that they would enjoy hearing the best singer alive, they moved back amidships from the stern. Arion dressed up in his full costume, took his lyre, stood on the quarterdeck and gave a complete rendition of "The Falsetto Song." When he finished the song, he threw himself into the sea just as he was, costume and all. They say that the crew sailed on for Corinth, but that a dolphin got under Arion and carried him to Taenarum. He got off the dolphin there, made his way in his costume to Corinth, and told the whole story when he arrived.

In disbelief, Periander put Arion under guard and did not let him go anywhere. Meanwhile, he watched closely for the seamen. As soon as they arrived, they were summoned and asked if they had any news about Arion. After they said that he was safe in Italy and that they had left him doing quite well in Tarentum, Arion appeared just as he had been when he jumped off the ship. They were so stunned that they could no longer, under cross-examination, deny what they had done. That is what the

---

7. A major Greek city on the Isthmus of Corinth, at the entrance to the Peloponnese.
8. A wild choral hymn, originally in honor of Dionysus.

9. The modern Cape Matapan, in the southernmost Peloponnese.
1. A town in the instep of the boot of Italy.

Corinthians and the Lesbians say, and indeed there is in Taenarum a small bronze offering from Arion of a man mounted on a dolphin.

Alyattes the Lydian died after the war against the Milesians, having reigned for fifty-seven years. After Alyattes recovered from his illness, he became the second of his line to make offerings at Delphi—a huge silver bowl and a welded iron stand, which is worth seeing above all the offerings in Delphi. It is the work of Glaucus the Chian, who alone, out of all mankind, invented the welding of iron.

When Alyattes died, his son Croesus inherited the kingdom at the age of thirty-five, and the first Greeks that he attacked were the Ephesians. When the Ephesians were being besieged by him, they dedicated their city to Artemis by tying a rope from the temple to the wall of the city. It is nearly a mile from the old city, which was then under siege, to the temple. Croesus attacked the Ephesians first and later each of the cities of Ionia and Aeolia in turn. He made different accusations against each city. He made greater accusations against those he found to have given greater cause, but he accused others even on petty grounds.

Now, when all the Greeks in Asia had been subjected to the payment of tribute, he took it into his head to build ships and attack the islanders. Some say that Bias of Priene came to Sardis when everything was ready for shipbuilding—although others say that it was Pittacus of Mytilene—and that when Croesus asked him whether he had any news about Greece, he put an end to the shipbuilding by saying this: "The islanders are joining together to buy ten thousand horses, Your Majesty, with the intention of making war on you in Sardis."

Croesus, thinking that he was telling the truth, said, "If only the gods would put it into the heads of the islanders to come against the sons of Lydia with horses!"

The other answered, "It's obvious to me, Your Majesty, that you pray for the chance to catch the islanders on horseback on the mainland, and you are right. And the islanders, ever since they found out that you intend to build ships against them, what do you think they are praying for but the chance to catch Lydians at sea so that they can get even with you for the mainland Greeks whom you have enslaved?"

Croesus was very pleased with this shrewdly argued object lesson, and he was in this way persuaded to stop building ships and to make an alliance with the Ionians who lived on the islands.

In the course of time, almost everybody living on this side of the Halys River was conquered. Except for the Cilicians and the Lycians, Croesus had subjected everyone else to himself—namely, the Lydians, the Phrygians, the Mysians, the Mariandynians, the Chalybes, the Paphlagonians, the Thynian and Bithynian Thracians, the Carians, the Ionians, the Dorians, the Aeolians, and the Pamphylians.

After Croesus added these conquered people to the Lydian empire, all the sages living in Greece at that time began to visit Sardis at the height of its wealth. Each came for his own reasons, especially Solon the Athenian, who had written laws for the Athenians at their command, and had then gone abroad for ten years. He sailed away on the pretext of seeing the world, but it was really so that he could not be compelled to repeal any of the laws he had laid down. That was something the Athenians were not able to do on their own, because they were bound by solemn oaths to obey for ten years whatever laws Solon had made for them.

So for these reasons—as well as to see the world—Solon left home to visit Amasis in Egypt and especially Croesus in Sardis. When he arrived, he was feasted in the palace by Croesus. Three or four days later, at Croesus' command, servants took Solon on a tour of the treasury and showed him how great and prosperous everything was. In due time, after Solon had observed and considered everything, Croesus asked, "Many stories have come to us, my Athenian guest, about your wisdom and your travels—how you have roamed around and seen so much of the world in your quest for knowledge. Well, this urge has come over me to ask you whether you have so far seen anybody you consider to be more fortunate than all other men."

He asked this expecting that the most fortunate of men would turn out to be himself. Solon did not use any delicate flattery, but told him the straight truth: "Tellus the Athenian, O King."

Croesus was amazed at what he said, and asked severely, "What makes you think that Tellus was so fortunate!"

Solon said, "In the first place, Tellus came from a thriving city and had honest, handsome sons. Also, he saw them all have children, all of whom survived. In the second place, he had a prosperous life, by our standards, and the end of that life was glorious. He came to the rescue during a battle between the Athenians and their neighbors in Eleusis[2] and died nobly after breaking the enemy's ranks. The Athenians honored him highly and buried him at the public expense right where he fell."

Solon had piqued Croesus with all that he had said about Tellus' good fortune, but Croesus, fully believing that he would at least come in second, asked who the next most fortunate might be.

Instead, Solon said, "Cleobis and Biton. They were Argives who made a good living and in addition to that had great physical strength. They were both prizewinning athletes, and this is the story most often told about them. The Argives were celebrating the feast of Hera, and it was absolutely necessary for their mother to be brought to the temple in her oxcart. But the oxen did not arrive from the field in time. Seeing that they were running out of time, the young men slipped in under the yoke themselves and dragged the wagon along with their mother riding in it.

---

2. A major city of Attica, bordering on Athens.

They arrived at the temple after covering over five and a half miles. Their action was seen by the entire congregation, and it was followed by the finest end a life can have. In it, god showed plainly through Cleobis and Biton that it is better for a man to die than to live.

"The Argive men gathered around congratulating the young men on their strength, while the women congratulated their mother. What sons she had! The mother was overjoyed both with the deed and with the praise. She stood before the statue of Hera and prayed that the goddess would give to her sons, Cleobis and Biton, who had honored her so highly, the very best thing that it was possible for a human being to have. After this prayer, while everyone was sacrificing and feasting, the young men lay down to sleep in that very same temple and never rose up again, transfixed in death. The Argives made the kind of statues of them that are made only for the very greatest men and dedicated them in Delphi."

Solon, then, gave the second prize for happiness to these two, and Croesus angrily said, "So then, my Athenian guest, as far as you are concerned, our prosperity amounts to nothing, and you do not even consider us on a par with private citizens!"

Solon said, "When you ask me about human affairs, you ask someone who knows how jealous and provocative god is. In the fullness of time, a man must see many things he doesn't want to see, and endure many things he doesn't want to endure. I'll set the limit of a person's life at seventy years. In those seventy years there are twenty-five thousand two hundred days, not counting any months thrown in. But if you make every other year longer by a month so that the seasons come around to the right place, then besides the seventy years there are thirty-five months, or one thousand and fifty days. All in all, then, these seventy years add up to twenty-six thousand two hundred and fifty days, and from one day to the next absolutely nothing happens the same way twice. Thus, my dear Croesus, humans are the creatures of pure chance.

"Now, you seem to me to be very rich and to be the monarch of many people, but I couldn't say anything about this question you keep asking me until I find out that you have ended your life well, because the rich man isn't any better off than the man who has enough for his everyday needs unless his luck stays with him and he keeps on having the best of everything until he dies happily. Many people who are super rich are unlucky, you know, while many lucky people are just moderately well-off. Now, the very rich but unlucky man has only two advantages over the lucky man, while the lucky man has many advantages over the unlucky rich man. First, the rich man is better able to gratify his desires, and second, he is able to afford the trouble they bring. The lucky man, on the other hand, is better off than the unlucky rich man in these ways: while he is not as able to afford desire and trouble, his good luck keeps these things away from him. He suffers no bodily harm, he doesn't get sick, he experiences no misfortunes, he has good children, and he is handsome. If, in addition to all this, he dies happily, then he is the one

you are looking for—the man who deserves to be called happy. Until he
dies, though, you must hold off and not call him happy—just lucky.

"Of course, it is impossible for a mere mortal to combine all these
things, just as no country is completely sufficient unto itself. It will have
this, but it will lack that. The one that has the most—that one is the
best. Thus, no one person is self-sufficient: he will have one thing, but
he will be lacking in another. To me, whoever has the most of these
things, and keeps on having them, and then happily ends his life, he is
the one, Your Highness, who rightly carries the title you seek. You have
to see how everything turns out, for god gives a glimpse of happiness to
many people, and then tears them up by the very roots."

Solon did not at all please Croesus with what he said, and Croesus
dismissed him without ceremony, thinking that someone who set aside
the present good and urged you to look at how things turned out was a
complete ignoramus.

After Solon left, though, Croesus got his great comeuppance from
god, I suppose because he thought that he was the happiest man in the
world. As soon as he fell asleep that night, a dream came to him which
showed him the truth about the disaster that would happen to his son.
Croesus had two sons. One was a cripple—a deaf mute—and the other
was by far the most outstanding young man of his generation. His name
was Atys. Now, the dream showed Croesus that he would lose Atys through
a wound from an iron spearhead. When he woke up, he gave this dreadful dream a great deal of thought. First, he chose a wife for his son.
Also, Atys had been accustomed to command Lydian military forces,
but Croesus no longer sent him anywhere on business of that kind. He
took spears and javelins and all such weapons of war out of the men's
living quarters and heaped them up in the women's bedrooms, lest one
of them fall from a wall onto his son.

While Croesus was busy with the arrangements for his son's wedding,
a man in the grip of a great misfortune came to Sardis, a man with blood
on his hands. He was of Phrygian descent and belonged to the royal
family. He came to Croesus' home and begged to be cleansed of his
guilt according to the customs of the country; and Croesus purged his
guilt away. The Lydian rite of purification is very similar to the Greek.
After Croesus performed the customary ritual, he asked him who he was
and where he came from, saying, "Who are you, stranger, and what
part of Phrygia have you come from to be a suppliant at my hearth?
What man or woman did you kill?"

He answered, "I am the son of Gordias, the son of Midas, Your Highness, and my name is Adrastus. I accidentally killed my own brother,
and I am here because I was driven away and completely disinherited by
my father."

Croesus replied: "You are descended from friends, and you have come
among friends. Remain with us, where you shall want for nothing. You
will gain all the more if you bear this misfortune as lightly as possible."

And so Adrastus lived with Croesus.

At the same time, a monster of a boar appeared on Mount Olympus, in Mysias. He kept coming down from the mountain and destroying the fields and crops of the Mysians. The Mysians often went after him, but they could never do him any harm—he harmed them instead. Finally, some Mysian messengers went to Croesus and said, "A monster boar has appeared on our land, Your Majesty, and destroys our crops. We have tried our hardest to catch him, but we can't. We beg you to send your son with some dogs and some handpicked young men back with us so that we can drive this animal from our land."

That is what they asked for, but Croesus remembered the message of the dream and said this to them: "Forget about my son—I couldn't send him with you. He is newly married, and that's what's on his mind now. I will, though, send the picked men and my whole pack of hunting dogs, and I'll order everyone who goes with you to do his utmost to rid your land of this beast."

That was his answer, and the Mysians were satisfied with it, but Croesus' son went up to him after hearing their request. Because Croesus was refusing to send him with them, the young man said, "The finest and noblest thing I once had was my reputation for hunting and fighting. But now you keep me away from both of them, though you don't see any cowardice or lack of enthusiasm in me. What kind of face am I supposed to wear when I go in and out of the marketplace? How do you suppose I look to my fellow citizens—to my bride! What kind of man will she think she's living with? Now, you must either let me go out after this animal or give me a good reason why what you have done is better for me."

Croesus said, "Son, I'm not doing this because I see any cowardice or other fault in you. A dream vision hovered over me in my sleep and said that you would have a short life because you would be killed by an iron spearpoint. It was because of this vision that I hurried up your marriage and will not send you out on this mission. I'm protecting you so that maybe I can steal you away from death while I live. You are my only son—I don't count that cripple as mine."

The young man answered, "I excuse you for protecting me after seeing such a vision. But you didn't understand it—the dream's meaning escaped you, and it's right that I should explain it to you. Now, you say that the dream told you that I would die because of an iron spearpoint. But what kind of hands does a boar have, and what kind of iron spearpoint are you so afraid of? If the dream had said that I would be killed by a tusk or by something else that belongs to this animal, then you would have to do what you are doing. But it was by a spear! So since this is not a battle against men, let me go."

Croesus answered, "Somehow, son, you've gotten the best of me with your interpretation of this dream, and since I've lost, I'll change my mind and let you go on the hunt."

After saying this, though, Croesus sent for Adrastus the Phrygian, and when he arrived, Croesus told him, "Adrastus, when you were struck down by your terrible misfortune—for which I do not blame you—I purged your guilt, welcomed you into my home, and took care of all your expenses. Now you owe me a favor in return for the favor I did for you. I want you to be my son's bodyguard while he goes out on this hunt in case any highwaymen show up and try to do you any harm on the road. Besides, you ought to go where you, too, can shine by your deeds. That is your birthright, and, anyway, you have the strength for it."

Adrastus answered, "Ordinarily I would not go on this mission. It's not fitting for me, after my terrible experience, to go among successful men my own age. I don't want to—and there are many reasons why I'd keep myself away from it. But now, since you insist, and since I must please you (for I do have an obligation to return your favors), I am ready to do this, and you can expect that your son, whom you order me to guard, will return none the worse for my protection."

After he gave Croesus this answer, the party set out, provided with picked men and dogs. When they arrived at Mount Olympus, they started hunting for the beast, and when they found it, they stood around it in a circle and hurled their spears at it. At that moment the stranger, the one who had been purged of his homicide, the man called Adrastus, hurled his spear at the boar but missed it and hit the son of Croesus instead. Atys, struck with the point of the spear, fulfilled the prophecy of the dream.

Someone started running to Croesus to report the news. When he arrived in Sardis, this messenger told Croesus about the fight with the animal and the fate of his son. Croesus was utterly bewildered by his son's death and was especially outraged that the man who had killed him was the man he had purged of a homicide. He became so furious over the calamity that he bitterly invoked Zeus as "the Purifier," and called on him to witness what he had suffered from the stranger. Croesus also invoked the very same god under the epithets of "the God of Hospitality," and "the God of Friendship"—the God of Hospitality because he had unknowingly welcomed the stranger who was to be the killer of his son into his home and fed him, and the God of Friendship because he had sent that man as a protector and found him to be an enemy.

Later, the Lydians appeared bearing the corpse, with the killer following behind it. Then Adrastus stood in front of the body and with outstretched hands tried to surrender himself to Croesus, demanding to have his throat cut over the corpse. He talked about his first misfortune, and how on top of that he had destroyed the man who had cleansed him, and how he was not fit to live. Even though he was in his own private grief, Croesus pitied Adrastus when he heard these words and said, "I have all the justice I want from you, stranger, since you have pronounced a sentence of death on yourself. Besides, you are not the cause of my troubles; you just unwillingly brought them about. It was some god, who long ago foretold what the future would be."

Croesus gave his son a fitting burial. Then, after people had left, when all was quiet around the tomb, Adrastus, the son of Gordias, the son of Midas, he who was the killer of his own brother and, in a way, the killer of the man who had purged his guilt, believing himself to be the unluckiest man he had ever known, cut his own throat over the grave.

For two years, Croesus sat idle, in deep mourning over the loss of his son. Then, when the empire of Astyages, the son of Cyaxares, was destroyed by Cyrus, the son of Cambyses, the growing strength of the Persians put an end to Croesus' grief, and he began to ponder whether he could seize that growing Persian power before it became too great. As soon as he had formed this intention, he tested the oracles in Greece and the one in Libya. He sent messengers off in different directions— some to Delphi, some to Abae, in Phocis, some to Dodona. Some were sent to Amphiaraus and to Trophonius, and some to Branchidae in Milesia.[3] Those were the Greek oracles to which Croesus sent off messengers for consultation, while he dispatched others to consult the oracle of Ammon in Libya. He sent them to test what the oracles knew, so that if he found that they gave true opinions he could send to them a second time to ask whether he should try to make war on Persia.

He sent the Lydians to test the oracles after giving them the following command: beginning with the day they set out from Sardis, they should count the remaining days until they came to the hundredth day. Then they should consult the oracle, asking what Croesus, the son of Alyattes and king of the Lydians, happened to be doing. They should write down whatever prophecies each of the oracles gave and then bring them back to him. Now, no one can say what the other oracles prophesied, but at Delphi, as soon as the Lydians entered the temple to consult the god and ask the question they had been ordered to ask, the Pythian priestess, speaking in hexameters, said:

And I know the number of the sands and the dimensions of the sea,
And I understand the mute, and hear those who do not speak.
Into my brain comes the smell of the strong-shelled tortoise
Seething in bronze with the flesh of lambs,
Bronze spread beneath it and covered with bronze above.

The Lydians wrote down the prophecy of the priestess and set off for Sardis. When all the others who had been sent abroad were present with their prophecies, Croesus unfolded each of the writing tablets and read over its contents. None of them pleased him, but when he heard the one from Delphi, he immediately accepted it and said a prayer, in the

---

3. Important oracles in different regions of Greece.

belief that the only real oracle was the one in Delphi, because it had
figured out what he had been doing. You see, after he had sent his
messengers to consult the oracles, he came up with the following idea
while waiting for the appointed day—it was something no one should
be able to figure out or guess. He himself had chopped up a turtle and a
lamb and then boiled them together in a bronze pot topped with a bronze
lid.

That, then, is the oracle that was given to Croesus from Delphi. I
can't say anything about the answer the oracle of Amphiaraus gave the
Lydians after they performed the customary rites at the shrine (indeed,
the answer wasn't even reported), except that in it, too, Croesus thought
that he had found an undeceitful oracle.

After this, Croesus propitiated the Delphic god with enormous sacrifices. He sacrificed three thousand of every kind of sacrificial animal.
He piled up couches ornamented with gold and silver, along with golden
bowls and crimson cloaks and undergarments, and burned them in a
huge fire, all in the hope that in this way he might bring the god over to
his side. He also commanded every Lydian to sacrifice something that
he had.

When he had finished with the sacrifices, he melted down an immense
amount of gold and beat it into ingots. There were one hundred and
seventeen of them, and they were eighteen inches long, nine inches
wide, and three inches high. Four of them were pure gold, weighing
about one hundred and fifty pounds each. The other ingots were an
alloy of gold and silver, each weighing about one hundred and twenty
pounds.

He also made a statue of a lion out of pure gold; it weighed six hundred
pounds. When the temple in Delphi burned down, this lion fell off the
ingots—it had rested on top of them, you see. It is now in the Corinthian
treasury and weighs three hundred and ninety pounds because two
hundred and ten pounds of it melted away.

After he had made these offerings, Croesus sent other things to Delphi
along with the rest: two very large vats—one of gold and the other of
silver. The golden one is on the right as you enter the temple, and the
silver one is on the left. These were also moved after the fire in the
temple. The golden vat is in the Clazomenian treasury and weighs about
five hundred and twenty-two pounds, and the silver one is in the corner
of the chapel's vestibule and holds nearly five thousand four hundred
gallons. It is used for mixing water and wine by the Delphians at the
festival of the Epiphany of the God. The Delphians say that it's the work
of Theodorus the Samian, and I believe it, for it's not the sort of work
you come upon every day.

Croesus also sent four silver jugs, which are in the Corinthian treasury. He also dedicated two holy-water sprinklers, one gold and one
silver. It has been inscribed on the golden one that it is an offering of
the Lacedaemonians—who say so, too, though incorrectly, for this piece

also came from Croesus. It was inscribed by a Delphian who wanted to please the Lacedaemonians, and I know his name, but I won't mention it. (The statue of the boy whose hand the water runs through *is* from the Lacedaemonians, but neither of the sprinklers is.) Croesus sent other uninscribed offerings along with these, such as the round silver bowls, and especially the four-and-a-half-foot statue of a woman, which the Delphians say is the likeness of Croesus' baker. In addition, Croesus dedicated his wife's necklaces and belts.

Those are the things he sent to Delphi. After finding out about the courage and fate of Amphiaraus,[4] Croesus sent his shrine a shield of pure gold as well as a solid-gold spear with a golden shaft and a golden point. Both shield and spear were lying in Thebes when I was there, in the Theban temple of Ismenian Apollo.

Croesus commanded those who were going to deliver the gifts to the shrines to ask the oracles whether he should make war on Persia and whether he should conclude a friendly alliance with any other army. When they came to the oracles to which they had been sent, the Lydians dedicated the offerings and consulted the oracles, saying, "Croesus, king of the Lydians and of other peoples, in the belief that you are mankind's only true oracles, has given you gifts to match the discoveries you made and now asks you whether he should make war on Persia and whether he should conclude an alliance with any other army."

That is what they asked, and the oracles were of one mind: they prophesied to Croesus that if he made war on Persia, he would destroy a great empire. They also advised him to find out who the most powerful Greeks were and to befriend them.

When the answers were brought back to Croesus, he was overjoyed with the oracles and expected to destroy Cyrus' empire quickly. After finding out its population, he sent again to Pythia with gifts for the Delphians: two staters[5] of gold for each man. In return, the Delphians gave Croesus and the Lydians rights of first consultation without a fee, front-row seats at Pythian games and festivals, and the right, in perpetuity, for any Lydian who so desired to become a citizen of Delphi.

Having regaled the Delphians with these gifts, Croesus consulted the oracle for a third time, for after he had gotten the truth from the oracle, he used it to the full. He asked whether his monarchy would last for a long time. And the Pythian priestess said this:

> But when a mule becomes king of the Medes,
> Do not stay then, tender-footed Lydian,
> But flee to the many-pebbled banks of the Hermus
> And do not be ashamed to be a coward.

---

4. Amphiaraus was a hero from Argos. He was one of the seven warriors celebrated in Aeschylus' *Seven against Thebes.* He was swallowed up by the earth at the site of his oracle.

5. A stater was a coin containing about one-half ounce of gold.

When they returned with these verses, Croesus was more pleased with them than with anything else because he believed that a mule would never rule over the Medes instead of a man and that therefore neither he nor any of his descendants would ever cease to reign.

Next he thought to inquire who the most powerful Greeks were and to befriend them. He learned that the Lacedaemonians and the Athenians were preeminent, and that the former were of Dorian descent while the latter were Ionians. These were considered to be the two superior races, the Ionians being originally a Pelasgic and the Dorians being a Hellenic people. The Pelasgians have never left their country, while the Hellenes have migrated a great deal. During the time of King Deucalion, the Hellenes inhabited Phthia, but during the time of Dorus, the son of Hellen, they lived in the region called Histiaeotis, near Mounts Ossa and Olympus. They were forced to leave Histiaeotis by the Cadmeians and occupied Pindus, or what is now called Macedonia. From there, they moved again into Dryopis, and from Dryopis they migrated into the Peloponnese, where they came to be called Dorians.[6]

I cannot say for sure what language the ancient Pelasgians spoke, but if I can cite the evidence of the present-day Pelasgians who live above the Tyrrhenians in the town of Creston, and who were neighbors of the people now called Dorians when they lived in the territory now called Thessaliotis; and if I can cite the Pelasgians who founded Placia and Scylace, on the Hellespont, and who used to be neighbors of the Athenians, and cite, as well, others who inhabit towns which have changed their Pelasgian names; if, again, I may speak on the basis of this evidence, why, then, the Pelasgians spoke a barbarian language. For if these are examples of the Pelasgian language, then the Attic people, though Pelasgian, learned a different language at the same time that they were Hellenized. For the Crestonians do not now speak the same language as any of their neighbors, nor do the Placians, who do, however, speak the same language as the Crestonians. This plainly shows that the Placians and Crestonians retained the character of their speech when they moved to that region and that they continue to preserve it.[7]

It is clear to me that the Hellenic people have always used the same language since their origins. Although they were weaker when they were separate from the Pelasgians, they expanded their domain from something small into a mass of peoples. The Pelasgians, especially, assimilated themselves to the Hellenes, as did numerous other barbarian peoples. Furthermore, it seems to me that the Pelasgians, a barbarian people themselves, never grew to a very great number.

6. A region in north central Greece.

7. This paragraph is difficult in the original Greek, with variant readings about which experts disagree. There is even dispute about the locations of the places Herodotus mentions. Some say they are in Thrace, near modern Bulgaria; others say they are in Italy. In general, Herodotus is attempting to show what the original language of a people must have been from survivals of that language in his own day. This continues to be a method of modern historical linguistics.

Now, as to these people, Croesus learned that after having been torn by civil strife, Attica was held in subjection by Pisistratus, son of Hippocrates, who was at that time the tyrant in Athens. It all began when a great omen came to Hippocrates when he was a private citizen attending the Olympic Games. While he was offering up the sacrificial animals, the pots, which were standing on their tripods and which were full of meat and water, began to bubble and boil over without a fire. Chilon the Lacedaemonian happened to be present and to see the omen, and he advised Hippocrates not to marry a fertile woman and bring her into his home, whereas if he was already married, he should divorce his wife and renounce his son, if he had one. Hippocrates refused to follow Chilon's advice. Later this Pisistratus was born.

When there was a struggle between the Athenians who lived near the sea, led by Megacles, the son of Alcmaeon, and those who lived on the plain, led by Lycurgus, the son of Aristolaides, Pisistratus formed a third party with the intention of setting up a tyranny. He got together his supporters, and after coming forward ostensibly on behalf of the people who lived in the hills, he concocted the following plot. He wounded himself and his mules and then drove his mule team into the marketplace as if he had just escaped from his enemies, who, so his story went, had tried to kill him while he was driving into the country. He asked the people to provide him with some sort of guard, since he had distinguished himself when he was a general in the campaign against Megara by taking Nisaea [8] and performing other great deeds. The Athenian people were completely deceived and gave him a bodyguard of men selected from the citizenry. They were not the usual "spearmen" but his "clubmen," since they walked behind him carrying wooden clubs. These men joined in a revolt with Pisistratus and took the Acropolis. Pisistratus became the ruler of the Athenians, but he did not shake up the system of government or change any of the laws—he governed according to the already established laws and administered the city fairly and well.

Not long afterward, the supporters of Megacles and Lycurgus entered into an alliance and deposed him. Thus, Pisistratus seized Athens the first time and then lost his supreme power before it was securely rooted. Meanwhile, those who had deposed Pisistratus started quarreling with one another all over again. Harried by the constant feuding, Megacles sent a message to Pisistratus asking whether he wanted to marry his daughter with a view of getting the tyranny back. Pisistratus accepted the proposal and agreed to the conditions, and then he and Megacles came up with what is far and away the most simpleminded plot to put him back in power that I have ever heard of, considering that from the very earliest times the Greeks have been distinguished from the barbarians by their intelligence and freedom from simpleminded foolishness—if, that

8. The port of Megara, on the Saronic Gulf.

is, these two actually did play this trick on the Athenians, who are said to be the foremost Greeks when it comes to brains.

There was a woman in the village of Paeania whose name was Phya. She was tall—about five ten—and good-looking in other ways also. They decked this woman out in full battle gear, and after showing her how she should pose to seem her most beautiful, they put her in a chariot and drove toward the city with criers sent running on ahead. As they approached the city, the criers, as ordered, shouted, "Athenians! Give a warm welcome to Pisistratus! Athena has honored him above all other men and is herself bringing him back to her own acropolis!" The criers went from place to place saying this. Word immediately spread from village to village that Athena was bringing Pisistratus back, and even the city dwellers, in the belief that this woman was the goddess herself, worshiped a human being and welcomed Pisistratus.

After retaking power in this way, Pisistratus married the daughter of Megacles in keeping with their agreement, but since he already had adolescent sons, and since it was said that the Alcmaeonid family was under a curse, Pisistratus did not want to have any children by his bride and had sex with her in unconventional ways. At first, the woman said nothing about this, but then she told her mother—who may or may not have asked about it—and her mother told her father. Megacles was furious over this insult from Pisistratus, and in the heat of anger he settled his differences with his opponents.

When Pisistratus found out about the conspiracy against him, he left the country altogether, and when he arrived in Eretria, he had a meeting with his sons. The opinion of his son Hippias won out—that they should get their power back—and so they collected contributions from whatever cities were under any obligations to them. Many cities supplied large sums of money, but Thebes stood out in the amount it gave. To make a long story short, time went by and everything was ready for their return: Argive mercenaries arrived from the Peloponnese, and a volunteer named Lygdamis came from Naxos bringing both money and men and generating a great deal of enthusiasm in everyone. The Pisistratids set out from Eretria during the eleventh year of their exile and made their way home.

The first place they took in Attica was Marathon. Their supporters in that city joined them while they were camped in the vicinity, and others streamed to them from the villages—everyone, that is, to whom tyranny was more welcome than freedom.

The Athenian citizens paid no attention to Pisistratus while he was collecting his war chest, and not even when he later took Marathon. But when they learned that he was making his way to their city from Marathon with a gathering force, *then* they marched out to attack him. They marched in full strength against the returning exiles, while the supporters of Pisistratus who had set out from Marathon marched on Athens. They met at the temple of Athena Pallenis and took up positions opposite each other. There, Amphilytus the Acarnanian, a fortune-teller, experienced a divine impulse. He went up to Pisistratus, stood beside him, and uttered this prophecy in hexameter verse:

> The net has been cast—it is spread wide.
> The tunas will dart through the moonlit night.

That is what he was inspired to prophesy. Pisistratus understood the prophecy, said that he accepted it, and led his army to the attack. The Athenians from the city were having their lunch just then, though some had finished lunch and were playing dice or taking a nap. Pisistratus and his supporters fell on the Athenians and routed them. While they were fleeing, Pisistratus thought of a very clever tactic to keep the widely scattered Athenians from regrouping. He got his sons on horseback and sent them on in advance. They caught up with the fugitives and repeated what Pisistratus had told them to say, commanding them not to be afraid and to go back to their homes.

The Athenians obeyed, and so for the third time Pisistratus took Athens. He firmly planted his tyranny with the help of a great many mercenaries and with the revenues which came in from Athens itself and from the area around the Strymon River. In addition, he seized the children of those who had not immediately fled but had stood their ground in the battle, and held them hostage on Naxos—for Pisistratus had also captured this island in the war and had turned it over to Lygdamis. Furthermore, on instructions from the oracles, he purged the island of Delos in the following way: he dug up the corpses from all the land the eye could see from the temple and moved them to another part of the island. And so Pisistratus became the absolute ruler of Athens. As to the Athenians, some had fallen in the battle, while others fled their homeland along with the Alcmaeonids.

Thus, Croesus found out about the repression of the Athenians during that time. Meanwhile, he learned that the Lacedaemonians had just gotten over a very troubled period and had already gained the advantage in their war with the Tegeans.[9] During the reigns of King Leon and King Hegesicles in Sparta, the Lacedaemonians had been successful in their other wars and had faltered only against Tegea. But long before these two kings, the Lacedaemonians were the worst governed of almost all the Greeks and had nothing to do either with foreigners or with each other. This is how they made the change to good government: Lycurgus, a highly respected Spartan, went to the oracle at Delphi, and as soon as he had entered the inner sanctum, the Pythian priestess said,

> You come, Lycurgus, before my rich shrine
> Dear to Zeus and to all who dwell in the halls of Olympus.
> I doubt whether to call you a man or a god,
> But rather a god, I think, Lycurgus.

---

9. A town in southeast Arcadia, a mountainous region in the central Peloponnese.

Some say, in addition, that the priestess taught him what is now the Spartan way of life, but as the Lacedaemonians themselves say, Lycurgus brought it in from Crete when he became the regent for his nephew Leobotes, king of Sparta, because as soon as he became regent, he changed all the laws and saw to it that the new ones were obeyed. Next Lycurgus changed the military institutions and established the sworn companies, the thirty-man platoon system, and the common messes. In addition, he established the Ephors and the council of elders.

The Spartans had an orderly government after these changes, and when Lycurgus died they built a temple to him where they revere him deeply. Because their land was rich and not thinly populated, they quickly sprang up and prospered and, of course, stopped being content with going about their own business. In the arrogant belief that they were stronger than the Arcadians, they consulted Delphi about the conquest of the whole of Arcadia. The priestess gave them this answer:

> You ask me for Arcady? You ask for much. I will not give it.
> Many are the acorn-eating men of Arcady—
> They will stop you. But I will not begrudge you:
> I will give you foot-tapped Tegea to dance on
> And her fair plain to measure with the surveyor's line.

The Lacedaemonians heeded this message when it was brought back and stayed away from the rest of Arcadia. They marched on Tegea carrying fetters, though, trusting in the deceptive oracle and expecting that they would lead the Tegeans into captivity. But they were defeated in the battle instead, and those who were taken alive ended up wearing the fetters they had brought and were put to work measuring the Tegean plain with surveyor's lines. The very same fetters in which they had been chained were still intact in Tegea when I was there, hung up around the temple of Athena Alea.

During the earlier war, then, the Spartans had constantly come off badly in their struggle with the Tegeans, but by the time of Croesus and in the reigns of Anaxandrides and Ariston in Lacedaemon, the Spartans had already gained the advantage, and they did it in the following way: because they were always being defeated in battle by the Tegeans, the Spartans sent ambassadors to Delphi to ask which god they should propitiate so that they could get the upper hand over the Tegeans. The priestess answered that they had to bring home the bones of Orestes, son of Agamemnon. When they could not find his grave, though, they again sent ambassadors on the road to the god, asking what country Orestes might be resting in. After the ambassadors asked this, the Priestess said,

> There is a place—Tegea—on a plain in Arcady,
> Where two winds are blown by mighty force,
> Where beat responds to beat and pain is heaped on pain.
> There, the life-giving earth holds fast Agamemnon's son.
> Bring him away, and be master of Tegea.

Although they looked everywhere, the Lacedaemonians were no closer to finding the tomb even after hearing this oracle until it was found by Lichas, one of the so-called Spartan "Benefactors." These Benefactors are always made up of the oldest citizens who leave the corps of the knights. There are five each year, and for the year that they serve, they are constantly being sent from one place to another on behalf of the state.

Now, one of these men, Lichas, found the grave in Tegea through a combination of shrewdness and luck. At a time when there happened to be a truce with Tegea, he went to a blacksmith's shop where he observed iron being beaten out and was amazed at the process. When the blacksmith saw his amazement, he stopped working and said, "You may be amazed at the manufacture of iron, my Laconian friend, but you would be really amazed if you could see what I've seen. I wanted to dig myself a well in this very courtyard, so I began to dig and came on a coffin over ten feet long! Well I couldn't believe that people were ever taller than they are now, so I opened it and saw a corpse as long as the coffin. I measured the corpse and then filled the hole back up again."

After the blacksmith told him what he had seen, Lichas thought about what had been said, and figured out on the basis of the oracle that the corpse must be that of Orestes. He figured it out in this way: the blacksmith's two bellows were the winds; the hammer and the anvil were the "beat answering beat"; and the finished iron was the "pain heaped on pain," which he inferred from the fact that the discovery of iron had been harmful to humanity. After coming to these conclusions, he returned to Sparta and explained the whole thing to the Lacedaemonians. They pretended to indict him on a made-up charge and to send him into exile. He went to Tegea and tried to rent the courtyard, after explaining his "misfortune" to the blacksmith. At first, the blacksmith didn't want to rent it, but Lichas eventually persuaded him. He moved in, dug up the grave, collected the bones, and carried them back to Sparta. Whenever they fought with one another after that, the Lacedaemonians got the upper hand, and most of the Peloponnese had now been conquered.

When Croesus had found out all this information, he sent ambassadors bearing gifts to Sparta to ask for an alliance, and he told them just what they should say. When they arrived, they said, "Croesus the king of the Lydians and of other nations sent us, and he says, 'Lacedaemonians! The god has commanded us through an oracle to make friends with the Greeks, and since I have learned that you are the leader of the Greeks, I call on you in conformity with the oracle, desiring to be your friend and ally without trickery or deceit.' "

Croesus sent this message through his ambassadors, but the Lacedaemonians had already heard about the oracle to Croesus. They were very happy over the arrival of the Lydians, and they took oaths of amity and alliance. And in fact, they were already obliged to Croesus for some good turns he had done them in the past, because when the Lacedaemonians had sent buyers to Sardis to try to buy some gold they wanted to use in a statue—the one of Apollo now standing on Mount Thornax, in Laconia—Croesus gave the gold to them as a gift.

For these reasons, the Lacedaemonians accepted the alliance, and also because Croesus had chosen them out of all the Greeks to be his friends. They stood ready to help him when he called on them, and they also made a bronze vat, holding two thousand seven hundred gallons and crowded with figurines on the outer rim, and shipped it to Croesus with the intention of giving it to him in return for his kindnesses. The vat never reached Sardis, and two different reasons were alleged for this. The Lacedaemonians say that when the vat was being transported to Sardis, it had to pass Samos, and that when the Samians found this out, they sent long warships after it and stole it. The Samians themselves, on the other hand, say that the Lacedemonians who were transporting the vat were behind schedule, learned that both Sardis and Croesus had been captured, and then sold the vat in Samos to private citizens, who bought it and dedicated it to the temple of Hera. On returning to Sparta, the sellers probably said that the vat had been stolen by the Samians.

And that's the way it was with the vat.

Croesus, meanwhile, having misinterpreted the oracle, led a force into Cappadocia [1] in the belief that he would destroy both Cyrus and the power of Persia. But while Croesus was preparing to march on the Persians, a Lydian who was already thought of as wise acquired an even greater reputation among the Lydians because of the following opinion. His name, by the way, was Sandanis, and this is the advice he gave Croesus: "Your Majesty, you are getting ready to make war on the sort of men who wear cowhide pants and cowhide everything else, too. They don't eat what they want but what they have, and they live in very rugged country. Furthermore, they don't make wine but drink water instead. They don't even have figs to snack on, or any other good thing of any kind. Now, on the one hand, if you win, what will you take away from them—they who have nothing? On the other hand, if you are defeated, think of the good things you will be throwing away. Once they get a taste of our comforts, they will cling to them, and it will be impossible for us to get rid of them. As for me, I thank the gods that they did not put it into the Persians' heads to make war on the Lydians."

That is what he said, but he did not persuade Croesus.

Before the Lydians were conquered, the Persians had neither delicacies nor comforts whatever.

The Cappadocians are called Syrians by the Greeks. At this time, the Syrians were subject to Cyrus, but before Persian rule, they were subject to the Medes. The boundary between the Median and the Lydian empires was the Halys River, which flows from the Armenian mountains through Cilicia and then separates the Matieni on its right bank from the Phrygians on its left. After passing these, it flows up toward the north wind,

---

1. The name for the central and east central region of Asia Minor.

where it separates the Cappadocian Syrians from the Paphlagonians on its left bank. Thus the Halys River cuts off almost all of lower Asia from the waters opposite Cyprus to the Euxine Sea. This region is the neck of the whole country, and it takes a man in good condition five days to cross it.

Croesus made war on Cappadocia because he longed to annex more land to his own domains, but especially because he trusted the oracle and wanted to avenge Astyages on Cyrus. You see, Cyrus, the son of Cambyses, had defeated Astyages, son of Cyaxares, the king of the Medes and the brother-in-law of Croesus. Astyages had become Croesus' brother-in-law in the following way. A rebel troop of nomad Scythians emigrated into Median territory. Cyaxares, the son of Phraortes and grandson of Deioces, ruled over the Medes at that time, and at first he treated the Scythians well since they were refugees. Because he also had a high opinion of them, Cyaxares entrusted his sons to them to learn their language and their skills at archery.

Time passed, and the Scythians were always going hunting and always bringing something back to Cyaxares. Once, though, it happened that they didn't catch anything, and when they came back empty-handed, Cyaxares (who was clearly hot-tempered) gave them a vicious beating. They felt that they did not deserve to be treated by Cyaxares in this way, so they decided to chop up one of the boys who was with them as a pupil, to prepare him the way they used to prepare their catches, and to present him to Cyaxares as if he were game. Then, after making their present, they would get away as fast as possible to Alyattes, son of Sadyattes, in Sardis. And that is just what happened, because Cyaxares and his dinner guests ate this meat, and the Scythians who had committed the deed became refugees at the court of Alyattes.

Later, because Alyattes did not surrender the Scythians on Cyaxares' demand, a five-year war broke out between the Lydians and the Medians, in which the Medians often defeated the Lydians and the Lydians just as often defeated the Medians. Once, they fought a kind of night battle, for it happened as they continued fighting this seesaw war into its sixth year that a battle took place in which day suddenly became night. Thales the Milesian had predicted to the Ionians that this change from day to night would occur, and he set as the outer limit of its occurrence the very year in which the change took place. As soon as the Lydians and the Medians saw day becoming night, they stopped fighting and were both very eager that there should be peace between them. The men who brought them together were Syennesis the Cilician and Labynetus the Babylonian. These were the ones who urged the two sides to make a sworn agreement, and they also arranged for an exchange of marriages. They determined that Alyattes should marry his daughter Aryenis to Astyages, the son of Cyaxares, for agreements can't remain strong without strong obligations. These people take oaths in the same way as the Greeks, but in addition they have to cut into the skin of their arms and lick up each others' blood.

Now, Cyrus overthrew this very Astyages, his own maternal grandfather, for reasons which I will give in a later narration.[2] Croesus held this against Cyrus and sent to the oracle to see whether he should make war on Persia. The deceptive oracle arrived, of course; he thought that it was favorable to him; and he invaded Persian territory.

In my opinion, when Croesus came to the Halys River he brought his army across on the already existing bridges, although according to most Greek accounts, Thales the Milesian brought the army over for him. They say that Croesus did not know how his army would get across the river, because the bridges were not there then, and that Thales—who was in the army camp—made the river, which was flowing on the left of the army, flow on its right also. He did it in the following way: beginning upstream from the army camp, he dug a deep, crescent-shaped canal so that the river would detour from its original channel and pass behind the encamped army into the canal. After skirting the camp, the river would return to its old channel. Thus, as soon as the river was split in two, it would be fordable on both sides. Some even say that the original channel was completely dried up, but I don't believe this either, because then how would they have crossed the river on their way back?

After Croesus crossed over with his army, he entered the region of Cappadocia known as Pteria (the most impregnable part of the country near Sinope on the Euxine Sea), where he camped and destroyed Syrian farmsteads. He also captured the capital of Pteria and sold its people into slavery. He captured its suburbs, as well, and drove the Syrians from their homes although they had done him no wrong. In turn, Cyrus mobilized his own army and, recruiting everyone who lived along the way, went to meet Croesus. (Before Cyrus led his army out, however, he sent envoys to the Ionians to see whether they could be induced to revolt from Croesus, but the Ionians were not persuaded to do so.)

When Cyrus arrived, he took up a position opposite Croesus, and there, in the Pterian country, they attacked each other in full strength. A furious battle took place, and many fell on both sides; but in the end neither side won a victory, and they disengaged at nightfall.

That was the kind of battle these armies fought. Croesus, however, faulted the size of his army (his attack force was much smaller than that of Cyrus), and so when Cyrus did not offer battle again on the next day, Croesus withdrew to Sardis with the intention of calling on the Egyptians to keep their promise—for he had made an alliance with the Egyptian king Amasis even before the one he made with the Lacedaemonians. He would send for the Babylonians, too, for an alliance had also been made between him and them while Labynetus was the ruler of the Babylonians, and he would also send a message to the Lacedaemonians telling them to come at an appointed time. His idea was to gather these

2. See book 1, chapters 107ff.

forces as well as to collect his own army, and then to wait out the winter and make war on Persia in the spring.

With this in mind, he sent messengers to his allies when he arrived in Sardis ordering them to gather there at the end of four months. He dismissed all of the mercenary troops who had fought with him against the Persians and sent them home, never expecting that Cyrus would march on Sardis after such a close fight.

While Croesus was thinking all these matters over, the outskirts of the city began to crawl with snakes, and when they appeared, the horses would leave their usual pastures and go to eat them. When Croesus saw that this was actually happening, it seemed to him to be an omen, so he immediately sent messengers to consult the Telmessian soothsayers. The messengers arrived and found out from the Telmessians what the omen meant, but they were unable to return the message to Croesus, because Croesus had been captured before they could sail back to Sardis. Nevertheless, the Telmessians had interpreted the omen to mean that Croesus should expect a foreign army on his soil and that when it came it would conquer the native inhabitants, for the snake, they said, was a child of the soil, whereas the horse was a hostile intruder. The Telmessians had worked out this interpretation for a Croesus who had already been captured, although they knew nothing about the situation at Sardis or about Croesus himself.

As soon as Croesus withdrew after the battle at Pteria, Cyrus became aware that Croesus had marched away with the intention of disbanding his army, and after taking thought he realized that he must make it his business to march as quickly as possible on Sardis before the Lydian forces could be assembled for a second time. He immediately acted on his decision and drove his army into Lydia so rapidly that he needed no messenger to bring the news of the event to Croesus—he brought it himself. Croesus was now in an extremely difficult situation, for things had turned out so very differently from what he had expected. Nevertheless, he led his Lydians out to battle, and at that time, at least, there was no braver or more warlike people in all of Asia than the Lydians. They fought on horseback, they carried long spears, and they were first-class riders.

The armies met on the plain in front of Sardis. It is wide and bare, and several rivers, including the Hyllus, flow through it and crash together into the largest of the rivers, called the Hermus, which flows from the mountain sacred to Mother Dindymene and into the sea at Phocaea. As soon as Cyrus saw the Lydians lined up for battle, he feared their cavalry, and at the suggestion of a Median named Harpagus he employed the following tactic: he collected all of the camels which followed his army carrying food and equipment, and removed their loads. He equipped men with cavalry outfits, mounted them on the camels, armed them, and ordered them to advance on Croesus' cavalry in front of the rest of the army. He ordered the infantry to follow the camels, and lined up the cavalry behind the infantry. When everything was set, he ordered his men not to spare the lives of any of the Lydians in their path—but they must not kill Croesus himself, not even if he resisted capture. Those were his orders.

Cyrus arrayed the camels opposite Croesus' cavalry for the following reasons: the horse fears the camel and cannot stand either the sight or the smell of it. He devised this tactic so that Croesus' cavalry would be useless to him, and it was with their cavalry that the Lydians intended to shine. When they entered into battle, the horses reared back as soon as they smelled and saw the camels, and Croesus lost all hope. The Lydians by no means showed themselves to be cowards, however, and as soon as they realized what was happening, they jumped off their horses and fought with the Persians from the ground. In time, after many men fell on both sides, the Lydians turned and ran and were trapped behind their town walls, where they were besieged by the Persians.

Croesus thought that the siege would last a long time and sent other messengers through the walls to his allies. The messengers who had been sent earlier had ordered them to gather at Sardis at the end of four months, but he sent these to implore them to come to the rescue as quickly as possible since Croesus was under siege.

He sent to all his other allies, but particularly to Lacedaemon, which was, coincidentally, involved at that time in a dispute with Argos over a region known as Thyrea. Lacedaemon had annexed Thyrea even though it was a part of Argolid territory, which extended as far as Malea to the west and included the mainland, the island of Cythera, and the other islands as well. When the Argives came to retrieve their lost land, they conferred with the Lacedaemonians and agreed that three hundred men from each side would do battle, and that the land would belong to whichever side won. The rest of each army would return home so as not to be present during the battle—that way, neither army would stand by and come to the rescue when it saw its side being defeated by the other. They left on these terms, and the men chosen from each side to remain behind started to fight. They were so evenly matched that after the battle only three of the six hundred men were left—Alcenor and Chromios for the Argives and Othryades for the Lacedaemonians—and these were left only because night fell to end the battle!

On the assumption that they had won, the two Argives ran back to Argos; Othryades the Lacedaemonian stripped the Argive dead and carried their armor to his camp, where he took up his post. On the next day, both armies came back to make an inspection. Both sides began by declaring victory—the Argives insisted that more of their men had survived, and the Lacedaemonians pointed out that the Argives had run away whereas the Spartan had remained and stripped their dead. They ended up by falling to blows during the dispute and having a battle. Many fell on both sides, but the Lacedaemonians won. From that time on, the Argives have cut their hair short, whereas they had formerly been required to wear it long, and have passed a law decreeing that curses would fall on any man who grew long hair and also on any woman who wore gold before Argos won back Thyrea. The Lacedaemonians, on the other hand, passed the opposite law, because they did not grow their hair long before that time, whereas afterward they did. Meanwhile, they say that the one Spartan who survived out of the three hundred, Othryades, was so ashamed to return to Sparta when all of the other men in his company were dead that he committed suicide right there in Thyrea.

This was the state of affairs in Sparta when the messenger from Sardis arrived to ask them to come to the assistance of the besieged Croesus. The Spartans, nevertheless, were eager to help after they heard the messenger's news, but then, just when they were outfitted and their ships were ready to sail, another message arrived, saying that the Lydian fortifications had been taken and that Croesus had been captured alive. As a result, they gave up the expedition, although they regarded the capture as a great disaster.

This is how Sardis was taken: after Croesus had been under siege for fourteen days, Cyrus sent riders through his army, announcing that he would give a reward to the first man to climb the wall of the city. After this, the army tried to take the city by storm and didn't get anywhere. When the other men had pulled back, though, a Mardian man named Hyroeades started climbing the section of the acropolis where no guards had been stationed, because there was no fear that it could ever be taken. Here, the acropolis is so steep and impregnable that even Meles, the first king of Sardis, had not carried the lion that his concubine had given birth to around this section even after the Telmessian soothsayers had decided that, once the lion was carried around the wall, Sardis would be invincible.[3] Meles had carried it around the rest of the wall—to those parts where the acropolis was vulnerable—but he thought it was absurd to carry it there, since it was so impregnable and so steep. It is on the side of the acropolis facing Mount Tmolus. The day before the battle, though, this Hyroeades the Mardian had seen a Lydian climb down this section of the acropolis to pick up a helmet which had rolled down from the top. He thought about it; it stuck in his mind. Then, of course, after he had climbed it, the other Persians followed suit and climbed it also. So many went up that Sardis was taken and the whole city plundered.

As far as Croesus himself is concerned, this is what happened. As I said earlier, Croesus had a son who was normal in every respect except

<hr/>

3. The legend had it that King Meles' concubine gave birth to a lion and that carrying the animal around the walls of the city would render the city invulnerable. Since the lion was not carried around a section thought to be already invulnerable, it was at that spot that the city was weakest.

that he was mute. In the days of his prosperity, Croesus had done everything possible and sought every remedy for him, to the point of consult-
ing the Delphic oracle about him. The Pythian priestess said this:

> O Lydian, King of many, great silly Croesus,
> Never seek to hear this prayed-for voice of a son crying out
> In your home. So much better for you if that voice
> Holds back, for it will sound out first on an unlucky day.

After the city walls were taken, a Persian who thought Croesus was
someone else went after him to kill him. Croesus saw him coming, but
he was so overcome by his troubles that he didn't care. Though it made
no difference to him if he was stabbed to death with a sword, his mute
son burst into speech through grief and dread when he saw the Persian
coming on and said, "Don't kill Croesus!" That was the first thing he
ever said, and after this he talked for the rest of his life.

The Persians, therefore, captured Sardis and took Croesus alive. He
had ruled for fourteen years and had been under siege for fourteen days
and had, in keeping with the oracle, destroyed his own mighty empire.

After capturing him, the Persians led him away to Cyrus, who piled
up a huge heap of wood and mounted Croesus, bound in fetters, on top
of it, along with fourteen Lydian boys beside him. Cyrus did this either
because he had it in mind to make a burned offering of the firstfruits of
his victory to one or another of the gods, or because he wanted to keep
a vow—or maybe Cyrus mounted Croesus on the pyre because he had
heard that Croesus was a religious man and he wanted to find out whether
one of his gods would keep him from being burned alive.

That, anyway, is what Cyrus did, but they say that to Croesus, though
standing in such terrible trouble on that pyre, there came the wisdom of
Solon—spoken as if by the inspiration of a god—that no living man was
ever truly happy. When this thought came into his head, he moaned
and heaved a deep sigh, and after a moment of profound quiet called
out the name Solon three times.

When Cyrus heard this, he commanded his interpreters to ask who
Croesus was invoking. They approached him and asked. For a while,
Croesus kept silent and would not answer the question, but they finally
forced him to say, "A man I would give a great fortune to see talking
with all the tyrants of the earth." Since his words made no sense to
them, they again asked what he meant. They persisted and goaded until
he told them how Solon, an Athenian, had visited him in the past, and
how Solon had seen all of his prosperity and had belittled it in various
ways. He told them everything had happened to him just as Solon had
said, although it was as true for all of humanity as it was for him, and
especially for those who thought that they themselves were happy. Croesus told them all this after the pyre was lit and the outer rims were
burning. When Cyrus heard from his translators what Croesus had said,
he changed his mind, realizing that he, a man, was about to burn another

man alive—a man who had been no less prosperous than himself. In addition, fearing retribution and reflecting that nothing was sure in human affairs, he ordered that the fire be put out immediately and that Croesus and those who were with him be brought down. His men tried, but they could no longer control the fire.

The Lydians say that when Croesus realized that Cyrus had changed his mind—when he saw everyone trying unsuccessfully to put out the fire—he shouted an invocation to Apollo saying that if ever the god had been pleased with any of the gifts he had been given, he should stand beside him and protect him from the danger he was in. He appealed to the god with tears in his eyes, and then, suddenly, in a clear and windless sky, storm clouds gathered and burst and extinguished the fire with the most savage rain. After this, Cyrus knew that Croesus was a good man and that the gods loved him, so he took him down from the pyre and said, "Croesus, what man persuaded you to make war on my country and be my enemy instead of my friend?"

Croesus said, "I did it, Your Majesty, and it has worked out to your benefit and to my harm, but the cause of it all was the god of the Greeks, who incited me to make war. No one is so stupid that he would prefer war to peace, for in the one sons bury their fathers while in the other fathers bury their sons. But for some reason, this is what the god wanted to come to pass."

After Croesus said this, Cyrus untied him, gave him a seat near himself, and treated him with special respect—both he and everyone around him marveled at the sight of the man. But Croesus was silent, deep in thought. Eventually, though, he turned and saw the Persians plundering the Lydian city and said, "May I tell you what is on my mind right now, Your Majesty, or must I be quiet?"

Cyrus told him to say confidently whatever he liked, so Croesus asked, "What is that crowd over there so busy doing?"

"They are looting your city and carrying off your wealth," said Cyrus. But Croesus answered, "It's not my city or my wealth they're looting. None of it is mine any more. What they are looting and leading away belongs to *you*."

Cyrus became anxious over what Croesus had said, so he dismissed everyone else and asked Croesus what he thought he should do under the circumstances.

"Since the gods have given me to you to be your slave," said Croesus, "I think that when I understand something more fully than you do it is right for me to tell you about it. Persians are unruly by nature, and they are also poor. Now, if you ignore these people who are looting and amassing great wealth, you can expect that it will occur to whichever one of them has the most wealth to rise up against you. Now then, if you are satisfied with what I say, this is what you should do. Station your bodyguards at every gate. Have them confiscate all the loot and tell the looters that they are required to give a tithe to Zeus. This way, you won't be resented for taking their wealth by force, and they will willingly hand it over, knowing that you are doing the right thing."

Cyrus was very pleased with what he heard, since it seemed to be good advice. He praised it highly and, after commanding his bodyguards to carry out Croesus' advice, said, "Though you are a king, Croesus, you are ready to give useful service and advice. Ask for whatever reward you like, and it will instantly be yours."

"Master," said Croesus, "you will make me most happy if you let me send these fetters to the god of the Greeks, the one I honored above all other gods, and to ask him whether it is his custom to deceive those who serve him well." Cyrus asked him what complaint he had against the god in making this request. Croesus went back to the beginning and told him about his intentions, about the oracles' answers, and especially his offerings, and about how, encouraged by the prophecy, he had made war on Persia. After relating all this, he ended up by again asking to be allowed to blame the god for the whole thing. Cyrus laughed and said, "You will get this from me, Croesus, and anything else you want whenever you want it."

When Croesus heard this, he sent some Lydians to Delphi with instructions to lay the fetters at the threshold of the temple and to ask whether the god was not ashamed to have egged Croesus on with prophecies to make war on Persia when that meant that the power of Croesus would be destroyed—from which, they were to say as they showed the fetters, the god got firstfruits such as these. They should ask this, as well as whether it was customary for Greek gods to be so ungrateful.

It is said that the Lydians arrived and gave their messages and that the Pythian priestess told them this: "Even a god cannot avoid what has been foreordained. Croesus makes up for the crime of his ancestor five generations ago, that bodyguard of the Heraclids who truckled to a woman's guile, killed his master, and took a title that did not belong to him. Loxian Apollo would have liked the suffering of Sardis to happen in the time of Croesus' sons, and not in the time of Croesus, but he could not get around the Fates. Yet he granted as many favors as they allowed. He put off the fall of Sardis by three years—so let Croesus know that his capture came three years later than the appointed time. In addition to this, Loxias helped him when he was being burned alive. And, as far as the actual prophecy is concerned, Croesus complains about it unfairly, for Loxias prophesied to him that if he made war on Persia he would destroy a great empire. Now, if he was going to plan well, he ought to have sent someone to ask in response to this whether the god meant Cyrus' empire or his own. But he did not understand what was said and he did not ask any further questions, so he has no one to blame but himself. As to the last thing he consulted the oracle about, Loxias said what he said about the mule, and Croesus did not understand that, either. Cyrus was really the mule because he was born to two people who were not of the same race, and his mother was superior to his father. She was a Mede and the daughter of Astyages, king of the Medes, while his father was a Persian—their subject—who lived with his own queen though he was beneath her in every way."

That was the answer the Pythian priestess gave to the Lydians, who brought it back to Sardis and repeated it to Croesus. He heard it, and acknowledged that the fault was his and not the god's.

That's the way it was as far as both Croesus' empire and the first conquest of Ionia are concerned. By the way, Croesus made many other offerings in Greece and not just the ones I have already mentioned. There is a golden tripod in Boeotian Thebes, which he dedicated to Ismenian Apollo, and the golden cows and most of the columns in Ephesus, and the great golden shield in the shrine of Athena Pronaia in Delphi. These things had survived when I visited those places, but others have been destroyed. As to Croesus' offerings to the Branchidae in the Milesian territory, I hear that they are equal in weight and in other ways similar to the ones in Delphi. The things he dedicated in Delphi and in the shrine of Amphiaraus were his own, the firstfruits of what he had inherited from his father, while the other offerings had belonged to an enemy of his, a man who, before Croesus became king, had become his political opponent by actively supporting Pantaleon to be the ruler of the Lydians. Pantaleon was the son of Alyattes and the brother of Croesus, though not by the same mother: Croesus was the son of Alyattes' Carian wife, while Pantaleon was the son of his Ionian wife. When, at his father's bequest, Croesus ruled over the kingdom, he killed this opponent by stretching him on the rack. In any case, he had even before this promised the man's property before dedicating it in the way and to the places I have mentioned. So much for these offerings.

In comparison with other places, Lydia has no natural wonders worth writing about except for the gold dust washed down from Mount Tmolus. It does have, though, by far the greatest man-made attraction outside those in Egypt and Babylonia—the tomb of Croesus' father, Alyattes. Its foundation is made of huge stones, while the rest of the tomb is an earthen mound. It was built by market people, craftsmen, and street whores. When I was there, five pillars were still on top of the tomb, with engraved records of the work contributed by the three groups. Comparison showed that the whores had done the most work. You see, all of the daughters of the Lydian common people work as prostitutes, and they keep at it until they save up enough of a dowry to get married. They also decide for themselves who they will marry. The tomb is three thousand eight hundred feet in circumference and one thousand three hundred feet in diameter. There is a large lake near the tomb, which the Lydians say is always full. It is called Lake Gyges.

That, then, is what the tomb is like.

Except for prostituting their female children, the Lydians observe the same customs as the Greeks. They are the first people we know of to mint and use gold and silver coins, and they were the first retail tradesmen. The Lydians say that the games both they and the Greeks play were also a discovery of theirs. They say that they colonized Tyrrhenia

at the same time as the games were invented, and this is the story they
tell about it: in the reign of King Atys, the son of Manes, there was a
severe famine thoughout all of Lydia. For a while, the Lydians just
patiently endured it, but then, when it did not let up, they looked for
some relief, and different people came up with different solutions. That
is when dice and knucklebones were invented, along with ball playing
and every other kind of game except checkers—that, at least, the Lydians
do not claim to have invented. After having made these discoveries, this
is what they say they did about the famine: every other day, they played
games the whole day through to keep from thinking about food, and the
next day they would stop playing for long enough to eat.

They lived in this way for eighteen years, but when their hardship not
only did not abate but got even worse, why then their king divided the
Lydians into two groups by lot—one to stay and one to leave the country. The king put himself in command of the group whose lot was to
remain there, and he put his son, whose name was Tyrrhenus, in command of those who would have to leave. The group that was to migrate
went down to Smyrna, where they built themselves ships in which they
stowed everything useful that they could carry and set sail in search of
land and livelihood until, after bypassing many nations, they came to
Umbria,[4] where they built the cities they inhabit to the present day.
They changed their names from Lydians to the name of the prince who
had led them, and so call themselves Tyrrhenians.

And so Lydia was enslaved by the Persians.

Now, though, our story turns to Cyrus—to this man who undid the
monarchy of Croesus—and to the Persians and how they achieved the
leadership of Asia. I know three separate versions of the story of Cyrus
besides this one, but when I write, I will follow the example of those
Persians who do not try to embellish the story, but who tell it as it actually
happened.

The Medes were the first to begin a revolt from the Assyrians, who
had ruled over the upper part of Asia for five hundred and twenty years.
Somehow, in their struggle for independence from the Assyrians, the
Medes were transformed into a people noble enough to cast off slavery
and be free. Later other nations did the same thing as the Medes, but
after they all became self-governing throughout the mainland, they
reverted to tyrannies in the following way. There was a cunning man
named Deioces among the Medes, and he was the son of Phraortes.
Now, this Deioces was in love with power, and this is what he did to get
it. The Medes were settled in villages, and Deioces, who had always
been well known in his, became very eager to establish a reputation for
uprightness. He did this, however, because there was a great deal of
lawlessness throughout Media, and he knew that crime is inimical to
civilization. The Medes in his village observed his practices and elected

4. The region of central Italy.

him to be their judge. And he actually was honest and just—but only because he courted power! He received not a little praise from the citizens for his conduct, so much so that when people in other villages who had fallen foul of unfair judgments found out that Deioces was the only man handing down honest decisions, why, when they heard that, even they gladly traveled all the way to Deioces to have their cases judged, and in the end nobody would appeal to anyone else.

What with more and more people coming to consult him all the time and finding out that his decisions were equitable, Deioces realized that everything was ready for him, so he refused to preside where he used to when passing judgment or even to hold court at all—there was nothing in it for him, he said, to neglect his own business completely while settling cases for his neighbors all day long.

So when there was even more robbery and crime in the villages than there had been before, the Medians held a meeting to consider it and said the following about the situation (although I think it was mostly the friends of Deioces who were doing the talking): "We cannot live in this country under the present constitution. Come then. Let's set up a king over ourselves so that the country will be well governed and we can get back to work and not have to flee our homes because of crime."

With some such argument, they persuaded themselves to be ruled by a king. They immediately began to nominate candidates for the monarchy, and Deioces was nominated and praised by everyone until they agreed that he should be their king. He then commanded them to build him a house fit for a king and to empower him to have a bodyguard. And that is just what the Medes did, because they built him a large, fortified house in a part of the country he designated and allowed him to enlist his own bodyguard from among all the Medes.

As soon as Deioces had power, he forced the Medes to build a capital city and to maintain it while paying less attention to the other towns. The Medes obeyed this also and built large, strong circular walls—for the city now called Agbatana—where one wall is set within the circle of another. The walls are designed so that the summit of each circular wall is higher than the one outside it by just the height of its parapets. To some extent, the fact that the place is on a hill contributes to this layout, but it was mostly done by design. There are seven circles in all, and of course the palace and the treasury are inside the last one. The largest of the walls is about the size of the wall around Athens. The parapets of the first circle are white, those of the second circle black, of the third crimson, of the fourth navy blue, and of the fifth orange. The parapets of all of these circles are brightly colored with paint, but the parapets of the two last circles are plated, one with silver and the other with gold.

Thus Deioces built walls around himself and his palace and commanded the people to live outside the walls. After having built everything in this way, Deioces became the first king to ordain that no one could come into his presence, but must conduct all business through messengers; that the king could be seen by no one; and that in addition to this to even laugh and spit in the vicinity of the king was an insult no matter who did it. He put on these airs so that none of his friends—who had been brought up with him, came from homes just as good as his, and were no less manly—would see him, become angry, and conspire against him. If they could never see him, he would seem to be a different kind of being altogether.

After he ordained these rules and strengthened his dictatorship, Deioces was harsh in the administration of justice. People used to write down their lawsuits and send them in to him, and he would pass judgment and send out his verdicts. That was his practice as far as the cases were concerned, and he also made these other rules: if he found out that someone had shown him any disrespect, he would send for the man and punish him to the fullest extent of the law for each offense—and there were spies and eavesdroppers throughout all his domain.

Thus Deioces united the Median nation—and it alone—and ruled over it. These are the tribes of Medea: the Busae, the Parateceni, the Struchates, the Arizanti, the Budii, the Magi. That is how many Median tribes there are.

Deioces had a son, Phraortes, who assumed power when his father died after reigning for fifty-three years. After taking power, though, Phraortes was not satisfied with ruling over just the Medes, and so after marching into Persia, he attacked them and made them the first Median subjects. Then, controlling these two nations, both so powerful, he began the subjugation of Asia by moving from one nation to another until he made war on the Assyrians, and in particular on those Assyrians who held Nineveh and who had once ruled the world. At that time, though, the Assyrians had become isolated after having been deserted by their allies, although they remained prosperous in their own right. Phraortes himself, after ruling for twenty-two years, was killed along with most of his army during this war.

Cyaxares, the son of Phraortes, the son of Deioces, succeeded on the death of Phraortes. They say that he was even more warlike than his forebears. He was the first to separate the Asians into distinct, specialized regiments: that is, regiments of spearmen, archers, and cavalry. Before him, they had all been jumbled up together. He was the one who was fighting with the Lydians when day became night as they fought and the one who acquired for himself all of Asia beyond the Halys River. He gathered together all of his subjects and marched on Nineveh, intending to avenge his father and to wipe out the city. He did battle with the Assyrians and defeated them, but while he was besieging Nineveh, he was attacked by a large army led by Madyes, son of Protothyes and king of Scythia. The Scythians had invaded Asia while driving the Cimmerians out of Europe, and that's how they came into Median territory—by chasing the fleeing Cimmerians.

It is a journey of thirty days from Lake Maeotis[5] to the Phasis River and into Colchis for a man in good condition. It is not far from Colchis to Media—there is only one nation, the Saspires, between them, and once you've crossed this you are in Media. The Scythians, however, did not invade by this route but turned aside onto the much longer inland road, keeping the Caucasus Mountains on their right. The Medians then engaged the Scythians, and after their defeat in the battle their power was dissolved and the Scythians controlled all of Asia.

From there, the Scythians moved against Egypt, but as soon as they were in Syrian Palestine, Psammetichus, king of Egypt, went out to meet them with gifts and entreaties and persuaded them not to advance any farther. After retreating, the Scythians were in the Syrian city of Ascalon, and although most of them passed through it without doing any harm, a few of the stragglers stripped the temple of the Heavenly Aphrodite. This temple—as I have discovered through investigation—is the oldest of all the temples of this particular goddess because, as the Cyprians themselves say, the temple in Cyprus is based on this one, while the Phoenicians in Cythera are the ones who built that temple—and they come from Syria. The goddess afflicted the Scythians who stripped the temple in Ascalon and all their descendants with effeminacy. Even the Scythians admit that they became sick for this reason, while those who travel into the Scythian territory can see for themselves how it is with those whom the Scythians call the Sissies.

The Scythians ruled Asia for twenty-eight years, and all of it was devastated because of their violence and contempt, for in the first place they exacted tribute which they imposed on everyone, and aside from taking the tribute they rode around robbing whatever else anyone had. Cyaxares and the Medes invited most of them to a feast, got them drunk, and killed them, and in that way the Medes regained their power and recaptured their former domains. They captured Nineveh (I will show how they did so in another story), and they made the Assyrians subject except for the Babylonian district. Then Cyaxares died, having ruled for forty years—counting the years of the Scythian occupation.

Astyages, the son of Cyaxares, inherited the monarchy. Now, Astyages had a daughter to whom he gave the name Mandane. One night, Astyages dreamed that she urinated so much that she filled up his city and then overflowed all of Asia. He recounted this dream to his Magian dream interpreters and was terrified when they told him its true meaning. When this Mandane later reached marriageable age, Astyages, for fear of this vision, did not marry her to any of the Medes who was his equal in rank. He married her instead to a Persian named Cambyses, whom he found to be of good family and quiet disposition, although he considered him to be far below the level of a middle-class Median.

5. The modern Sea of Azov.

But in the first year after Mandane started living with Cambyses, Astyages had another dream. It seemed to him that a vine grew out of his daughter's vagina, and that the vine spread over all of Asia. After he saw this and related it to his dream interpreters, he had his now pregnant daughter brought back from Persia and kept her under guard with the intention of destroying her offspring—for his Magi had foretold from this vision that his daughter's male child would rule instead of him. Astyages was determined to prevent this, so when Cyrus was born, Astyages summoned Harpagus, a relative, the Mede he trusted most, and the steward of everything he owned, and said something like this: "Harpagus, under no circumstances are you to disregard my command, whatever it may be, or to deceive me and serve others, because if you do you'll only trip yourself up later. Take the child Mandane has just given birth to, carry it to your house, and kill it. Then bury it any way you want."

Harpagus answered, "Your Majesty, so far you have never seen *this* man do anything to offend you, and I will make sure that I do not offend you in the future, either. If it pleases you that this should come to pass, I will duly render what service I can."

That was the answer Harpagus gave, but he went home in misery after the baby was given to him dressed in burial clothes. When he arrived, he told his wife everything Astyages had said. She asked him, "What do you intend to do now?" and he answered, "Not what Astyages has commanded, not even if he goes crazier and more raving mad than he already is. I won't go along with his ideas or serve him in this kind of murder. There are many reasons why I won't kill the child. For one thing, he is my kin, and for another, Astyages is old and has no male offspring. Also, if after his death the tyranny should devolve to this daughter, whose son he is now killing through me, what else would there be for me from then on in but the gravest danger? This child must die for the sake of my present safety, but the murder has to be committed by one of Astyages' men and not by one of mine."

After saying this, he immediately sent a messenger to get a cowherd of Astyages. Harpagus knew that this man pastured his animals in the most beast-infested mountains—just the kind of place Harpagus wanted. The cowherd's name was Mitradates, and he was married to a fellow slave. This woman's name was Spaco in Median but Bitch in Greek. You see, the Medians call a bitch a "spaco." The foothills of the mountains where this cowherd kept his pastures are upwind north of Agbatana toward the Euxine Sea. There, near the Saspires, the Median territory is very mountainous and steep and densely covered with forest. The rest of Media is all flat.

When the cowherd hurriedly arrived after being summoned, Harpagus said, "Astyages commands you to take this child and put it in the remotest part of the mountains so that it will die as quickly as possible. And he has commanded me to say this: if you do not kill it, but protect it in any way, he will inflict the most horrible death on you. I have been ordered to see the child after it has been exposed."

The cowherd heard this, took up the child, and retraced his path back to his hut. Now, it turns out that his own wife had been expecting to give birth any day, and by the will of god it happened that she had a child while the cowherd was on his way to town. Both of them had each other very much in mind: he, because he was worried about his wife's childbirth, and the wife because Harpagus was not accustomed to sending for her husband. When she saw him return unexpectedly and stand beside her, the woman immediately asked why Harpagus had sent for him so eagerly. He said, "Woman, I went into the city and saw and heard what I wish I'd never seen and what should never have happened to our masters. Harpagus' whole house was full of weeping and wailing. I was scared to death, but I went inside. As soon as I go in, I see a child lying there, wriggling and screaming and all dressed up in embroidered silver and gold. When Harpagus saw me, he commanded me to pick up the child immediately and take it where the mountains are fullest of wild beasts and leave it there. He said that Astyages was the one who had imposed this on me, and he threatened all kinds of things if I didn't do it. So I picked the baby up and carried it away, thinking that it belonged to one of the house slaves. I would never have dreamed where it came from. Still, I was amazed to see it dressed up in gold and finery, and besides, there was all that wailing at Harpagus' house. Well, the minute we're on the road, I find out the whole story from a servant who hands over the baby after leading me out of the city—that, believe it or not, this is the son of Mandane, daughter of Astyages, and of Cambyses, son of Cyrus, and that Astyages has ordered him to be killed. And here he is."

As he was saying this, the cowherd uncovered the baby and showed it to his wife. When she saw the large, beautiful child, she burst into tears and, clutching her husband around the knees, begged him not to expose the child for anything. He said that he couldn't do otherwise, because Harpagus' spies would come around to make an inspection and that he would die horribly if he didn't do as he was told.

Since she couldn't persuade her husband, the woman then said, "Seeing that I can't persuade you not to expose the child, do this, since it's so necessary for the child to be seen after it's exposed. I gave birth, too, but I had a stillbirth. Put that baby out, and let's bring up the child of Astyages' daughter as if it were ours. That way you won't be caught doing wrong by your masters and we won't have obeyed an evil command. The dead child will get a king's burial, and the surviving one won't lose its life."

It seemed to the cowherd that his wife had given good advice under the circumstances, and he followed it immediately. He handed the child he was supposed to kill over to his wife, took his own dead child, put it into the urn in which he had carried the other child, dressed it in that child's clothes, and carried it to the remotest part of the mountains, where he set it down. When the child had been exposed for two days, the cowherd left one of his herdsmen behind to stand guard and went to the city. He came before Harpagus and said that he was ready to show the corpse of the child. Harpagus sent the most trustworthy of his body-guards and through them he "saw" and "buried" the cowherd's child. Thus the one child lay buried, while the cowherd's wife adopted and raised the child who would later be called Cyrus, although she gave him a name other than Cyrus.

Now, when the boy was ten years old, something like the following event happened which revealed who he really was. He was playing in the village where these pastures were, playing in the road with some of his friends. And while they played, they elected the supposed cowherd's son to be their king. He assigned some of them to build buildings, others to be his bodyguards; he made one his chief of police, while he conferred on another the honor of carrying messages. Each was given some assign-ment. One of these playmates, the son of Artembares, a respected Mede, just refused to do what had been assigned him by Cyrus, so Cyrus com-manded the other boys to tackle him. They obeyed, and Cyrus subjected the boy to a brutal whipping. As soon as he was released, the boy became furious over what he considered an indignity, went to his father in the city, and complained about the way he had been treated by Cyrus—not saying Cyrus, of course, because that wasn't his name then—but, any-way, by the son of Astyages' cowherd. Without waiting for his rage to calm down, Artembares took his son along with him to Astyages and said that he had suffered a shocking affront "from your *slave*, Your Maj-esty," he said "We have endured this insult from the son of your *cow-herd!*" And he uncovered the boy's shoulders.

Astyages listened and looked, and out of a desire to avenge the boy on account of Artembares' social position he sent for the cowherd and his son. When they both appeared, Astyages looked at Cyrus and said, "Have you, the son of a man like this, dared to subject the son of one of my foremost subjects to such an insult?"

This is how the boy answered: "I did what I did with justice on my side. While we were playing, the boys in our village—and he was one of them—set me up as their king: they thought I was the right man for the job. Now, the other boys obeyed their orders, but this one disobeyed and didn't pay any attention to me, and that's why he got his punish-ment. If I deserve your worst because of this, here I am."

After the boy said this, Astyages began to recognize who he was. He thought that the features of the boy's face bore a resemblance to his own . . . the answer was so outspoken . . . and the period between the expo-sure and the age of the boy seemed to correspond. He was speechless for quite some time, bewildered by these thoughts. But he wanted to dismiss Artembares so he could get the cowherd alone and cross-examine him. So he pulled himself together with great difficulty and said, "I will deal with this, Artembares, in such a way that you and your son will have nothing to complain about." Then Astyages dismissed Artembares while servants led Cyrus away at his command. When the cowherd had been left all alone, Astyages asked him just one question: Where did he get the boy, and who was the one who handed him over? The cowherd said that the boy was his own offspring and that the woman who had given him birth was still with him. Astyages said that it was not a good idea for him to be so eager to be tortured, and while the cowherd spoke, Astyages gave a sign to his bodyguards to seize him. When he was being led away to the torture—that was when he revealed the true story. He began at the beginning and told it truthfully through to the end. He concluded with entreaties and begged Astyages to put himself in his place.

Astyages was paying less and less attention to the cowherd even as he was revealing the true story. It was Harpagus he held most responsible, and he commanded his bodyguards to summon him.

When Harpagus appeared, Astyages asked him, "Harpagus, just how did you kill that child—the one my daughter gave birth to?" When Harpagus saw the cowherd there, he avoided taking any false steps so that he wouldn't be contradicted and caught. Instead, he said, "After I took the child, I thought about how I could remain blameless toward you and do what you had in mind and yet not be a murderer in the eyes of either you or your daughter. So this is what I did: I called for this cowherd and handed over the child, saying that you were the one who had commanded him to kill it. And when I said this, I wasn't lying—because you did order it. But I gave it to him on this condition: I ordered him to place it on a remote mountain and to stay there and watch it until it died. I threatened him with all kinds of things if he didn't execute these commands. When he had obeyed his orders and the child was dead, I sent my trustiest eunuchs, and through them I saw the child and buried it. That is what happened in this matter, Your Majesty, and that is how I killed the child."

Harpagus had indeed told the straight truth, but Astyages concealed the rage he felt toward him over what had happened. First, he told Harpagus the facts as he had heard them from the cowherd, and he ended the story by saying that the child had survived and that everything had happened for the best. "I was very troubled," he continued, "by what had been done to the child, and I didn't take it lightly when I was repudiated by my daughter. But since luck has done such a happy about-face, send your son over here to keep the newcomer company and then you be my guest at a feast, because I'm going to sacrifice an offering to those gods who deserve the thanks for saving this boy."

When Harpagus heard this, he prostrated himself, making much of the fact that his offense had turned out all right and that he had been invited to a feast of thanksgiving. He went home and rushed inside. He had an only son, who was about thirteen years old, and he sent him off to Astyages with instructions to do whatever Astyages commanded. And then, overjoyed, Harpagus told his wife everything that had happened.

As soon as the son of Harpagus arrived, though, Astyages cut his throat and tore him limb from limb, and, after roasting some of his flesh and boiling the rest, he prepared it for serving and kept it ready. Harpagus and the other diners arrived at dinnertime. Tables heaping with lamb were set in front of Astyages and the others. In front of Harpagus was his own son—everything, except for his head, hands, and feet. These had been set aside on a covered serving tray. When it looked as if Harpagus had had enough to eat, Astyages asked him whether he had enjoyed his meal. When Harpagus said that he had enjoyed it thoroughly, some servants to whom this task had been assigned carried over the covered head, hands, and feet, stood before Harpagus, and asked him to uncover the tray and take whatever he liked. Harpagus complied, and when he uncovered the tray he saw the remains of his son. He saw it, but he didn't flinch; he kept within himself. Astyages asked him if he recognized the animal whose meat he had eaten. Harpagus said that he did recognize it and that he was satisfied with everything the king did. After giving this answer, he picked up what was left of the body and went home, whereupon, I suppose, he must have gathered everything together and buried it.

That is the punishment Astyages imposed on Harpagus.

While considering what to do about Cyrus, Astyages called for the same Magi who had given him the interpretation of that dream. When they arrived, Astyages asked them to repeat their interpretation of it for him. They gave the same answer and said that the boy would have been a king if he had survived and had not died first. Astyages answered them by saying, "He survived and lives! He was living out in the woods, and the other boys in the village made him their king. He behaved in every way just as real kings do. He appointed bodyguards, gatekeepers, messengers, and all the rest of it, and he ruled. Now, what does that seem to mean to you?"

The Magi said, "If the boy indeed survives and did become a 'king' and it didn't happen through some plot, then you should be confident and take heart for this reason: he will not rule again. Even some of the oracles have amounted to very little for us, and the details of dreams can come to nothing in the end."

Astyages answered, "I am of pretty much the same opinion. Because the boy has been called a king, the dream has been fulfilled and this boy is no longer anything for me to be afraid of. Still, think it over carefully and advise me. What will be the safest course for my house and for you?"

The Magi answered, "Your Majesty, we, too, are very interested in the success of your reign. According to the other interpretation, power would be transferred to this boy—a Persian—and we, who are Medes, would be enslaved and count for nothing to the Persians, who are foreigners. As long as you, a fellow citizen, are firmly on the throne, we also share in rule and receive great honor through you. So it is up to us to look after you and your rule in every way. If we foresaw anything disturbing, we would by all means forewarn you, but now that this dream has dissipated into trivialities, we feel very confident and urge you to be confident too. Meanwhile, get this boy out of your sight. Send him away to his parents in Persia."

Astyages was very happy when he heard this, and after sending for Cyrus said this to him, "Boy, I did you wrong because of a vision in a dream that didn't come true. But it was your destiny to survive. Now go to Persia. I'll send an escort along with you. There you will find a father and a mother very different from Mitradates the cowherd and his wife."

After saying this, Astyages sent Cyrus away. When he returned to Cambyses' house, his parents admitted him. When they found out who he was, they greeted him joyfully—after all, they believed that he had died long ago—and they asked how he had managed to survive. He told them, explaining that he had not known previously and had had a very mistaken idea of who he was, and that he had found out about all of his misfortunes on the road home. He had thought that he was the son of Astyages' cowherd, but he had found out the whole story from his escorts on the way. He said that he had been raised by the cowherd's wife, whom he kept praising through his whole narration, referring to her always as the Bitch. His parents picked up on this name and spread the rumor that Cyrus had been exposed and nurtured by a bitch so that the Persians would think that their son had been saved for them through divine intervention. That was where this story got started.

When Cyrus reached manhood and became the bravest and most popular of his contemporaries, Harpagus made overtures to him by sending him gifts. Harpagus wanted to take revenge on Astyages. He foresaw, though, that he, as a private citizen, could not punish Astyages, so when he saw that Cyrus was fully grown, he kept trying to make an alliance by comparing Cyrus' suffering with his own. Even before this, though, Harpagus had taken the following measures: Astyages had turned cruel toward the Medes, so Harpagus had approached the leading Medes one by one and persuaded them that it was time to make Cyrus their leader and terminate Astyages' reign. The plan was laid and ready, but when Harpagus wanted to reveal his intentions to Cyrus, who was living in Persia, there was no way to do it, because all the roads were being guarded. So he came up with the following scheme. He prepared a hare by cutting open its belly and leaving it like that—he didn't skin it. He stuffed it with a papyrus on which he had written his plan and then sewed up the hare's belly again and give it in a net to his trustiest servant, who was dressed as a hunter. Harpagus sent the man to Persia with verbal instructions to give the hare to Cyrus and say that he should cut it up with his own hands with nobody around while he was doing it.

These instructions were carried out, and Cyrus took the hare and cut it open. He found the papyrus inside, removed it, and read it. It said, "Son of Cambyses, the gods watch over you. Otherwise you would not have been so lucky. Now it is your turn to punish Astyages for trying to murder you. If he had had his wish, you would be dead, but you survive because of the gods—and me. I think you found out long ago about everything I did for you and about what I suffered from Astyages because I didn't kill you but gave you to the cowherd instead. But now, if you will only do as I say, you will rule over all the dominions of Astyages. Just persuade the Persians to revolt, and then lead an army against Media. It will come out the way you want it whether I am appointed general by Astyages to oppose you or whether it is some other prominent Mede. They are the first to rebel against him—they are on your side and will try to depose Astyages. Everything is ready here, so act, and act quickly."

When Cyrus heard this, he gave some thought to the shrewdest way to persuade the Persians to revolt, and after thinking it over he found the most direct plan and began to implement it. He wrote what he had in mind on a papyrus and called a meeting of the Persians. Then he unrolled the papyrus and, reading it aloud, said that Astyages had appointed him general over the Persians. "Now then, men of Persia" he said, "I order each of you to return with a sickle." That was Cyrus' order.

Now, there are numerous Persian tribes, and Cyrus marshaled only some of them and persuaded them to revolt from the Medes. They are the ones on whom all the other Persians rely: the Pasargadae, the Maraphii, and the Maspii. Of these, the Pasargadae are the noblest, for within the Pasargadae is the clan of the Achaemenids, from which the kings of Persia are drawn. These are some of the other Persian tribes: the Panthialaei, the Derusiaei, and the Germanii. These are all farmers, but others, like the Dai, the Mardi, the Dropici, and the Sagartii, are nomads.

When they all appeared with the above-mentioned sickles, Cyrus— and I should say that they were in an area of Persia about two and a quarter to two and a half miles square which was covered with brambles—Cyrus ordered them to clear this area in one day. When the Persians had completed their assigned task, Cyrus ordered them to come back the next day all washed and clean. In the meanwhile, Cyrus gathered his father's flocks of goats and sheep and his herds of cattle in one place, slaughtered them, and prepared them for the Persian army along with all the wine and bread they would need. When the Persians arrived the next day, he made them sit down in a meadow and feast. When they had finished eating, Cyrus asked them whether they preferred what they had the day before or what they had today. They said that there was a big difference: yesterday everything had been bad; today everything was good. Cyrus picked up on the word "good" and bared his whole plan. He said, "Men of Persia, this is your choice! If you decide to obey me, you will have these and ten thousand other good things and never have to do the work of slaves, but if you decide not to obey me, you will have countless labors like those of yesterday. Follow me, then, and be free! I think that I was born by divine chance to set my hand to this task, and I believe that you are not inferior to the Medes in war or in any other way. That's how things are, so rise up against Astyages now!"

After the Persians had chosen their leader, they eagerly set about liberating themselves. They had long resented Median rule. As soon as Astyages learned what Cyrus had done, he sent a messenger to summon him. Cyrus told the messenger to take back the message that he would come to Astyages sooner than Astyages would wish. When Astyages heard that, he put all the Medes under arms and, because he was living in a delusion, appointed Harpagus general, forgetting what he had done to him. When the Medes marched against the Persians and began to do battle with them, some of the Medes who were not in on the conspiracy fought, others deserted to the Persians, and most fought badly on purpose and then ran away.

As soon as Astyages found out that the Median army had scattered in disgrace, he sent this threat to Cyrus: "You still have nothing to be happy about." First he impaled the Magian dream interpreters who had recommended letting Cyrus go, and then he armed the Medes who had been left behind in the city—the young boys and the old men. He led them out and was defeated in his encounter with the Persians; Astyages himself was taken alive, but the Medes he had led were killed.

After Astyages had become a prisoner of war, Harpagus stood in front of him, gloating over him and mocking and insulting him and in particular asking "whether he enjoyed" slavery in comparison with monarchy—referring to the feast in which Astyages had fed him the flesh of his own son. Astyages looked at him and asked in return whether he took responsibility for what Cyrus had done. Harpagus said yes, he had written the letter, and yes, credit for the thing rightly belonged to him. Astyages then demonstrated to him through logic that he was either the stupidest or the most unjust of men. He was the stupidest if, it being possible for him to be king himself—as it was if he was the one who had brought about the present state of affairs—he had then conferred power on someone else. He was the most unjust if he had enslaved the Medes on account of that feast, for if he absolutely had to confer the monarchy on someone else and not keep it for himself, then it would have been juster to bestow this valuable commodity on a Mede rather than on a Persian. The Medes, however, who had no guilt in this matter, had now become slaves instead of masters, while the Persians had now become the masters of the Medes whereas they had formerly been their slaves.

In this way, the monarchy of Astyages was brought to an end after he had ruled for thirty-five years. Because of his cruelty, the Medes had to bow before the Persians after they had ruled all of Asia beyond the Halys River for one hundred and twenty-eight years, not counting the Scythian rule. Later the Medes regretted what they had done and rebelled against Darius the Persian, but they were subdued again after being defeated in battle. In the time of Astyages, though, Cyrus and the Persians rose up against the Medes and ruled over Asia from then on. Cyrus did Astyages no other harm, but kept him with him until Astyages died. That, then, is how Cyrus was born, raised, got to be king, and later conquered Croesus, who began the wrongdoing, as I said before. But it was his conquest of Astyages that made Cyrus ruler over all of Asia.

These are the customs I know the Persians to observe. They are not allowed to build statues, temples, and altars, and in fact they accuse those who do of silliness, in my opinion because unlike the Greeks, they don't think of the gods as having human form. It is their custom to climb to the mountaintops and sacrifice to Zeus, which is the name they give to the full circle of the sky. They sacrifice to the sun and the moon and the earth, as well as to fire, water, and air. At first, they sacrificed only to these, but they later learned to sacrifice to the Heavenly Aphrodite— they learned this from the Assyrians and the Arabians. The Assyrians call Aphrodite Mylitta, the Arabians call her Alilat, and the Persians call her Mitra.

This is the way the Persians sacrifice to the above-mentioned gods: they make no altars and light no fires when they are about to sacrifice. They don't pour libations or play the flute or wear garlands or sprinkle barley on their victims. Whenever someone wants to sacrifice to one of the gods, he leads the victim to a ritually pure place and invokes the god while wearing his turban wreathed, preferably, with myrtle. It is not allowed for the sacrificer to pray, in private, for good things for himself. Instead, he prays for the well-being of all the Persians and of the king, for the sacrificer, after all, is included among all the Persians. When he has cut up the sacrificial victim into pieces and then boiled the meat, he spreads out the tenderest grass—preferably clover—and then places all of the meat on top of it. When he has arranged the meat piece by piece, a Magus stands near and chants a hymn on the origin of the gods— anyway, that's the kind of hymn they say it is. It is not their custom to perform a sacrifice without a Magus. The sacrificer waits a little while, then carries away the meat and does whatever he wants with it.

The day of all days they celebrate the most is their own birthday. On that day, the right thing to do is to serve a bigger meal than on any other day. On that day, their rich people serve up oxen, horses, camels, and donkeys that have been roasted whole in ovens, while their poor people serve smaller cattle, like sheep and goats. They eat few main dishes, but lots of appetizers, one after another, and for this reason the Persians say that the Greeks eat a main course and then stop when they are still hungry since after dinner nothing worth mentioning is brought out, though they wouldn't stop eating if it was. They love wine, but they are not allowed to vomit or to urinate in front of someone else. But though they have to be careful about that, they are accustomed to deliberate about their most important affairs when they are drunk, and then, on the next day, when they are sober, the master of the house they have been deliberating in proposes the decision that pleased them most. If they like it even when they are sober, they adopt it, but if not, they let it go. If they ever come to a provisional decision while sober, though, they then get drunk and reconsider it.

This is how you can tell if people who happen to meet each other on the street are social equals: instead of a verbal greeting, they kiss each other on the lips. If one is of slightly lower rank, they kiss each other's cheeks. If one is of a much lower rank, though, he prostrates himself and pays homage to the other. After themselves, Persians have the highest respect for the people who live closest to them, and next highest for those next closest, and so on. In accordance with this principle, they have the least respect for those who live farthest away. They consider themselves to be the best of people by far and others to share worth proportionally, so the people who live the farthest away are the worst. Subject nations ruled each other even under Median rule. That is, the Medes ruled over everything, but especially over those nearest to them, while those, in turn, ruled their neighbors, and so on. The Persians rank nations according to the same principle, by which each nation has a surrogate rule over the next one.

Nevertheless, the Persians are more inclined than other people to adopt foreign customs. For example, they wear Median clothes in the belief that they are more attractive than their own, and they wear Egyptian breastplates into war. They seek out and learn about all kinds of delights, and they even learned from the Greeks to have sex with boys. Each Persian man has many lawfully wedded wives, but many more mistresses.

Second only to being brave in battle, a man is considered manly if he has many sons to show for himself, and every year the king sends gifts to the man who shows off the most sons. They believe that there is strength in numbers. They educate their sons from the age of five to the age of twenty in only three things: horseback riding, archery, and telling the truth. The boy does not come into the presence of his father until he is five years old—until then he lives with the women. This is done so that if he should die while he is growing up he won't cause any grief to his father.

I approve of that custom, and I also approve of the one that forbids even the king to put someone to death on the basis of only one charge, and that forbids any Persian to do any of his household slaves any irreparable harm on the basis of one charge either. If, however, he finds on review that there are more and greater offenses than services, then he may give way to anger.

They say that no one has yet killed his own father or mother. It is inevitable, they say, that any such child who has ever been born will be found on investigation to have been either a changeling or a bastard. They say that it just isn't likely that a true parent will be killed by his own child.

Whatever they are not allowed to do, they are also not allowed to talk about. They consider lying to be the most disgraceful of all things. After that, it is owing money—for many reasons, but mostly, they say, because it is necessary for somebody who owes money to tell lies.

No citizen who is an albino or who has leprosy is allowed into the city or to mingle with other Persians. They say that he has committed some offense against the sun. Foreigners who catch these diseases are driven out of the country by posses. Even white doves are driven out, charged with the same offense.

They don't spit, urinate, or wash their hands in rivers, or allow anyone else to, for they especially revere rivers.

The Persians don't notice it, though we do, but this also happens to be true of them: their names, which refer to their physical characteristics or to their social importance, all end in the same letter, which the Dorians call san and which the Ionians call sigma. If you look into it, you will find that Persian names end in this letter—not some here and some there, but *all* of them.

I am able to say these things with certainty because I know them for a fact. There are things about the dead, though, which are concealed or referred to obliquely—for example that the corpse of a Persian man is not buried until it has been torn at by a bird or a dog. I know for sure, though, that the Magi practice this—because they do it openly—and that the Persians cover a corpse with wax before putting it in the ground. The Magi are very different from other people, including the Egyptian priests. The Egyptian priests refrain from killing any living thing, except what they ritually sacrifice. The Magi, however, will kill everything but dogs and people with their own hands. In fact, they make a point of killing things, and go around killing ants and snakes and anything else that creeps, crawls, and flies. Well, that's how they've been practicing this custom since the beginning, so let it stay that way.

I'll resume my earlier narrative.

As soon as the Lydians had been conquered by the Persians, the Ionians and the Aeolians sent ambassadors to Cyrus in Sardis offering to become his subjects on the same terms as they had when they were subject to Croesus. He listened to their proposal and then told them a story. He said that once upon a time there was a flutist who saw some fish in the sea and who played his flute thinking that they would march up onto the land. But when his belief turned out to be false, he got a net, threw it over a large number of fish, and pulled them out. When he saw the fish flapping around, he said, "Stop dancing! You didn't want to come out and dance when I was playing my flute!" Cyrus told this story to the Ionians and the Aeolians for this reason: Cyrus had once asked the Ionians, through ambassadors, to rebel against Croesus, and they had refused. But now that all his work was done, they were ready to obey him! When this story was brought back to their cities, and the Ionians heard what Cyrus had said in his anger, all the cities built walls around themselves and then assembled in the Panionium[6]—all except the Milesians. They were the only ones Cyrus made a treaty with on the same terms as they had had with Lydia. By common consent, the rest of the Ionians decided to send ambassadors to Sparta asking it for help.

These Ionians—the ones to whom the Panionium belongs—happen to have built their cities in the best climate with the fairest seasons of any people we know. Neither the country to the north nor to the south of it affects its people like Ionia. In the north they are hampered by the cold and the damp, and in the south by the heat and the aridity. The Ionians don't all use the same language. There are four different dialects. Miletus is the most southerly city, and then Myus and Priene. These cities are located in the province of Caria, and the people there talk to one another in the same dialect. The following cities are in Lydia: Ephesus, Colophon, Lebedos, Teos, Clazomenae, and Phocaea. These cities speak the same language, but it bears no resemblance to that of the cities mentioned above. There are three remaining Ionian cities, of which two are located on the islands of Samos and Chios, whereas one, Erythrae, was built on the mainland. The Chians and the Erythraeans speak the same language, while the Samians have a language unto themselves.

These, then, are the four dialects of Ionia.

Now, of these Ionians of the Panionium, the Milesians were safe from danger because they had made that treaty with the Persians. Also, there was no danger whatever to the islanders, because the Phoenicians were not yet subjects of the Persians, and the Persians were not a seafaring people. These Ionians of the Panionium were not distinguished from the other Ionians in any other way. The whole Greek race was weak at that time, but the Ionian peoples were by far the weakest and most insignificant. Except for Athens, there was no other important Ionian city. As a matter of fact, the other Ionians and the Athenians did not want to be called Ionians and avoided the name, and most of them seem to me even now to be ashamed of the name, whereas, on the other hand, these twelve Panionian cities take pride in it and have built a temple for themselves, called the Panionian Temple, which they have decided not to share with any other Ionians—not that any of them wanted to share it, of course, except for the Smyrnans. It is like the Dorians of the region of the Five Cities, which used to be called the region of the Six Cities, who make sure not to admit any neighboring Dorians into the Tripian Temple and even exclude from membership those of themselves who have broken the rules of the temple. You see, in antiquity they gave bronze tripods to the winners of the athletic games dedicated to the Triopian Apollo. For their part, the winners were not allowed to take the tripods out of the temple, but had to dedicate them to the god right

6. The meeting place where the twelve cities of Ionia gathered to discuss common policy.

there. Now, a man from Halicarnassus named Agasicles once won and then ignored the custom by taking his tripod home and nailing it up on a wall. Because of this offense, the five cities of Lindus, Ialysus, Camirus, Cos, and Cnidus excluded the sixth city, Halicarnassus, from membership in the temple. That was the penalty they imposed on Halicarnassus.

I think the reason that the Ionians formed twelve cities and did not want to admit any more is that they were divided into twelve groups when they lived in the Peloponnese, just as the Achaeans who drove them out are divided into twelve: first, Pellene, near Sicyon; then Aegira; then Aegae, the site of the always flowing river Crathis, from which the river in Italy got its name; then Bura; then Helice, where the Ionians fled after being defeated in battle by the Achaeans; then Aegium; then Rhypes; then Patrees; then Pharees; then Olenus, site of the great Pirus River; then Dyme; and then Tritaees, the only inland city of the twelve. These are the twelve present-day divisions of the Achaeans, as they were of the Ionians in the past.

That is really why the Ionians formed twelve cities. It is ridiculous to say, therefore, that they are more Ionian than the other Ionians or that they are more nobly born. The Abantes of Euboea, after all, compose no small number of their citizens, and they are not even called Ionian. Meanwhile, the Orchomenian Minyans have intermarried with the Ionians, as have the Cadmeians, the Dryopians, the Phocian colonists, the Molossians, the Pelasgian Arcadians, the Dorian Epidaurians—and lots of others. As to those who came from the town hall in Athens, and who consider themselves to be the "purest" Ionians—well, they didn't bring wives along to their colonies but took Carian women whose parents they had murdered. It was because of this murder that these women established the custom—which they bound themselves to under oath and passed on to their daughters—of never eating at the same table with their husbands and never calling their husbands by name. That's why—because those men killed their fathers and husbands and sons, and then, after having done this, forced the women to live with them. Those events took place in Miletus.

Some of these Ionians chose their kings from Lycian descendants of Glaucus, son of Hippolochus; some chose from the Caucones of Pylus, descended from Codrus, son of Melanthus; and others chose from both. But they, more than the other Ionians, want to hold on to the name Ionian, so let them be the "thoroughbred Ionians." The fact is, though, that an Ionian is anybody of Athenian descent who observes the festival of Apaturia.[7] All Ionians observe it except the Ephesians and the Colophonians. These are the only Ionians who do not observe the Apaturia, and they use some excuse having to do with a murder.

7. A festival characteristic of Ionians and Athenians, in which, among other things, newly born children were introduced into society and granted their civil rights.

The Panionium is a sacred place in Mycale. It faces north and was jointly dedicated by the Ionians to the Heliconian Poseidon. Mycale is on a promontory of the mainland, heading toward Samos and the west wind, and the Ionians used to gather there from their cities and celebrate a festival to which they gave the name Panionia. (Not only Ionian festivals, by the way, but all Greek festivals have names that end in *a*, just as all Persian proper names end in the same letter.)

Those, then, are the cities of Ionia. These are the cities of Aeolia: Cyme, which is known as Phriconis; Lerisae; New Wall; Temnus; Cilla; Notium; Aegiroessa; Pitane; Aegaeae; Myrina; Grynea. These are the eleven ancient cities of Aeolia. They, too, used to have twelve cities on the mainland, but one of them, Smyrna, was annexed by the Ionians. Now, the Aeolians settled on land better than that of the Ionians, but they didn't do as well with the climate.

This is how the Aeolians lost Smyrna. The Smyrnaeans admitted some Colophonian men who had been defeated in a civil war and exiled from their country. Later, the Colophonian exiles waited for the Smyrnaeans to hold a festival to Dionysus outside the city walls, and then locked the gates and seized the city. All Aeolia came to the aid of the Smyrnaeans and reached an agreement whereby the Colophonians would return the Smyraeans' movable goods to them and the Aeolians would abandon Smyrma. After the Smyrnaeans left, the other eleven cities apportioned the Smyrnaeans among themselves and made them citizens.

These, then, are the Aeolian cities of the mainland, aside from those settled in the Ida region, which are a separate entity. As to the island cities, there are five on Lesbos (the Methymnaeans enslaved the sixth Lesbian city, Arisba, whose inhabitants were their own blood relatives); there is one city on Tenedos, and another in the so-called Hundred Islands. There was no danger whatever from the Persians to the Lesbians and the Tenedonians, or to the Ionian islanders. The remaining cities jointly agreed to follow wherever the Ionians might lead.

When the Ionian and Aeolian ambassadors arrived in Sparta—and this business was undertaken very quickly—they elected a Phocaean named Pythermus to speak for them. He wrapped himself in a blood-red cloak, so that as many Spartans as possible would hear about him and attend his speech, and spoke at length and with great composure asking the Spartans to help them. But the Lacedaemonians did not go along—they decided not to help the Ionians. So the Ionians left, but although the Lacedaemonians had rejected the Ionian ambassadors, they still sent off some men in a penteconter[8] to keep an eye (as I believe) on what happened between Cyrus and Ionia. When these observers arrived in Phocaea, they sent their most respected member, whose name was Lacrines, to deliver the Spartan message to Cyrus not to destroy a single Greek city, because the Spartans would not stand for it.

8. A ship with fifty oars.

They say that after the envoy made his announcement, Cyrus asked some Greeks in his entourage who these Spartans were and how many of them there were that they should give him orders. When he found out, he said to the Spartan envoy, "I've never yet been afraid of the kind of men who have a specially appointed place, set apart in the middle of their city, where they get together and make false promises to each other. If I stay healthy, the Spartans won't be talking about the troubles in Ionia, but about their own."

Cyrus really hurled these words at all the Greeks, because they all have markets where they buy and sell. The Persians are not used to markets and don't have a single market anywhere. After this, Cyrus turned Sardis over to Tabalus, a Persian, left the gold of Croesus and the other Lydians to be carried by Pactyes, a Lydian, and marched off to Agbatana, taking Croesus along with him but not making Ionia his primary objective. It was Babylon that was in his way now, Babylon and the Bactrian people, along with the Sacae and the Egyptians. He would lead an army against them personally, and send some other general against the Ionians.

As soon as Cyrus marched out of Sardis, Pactyes induced the Lydians to revolt against Cyrus and Tabalus. Since he had all the gold of Sardis, Pactyes went down to the coast, where he hired mercenaries and persuaded the coastal inhabitants to join in the war with him. Then he marched on Sardis and besieged Tabalus, who was trapped in the acropolis.

Cyrus found out about these events en route to Agbatana and said to Croesus, "When am I going to see the end of this, Croesus? It looks like the Lydians are never going to stop making trouble for me and for themselves. It occurs to me that maybe the best thing would be to just sell them all into slavery. I think I'm like someone who has killed a father but spared the children. I captured you and led you away, you who are more than a father to the Lydians, but then I turned the city back over to them and now I'm surprised that they rebel against me!"

After Cyrus said what was on his mind, Croesus fearing that Cyrus would evacuate Sardis, said, "What you have said is understandable. But please, Your Majesty, do not completely give way to anger and destroy an ancient city that is not responsible for what happened before or now. I was responsible the first time, and I have the dust and ashes on my head to show for it. Pactyes is the wrongdoer now—and remember that *you* entrusted him with Sardis. Punish him, then.

"Pardon the Lydians, but impose this condition on them to prevent them from rebelling or from ever being a threat: send them a message prohibiting them from owning weapons. Order them to wear tasseled underwear and to take up acting. Command them to spend their time playing the lute and the harp and to teach their children to be merchants. You will see them quickly transformed, Your Majesty, from men into women, and they will never rebel against or be a threat to you again."

Croesus made this suggestion to Cyrus in the belief that the Lydians would prefer it to being enslaved and sold; in the knowledge that if he didn't offer Cyrus a good argument, he would not persuade him to change his mind; and in the fear that even if the Lydians should get out of their current situation, they might once again rebel against the Persians in the future and be utterly destroyed. Cyrus was pleased with the suggestion, relented from his anger, and said that he was persuaded. He called to Mazares, a Mede, and ordered him to issue the commands to the Lydians which Croesus had suggested and, in addition, to sell into slavery everyone who had marched on Sardis, while making sure that Pactyes was brought back to him alive.

Cyrus gave this order on the march into Persian territory. When Pactyes learned that an army sent against him was nearby, he became frightened and ran away to Cyme. Mazares the Mede marched into Sardis with some part of Cyrus' army (I am not sure of the size), and when he found out that the supporters of Pactyes were not there any longer, the first thing he did was to force the Lydians to begin to carry out Cyrus' instructions. Because of this command, the Lydians changed their whole way of life. Next, Mazares sent messengers to Cyme demanding that they surrender Pactyes. The Cymaeans decided to take the matter to the god in Branchidae for his advice. There was an ancient oracle there which all the Ionians and the Aeolians used to consult. The place is in Milesia above the port of Panormus.

The Cymaeans, therefore, sent envoys to ask what they should do about Pactyes that would be most pleasing to the god, and in answer to their question came an oracle that they should surrender Pactyes to the Persians. When this message was brought back and the Cymaeans heard it, they were eager to give him up, but Aristodicus, the son of Heracleides, a man respected among the citizenry, kept the people of Cyme from doing it until some other envoys, including himself, could go to ask about Pactyes for a second time. Aristodicus disbelieved the oracle's response and thought the envoys were not telling the truth. When they arrived in Branchidae, Aristodicus spoke for the others and said this to the oracle: "Lord, a suppliant, Pactyes the Lydian, came to us fleeing violent death from the Persians. They want him back, and they have ordered us, the Cymaeans, to send him. Although we fear the power of Persia, we have not yet dared to give him up until you make it infallibly clear to us what we should do." That is what he said, but the god again revealed to them the same oracle telling them to give Pactyes up to the Persians. In view of this answer, Aristodicus did something he had decided on in advance: he went around the temple removing the sparrows and any other species of birds that nested there. They say that as Aristodicus was doing this, a voice wafted toward him from the inner sanctum of the temple saying, "Most blasphemous of men, how dare you! You are stripping my temple of its supplicants!"

Aristodicus was prepared for this and said, "Lord, this is how you come to the aid of your supplicants, and yet you command the Cymaeans to surrender theirs!"

They say the god answered, "Yes, I do command it, so that you will commit an impiety and quickly be destroyed for it and never come here in the future to consult this oracle about the return of supplicants!"

When this news was brought back and the Cymaeans heard it, they didn't want to give Pactyes up and be destroyed or keep him and be besieged, so they sent him off to Mytilene. When Mazares sent *them* the message to give up Pactyes, they actually got ready to do it—for a price. I can't say for sure how much it was, because the deal was never worked out. The reason is that when the Cymaeans found out what the Mytilenaeans were doing, the sent a ship to Lesbos to transport Pactyes to Chios. There, he was dragged away by the Chians from the temple of Athena the City Guarder and surrendered to the Persians. The Chians surrendered him in exchange for Atarneus, a place in Mysia opposite Lesbos. The Persians took custody of Pactyes and kept him under guard, intending to deliver him to Cyrus. It was a long time before any Chian would sprinkle a sacrificial offering of barley that came from Atarneus to any of the gods, nor would anybody bake wafers with flour that came from there. Indeed, they kept anything that might come from this place away from anything having to do with religion.

Thus the Chians gave up Pactyes. Then Mazares attacked those who had joined in the siege of Tabalus. Next he sold the Prieneans into slavery, went rampaging and pillaging with his army over the whole plain of the Maeander, and then did the same in Magnesia. Right after this, he died of an illness.

After he died, Harpagus succeeded him in command. Harpagus was also a Mede, and was the one for whom Astyages, king of the Medes, had set that savage table, the one who had helped Cyrus to the throne. This man, then, had been appointed general by Cyrus, and when he arrived in Ionia he set about capturing its cities through the use of mounds. Whenever he mounted a siege, he would pile a mound up against the city wall, climb over it, and capture the city.

The first Ionian city he attacked was Phocaea. Now, the Phocaeans were the first Greeks to make long sea voyages and were the ones who opened up the Adriatic, Tyrrhenia, Iberia, and Tartessus.[9] They made their voyages not in round boats but in penteconters. When they landed in Tartessus, they became friendly with the Tartessan king, whose name was Arganthonius. He had ruled over Tartessus for eighty years, and he lived for one hundred and twenty years in all. The Phocaeans became

---

9. Phocaea was the northernmost Ionian city on the coast of Asia Minor. Tyrrhenia was an Etrus-   can region in northwestern Italy, and Tartessus is probably the Tarshish of the Old Testament.

such good friends with this man that he asked them to leave Ionia and settle wherever they liked in his country. Then, since he could not persuade the Phocaeans to do this, when he found out from them how Persia was expanding, he gave them money so that they could build a wall around their city. And he gave generously, because the wall is quite a few furlongs in circumference, and it is made entirely of huge, well-joined stones.

That, then, is how the Phocaean wall came to be built.

After Harpagus marched his army up to it and besieged the city, he sent word that it would be enough if the Phocaeans just knocked down one of the wall's towers and sacrificed just one house as a sign of submission. The Phocaeans, appalled by the idea of slavery, said that they wanted a day to think it over, and that they would give their answer then. They asked him, though, to withdraw his army from the wall while they were deliberating. Harpagus said that he knew very well what they were about to do, but he let them have their "deliberation" anyway. Now, in just the time it took Harpagus to lead his army away from the wall, the Phocaeans dragged their fifty-oared ships down into the water, boarded their wives and children, and stowed their movables along with the statues from their temples and their other temple offerings—not counting bronze, stonework, or painting, but everything else—and then they got in themselves and set sail for Chios. The Persians captured a completely deserted Phocaea.

The Phocaeans tried to buy the so-called Oenussae Islands, but the Chians would not sell them, for fear that the islands would be turned into a market and that they would thereby shut off their own trade. Therefore, the Phocaeans prepared to go to Cyrnus[1] because they had founded a city named Alalia there twenty years earlier by oracular command. (Afganthonius, by the way, had already died.) They were preparing to go to Cyrnus, but first they sailed into Phocaea and killed the Persian guard which stood watch after taking command of the city from Harpagus. Then, after they had accomplished their mission, the Phocaeans laid implacable curses on anyone in their expedition who stayed behind. In addition, they dropped a lump of iron into the sea and vowed that they would never return to Phocaea until that lump should reappear. But as they were making for Cyrnus, a nostalgic longing for their city and for its familiar scenery overcame more than half of the citizens, and they broke their promise and sailed back to Phocaea. The rest kept their promise, and sailed on after setting out from Oenussae.

When the Phocaeans reached Cyrnus, they lived together for five years with the first settlers and built a temple. But because the Phocaeans kidnapped and plundered their neighbors, the Etruscans and the Carthaginians formed an alliance and attacked them with sixty ships each. The Phocaeans manned their own ships—they had sixty—and went out

1. Cyrnus is the modern Corsica.

to confront their attackers in the so-called Sardinian Sea. The naval battle was joined, and the Phocaeans won a pyrrhic victory. Forty of their ships were destroyed, and the remaining twenty were useless to them as warships because their rams had been bent back. They sailed to Alalia, picked up their wives and children and all the other possessions their ships could carry, and, leaving Cyrnus behind, sailed for Rhegium.

The Carthaginians and the Etruscans drew lots for the crews of the wrecked ships. The town of Agylla got the largest number of them. Its people led the men away and stoned them to death. After this, though, anything, whether cattle, yoke oxen, or people, which passed by the place where the stoned Phocaeans had lain became palsied, twisted, and lame. Wanting to rectify their mistake, the Agyllaeans sent messengers to the Delphic oracle. The Pythian priestess commanded them to do what they continue to perform to the present day, which is to make large offerings to the dead Phocaeans and to hold gymnastic contests and horse races in their honor.

That is the fate those Phocaeans met with. The ones who ran away from there and made for Rhegium built the city in the Oenotrian territory which is now known as Hyele. They built it because they had learned from a Posidonian man that the Pythian priestess had meant not that they should found a colony on Cyrnus, the island, but that they should found a shrine for the worship of Cyrnus, the heroic son of Heracles.

And that's what happened to the Phocaeans of Ionia.

Something similar happened to the Teians, because when Harpagus got over their wall with a mound, all of them boarded their ships and sailed to Thrace, where they rebuilt the city of Abdera, which had been founded by Timesius of Clazomenae—although Timesius couldn't do anything with it, because he was driven away by the Thracians. Nowadays, Timesius is honored by the Teians of Abdera as a hero.

These were the only Ionians who left their native land because they would not endure slavery. The other Ionians, except for the Milesians, met Harpagus in battle just as the emigrants had done, and although they proved themselves to be brave as each man fought for his own city, when they were defeated and captured, they stayed where they were and followed orders. As I have already said, the Milesians had made a treaty with Cyrus and held their peace.

Thus was Ionia enslaved for the second time.

When Harpagus had the Ionians on the mainland in his hands, the island-dwelling Ionians, dreading destruction, surrendered themselves to Cyrus.

Although defeated, the Ionians nonetheless continued to meet at the Panionium, and I have learned that Bias, a Prienean, put forward a proposal so useful that if the Ionians had adopted it, it would have given them the opportunity to be the most successful of the Greeks. He told them to rise up en masse from Ionia, sail to Sardinia, and then found an all-Ionian city. In that way they would rid themselves of slavery and become rich because they would occupy the largest of all the islands and rule over the others. He said that if they remained in Ionia, he could not foresee that they would ever be free.

Bias of Priene's opinion was proposed to a defeated Ionia, but even before the destruction of Ionia a useful proposal came from Thales the Milesian, whose people were originally from Phoenicia. He told the Ionians to establish one administrative body in Teos (because Teos is right in the middle of Ionia) which would regard the other cities as no more than dependent local governments.

These, then, were the opinions those men advanced.

After conquering Ionia, Harpagus formed an expeditionary force against the Carians, the Caunians, and the Lycians and took some Ionians and Aeolians along with him. Now, the Carians came to the mainland from the islands. In antiquity, they were called Leleges, and they controlled the islands even though they were the subjects of Minos. As far as I can tell from what I have heard, they paid no tribute, but did have to man Minos' ships whenever he wanted them to. Since Minos was lucky in war and conquered a great deal of territory, the Carian nation was by far the most respected of them all at that time. They invented three things which the Greeks use. They introduced the practice of tying plumes to the top of helmets, as well as that of putting designs on shields. They were also the first to attach handles to shields. Before them, everyone who used a shield carried it without a handle—he would maneuver it with a leather strap wrapped around the neck and left shoulder. Much later, the Ionians and the Dorians evacuated the Carians from the islands, and that is how they came to the mainland. That, anyway, is what the Cretans say about where the Carians came from. The Carians, themselves, however, do not agree with the Cretans but believe that they are indigenous mainlanders and that they have always had the same name as they have now. They point out that there is an ancient temple to the Carian Zeus in Mylasa and that it is shared with the Mysians and the Lydians because of their kinship with the Carians. They say that Lydus, Mysus, and Car were brothers. The Carians, then, share the temple with them, but they do not share it with any other people even though those people may have learned to speak the Carian language.

On the other hand, I believe that the Caunians are indigenous even though they say that they came from Crete. Their language has come to resemble that of the Carians (or else Carian has come to resemble their language—I can't decide about this for sure) but their customs are very different from those of other people, including those of the Carians. What they like best is to get together in groups of friends of the same age and drink—men, women, and children. They once built temples to foreign gods, but they changed their minds and decided to worship only the gods of their fathers, so all adult Caunians put on their war gear and marched as far as the boundaries of Calynda while stabbing the air with their spears and saying that they were expelling all the foreign gods.

These, then, are the kinds of habits the Caunians have.

The Lycians, on the other hand, originally came from Crete. In antiquity, all of Crete was occupied by barbarians. Sarpedon and Minos, the sons of Europa, quarreled in Crete over the kingship, and when Minos won the civil war he drove Sarpedon and his followers out. After their expulsion, they went to the Milyan territory in Asia. You see, where the Lycians live now used to be Milyas in antiquity, and the Milyans were called Solymi at that time. While Sarpedon ruled, the Lycians called themselves the Termilae, which was the name they had then and which they are still called by their neighbors. When Lycos, the son of Pandion, was driven out of Athens by his brother Aegeus he went to Sarpedon, in Termila, and thus, in time, the Lycians got their name from Lycos. They have customs which are partly Cretan, partly Carian, but they have one custom so idiosyncratic that it is not shared by any other people in the world: they get their names from their mothers and not from their fathers. If you ask one of them who he is, he will give you his genealogy, starting with his mother and going back through his mother's mothers. And if a woman who is a citizen marries a slave, her children will be considered legitimate, but if a male citizen, even the foremost of them, should marry a foreign woman or a concubine, his children will have no civil rights.

The Carians did not perform any shining deeds as they were being enslaved by Harpagus—neither they nor any of the other Greeks who live in this region. Among the others who live there are the Cnidians, who are colonists from Lacedaemon and whose land—called Triopium—faces the sea. Beginning at the Bybassian Chersonese, all but a little bit of Cnidus—somewhat more than half a mile—is surrounded by water. It is bounded by the Gulf of Ceramicus to the north and by the sea of Syme and Rhodes to the south. While Harpagus was conquering Ionia, the Cnidians started to dig a canal through that little bit of dry land with the idea of turning their country into an island. Large numbers of them set to work. They were digging their canal just at that point where the isthmus meets the mainland, and they were making progress in turning themselves into an island, except that many of the Cnidians seemed to suffer more injuries than normal from flying chips of stone striking all over their bodies, but especially around their eyes. So they sent messengers to the Delphic oracle to ask what the trouble was. According to the Cnidians themselves, the Pythian priestess answered in iambics:

> Dig no canals and build no walls;
> Zeus would have made an island had he wished.

After the Pythian priestess gave this answer, the Cnidians abandoned the canal and surrendered themselves without a struggle to Harpagus and his advancing army.

The Pedasians lived in the interior above Halicarnassus, and whenever anything bad was about to happen either to them or to their neighbors, their priestess of Athena would grow a long beard. This happened three times. These are the only people near the Carians who held off Harpagus for any length of time; they gave him the most trouble by fortifying a mountain called Lida.

In time, though, the Pedasians were wiped out.

On the other hand, when Harpagus marched his army into the plain of Xanthus, the outnumbered Lycians went out to meet them and showed great bravery in battle. After they were defeated and trapped inside their city, though, they gathered their wives, children, possessions, and household slaves into the acropolis, set it all on fire, and burned it down. The men of Xanthus all took solemn oaths after they did this and then charged back out and died in battle. Except for eighty families, most of the Lycians who say they are Xanthians are really immigrants. The eighty families happened to be away from the city at the time of the battle and thus survived. That is how Harpagus captured Xanthus, and he captured Caunus in a similar way because the Caunians by and large imitated the Lycians.

Thus Harpagus devastated lower Asia. In upper Asia, it was done by Cyrus himself, conquering every nation and bypassing none. I will bypass most of them, however, and mention only those that gave the most trouble and are most worth describing.

When Cyrus had all of the mainland in his hands, he attacked the Assyrians. Now, there may be other great cities in Assyria, but the mightiest and most famous, the one where the royal palace was established after the abandonment of Nineveh, that city was Babylon, and it is something like this: it lies in a great plain, and each of its sides is fifteen miles long. It is square, so altogether the trip around the city is sixty miles long! Such, then, is the size of the city of Babylon, and it was designed like no other city that we know of. First, a deep, wide moat full of water runs around it, and second, its wall is fifty royal cubits thick and two hundred royal cubits high. (The royal cubit is two inches longer than the ordinary one.)

I must, in addition, describe what was done with the earth that was dug out in making the moat and how the wall was built. At the same time that they excavated the moat, they were making bricks with the earth they carried out of it, and when they had formed enough bricks, they baked them in ovens. Then, using hot tar as mortar, and stuffing mats of reeds between every thirtieth layer of bricks, they built the banks of the moat first and then the wall itself in the same way. On top of the wall and along its edges, they built one-room houses which faced each other, with space enough in between them to drive a four-horse team. There are one hundred gates built into the circuit of the wall, all of them made of bronze, as are the doorjambs and lintels.

There is another city eight days' journey from Babylon. Its name is Is. A not very large river flows through it, and the name of the river is also Is. It discharges its waters into the Euphrates. Many lumps of tar spring up with the waters of the river Is, and they are the source of the tar in the wall of Babylon.

That, then, is how the Babylonian wall was built.

The city itself has two sections. It is divided in half by a river, a large, swift, and deep river called the Euphrates, which flows out of Armenia and disembogues into the Red Sea.[2] The two outer city walls curve down into the river, and from the points where the city walls meet the river two other lower walls of baked brick run through the town along each bank of the river at right angles to the city walls. The road cuts in this city full of three- and four-story buildings are perfectly straight and parallel to the river and are intersected by straight streets leading to the river. At the end of each street there was a little gate—one gate for each street. These gates were also bronze, and opened right onto the river.

This outer wall, then, is like a breastplate, but there is yet another, inner wall running parallel to it which is not much weaker than the outer wall and just a little thinner. Right in the middle of one section of the city, and surrounded by a large, strong wall, is the royal palace, while in the other section is the square, bronze-gated temple of Zeus Belus, a quarter mile to a side, which was still there when I visited it. A solid tower is built in the middle of the temple. It is an eighth of a mile in length and breadth, and on it is mounted another tower, and yet another on that, until there are eight towers in all. You ascend by an external spiraling stairway built into the towers. People going up can stop and sit down on benches on a landing halfway up the stairway. There is a large shrine on top of the last tower, and inside the shrine is a huge, richly covered bed with a golden table standing beside it. No statue of any kind has been set up there, and no human sleeps there at night except one lone native woman whom the god has chosen from all the others—this according to the Chaldaeans who are the priests of the god.

I don't believe them, but these priests also say that the god himself frequents the shrine and rests on the bed, just as, according to the Egyptians, the same thing happens in the same way at Egyptian Thebes, because there, too, a woman sleeps in the temple of Theban Zeus, and because in both places they say that the women never have intercourse with mortal men. The same thing happens whenever there is a prophetess of the god in Lycian Patara. The god isn't always there, you see, but when he is, the woman is locked into the temple at night with him.

2. The Euphrates converges with the Tigris River
to form the Shatt-al-Arab, which in turn flows into
the Persian Gulf.

There is yet another shrine at ground level in the temple of Babylon. Inside, there is a huge golden statue of a seated Zeus; he is on a golden throne on a golden base and there is a golden table beside him. According to the Chaldaeans, these things were made from forty-six thousand four hundred pounds of gold. There is a golden altar outside of the shrine, but there is also another huge altar on which they sacrifice the full-grown cattle, because it is not allowed to sacrifice anything but suckling animals on the golden altar. On the larger altar, also, the Chaldaeans burn fifty-eight thousand pounds of frankincense every year when they celebrate the festival of this god. At the time Cyrus conquered Babylon, there was also an eighteen-foot-high solid-gold statue of a man in this sacred precinct. I didn't see it: I'm just saying what the Chaldaeans say. Darius, the son of Hystaspes, had some ideas about taking this statue, but he didn't dare to do it; Xerxes, the son of Darius, did take the statue and killed the priest who was forbidding him to move it.

That is how this temple was adorned. There are, in addition, many private offerings.

Many other Babylonian monarchs made additions to the walls and the temples, and I will describe them in my narratives on Assyria. Two of the monarchs were even women. The first of these to rule, Semiramis, lived five generations earlier than the second. She was the one who built the dikes all over the plain, and they are well worth seeing. Before her, the river used to rise over the plain and flood it all.

The name of the second queen was Nitocris, and she was more intelligent than the first. To begin with, she left behind accomplishments which I will describe in a moment, but more important, she watched the great, restless Median power constantly annexing cities to itself, including even Nineveh, and she prepared the strongest defenses against them that she possibly could. Before Nitocris, the Euphrates River, which runs right through the middle of Babylon, used to be perfectly straight, but she dug canals above the city which made the river so meandering that it actually flows through the same Assyrian village three times! The name of this village is Ardericca, and even now anyone who wants to travel from our sea to Babylon will sail down the Euphrates and arrive in this very village three times in the course of three days. So she did that; but she also built up dikes along the banks of the river which are really astonishing—that's how extensive and high they are. Far above the city, Nitocris excavated a reservoir, stretching along the river at a little distance from it. She dug it down to the water table. The reservoir is wide and has a circumference of fifty miles. She used the earth taken from this excavation for the dikes along the banks of the river. When the reservoir was dug out, she had stones brought in and made a rim running around it. Nitocris did both of these things—making the river crooked and the reservoir all marshy—so that the river would be broken into many bends and flow more slowly, and so that there would be a meandering journey toward Babylon followed by a long sail through the reservoir. She remade the terrain in just the region of the mountain passes where there is the shortest road from Media so that the Medes could not mingle with her people and find out about her government.

Nitocris built these defenses out of deep strategy, but other, minor works developed from them. The city is divided into two sections, with the river flowing between them, so under former monarchs whenever someone wanted to cross from one section over to the other he had to get in a boat, which I imagine must have been a nuisance. So Nitocris provided for this, too, because when she had finished excavating the reservoir, she used that work to leave behind yet another monument. First, she quarried huge stones. Then, when the stones were ready and the reservoir was excavated, she completely diverted the flow of the river into it. While the reservoir was filling up, the old riverbed became dry, and then, using baked bricks in the same type of construction as the city wall, she built the embankments running along the river through the city and the stairways from the gates down to the river; at the same time, she used the stones she had quarried to build a bridge just about in the middle of the city and held the stones together with iron and lead. (Every day at daybreak, square planks of wood were laid on the bridge so that the Babylonians could cross over on them. At night, the planks were removed so that the people couldn't go back and forth and steal from each other.) After the excavated reservoir had been filled up by the river and the finishing touches had been put on the bridge, the Euphrates was rerouted from the reservoir back to its old bed. Thus the reservoir, which had served its purpose, became a marsh, and a bridge was built for the citizens.

This very same queen played a trick that went something like this: she built a tomb for herself over the most crowded gate of the city—right out in the open on top of the gate. She had an inscription carved on the tomb which read, "If one of the kings of Babylon who succeeds me ever needs money, let him open my tomb and take what money he wants; but do not open it without need, for then it will do no good." Now, this tomb was inviolate until Darius came to the throne. Darius thought it was wrong that he could never use this gate and that he couldn't take the money when it was lying up there and even the inscription was inviting him to do it. (He never used the gate, because there would be a corpse over his head as he drove through.) He opened the tomb, but he didn't find any money. He found the corpse and another inscription, saying, "If you were not shamelessly greedy and insatiable for money, you would not have opened the coffins of the dead."

That's the kind of queen they say she was.

Cyrus made war on the son of this woman. He had his father's name, Labynetus, and he had inherited the throne of Assyria. Now, Cyrus, the Great King,[3] is well stocked with food and cattle from back home when

3. Great King is the usual name for the king of Persia.

he makes war; he even takes along water from the Choaspes River, which flows alongside Susa, for Persian kings drink from this and from no other river. Many mule-teamed wagons carry the boiled water of the Choaspes in silver buckets and follow the king wherever he leads.

When Cyrus reached the Gyndes River on his march to Babylon, the river whose source is in the Matieni Mountains, and which flows through Dardanus and into the Tigris, which in turn flows alongside the town of Opis and disembogues into the Red Sea—when Cyrus, then, was trying to cross this river (which is navigable) one of his sacred white horses galloped overconfidently into the river and tried to swim across, but the river sucked him under and swept him away. Cyrus was so angry with the violence of the river that he vowed to make it so weak that from then on even women could easily cross it without getting their knees wet. After making this vow, he put off his campaign and divided his army in two, and then marked out one hundred and eighty straight channels on each bank of the Gyndus, all pointing in a different direction, and after positioning his men, he ordered them to start digging. What with the large number of men, the job was finished; nevertheless, they spent the whole summer working on it.

Thus Cyrus took vengeance on the Gyndus River by breaking it up into three hundred and sixty channels, and at the first blush of the next spring he marched on Babylon. The Babylonians had marched out and were waiting for him. They gave battle when Cyrus was near the city, but they were defeated and were forced back behind their walls. Since they had long known that Cyrus was not peaceful, and had seen him attack every other nation indiscriminately, the Babylonians had already packed in supplies to last them for many years. Therefore they did not take the siege seriously, and Cyrus was in a bind because more and more time was passing and he wasn't making any progress with his campaign.

But then—whether somebody suggested a way out of his quandary, or whether he himself realized what he had to do—he took the following action: he positioned his main army at the point where the river enters the city and stationed some others at the point where it leaves and gave his men the order to penetrate the city by the riverbed when they saw that the river had become fordable. Then, leaving his men in place with their orders, he marched away with his support troops to the reservoir and did just the same thing with the river and the reservoir as the queen of Babylon had done. He diverted the river by a canal into the marshy reservoir and made the original riverbed fordable when the water subsided. When this happened, and the water had subsided to where it reached to about the middle of a man's thigh, the troops who had been positioned along the Euphrates for just that reason entered Babylon via the riverbed. Now, if the Babylonians had known anything in advance or found out about what Cyrus had done, they would have allowed the Persians to enter the city and then cruelly destroyed them. They would have shut all the gates leading down to the river and then climbed up onto the walls running along the banks of the river and caught the Persians like fish in a trap. But now, without their expecting it, the Persians were standing right next to them. Because of the great size of the city, as those who live there say, the residents in the middle of Babylon did not know that the people at the ends had been taken prisoner, and because a festival happened to be going on, they were dancing and enjoying themselves during the whole time until, of course, they learned the news only too well.

And that's how Babylon was captured the first time.

I will show by many examples how extensive the wealth of the Babylonians is, beginning with this: apart from tribute, all the land the Great King rules over is divided up for his maintenance and that of his army. Babylonia maintains the king for four of the twelve months of the year, while all the rest of Asia maintains him for the remaining eight. Therefore, Assyria has one-third the wealth of Asia, and the administration of this territory, which the Persians call a satrapy, is by far the most powerful of all, considering that the daily income of Tritantaechmes, the son of Artabazus, who governs the province in the name of the king, is one artaba full of silver. (The artaba is a Persian measure equal to nearly thirteen Attic gallons.) Aside from warhorses, Tritantaechmes had a private stable of eight hundred stallions and sixteen thousand brood mares. Each stallion mounted twenty mares. He kept such a large number of Indian hunting dogs that four of the large villages in the plain were otherwise untaxed except for having to provide food for the dogs. And that was merely the income of the man who *governed* Babylonia!

It rains little in Assyria, just enough to make the seeds of grain sprout. The corn ripens and the grain grows with water that comes from the river, brought by hand or by shadoof, and not, as in Egypt, with the river itself rising in flood over the fields. All of Babylonia, like Egypt, is intersected by canals, and the largest of the canals is navigable, bearing southeast from the Euphrates in the direction of the rising winter sun, and opening into the Tigris, beside which Nineveh was settled. Of all the countries we know, this is the best at bringing forth the fruits of Demeter.[4] The land doesn't even try to produce other plants—not fig trees, or vines, or olive trees—but it brings forth grain so plentifully that its yield is two hundred–fold and, when it surpasses even itself, three hundred–fold. The blades of corn and barley are easily four fingers wide. I know how big the millet and sesame plants get, but I won't mention it, because I know very well that even what I have said about the yields of grain is not going to be believed by those who have not visited Babylonia. They don't use olive oil, but get their oil from sesame seeds. There are date palms growing all over the plain, most of them fruit-bearing, and they make flour, wine, and honey from the fruit. They

---

4. Sister of Zeus and goddess of agriculture, fertility, and marriage.

cultivate the date palms pretty much like figs, particularly in the way they tie the fruit of what the Greeks call the "male" palm to the "female," or date-bearing, palm so that the date wasp can get into the female palm, fertilize the date, and keep it from falling off the plant. You see, the male palms carry the wasps in their fruit—just like wild figs, in fact.

I will now describe what is to me the greatest Babylonian marvel of all—after the city itself, that is. They have these round boats, made completely of leather, which traffic the river to Babylon. When they are upstream from Assyria, among the Armenians, they cut strips of willow and form them into ribs for the boats. Then they stretch watertight hides around the ribs and make a hull which is not pinched at the stem or widened at the stern. Instead, they make the boat round and concave, like a shield, fill the bottom with straw, set it afloat on the river, load it with freight—especially with kegs full of date wine—and then bring it downstream. The boat is steered with two oars worked by two standing men. The man in front draws his oar through the water toward the boat, and the man in back pushes his oar away from it. Some of the boats are very large indeed, others less so, but the largest of them will carry a cargo of over one hundred and forty tons. There is at least one live donkey in each boat, more in the bigger ones. After they have floated into Babylon and disposed of their cargo, they sell off the ribs of the boat and all the straw, load the hides onto the donkeys, and head back to Armenia. There is absolutely no way to sail back up the river, because of the swiftness of the river, which is why the boats are made not from wood but from hides. They make another boat in the same way after they get back to Armenia with their donkeys.

That's what their boats are like; this is the kind of clothing they wear: first, a long linen tunic reaching to their feet. On top of that they wear another woolen tunic with a little white cloak wrapped around it. They wear native open-toed sandals similar to the Boeotian slipper. They grow their hair long and knot it up under an oriental headdress, and they cover their whole body with perfume. Every man has a cylindrical signet and carries a handmade walking stick, and on top of each walking stick there is a carved apple, or rose, or lily, or eagle, or something. It's not customary for anybody to have a stick without his insignia on top of it.

Those are the ornaments of their bodies; these are their settled customs. In my opinion, their shrewdest custom was one which, as I have discovered, they shared with the Veneti of Illyria. [5] This is what they always did in every village once a year. When the virgin girls had reached marriageable age, they were all gathered together and led en masse to a place where a crowd of men stood around them. A town crier would stand the girls up one by one and auction them off, starting with the most beautiful of them all; after she had fetched the highest price and

5. Illyria was the region around present-day Venice.

was sold, the crier would call up the next-most beautiful one. They were sold not into slavery, mind you, but into marriage. The rich young Babylonian men would keep upping the bid on each other to buy the most beautiful girls while the poorer men, for whom good looks didn't matter, would take the uglier virgins along with some money. You see, when the town crier had gone through the sale of the most beautiful virgins, he would then stand up the ugliest, or even one who was crippled, and auction her off to whoever would take the least amount of money to marry her—and that's the one she would belong to, the one who accepted the least. The money came from the sale of the beautiful virgins, and in this way the beautiful married off the ugly and the lame. It was forbidden for a man to marry his daughter to whomever he wanted to or to take away a newly purchased virgin without a bondsman. He had to find a bondsman who would guarantee that he would actually live with her—and then he could take her away. It was permitted for someone who wanted to buy a wife to come from another village. If the couple did not get along, the law required that the money be returned so that the women would not be harmed or carried off to yet another city. This was their very best custom, although they don't observe it any more and have recently come up with a new practice. Because they have fallen on hard times and financial ruin since their capture, all the ordinary people who cannot make a living are forcing their daughters into prostitution.

This is the second-wisest custom they have: they carry their sick people out into the marketplace. You see, they don't consult doctors. Then people go up to the patient and talk to him about his illness to see if anyone has himself suffered from what the patient has or knows someone else who has suffered from it. So they go up and talk to the sick and recommend whatever they or the person they know did to escape from a similar disease. You are not allowed to walk silently by a sick person without first asking him what disease he has.

They bury their dead embalmed in honey, but their wakes are similar to those in Egypt. After a Babylonian man has had sex with his wife, he sits down next to burning incense while his wife does the same thing opposite him. In the morning, both of them wash themselves—they can't touch any cups or jars until they have washed. The Arabians, by the way, do the same thing.

This is the most disgraceful of the Babylonian customs: every native woman has to sit in the temple of Aphrodite once in her life and have sex with a strange man. Many rich, snobbish women who don't deign to associate with the other women drive to the temple in covered wagons, followed by a large retinue of servants, and stop in front, but most of the women sit in the temple of Aphrodite wearing wreaths of string around their heads. The women come and go. There are straight passages running every which way through the crowd of women, and the men walk by making their choices. Once a woman has sat down, she may not go back home until one of the strangers has tossed silver into her lap and then had sex with her outside the temple. While he is tossing the money, he has to say, "I claim you in the name of the goddess Mylitta." (The Assyrians call Aphrodite "Mylitta.") The amount of money doesn't matter, because the woman absolutely may not refuse it; that is against the law because the money is sacred. The woman has to follow the first man to throw her money and cannot reject anyone. Once she has had sex and done her duty to the goddess, she goes home, and after that you can't have her, no matter how much money you give her. Tall women with pretty faces go home quickly, but the ugly ones wait a long time without fulfilling their obligation. Some of them even wait as long as three or four years. There is a custom similar to this one in some parts of Cyprus.

These, then, are the set customs of the Babylonians.

They have three clans which eat nothing but fish. After they have caught the fish and dried them in the sun, they put them in a mortar, grind them with a pestle, and then drain them through linen. Some prefer to eat this right after it has been kneaded into a cake, while others bake it first, like bread.

After this nation, too, became subject to Cyrus, he set his heart on having the Massagetae under his control. They say that this is a large and courageous nation living in the east toward the rising sun, beyond the Araxes River and neighboring the men of Issedonia. There are those who say that the Massagetae are a Scythian nation.

Some say that the Araxes is longer than the Ister and others that it is shorter. They say that there are numerous islands in it close in size to Lesbos and that there are people on the islands who dig up all kinds of roots in the summer and eat them and that they collect and store the edible ripe fruit of trees and bushes and eat it in the winter. These people are supposed to have discovered a plant with a fruit that has such properties that when they get together in groups for this very purpose, light a fire, sit around it in a circle, and then throw the plant into the fire and smell the smoking fruit, they get as drunk with the smell as Greeks get with wine—and the more they throw in, the drunker they become, until they get up and dance and even sing. Anyway, that's what they say the life of these people is like.

The Araxes River flows down from the Matieni Mountains, just like the Gyndes, the one Cyrus broke up into three hundred and sixty canals. The Araxes discharges its flow into forty mouths, of which all but one are marshes and lagoons, where they say people live who eat raw fish and ordinarily wear sealskin clothes. The Araxes flows from that one mouth, though, clean through to the Caspian Sea. The Caspian Sea is self-contained and does not mix with any other sea. All of the seas the Greeks navigate, along with the sea beyond the Pillars of Heracles—known as the Atlantic—as well as the Red Sea, are really all one and the same sea.

But the Caspian is separate and self-contained. It takes fifteen days to row its length and eight days to row across it at its widest. Along the western shore of the Caspian stretch the Caucasus Mountains, of all mountain ranges the highest and the most extensive. The Caucasus sustains many peoples of all kinds, most living off the wild forest, where, they say, there is a kind of tree leaf that they grind up and mix with water and use to paint pictures onto their clothes, pictures that don't wash out but age with the wool just as if they had been woven in to begin with. They say these people have sex out in the open like cattle.

The Caucasus, then, bounds the western shore of this sea they call the Caspian, while toward the east and the rising sun there is an endless plain for as far as the eye can see. Now, the Massagetae, on whom Cyrus had a hankering to make war, inhabit no small part of this huge plain. [6] There were many powerful forces stirring him up and spurring him on. First, there was his birth—the belief that he was more than a mere mortal—and second, there was his luck in war, for wherever Cyrus had set out to do battle, it was useless for that people to try to escape.

The queen of the Massagetae was a widow. Her name was Tomyris. Cyrus sent ambassadors to her, ostensibly to woo her and to say that he wanted her to be his wife. But Tomyris understood that he was wooing not her but the throne of the Massagetae and rejected his advances. Next, since deceit didn't get him anywhere, Cyrus marched to the Araxes and openly began to mount his expedition against the Massagetae. He started to bridge the river so that his men could cross it and to build towers on the ferries plying the river. While he was in the middle of this work, Tomyris sent him a messenger, who said, "King of the Medes, stop rushing ahead so eagerly: you cannot know if the end of all this will be good for you. So stop. Rule over your own dominions and put up with seeing us rule over ours. . . . But no, you won't want to accept this advice—you will do anything rather than be at peace. Come on, then, since you so desperately yearn to put the Massagetae to the test. Don't bother to bridge the river. Cross over into our territory after we retreat from the river for three days. Or, if you would rather admit us to your country, you do the same thing."

After Cyrus heard this message, he called the foremost Persians together for a meeting and openly laid out the situation to get advice about what he should do. They all had the same opinion, urging him to receive Tomyris and her army into his territory.

Croesus the Lydian was there, and he objected by putting forward just the opposite opinion. He said, "Your Majesty, I once said that because Zeus gave me to you, if ever I saw any harm coming to your house, I would try to turn it aside with all my strength. I have learned from my suffering. If you think you are immortal and command an immortal army, it would be pointless for me to tell you my opinion, but if you

6. The present-day Ust Urt Plateau.

know that you, too, are a man in command of other men, then the first thing you must learn is that human events are like a turning wheel that does not allow the same people to prosper all the time. Now then, I have an opinion about the present situation that is opposed to the opinion of your other advisers. If we allow the enemy into our territory, there is this danger in it: if you are defeated, you will lose your whole kingdom. It's obvious that the victorious Massagetae will not run away, but will move forward against your empire. Also, if you win, you won't win as much as if you cross the river into their territory, defeat the Massagetae, and pursue them as they flee. Then the opposite will happen—if you defeat your opponents, you will march right through the kingdom of Tomyris. And aside from all that, it would be disgraceful and intolerable for Cyrus, the son of Cambyses, to retreat and give ground to a woman. So then, I think that you should cross over, advance as far as they withdraw, and then try to get the better of them by doing the following. To my knowledge, the Massagetae have never experienced Persian comforts or enjoyed life's great pleasures. Let's butcher our cattle unsparingly and prepare a banquet in our camp for your men—along with overflowing bowls of undiluted wine and all kinds of other food. After we do this, leave the preparations with your most expendable troops and then withdraw toward the river with the rest. If I'm not mistaken, the Massagetae will see all these good things and be drawn to them, and that will give us the chance to do some mighty deeds."

Of the two opposing opinions, Cyrus rejected the first and chose Croesus'. He announced to Tomyris that she should withdraw since he was going to cross over into her territory, and she in fact did withdraw as she had initially promised. Then Cyrus entrusted Croesus with his son Cambyses, to whom he intended to bequeath the kingdom, and told Cambyses to honor Croesus and treat him well even if crossing the river against the Massagetae did not succeed. With these instructions, he sent them back to Persia, and then he and his army crossed the river.

When he was on the other side of the Araxes, Cyrus fell asleep at nightfall and had this dream in the land of the Massagetae: in his sleep, Cyrus thought he saw the oldest son of Hystaspes with wings on his shoulders, one casting a shadow over Asia; the other, over Europe. Now, Darius was the oldest son of Hystaspes, the son of Arsames—a man of the Achaemenid clan. Darius was then around twenty and had been left in Persia because he was not old enough to go to war. Cyrus thought this dream over as soon as he woke up, and because he thought it was significant, he summoned Hystaspes and said to him when he had him alone, "Hystaspes, your son has been caught in the act of conspiring against me and my kingdom. I will tell you how I can be so sure of this. The gods care about me and reveal everything that is coming to pass, and so while I was sleeping last night I saw your oldest son with wings on his shoulders—one casting a shadow over Asia and the other over Europe. There is no way at all that he isn't conspiring against me—not after this dream. So you have to return to Persia as fast as you can and see to it that—when I go back there after conquering this place—you bring your son before me for questioning."

Cyrus said this in the belief that Darius was a conspirator, but, really, god had revealed to Cyrus that he was going to die right where he was and that his kingdom would devolve on Darius.

Hystaspes answered, "Your Majesty, let no living Persian ever conspire against you, but if there is one, let him die immediately! For you have made the Persians free instead of slaves, and the rulers instead of the ruled. If a dream has told you that my son is planning a revolution against you, I myself will hand him over to you to do with as you like." After giving this answer, Hystaspes crossed back over the Araxes, went to Persia, and put his son Darius under guard for Cyrus.

Cyrus marched inland from the Araxes for a day and did as Croesus had advised. Then Cyrus went back to the Araxes with his fittest Persian troops, leaving an expendable force behind, and one-third of the Massagetan army attacked and slaughtered this remnant of Cyrus's army—although it did put up a fight. After defeating their enemies, the Massagetae saw the banquet that had been laid out, so they relaxed and feasted, and, filled with food and drink, they slept. Then the Persians attacked and killed many of them but took even more of them alive, including the Massagetan general, whose name was Spargapises and who was the son of Queen Tomyris.

When she found out about what had happened to her army and to her son, she sent a messenger to Cyrus saying, "Cyrus! You! Insatiable for blood! Don't exult over what you've just done. It was by the fruit of the vine, with which you Persians glut yourselves to madness so it flows down into your bodies and rises up as obscenities—it was by this drug that you deceived and defeated my son and not by a battle's test of strength. Now take my advice: give me back my son and get out of this country unscathed even though you have humiliated a third of our army. If you don't, I swear by the sun-god, lord of the Massagetae, that greedy though you be, I will quench your thirst for blood!"

Cyrus paid no attention whatever to this message.

When the wine wore off Spargapises, son of Tomyris, and when he realized the trouble he was in, he successfully implored Cyrus to free him from his chains and killed himself as soon as he had the use of his hands. That, then, is how Spargapises died.

When Cyrus didn't listen to Tomyris, she gathered together all of her forces and attacked him. This battle was the fiercest that has ever been fought between barbarian peoples, and I have learned that it took place in the following way. It is said that at first they stood apart and shot arrows at each other and that then, when their arrows were used up, they fell to hand-to-hand combat with spears and daggers. They stood fighting together for a long time, with neither side wanting to turn and run, but in the end the Massagetae prevailed. Most of the Persian army was killed right there in battle, and yes, even Cyrus died, after having ruled for twenty-nine years. Then Tomyris filled a wine sack with human blood and searched through the Persian dead for the corpse of Cyrus. When she found it, she shoved his head into the sack and, while mutilating his corpse, she said, "Even though I have lived to defeat you in battle, you have destroyed me by tricking and capturing my son. But still, as I promised, I will quench your thirst for blood."

To me, of all the many stories that are told about the end of Cyrus's life, this is the most believable.

The Massagetae are similar to the Scythians both in their clothes and in their way of life. They use cavalry and infantry, and both archers and spearmen; they usually carry battle-axes. They make all kinds of things out of bronze and gold. When it comes to spearpoints, arrowheads, and battle-axes, they always use bronze, though, and they decorate their headgear, belts, and chest bands with gold. In the same way, they put bronze breastplates on the breasts of their horses and make the bridles, bits, and cheekpieces out of gold. They do not use iron or silver at all, and don't even have any in their country, although there is an abundance of bronze and gold.

These are the customs they observe. Each man marries a wife, but they have sex with their women in common. The Greeks say it is the Scythians who do this, but it isn't the Scythians—it's the Massagetae. Any man who has a hankering for a Massagetan woman just hangs his quiver up in front of her wagon and has sex with her undisturbed. This is the only limit they put on the number of a man's years: when he is very old, his relatives gather together and sacrifice him and some cattle along with him. They stew the meat and feast on it. This is considered to be the happiest way to die. They don't eat someone who dies of illness, but bury him in the ground instead and lament that he didn't live long enough to be sacrificed. They have no agriculture, but live off cattle and off the fish which are abundant in the Araxes River. They drink milk. The only god they worship is the sun, to whom they sacrifice horses. The reasoning behind this is that they are setting aside the swiftest of mortal things for the swiftest of the gods.

Book 2

The interest Herodotus showed in book 1 about the origins of war expands in book 2 to embrace the question of origins more broadly. This is probably how we should construe the attention Herodotus devotes to speculation about the source of the Nile, as well as the attempt by Psammetichus to identify the oldest of peoples, a project that also entailed investigation into the origins of language. The antiquity of Egyptian civilization, and the opportunity it presented for comparative study, captured Herodotus' imagination. His stress on the antiquity of Egyptian civilization was in part a message to his fellow Greeks that their smug belief in the originality of their own culture was greatly exaggerated. Herodotus suggests that many practices—and even some gods—claimed by the Greeks as their own were actually borrowed from the Egyptians. Book 2 also demonstrates Herodotus' characteristic curiosity about the customs of non-Greek peoples and about questions of cultural transmission. As he did in book 1, Herodotus evinces an uncommon interest in women's lives as well as in those of men.

Although at times Herodotus seems too trusting of his native informants, many of the stories he relates here and elsewhere show the hesitance of the oral historian to place too much faith in any one source. He is often sharply analytical in his approach to local lore—for example, in his discussion of the "doves" who served as priestesses at the shrine of Zeus at Dodona. He suggests these were foreign women who seemed like birds to the natives because they spoke an alien tongue. He is also perfectly prepared to thumb his nose at tradition, as in his refusal to participate in the culturally prescribed reverence for Homer as a historical source. He argues that Helen could not have been in Troy during the Trojan War, since the Trojans would surely have returned Helen to avoid the war if she had been theirs to give.

Chapters 1–98

When Cyrus died, Cambyses inherited the kingdom. He was the son of Cyrus and Cassandane, the daughter of Pharnaspes. When she died young, Cyrus himself grieved deeply and commanded everyone he ruled over to go into mourning. Now, as the son of Cyrus and this woman, Cambyses considered the Ionians and even the Aeolians to be his hereditary slaves, so when he gathered a military expedition against Egypt, he conscripted his other subjects, but particularly the Greeks he had in his power.

As to the Egyptians, before Psammetichus[1] became king, they assumed that they were the very first people who ever existed. But when Psammetichus came to the throne, he wanted to know for sure who the first were, and ever since Psammetichus the Egyptians believe that the Phrygians preceded them, whereas they precede everybody else. Since Psammetichus could not find out who came first by asking questions, he devised this experiment: he gave two children chosen from the common people to a shepherd to raise among his sheep. He commanded that no one should make any sound in their presence, but that they should be kept to themselves in a solitary pen and should be brought she-goats from time to time, have their fill of milk, and be otherwise provided for. Psammetichus devised this experiment and gave this order because he wanted to find out—apart from meaningless babble—just what word first broke from the children.

And that's just what happened. After two years had gone by, this is what happened to the shepherd as he followed his routine: when he opened the door and went in, both children fell down before him and reached out their hands, saying "baakos!" The first time he heard this, the shepherd kept quiet about it, but since he heard the word every time he went there to do his chores, he mentioned it to his master and, at his master's command, led the children into his presence. When Psammetichus heard them for himself, he asked which people called something "baakos," and found out that it was what the Phrygians called bread. Calculating on the basis of this experiment, the Egyptians conceded that the Phrygians were older than they. I heard that is the way it was from the priests of the temple of Hephaestus in Memphis. (The Greeks talk a lot of nonsense, such as that Psammetichus cut out the tongues of some women and arranged for the children to live among these women.)

This is what they said about the upbringing of the children, but I heard other things in Memphis when I went there to confer with the priests of Hephaestus. I even went to Thebes and to Heliopolis since I wanted to know whether they would agree with the stories that came out of Memphis, because the Heliopolitans are said to be the most learned of all Egyptians when it comes to stories.

Now, I am not eager to relate what I heard about religion in these stories, except only for the names of the gods, since I believe that all men know the same things about gods, whatever they call them. If I do mention anything, it will be a necessary part of the story I am telling.

As to human affairs, however, all the priests agree about this: the Egyptians were the first of all mankind to discover the year, dividing the seasons into the twelve parts which make it up. They said that they figured this out from the stars. It seems to me that they went about this

1. Psammetichus (Psamtik I) ruled Egypt from 663 to 609 B.C.

more intelligently than the Greeks, because the Greeks insert a month every other year on account of the seasons, whereas the Egyptians make up twelve thirty-day months and add five days to that number every year so that the circle of the seasons will come around to the same place every time. In addition, the priests said that the Egyptians were the first to regularly call the gods by twelve names, and that the Greeks adopted this practice from them. Furthermore, they were the first to assign altars and statues and temples to the gods, and to chisel pictures into stone. They outright proved to me that most of these things were so, but they merely asserted that the first human to rule Egypt was called Min.

In his time, they said, all of Egypt except for the province of Thebes was a marsh, and none of what is there now existed below Lake Moeris, to which it is a seven-day sail up the river from the sea. It seemed to me that what the priests said about this land was true. For it is as plain as plain can be even to someone who has not heard about it in advance but just seen it—to someone, that is, who has any brains—that the Egypt into which the Greeks navigate is recent landfill for the Egyptians, a gift from the river. It is also true that the region above this lake, to a distance of three days' sail, is land of the same kind, although the priests did not say anything about this. For this is the nature of the land of Egypt: when you first sail toward it, if you let down a sounding line when you are still a day's run from shore, you will draw up mud even if you are in eleven fathoms of water. This shows that there is silt from the land even this far out.

The length of Egypt itself along the coast is sixty reels of string, in keeping with our demarcation of Egypt from the Plinthine Gulf to Lake Serbonis, along which stretches Mount Casius: the sixty reels extend between these two points. Men who are poor in land measure their tracts in yards; those who are less poor, in furlongs; those who have a great deal, in miles; and those who have a boundless quantity, in reels of string. A mile is eight furlongs, and the reel—a measurement peculiar to Egypt—equals sixty furlongs. Thus Egypt would run thirty-six hundred furlongs along the coast.

From here to as far as Heliopolis in the interior, Egypt is wide, and all muddy, flat, and wet. The distance up to Heliopolis from the sea is about the same as the length of the road out of Athens from the altar of the Twelve Gods to Pisa and the temple of Olympian Zeus. Someone computing the difference between these two roads would find it slight: they fall short of being equal by not more than fifteen furlongs, for the road from Athens to Pisa falls fifteen furlongs short of fifteen hundred, while the road to Heliopolis from the sea is fully that number.

When you travel up from Heliopolis, you will find Egypt to be narrow. The Arabian mountains extend along one side, bearing from the north to the zenith and the south, and stretching ever upward to the so-called Red Sea. The quarries which were cut to make the pyramids in Memphis are in these mountains. At this point, the mountains leave off, turning away toward the places I have mentioned. As I found out, it takes two months of traveling from east to west to cross the mountain range at its broadest point. At the eastern verge, the land yields frankincense.

That is what those mountains are like, while on the Libyan side of Egypt, where the pyramids are, there stretches another rocky mountain range, covered with sand and carved out in the same way as the one which bears south on the Arabian side. Now, by Egyptian standards there isn't really very much territory beyond Heliopolis, just a four-day sail up a narrow stretch of land. Between these mountains, the land is flat, and at its narrowest it seemed not much more than two hundred furlongs from the Arabian to the so-called Libyan Mountains. From there on, Egypt is wide again.

This, then, is the nature of the land.

It is a nine-day sail from Heliopolis to Thebes over a distance of four thousand eight hundred and sixty furlongs, or eighty-one reels. Added together, this is the total number of furlongs in Egypt: I have already shown that there are three thousand six hundred furlongs along the coast. I will now tell you the distance from the sea into the interior as far as Thebes: it is six thousand one hundred and twenty furlongs. From Thebes to the so-called Elephant City[2] it is one thousand eight hundred furlongs.

According to the priests, most of the above-mentioned land was landfill, and I think so too. The land between those mountains above Memphis seemed to me to have been a gulf of the sea at one time, like the land around Ilium, Teuthrania, Ephesus, and the plain of the Maeander—to compare small things with great. For when it comes to size, not one of the rivers that built up these lands is worthy of comparison to a single mouth of the Nile—which has five mouths! There are other rivers—though not of the Nile's magnitude—which have performed great works. I could give the names of several, and not least of the Achelous, which, flowing through Acarnania, issues into the sea and has already made half of the Echinades Islands into mainland.

Not far from Egypt, a gulf of the so-called Red Sea penetrates into Arabian territory, and I will now describe how long and narrow it is. As to length, beginning at its innermost point and rowing to the open sea, the voyage takes forty days; while as to width, it is a half day's journey at the gulf's widest point. The tide ebbs and flows in it every day. I believe that Egypt was once a gulf just like this, on one side entering from the North Sea into Ethiopia, and on the other, bearing from the south into Syria, and almost boring their way through to each other at their innermost reaches, leaving only a little bit of land between them. Now, if the Nile ever chose to divert its flow into this Arabian Gulf, what would

2. Elephant City, often referred to as Elephantine, was a military and commercial center located on an island below the first cataract of the Nile.

prevent it, considering its flow, from filling the gulf with silt in twenty thousand years? Really, I myself believe that it could fill it up in ten thousand. In all the time, therefore, which went by before I was born, why couldn't a far greater gulf even than this one have been filled in by such a mighty and active river?

Now, I believe these statements about Egypt and those who make them, and I myself am firmly convinced that they are so, because I have seen Egypt projecting from the surrounding terrain, and shells appearing on mountains capped with brine—which even corrodes the pyramids— while the only sandy mountain in Egypt is the one beyond Memphis. In addition, Egypt is not even remotely like neighboring Arabia or Libya or even Syria (the Syrians inhabit the area of Arabia along the sea), but instead has black and crumbly land—as it would have if it were mud and silt carried down from Ethiopia by the river. We know that Libyan soil is redder and sandier, while Arabia and Syria are more clayey and rocky.

The priests gave me this important piece of evidence about the country: in the reign of King Moeris, whenever the river rose to at least twelve feet, it watered Egypt below Memphis. And Moeris had not even been dead for nine hundred years when I heard this from the priests! But nowadays, if the river does not rise at least twenty-three or twenty-four feet it will not overflow into the country. It seems to me that if this same region continues to increase in height like this without giving back a similar amount in extent, and if ever the Nile stops inundating it, those Egyptians below Lake Moeris who inhabit the rest of the country and the so-called Delta will forever suffer the same thing they once said the Greeks would suffer. You see, when they learned that it rains on all the land of the Greeks, and Greece is not watered by rivers like theirs, the Egyptians said that if the Greeks were ever disappointed in their great hope of rain they would starve miserably. What this meant was that if the god ever stopped raining on them and started bringing drought instead, the Greeks would be gripped by famine, because they really have no other recourse to water whatever except what they get from the god.

What the Egyptians say about Greece is quite true, but bear with me while I explain how it also applies to the Egyptians themselves.

If, as I said earlier, the land below Memphis (for this is the area that is growing) were to rise to a height proportional to its rate over past time, what else can the Egyptians who live there do but starve if the land never brings them rain and the river becomes unable to overflow onto the fields?

For the time being, though, the farmers of the Delta reap the fruits of the earth more easily than all the other Egyptians and indeed than all the rest of mankind, for they neither have the hard work of breaking furrows with plows or hoes, nor do they labor, toiling over their crops like other people; but when the river, rising on its own, waters their fields and, having watered, recedes again, then everyone seeds his own field and turns a pig loose on it, and when the seed is trampled in by the pig, the farmer just waits for the harvest and garners it after using the pig to thresh the grain!

Now, if we want to apply the theory of the Ionians, who argue that Egypt is only the Delta, and who say that it goes from the so-called Lookout of Perseus along the coast as far as the Pelusian pickling factories, a distance of forty reels, and that it stretches from the sea into the interior as far as Cercasoropolis, where the Nile splits and flows toward Pelusium and Canobus, and who say, furthermore, that the rest of Egypt is Libya on the one hand and Arabia on the other—what we would prove if we applied this argument is that the Egyptians did not originally have a country. For as the Egyptians say and as I believe, the Delta actually is alluvial and, so to speak, newly brought to light. If, however, they had no original country, why did they make such a big to-do about the idea that they were the first people to come into existence? They need not have conducted that experiment with the children, to see which language they uttered first. No, I think that the Egyptians did not appear along with what the Ionians call the Delta, but that they have been here since the human race came into existence, and that as the land spread forward many of them stayed behind, while many gradually fanned out along with it. In antiquity, by the way, Thebes used to be called Egypt, and measured six thousand one hundred and twenty furlongs around.

Now, if our opinion about the Egyptians is right, that of the Ionians is wrong. If, however, the opinion of the Ionians is right, I can prove that the Greeks and the Ionians themselves do not know how to compute—those, that is, who say that the whole world is divided into three parts: Europe, Asia, and Libya. For they must add the Egyptian Delta as a fourth part, since it belongs neither to Asia nor to Libya: after all, according to their argument, isn't it the Nile that separates Asia from Libya? Since the Nile breaks up at the apex of this Delta, though, and flows on either side of it, the Delta would have to be somewhere *between* Asia and Libya.

Let us bid farewell to the Ionian theory. We say something like this about these matters: Egypt is all of that which is inhabited by Egyptians, just as Cilicia is what is inhabited by Cilicians, and Assyria by Assyrians. Strictly speaking, we know no boundary between Asia and Libya except the boundaries of Egypt—while if we adopted the opinion of the Greeks, we would have to think that all of Egypt, beginning with the first cataract and Elephant City, is split in half and is named after both continents: this part after Libya, and that part after Asia, because the Nile, beginning at the cataracts, splits Egypt in half and flows to the sea. [3]

---

3. The boundaries of Egypt were extremely important to Herodotus, who wished to convey what was known about the world's geography, and particularly about the demarcations of the continents.

Herodotus was not only the West's first historian but also one of its first geographers, ethnographers, and naturalists.

Now, the Nile flows as one river as far as Cercasoropolis, but below this city it breaks up into three channels. One turns toward the dawn, and this mouth is called the Pelusian. The other holds toward the setting sun, and this mouth has been called the Canobicus. The Nile's straight course flows like this: bearing down from the land above, it arrives at the apex of the Delta, and from there, cutting through the middle of the Delta, it flows into the sea. It contributes not the least share of the river's waters, nor enjoys the least part of its fame. It is called the Sebennyticus. Two other branches break off from the Sebennyticus toward the sea, and their names are the Saitic and the Mendesian. The Bolbitine and the Bucolic are not natural mouths of the river but rather canals.

Evidence in support of my theory—that Egypt is what I have argued it to be—is an oracle from Ammon which I found out about after I had formed my own theory. People from the cities of Marea and Apis, who live on the border of Egypt with Libya, considered themselves to be Libyans and not Egyptians. Also, upset over rituals involved in sacrifices, and not consenting to be prohibited from eating cows, these people sent to Ammon saying that they had nothing in common with the Egyptians, since they lived outside the Delta, agreed with them about nothing, and wanted to be allowed to eat anything they liked. The god did not permit them to do this, saying that Egypt was what the Nile watered and that Egyptians were those who lived below Elephant City and drank from the river. This was the answer the oracle gave them.

When the Nile is in flood, it overflows not only the Delta, but also the so-called Libyan and Arabian territories, in some places up to a two days' journey on both sides, in some places even more than this, and in some less. I was unable to find out about the nature of the river either from the priests or from anyone else. I was especially eager to learn this from them: why the Nile's flood comes down after the summer solstice for a period of about a hundred days and then begins to recede, abating its flow, so it stays shallow for the whole winter until the summer solstice comes again. Now, I was unable to find out about these things from any of the Egyptians when I asked them what it was about the Nile that made it behave the opposite of all other rivers. I made these inquiries because I really wanted to know about these matters, as well as about why it, alone of all rivers, does not blow with river breezes.

Some Greeks, however, wanting to get a reputation for learning, have delivered themselves of three separate opinions about this body of water. I don't consider two of these worth mentioning, but I do just want to show what they are. One of these opinions states that the annual winds are the reason why the river swells, since they prevent the Nile from flowing out into the sea. Frequently, though, the annual winds do not blow, while the Nile still behaves in the same way. Furthermore, if the annual winds were the cause, it would be necessary for other rivers which flow against these winds to undergo the same thing that happens to the Nile and, indeed, to the extent that they are lesser rivers, to produce an even weaker flow. But there are many rivers in Syria, and many in Libya, which do not undergo anything like what happens to the Nile.

The other opinion is even more unscientific than this one, though it is more exotic to relate, for it states that the Nile produces these effects after flowing from the Ocean, and that the Ocean flows around the whole world!

The third view is especially deceptive because it is by far the most plausible. For this one utters pure nonsense when it says that the Nile derives from melting snow, of all things—the Nile, which flows from Libya through the middle of Ethiopia and issues into Egypt. Now, how could it possibly flow from snow when it flows from the hottest of places and into a generally cooler climate? To anyone who is capable of reasoning about these matters—namely, how unlikely it is that the river flows from snow—the first and most important evidence is provided by the hot winds which blow from these lands. The second is that the country never has rain or frost, although it is absolutely necessary for it to rain within five days of a snowfall, so that if it snowed, it would also rain. Third, the people are black from the burning heat. Also, kites and swallows stay all year round and do not migrate, while cranes flee the cold weather of Scythia and flock to these regions for the winter. If, however, it snowed even the least little bit on this land through which the Nile flows and from which it springs, none of these things would be true, as necessity proves.

The explanation which adduces Ocean and refers the unknown to the realm of legend cannot be disproved. I do not know of any river named Ocean, though I believe that Homer or one of the earlier poets invented this name and brought it into poetry. [4]

If, however, it is necessary for one who finds fault with prevailing theories to make known his own theory about unknown things, I will explain why I think the Nile floods in the summer. During the winter season, the sun, driven out of its original orbit by winter storms, moves upland into Libya. Now, to explain things in the fewest words, this says it all: it is natural for whatever region this god is in or near to be especially parched, and for the streams of its local rivers to dry up.

To explain things at greater length, this is the formulation. As the sun traverses the interior of Libya, it produces the same results as it does in the summer, when it passes through the middle of the sky. Because the Libyan air is always clear throughout the entire country and because the land is open to the sun and without cold winds, the sun draws water up to itself and then displaces it inland, where the winds take hold of it and scatter its mists. It is only natural, therefore, that the south and southwest winds which blow from those regions are the rainiest of all. Now,

4. Homer imagined Ocean as a river encircling the earth to which all other rivers were tributary. Herodotus objects to this geographical conception on the grounds that there is no empirical evidence for it.

it seems to me that the sun does not disperse all the water it draws up from the Nile every year, but that it keeps some for its own nourishment. As the winter abates, the sun moves back to the middle of the sky, whereupon it evaporates the water equally from all the rivers. The other rivers flow mightily for as long as a lot of rainwater pours into them and the rain cuts rivulets into the land, but, during the summer, when they are abandoned by the rains and evaporated by the sun, the other rivers are weak. The Nile, though, is the only river on which it does not rain during the winter, and it naturally flows much more weakly than usual while its sources are being evaporated by the sun than during the summer, for *then* it is evaporated at a rate equal to that of all the other waters, while it alone is constricted in the winter. Thus I have concluded that the sun is the cause of these phenomena. According to my theory, the sun is also the reason why the air is dry in Ethiopia: since it burns its way through its own orbit, there is always summer inland from Libya. Now, if the positions of the seasons were changed in the sky, so that the south wind and the summer were where the north wind and the winter now are, and the north wind were where the south wind is—if this were the case, the sun, driven from the middle of the sky by the winter and the north wind, would move to the interior of Europe just as it now moves to the interior of Libya, and I expect that as it passed over all of Europe, it would affect the Ister in the same way that it now operates on the Nile.

Now, as to the river breezes—that they don't blow—I have this theory: it is extremely unlikely for any breeze to blow in hot countries. Breezes like to blow from cool spots. But let these things stay as they are and as they have been since the beginning of time.

As to the sources of the Nile, none of the Egyptians, Libyans, or Greeks who discussed it with me claimed to know what they were, except the scribe at the holy treasury of Athena in the Egyptian city of Sais— but I thought he was playing a joke on me when he said that he knew for sure. This is what he said: between Theban Syene and Elephant City, there are two mountains whose peaks come to a tip, and whose names are Crophi and Mophi. The springs of the Nile, which are unfathomable, flow from between these two mountains, and half of this water flows toward Egypt and the north wind, while the other half flows toward Ethiopia and the south. As to the springs' being fathomless, he said that Psammetichus, king of the Egyptians, had gone there to test it. Psammetichus plaited many thousands of fathoms of rope and let it down into the spring, but it did not reach the bottom. In my opinion, what this scribe showed, if he spoke the truth at all, was that there were powerful, back-flowing eddies in this place, so when the water was forced out into the mountains the sounding line could not descend to the bottom.

I was unable to learn anything from anyone else on this subject, but I learned about other things at the greatest length, as an eyewitness as far as Elephant City, and beyond this point by asking questions and listening carefully.

The land is steep as you go up past Elephant City. In this region, you have to tie each side of your boat as if it were an ox and pull it upstream. If the rope breaks, the boat is swept away by the strength of the current. It takes four days to sail through this region, and the Nile is as winding there as the Maeander. You must sail in this way for a distance of twelve reels, and after that you come to a smooth plain where the Nile flows around an island called Tachompso. Ethiopians begin to occupy the region above Elephant City, as well as half of the island, while Egyptians occupy the other half. Not far from the island is a great lake around which Ethiopian nomads live. You sail across it and return to the Nile's current, which flows into this lake. Then you have to disembark and make your way on foot along the river for forty days because sharp rocks stick out of the water and there are many submerged rocks as well, which it isn't possible to sail through. After passing through this country in forty days, you get back into another boat and sail for twelve days until you come to a large city named Meroe. This is said to be the capital city of all the Ethiopians. Here, the only gods they worship are Zeus and Dionysus, but they revere these two greatly and have established an oracle of Zeus. They make war whenever and wherever this god commands them to in his oracles.

Sailing from this city, you get to the Deserters in the same amount of time as it takes to get from Elephant City to the Ethiopian capital. These Deserters are called the Asmach, which in Greek means "those who stand to the left of the king." Two hundred and forty thousand Egyptian warriors deserted to the Ethiopians for the following reason. In the reign of King Psammetichus, security forces were stationed against the Ethiopians in Elephant City. There was another force in Pelusian Daphne against the Arabians and the Syrians, and yet another in Mare against the Libyans. (Even when I was there, Persian forces were on the same duty as the soldiers in the reign of Psammetichus, for the Persians are on guard in both Elephant City and Daphne.) No one relieved the Egyptians after three years of garrison duty. They had a meeting and by common consent deserted Psammetichus and crossed into Ethiopia. Psammetichus pursued them as soon as he found out about it. When he caught up with them, he implored them with many arguments and tried to persuade them not to abandon the gods of their forefathers and their women and children. It is said that one of the soldiers pointed to his penis and said that wherever *that* was, there would be plenty of women and children.

When the Deserters reached Ethiopia, they put themselves in the power of the Ethiopian king. He gave them this in return: there were some Ethiopians who had been differing with him. He commanded the Deserters to drive them out of their land and to live in it. Since these men settled in Ethiopia, the Ethiopians have learned Egyptian ways and become more civilized.

The Nile is known to exist for up to a four-month journey by land and water beyond the appearance of its current in Egypt. It will take you

that many months, traveling out of Elephant City, to get to the Deserters. There, the river flows from the west and the setting sun. No one
can give a clear account of what happens after this point, since the land
is desolate because of the burning heat. But I did hear this from some
Cyrenaean men who said they had gone to the oracle at Ammon and
had entered into a conversation with the Ammonian king, Etearchus.
They talked about things in general until they began to chat about the
Nile, and about how nobody knew its source, when Etearchus said that
he had once been visited by some Nasamonian men. They are a Libyan
people, and inhabit the Syrtis and a little bit of the Syrtis' more eastward
regions.

After the Nasamonians arrived, they were asked whether they had
anything to add to the general knowledge about the Libyan desert. They
said that their chiefs had once produced a generation of unusually ram-
bunctious sons who made all sorts of extravagant plans when they came
of age, in particular to select five of themselves by lot to explore the
Libyan desert to see whether they could find out anything more about
its farthest reaches than what was already known. Now, except for some
Greeks and Phoenicians, many Libyans and Libyan tribes are stretched
along the whole northern coast of Libya, from Egypt, where it begins,
to the Soloian promontory, where it ends. Inland, and beyond those
who are settled along the seacoast, Libya is infested with wild animals;
and beyond this animal-infested zone is a terribly dry, sandy desert, barren of any living thing. Now, after these youths, who were well supplied
with food and water, were sent forth by their friends, they traveled through
the inhabited country first. When they had crossed through this, they
came to the wild-animal zone and then crossed into the desert, making
their way toward the west wind. They covered a lot of sandy ground, but
after many days they saw some trees growing on a plain. They went over
to them to pick the fruit that was on them, but as they picked, some
little men—men, that is, who were smaller than normal—crept up on
them, captured them, and led them away. The Nasamonians did not
know who was leading them, and did not understand their language.
They led the Nasamonians through a hugh marsh, and when they had
crossed it, the Nasamonians arrived at a city in which everybody was the
same size as their captors. Their skin was black. A great river flowed
along the city. It flowed from the west toward the rising sun, and you
could see crocodiles in it.

Enough said about the story of Etearchus the Ammonian, except that,
according to the Cyrenaeans, he alleged that the Nasamonians returned
home, and that the men they had gone among were all wizards. He
concluded that this river—the one that flows along the city—must be
the Nile, and indeed the story proves as much. For the Nile flows out
of Libya and cuts Libya in half, and, as I conclude by bringing the
evidence of what is known to bear on what is not known, the Nile runs
the same distance as the Ister. The river Ister begins at the city of Pyrene,

in the land of the Celts, and flows through the middle of Europe. The Celts live outside the Pillars of Heracles, and border on the Cynesians, who live in that part of Europe where the sun sets at the end of the earth. After flowing through all of Europe, the Ister ends up in the Euxine Sea at Istria, a town inhabited by Milesian colonists. [5]

Now, the Ister flows through populated territory and is known by many people, whereas no one is able to say anything about the source of the Nile, since the part of Libya it flows through is barren and uninhabitable. I have said as much about its flow as I could ascertain after the most extensive inquiries. The river flows into Egypt, and Egypt lies more or less opposite the mountainous part of Cilicia. [6] From there to Sinope in the Euxine Sea is a five-day journey on a straight road for a man in good condition, and Sinope is opposite the point where the Ister flows into the sea. Thus, I believe that the Nile, where it traverses all of Libya, is equal in length to the Ister.

Enough said about the Nile.

I go on at such length in this section on Egypt because it offers the most wonders of any place in the whole world and because there are impressive human works throughout the land which are greater than words can say. For these reasons, I will say still more about it.

The Egyptians, along with having their own peculiar climate and a river with a nature different from all other rivers, have established many habits and customs which are almost the complete opposite of the rest of mankind. For example, the women go to market and keep shop, while the men stay home and weave. Meanwhile, others push the woof upward when they weave, but the Egyptians pull it down. It is the men who carry burdens on their heads, while the women carry them on their shoulders. Women urinate standing up; men do it squatting down. They relieve themselves in their own homes, but they eat out in the street. The logic behind this is that one must perform shameful necessities secretly and those that are not shameful openly. There are no priestesses whatever, for either male or female gods; only male priests for gods of both sexes. Sons never have to take care of their parents if they don't want to, but daughters must, whether they like it or not. In other places, the priests of the gods wear their hair long, but in Egypt they shave their heads. Among other people, it is the custom for those most touched by grief to shave their heads, but the Egyptians honor the dead by letting the hair on their heads and their faces grow. The rest of the time, they shave it all off. Other people live apart from their animals, but Egyptians live among their animals. Others live on wheat and barley, while it is

5. The Ister is the present-day Danube. Pyrene was a town at the foot of what are now called the Pyrenees. The Pillars of Heracles are otherwise known as the Straits of Gibraltar. Istria was in what is now western Romania.

6. The eastern half of the southern coast of Asia Minor.

the greatest disgrace for an Egyptian to make his food from these things—instead, they make bread with horse fodder, a grain some call zeia. They knead flour with their feet, but they pick up mud and dung with their hands. Other people (except those who learned from the Egyptians) leave their genitals in their natural state; the Egyptians practice circumcision. Every man has two garments, but every woman only one. Others tie the ringbolts and reefing ropes to the outside of the ship, but the Egyptians tie them inboard. Greeks write and work the abacus by moving their hands from left to right, the Egyptians from right to left; but they call that writing forward, while the Greeks call it writing backward. They use two scripts, one called sacred and the other popular.

As the most exceedingly devout people in the world, the Egyptians practice such rituals as these: they drink from bronze cups and wipe them clean every day—not just some people but *everybody*. They make a special point of always wearing freshly washed linen clothing. They circumcise the penis for the sake of purity, and so esteem purity more than beauty. Priests shave their entire body every other day so that neither lice nor any other abomination will ever be on them when they are worshiping the gods. The priests wear clothes made only of linen, and sandals made of papyrus. It is not permitted for them to wear any other kind of clothing or sandals. They wash in cold water twice a day and twice a night.

While the priests perform what seem like thousands on thousands of rituals, they also enjoy many benefits. They do not have to deplete their property or spend their money. Sacred bread is baked for them, and each gets an abundance of beef and goose every day. They are also given grape wine. They are not, however, allowed to eat fish. Egyptians do not plant beans on their land, and they neither cook the ones that grow wild nor eat them raw. Priests cannot even stand the sight of them, and think that legumes make them impure. There is not just one priest for each of the gods but many. Of these, one is an arch-priest, and when he dies, his son takes his place.

They believe bulls are sacred to Epaphus, and for this reason they subject them to such intense scrutiny that if they see so much as a single black hair growing on one of them, they do not consider it to be pure. A priest specially appointed for this purpose searches the animal both when it is standing up and when turned on its back, and even pulls out its tongue to see whether it is free of those recognized marks of the Apis which I will relate in another narrative. [7] Moreover, he inspects the hairs of the tail to see whether they are normal. If the bull is pure in all of these respects, the priest certifies it by wrapping papyrus around its horns and plastering it on with a sealing clay. He stamps this with his signet

7. Herodotus keeps this promise in a section of book 3 not included in this text. The Apis was a sacred bull worshiped in Egypt.

ring, and they lead the bull away. The penalty for sacrificing an uncertified bull is death.

That, then, is the method of examining the animal; here is the method of sacrificing it: they lead the certified bull to the altar where it will be sacrificed and start a fire. Then they pour wine on the victim and cut its throat as they invoke the god. After cutting its throat, they cut off its head. Next they skin the carcass of the animal and carry the head away as they revile it with curses. In those places where there is a market and resident Greek traders, they carry it into the market and sell it. Where there are no Greeks, they throw the head into the river. They lay these curses on the head so that if any evil is in store either for those who are doing the sacrifice or for Egypt in general, the evil may be turned onto the head instead. The Egyptians practice the rituals involving the head of the sacrificed cattle and the pouring of the wine in exactly the same way no matter what kind of animal is to be sacrificed, and as a result no Egyptian will ever eat the head of any living thing. The way the animal is disemboweled and burned, however, is different with each kind of victim.

I will now talk about which goddess they consider to be the greatest and about the religious festival they observe in her name. They skin the bull and then they say a prayer and pull out all of its intestines, although they leave the lard and the internal organs in the body. They cut off the legs, the rump, the shoulders, and the neck. When this is done, they stuff what is left of the bull's body with purified loaves of bread, honey, raisins, figs, myrrh, frankincense, and other spices. When they have stuffed it with these ingredients, they roast it, basting it with huge amounts of olive oil. They fast before they perform this sacrifice, and while the victims are roasting, they beat themselves with their hands. When they have finished beating themselves, they set out a banquet of what is left of the sacrifice.

All Egyptians sacrifice ritually clean bulls and calves, but it is forbidden to sacrifice cows since they are under the protection of Isis. The statue of Isis is of a woman with the horns of a cow—like the Greek depictions of Io—and all Egyptians alike revere cows far and away more than all other cattle. For this reason, no Egyptian man or woman will ever kiss a Greek man on the mouth, or use a Greek's knife or fork or kettle. They will not even eat a piece of ritually clean beef which has been cut up with a Greek knife.

This is how they bury dead cattle: they throw the cows into the river, but each city buries the bulls on the outskirts of town, leaving either one or both horns sticking out of the ground as a marker. When the body has rotted away, a barge following its appointed rounds comes to each city from the so-called Prosopitis Island. This island is in the Delta, and it has a circumference of nine reels. There are various cities on Prosopitis Island, but the one from which the barges set out to collect the bones of the bulls is called Atarbechis. A temple sacred to Aphrodite has

been built there. Many people from this city travel around to other cities, and all of them dig up the bones and bury them in one spot. They
bury other dead cattle in the same way as the bulls. These customs have
been laid down among them concerning these other animals, because
the Egyptians do not kill them either.

All those who build temples to Theban Zeus or who come from the
province of Thebes sacrifice goats but refrain from sacrificing sheep.
(You see, Egyptians do not all worship the same gods, except for Isis and
Osiris, who they say is Dionysus. They *all* worship these two.) Those
who have a temple to Mendes, or who come from the province of Mendes,
abstain from goats but sacrifice sheep. Now, the Thebans and those who
abstain from sheep because of the Theban influence say that this rite
was established among them in this way: Heracles wanted very much to
see Zeus, who did not wish to be seen by him. In the end, since Heracles
kept imploring him, Zeus came up with a solution. He skinned a ram
and cut off its head and, getting into the ram's skin and holding its head
in front of him, showed himself to Heracles. Because of this, the Egyptians make their statutes of Zeus with a ram's face, and the Ammonians
follow them in this since they are colonists of the Egyptians and the
Ethiopians and speak a language which is a blend of the two. Now, in
my opinion, the Ammonians have named themselves after this god. The
Egyptians, you see, call Zeus Ammon. For this reason, the Thebans do
not sacrifice rams, which are sacred to them. One day every year, however, during the feast of Zeus, they skin a ram and cut it in pieces and
dress the statue of Zeus just as Zeus had dressed himself, and then carry
a statue of Heracles toward it. After they have done this, everyone around
the temple beats himself in grief for the ram, which they then bury in a
sacred coffin.

I heard the thesis that Heracles was one of the Twelve Gods. I never
heard of the other Heracles, the one the Greeks know, anywhere in
Egypt. Indeed, I have a great deal of evidence that the Egyptians did not
borrow the name from the Greeks, but that the Greeks got it instead
from the Egyptians, and that whoever gave the name Heracles to the
son of Amphitryon got it in turn from the Greeks. For example, both of
Heracles' parents—Amphitryon and Alcmene—were of Egyptian descent,
while the Egyptians say that they do not so much as know the names of
Poseidon and the Dioscuri, and that these gods are not accepted in their
pantheon. Furthermore, if they had indeed ever taken the name of any
god from the Greeks, they would remember these most, and not least,
of all—if, as I rather suspect is the case, they ever went to sea in those
days and there ever was a Greek seaman. So that the Egyptians would
know the names of these gods by heart, and not that of Heracles.

And yet, Heracles is one of their ancient gods, for as they say, it has
been seventeen thousand years since the reign of Amasis, when the Twelve
Gods, of whom they believe Heracles to be one, were generated by the

original Eight Gods. Now, since I was eager to get a clear understanding of these matters from the people who know them best, I even sailed as far as Phoenician Tyre when I learned that it had a temple sacred to Heracles. I saw it. It was very richly bedecked with a great many offerings, and especially with two pillars—one of refined gold and the other of an emerald so large that it shone luminously in the night. I had a conversation with the priests of the god and asked how long it had been since the temple was built. I found out that even they did not agree with the Greeks, for they said that the temple had been built at the very same time as the founding of Tyre itself, and that it had been twenty-three hundred years since then.

I saw in Tyre yet another temple to Heracles, this one called the Thasian Heracles. So I also went to Thasos, where I found a temple to Heracles built by Phoenicians who founded Thasos after setting sail in search of Europa—as much as five generations of men before Heracles, the son of Amphitryon, appeared in Greece! My research clearly shows, then, that Heracles is an ancient god. Thus the most orthodox Greeks seem to me to be those who have set up shrines to two separate Heracles, sacrificing to one in the manner appropriate to an immortal Olympian, and to the other as befits a mortal hero.

The Greeks say a great many things that do not stand up to scrutiny. One of the most foolish of these is the tale they tell about how the Egyptians crowned Heracles when he came to Egypt and led him out in a procession to sacrifice him to Zeus. He went along quietly at first, they say, but when the Egyptians led him to the altar, he summoned his great strength and killed them all. It seems to me that the Greeks who say this have no experience whatever of the character and customs of the Egyptians. People for whom it is a sacrilege to sacrifice any cattle except such sheep and bulls and calves as are ritually pure—oh yes, and geese—how could such people ever sacrifice humans? Besides, being but one person, and that a mortal man, as the Greeks insist, how could Heracles have the strength to kill tens of thousands of people?

May the gods and heroes show us their favor, though we say such things about them!

This is the reason the Egyptians I have mentioned eat neither male nor female goats: the Mendesians count Pan among the Eight Gods, and they say that these Eight Gods existed before the Twelve Gods. Painters and sculptors draw and carve the images of Pan as the Greeks do, with the face and legs of a goat, not that they think he is really like that. They think he is like the rest of the gods, but I do not care to say why they draw him in this way. The Mendesians revere all goats, though males much more than females, and among Mendesians goatherds enjoy great esteem. The chief goatherd is especially honored, and when he dies there is a period of great mourning throughout the Mendesian province. In Egyptian, the word for both "goat" and "Pan" is "Mendes."

Something monstrous happened in my presence in this district, though—
a woman openly had sex with a billy goat. It showed me something
about humanity.

The Egyptians consider pigs to be unclean animals, so much so that
if someone merely touches a pig in passing, he immerses himself in the
river, clothes and all. Furthermore, although swineherds are full-blooded
Egyptians, they alone, of all the people in Egypt, are not allowed into
any temple. No one will give his daughter to, or marry the daughter of,
a swineherd. Instead, swineherds intermarry among themselves. The
Egyptians do not think it is right to sacrifice pigs to any of the other gods,
but solely to Dionysus and the moon, and to both at the same time—
the time of the full moon. Then those who sacrifice the pigs eat their
meat. The Egyptians tell a story about why they abominate pork at other
feasts but eat it at this one, and although I know what it is, it is not
appropriate for me to talk about it. [8]

This is how they sacrifice pigs to the moon. They take the tail, together
with the spleen and the peritoneum, wrap it up in the fat around the
stomach, and burn it in the fire. They eat the rest of the meat on the
very night of the full moon on which they sacrifice the victims—they
would not eat it on any other day. For lack of money, the poor mold
flour into the shape of a pig, which they then bake and sacrifice.

On the eve of the feast of Dionysus, everybody slaughters a piglet in
his front doorway and gives it back to the swineherd he bought it from.
The Egyptians conduct the rest of the feast of Dionysus in almost the
same way as the Greeks, except for the dances. Also, instead of a phal-
lus, women carry around an eighteen-inch, string-operated puppet from
village to village, and make its penis—which is not much smaller than
the rest of its body—bob up and down. A flutist leads the procession,
and the women follow singing the praises of Dionysus. There is a sacred
story which explains why the puppet has such a large penis and why it
is the only part of the body which moves.

It seems to me, in any event, that Melampus, the son of Amythaon,
was not ignorant of this sacrifice but had some experience of it. For
Melampus was the one who introduced to the Greeks the name, sacrifice, and phallic procession of Dionysus. His exegesis of the myth did
not infallibly bring all of its elements together, although other divines
who followed him made it more clear. Nevertheless, Melampus is the
one who instituted the phallic procession to Dionysus, and having learned
it from him, the Greeks now do . . . what they do. In fact, I now declare
that Melampus was a clever fellow who acquired some techniques of
prophecy and that, having learned a great many things from the Egyptians, including the Dionysian rites, he introduced them to the Greeks

8. Here as elsewhere in this book (see, for example, chapter 65), Herodotus is reluctant to discuss the reasons for religious practices. His hesitance may derive from religious piety, or perhaps from prom-ises made to his informants (particularly to Egyptian priests) to keep some of what they told him confidential.

with few changes. For I absolutely deny any mere coincidence between the rites for this god in Egypt and those among the Greeks. If that were the case, they would be indigenous to the Greeks and not recently introduced. I further deny that the Egyptians ever adopted this or any other ritual from the Greeks. In my opinion, rather, Melampus learned the Dionysian ritual from Cadmus of Tyre and from those who came along with him from Phoenicia into what is now called Boeotia.

Furthermore, practically all the names of the gods came into Greece from Egypt. I have made inquiries and found that they came from barbarian lands, but I believe that they come from Egypt above all. Except, of course, for Poseidon and the Dioscuri, as I said before, as well as Hera, Hestia, Themis, the Graces, and the Nereids, the names of all the other gods have always existed in the land of Egypt. I say only what the Egyptians say themselves. Those gods whose names the Egyptians deny knowing seem to me to have been named by the Pelasgians, except for Poseidon. The Greeks found out about this god from the Libyans. Except for the Libyans, who have always worshiped him, no one else has known the name of this god from the beginning. The Egyptians do not worship heroes at all.

As I will show, the Greeks have adopted these and other beliefs from the Egyptians. They did not, however, learn from the Egyptians how to make statues of Hermes with an erect penis. Instead, the Athenians were the first Greeks to borrow this practice from the Pelasgians, while everyone else got it from the Athenians. The Athenians already counted as Greeks when the Pelasgians came to live in their land, and as a result the Pelasgians also began to be considered Greek. Whoever has been initiated into the Cabirian secret rites, which the Samothracians practice and which they adopted from the Pelasgians—he knows what I am talking about. (You see, the Pelasgians, the ones who later went to live among the Athenians, first lived in Samothrace, where the Samothracians adopted their rites.) The Athenians, then, are the first Greeks to learn from the Pelasgians how to make statues of Hermes with an erect penis. The Pelasgians have a sacred explanation for this, which is revealed in the Samothracian mysteries.

At first, the Pelasgians called out to the gods in prayer while performing all their sacrifices, although, as I know from what I heard in Dodona, they prayed without giving any of the gods either a name or an epithet. They hadn't heard any yet. The Pelasgians called them "gods" because they put everything in order and owned all the pastureland—or for some such reason. After a very long time, they learned the names, newly arrived from Egypt, of all the gods except Dionysus, which they learned much later. They soon consulted the oracle in Dodona about the names. This particular oracle is considered to be the oldest of all the oracles in Greece and was, at that time, the only oracle. After the Pelasgians had consulted in Dodona about whether they should adopt names which had come over to them from barbarians, the oracle answered that they should.

From then on, the Pelasgians invoked the names of the gods when they sacrificed, and the Greeks later learned the names from them.

Where each of the gods came from, whether they have all always existed, what they look like—these things were unknown until only yesterday, so to speak, or the day before. In my opinion, the generation of Homer and Hesiod came four hundred years before mine and no more. They are the ones who created a theogony for the Greeks. They gave names to the gods, decided what their special skills were and what honors they should be given, and described their appearance. It seems to me that the poets said to predate these men really came later. (The Dodonian priestesses relate the first part of this subject, [9] while I take responsibility for what I say in the later material on Hesiod and Homer.)

Now, on the subject of oracles, the Egyptians have this story to tell about the one in Greece and the one in Libya. The priests of Theban Zeus said that two priestesses were abducted from Thebes by Phoenicians. [1] They learned that one of them was sold in Libya and that the other was sold to the Greeks. These were the women who first established oracles among these peoples, respectively. When I asked the priests how they could be so sure about what they were saying, they said that they had conducted a great search for these women, and that while they had been unable to find them, they had later discovered the facts which they related about them.

That's what I heard from the priests in Thebes. This, now, is what the prophetesses at Dodona say: two black pigeons flew out of Egyptian Thebes, and one went to Libya while the other came to them. Perching on an oak tree, she cried out in a human voice that there had to be an oracle of Zeus on that very spot. They surmised that this was a divine message to them, and they therefore built the oracle. Meanwhile, they say, the other pigeon went to Libya and commanded the Libyans to build an oracle of Ammon, which is the same as an oracle of Zeus. The Dodonian priestesses—the oldest was named Promeneia, the next Timarete, and the youngest Nicandra—all said this, and all the other Dodonians involved in the temple agreed with them.

I have the following theory about this subject. If the Phoenicians truly did take these holy women and sell one of them into Libya and the other into Greece, then it seems to me that the woman of what is now Greece (formerly called Pelasgia) was sold to the Thesprotians. There, in slavery, she set up a shrine of Zeus where an oak was growing since it was

9. Herodotus presumably refers here to the mythical poets Musaeus, Orpheus, and Linus. Some myths claimed that Apollo was Linus' father; others, that he was taught by Heracles. Musaeus was said to have taught cures for diseases and pronounced oracles. Orpheus the Thracian is still known today for his unsuccessful attempt to bring back his wife, Eurydice, from the dead, and he

became the object of the classical cult of Orphism, which taught abstention from animal flesh and other rituals of purification in preparation for the rebirth of the soul.
1. The priestesses to whom Herodotus refers are the Dodonian priestesses mentioned in the previous paragraph. The oracle of Dodona was located in Epirus, in northern Greece.

natural for one who had been a servant at the temple of Zeus in Thebes to have a memorial to him wherever she went. She introduced the oracle later, after she had learned Greek. She also said that her sister had been sold into Libya by the same Phoenicians by whom she had been sold. It seems to me that the women were called pigeons by the Dodonians because they were barbarians and seemed to the Dodonians to chirp like birds. They say that the pigeon cried out in human language after a while—when, that is, she spoke to them intelligibly. For so long as she spoke her barbarian language, however, she seemed only to chirp like a bird, since how on earth could a pigeon ever speak in a human voice? They show that the woman was an Egyptian when they say that the pigeon was black. In addition, the methods of divination in Egyptian Thebes and in Dodona are very similar to each other, and therefore the practice of divining from victims is also an Egyptian import.

Now, the Egyptians were the first people to create religious gatherings, parades, and processions, and the Greeks learned these from them too. My evidence for this view is that their ceremonies appear to have been developed over a long period of time, whereas the Greek versions are newly formed.

The Egyptians have religious gatherings not just once a year but frequently, especially and most enthusiastically in the city of Bubastis in honor of Artemis. Their second-favorite city is Busiris, where they go to honor Isis. The greatest temple of Isis is in this city, which is built in the middle of the Egyptian Delta. In the Greek language, Isis is Demeter. Third, they gather in Sais for Athena; fourth, in Heliopolis for the sun; fifth, in the city of Buto for Leto; and sixth, in Papremis to honor Ares. [2]

This is what they do when they travel to Bubastis: men actually travel together with women, and large numbers of both travel in each boat. Some of the women have rattles, which they shake, while some men play the flute during the whole voyage. The rest of the men and women sing and clap their hands. Whenever they sail near any other city, they bring their barge close to shore and do this: some of the women do as I have just said, while others jeer and shout at the women in that city; some dance, while still others stand up and hoist their skirts. They do these things along the riverfront of every city. When they arrive at Bubastis, they celebrate huge sacrifices and have a feast. They drink more grape wine during this feast than in all the rest of the year. Any man or woman (but not children) can make this pilgrimage, and according to the locals, up to seven hundred thousand do so.

That is what is done there. (I have already said how they conduct the feast of Isis in Busiris.) All the men and women, tens of thousands of people, beat themselves after the feast, although it would be sacrilegious

---

2. All the towns Herodotus mentions were in the region of the Nile Delta. It is not always clear to whom the Greek gods Herodotus mentions correspond in Egyptian theology.

of me to say how they do it. Now, the Carians who live in Egypt go so far in this that they even cut their foreheads with a knife, and in doing so they make it plain that they are foreigners and not Egyptians.

At Sais, on the night when they are gathered together for the sacrifice, they all leave many lamps burning outdoors in a circle around their houses. The lamp is a saucer full of salt and oil. The wick itself is on top, and it burns all night long. The name of this feast is the Lamp Burning. The Egyptians who do not go to this gathering all observe the night of the feast by lighting the lamps, and so it is not only in Sais that they burn but throughout all Egypt. There is a sacred story to explain why this night was chosen to be honored with light.

In Heliopolis and Buto people gather only to perform sacrifices. In Papremis they perform sacrifices and rites as in other places, except that when the sun is on its way down, a few of the priests are busy with the statue,[3] while most of them stand at the entrance to the temple holding wooden clubs. In accordance with a vow they have taken, others—more than a thousand men also holding clubs—take up a position opposite them. (Now, on the day before this event, the priests move the statue in its shrine of gold-plated wood from its usual sacred chamber to another one.) The few priests who have been left with the statue start pulling a four-wheeled wagon carrying the shrine and the statue inside it. Those who are standing at the entrance do not allow the wagon to enter, while those who are bound by their vow come to the defense of the god and attack the resisters. Then a furious fight with clubs begins, skulls are fractured, and, as I believe, many die of their wounds. The Egyptians, however, deny that anyone is ever killed. The natives say that this gathering has become a custom for this reason: the mother of Ares used to live in this temple, and Ares, who had been reared away from home, returned as a grown man with the desire to have sexual intercourse with his mother. His mother's attendants, who had never seen him before, would not allow him to enter and kept him out. Then he brought in some men from another city, brutally beat up the attendants, and raped his mother. That is why this customary battle is conducted on the feast of Ares.

The Egyptians are also the first to observe the rule that one should not have sex with a woman in temple precincts or participate in rituals after having come unwashed from a woman. Almost all other people, except the Egyptians and the Greeks, have sex in temples, or get right up off a woman and go into the temple without washing, since they think that people are just like other animals. "After all, we see all the animals and all the species of birds copulating in the temples and sacred precincts of the gods. If this were not to the god's liking, the animals would not do it." This is how they explain what they do, but such argu-

3. In chapter 59 Herodotus indicates that this was a statue of "Ares," the Greek god of war, although it is not clear to which Egyptian god Herodotus' Ares corresponds.

ments are unacceptable to me. Anyway, the Egyptians scrupulously observe all the regulations concerning the temple, and this one in particular.

Although Egypt borders on Libya, it is not especially infested with wild animals, but they consider all those that are there to be sacred, both those that are domesticated and those that are not. If I were to give the reasons why they are consecrated, though, I would bring the discussion around to the subject of divine matters, which I especially want to avoid talking about. Whatever I have said in touching on that subject, I have said because I absolutely had to.

These, though, are their customs when it comes to animals. Both male and female Egyptians are appointed as keepers to care for each different kind of animal, and the office is handed down from parent to child. In each city every person performs these vows: before praying to the god to whom the animal is dedicated, they shave either all, or a half, or a third of the heads of their children, and then they take the weight of the hair in silver. They give whatever it weighs in silver to the woman who tends the animals. She uses it to buy fish, which she cuts up and gives to the animals for food. That is the kind of food they eat. If someone willfully kills one of these animals, the penalty is death; if he does it unwillingly, he pays whatever penalty the priests impose. If someone kills an ibis or a hawk, whether willfully or not, he must die.

A great many animals live with people, and there would be even more if the following did not happen to the cats. After the females litter, they do not have anything to do with the males, who seek unsuccessfully to mate with them. To achieve this aim, the males come up with the practice of snatching the kittens from the females, stealing them away, and killing them. Although they kill them, however, they do not eat them. Thus the females, bereft of their kittens and yearning for more, return to the males, for this animal loves her offspring. When a fire breaks out, something strange happens to the cats. The Egyptians, uninterested in putting out the fire, form a chain and keep a lookout for cats. The cats, though, dodge between and jump over the people and leap into the fire. The Egyptians feel great sorrow whenever this happens. In any home where a cat dies a natural death, all the residents shave off their eyebrows only, but where a dog dies, they shave the whole body including the head. They carry the dead cats away to sacred buildings in Bubastis, where they are embalmed and buried; but they bury bitches in their own city in a sacred coffin. The mongoose is buried in the same way as the dog. They carry the shrews and the hawks to Buto and the ibises to Hermopolis. Bears being scarce, and wolves being not much bigger than foxes, these animals are buried wherever they are found lying.

This is what the crocodile is like: during the four wintriest months, it eats nothing. It is four-footed and lives on the land and in the water, for it lays and hatches its eggs in the earth, and spends most of the day on dry land, but all night in the river. This is because the water is actually warmer than the air or the dew. Of all the animals we know, this one grows from the smallest to the largest size, for it lays eggs not much bigger than goose eggs, and the newborn is proportional to the size of the egg—but it grows to a length of twenty-six feet and even longer. It has the eyes of a pig, and huge teeth as well as tusks, though it is the only animal which does not grow a tongue. Also, it does not move its lower jaw, but, again alone among animals, it brings its upper jaw down on top of the lower. It has powerful claws, and scaly, unpierceable skin on its back. It cannot see in the water, but in the open air it is the most sharp-sighted of all. Because the crocodile spends so much time in the water, the inside of its mouth is entirely filled with leeches. While the other birds and beasts flee the crocodile, though, the plover is on friendly terms with it, since it benefits from the bird. Whenever the crocodile comes out of the water onto the land and then keeps its mouth open— as it usually does turned toward the west wind—why then the plover goes into its mouth and gobbles down the leeches. The crocodile enjoys and benefits from this service and does nothing to harm the plover.

The crocodiles are sacred to some of the Egyptians, but not to others, who treat them like downright enemies. Those who live around Thebes and Lake Moeris consider them to be very sacred indeed. Each of these places raises one crocodile out of all the rest. They tame it and put pendants of gold and rhinestones in its ears and ankle bracelets on its front legs. They feed it special food and sacrificial offerings and treat it extremely well while it is alive. When it dies, they embalm it and bury it in a sacred coffin. Those who live around Elephant City, however, do not consider crocodiles to be sacred, and even eat them.

In Egypt, by the way, they are called not crocodiles but champsae. It was the Ionians who named them crocodiles, comparing their shapes to the crocodiles, or lizards, on their walls.

There are all kinds of ways of catching them. I will write about the one that seems to me most worth describing. After the crocodile hunter has baited a hook with the back of a pig, he casts it into the middle of the river. Then he begins to beat a suckling pig he is holding at the bank of the river. After hearing the squealing, the crocodile rushes toward it. When it comes upon the bait, it swallows it down, and then it is hauled in. After it has been pulled onto the land, the first thing the hunter does is to smear the crocodile's eyes with mud. After he does this, he can handle the animal very easily from then on, but only with great difficulty if he doesn't.

Hippopotamuses are sacred in the Papremitian district, but not in the rest of Egypt. This is what they look like: they are four-footed, and cloven-footed, with hoofs like those of an ox; they are snub-nosed, have a horse's mane, prominent tusks, and the tail and neigh of a horse. They are about the size of the largest ox. Their skin is so thick that when it is dry a spear shaft can be made out of it.

There are also otters in the river, and the Egyptians hold these sacred too. Of the fish, they believe that the so-called scaly carp and the eel are sacred, and of the birds, the Egyptian fox goose. These, they say, are the animals sacred to the Nile.

There is yet another sacred bird, called the phoenix. I have not seen him, except in pictures, for he appears at rare intervals indeed—according to the Heliopolitans, every five hundred years. They say that he comes whenever his father dies. He looks more or less like this, if, that is, he resembles the pictures: some of the plumage on his wings is golden and some red. In shape and size, he most closely resembles the eagle. This is what they say he does, though what they say doesn't seem very believable to me. The phoenix sets off from Arabia for the temple of the Sun carrying his father, whom he has stuffed in myrrh, and buries him in the temple. He carries him like this. First he forms an egg out of myrrh, making it heavy as he can possibly bear. Then he tries it out and carries it. After this test flight, the bird hollows out the egg and puts his father inside, stuffing with yet more myrrh the hollowed-out area into which he has placed his father, so that it has the same weight with his father lying stuffed inside as it did before. Then he carries him into Egypt and the temple of the Sun. That is what this bird does, or so they say.

There are some sacred snakes around Thebes which are not at all harmful to people. They are small, have two horns growing out of the tops of their heads, and are buried in the temple of Zeus when they die, for they are said to be sacred to this god.

There is a place in Arabia located in the vicinity of Buto, [4] and I went there to find out about the winged snakes. When I arrived, I saw snake bones and spines in quantities impossible to describe, but there were large, medium, and smaller heaps of spines and lots of them. This place, in which the spines are piled, is like this: there is a pass through dense mountains into a great plain, and this plain joins with the Egyptian plain. The story goes that winged snakes fly out of Arabia and into Egypt in the spring, and that ibises oppose the snakes at the pass into this place and do not let them through but kill them instead. The Arabians say that the ibis is greatly honored by the Egyptians for this deed, and the Egyptians agree that this is why they honor these birds.

This is what the ibis looks like: it is deep black all over, and has the legs of a crane. Its beak is extremely hooked, and it is about the size of a corncrake. This is the appearance of the black ibises that do battle with the snakes. Those that cluster around people's legs instead (for there are two kinds of ibis) look like this: the head smooth, along with the whole neck; the plumage white, except for the head, the neck, the wing tips,

4. This is not the same Buto mentioned in chapter 59. It is not clear what place Herodotus has in mind.

and the tail (for these, as I said, are extremely black). Its legs and beak are like those of the other ibis. As to the snake, its shape is like the water snake's. Its wings are not feathered, though, but more or less resemble those of a bat.

So much for the subject of sacred animals.

The Egyptians who live in Egypt's farmland have the most practiced memories of any people in the world, and have more tales to tell by far than anyone else I have ever questioned. This is their way of life: they drink radish juice and salt for three consecutive days every month to make themselves throw up. They pursue health through emetics and enemas, since they believe that all the diseases of mankind are caused by what they eat. After the Libyans, the Egyptians are the healthiest of people even without this regimen—in my opinion because of the climate and the fact that the seasons do not change. For diseases especially afflict people at times of change, and above all during changes of season. They eat bread—which they call cyllestis—and make it out of a horse fodder or spelt. They drink a wine made from barley, for there are no grapevines in the country. They eat their fish raw, some after drying it in the sun and some after it has been preserved in salt. Of the birds, they eat quails, ducks, and the smaller fowl raw, also after preserving it. Whatever other fish or birds they have, except what has been declared to be sacred, they eat either roasted or boiled.

After dinner at the parties of the wealthy Egyptians, a man carries around a coffin containing a wooden corpse. The corpse is an accurate model, in both its carving and its coloring, and is from eighteen inches to three feet long. He shows it to each of the guests and says, "Look at this, drink and be merry, for this is what you will be like in death." This is what they do at their drinking parties!

They observe their ancestral customs and do not adopt any others. They have a number of noteworthy pastimes, and one in particular— "The Song of Linus," a man who is sung about in Phoenicia, Cyprus, and elsewhere. He happens to be the same person whom the Greeks call Linus and sing about, although each people has its own name for him. So many things amaze me about things Egyptian, and one is where they got the Linus melody from. It is obvious that they have always sung this song, though in Egyptian, Linus is called Maneros. The Egyptians said that he was the only son of their first king and that when he died young, he was honored by them with this dirge, and that it was their first and only song.

The Egyptians happen to have this other custom in common only with the Lacedaemonians: when the young meet their elders, they turn aside and yield them the right of way; they also get up and give them their seats in deference. The Egyptians share this next custom, however, with none of the Greeks: instead of calling to each other in the road, they bow low to each other and bring their hand down to their knee.

They wear tasseled linen underwear, which they call calasiris, hanging down around their legs, and they wear white woolen cloaks thrown over this. They do not, however, wear wool into the temple, nor is it buried along with them. That is a sacrilege. This custom agrees with the so-called Orphic and Bacchic rituals, which are really Egyptian and Pythagorean, since it is also a sacrilege for a communicant in these rites to be buried in woolen clothing. A sacrosanct story is told about these matters.

Another thing that the Egyptians have discovered is that there is a day and a month for each of the gods, along with what sort of person you will be like if you are born on a given day, and the kinds of things that you will meet with in life, and how you will end up. (Greek poets have made use of all this, by the way.) They have found out about more omens and portents than all the rest of mankind has. For when an omen occurs, they keep track of it and write down the outcome, and then, when something similar to it happens later on, they conclude that it will come out in the same way.

This is how prophecy is instituted among them: the skill is not conceded to any individual person but to various gods. There are oracles in the country to Heracles, Apollo, Athena, Artemis, Ares, Zeus, and to the oracle they hold in the highest esteem of all, that of Leto in Buto. The methods of divination are not all the same, however; on the contrary, they are all different from each other.

The practice of medicine is assigned in this way: each physician specializes in one illness and no more, so there are all kinds of doctors—for the eyes, for the head, for the teeth, for the stomach, and for the vague, unspecific malaise.

This is what their wakes and funerals are like: when a person of any importance in a household passes away, all the females in the household smear their heads and even their faces with mud, and then, leaving the corpse in the house, they, and all their relatives along with them, wander around the city beating themselves and pulling their clothes down to their belts to expose their breasts. Elsewhere, the men also beat themselves and pull down their clothes. After they have done this, they take the corpse to be embalmed.

People skilled in embalming are set up in business for this very purpose. After a corpse has been brought to them, they show the people who brought it some realistically painted wooden models of corpses. They tell them that the best of these is a model of one whose name it would be sacrilegious of me to use in this sort of context. Next they display a model cheaper and less finished than the first, and third, they show the least expensive of all. Having explained everything, the embalmers find out from the relatives how they would like the corpse to be prepared for them. Once the relatives agree on the price and get that out of the way, they depart.

Meanwhile, the embalmers remain in their shop and go about the most elaborate embalming job in the following way: first, using an iron corkscrew, they pull the brain out through the nostrils. They get out as much as they can in this way, and the rest they dissolve by pouring chemicals into the nose. Next, using a sharp Ethiopian stone, they make an incision along the flank, through which they draw out all of the intestines. They thoroughly clean out the cavity and flush it first with palm wine and then with a solution of ground herbs and fragrant spices. Then they fill the abdomen with ground virgin myrrh, cassia, and all sorts of incense, except frankincense, and having filled it, they sew it back up again. When they have done this, they pickle the body by completely covering it with saltpeter for seventy days. It is not possible to pickle it for longer than this. When the seventy days are up, they wash the corpse and wrap linen bandages of the finest muslin all around it— after having smeared the bandages with a gum they call commi, which the Egyptians use instead of glue. Then the relatives take the body back and make a human-shaped wooden casket, close up the corpse in it, seal it, and store it standing up against a wall in a burial chamber.

That is their most expensive way of preparing corpses. This is the method of preparation for those who, wishing to avoid the expense, make the second choice. The embalmers prepare a syringe with a cedar resin and then fill the intestines of the corpse with it. They neither cut him open nor draw out his guts, but squirt the resin into his anus, which they then plug up so that the enema cannot dribble back out. Embalming goes on for the necessary amount of time, at the end of which they drain the original cedar resin out of the abdomen. This resin is so potent that it brings out the dissolved stomach and innards along with it. The saltpeter then dissolves the internal musculature, leaving only the skin and bones. When this has been done, they return the body without performing any additional operations.

The third method of embalming—the one they provide for those who have the least amount of money—is to embalm for the seventy days after washing out the innards with an enema, and to return the body to be taken away.

When the wives of prominent men die—or women who are very beautiful or otherwise notable—they are not immediately given out for embalming. Instead, they are given to the embalmers only after three or four days have passed. The Egyptians do this so that the embalmers will not have sex with the women, for they say that an embalmer, on the information of his co-worker, was once caught in the act with the fresh corpse of a woman.

Whenever someone—whether Egyptian or foreigner makes no difference—is carried away by a crocodile, or appears to have died because of the river, it is the responsibility of whatever city onto which he has been washed up to embalm him and to prepare him as beautifully as possible for burial in a sacred coffin. No one—not even his relatives or friends—

is allowed to so much as touch him. The Nile priests themselves handle and bury him, since his corpse is considered more than human.

Egyptians avoid adopting Greek customs and, in general, the customs of any other people whatever. Now, while most Egyptians do hold to their ways, there is the large city of Chemmis in the Theban district near New City. In this city there is a square shrine of Perseus, the son of Danae. Palm trees grow around it, and it has a very large stone gateway, at which stand two large stone statues. In this enclosure there is a temple, in which stands a statue of Perseus. Now, these Chemmites say that Perseus has frequently appeared to them around their territory, often in the temple, and that occasionally one of his worn-out three-foot-long sandals is found—and whenever it appears, all of Egypt prospers. That is what the Chemmites say, and these are the Greek customs which they practice in honor of Perseus: they have established gymnastic contests in every category, and award prizes of cattle, cloaks, and skins. When I asked why they were the only ones Perseus appeared to, and why they set themselves apart from the rest of Egypt by organizing gymnastic contests, they said that Perseus had derived from their own city, because Danaus and Lynceus, who were Chemmites, had sailed to Greece. From these two, they trace a genealogy down to Perseus. When Perseus came to Egypt for the reason the Greeks themselves give—to carry the Gorgon's head out of Egypt—they say that he came among them and recognized all of his kin. He had been thoroughly familiar with the name of Chemmis when he came to Egypt, because he had learned it from his mother. It was he who commanded the Chemmites to hold the gymnastic contests. [5]

All those are the customs of the Egyptians who live above the swamplands. The people who live in the swamplands observe the same customs as the rest of the Egyptians, such as that—like the Greeks—each of them lives with one woman. They have, though, discovered this means to reduce the cost of food. When the river becomes full and the fields are inundated, a great many lilies, which the Egyptians call lotuses, grow in the water. They pluck these, then dry them in the sun. Then they grind the stuff in the heart of the lotus, which resembles poppy seeds, and make loaves from it, which they bake in the fire. The root of the lotus is edible and fairly sweet tasting; it is round and about the size of an apple. There are other lilies like roses—and these, too, grow in the water—whose fruit comes from a calyx growing up alongside the flower from the root. It looks most like a wasp's comb. In it, there are numerous seeds about the size of olive pits, which they munch on either fresh or dried. When they pull the annual papyrus crop out of the swamp, they cut off the top of the plant and use it for other purposes, but the remaining eighteen-or-so-inch bottom section they eat or sell. Those who want

5. Perseus was the son of Danae by Zeus, and was chiefly famous for slaying the Gorgon Medusa with Athena's help. There is no known connection between Perseus and any Egyptian god.

to enjoy the papyrus at its best stew it in a red-hot pot and eat it that way. Some of the swamp dwellers live on fish alone. They dry them in the sun after they have caught them and taken out the guts, and then eat them dried.

River fish do not usually swim in schools, but those that live in the lakes do. When the mating frenzy comes over them, they swim out into the sea in schools. The males lead the way, spraying out their semen; the females follow, swallow it down, and in this way conceive. When the females grow pregnant in the sea, the fish swim back to their regular habitat. This time, the males no longer lead, however; rather, the leadership falls to the females. They lead the schools and do just as the males had done, for they spray out their eggs, a few at a time, like tiny seeds, while the males gulp them down as they follow. Now, these little seed-like eggs are really fish, which is what those that are not eaten and survive to maturity become.

Fish that are caught swimming out to sea show scrapes on the left side of their heads, while those swimming back have been scraped on the right. This happens to them for the following reason: they keep close to the land on the left as they swim down into the sea and hug the same bank on the way back, drawing near it and touching it as much as possible so that they do not lose their way on account of the current.

When the Nile begins to flood, pools and marshes in the land near the river begin to fill up as water spills in from the river, and no sooner are they filled than they all instantly teem with tiny fish. Now, it seems to me on reflection that this is their most likely origin: in the previous year, when the Nile is receding, the fish drop eggs in the mud as they swim away with the last water. When the time comes around again for the river to rise, these fish are instantly hatched from the eggs.

And that's the way it is with the fish.

The Egyptians who live around the marshes use an oil made from the castor oil plant—from its fruit, that is. They call it kiki, and this is how it is made: they cultivate this plant, which grows wild in Greece, along the banks of their rivers and lakes. In Egypt, the plant yields fruit which is abundant but foul smelling. After it has been harvested, some cut it up and crush it, while others roast it, boil it, and collect the liquid that comes out. The oil is rich and no less suitable for lamps than olive oil, although it has a pronounced odor.

They have worked out this way of dealing with the unlimited swarms of mosquitoes: towers help those who live inland from the swamps— they climb up and go to sleep, and the mosquitoes are prevented by the breezes from flying that high. Something other than towers has been devised for those who live in the swamplands. Every man owns a net with which he catches fish during the day and which is also useful at night, because he hangs the net around his bed and goes to sleep after climbing in under it. If he sleeps wrapped up in a cloak or in a linen sheet, the mosquitoes are able to bite through them, but they don't even try to bite through the net in the first place.

Their transport ships are made of the acacia, whose shape is similar to that of the Cyrenaean lotus, and whose sap—which flows like tears—is that "commi" gum. Now, from this acacia they cut planks about three feet long and fit them together like bricks, building their ships in the following way: they fix the three-foot planks around long, close-set tenons. When they have built the ship in this way, they stretch crosspieces over the planks. They use no ribs. They caulk the seams from within with papyrus. They make one rudder, which they thrust through the keel. They use an acanthus mast and papyrus sails.

This ship cannot sail upriver unless a keen wind is blowing. Instead, it is pulled up from the shore. This is how it is brought downstream. They take a raft made of tamarisk wood tied together with a rush matting of reeds, and a stone weighing about one hundred and twenty pounds with a hole bored through it. The raft is tied to the fore of the ship with a rope and sent downstream in front, while the stone is tied astern with another rope. The raft, of course, moves rapidly in the rush of the current, and drags the *baris* along (for that is the name of these vessels), while the stone drags from the depths behind and steadies the course. They have a great many of these boats, and some can transport huge tonnages.

When the Nile floods the land, only the cities rise above it, a lot like the islands in the Aegean. Only the cities rise above it, and all the rest of Egypt becomes a sea. When this happens, people no longer sail along the current of the river, but right over the middle of the plains. You can sail past the pyramids themselves from Naucratis to Memphis, although people usually sail by the apex of the Delta and Cercasoropolis. Sailing over the plain you can reach Naucratis from Canobus and the sea via Anthylla and the so-called City of Archandrus.

Of these two cities, Anthylla is notable for having been chosen to provide shoes to the wife of whoever reigns over Egypt. This practice began after Egypt became subject to the Persians. The other city seems to me to have been named after the son-in-law of Danaus—Archandrus, the son of Phthius, the son of Achaeus. So it is called the City of Archandrus. But there may have been some other Archandrus. Anyway, the name is not Egyptian.

*   *   *

Chapters 112–120

They said that a man from Memphis whose name, in Greek, was Proteus inherited the Egyptian throne from Pheros. His sacred precinct is in Memphis. It is richly ornamented and very beautiful and lies to the south of the temple of Hephaestus. Phoenicians from Tyre live around this precinct, and the whole region is called the Tyrian Quarter. There is a temple of the so-called Foreign Aphrodite in the precinct of Proteus. I suspect that this temple belongs to Helen, the daughter of Tyndareus, in part because of a story I heard that Helen had stayed with Proteus,

but mostly because the temple is named for the Foreign Aphrodite. You
see, no other temple to Aphrodite is called foreign.

The priests told me when I inquired that these were the circumstances
surrounding Helen. After Alexander had abducted Helen from Sparta,
he sailed away toward his own country; but when he was in the Aegean
the winds blew him off course and forced him into the Egyptian Sea.[6]
From there (for the winds did not abate) he came to Egypt, that is, into
what is now called the Canobic mouth of the Nile and its salting factories. On the shore there was, and still is, a temple to Heracles, and if
the servant of any man whatever flees there he may not be seized, provided he is branded with the sacred branding iron and dedicates himself
to the god. This custom has been practiced in the same way from the
very beginning to my own time. Now, some of Alexander's servants
found out about the custom in this temple and deserted him. They sat
as supplicants before the god and intended to harm Alexander by
denouncing him and revealing the whole story about Helen and the
injustice he had done Menelaus. They made these accusations before
the priests and before Thonis, the officer in charge of this mouth of the
Nile.

Thonis heard them out and immediately sent a message to Proteus in
Memphis, saying, "A stranger from the tribe of Teucer has arrived after
having been driven to your land by the winds. He has committed an
impious deed in Greece, for he has seduced the wife of his own host and
carried her and a great deal of wealth away from him. Should we allow
him to sail away unharmed, or should we confiscate his cargo?" Proteus
responded by saying, "Whoever this man who has committed such
impious deeds against his own host may be, arrest him and bring him to
me so that I may hear what he has to say."

When Thonis heard this, he arrested Alexander, impounded his ships,
and then led him, Helen, and the property to Memphis. He also brought
the supplicants. After they all arrived, Proteus asked Alexander who he
was and where he had sailed from. Alexander recited his lineage, gave
the name of his native land, and disclosed where he had begun his
voyage. Then Proteus asked him where he had gotten Helen, and when
Alexander was evasive in his story and did not tell the truth, he was given
away by the supplicants, who told the whole story of the crime. Finally,
Proteus passed this sentence on them: "If I did not make it a rule never
to kill a stranger, especially one who has come to my land after being
blown off course by the wind, I would punish you for what you have
done to this Greek, you, you vilest of men, who have repaid the hospitality you received with a most unholy deed. You lay with the wife of
your own host, but that wasn't even enough for you, because you have
carried her away with you on the wings of seduction. And not even that

6. Alexander was an alternative name for King   tion of Helen, the wife of the Spartan king Mene-
Priam's son Paris, the Trojan prince. Paris' abduc-   laus, was believed to have begun the Trojan War.

was enough, for you come here after looting your host's house! Now then, though it is my policy not to kill strangers, I will not allow you to take away this woman and these goods. Instead, I will hold them in safekeeping for the Greek stranger until he himself comes and takes them away. As for you and your fellow sailors, I command you to change your moorings within three days to some land other than mine. If you do not, I will treat you as enemies."

The priests said that this is how Helen came to Proteus, and it seems to me that Homer knew this story, but that it wasn't as suitable to his epic as the one he used. So he set the story aside, but made it clear that he knew it anyway. It is clear that in the *Iliad* he let slip his knowledge of the wanderings of Alexander (and this is the only place where he trips himself up), where he says that Alexander carried away Helen and wandered to many places, including Phoenician Sidon. He refers to this in the Exploits of Diomedes where he says,

> There were the robes, richly wrought, the work of Sidonian
> Women, robes Alexander, in from like a god, himself fetched
> From Sidon while sailing the wide sea
> When he led away well-born Helen. [7]

And in fact he mentions it also in these lines in the *Odyssey:*

> The daughter of Zeus had such excellent subtle drugs,
> The gift of Polydamna the Egyptian, the wife of Thon.
> For there the grain-giving fields yield many drugs,
> Many prepared for good, and many for evil. [8]

And again, Menelaus speaks this other line to Telemachus:

> The gods held me in Egypt, though I yearned to be home
> Because I had not given them perfect hecatombs in sacrifice. [9]

In these lines, Homer makes it clear that he knew of Alexander's straying into Egypt, for Syria borders on Egypt, and the Phoenicians—to whom Sidon belongs—live in Syria. The lines in these passages are the greatest proof that the Cyprian epic is not by Homer but by someone else, for in the *Cypria* it is said that Alexander took advantage of a fair wind and a smooth sea to arrive at Ilium with Helen on the third day after leaving Sparta, while in the *Iliad* it says that he wandered around with her.

But let us bid adieu to Homer and the Cyprian epic.

When I asked the priests whether the story the Greeks tell about what happened at Ilium is a mere fiction or not, they told me what they said they knew from asking Menelaus himself. After the abduction of Helen, a large Greek army went to Troy on behalf of Menelaus. The Greeks

7. *Iliad*, 6.289–92.
8. *Odyssey*, 4.227–30.
9. *Odyssey*, 4.351–52.

disembarked, set up camp, and sent messengers to Ilium, among them Menelaus himself. When they had entered the walls of the city, they demanded the return of Helen and of the property which Alexander had stolen. They also demanded damages for the harm that had been done. The Trojans said the same thing then as later, sometimes on their oath and sometimes not: they had neither Helen nor the money in question. It was all in Egypt, they said, and it wasn't right for them to be responsible for damages on what Proteus the Egyptian was holding. The Greeks, thinking they were being trifled with, besieged the city until they captured it. When there was still no Helen after they had stormed the walls of Troy, and they heard the same story as they had at first, the Greeks believed the original story and sent Menelaus to Proteus.

Menelaus arrived in Egypt and sailed upriver to Memphis. After truthfully describing the situation, he was richly entertained and received Helen—and all of his property—back unharmed. After all this, however, Menelaus did the Egyptians a wrong. You see, although he was eager to sail, he was detained by contrary winds. When this situation lasted for a long time, he came up with an unholy solution. He kidnapped two infants belonging to native men and sacrificed them as propitiatory offerings. He was hated and pursued when his deed became known, and he fled with his ships straight for Libya. The Egyptians could not say where he went next. They told me that they knew about some of this story through inquiry, while they could speak with certainty about what had happened in their own country.

This is what the Egyptian priests said. I myself agree with their version of the Helen story for the following reason. If Helen had been in Ilium, she would have been returned to the Greeks whether Alexander liked it or not, for neither Priam[1] nor his relatives were so addlebrained that they would risk their city and their own lives and the lives of their children just so that Alexander could live with Helen. If they had any such idea in mind at first, after seeing that so many Trojans died whenever they had a melee with the Greeks, and that there was not an occasion when two, three, or even more of Priam's own sons did not die in battle (if we may believe the epic poets)—why, all these things being so, I expect that even if Priam himself had been living with Helen he would have given her back to the Achaeans if there was any chance of getting out of the trouble they were in. Nor did the throne even devolve on Alexander, which would have left the affairs of state up to him, in view of Priam's age. Instead, Hector, who was older and much more of a man than Alexander was, would inherit the throne on the death of Priam, and it was not fitting for Hector to give in to his outlaw brother, especially when Alexander was the cause of so much misery to Hector personally and to all the rest of the Trojans combined. But the fact is that

---

1. The king of Troy, or Ilium.

the Trojans did not have Helen to give back, and that the Greeks did not believe them when they told the truth. Because—and I'm now declaring my own theory—the gods arranged things so that the Trojans, through their total annihilation, would make it perfectly clear to all mankind that great wrongs bring great retributions from the gods. This is said in keeping with my own beliefs.

* * *

Book 3

In book 3, Herodotus recounts the conquest of Egypt by Cyrus' son Cambyses and the difficulties Cambyses brought on himself by his foolishly self-destructive behavior. Like many powerful men in Herodotus' *Histories*, Cambyses acts hastily and injudiciously, misunderstanding the signs of dreams and having his own brother put to death under the misapprehension that he was plotting against him. Cambyses also shows a dangerous disrespect for Egyptian cultural norms in attacking the revered god-calf Apis. Herodotus considers it divine justice that Cambyses eventually dies from a wound in the thigh, precisely the place where he had struck Apis.

Herodotus sees Cambyses' disregard of Egyptian religious customs as clear evidence that he must have been insane, an argument that leads into one of the most famous passages in Herodotus' work. Only a crazy person, Herodotus reasons, would fail to see that all peoples believe their native customs to be the best. He cites as evidence for this the story of Darius, king of Persia, who asked some Greeks how much money they would take to eat the dead bodies of their fathers. The Greeks replied that no amount of money would persuade them to do such a thing. Later on, in the presence of the Greeks, Darius asked some Indians, who by custom ate the dead bodies of their parents, how much money they would have to be paid in order to burn them instead. The Indians were scandalized, and made the same reply as the Greeks. One can learn from this, Herodotus concludes, that his contemporary Pindar was right when he said that custom was "king of everything."

Book 3 also contains the famous debate on government, the first extended discussion of the subject in Western literature. After the death of Cambyses, Herodotus writes, several Persian nobles compared the merits of three different kinds of government—monarchy, aristocracy, and democracy. Although it may not be historically accurate, this discussion reflects the ways in which a thinker of Herodotus' day might evaluate a government. Indeed, at the time Herodotus was writing, the Athenian democracy was in the process of overturning entrenched assumptions about the privileged position of the rich and wellborn.

* * *

Chapters 39–43

While Cambyses was making war on Egypt, the Lacedaemonians also mounted a campaign against Samos and particularly against Polycrates, son of Aeaces, who had taken control of Samos in a revolution. The first thing Polycrates did was to divide the city into three parts and share them with his brothers Pantagnotus and Syloson. Later, though, he killed his older brother, exiled Syloson, the younger, and took all of Samos after forming an alliance with Amasis, king of Egypt, which was sealed by an exchange of gifts. The power of Polycrates grew in such a very short time that it made a noise throughout Ionia and the rest of Greece. Wherever he set out on a campaign, his good luck made everything go his way. He had a hundred penteconters and one thousand archers. He carried off booty and captives from friend and foe alike, and said that you make your friends happier by giving back what you have taken than by never taking anything in the first place. He conquered numerous islands and many cities on the mainland. In a naval battle, he also defeated the Lesbians, who had gone out in full force to relieve the Milesians and who, in chains, later dug the whole trench around the Samian wall.

Amasis couldn't help noticing that Polycrates was having such huge success, and it made him a little anxious. When Polycrates' success became even greater still, Amasis wrote this letter on a piece of papyrus and sent it to Samos: "This is what Amasis has to say to Polycrates. It is usually pleasing to find out that a dear friend and ally is prospering, but your immense good luck does not please me, because I know that god is a jealous god. Now, I prefer that I and those I care about succeed in some things and fail in others, thus passing our lives with changing fortunes rather than with complete success. I have never heard tell of any totally lucky man who didn't finally end up in utter misery. Now, listen to me, and do the following about all this good luck: give some thought to what you regard as your most valuable possession—the one that it would give your heart the most pain to lose—and then throw it where no man can ever get to it again. If the good luck doesn't fall into a rhythm with the bad after you do this, then just keep following my prescription and you'll be cured."

After reading this letter and realizing that Amasis had given him good advice, Polycrates tried to figure out which of his heirlooms it would most vex his heart to lose, and after thinking it over, he realized that it was a signet ring he used to wear, an emerald set in gold, and the work of a Samian—Theodorus, son of Telecles. After he decided that this was what he was going to throw away, here is what he did: he manned a fifty-oared ship, boarded it, and ordered that it make for the open sea. When it was far from the island, he took off the ring and, with all of the sailors looking on, threw it into the sea. After doing this, he sailed back and became very despondent when he reached home.

Five or six days after these events, the following took place: a fisherman caught a beautiful huge fish, one he thought worthy of being given to Polycrates. So he brought it to the palace gates and said that he wanted to be admitted to Polycrates' presence. He succeeded in gaining admission, and as he presented Polycrates with the fish, he said, "Your Majesty, after I caught this fish, I didn't think it would be right to take it to the marketplace, even though I am a man who has to earn his own living. Instead, I thought it was worthy of you and your power, so I have brought it here and offer it to you."

Polycrates was delighted with the words of the fisherman and answered, "Thank you very much. You will be rewarded twice over both for your words and for your gift. You are even invited to dinner!"

Deeply honored, the fisherman went home while Polycrates' servants cut open the fish and found the signet ring in its guts. As soon as they saw the ring, they removed it, gleefully took it to Polycrates, and handed it over to him while they told him how it had been found. When he realized that this was the work of god, he wrote down on a papyrus how everything he had done had turned out and sent the letter off to Egypt.

After Amasis had read over Polycrates' letter, he understood that it was impossible for one man to save another from what had to be, and that Polycrates—so lucky in every way—was not destined to come to a happy end when he even found the things he threw away! Then Amasis sent a messenger to Samos and said that he was dissolving their alliance. He did this so that his spirit would not be pained over a friend when Polycrates was in the grip of a great and terrible circumstance.

* * *

Chapters 61–88

Two Magian brothers—one of whom Cambyses, son of Cyrus, had left behind as his household steward—rebelled against Cambyses while he dawdled in Egypt after going out of his mind. Now, this rebellious steward had learned that Smerdis had been secretly murdered and that very few Persians actually knew Smerdis, while at the same time most thought that he was alive. In view of this, the steward devised a plan for taking over the throne. He had a brother—the one I said rebelled along with him—who looked very much like Smerdis, son of Cyrus, whom Cambyses killed even though he was his own brother. And not only did he resemble Smerdis in appearance; he even had the same name: Smerdis! The Magus Patizeithes persuaded his brother that they could get away with this plot and seated him on the royal throne. After doing so, he sent messengers everywhere, even Egypt, to announce to the army that they should obey Smerdis the son of Cyrus from now on and not Cambyses.

Now, the other messengers made this announcement, as did the one who had been ordered to Egypt. He found Cambyses and his army in Agbatana, in Syria, and announced the Magi's order while standing right in the middle of the troops. Cambyses heard the messenger and thought that what he was saying was the truth and that he had been betrayed by Prexaspes. (You see, Cambyses had sent Prexaspes to kill Smerdis, and now Cambyses thought that Prexaspes hadn't done it.) He looked at Prexaspes and said, "Prexaspes, is this the way you handled that matter I gave you?"

Prexaspes answered, "It isn't true, Master, that your brother Smerdis has rebelled against you or that you will ever have any problem from him again—big or small. I myself did what you commanded, and I buried him with my own hands. If the dead are rising up nowadays, you can expect that even Astyages the Mede will be resurrected! But if things are still the way they were before, nothing new is going to be sprouting out of your brother. Now, I think that we should go after this messenger and cross-examine him about who he comes from with his announcement that we should obey 'King Smerdis.' "

Cambyses liked what Prexaspes said, and the herald was immediately pursued. When he was brought back, Prexaspes questioned him. "You say, my man, that you are a messenger from Smerdis the son of Cyrus. Now, just tell the truth and you can go in peace. Was it Smerdis himself who told you this to your face, or was it one of his underlings?"

The messenger said, "I myself have not seen Smerdis the son of Cyrus since King Cambyses marched into Egypt. The Magus, the one Cambyses entrusted his house to, he is the one who gave this order and who said that Smerdis the son of Cyrus had commanded me to say this to you." The man had told them the unadorned truth, and Cambyses said to Prexaspes, "You followed orders like a trusty man; you are free of blame. But what Persian has rebelled against me and is using the name of Smerdis?"

Prexaspes said, "I think I understand what has happened, Your Majesty. The Magi are the ones who have rebelled against you—Patizeithes, whom you left in charge of your household, and his brother, Smerdis." And then, when Cambyses heard the name Smerdis, he was struck by the truth both of these words and of his dream, in which he thought someone had given him the message that Smerdis would sit on the royal throne and touch the sky with his head. When he realized that his brother had died in vain, he mourned for Smerdis, and in his grief and vexation over the whole disaster he leaped on his horse with the idea of going to Susa and attacking the Magus immediately. But just as he was leaping on his horse, the tip of his sword sheath fell off and his naked sword stabbed his thigh. He was wounded in the very place where he had once struck the Egyptian god Apis, and because he thought he might have received a mortal wound, Cambyses asked the name of the city they were in. They told him that its name was Agbatana. Now, he had once been told by the oracle at Buto that he would end his life in Agbatana. He had of course thought that he would die of old age in Agbatana in Media, the seat of his government, but—lo and behold!—the oracle meant Agbatana in Syria. And then, when he found out the name of the city, what with the shock of the wound and the Magian disaster, he regained his sanity. He grasped the meaning of the oracle and said, "This is where Cambyses, son of Cyrus, is destined to die."

That was all, for then, but about twenty days later, Cambyses sent for the foremost Persians who were there and said, "Men of Persia, it falls to me now to reveal the deed I have done my best to hide. When I was in Egypt, I saw a vision in my sleep, and oh how I wish I had never seen it! I thought a messenger had come from my home to say that Smerdis was sitting on the royal throne and touching the sky with his head. Out of fear that my kingdom would be stolen by my brother, I acted with more haste than wisdom because, after all, human nature cannot turn aside what is to come. But fool that I was, I sent Prexaspes to Susa to kill Smerdis. I lived without fear after the evil deed was done, never reflecting that somebody else might revolt against me even though Smerdis had been done away with. I was mistaken in what was to be, I needlessly became a brother-killer; yet even so I have lost my throne. Because clearly Smerdis the Magus was the one who god foretold would revolt against me in that dream. But I have done the deed. Think not of Smerdis, son of Cyrus. He is no more. It is your Magi who control the royal palace! The man I left in charge of my household and his brother, Smerdis! And the one who ought most to help me now, as I suffer this outrage from the Magi, has met an unholy fate at the hands of his own kin. He is no more. Therefore it is on you, O men of Persia, that I must henceforth enjoin those things I would see done as I end my life. In the name of our royal gods, I call on you, all of you, but especially the Achaemenids, who are here not to allow power to return to Media again but to take it back by guile if they get it by guile, or to recover it by brute force if it is force they use to win it. If you do this, may your land bring forth fruit, and your women give birth and your cattle multiply, and may you be now and forever free. But if you do not recover or try to recover the kingdom, I pray that it may be the reverse for you, and that in addition, for each and every Persian, the end of his life shall be as my own." And as he said this, Cambyses bitterly regretted all his deeds.

When the Persians saw their king weeping, they tore their clothes and set up an unceasing wail. Then, right after his bone became gangrened and his thigh began to decay, the wound carried off Cambyses the son of Cyrus after he had ruled for seven years and five months in all without leaving any children, either male or female. Yet a deep skepticism welled up in the Persians who were there that the Magi had really taken over the government; instead, they thought that Cambyses had said what he did about the death of Smerdis in order to defame his brother and to foment war throughout Persia against him.

They thought that Smerdis the son of Cyrus was sitting on the throne because Prexaspes heatedly denied that he had killed Smerdis: now that Cambyses was dead, it wasn't safe to say that he had killed the son of Cyrus with his own hands. Thus, after Cambyses died, the Magus used the name of Smerdis son of Cyrus and ruled with impunity for the seven months that were left to complete the eighth year of Cambyses' reign. During that time, the Magus showed himself to be a great benefactor of his people, so that everyone in Asia except for the Persians mourned him when he died. You see, the Magus had announced to all the peoples of Asia that they would be exempt from a military service and taxes for three years.

He made this announcement as soon as he took power, but eight months later he was found out in the following way. Otanes was the son of Pharnaspes, [1] and by birth and wealth he was the equal of any Persian in the land; and it was this Otanes who first suspected that the Magus was not Cyrus' Smerdis but the man who, in fact, he really was. He figured it out because the Magus never left his fortress and because he never called any of the foremost Persians into his presence. Otanes acted on his suspicions in the following way: Cambyses had married his daughter, and her name was Phaedima. Now, the Magus took her over and lived with her along with all the other wives of Cambyses, so Otanes sent a message to this daughter to find out who she slept with, Smerdis the son of Cyrus or somebody else. She sent back saying that she didn't know, because she had never seen either the son of Cyrus or the man she was living with. Otanes sent a second message, which said, "If you don't know Smerdis the son of Cyrus, find out from Atossa, since both of you live with him. Surely she will recognize her own brother." She answered, "I can't get to talk to Atossa or to see any of her ladies-in-waiting. As soon as this man, whoever he is, took over the throne, he scattered us around to different places." And when Otanes heard this, the situation became even more clear to him.

He sent her yet a third message, which said, "Your noble birth obliges you, my daughter, to run this risk that I, your father, call on you to undertake, because if this man really is not Cyrus' Smerdis, but the one I suspect him to be, then he must be brought to justice and not be allowed to get away with taking you for his wife and seizing the power of Persia. So do this: the next time he goes to bed with you and you know that he is asleep, reach out and feel for his ears. If he has ears, consider yourself married to Smerdis the son of Cyrus, but if he does not have them, it is to Smerdis the Magus."

Phaedima sent back saying that she would be running a great risk indeed in doing it because she knew very well that he would do away with her if he didn't have ears and caught her feeling for them. Still, she would do it; she promised her father that she would get what he wanted. (You see, during his reign, Cyrus the son of Cambyses had cut off the ears of this Smerdis the Magus for a very serious offense.) This Phaedima, as became the daughter of Otanes, did everything she had promised her father, because when it was her turn to visit the Magus (Persian women take turns going to bed with their husband), she went and lay down beside him and, when the Magus was fast asleep, reached out and felt for his ears. It wasn't hard, really; she easily found out that the man had no ears, and as soon as it was day she sent a message to tell her father what had happened.

Then Otanes joined forces with Aspathines and Gobryas, two of the foremost Persians and two of his most trusted advisers, and explained the

---

1. Herodotus seems to have made a mistake here. Evidently Otanes' father was really Socris.

whole situation to them. They themselves had suspected that this was the way things were, but they accepted it only when Otanes made the argument. They decided that each of them should enlist the Persian he trusted most as a coconspirator. Otanes brought in Intaphernes, Gobryas Megabyzus, and Aspathines Hydarnes. After this group of six was formed, Darius, the son of Hystaspes, arrived in Susa from Persia, where his father was the satrap. After he arrived, the six decided that they should also bring him into the conspiracy. This group of seven met to exchange confidences and opinions. When it was Darius' turn to speak his mind, he said, "I thought I was the only one who knew that the Magus was reigning and that Cyrus' Smerdis was dead. And that's exactly why I came here in such a hurry—to arrange for the death of the Magus. When it turned out that you also knew and not just me, I decided that the best thing we could do was to act immediately and not delay."

Otanes responded to this by saying, "Son of Hystaspes, you are the son of a noble father and look as if you will be no less a man than he is; but you mustn't rush an attack like this without a plan; you have to make the assault more cautiously, and it seems to me that there must be more of us before we can undertake it."

And Darius responded to this by saying, "Everyone here should know that if you follow the course set forth by Otanes, you will die a miserable death because someone will betray us to the Magus for his own, private gain. You should be attacking right now, on your own; but since you saw fit to bring in others and to ask my advice, then either do it today or know that if you let this day go by, no one will beat me to making an accusation, because I will reveal the plot to the Magus myself."

When Otanes saw what a hurry Darius was in, he said, "Since you are forcing us to rush forward and won't allow us to delay, come, show us how we can get into the royal palace and attack them. You know that there are guards posted everywhere—at least you've heard about them, even if you haven't seen them—and how are we going to get past them?"

Darius answered, "Otanes, many things can't be shown through words, but through deeds, while other things are possible in words though nothing clear ever comes of them. You know that it isn't hard to walk right past stationed guards. Considering who we are, no guard will prevent us from passing through, partly out of respect for us and partly out of fear. Anyway, I have a plausible reason to go in. I'll say that I have just arrived from Persia and that I have a message from my father for the king. When you have to tell a lie, tell it! We strive for the same thing whether we lie or tell the truth. Some lie when it's likely that they will gain something by persuading others of their lies, and others tell the truth so that they can use it to attract some advantage and so that things will be more likely to go their way. Thus, without using the same means, we gain the same end. If there was nothing to be gained, the truth teller would be just as likely to be false as the liar to be true. In the long run, any gatekeeper who freely lets us through will be better off; whoever tries to stop us shows by that act that he is an enemy—let us push him aside and fall to our work!"

After this Gobryas said, "My friends, will there ever be a better time for us to regain power, or, if we can't get it back, to die trying? Here we are, Persians, ruled by a Median Magus, and a man without ears, at that! Those of us who were at the side of the sick and dying Cambyses must remember the deathbed curse he laid on us Persians if we didn't try to recover the throne. At the time, we didn't accept what Cambyses said; we thought he was talking slander. But now I cast my vote to heed Darius and not to adjourn this meeting except to go up against the Magus immediately." That's what Gobryas said, and everyone agreed.

While they were plotting, other things had been happening quite by chance. The Magi decided to befriend Prexaspes because he had suffered an outrage at the hands of Cambyses, who had killed his son with an arrow;[2] and also because he was the only one who knew Smerdis the son of Cyrus was dead, having killed him with his own hands; and finally because he was held in the highest esteem in Persia. For these reasons, they summoned him, offered him friendship, and promised him a thousand thousand gifts if he gave oaths and pledges that he would, so help him, keep to himself the lie they had foisted on the Persians and not disclose it to another human being. After Prexaspes promised to do what the Magi had urged, they made a second proposal, which was that he call the Persians to the palace wall and that he mount the tower and proclaim that they were being ruled by Smerdis the son of Cyrus and by no one else. They asked him to do this because he was, believe it or not, the most trusted man in Persia—one who frequently expressed the opinion that Cyrus' Smerdis was alive and at the same time categorically denied killing him.

When Prexaspes said that he was prepared to do this, the Magi called the Persians together, mounted Prexaspes on the tower, and ordered him to make his announcement. He disregarded the promises they had extracted from him in advance and talked about the ancestors of Cyrus, beginning with Achaemenes. Then, when he got to Cyrus, he concluded the genealogy by describing all the good things Cyrus had done for the Persians, and, after going through these, he revealed the truth, saying that he had concealed it at first because it wasn't safe for him to say what had happened, but that now, under the circumstances, he was forced to make it known; and so he said that he had killed Smerdis the son of Cyrus—Cambyses made him do it—and that the Magi ruled Persia. He called many curses down on the heads of the Persians if they did not get back the throne and punish the Magi, and then threw himself from the tower head first. That is how Prexaspes, who had always been such a reliable man, died.

---

2. In book 3, chapter 35, Herodotus relates how Cambyses tried to prove that he was not crazy and that he could hold his liquor by shooting the son of Prexaspes with an arrow.

After the seven decided to attack the Magi immediately and not delay, they went to pray to the gods knowing nothing of what Prexaspes had done. They had marched halfway to the palace when they heard of the events surrounding Prexaspes. They got off the road and once again deliberated among themselves, with Otanes and his followers urging them to wait and not to make their attempt in this swell of events, and with Darius and his followers urging them not to delay and to go on and do what they had decided. They were beginning to push and shove each other when there appeared seven pairs of hawks chasing, plucking, and mangling two pairs of vultures. When the seven saw this, they all agreed with Darius and once again headed for the palace, heartened by the omen of the birds.

When they stood at the gates, it turned out just as Darius had thought. The guards stood in awe of such prominent Persians, and, never suspecting what they were about to do, the guards let these men (who were under divine escort)[3] pass without asking a single question. When they had gone as far as the inner court, they met the eunuchs who brought messages into the magi; the eunuchs asked why they had come and what they wanted. The eunuchs were simultaneously asking these questions, reprimanding the guards for letting the seven through, and trying to restrain them as they attempted to go even farther. Then the seven egged each other on, and, drawing their daggers there and then, they all stabbed the eunuchs who were holding them and ran into the men's quarters.

The Magi happened to be inside at the time, talking over the Prexaspes situation, but when they heard a commotion and shouting among the eunuchs, they both got up hurriedly and, when they found out what was happening, prepared to defend themselves. One Magus was able to get to his bow while the other ran for a spear. Then they came to close quarters with the seven. The Magus who had taken up the bow found that it was useless to him because the attackers were too close and pressing too hard; the other one defended himself with the spear and stabbed Aspathines in the thigh and Intaphernes in the eye. Intaphernes lost his eye because of this wound, though he did not die of it. Thus one of the Magi wounded these men, while the other, when his bow turned out to be useless to him, fled into a room off the men's quarters and was trying to shut the doors when two of the seven, Darius and Gobryas, crashed through the doors together. Gobryas fell into a tussle with the Magus on the floor, and Darius was at a loss for what to do as he stood over them in the dark. He was afraid of hitting Gobryas, but when Gobryas saw him standing there doing nothing, he asked, "Why don't you use your sword hand?"

Darius said, "I'm afraid to. I don't want to hit you."

But Gobryas answered, "Run your sword through both of us!"

_____

3. Herodotus means that events were turning out according to divine will.

Darius obediently made a sword thrust and somehow managed to hit the Magus.

After they killed the Magi and cut off their heads, the remaining five left behind their wounded, who were weak but who could still guard the acropolis, and ran out with the heads of the Magi, shouting and carrying on and calling to the other Persians in order to explain what had happened and to show them the heads. At the same time, they killed every Magus who came their way. When the Persians found out about the imposture of the Magi and about what the seven had done, they saw fit to do likewise and drew their daggers and killed every Magus they could find. If nightfall had not stopped them, not a single Magus would have been left alive. The Persians commemorate this day more than any other and hold a great festival on it. The Persians call it the Magophonia, or the Slaughter of the Magi, and on that day no Magus is allowed to show his face—they must keep to their houses all day long.

Five days after the turmoil died down, the seven who rebelled against the Magi had a meeting to debate their form of government. Speeches were made which some Greeks find impossible to believe—but they were made, all right. Otanes demanded that the government be left up to the Persian people, and said:

"I don't think that we should have a monarchy any longer. It is neither agreeable nor advantageous. You have seen what pitch the arrogance of Cambyses soared to, and you have also had your share of the arrogance of the Magi. How could monarchy be a well-ordered thing when the monarch is able to do whatever he wants without accountability to anyone? Even the noblest of men would change his way of thinking if he had that kind of power. Arrogance would develop from his good qualities themselves, while envy has been natural to mankind from the very beginning; and when the monarch has these two things he has all he needs to do evil, for, glutted with arrogance and envy, he will commit the most monstrous atrocities. Now, the tyrant ought not to feel any envy, since he has all the good things he wants, but he is really just the opposite in the way he treats his subjects. He envies the best of them simply for being alive, while he delights in his most contemptible subjects and loves, above all, to listen to slanderous gossip. And the most incongruous thing of all: if you admire him appropriately, he is angry because you are not totally subservient to him; but if you are totally subservient, he is angry at you for being a flatterer. But I have yet to mention the worst things: he will disrupt the settled customs of our ancestors, rape our women, and murder indiscriminately.

"Majority rule, on the other hand, is called by the fairest of terms: Equality before the Law. Next, it requires something the tyrant never allows: people hold office by lot, they are accountable for the actions of their administrations, and their deliberations are held in public. I propose, therefore, that we abolish the monarchy and increase the power of the people, for in the many is all our strength."

Otanes, then, advanced this position, but Megabyzus exhorted them to adopt an oligarchy. He said:

"I agree with Otanes when he says that we must abolish the monarchy, but he misses the mark when he urges us to hand power over to the people, because there is nothing stupider or more arrogant than an idle mob. It would be absolutely unbearable to flee the arrogance of a tyrant and to fall prey to the arrogance of the unbridled masses. At least the tyrant knows what he is doing; the common people don't know anything. How could they know when they are uneducated and have never learned anything on their own and when, like a raging river, they mindlessly rush in and sweep away the business of government? Let those who bear ill will toward the Persians be governed by the people; let us select a group of the best men and give power to them, for we ourselves will be in that group, and it is natural for the best men to produce the best counsels."

This, then, was the opinion Megabyzus advanced. Darius expressed yet a third opinion, and said:

"I think Megabyzus is right in what he said about the majority but wrong in what he said about an oligarchy. For of the three forms of government set forth in debate as the best—democracy, oligarchy, and monarchy—I say that monarchy is far and away superior. After all, no one could be better than the one best man, and in the implementation of his own best counsel the monarch can faultlessly govern his people and keep his own secrets while carrying out his plans against his enemies. Powerful private hatreds always arise in an oligarchy when a large group of men vies for preeminence before the public. When each man wants to be the leader and wants his opinions to prevail, all come to hate each other immensely, and from this comes civil strife, and from civil strife comes bloodshed, and after the bloodshed you end up with a monarchy—and in this way it becomes clear how much better the monarch is.

"It is impossible for a democracy to avoid corruption, but when corruption arises in government, it engenders strong friendships instead of hatreds because those who huddle to corrupt the government have to act together. This goes on until a man of the people comes forward and puts a stop to it. As a result, he becomes the admiration of the people, and after being an object of admiration he shows himself, of course, to be a monarch. In this way he, too, makes it clear that monarchy is the best form of government. One word sums it all up: Where did our freedom come from? Who gave it to us? Was it from the people or from an oligarchy or from a monarchy? I believe that since we were liberated by one man, we should preserve the monarchy and that we should, in addition, retain the ancestral customs which have served us so well. This is our best course."

These three proposals were advanced, and four of the seven chose that of Darius. When Otanes was defeated after urging the view that the

Persians should adopt a government of equality before the law, he openly made this announcement to the group:

"It is as plain as can be, my fellow revolutionaries, that one of us is going to be king, whether we choose him by lot, leave it up to the Persian people to elect him, or find some other way. I will not compete with you for it, though. I will neither rule nor be ruled. But I give up all claim to the throne on one condition, the condition that I will never be subject to any of you, neither I myself, nor any of my offspring forever." The seven went along with what he had proposed, and he did not, indeed, compete with them but maintained a strict neutrality. To this day, only the house of Otanes continues to be free in Persia and, without breaking any of the laws of Persia, only obeys the king to the extent that it chooses.

The rest of the seven deliberated about the fairest way to institute a monarchy. But first they decided that if one of them became king, Otanes and his offspring would forever annually be given the choicest Median wardrobe and all the other most cherished gifts of Persia. They decided that he should be given these things because he was the first to plan the coup and to bring the seven together. These privileges were set aside for Otanes, but the following rules were to apply to them all. Any one of the seven could enter the royal palace without announcing it in advance, unless the king was in bed with one of his wives. Also, the king would not be permitted to marry anyone outside the families of his corevolutionaries. As to the question of who should get the throne, this is what they decided: they would all mount their horses and ride out to the city limits, and that man would have the throne whose horse was the first to neigh after sunrise.

Now, Darius had a shrewd groom whose name was Oebares, and after the meeting broke up, this is what Darius said to the man: "Oebares, this is what we've decided to do about who gets the throne. The first one of us whose horse neighs when we're riding at sunrise is going to be king. So if you have the skill to do it, work out a way for us, and not somebody else, to win this prize."

Oebares answered, "Well, Master, if that is what being king or not being king depends on, take heart and don't worry, because no one will be king but you. I have just the medicine we need."

And Darius said, "If you know some trick, waste no time and play it now, because we're going to have our contest tomorrow."

After Oebares heard this, he did the following: he took the mare Darius' horse loved best and led her out to the city limits. He tethered her there, and then brought out Darius' horse and led him around and around the mare, getting closer every time, until finally the groom allowed him to cover her.

With the first rays of dawn, the six arrived on their horses, as agreed. They rode out to the city limits, toward the very place where the mare had been tethered the night before. Suddenly, Darius' stallion galloped ahead and began to neigh, and at the same moment as the horse did so, there was thunder and lightning in a perfectly clear sky. This unexpected event confirmed Darius as if by some covenant, and the others sprang down from their horses and prostrated themselves before him.

That is what some say about the trick Oebares played, but others say— and both stories are told by the Persians—that he rubbed the mare's vagina with his hand, which he then kept hidden in his pants. As the horses were about to be released at sunrise, this Oebares pulled his hand out of his pants and brought it up to the nostrils of the horse, who began to snort and neigh as soon as he recognized the smell.

Thus was Darius, the son of Hystaspes, chosen king and, because it had been conquered first by Cyrus and then again by Cambyses, all of Asia except Arabia was subject to him. The Arabians never submitted to be Persian slaves, but they did become allies when they allowed Cambyses to pass into Egypt. Without the cooperation of the Arabians, the Persians could never have invaded Egypt. The first marriages Darius made were with Persian women—Atossa and Artystone, the daughters of Cyrus. Atossa had been previously married to her brother, Cambyses, and then later to the Magus, while Artystone was a virgin. In addition, he married a daughter of Smerdis the son of Cyrus. Her name was Parmys. He also married the daughter of Otanes, the one who had exposed the Magus. His power was felt everywhere. The first thing he did was to erect a stone relief with the figure of a man on horseback carved into it. An epigraph said, DARIUS THE SON OF HYSTASPES AIDED BY THE HIGH SPIRITS OF HIS HORSE (and here he gave the horse's name) AND BY HIS GROOM OEBARES WON THE THRONE OF PERSIA.

*   *   *

Chapters 98–105

This is how the Indians get the large quantities of gold from which they bring the king of Persia the gold dust I have mentioned. [4]

India is all sand dunes toward the rising sun. [5] Judging both by what we know and by what is reliably reported, the Indians are the first people to inhabit Asia toward the East and the rising sun, for it is sandy desert from where they live to where the sun rises. There are many Indian peoples, and they don't speak the same language to one another. Some of them are nomads, while others are not, and yet others live in river marshes and eat raw fish which they catch from bamboo boats—where each boat is made from the single joint of a huge bamboo shoot! These Indians wear clothes made of reeds. After they gather the reeds from the

4. Herodotus mentions this in earlier passages on the tribute various peoples paid to the Persians.
5. Herodotus had heard of what is now India from the lower Indus Valley to the Punjab. He knew that India had a huge population and thought that India was the most easterly land on earth and that the sun rose at its easternmost border.

river and pound them flat, they weave them like a mat and wear them like a chest protector.

Other eastern Indians are nomads; they eat raw meat and are called the Padaei. It is said that they observe the following customs: whenever one of the natives gets sick, be it a man or a woman, his best friends kill him (that is, in the case of a man) on the grounds that he is wasting away from the disease and spoiling their meat. He always denies that he is sick, but they kill him without pity and feast on his flesh. Women treat a woman who gets sick in the same way the men treat a man. As to someone who reaches old age, they sacrifice him and feast on his flesh, but few achieve this distinction, because they kill everyone who falls sick before he can grow old.

There is yet another group of Indians with yet other customs. They neither kill any living thing nor sow crops, nor is it their custom to build houses. They eat grasses, though, and they have a grain in a husk about the size of a millet seed which grows wild in the land; they gather this, boil it husk and all, and eat it. Whoever among them falls sick goes and lies out in the desert: nobody gives any thought to his own sickness or death.

All of the Indians I have mentioned have sexual intercourse out in the open, like cattle. They all have the same skin color, which is similar to that of the Ethiopians. The semen they ejaculate into their women is not white like other people's, but black like the color of their skin. The Ethiopians also ejaculate the same colored semen. This whole group of Indians lives far to the south of Persia and was never subject to King Darius.

There are other Indians bordering on Caspatyrus City and the Pactyic territory who live toward the north wind and the constellation of the Bear. [6] Their way of life is similar to that of the Bactrians. These are the most warlike Indians and the ones who send out parties to explore for gold in the region of the sandy desert. You see, in the sand of this desert there are ants which are smaller than dogs but larger than foxes. Some of them have even been caught and brought to the king of Persia. Now, when these ants dig their colonies underground, they carry out sand just like the ants in Greece, and they do it in the same way—why, they even look like Greek ants—except that the sand they carry up is full of gold! The Indians make forays into the desert for this sand, with each man harnessing three camels together—two males in traces on the outside and a female in the middle. The Indian rides atop the female, seeing to it that he harnesses only one who has been dragged away from her newly dropped young. Their camels are no slower than horses, and they are, in addition, better able to carry heavy loads. Since the Greeks know what a camel looks like, I won't describe it, but I will point out what they

---

6. This is probably the region of northeast Afghanistan.

don't know about it: it has two leg bones and two knees in each of its hind legs, and its genitals are turned outward from its hind legs toward its tail.

In this way, then, and using this kind of animal team, the Indians go after the gold, timing it so that they make their raid when the sun is at its hottest because the ants disappear underground then on account of the heat. For these people, the sun is hottest at dawn and not at midday as it is for others, and the sun keeps rising until the market closes at midmorning. It is much hotter during all this time than it is at midday in Greece—so much so that they are drenched in sweat the whole time. At midday it is almost as hot for everybody else as it is for the Indians. As the sun descends from the zenith, it gets to be as the dawn is for other people. It keeps getting colder as the sun goes lower, until it is very cold at sunset. [7]

When they arrive at the place where the gold dust is, the Indians fill the little sacks they carry with the dust and then race back as fast as they can, according to the Persians, the ants start chasing them as soon as they become aware of their smell. These ants are like no other animal for speed—so much so that if the Indians did not get a head start while the ants were assembling, not a single one of them would get back alive. Now, the male camels run more slowly than the female, and when they begin to flag they are cut loose, though not both at the same time. The females remember the foals they left behind and do not slacken for an instant.

According to the Persians, this is how the Indians get most of their gold. A small quantity is mined in their own country.

* * *

7. Herodotus thought the earth was a flat disk. It would be hottest at dawn in India because the sun would be close to the land at sunrise. By the same token, the sun would be hot at sunset in the west-ernmost regions of the earth as the sun again approached the earth in its descent. Since the western sun would be farthest from India, India would be very cold at sunset.

Book 4

In book 4, Herodotus takes the occasion of Darius' attack on Scythia to discuss the customs of the Scythians in much the same way he discussed those of the Egyptians. He also introduces the history of the Amazons, with whom the Scythians were reported to have intermarried. A legendary tribe of fierce warrior women, the Amazons represented to the Greek mind everything that was alien to their culture. Herodotus also relates with some skepticism what was known to him concerning the Hyperboreans, another legendary race, who lived in the far north and were associated with Apollo. Herodotus seems inclined to believe in the historicity of the Amazons as well as of the entirely bald race to the north of the Scythians, the Argippaei, who subsist on a kind of cherry and are regarded as sacred; he rejects the story the Argippaei tell of a goat-footed race and of people to the far north who sleep six months of the year (presumably a confusion derived from the extreme length of winter nights in the Arctic region). He also comments on the common sense of the Issedones, a Scythian tribe that accorded equal authority to men and women.

The Persian expedition to Egypt affords Herodotus an opportunity for a digression on the cultures of North Africa and their history. He also describes a number of practices which he believed the Greeks had derived from the North Africans, such as the dress in which the goddess Athena was represented, the custom of women weeping at funerals, and the harnessing of four horses to a chariot. The book ends with the death of Queen Pheretima, one of the powerful female monarchs so common in Herodotus' narrative. Altogether, book 4 shows Herodotus' keen interest not only in geography but in cultural differentiation and transmission.

* * *

Chapters 36–44

Enough about the Hyperboreans. I won't tell the story about Abaris the so-called Hyperborean, that is, how he carried an arrow around the whole world without ever eating anything. If there are Hyperboreans, though, there must be Hyperaustralians too.

It makes me laugh to see so many people drawing maps of the world without any rational idea of what they are doing. They make maps of Ocean flowing around a world as circular as if it had been drawn with a compass, and they make Asia the same size as Europe. I, however, will briefly show how big each one really is, and what each looks like on a map.

The Persians have spread as far as the southern sea—the so-called Red Sea.[1] Above the Persians in the direction of the north wind live the Medes, and above the Medes the Saspires, and above them the Colchians, who have spread to the northern sea, into which the Phasis River flows. These four peoples occupy all the territory from sea to sea. I will now describe how two great peninsulas extend west from this territory into the sea. The upper rim of the northern peninsula stretches into the sea from the Phasis along the Pontus and the Hellespont as far as Sigeum in the Troad; the southern rim of this same peninsula runs from the Myriandic Gulf, which is near Phoenicia, to Cape Triopium. Thirty distinct peoples live in this peninsula.

So much for one of the peninsulas. The other begins in Persia and extends into the Red Sea. It contains first Persia, then Assyria, then Arabia, and ends—or is customarily represented as ending—in the Arabian Gulf, into which Darius dug a canal from the Nile. The country from Persia to Phoenicia is vast and flat, and from Phoenicia this peninsula extends along our sea through Palestinian Syria and Egypt, where it ends. There are only three peoples in this peninsula.

That is how much of Asia there is from Persia to the west. Inland, toward the east and the rising sun, the Red Sea adjoins the Persians, the Medes, the Saspires, and the Colchians. North of Asia is the Caspian Sea and the Araxes River, which flows toward the sunrise. Asia is inhabited as far as India. It is uninhabited beyond this to the east, and there is no one who can say what it is like there.

That, then, is the size and shape of Asia. Libya is actually a part of the second peninsula because it extends from Egypt. At Egypt this peninsula forms a narrow stretch of land about one hundred and twenty-five miles long between our sea and the Red Sea, and the extremely flat peninsula known as Libya is attached to this narrow stretch.

Now, I am amazed at the way mapmakers delimit and divide Libya, Asia, and Europe, because the differences between them are by no means small. Europe runs along the whole length of both Libya and Asia, and I don't think it's worth even trying to guess at its width. It is obvious that Libya is surrounded by water, except at that narrow point where it is attached to Asia. Neco, the king of Egypt, is the first person we know of to discover this fact.[2] After he stopped the excavation of the canal from the Nile to the Arabian Gulf, he sent some Phoenician men out in ships from the gulf with orders to keep sailing until they sailed through the

1. The Red Sea is the Persian Gulf and the Indian Ocean, and the land Herodotus refers to as extending from Persia to Colchis is the region that stretches north from present-day Iran to the Black Sea. Herodotus seems to have thought of western Asia and Asia Minor as peninsulas like Iberia, Italy, and Greece. The "upper rim" of the northern peninsula is the north coast of Asia Minor to the Hellespont. The southern rim is the coast from the Bay of Issus to the southwest corner of Asia Minor. The southern peninsula extends into the "Red Sea" and is made up of Syria, Arabia, and Phoenicia, with Persia as its base. It is joined to Libya (or Africa) at the Isthmus of Suez and comprises most of what we think of in the present day as the Middle East. The "peoples" are the Assyrians, the Arabians, and the Phoenicians.
2. Neco, son of Psammetichus, attempted to build a canal across the Isthmus of Suez.

Pillars of Heracles into our northern sea and back to Egypt again. The Phoenicians set forth from the Red Sea and kept sailing down the southern sea. In the autumn they would come ashore, plant some crops wherever in Libya they happened to be, and wait for the harvest. Then they would reap their crops and sail on. Two whole years went by, and in the third year they rounded the Pillars of Heracles and returned to Egypt. They reported all sorts of things I don't believe, such as that when they rounded Libya the sun was on their right. [3]

That is how Libya's true nature was first understood. Our next witnesses are the Carthaginians, since Sataspes, son of Teaspes, an Achaemenid, could *not* circumnavigate Libya, although he had been sent out to do just that. [4] He returned home, fearing the length and the loneliness of the voyage, and could not endure the ordeal his mother had imposed on him. You see, he had raped the virgin daughter of Zopyrus, son of Megabyzus. When he was about to be impaled for this crime by King Xerxes, his mother, who was the sister of Darius, interceded on his behalf saying that she would impose a greater penalty on him than Xerxes would: Sataspes would have to sail around Libya until he returned to the Arabian Gulf. Xerxes was amenable to these terms, and Sataspes went to Egypt, selected a boat and Egyptian sailors, and headed for the Pillars of Heracles. He sailed through them, rounded the Libyan cape known as Cape Soloeis, and sailed south. He crossed vast seas over many months, but there was always more to sail, so he turned back and sailed to Egypt. He returned to King Xerxes from Egypt and said that at the farthest point they reached they had sailed past tiny people wearing clothes made of palm leaves who fled their villages and headed for the hills whenever he and his men brought their ship ashore. He said that they did them no wrong after landing except to make off with some of their cattle. Sataspes said that the reason they were unable to complete the circumnavigation of Libya was that it had become impossible to make way against headwinds. But Sataspes had not endured the ordeal that had been imposed on him, so Xerxes showed him no sympathy even though he spoke the truth. Xerxes imposed the original punishment and impaled him. As soon as he learned that his master was dead, Sataspes' eunuch fled to Samos with a large sum of money, which a Samian then stole. I know the Samian's name, but I purposely forget it.

Most of Asia was explored by Darius. He wanted to find out whether the Indus River—which is the only other river in the world with crocodiles in it—whether it flows into the sea; so he shipped out men he trusted to report the truth, particularly Scylax the Caryandean. They set forth from Caspatyrus City, in the Pactyic territory, and sailed the river eastward toward the rising sun and into the sea. Then they sailed this

---

3. This report, which Herodotus does not believe, is the strongest evidence for a Phoenician circumnavigation of Africa. The sun would be on the right as one sailed west past the Cape of Good Hope.

4. The Achaemenids were the Persian royal family from which Cyrus and Darius were descended.

sea westward for thirty months and arrived at the place from which I earlier said the Egyptian king had dispatched the Phoenicians on the circumnavigation of Libya. After the voyage of these men, Darius conquered India and regularly sailed this sea. Thus Asia—except for the region toward the rising sun—was found to be very similar to Libya.

The nature of Europe is not clearly understood by anybody, because it is not known whether it is surrounded by water toward the rising sun or toward the north. It is known, though, that Europe extends along the length of both Libya and Asia. Nor can I figure out why three names are given to the parts of one landmass—and the names of women at that—or how the borders of these divisions came to be the Egyptian river Nile, or the Colchian river Phasis (though some say it is the Maeotic river Tanais and the Straits of Cimmeria). I have not been able to find out who made the divisions, or where they got the women's names from. Most Greeks say that Libya took its name from a native woman, while Asia got its name from the wife of Prometheus. A claim on this name is also made by the Lydians, though, who say that Asia is named after Asies, the son of Cotys, the son of Manes, [5] and not after Asia, the wife of Prometheus. It is after this Asies that the Lydian clan of Asias in Sardis was named. As to Europe, it is not known by any human being whether it is surrounded by water, or where it took its name from, or who bestowed the name—unless we say that the continent took its name from Europa of Tyre. Before her, of course, it would have had no name—just like the other continents. That woman, though, appears to have been from Asia and not to have gotten to the land which the Greeks now call Europe, but only as far as Crete from Phoenicia and then as far as Lycia from Crete. So much for this subject, though, because I will continue to use the traditional names for the continents. [6]

*   *   *

---

5. Members of the mythical royal family of Lydia.
6. Herodotus continues his discussion of the Scy-
thians and then moves on to the history of the peoples of North Africa.

Book 5

Book 5 is an invaluable source for the history of the Greek city-states during the seventh and sixth centuries B.C. Here Herodotus discusses both the internal political development of the city-states and relations among them. He also moves the reader significantly closer to the outbreak of war between Greece and Persia.

In 499 B.C. the cities of Ionia—the Greek-speaking western coast of Asia Minor—resolved to revolt from their Persian overlords. (Formerly part of Lydia, the Ionian cities had been incorporated into the Persian empire through Cyrus' conquest of Croesus.) Herodotus' account of the Ionian rebels' attempt to enlist the support of Sparta and Athens gives him occasion to discuss the history of the mainland Greek states, and to contrast the Spartans' fear of involvement in a campaign far from home with the Athenians' adventurousness and commitment to Greek freedom. This was a charged question at the time Herodotus was writing, when Athens' maritime strength had built a powerful, far-flung empire and Sparta, in opposition to Athens, had come to bill itself as the champion of Greek autonomy.

Whereas the Spartans refused to become involved in the Ionian rebellion, the people of Athens and of Eretria (north of Athens) furnished ships. In the end the rebellion failed, but in the course of it the Persian capital city of Sardis caught fire. Whether or not Greek involvement in the burning of Sardis actually prompted Darius' war against the Greeks, as Herodotus seems inclined to believe, it served as a plausible pretext for the campaigns that culminated in the Battle of Marathon in 490 B.C.

* * *

Chapters 48–105

That, then is how Dorieus[1] died. If he had remained in Sparta and been able to endure being ruled by Cleomenes,[2] he would have ended up as king of the Lacedaemonians because Cleomenes did not rule for very long and died without an heir, leaving only a daughter named Gorgo.

Now, Aristagoras, the tyrant of Miletus, arrived in Sparta when Cleomenes was in power. According to the Lacedaemonians, Aristagoras brought to their meeting a bronze tablet on which had been etched a map of the whole world, along with all its seas and rivers. At the meeting, this is what Aristagoras said to Cleomenes: "In view of the situation,

---

1. Younger half brother of the Spartan king Cleomenes.

2. King of Sparta from 519 to 490.

you must not be surprised at my haste in coming here. That the sons of Ionia are slaves rather than free men brings the greatest pain and disgrace to us, of course, but after us, to you, who are the leaders of Greece. In the name of the gods of Hellas, therefore, rescue the Ionians from slavery now, for they are your blood kin. It will be easy for you to accomplish this, because the barbarians are not very valorous, while you have reached the highest pitch of bravery in war. They fight with bows and short spears, and they wear baggy pants and turbans to battle! That should make them easy enough to handle. Also, the people who live on that continent have riches like no one else in the world, beginning with gold and including silver, bronze, fine clothes, beasts of burden, and slaves. If you really wanted these things, you could have them.

"Let me describe their geographical relationship to each other. These Lydians here are right next to these Ionians—they have lots of money and live on good land." As he said this, he pointed at the map of the world etched on the tablet he carried. "After the Lydians," continued Aristagoras, "the Phrygians occupy this land to the east. They have more cattle and richer harvests than any people I know. After the Phrygians you have the Cappadocians—only we call them Syrians—and bordering them are the Cilicians, who extend down to this sea here, where the island of Cyprus is. They send fifteen tons of tribute to the king of Persia every year. Next to the Cilicians, there are the Armenians—they have lots of cattle, too—and after the Armenians the Matieni occupy this territory here. Here is Cissia, and the Choaspes River here, and that's the famous Susa lying along it. That's where the Great King lives, and where his treasure houses are. Take this city, and from then on you can confidently rival Zeus himself for riches!

"So why must you risk battles with the equally matched Messenians and with the Arcadians and the Argives,[3] people who have no gold or silver at all—those things many a man has passionately fought and died for—over a little patch of land with insignificant borders not nearly as valuable as what I have shown you, when it is possible for you easily to become the masters of Asia? What's there to choose?"

That is what Aristagoras said. Cleomenes answered, "I will wait, my Milesian friend, until the day after tomorrow to give you an answer." That was as far as they got that day.

When the day for the answer came and they had gone to the appointed meeting place, Cleomenes asked Aristagoras how many days' journey it was inland from the coast of Ionia to the king of Persia. After having otherwise so successfully and cleverly fooled Cleomenes, this is where Aristagoras tripped up, because he should not have told Cleomenes the truth if he wanted to lure him into Asia. But tell the truth he did: he said the journey inland took three months. At that point Cleomenes cut

---

3. These were all neighboring states with which Sparta was in dispute.

short any further comment Aristagoras was about to make and said, "Leave Sparta before sundown, my Milesian 'friend.' Nothing you say sounds good to us Spartans any more, since you want to lead us on a three-month march inland from the sea."

After saying this, Cleomenes went home, but Aristagoras got hold of an olive branch and followed him. He entered Cleomenes' home as a supplicant and asked Cleomenes to send his child away and hear him out. You see, Cleomenes' daughter was standing next to him. Her name was Gorgo. She was his only child, and she was eight or nine years old. Cleomenes told Aristagoras to say whatever he wanted and not to hold anything back on account of the child. Aristagoras began by promising nearly six hundred pounds of precious metals if only Cleomenes would do what he had asked. When Cleomenes turned up his nose at this, Aristagoras kept increasing the amount of money until he was finally offering nearly thirty thousand pounds! Then the child cried out, "Father! If you don't get up and go away, this stranger will corrupt you!" Cleomenes was delighted with his child's advice and went into another room; Aristagoras left Sparta for good and never did get the chance to point out anything more about the road to the Great King on his map.

Here is what that road is like. There are royal way stations and fine inns all along the way, and the whole road runs through safe, inhabited territory. There are twenty way stations on the three-hundred-seventy-seven-and-a-half-mile stretch from Lydia to Phrygia. The Halys River is on the Phrygian border. Gates stand at the river crossing, and it is absolutely necessary to pass through them to cross the well-guarded river. After you cross over into Cappadocia, [4] there are twenty-eight way stations as you make your way from there to the Cilician [5] border, a distance of four hundred and sixteen miles. At the border, you have to go through two gates and pass two guard posts. After you pass through all this and follow the road through Cilicia, there are three way stations over a distance of fifty-nine and one-half miles. At the border between Cilicia and Armenia is a river called the Euphrates, which is crossed by ship. In Armenia, there are fifteen stations or rest houses over the course of two hundred twenty-five and one-half miles. There is also a guard house at this border. There are four rivers you cannot avoid crossing in Armenia, and you have to cross them by boat. The first is the Tigris; the second and third are called the Zabatus, although they are not the same river and do not flow from the same source. [6] The first river Zabatus is said to flow from Armenia itself; the second, from Matiene. [7] The fourth river is called the Gyndes [8] and is the one Cyrus once broke up into three hundred and sixty canals. When you leave this part of Armenia and

---

4. East central Asia Minor.
5. The eastern half of the southern coast of Asia Minor.
6. These are the Greater and the Lesser Zab rivers.

7. The Matiene in this passage is roughly the area of modern Turkish and Iranian Kurdistan.
8. The modern Diyala, which flows into the Tigris.

cross over into the Matienian country, there are thirty-four way stations over five hundred and forty-eight miles. From here, you pass into Cissia, where there are eleven stations over one hundred and sixty-eight miles until you get to the Choaspes River, which must also be crossed by boat and on which the city of Susa has been built. That makes one hundred and eleven stations in all—one hundred and eleven stopping places as you go up from Sardis to Susa!

If the royal road has been correctly measured in miles and if there are about eight furlongs in a mile, as indeed there are, then from Sardis to the palace of Memnon, as it is called, there are about eighteen hundred miles or fourteen thousand four hundred furlongs. If you travel one hundred and sixty furlongs every single day, it will take exactly ninety days to get there.

Thus Aristagoras the Milesian was telling Cleomenes the Lacedae-monian the truth when he said that the journey up to the Great King took three months. But if one is looking for something even more accu-rate than this, I will compute that also, because it is necessary to add in the trip from Ephesus to Sardis. Therefore I say that from our Greek sea to Susa (which is what the city of Memnon is called), there are in all fourteen thousand eight hundred and eighty furlongs, because there are four hundred and eighty from Ephesus to Sardis. Thus the three-month journey is lengthened by three days.

After Aristagoras was driven out of Sparta, he went to Athens, which had been freed from tyranny in the following way. After Aristogeiton and Harmodius, who were Gephyraeans by blood, killed Hipparchus, the son of Pisistratus and the brother of the tyrant Hippias (and Hippar-chus had had a perfectly clear dream vision of his own death in his sleep, by the way)—after that, the Athenians lived for another four years under a tyranny which was not better but even worse than it had been before the murder. Now, this was the dream vision of Hipparchus: on the night before the Panathenaic festival, Hipparchus thought he saw a tall, hand-some man standing in front of him speaking this riddle:

> Lion! suffer the insufferable in your suffering heart;
> No one fails to pay the fine for his injustice.

As soon as it was day, Hipparchus is known to have discussed this dream with some dream interpreters, but then, after talking out the dream, he went to marshal the procession in which, of course, he was killed.[9]

---

9. Aristogeiton and Harmodius were members of the ancient Athenian family of the Gephyraeans. For personal reasons, they plotted to kill the tyrant Hippias in 514 B.C. At the last moment, they believed that their conspiracy had been betrayed, so they killed Hipparchus, the brother of Hippias, and not the tyrant himself. Decades later, Atheni-ans came to believe that the assassination had been politically and not personally motivated, that Hip-parchus and not Hippias had been the tyrant, and that Harmodius and Aristogeiton had liberated Athens from tyranny. Athenians continued to hold this view even after it had been refuted by both Herodotus and Thucydides. (See the selection from Thucydides below, p. 256.)

According to the Gephyraeans themselves, from whom the murderers of Hipparchus were descended, they originally came from Eretria; but as I have discovered after investigation, the Gephyraeans derive from the Phoenicians who came with Cadmus into the country now called Boeotia.[1] Their share of the country was the Tanagran region, where they lived. But the Argives drove out the Cadmeians, and the Boeotians drove out the Gephyraeans, who then fled to Athens. The Athenians accepted them as fellow citizens on certain conditions: they were denied a few minor civil rights not worth mentioning.

These Phoenicians who came to live in this country with Cadmus and who were the ancestors of the Gephyraeans brought many useful skills into Greece—especially writing, which the Greeks did not, in my opinion, previously have. At first, the writing was the same as that used by Phoenicians everywhere, but with the passage of time, the shape of the letters changed along with the sounds of words. Ionian Greeks neighbored much of the Phoenician district back then. They learned the alphabet from the Phoenicians and adopted it with few changes. They called the letters phoenicians, and rightly so, since the Phoenicians had brought them into Greece. Since antiquity, the Ionians have referred to papyrus as "hide," because at one time, when papyrus was rare, they wrote on goat and sheepskin. To this day, in fact, many barbarians write on such hides.

I myself saw writing from the time of Cadmus[2] carved on three tripods in the temple of Ismenian Apollo in Boeotian Thebes—it closely resembled Ionian writing. This epigraph was on one of the tripods:

AMPHYTRYON DEDICATED ME HE PLUNDERED ME FROM
THE TELEBOAE

This would date it to around the time of Laius, the son of Labdacus, the son of Polydorus, the son of Cadmus. There is a hexameter inscription on another tripod which reads:

SCAEUS THE BOXER WON HIS FISTFIGHT HE DEDICATES THIS
FINE GIFT OF MYSELF TO YOU SURESHOOTING APOLLO

This Scaeus would have been the son of Hipokoon, if indeed it is he who dedicated it and not someone with the same name as the son of Hippocoon. It would be from the time of Oedipus, the son of Laius.

The third tripod also had a hexameter inscription:

LAODAMAS THE MONARCH HIMSELF DEDICATES THIS FINE GIFT OF A TRIPOD
TO YOU SHARPEYED APOLLO

It was during the reign of this Laodamas, the son of Eteocles, that the Cadmeians were expelled by the Argives and fled to the Encheleis. The

1. A region of Greece north of Attica whose principal city was Thebes.

2. The mythological founder of Thebes, who was said to have introduced the alphabet into Greece.

Gephyraeans stayed behind, but they later migrated to Athens because of the Boeotians. They have temples in Athens, which are not among the Athenian temples but are set apart from the rest. Their foremost temple is dedicated to Demeter of the Sorrows for her secret rites.

Now that I have talked about Hipparchus' dream vision and about the origins of the Gephyraean clan, from which the murderers of Hipparchus came, let me pick up on the story I began to tell—how the Athenians freed themselves from tyranny. Hippias had become more and more resentful and tyrannical toward the Athenians because of the death of Hipparchus. The Alcmaeonids, a family of pure Athenian descent who had gone into exile to avoid the Pisistratids, had tried—along with other exiles—to return to Athens and free the city by force. They failed miserably, so they withdrew to Lipsydrium in the Paeonian district and fortified the place. From there, they did everything they could think of to undermine the Pisistratids. For example, they accepted a contract from the Amphictyons to build the present temple in Delphi, which did not exist in those days. Since the Alcmaeonids were rich and illustrious, and had been for generations, they made the temple even more beautiful in several ways than the plans called for. For example, they had agreed to use limestone in building the temple, but they built the façade out of Parian marble instead.

According to the Athenians, while the Alcmaeonids were in Delphi, they bribed the Pythian priestess to suggest to any Spartans who came to consult the oracle either as private citizens or on behalf of the state that they should liberate Athens. Since the Lacedaemonians were always getting the same oracular message, they sent one of their foremost citizens, Anchimolius son of Aster, with an army to drive the Pisistratids out of Athens. The Spartans did this even though the Pisistratids were very close allies: they put the wishes of god before those of men.

The Spartans sent this force by sea. Anchimolius put in at Phalerum and disembarked his troops. Meanwhile, the Pisistratids had had advance news of this landing and called on the Thessalians for help. (They had earlier made an alliance with them.) At the request of the Pisistratids, then, and with the consent of the people, the Thessalians dispatched a thousand cavalrymen along with their king, Cineas the Coniaean. This is what the Pisistratids did after their allies arrived: they cleared the field of Phalerum and made it fit for cavalry operations and then sent the cavalry against Anchimolius' camp. They fell on the Lacedaemonians, killed many of them, including Anchimolius, and drove the survivors back to their ships. That, then, is how the first Lacedaemonian expedition fared. Anchimolius has a tomb in Alopecae, in Attica, near the temple of Heracles in Cynosarges.

Then the Lacedaemonians outfitted a larger expedition and sent it against Athens. They appointed their king, Cleomenes, the son of Anaxandrides, as general—and this time they sent the army not by sea but by land. As soon as they crossed into Attica, they were attacked by the

Thessalian cavalry, which was quickly forced back with a loss of over forty men. The survivors galloped straight to Thessaly without further ado. When Cleomenes reached the city, he and the Athenians who wanted to be free besieged the tyrants who were hemmed in behind the Pelargic wall on the Acropolis.

The Lacedaemonians could not force the Pisistratids out, and they had no intention of setting up an extended siege, because the Pisistratids were well supplied with food and water, so they would probably have kept up the siege for a few days and then returned to Sparta. But then a chance event happened which, though it was one and the same event, hurt one side and helped the other: the children of the Pisistratids were captured as they were being smuggled out of the country. As soon as this happened, the situation of the Pisistratids was thrown into utter confusion and they surrendered in exchange for their children and on the condition, determined by the Athenians, that they would leave Attica within five days. They left for Sigeum, on the Scamander River, after having ruled over Athens for thirty-six years. The Pisistratids were descended from Neleus, king of Pylos, as were the families of Codrus and Melanthus, who were originally immigrants but who became kings of Athens. That is why Hippocrates gave his son the name Pisistratus—in memory of Pisistratus the son of Nestor.

This is how the Athenians rid themselves of the tyrants. I will now relate whatever is worth mentioning about what they did and experienced after they became free, and before the Ionians revolted from Darius and Aristagoras the Milesian came to Athens to ask for their help.

Athens had been an important city before, but it became even more important after it got rid of the tyrants. Two men wielded power in the city: Cleisthenes the Alcmaeonid—the one they say bribed the Pythian priestess—and Isagoras, son of Tisander, who came from a prominent family, although I cannot speak for his ancestry. In any case, his relatives sacrifice to Carian Zeus. These two were engaged in a power struggle, and when Cleisthenes was defeated he allied himself with the common people. He divided the Athenians into ten tribes, whereas there had previously been four. They had been named after the four sons of Ion: Geleon, Aegicores, Argades, and Hoples; but he changed those names and substituted the names of local heroes—except for Ajax, who was included because he was a neighbor and an ally even though he was a foreigner. It seems to me that in making this change, Cleisthenes was imitating his maternal grandfather, Cleisthenes, tyrant of Sicyon.

After Cleisthenes the tyrant finished his war with Argos, the first thing he did was to put an end to competitions in Sicyon in which singers chanted the epic poems of Homer because the poems constantly celebrate Argos and the Argives. Also, there was—and still is—a hero's shrine for Adrastus, the son of Talaus, in the market place of Sicyon, and the next thing Cleisthenes wanted was to send it out of the country because Adrastus was an Argive. So he went to Delphi and consulted the oracle about whether he should banish Adrastus, but the Pythian priestess said that Adrastus was a king of Sicyon while he, Cleisthenes, was only an oppressor. Since the god would not grant his wish, Cleisthenes tried, on the way home, to think of a way to get Adrastus to leave on his own. When he thought he had found it, he sent a message to Boeotian Thebes saying that he wanted to bring the cult of Melanippus, son of Astacus, into his country—and the Thebans permitted it. So Cleisthenes invoked Melanippus and set up his statue in a sacred area designated for him right there in the best-guarded part of the town hall. It should be said that Cleisthenes invoked Melanippus because he had killed Adrastus' brother Mecistes and his son-in-law Tydeus, and was therefore Adrastus' mortal enemy. After the shrine was set up, Cleisthenes took the sacrifices and feastdays away from Adrastus and consecrated them to Melanippus.

Now, the Sicyonians, for their part, had always deeply revered Adrastus. The country itself had once belonged to Polybus, and Adrastus was the son of Polybus' daughter. When Polybus died without a male heir, he left the throne to Adrastus. The Sicyonians honored Adrastus in many ways, but particularly by commemorating his sufferings in tragic choruses. It was Adrastus they honored in tragedy, and not Dionysus! Yet Cleisthenes reassigned the choruses to Dionysus and the sacrifices associated with them to Melanippus.

That's what he did to Adrastus. As to the tribes, he changed their names so that they wouldn't be the same for the Sicyonians as for the Argives. In this more than in any other way, he humiliated the Sicyonians. He attached the suffixes of their tribal names (except for his own tribe) to words for "pig" and "ass." To his own tribe, he gave a name that signified his rule: he called them "the Rulers." But the others became "the Porkies," "the Donkeymen," and "the Piglets." The Sicyonians used these names for their tribes not only while Cleisthenes was alive but for sixty years after his death. After that, though, they thought it over and changed to the Argive names of the Hylles, the Pamphyli, and the Damanatae. They imposed the name of Aegialeus, son of Adrastus, on the fourth tribe—Cleisthenes' tribe—and made them be called the Aegiales.

Those are the things that Cleisthenes of Sicyon had done. Meanwhile, the Athenian Cleisthenes seems to me to have had contempt for the Ionians, because in not allowing the Athenians to have the same tribal names as the Ionians, Cleisthenes imitated his maternal grandfather and namesake, Cleisthenes the Sicyonian. Once he had won the previously despised Athenian people over to his side, he changed the names of the tribes and expanded their number. He appointed ten tribal leaders instead of the previous four, and he distributed the city's wards among the tribes so that each tribe would include ten of them. After gaining the support of the people, Cleisthenes became much more powerful than his opponents. But now that it was his turn to be defeated,

Isagoras developed a counterstrategy: he called in Cleomenes the Lacedaemonian, who had become an ally of his because of the siege of the
Pisistratids. Cleomenes, by the way, had been accused of having an
affair with Isagoras' wife. Cleomenes first sent an envoy to Athens banishing Cleisthenes and many other Athenians along with him. They
were specifically referred to as "the Polluted Ones." They were referred
to in this way on instructions from Isagoras, because the Alcmaeonids
and their supporters were guilty of the murder in question, while neither
Isagoras nor his friends had had any part in it.

This is how the "polluted" Athenians got their name: Cylon was an
Athenian Olympic champion who had set his sights on becoming a tyrant.
He formed a junta of men his own age and tried to seize the Acropolis,
but when he couldn't gain control of it he sat down in front of the statue
of Athena as a supplicant. The board of magistrates which governed
Athens in those days got them to leave on condition that they would
receive a punishment short of the death sentence. They were killed,
though, and the blame for it fell on the Alcmaeonids. All this happened
before the era of Pisistratus.

After Cleomenes sent the order banishing Cleisthenes and "the Polluted Ones," Cleisthenes slipped out of town by himself. Nevertheless,
Cleomenes later appeared in Athens with a small force and, on the advice
of Isagoras, expelled seven hundred families as moral polluters of the
city. The next thing he did was to try to dissolve the assembly and to put
power into the hands of three hundred supporters of Isagoras. When the
assembly resisted and would not obey, Cleomenes and Isagoras and his
supporters took control of the Acropolis. The rest of the Athenian people
were of one mind and besieged them for two days; on the third day, the
Lacedaemonians were allowed to leave under a truce. The warning given
to Cleomenes was thus made good. You see, after he had climbed up to
the Acropolis to take control of it, he was about to go into the sanctum
sanctorum of Athena to address the goddess. The priestess stood up from
her seat, and before he could get through the door, she said, "Go back,
Spartan friend, and do not enter the temple! No Dorian is permitted to
enter here." He said, "I am an Achaean, woman, not a Dorian." He
ignored the warning, went ahead with his attempt on the acropolis, and
was thrown out with the rest of the Lacedaemonians. The others were
imprisoned on capital charges. Among the prisoners was Timesitheus of
Delphi. Ah! I could tell the most wonderful tales of his feats of strength
and courage!

After the prisoners were put to death, the Athenians sent for Cleisthenes and the seven hundred exiled households; next they sent ambassadors to Sardis. They wanted to make an alliance with Persia because
they knew that Cleomenes and the Lacedaemonians were still bent on
war with them. After the ambassadors arrived in Sardis and delivered
their messages, Artaphernes, the son of Hystaspes and satrap of Sardis,
asked the Athenians who they were and where they came from that they

should want an alliance with Persia. When he got this information from the ambassadors, he summed it up for them this way: the alliance would be concluded if the Athenians gave King Darius both land and water; if not, he told them that they could go away. The ambassadors wanted the alliance to be made, so they took it on themselves to say that land and water would be given. They were, however, severely reprimanded for this after their return to Athens.

Cleomenes knew that he had been humiliated by the Athenians in word and deed, so he assembled an army from all over the Peloponnese without telling them why he was doing so, although what he wanted to do was punish the Athenian democrats and set Isagoras up as tyrant. You see, Isagoras had left the Acropolis along with him. Cleomenes attacked Eleusis with a large force while the Boeotians took the outermost wards of Attica—Oenoe and Hysiae—by a prearranged plan. Meanwhile, the Chalcidians marched in and devastated the other side of Attica. Although the Athenians were attacked on two fronts, they decided to deal with the Boeotians and Chalcidians by and by and to take their stand against the Peloponnesians in Eleusis.

Just before the two camps were about to join in battle, the Corinthians were the first to realize that they weren't doing the right thing, so they did an about face and left. Demaratus, the son of Ariston and the other of Sparta's two kings, followed them although he had led the army out of Lacedaemon and had not disagreed with Cleomenes in the early going. After this dissension, a law was passed in Sparta forbidding both kings from accompanying the army at the same time. Until then, both used to go out on campaigns, but now, when one was away, the other had to remain in Sparta—he, and one of the statues of Castor and Pollux. Before this law, both statues also went along as guardians of the army. But on that day in Eleusis, when the other allies saw the kings of Sparta disagreeing while the Corinthians abandoned the formation, they, too, backed off and left.

This was the fourth time the Dorians went into Attica—twice to make war, and twice for the good of the Athenian people. The first time was when Megara was founded, and this expedition is rightly said to have taken place when Codrus was king of Athens. The second and third times were when they came from Sparta to expel the Pisistratids, and the fourth time was this one, when Cleomenes invaded Eleusis with a force of Peloponnesians.

That, then, was the fourth time the Dorians attacked Athens.

The Athenians wanted revenge after this army disbanded so ingloriously, and they formed a force to attack the Chalcidians first. The Boeotians came to the aid of the Chalcidians at the Euripus Strait. When the Athenians saw the relief force, they decided to attack the Boeotians first and not the Chalcidians, so they took on the Boeotians and completely defeated them, killing a great many and taking seven hundred prisoners. On the very same day, the Athenians crossed into Euboea and fought with the Chalcidians, whom they also defeated. Then they left four thousand settlers on the land of the knightly Chalcidian horse ranchers—"horse ranchers" was what the Chalcidian rich were called. The Athenians fettered both the Chalcidian and Boeotian prisoners and kept them under guard. They were eventually released at a price of two hundred drachmas a head. The chains they were fettered in were hung up on the walls of the Acropolis, and they were still there in my time— hanging on walls that had been charred in Persian fires—opposite the great westward-facing temple of Athena. They made a bronze four-horse chariot with one-tenth of the ransom money and dedicated it to the goddess. It stands on the left as you first enter the gateway to the Acropolis, and it has this inscription on it:

THROUGH THEIR EXPLOITS IN WAR THE SONS OF ATHENS SUBDUED THE BOEOTIAN AND CHALCIDIAN NATIONS, QUENCHING THEIR INSOLENCE IN IRON JAILS OF GRIEF AND CONSECRATING THIS TITHE OF HORSES TO PALLAS ATHENA.

Athens really began to thrive now. It shows, not just in one way, but in every way, that equality before the law is a goodly thing, since under the tyrants the Athenians were no better than their neighbors in battle, whereas after they got rid of the tyrants they became by far the best; it shows that when they were downtrodden they slacked off, since they were toiling for a despot, but that when they became free, each and every one eagerly strove for his own success.

After the Athenians performed these feats, the Thebans consulted Apollo because they wanted to take revenge on Athens. The Pythian priestess said that "their revenge would not come from themselves." She told them to take the matter out "to the place of many voices," and ask "those who were nearest to them" for help. When the envoys returned, they brought the oracle before the full Theban assembly, and when the Thebans heard what they said about "asking those who were nearest to them," they said, "Aren't the people who live nearest to us the Tanagrans, the Coroneans, and the Thespians?"

"But they already do willingly fight our wars with us, right through to the end."

"What would we ask them for?"

"The oracle must mean something else."

They were talking along these lines when somebody suddenly got it and said, "I think I know what the oracle is trying to tell us! They say that Asopus had two daughters, Thebe and Aegina. Because these two were sisters, I think that the god is telling us to ask the Aeginetans to be our allies."

Since no better opinion presented itself, they immediately sent to the Aeginetans, calling on them to help "as their nearest," in the words of the oracle. In response to this request, the Aeginetans said that they would send their statues of Aeacus and his sons to guard the Thebans in battle. The Thebans tried an attack with their statue allies, but when they got rough treatment at the hands of the Athenians, they sent the statues back to the Aeginetans and asked for some real men instead. The Aeginetans were then feeling the confidence of a period of great prosperity; they also remembered their ancient animosity against the Athenians. So, at the request of Thebes, they launched an undeclared war against Athens. For example, while the Athenians were attacking the Boeotians, the Aeginetans sailed over to Attica in long ships and raided Phalerum and other coastal towns. These actions inflicted great damage on the Athenians.[3]

This longstanding, unappeased Aeginetan hatred of the Athenians had the following origin. There was once a time when the land yielded up no harvest to the Epidaurians, and they consulted the Delphic oracle about this calamity. The Pythian priestess commanded them to build statues of Damia and Auxesia—things would get better for them after the statues were erected. The Epidaurians asked whether they should make the statues out of bronze or stone; the priestess forbade them to use either—only the wood of cultivated olive trees. In the belief that Athenian olive trees were the most sacred of all, the Epidaurians asked the Athenians for some trees to cut down. It is even said that in those days there were no olive trees in any part of the world except Athens. The Athenians said that they would give them the trees on condition that they bring offerings to Athena of the City and to Erechtheus every year. The Epidaurians agreed to these terms; they got the olive wood they wanted, and they installed the statues they built with it. Their land yielded fruit again, and they kept their agreement with the Athenians.

At this same time—and even before—the Aeginetans gave their allegiance to Epidaurus and also went over there to have the Epidaurians settle their legal disputes for them. Some time later, though, the Aeginetans built a navy and ungratefully rebelled against the Epidaurians. The Aeginetans had control of the sea, and their hostility led them to do the Epidaurians a great deal of harm. They even stole the statues of Damia and Auxesia, brought them over to Aegina, and set them up in the interior of the island—in a place called Oea, about two and a half miles from the city. Then they worshiped the statues of these deities with sacrifices and with women's troupes performing carnival dances and satirical songs. They appointed ten men per statue to train and direct the women, who did not satirize any men, but only the local women. The Epidaurians had practiced the same rites, although they also had other, secret rites.

After the statues were stolen, the Epidaurians stopped honoring their agreement with the Athenians. Athens sent a protest to the Epidaurians,

3. War was declared when one side sent a herald to the other to announce the existence of a state of war. During the war, the safety of heralds was assured by both sides so as to keep lines of communication open. Undeclared war began with surprise attacks and was a sign of the bitterest enmity.

who took the position that they had done nothing wrong. They said that they had kept the agreement for so long as the statues were in their country, but now that they had been stolen, Athens had no grounds to make charges against them; so they told Athens to get the offerings from the Aeginetans, who had the statues. In view of this, the Athenians sent Aegina a request that the statues be returned. The Aeginetans responded by saying that they had no obligation whatever to Athens.

The Athenians say that after this request was made, the people manned a single trireme[4] and sent it to Aegina. When the ship arrived, its crew tried to lift the statues off their mountings and bring them home on the grounds that they were made of Athenian wood. When the men couldn't get them off in this way, they threw some ropes around the statues and tried to pull them down, but as they were pulling they were met by thunder and, along with the thunder, an earthquake. After these shocks, the crew that was pulling down the statues went berserk and began to kill each other like enemies in battle until only one was left to be brought back to Phalerum.

That is how the Athenians say it happened. The Aeginetans, on the other hand, say that the Athenians didn't come in just one ship. (They say that if there had only been one, or even just a few, they would have been able to defend themselves easily—even if they didn't happen to have any ships of their own.) No, the Athenians bore down on their island with a large fleet and they gave way without a fight. Their statements don't make it clear whether they gave way because they realized that they were outnumbered in a naval battle or whether they had planned to do as they did. According to the Aeginetans, when no one opposed the Athenians in battle, they disembarked from their ships and made their way to the statues. When they couldn't get the statues off their mountings, they threw some ropes around them and started to pull. The Aeginetans say that while they were being pulled, both statues did exactly the same thing. What they say is not credible to me, though it may be to others, because they say the statues fell on their knees before the Athenians and stayed that way forevermore. The Aeginetans also say that they had found out in advance that the Athenians intended to make war on them and had obtained the help of Argos. When the Athenians landed on Aegina, the Argives were there. They had crossed over to the island from Epidaurus unnoticed and then attacked the unsuspecting Athenians, cutting them off from their ships, while thunder and earthquake struck at the same time.

This is what is said by the Argives on the one hand, and the Aeginetans on the other.

The Athenians agree that just one of them survived to return to Attica— only the Argives insist that he escaped after they had destroyed the Athe-

---

4. A trireme was a fighting ship with three banks of oars.

nian forces, while the Athenians say it was an act of god. That one man didn't really survive, though. He died in the following way: after he was brought to Athens, he gave an account of what happened, and when the wives of the other men who had attacked Aegina heard it, they were furious that only one out of all those men should survive. So they surrounded the man and grabbed him and stuck him with the pins that help up their dresses while each woman asked him where her husband was. That is how he was killed, and the Athenians regarded what the women did as even more terrible than what had happened to the other soldiers. They couldn't really punish the women in any other way than to make them adopt an Ionian style of dress. Before that time, the women of Athens had worn Dorian-style clothes—very similar to the Corinthian—but they were made to switch to linen tunics to keep them from using pins. (To be strictly accurate, this garment was not originally Ionian but Carian, since the style of all Greek clothing for women was originally the same as what we now call the Dorian style.)⁵

This same event led to the Argives and the Aeginetans to change their customs. Both of them made dressing pins half again as large as their normal size used to be, and women's favorite offerings to their gods became pins and brooches. They stopped bringing anything made in Attica—even ceramics—to their temples, and from that time on it became the custom to drink only from locally made ceramic cups. And even in my day, Argive and Aeginetan women wore pins that were larger than they used to be because of their feud with Athens.

That, then, is how the enmity of the Aeginetans toward the Athenians began. Therefore, when the Thebans asked them for aid, the Aeginetans called to mind the events connected with the statues and willingly helped them.

So the Aeginetans ravaged the seacoast of Attica, and just as the Athenians were about to send an army out to make war on Aegina, they received an oracle from Delphi: if they held off from doing anything about the Aeginetan affront for thirty years, and in the thirty-first year dedicated a temple to Aeacus, and *then* began the war with Aegina, they would achieve everything they wanted; but if they marched off immediately, they would suffer much and accomplish much over the years, though they would in fact finally conquer Aegina. The Athenians listened to the message, and dedicated the temple to Aeacus, which is still in the marketplace; but they didn't wait the thirty years they were supposed to—they felt that they had suffered too great an atrocity from the Aeginetans.

While the Athenians were preparing their punitive attack, a problem with the Lacedaemonians came up and stood in their way. The Lace-

5. "The Ionian chiton was a long linen garment like a night-gown, with full sleeves to the elbow." See W. W. How and J. Wells, A *Commentary on* *Herodotus* (Oxford, 1928), p. 48. The Dorian costume was a square woolen cloth folded around the body and fastened at the shoulder with a pin.

daemonians had found out about the Alcmaeonid bribery of the Pythian priestess and about her lying oracles to them concerning the Pisistratids, and they were doubly upset over it—first, because they had driven their own allies out of Athens and, second, because after they had done so they got no thanks whatever from the Athenians. In addition to this, they were motivated by oracles saying that "they would be the object of all sorts of hostilities from Athens." They had known nothing of these oracles before, but they were able to study them carefully after Cleomenes brought them to Sparta: he had gotten possession of them in the Athenian Acropolis, where they had been kept by the Pisistratids. They left the oracles in the temple when they were driven into exile and Cleomenes picked them up after they had been left behind.

As soon as the Lacedaemonians had the oracles, they saw how the power of Athens had grown, and that the Athenians weren't about to submit to them under any circumstances. The Lacedaemonians realized that if the Attic people were free, they would weigh equally in the balance of power with Lacedaemon, while if they were crushed by a tyrant, they would be obedient and weak. When the Lacedaemonians understood all this, they recalled Hippias from Hellespontic Sigeum, where the Pisistratids had gone into exile. After Hippias answered their summons, the Spartans sent for the representatives of their allies and said, "Friends, we must admit that we have made a mistake. We were encouraged by lying oracles to drive good friends and allies out of their fatherland—men who allowed us to take the affairs of Athens in our hands. Then, after we did this, we gave the city to a thankless mob which insulted and expelled our king once it lifted up its head in the freedom we gave it. Athens expands with a swelling spirit, as their neighbors the Boeotians and the Chalcidians know better than anyone—though others may yet make the mistake of finding out. But since we have mistakenly created this condition, we are now going to try to cure it—with your help. That is why we have summoned you, and Hippias here, from your cities: so that we can with one mind and one body return him to Athens and restore to him what we have taken away."

That's what they said, but the majority of their allies did not accept their argument. They all held their peace, though, except Socles the Corinthian. This is what he said: "Well now! Next the sky will be under the earth, and the earth will be suspended above the sky; men will hold sway in the sea, and fish will haunt the realm of men, for you, O Sparta, are destroying republics and preparing to restore to our cities those tyrannies than which humanity knows nothing more unjust or fouled with blood. But if it seems so worthwhile to you for cities to be ruled by tyrants, why don't you set one up among yourselves first, before you seek to impose them on others? The fact is, though, that while you have no experience with tyrants and take every precaution to keep this terror from Sparta, you will use it as a means to an end among your allies. If you *were* experienced with it, as we are, you would come up with better ideas about it than you have now.

"At one time, the Corinthians had an oligarchic constitution. The clan of the Bacchiadae governed the city, intermarrying among themselves. But one of these men, Amphion, had a lame daughter—in fact, her name was Labda. None of the Bacchiadae wanted to marry her, so she was taken by Eetion, son of Echecrates, who was from the village of Petra—although he was descended from Caeneus the Lapith. He had no children by this wife, though, or by any other, so he went to Delphi to ask about getting offspring. Just as he was entering the oracle, the Pythian priestess greeted him with these verses:

Eetion, no one honors you, honorable though you are.
Labda is pregnant and will give birth to a stone
That will roll over the oligarchs and pass judgment on Corinth.

"Somehow, the Bacchiadae were informed of this oracle. They had previously found another oracle about Corinth to be incomprehensible, but it prophesied the same thing as the one to Eetion. It said:

An eagle conceives in the rock; it will bear a lion,
Raging, ravenous, to loosen the sinews of many a knee.
Take care, Corinthians, you who live near fair Peirene
And the deep-browed cliff of Corinth.

"The Bacchiadae didn't have a clue to the meaning of this oracle, but as soon as they heard the oracle to Eetion, they immediately understood that the first one jibed with his. Although they understood, though, they kept quiet about it because they wanted to kill Eetion's as yet unborn child. As soon as the woman gave birth, they sent ten men from their own clan into Eetion's village to kill the child. After they arrived in Petra, they went to Eetion's house and asked to see the baby. Labda had no idea of why they were really there. She thought they were asking to see the baby because they were friends of its father, so she carried it over to one of them and put it in his arms. Now, on the way to Petra the men had decided that the first one of them to hold the baby should smash it against the ground. But by the luck of the gods, as soon as Labda handed over the baby, it smiled at the man who took it. When he saw this, such pity came over the man that he couldn't kill the child. He handed it over to the second man, who passed it in pity to the third. The baby was handed from one to the other until it made the rounds of all ten. None of the men wanted to destroy it. Finally, they gave the child back to its mother and went outside. They stood at the door collaring and blaming each other, but especially the first one to hold the baby because he hadn't carried out the plan. They kept this up for quite a while, until they decided to go back inside, where all of them would take a hand in killing the infant.

"But the seed of Eetion was destined to bring forth evil fruit for Corinth. Labda was standing by the door and heard everything. She was afraid that they really had changed their minds and that they really would kill the baby once they got hold of it the second time around, so she took the child and hid it in a large jar, which seemed to her to be a place nobody would ever think of. She knew that they would ransack everything if they came back in for a search—which is just what happened. When the men couldn't find the baby after going in and searching, they decided to leave and tell the people who had sent them that they had followed their orders to the letter. And so they did.

"The child grew up, and Eetion called him Cypselus—the name for the kind of jar in which he had escaped danger. When Cypselus became a man, he consulted the Delphic circle and was given a double-edged prophecy he trusted in so much that he got to work and eventually seized power in Corinth. This was the prophecy:

> This man who comes down into my house is lucky
> —Cypselus, son of Eetion, king of splendid Corinth—
> He and his sons, but not the sons of his sons.

"This was what the oracle said, and after he took power, this is the kind of man Cypselus became: he exiled many Corinthians, and he stripped many of their property and many more of their lives. He ruled for thirty years, and after he successfully finished the web of life, his son Periander followed him in power. Now, Periander was at first more benign than his father, but then, after he became acquainted through his ambassadors with Thrasybulus, tyrant of Miletus, he steeped himself in blood more deeply even than Cypselus.

"Periander had sent an envoy to Thrasybulus to find out the surest way for him to set up a government so that he might best administer the affairs of the city; but Thrasybulus led Periander's envoy out of town and into a field of grain, and as they walked through the wheat, Thrasybulus kept stopping the envoy and asking him questions about his trip from Corinth. Meanwhile, whenever Thrasybulus saw some especially tall spikes of wheat he would cut them off and throw them away until he had destroyed the finest and tallest plants in the crop. After they had walked through the whole field in this way, Thrasybulus dismissed the envoy without a word of advice.

"After the man returned to Corinth, Periander was eager to find out what Thrasybulus' advice was. The envoy said that Thrasybulus hadn't given him any advice. In fact, the man was surprised that Periander should send him to such a person—a lunatic who went around gleefully destroying his own crops. And then the envoy described what he had seen Thrasybulus doing.

"Periander understood Thrasybulus' actions and realized that he was advising him to kill the most outstanding men in Corinth; and from that day on Periander exhibited every form of wickedness to his fellow citizens. Indeed, he finished off anyone Cypselus had neglected to banish or kill, and there was one day in particular when he stripped naked every Corinthian woman on account of his wife, Melissa. You see, Periander had sent ambassadors to the necromancers in Thesprotia on the Acheron River to be reminded of where he had buried some treasure belonging to a friend. The ghost of his wife, Melissa, appeared and said that she wouldn't tell them where the treasure was either in words or in signs, because she was naked and cold. She said that her clothes had been buried along with her and that they were no use to her unless they were also burned. "Tell Periander that he shoved his loaf into a cold oven," she said, "and he'll know that I'm an honest ghost." This message was brought back to Periander, and he knew that the clue was reliable—he who had had sex with Melissa's dead body. Immediately after he got the message he sent out the announcement that all Corinthian women must gather in the temple of Hera. They all went, as if to a festival, wearing their finest, but Periander's bodyguards were hiding in the temple and stripped them one and all, free women and slaves alike. Then Periander put the clothes in a pit, said a prayer to Melissa, and burned them all up. After he did this, he sent to the necromancers a second time and the ghost of Melissa reminded him where he had buried the treasure of his friend.

"That's tyranny for you and those are its actions, my Spartan friends. Astonishment seized us Corinthians when we saw you summoning Hippias, and we are even more astonished over what you have said. We invoke the gods of Greece as we solemnly entreat you not to establish tyrannies in our cities. Will you not forbear? Must you try unjustly to restore Hippias to power? If you do, know that we Corinthians will never consent to it!"

That was the speech of Socles, ambassador from Corinth. Hippias answered him by invoking the very same gods as he did and by saying that the Corinthians would miss the Pisistratids more than anyone else when the day came—as it inevitably would—that they were brought to grief by the Athenians. Hippias gave this answer with a surer understanding of the oracles in question than anyone else. The other allies had been holding their peace all this time, but after they heard Socles speaking so freely, every one of them called out to adopt the Corinthian viewpoint and implored Sparta not to foment revolution in any Greek city.

The plan was dropped. After Hippias was sent away, Amyntes the Macedonian offered him Anthemus while the Thessalians offered him Iolcus. He didn't accept either of these, though, and returned instead to Sigeum, which Pisistratus had taken from the Mytilenaeans by force. After Pisistratus had control of it, he set up Hegesistratus—his illegitimate son by an Argive woman—as its tyrant. It was not without a struggle that Hegesistratus held on to what he had inherited from Pisistratus, because for a long time Mytilenaeans from a city near the tomb of Achilles and Athenians from Sigeum made war on each other: the Mytilenaeans demanded the territory back, but the Athenians wouldn't acknowledge the demand and argued from the text of Homer that the Aeolians had no more right to Troy than the Athenians or anybody else who had helped Menelaus to avenge the abduction of Helen.

All sorts of things happened in battle during this war. During one encounter, which the Athenians won, Alcaeus the poet ran for his life. The Athenians captured his battle gear and hung it up in front of the temple of Athena in Sigeum. Alcaeus wrote a lyric poem describing his experience and sent it to Melanippus, his comrade-in-arms in Mytilene.

Periander the son of Cypselus reconciled the Mytilenaeans and the Athenians after they appealed to him to act as arbitrator. The terms of the agreement were that each side should remain in the territory it occupied. Thus Sigeum fell under Athenian control.

Hippias went back to Asia after leaving Lacedaemon and was constantly busy denouncing the Athenians to Artaphernes and doing everything he could to see to it that Athens became subject to him and Darius. When the Athenians found out that Hippias was actually doing this, they sent ambassadors to Sardis forbidding the Persians to aid the exiles. Artaphernes ordered them to take Hippias back—if they knew what was good for them. The Athenians, of course, didn't accept this answer, and by not doing so, they had decided openly to become the enemies of Persia.

Just at the time when the Athenians had reached this decision and were at odds with the Persians, Aristagoras the Milesian, who had been driven out of Sparta by Cleomenes the Lacedaemonian, arrived in Athens. It was, after all, the most powerful of the remaining Greek cities. Aristagoras went to the people's assembly and told them the same thing he had said in Sparta about the riches of Asia and about Persian fighting tactics, such as that since they did not typically use shields or spears it would be easy to get the upper hand over them. He added that it would be appropriate for the Athenians, with their great power, to come to the aid of the Milesians, who had been Athenian colonists. There was nothing he did not promise in return for what he asked. It would seem to be easier to deceive many people than one person: Aristagoras had not been able to deceive the lone Cleomenes the Lacedaemonian, but he managed to do it with thirty thousand Athenians. After the Athenians were won over, they voted to send twenty ships to the aid of Ionia, and they placed them under the command of Melanthius, a citizen who was highly regarded in every way. These ships were the beginning of trouble between the Greeks and the barbarians.

Aristagoras sailed on ahead, and after arriving at Miletus he devised a plan from which no benefit whatever was destined to come to Ionia (not that he did it for any other reason than to irritate King Darius). He sent a man into Phrygia, to the Paeonians from the river Strymon who had fallen prisoner to Megabazus and who had settled in the Phrygian territory and had a village to themselves. When this man reached the Paeonians, he said, "Aristagoras, tyrant in Miletus, has sent me, O men of Paeonia, to offer you an escape—if, that is, you decide to accept it. All Ionia has now revolted from the king, and it is possible for you to return to your lands there. All you have to do is get to the coast. Let us worry about the rest."

The Paeonians were overjoyed to hear this, and, taking up their wives and children, they fled to the sea, though some of them stayed behind out of fear. After reaching the coast, the Paeonians crossed over to Chios. They were already in Chios when a large contingent of Persian cavalry that had been hot on their heels arrived at the coast. Seeing that they had not caught them, they sent a message to Chios telling the Paeonians to come back. The Paeonians rejected the proposal, and the Chians conveyed them to Lesbos and the Lesbians to Doriscus. From there, they made their way on foot to Paeonia.

Now, Aristagoras, after the Athenians arrived with twenty ships and five Eretrian triremes, which did not come along on the expedition as a favor to the Athenians but as a way of returning a favor to the Milesians, who had in turn once helped the Eretrians carry on a war against the Chalcidians when the Samians aided the Chalcidians against the Eretrians and Milesians—Aristagoras, I say, formed an expedition against Sardis once the Athenians had arrived and all the other allies were together. He did not campaign in person, of course. He remained in Miletus and appointed others to command the Milesians—his brother Charopinus, and Hermophantus, an ordinary citizen.

When the Ionians reached Ephesus with this force, they left the ships in Ephesian Coresus, appointed Ephesian guides, and marched inland with a large army. They made their way along the Cayster River and from there went up and over Mount Tmolus and took Sardis without opposition—all of it, that is, except the acropolis. Artaphernes himself defended the acropolis with a not inconsiderable body of men.

This is what kept the Ionians from plundering the captured city. Most of the houses in Sardis were made of straw, and those that were made of brick had straw roofs. A soldier set one of these houses on fire, and the flame spread from house to house until the whole city had caught fire. When the city was burning, the Lydians and such Persians as were in the acropolis found themselves hemmed in by a ring of fire, and since they had no escape route from the city they streamed into the marketplace and down to the Pactolus River, which carried gold nuggets down from Mount Tmolus, flowed through the middle of the marketplace, and merged with the Hermus on its way to the sea. After gathering at the river and in the market, then, the Lydians and the Persians were forced to stand and fight. When the Ionians saw some of their enemies taking up defensive positions and large numbers of others getting ready to attack, they nervously retreated to Mount Tmolus and slipped away from there to the ships as night fell.

Not only was Sardis burned to the ground, but along with it a temple sacred to Cybebe, a local goddess. The Persians later used this fact as an excuse for burning down Greek temples in retaliation.

The Persians with provinces on this side of the Halys River had early knowledge of Ionian movements and raised a force to come to the aid of the Lydians. As the Ionians were no longer to be found at Sardis, though, they followed their trail until they caught up with them at Ephesus. The Ionians positioned themselves to fight and were seriously defeated in the battle. The Persians killed many of them and even some who were famous, including the Eretrian general Eualcides, who had won the laurel wreath in many an athletic event and been highly praised by Simonides of Ceos. Some of the Ionians deserted the battle and dispersed through the cities.

That was what the fighting was like at that time. Later, the Athenians completely abandoned Ionia and refused to help Aristagoras, although his messengers often called on them to do so. The Ionians were deprived of the Athenian alliance, but they had gone so far in their actions against Darius that they nonetheless continued their war with the king. They sailed through the Hellespont in order to subject Byzantium and all the other cities in the region to themselves; and they sailed out of the Hellespont to win most of Caria over to an alliance. Caunus had not wanted an alliance at first, but when Sardis was burned down, it too came over to the Ionians. Except for the Amathusians, all of Cyprus went over to the Ionians.

* * *

The message was brought to King Darius that Sardis had been captured and burned by the Ionians and Athenians and that the leader of the conspiracy which had woven the plot had been Aristagoras the Milesian. They say that when Darius learned these things, he was not interested in the Ionians, since he well knew that they could not rebel with impunity. He did, though, ask just who these Athenians might be, and when he found out he asked for his bow. He took it, drew an arrow, and shot it into the air, and as he shot at the sky, he said, "O Zeus, may it be possible for me to punish the Athenians." So saying, he commanded one of his servants to say three times whenever serving dinner, "Master, remember the Athenians."[6]

* * *

6. In the twenty-one chapters that follow to the end of book 5, Herodotus tells of the progress of the Ionian rebellion.

Book 6

The focus of book 6 is the stunning Greek victory on the plain of Marathon, north of Athens, where, Herodotus maintains, the Greeks lost under two hundred men while Darius lost over six thousand. Greatly outnumbered by the attacking Persians, the Athenians dispatched the runner Philippides (sometimes called Pheidippides) to Sparta to seek aid—Herodotus claims Philippides covered the distance of about 150 miles in two days—but the Spartans were unwilling to march because of an ongoing religious festival. (A later story developed by the Greek writer Lucian under the Roman empire maintained that Philippides ran to Athens to announce the victory at Marathon and dropped dead upon his arrival. The long-distance race known as the marathon was devised in honor of Philippides' supposed feat of dedication.) In the end, nearly all the Greek troops at Marathon were Athenian, and Herodotus ascribes their victory in large part to the vigorous leadership of Miltiades, a great Athenian military hero.

Miltiades by his checkered career reveals a great deal about the difficulties the developing Athenian democracy was having in defining itself. In chapters at the end of book 6 (not included here), Miltiades' uncle, also named Miltiades, had been sent by the Athenian ruler Pisistratus to administer the area of the Chersonese, by the Black Sea; when Miltiades the Younger—the Persian War hero—succeeded his uncle, he found himself impeached by political enemies at home for misconduct, something people could hardly have been concerned about in any genuine way, since the people whom he was accused of abusing were not Athenians. After the Persian Wars, his great reputation persuaded the Athenians to grant him ships and money to undertake a secret mission he promised would enrich them. He sailed against the island of Paros, but when the expedition culminated not in wealth but in disaster, he was impeached and heavily fined. Athens had no president or prime minister, and in a rising democracy that had no officials higher than its board of ten generals, it was important for the assembly to keep a close watch on military men and politicians alike. This vigilance, however, sometimes opened the door to attacks by professional and personal enemies who were able to manipulate the strong Athenian concern for accountability to their own advantage. After Miltiades died of a wound sustained in the unsuccessful attack on Paros, his fine was reduced and paid by his son Cimon, who became the most distinguished general in the Athenian maritime confederacy that grew out of the war.

* * *

Chapters 98–117

After doing this, Datis sailed away to Eretria with his army and took some Ionians and Aeolians with him.[1] There was an earthquake in Delos after he left, and according to the Delians it was the first and last seismic event in their history so far. Through it, surely, god gave a sign to mankind of the evil that was to come; for in the three successive generations of Darius the son of Hystaspes, Xerxes the son of Darius, and Artaxerxes the son of Xerxes, there was more woe for Hellas than in the twenty generations that went by before Darius—some of it brought on Greece by the Persians, and some by the leading cities of Greece warring among themselves for supremacy. Thus it was fitting that there should be an earthquake in Delos when there had never been one before. (By the way, there was a prophecy on record about this which said, "I will shake Delos, unshaken though it has been." Also, in Greek, the Persian names Darius, Xerxes, and Artaxerxes mean, respectively, "the Doer," "the Warrior," and "the Great Warrior," and if those were the names the Greeks gave these kings they would be very appropriately named indeed.)

After they set sail from Delos, the barbarians stopped off at the islands, where they conscripted an army and took the children of the islanders hostage. They also stopped at Carystus[2] as they went from one island to another, and because the Carystians would not give them hostages and refused to make war on neighboring cities—meaning Eretria and Athens—the barbarians besieged them and scorched their earth until the Carystians came around to the Persian way of thinking.

When the Eretrians learned that the Persian army was sailing against them, they called on the Athenians for help. The Athenians did not refuse aid—they sent those four thousand settlers from the "horse-ranching" country of Chalcis as reinforcements. But the Eretrians who had sent for the Athenians didn't have a sound policy and were of two minds about what to do. Some of them wanted to abandon the city and head for the Eretrian hills, while others expected to profit personally from the arrival of the Persians and were preparing to betray the city. Aeschines, son of Nothon, was one of the foremost Eretrians, and as soon as he found out about these two prevailing views he explained the situation to the newly arrived Athenians and urged them to go back where they came from to avoid getting killed along with everybody else. The Athenians followed Aeschines' advice.

1. Datis and Artaphernes were generals sent by Darius to reduce Athens and Eretria to slavery. We take up the narrative after Datis has made an offering at Delos.

2. Carystus, Eretria, and the other cities mentioned here were on the long island of Euboea (the modern Evvoia).

While the Athenians were saving themselves by crossing over to Oropus, the Persians sailed in and landed their ships along the Eretrian coast at Tamynae, Choereae and Aegilia. As soon as they had landed, they put their horses ashore and got ready to take the fight to their enemies; but the Eretrians had no intention of going forth and doing battle with the Persians. What they were worried about was finding a way to defend their city walls—since the idea of not abandoning the city had won out. There were furious attacks on the wall for six days, and many fell on both sides. On the sixth day, two of Eretria's leaders—Euphorbus, son of Alcimachus, and Philagrus, son of Cyneas—betrayed the city to the Persians. After they entered the city, the Persians robbed and burned the temples to take vengeance for the temples that had been burned down in Sardis, and then, as Darius had ordered, they enslaved the whole population.[3]

The Persians stayed on for a few days after Eretria was completely under their control, and then they sailed full speed ahead to Attica with the idea of doing the same thing to the Athenians that they had done to the Eretrians. Because it was close to Eretria, and because it was the best place in Attica for cavalry operations, Hippias, son of Pisistratus, guided the Persians to Marathon.

When the Athenians found out about this, they set up a war cry and then they, too, headed for the plain of Marathon. They were led by ten generals. The tenth—and the commander in chief—was Miltiades, whose father, Cimon, son of Stesagoras, happened to have been banished from Athens by Pisistratus, son of Hippocrates. In exile, Cimon won an Olympic victory in the four-horse chariot event, exactly the same prize as his half brother Miltiades. He won at the next Olympics with the same mares, but he allowed Pisistratus to be heralded as the winner. For transferring the victory to Pisistratus, Cimon was allowed to return home unhindered. After Cimon won yet another Olympic victory, still with the same mares, he was killed by the sons of Pisistratus, who was no longer living. Their assassins ambushed him at night in the city hall. Cimon was buried, right outside the city, across the road that leads to the so-called Hollow. The mares that won three Olympic victories were buried opposite him. (No other mares have ever performed this feat except those of Euagoras the Laconian.) At the time of the murder, Cimon's oldest son, Stesagoras, was being brought up by his uncle Miltiades in the Chersonese, while the youngest was living with his father in Athens. His name was Miltiades, after the uncle who had founded the colony in the Chersonese.

Now, it was this Miltiades who had become commander in chief of the Athenian forces after fleeing the Chersonese and escaping death twice.

3. For the burning of Sardis, see book 5, chapter 101.

He had been pursued as far as Imbrus by the Phoenicians, who did everything they could to catch him and bring him to the Great King, and then, after he had returned home in the belief that he was finally safe, his enemies, who had been lying in wait for him, hauled him off to court and prosecuted him on a charge of having been a tyrant in the Chersonese. But he escaped them, too, and was appointed an Athenian general after an election by the people.

While they were still in the city, the first thing the generals did was to send Philippides the herald to Sparta. He was an Athenian who kept himself in constant training as a long-distance runner. To hear Philippides tell it—and he did tell it to the Athenians on his return—the god Pan fell in with him on Mount Parthenium, up over Tegea. Pan shouted out his name—"Philippides!"—and commanded him to bring a message to the Athenians, asking them why they didn't ever worship him, since he had good will toward them and had been useful to them in all sorts of ways in the past and would be again in the future. The Athenians believed this story, and, because of this message, when things finally returned to normal they built a temple to Pan under the Acropolis, where they worship him with annual sacrifices and torch races.

This Philippides was in Sparta the day after being sent off from the city of Athens by the generals on the mission during which he says that Pan appeared to him. As soon as he arrived, he said to the Spartan officials, "Lacedaemonians! The Athenians call on you to come to their aid and not to allow the most ancient city in Greece to be enslaved by barbarians. Eretria is even at this very moment enslaved and Hellas has become weaker by one important city." After Philippides delivered his message, the Lacedaemonians told him that they would be happy to help the Athenians but that it was impossible for them to do it just then, because they didn't want to break the law: it was the ninth day of the month, and they said that they couldn't go out to battle on the ninth unless the moon was full.[4]

So they waited for the full moon while Hippias, son of Pisistratus, was leading the barbarians to Marathon. The night before they got there, Hippias had a dream. He dreamed that he had gone to bed with his own mother. He interpreted the dream to mean that he would return to Athens, regain his power, and die of old age in his own land. That was how he interpreted this dream! The next day, he guided the Persians to the Styrean island known as Aegilia, where he dropped off the Eretrian captives. Next, he led the ships to Marathon, where he brought them to anchor, and then he positioned the barbarians for battle as they came ashore. While he was doing this, an unusually severe fit of sneezing and coughing came over him. Now, since he was on the old side, most of

---

4. The Spartans were celebrating the Carneia, a festival in honor of Apollo during which all Dorians refrained from warfare unless the moon happened to be full.

his teeth were loose, and when one of them was forced out by a violent cough and fell into the sand, he looked high and low for it. When the tooth didn't turn up, he sighed deeply and said to the people who were standing near him, "This land isn't ours, and we won't be able to conquer it. Now my tooth is taking a bite out of any share of it I ever had." Hippias concluded, then, that this was the fulfillment of his dream.

The Athenians had taken up a position at the temple of Heracles, and the Plataeans came to their aid in full strength. Actually, the Plataeans had long before given up their freedom to Athens, which has since borne many a burden for them. The Plataeans gave up their independence in the following way. Because they were being ground down by the Thebans, the Plataeans first offered their fealty to Cleomenes, son of Anaxandrides, and his Lacedaemonians, who happened to be on Plataean territory at the time. They rejected the offer, though, and said this: "We live so far away from you that any help from us would arrive too late. You'd be carried off into captivity many times over before any of us even found out about it. We advise you to swear your allegiance to the Athenians. They live nearby, and they're not bad fighters." The Lacedaemonians gave this advice not so much out of goodwill toward the Plataeans as because they wanted the Athenians to have the burden of a constant conflict with the Thebans. In any case, that was the advice the Lacedaemonians gave the Plataeans, and the Plataeans followed it. While the Athenians were sacrificing to the Twelve Gods, Plataean ambassadors sat as suppliants at the altar and offered their fealty to Athens. When the Thebans found out about this, they made war on Plataea—and Athens came to its defense. Just as they were about to do battle, a Corinthian force which happened to be in the vicinity stepped in and, at the request of both sides, imposed a settlement which created a border between Thebes and Plataea on condition that Thebes would not stand in the way of any Boeotians who did not want to belong to the Boeotian confederacy. The Corinthians left after rendering this judgment. Then the Boeotians attacked the departing Athenians, who defeated them in the battle that followed. The Athenians crossed the border the Corinthians had just set for Plataea and determined that the Asopus River was now the border between Thebes on one side and Plataea and Hysiae on the other.

The Athenian generals were of two minds. There were those who opposed giving battle, saying that they were too few to fight with the Persian army, while others, including Miltiades, urged it on. Because opinion was evenly divided, and because the worse course was about to be adopted by default, Miltiades went to talk to the war chief, Callimachus of Aphidnae. He was an eleventh Athenian officer who was chosen by lot, and in those days the Athenian people empowered the war chief to cast the decisive, tie-breaking vote. Miltiades said to him, "Callimachus, it is up to you, *right now*, to enslave Athens or to make her free, and to leave for all future generations of humanity a memorial to yourself such as not even Harmodius and Aristogeiton have left. *Right now*, Athens is in the most perilous moment of her history. Hippias has already shown her what she will suffer if she bows down to the Medes, but if this city survives, she can become the foremost city in all of Greece. Now, I'll tell you just how this is possible, and how it is up to you—and only you—to determine the course of events. We ten generals are split right in two, with half saying fight and the other half not. If we don't fight now, I am afraid that a storm of civil strife will so shake the timber of the Athenian people that they will go over to the Medes. But if we fight now, before the cracks can show in some of the Athenians, and provided that the gods take no sides, why then we can survive this battle. All this depends on *you*. It hangs on your decision—*now*. If you vote with me, your fatherland will be free and your city will be first in all of Hellas, but if you choose the side of those who urge us not to fight, then the opposite of all the good I've spoken of will fall to you."

Miltiades won over Callimachus with these words. With the support of the war chief the decision to fight was made. Then, since command rotated from general to general on a daily basis, the generals who were in favor of a battle relinquished their commands to Miltiades. He accepted them, yet he didn't fight until it was his regular day to command anyway.

When his turn came up, the Athenians got into position for battle. Callimachus, the war chief, commanded the right flank of the army. That was the custom in those days—for the war chief to command the right flank. Beginning at the right, the other tribes were stationed one beside the other in their official order, ending with the Plataeans, who held the left flank. And ever since this battle at Marathon, whenever the Athenians offer sacrifices at the national festivals they hold every four years, the Athenian herald prays for the blessing of the gods to light on the Plataeans as well as on the Athenians. The Athenian formation at Marathon that day was something like this: their line was the same length as the Persian line, but their center was only a few rows deep. In fact, the center was the weakest part of the line, while each flank had been reinforced in great strength.

After they had taken up their positions, they kept cutting the throats of sacrificial animals until the omens looked good; then the Athenians were unleashed, and they furiously charged the barbarians. There was a distance of no less than one mile between their spearpoints. When the Persians saw them advancing on the double, they started preparing to take the charge, and when the Persians saw how few they were, charging impetuously without horses or archers, they thought the Athenians were rushing insanely to their complete and utter destruction. Well, that's what they thought. But when the Athenians came to grips with the barbarians, what a fine account they gave of themselves! They were the first of all the Greeks we know of who used the tactic of charging the enemy line; they were also the first who could bear up under the sight of Persian uniforms and the men wearing them. Until that day, merely to hear the word "Persian" was terrifying to the Greeks.

Long they fought at Marathon. The barbarians eventually won the battle in the center of the line, which is where the Sacae and the Persians themselves were positioned. After this seeming victory, the barbarians broke through and started chasing the Athenian center inland; meanwhile, the Athenians and Plataeans won at both flanks. They allowed the beaten barbarians to turn and run. Then the two flanks of the Athenian army joined forces, advanced against the Persian troops that had broken through in the middle, engaged them in battle, and defeated them. They chased the routed Persians, cutting them to pieces until they reached the sea, and then they took hold of the retreating Persian ships and called out for fire.

In this battle for the ships, Callimachus, the war chief, was killed, a valiant man, along with one of the generals, Stesilaus, son of Thrasylaus. Cynegirus, son of Euphorion, fell there, too—his hand chopped off with a battle-ax as he grabbed hold of the figurehead of a ship; and there fell, too, many other Athenians of great renown.

The Athenians captured seven of the ships in this way, but the barbarians managed to push away from shore in the rest. Then they picked up the Eretrian captives they had left on the island and rounded Sunium with the intention of beating the Athenians to the city. The accusation was made in Athens that the Alcmaeonids had devised this strategy and that, by a prearranged signal, they had flashed a shield at the Persians after they had gotten back in their ships.

Be that as it may, the Persians were sailing around the headland of Sunium, and the Athenians ran to the rescue of their city as fast as their legs could carry them. They got there before the barbarians did and bivouacked near the temple of Heracles in Cynosarges after having come from the other temple of Heracles in Marathon. The barbarians lay out to sea in their ships opposite Phalerum, which used to be Athens' harbor in those days, but after riding at anchor for a while they sailed back to Asia.

Sixty-four hundred barbarians died at the Battle of Marathon as opposed to one hundred ninety-two Athenians. Those are the numbers of the fallen. But an amazing thing happened at Marathon. Epizelus, son of Cuphagoras, an Athenian who was bravely fighting in the battle, lost his eyesight without being struck by a sword or missile anywhere on his body. From that day on, he remained blind for the rest of his life. I hear that he always used to tell this story about his misfortune: he thought a gigantic, heavily armored warrior was coming at him, a man so big that his beard cast a shadow over his whole shield; but the apparition passed him by and killed his buddy. Anyway, that's what they tell me Epizelus always said.

*   *   *

Book 7

Book 7 shows Herodotus' enormous interest in military decision making, especially the gathering of intelligence and the weighing of information and arguments. Advisers such as Artabanus, Mardonius, and Artemisia represent the different perspectives Xerxes was forced to consider in planning his campaign. Although Herodotus had no way of knowing the precise words spoken at the Persian court—and modern readers may be bemused by the notion of a powerful monarch mapping strategy according to dreams—the story of Xerxes' interchange with Artabanus and the dreams that followed conveys Xerxes' ambivalence about the huge campaign he was undertaking. Herodotus' use of dreams to reflect the hesitations of a fearful commander draws on the tradition of Homer, who in book 2 of the *Iliad* had expressed Agamemnon's apprehensions about the siege of Troy through a dream. The Homeric tradition is also evident in Herodotus' sonorous catalog of the various armed contingents, which evokes Homer's catalog of ships, also in book 2 of the *Iliad*. The careful descriptions of weapons and uniforms that attire the assorted nationalities who march with Xerxes underline the variety of peoples involved in the war and add vividness and particularity to the narrative.

Chapters 1–57

King Darius, son of Hystaspes, was already in a sharp mood toward the Athenians because of their attack on Sardis, but when the news about the battle that had taken place at Marathon arrived, why then he became much more furious and was more eager than ever to make war on Greece. He immediately sent heralds from city to city announcing that they should muster an army—only this time he demanded far more men than they had supplied before—along with warships and transports, horses and food. After this call went out, Asia was in a commotion for three years as they selected and trained their best men for the assault on Greece. In the fourth year, though, the Egyptians, who had been enslaved by Cambyses, rebelled against the Persians, whereupon Darius actually chafed to make war on both Greece and Egypt.

But just as Darius was about to set out against Egypt and Athens, a major conflict developed among his sons over the succession, since under Persian law the king had to appoint a successor before he could go on a campaign. Before he became king, Darius had had three sons by his first wife, the daughter of Gobryas, and then another four after he became king by Atossa, the daughter of Cyrus. Artabazanes was the oldest of the first group; Xerxes, of the second. These two sons of different mothers quarreled—Artabazanes on the grounds that he was the oldest of all of Darius' progeny, and that it was customary among all people for the oldest to inherit the throne; Xerxes on the grounds that he was the son of Atossa, daughter of Cyrus, and that Cyrus was the one who had made Persia free.

At the time of these events, but before Darius had made his decision known, Demaratus, the son of Ariston, happened to have gone up to Susa after losing his throne in Sparta and going into self-imposed exile from Lacedaemon. Rumor has it that this man found out about the dispute between Darius' sons and that he approached Xerxes and advised him to add to the arguments he had already made the point that Darius had him when he was already in power as king of Persia, whereas Artabazanes was born while Darius was still a private citizen. Therefore, added Demaratus, it was neither fitting nor just that anyone should take precedence over him, since it was the custom even in Sparta that if the older children were born before their father became king, while the younger was born afterward, the royal succession fell to the latecomer. Xerxes followed Demaratus' advice, and Darius realized that what he said was just and appointed him king. In my opinion, though, Xerxes would have become king even without this advice because Atossa was all-powerful. After proclaiming Xerxes king of Persia, Darius hurried up his preparations for war. But in the thirty-sixth year of his rule, in the year after the Egyptian rebellion and the succession struggle, and while he was still busy with his preparations, it came to pass that Darius died without ever getting the chance to punish either the Egyptian rebels or the Athenians. After the death of Darius, royal power was transferred to Xerxes.

Now, Xerxes at first had no enthusiasm at all for an expedition against Greece, although he did continue to muster an army for an attack on Egypt. But Xerxes' most influential Persian adviser, his ever present cousin Mardonius, son of Gobryas and of Darius' sister, kept repeating an argument that ran like this: "Master, it doesn't look good when the Athenians can do all kinds of damage to us Persians with impunity. If you would only do what you now have the power to do! Tame the impudent Egyptians and then lead your armies against Athens so that you will have some respect in the world and so that people will think twice later on about making war on your soil." It was basically an argument for vengeance, but it was always made with the addition that Europe was a very beautiful continent, with all sorts of crops of unsurpassed fertility under cultivation, a place which the king more than any other mortal should possess.

Mardonius said all this out of a craving for gratuitous change and because he himself wanted to be the satrap of Hellas. Mardonius worked on Xerxes for a long time and finally persuaded him to do it, but it happened that other events conspired to persuade him also. First, Thessalian ambassadors came from the Aleuadae (a Thessalian princely family) offering the king their complete support and appealing to him to attack Greece. Then there were the Pisistratids who had gone up to Susa and were making the same arguments as the Aleuadae—and they even had something more to offer than arguments. They had patched up their differences with Onomacritus and brought him along with them. Onomacritus was an Athenian oracle collector who had compiled and edited the oracles of Musaeus; but he had been banished from Athens by Hipparchus, son of Pisistratus, when Lasus of Hermione caught him redhanded as he was altering the text of Musaeus by inserting an oracle which said that the islands off the coast of Lemnos would disappear under the sea. As a result, Hipparchus banished him, although they had previously been close friends.

At this time, though, Onomacritus accompanied the Pisistratids to Susa, and, whenever he came into the presence of the king with them, they would solemnly mutter his praises while he expounded oracles. Onomacritus didn't even mention the oracles that portended failure for the barbarian. He selected only the most auspicious ones and recited them—such as how "the Hellespont must be yoked by a Persian"—after which he would go into the details of the expedition. What with Onomacritus chanting prophecies and the Pisistratids and Aleuadae pushing their arguments, Xerxes was finally persuaded to make war on Greece.

First he attacked the rebellious Egyptians—two years after the death of Darius. After he subdued them and reduced all of Egypt to even greater slavery than they had known under Darius, he turned the country over to his brother Achaemenes, son of Darius. Many years after Achaemenes became satrap of Egypt, he was killed by a Libyan, Inarus, son of Psammetichus.

After the conquest of Egypt and just before taking command of the expedition against Athens, Xerxes called a special assembly of Persian nobles so that he could learn their views and personally brief them all on his plan. When they were convened, this is what Xerxes said: "Men of Persia! I am not introducing new ways among us; I have inherited our ways of conquest, and I will follow them. I hear from our most senior citizens that we Persians have not been idle for one moment since Cyrus deposed Astyages and we took power away from the Medes. On the contrary. God directs things in such a way that the more active we are, the better they turn out. Cyrus, Cambyses, and my father, Darius, conquered other peoples and annexed them to us . . . but you know this very well, there's no point in telling it to you. And since I inherited this throne, I have thought about how to avoid falling short of my forebears in this office or acquiring less power for Persia; and having taken thought, I have found a way to add to our glory and to conquer a territory not poorer but richer and at least as vast as what we already have—while we punish and avenge our foes all at the same time. That is why I have convened you today, to tell you what I intend to do.

"I am going to build a bridge over the Hellespont and march an army across Europe into Greece in order to take vengeance on the Athenians for what they did to Persia and to my father. You yourselves saw Darius getting ready to make war on those people. He died and wasn't able to take revenge, but on behalf of him and of all Persians I will not rest until I capture Athens and burn it down—for the Athenians were the ones who started this trouble by wronging my father and me. First they entered Sardis with Aristagoras the Milesian—our slave!—and burned its sacred groves and temples. Then there's what they did to us when we landed on their soil, when Datis and Artaphernes were in command. But you all know about that. For all these reasons, then, I am determined to go to war; and when I think about it I find that war will bring these advantages: if we conquer the Athenians and their neighbors—the ones who live in the land of Pelops the Phrygian—we will create a Persia that borders on the very sky of god. For the sun will not look down on any country that borders on ours; instead, I will, with your help, pass through all of Europe and make its lands one land. They tell me this is the way things are: there won't be a human city or nation of mankind left that will be able to oppose us once we have disposed of the people I've mentioned. Thus both the guilty and the guiltless will wear our yoke of slavery.

"It would please me if you would do the following: when I tell you when you have to report for duty, it would be best if each and every one of you showed up enthusiastically. I will bestow the most highly prized gifts our society has to offer on whoever arrives with the best equipped army. That, then, is what must be done. But, so that I won't seem to you to be making all these decisions myself, I'm opening up the whole subject to discussion, and I urge any one of you who so desires to make his opinions known." And with these words, he ended.

Mardonius spoke after him. "Master," he said, "you are not only the noblest Persian who has ever lived but the noblest who will ever live, you who have scaled the heights of nobility and truth in your speech and who will not allow those base European Ionians to make light of us. Just because we wanted to expand our power, we have enslaved the Sacae, the Indians, the Ethiopians, the Assyrians, and other great and numerous peoples who have done us no wrong. So it would be very strange indeed if we did not punish the outlaw Greeks. What should we fear? The size of their army? The influence of their wealth? We know how they fight, and we know how weak they are. After all, we have defeated their sons in battle—the ones who have settled on our soil and are called Ionians, Aeolians, and Dorians. I have campaigned against these men on orders from your father, and I have marched as far as Macedon, not far from Athens itself, without anyone's opposing me in battle.

"Meanwhile, I hear that the Greeks are in the habit of fighting poorly planned wars through stubborn stupidity. Whenever they declare war on

each other, they look for the finest, flattest field and go there to fight—
which means that the victors leave with huge casualties. I won't even
mention the losers; they're just completely destroyed. Since they all speak
the same languages, they ought to use envoys and ambassadors to settle
their differences—or do anything rather than fight. But if they absolutely
have to make war on each other, they ought to find places where it
would be hard to get at one another, and fight there. It was probably
because the Greeks use these inefficient tactics that I could march as far
as Macedon without its entering their minds to fight with me.

"So who, Your Majesty, is about to oppose you or threaten war when
you lead all your fighting hordes and navies out of Asia? In my opinion,
the Greeks aren't organized enough to be so bold. But if I'm wrong,
and, aroused by folly, they come out to meet you in battle, they'll find
out that we are the best fighters in the world. Anyway, let's leave no
stone unturned. Keep trying and all things come to you, but nothing
will come on its own."

After thus taking the rough edges off of Xerxes' plan, Mardonius ended
his speech. The other Persians kept silent, not daring to put forward an
opposing view, but Xerxes' uncle Artabanus, son of Hystaspes, believed
that his relationship with the king would protect him and said this: "Your
Majesty, when there is no debate of opposing views, it isn't possible to
choose the best course—you must adopt whatever has been proposed.
But when there is debate, you have a choice. In the same way, you can't
assay gold just by looking at it; but when you rub it against another piece
of gold, you find out which is purer. I told your father—my brother
Darius—not to make war on the Scythians, men who don't live in any
city on this earth, but he expected to conquer the Scythian nomads and
didn't listen to me. He waged his war and got away only after losing
many of his best troops. Yet you, Your Majesty, are about to make war
on men who are far superior to the Scythians, men, they say, who excel
on both land and sea. It's only right for me to point out to you how
dangerous they are.

"You say that you are going to bridge the Hellespont and march an
army across Europe and into Greece. Now, let's just say that you are
defeated on land or sea—or even on both. After all, they say these are
brave men, which you could figure out for yourself from the fact that
the Athenians single-handedly wiped out the army that went to Attica
with Datis and Artaphernes. But say you aren't defeated on both—even
if they just ram our ships and defeat us in a naval battle and then sail to
the Hellespont and destroy the bridge, why that, Your Majesty, that
would be really dangerous. And I'm not just making this up out of my
own imagination. We almost suffered a tragedy like it once when your
father built bridges over the Thracian Bosporus and the Ister and then
crossed into Scythia. The Ionians had been entrusted with guarding the
bridge over the Ister, and the Scythians tried everything to get them to
undo it. And if Histiaeus the tyrant of Miletus had gone along with the

opinion of the other tyrants without opposition, the military might of Persia would have been done for. It's terrifying to so much as hear it said that our king's whole empire depended on one man!

"You must not under any circumstances put yourself into such danger when there is no reason to. Trust me. Dissolve this assembly now. Think it over by yourself later, and then, when you decide the time is right, announce what you think the best course is. I have found that good planning gives you a tremendous advantage. Then, if something gets in the way of the plan, it was nonetheless a good plan; it was just thwarted by bad luck; but if someone plans sloppily, it's still a bad plan even if he gets lucky and has a windfall success. You see for yourself how god strikes oversize beasts with lightning and doesn't let them show themselves off, while the little ones don't bother him at all. You see for yourself how he always hurls his lightning shafts at the tallest buildings and trees. God loves to lop off everything that gets too big. Thus large armies are defeated by small ones when god in his resentment of them casts thunder and panic in their midst, and they perish, so unworthily, in disgrace. You see, god doesn't allow anyone but himself to have grand plans. Everything stumbles when it hurries too much, and from such falls the greatest injury always comes. There are advantages in delay; you may not see them immediately, but you'll find them out in time.

"That's the advice I have for you, Your Majesty. As for you, Mardonius, son of Gobryas, stop talking nonsense about the Greeks; they don't deserve to be belittled. You are only maligning them to incite the king to war. That's what I think you really want. But may that never happen! Slander is a most terrible thing. In it, two men do an injury and one is injured. The slanderer does an injury by accusing someone behind his back, and his listener does one by believing the hearsay before he knows it for a fact. The victim, who has no part in the discussion, is wronged because he is slandered by the one and considered to be wicked by the other.

"But come, Mardonius, if it is absolutely necessary to make war on those people, let the king stay home, here in Persia, while you and I bet our children on the outcome. Command the army. Choose whatever men you want, and make the army as large as you think necessary. If the war turns out as you say it will for the king, then let my children be killed, and me along with them. If it's as I predict, though, then let your children suffer the same fate, and you, too, if you ever return. But if you don't want to take on this bet, and if you must steer the armada to Greece, then I predict that some of those who stay behind here will hear that Mardonius brought a great disaster on Persia and is being scattered piecemeal by dogs and birds somewhere in Athens or Lacedaemon—if, that is, it doesn't happen to you along the way first, and you learn the kind of men you are advising the king to fight with."

After Artabanus said this, Xerxes answered in a rage, "You are my father's brother. That will save you from receiving the payment you

deserve for your foolish words. The disgrace I will inflict on you for
being so cowardly and craven is that you will not campaign with us but
stay here with the women. I will do without you what I have said must
be done. May I not be the descendant of Darius, Hystaspes, Arsames,
Ariaramnes, Teispes, Cyrus, Cambyses, Teispes, and Achaemenes if I
do not punish the Athenians, because I know very well that if we lie still
and they do not, then, judging by what they have already done, they
will be the ones who are making war on us, they who have already
advanced into Asia and burned Sardis to the ground. There's no retreating for either side; the struggle is joined, to suffer or to act; either we will
be subject to the Greeks or they to us, for there is no compromise in
hatred. It's a good thing we were the first ones who were wronged and
have the chance to take revenge, so that I can find out about this terrible
calamity I'm going to suffer in making war on men like the Greeks—
men whom Pelops the Phrygian, the slave of my ancestors, conquered
so completely that to this day these men and their land still bear the
name of their master."[1]

That was what was said on the subject. Later, though, in the still of
the night, Artabanus' opinion kept troubling Xerxes. As he thought it
over that night, he realized that invading Greece really wasn't the best
thing for him to do. He fell asleep after he reached this new conclusion,
and then, or so the Persians say, he had a dream something like this:
Xerxes thought he saw a tall, handsome man standing over him who
said, "So then, Persian, have you decided not to lead a campaign against
Greece after commanding the Persians to muster an army? But you don't
do well to change your mind, and there is no one near who will excuse
you. No, do as you decided to do today; go on down that path." After
the man said this, Xerxes thought he flew away.

When it was broad daylight again, though, Xerxes paid no attention
to this dream and reconvened the same assembly. He said, "Men of
Persia! Excuse me for changing my plans so suddenly. After all, I haven't
yet reached the height of my mental powers, and the people who urge
me to take this action are never away from me for a minute. Still, my
youthful spirit did boil up as soon as I heard Artabanus' opinion, so that
I spewed out ruder language than I should have at an older man. Now,
though, I agree with him, and I'm going to take his advice. So you can
relax: I've changed my mind about invading Greece."

When the Persians heard this, they joyously prostrated themselves
before him.

But then, that night, the same apparition again stood over the sleeping
Xerxes and said, "Son of Darius! Have you really, in front of the Persians, openly renounced the campaign and disregarded my words as if

1. In mythology, Pelops was the son of Tantalus, a Lydian king. Xerxes' reasoning is that since Pelops, the eponymous founder of the Peloponnese, had been an Asian subject, Sparta and hence Greece were also subject to Asia.

they came from a nobody? You'd better understand the consequences of your actions: if you don't start that campaign immediately, you will be brought low just as fast and in just as short a time as you became great and powerful."

Xerxes jumped out of his bed in terror after he saw this vision and sent a messenger to get Artabanus. When he arrived, Xerxes said, "Artabanus, I wasn't thinking clearly when I spoke nonsense to you on the spur of the moment about your valuable counsel. Not much later, though, I changed my mind, and I realized that I had to do what you had advised. But now it seems that I can't just do that even though I want to. You see, since I turned it over in my mind and then changed my plan, a dream figure has been visiting me and absolutely refusing to allow me to change. He has just gone away now, in fact, after violently threatening me. If it's god who is sending this dream and who can only be made happy by an invasion of Greece, then the dream will also fly over to you and give you the same order it gives me. I suspect that this would happen if you were to put on my royal costume, sit on my throne, and then later go to sleep in my bed."

Although Xerxes told him to do this, Artabanus did not at first obey the order, because he didn't think it was right for him to sit on the royal throne. But he was finally pressured into doing it, and this is what he said before obeying the order: "As far as I'm concerned, Your Majesty, it makes no difference whether one plans well oneself or is willing to listen to good advice. You are able to do both, but you are frustrated by your association with unworthy people—just as the sea, which is the most useful of all things to mankind, is thwarted, or so they say, by the blasts of wind which fall on it and will not allow it to be itself. The pain of hearing your reproaches didn't gnaw at me so much as the fact that when two courses were open to Persia—one which swelled our insolence, and the other which suppressed it and said that it was evil to teach the spirit to always look for more than it has—of these two courses, you chose the worse for yourself and for Persia.

"But now that you have opted for the better choice, you say that since you gave up the idea of an expedition against Greece, a dream sent by some god keeps visiting you and not allowing you to disband the army. But dreams don't come from god, my dear boy. The drifting dreams that haunt people are such as I will teach you, I who am so many years older than you are. The dream visions that orbit our minds usually come from what we have been thinking about during the day, and our days have been very busy with this invasion recently.

"But look, if this isn't as I say, and does have something to do with god, then you yourself have said it succinctly: let the image come and give his command to me, as he has to you, although, really, if he wants to appear to me, he will do it anyway, whether I'm wearing my clothes or yours or sleeping in my bed or yours. Whatever it is that appears to you in your sleep, it's not so stupid as to think I'm you when it sees me just because I'm wearing your clothes! But if it pays no attention to me and won't deign to appear to me, whether I'm in your clothes or mine, but will only visit you . . . well, that's what we have to find out now. If it really does continually visit the same place, though, then even I would say that it comes from god.

"If there is no getting away from it, and it's been decided that I must sleep in your bed, let's go. I will do it all, and then let the vision appear to me, too. In the meanwhile, I'll stick to my opinion."

After saying this, Artabanus did as he was told, expecting to show Xerxes that his idea was wrong. He put on Xerxes' clothes and sat on the royal throne, and then, after he had gone to bed and was fast asleep, the same vision that had come to Xerxes came to him. It stood over him and said, "So you are the one who is so very, very anxious for Xerxes that you try to deter him from making war on Hellas. But you won't escape the consequences of trying to avert what must be, not now and not in the future; and as for Xerxes, he has already been shown what he must suffer if he disobeys."

After the vision made these threats, Artabanus thought that it was about to burn out his eyes with a hot iron. Screaming, he jumped up and went and sat next to Xerxes and told him everything he had seen. Then he said, "I tried to keep you, Your Majesty, from giving way completely to your youthful spirit because I am a man who has seen many large and powerful armies brought low by smaller ones, and who knows that it is evil to covet things. I remember Cyrus' campaign against the Massagetae, and how it fared; I remember Cambyses' campaign against the Ethiopians, too; and I marched with Darius against the Scyths. And because I know all this, I thought that if you only held still, you would be the happiest man in the world. But since this impulse comes from god and since, it seems, some heaven-sent ruin is hunting out the Greeks, then I hereby alter course and change my opinion. Tell the Persians the message god sent; command them to supply the provisions you originally required; then act in such a way that, god willing, you yourself are not found wanting."

That was what was said, and so encouraged were they by the vision that as soon as it was day Xerxes explained everything to the Persians, while Artabanus, who had formerly been the only one to openly oppose the war, was now as openly urging it on.

Later, after he decided to lead his army into the field, yet a third vision appeared to Xerxes in his sleep, and when the Magi heard it they interpreted it to mean that he would enslave the whole world and all its people. This was the dream: Xerxes seemed to be crowned with the young shoots of an olive tree while the branches of the tree overspread the whole earth; then the crown on Xerxes' head disappeared. After the Magi gave the dream this interpretation, every Persian nobleman from the assembly rushed to his province eager to meet his military quota— each one wanting to win the gifts which Xerxes had promised—while

Xerxes scoured every stretch of the continent mustering men for his army.

Xerxes spent four full years after the conquest of Egypt preparing an army and the provisions for that army, and during the fifth year he started on his campaign with a huge body of troops. To my knowledge, this was by far the largest military force that has ever existed, so that the army Darius took against the Scyths was as nothing in comparison, and neither was the Scythian army which pursued the Cimmerians, invaded Media, and conquered and occupied nearly all of upper Asia—for which Darius was later trying to take revenge. Neither was the army they tell us the Atreidae took against Ilium, or the army of Teucrians and Mysians who crossed into Europe via the Bosporus before the Trojan War, and then conquered all of Thrace, went down the coast of the Ionian Sea, and marched as far south as the Peneus River.

Not all these armies together or any others equaled this single expedition. For what nation did Xerxes not lead out of Asia against Greece? Except for the very greatest rivers, what river did his army not drink dry? Some supplied ships; others joined the infantry; some had to provide horses; and some both horse transports and men; some furnished long ships for the bridges, and some both ships and food.

By the way, because of the disaster to the first fleet that had tried to sail around Mount Athos, advance preparations had been going on there for about three years.[2] Triremes anchored off Elaeus, in the Chersonese, and army troops of different nationalities set off from there in relays to be whipped into digging a canal. The people who lived at Athos also dug. The project was overseen by two Persians, Bubares, son of Megabazus, and Artachaees, son of Artaeus. Athos is a high, famous, inhabited mountain which extends right down to the sea. The mountain ends at a peninsular neck of the mainland about one and a half miles wide. This region is flat with little hillocks on it and is bounded by the sea at Acanthus on one side and by the sea off Torone on the other. On the neck of land where Mount Athos ends is the Greek town of Sane. There are towns outside of Sane, on Athos itself, whose inhabitants the Persians changed from mainlanders to islanders. These towns are Dium, Olophyxus, Acrothoon, Thyssus, and Cleonae.

Those are the towns on Athos, and this is how the barbarians excavated the isthmus. After they stretched a straight line from Sane, each nationality was assigned its own segment of the land to work on. When the canal began to get deep, the men at the bottom kept digging, while others constantly handed up the soil as it was dug out to others standing on stages higher up the trench, and these to yet others until it got to the men on top. These carried it out and threw it away. All the groups of workers except the Phoenicians had to do double labor because the sides

2. In 492 B.C. a large Persian fleet bound for Greece was destroyed off Athos by a storm. See book 6, chapters 44ff. (not included in this edition).

of the trench kept caving in on them. Now, this was bound to happen because they were making the opening at the top of the trench the same width as that at the bottom. The Phoenicians are always showing their expertise at doing things, but never more so than in this: after they were assigned their stretch of canal to dig, they began to excavate by making the top of the trench twice as wide as the canal itself had to be and they kept narrowing the width as they got progressively deeper until it was equal to the width of the other trenches when they got to the bottom. Markets and food stalls were set up at a nearby meadow, and large quantities of ground grain were brought to them from Asia.

I have thought it over and come to the conclusion that Xerxes ordered this canal to be dug because of his towering ambition. He wanted to display his power and leave behind a monument to himself, because while it would have been possible to drag the ships across the isthmus without any trouble, he ordered a sea channel to be dug wide enough for two triremes to row across it side by side. Xerxes had also ordered the same crew that dug the canal to build a bridge across the Strymon River.

While the canal was being built, the Egyptians and the Phoenicians were required to provide papyrus and flaxen cables for the bridges; also, food was stored so that neither the army nor the pack animals would go hungry as they made their way to Greece. Xerxes had the route scouted, and ordered supplies to be brought from all over Asia by merchant ships and ferries and stored where they would be needed most along the way. Most of the supplies were brought to a place called White Point in Thrace, but some were earmarked for Tyrodiza, in Perinthia, Doriscus, Eion-on-Strymon, and Macedonia.

While these forces were performing their assigned tasks, Xerxes set out for Sardis with his entire infantry from Critalla, in Cappadocia, where the continental forces that were scheduled to march with Xerxes had been ordered to assemble. Now, I can't say which satrap carried away the gifts the king had offered for bringing the finest army—I don't even know whether it was ever decided in the first place. After they crossed the Halys River, the army was in Phrygia. They made their way through Phrygia to Celaenae, where the springs of the Maeander River rise, and of another river, too, no smaller than the Maeander, whose name happens to be the Cataract. It rises right in the middle of the marketplace in Celaenae and flows into the Maeander. The skin of Marsyas, son of Silenus, is hanging in this marketplace—the one the Phrygian story says was flensed off Marsyas and hung out by Apollo.[3]

In this same city, a Lydian—Pythius, son of Atys—was waiting for Xerxes and feted the king's army and the king himself with entertainment on a grand scale. He also announced that he wanted to contribute money for the war. After Pythius' offer of money was made, Xerxes asked

3. In mythology, Marsyas was a satyr who challenged Apollo to a contest in music on condition that the winner could do as he liked with the loser. Apollo won and skinned Marsyas alive.

his Persian attendants who this Pythius was and how much money he had that he was able to make this kind of offer. They said, "This is the man, Your Majesty, who gave your father, Darius, the gold plane tree and the golden vine and who remains the richest man in the world that we know of after you."

Xerxes was so astonished by this last comment that he himself asked Pythius how much money he had. "Your Majesty," he said, "I won't hide it from you or pretend that I don't know my own wealth. I do know it, and I will give you an exact accounting of it. As soon as I found out that you were going down to the Greek coast, I wanted to offer money to pay for the war, so I made a careful audit of my assets. I added it all up and found that I have fifty-eight tons of silver, and I'm only seven thousand gold *staters* shy of four million.[4] That's what I'm offering you. As for me, I have enough of a livelihood from my land and my slaves."

Xerxes was overjoyed by this statement and said, "My Lydian friend, since I left Persia I haven't met a single man until now who wanted to offer hospitality to my army or who would come into my presence on his own to contribute money toward the war—except you. You have not only lavishly hosted my army but offered a huge sum of money. So, in return, I give these presents to you: I hereby make you my friend and ally and offer you, out of my own funds, the seven thousand staters you need to have four million; that way, you won't be seven thousand shy of the four million, but will have a full, round number, thanks to me. Keep what you already have, and remember always to be the kind of man you are now—you won't regret such acts as this, either now or in the future."

After making good on these words, Xerxes kept marching onward, ever onward. He passed by the Phrygian town known as Anaua and a salt-producing lake and arrived in the large Phrygian city of Colossae, where the river Lycus crashes into a chasm and disappears. It reappears a little over half a mile away, and then it, too, flows into the Maeander. From Colossae, the army set out for the border between Phrygia and Lydia and arrived at the town of Cydrara, where a pillar, erected by Croesus, with a written description of the borders, is set into the ground.

The road forks as it enters Lydia from Phrygia. On the left, it leads to Caria, and to Sardis on the right. If you take the right fork, you must cross the Maeander River and pass the town of Callatebus, where specialists make honey from tamarisk and from wheat. As Xerxes was traveling this road, he saw a plane tree so beautiful that he decorated it with gold ornaments and appointed a man to be its perpetual custodian. On the second day, he arrived in the capital city of Lydia. The first thing he did after he arrived in Sardis was to send envoys into Greece demanding earth and water and giving advance notice that they should prepare a banquet for the king. He sent men everywhere to fetch land and water,

---

4. A stater was a gold or silver coin which had different values depending on where it was minted.

everywhere except Athens and Lacedaemon. This is why he sent for land and water yet a second time: he was quite sure that those who would not give it earlier when Darius had demanded it would give it out of fear now. Anyway, he just wanted to find out if he was right.

Next he prepared to march to Abydos. There, Asia had just been yoked to Europe by a bridge across the Hellespont. Between Sestos and Madytus, in the Hellespontic Chersonese, there is a rocky promontory stretching into the sea opposite Abydos. (Here, not much later, Athenian forces under general Xanthippus, son of Ariphron, captured Artayctes, the Persian satrap of Sestos, and nailed him alive to a plank for bringing women into the temple of Protesilaus in Elaeus and having orgies with them.)

Starting from Abydos, the men responsible for this phase of operations brought their bridges of cable to the promontory—with the Phoenicians using cables of flax and the Egyptians cables of papyrus. It is seven furlongs across from Abydos. After the strait was bridged, though, a violent storm loosened the whole thing and broke it up.

When Xerxes heard this, he became furious and ordered that three hundred lashes be laid on the Hellespont with a whip and that a a pair of fetters be thrown into the water. I have even heard that he sent along men with branding irons to brand the Hellespont! Be that as it may, he ordered the men to say these atrocious, barbarous words while flogging the stream: "Your master imposes this punishment on you, O bitter water, because you did him wrong though you suffered no wrong from him. King Xerxes will cross over you whether you like it or not. No one sacrifices to you, and rightly so, you briny, muddy stream!" That, then, is the punishment Xerxes imposed on the water; as to the men in charge of bridging the Hellespont, he ordered that their heads be chopped off.

The men who had been assigned to this thankless detail carried out their orders, and other engineers went ahead with building the bridges. This is how they did it: penteconters and triremes were anchored in a row under the cables. There were three hundred and sixty under the cable nearer the Euxine Sea, and three hundred and fourteen under the other. In order to keep the tension on the gear slack, the cables were at right angles to the Pontus, and the ships were parallel to the current of the stream. When the ships were in a row under the cables, huge anchors were let down, toward the Pontus on one side because of the winds blowing from the Euxine, and toward the west and the Aegean on the other side because of the south and west winds. Narrow openings or passages were left between the penteconters in three places so that people could sail in and out of the Pontus in small craft. After all this was done, the cables were tightened from the shore with wooden winches, only this time each bridge was made with not just one kind of cable. Instead, two flaxen cables and four papyrus cables were used per bridge. The two cables were of equal thickness and quality, but the flax was proportionately heavier and weighed about one hundred and sixty pounds per meter.

When the strait was bridged, they sawed logs equal to the width of the pontoons, laid them in even rows over the tightened cables, and then fastened them on top. Then brushwood was laid evenly in the interstices and earth packed down on top of the brushwood. A fence was built on either side high enough that the pack animals would not panic by looking over the bridge at the sea.

When everything was finished—the bridges, the breakwaters which were built at the mouths of the Athos canal to keep the water from flowing in and refilling them with silt—and when the message came that, in fact, the whole canal had been completed, the fully equipped army set out for Abydos at the beginning of the spring after wintering in Sardis. On an especially clear and cloudless day, though, just as they were setting out, the sun abandoned its usual place in the sky and disappeared, and instead of day it became night. Xerxes became very nervous when he saw and understood what was happening, and he asked his Magi what the portent meant. They said that the sun god was foretelling that the Greeks would abandon their cities, because, as they explained, the sun was an omen for the Greeks—theirs was the moon.

When Xerxes heard this, he was overjoyed and marched on, but as he was doing so, Pythius the Lydian, dreading the portent in the sky and encouraged by the gifts he had received, went to Xerxes and said, "I have something to ask of you, Master, which I hope you will grant. It will be just a small favor to you, but a very great one to me." Xerxes—expecting him to ask for anything but what he in fact wanted—said that he would do the favor and told him to speak up and say what he wanted. Pythias, emboldened by what he heard, said, "Master, I have five sons, and it so happens that all of them are marching against Greece with you. Take pity, Your Majesty, on my advanced age and release one of my sons—the oldest—from the army so that he can care for me and my possessions. Take the other four along with you, and may you return home safely after accomplishing everything you have in mind."

Xerxes went into a rage and said, "You wretch! You dare, when I myself am going to war against Greece at the head of my sons, brothers, relatives, and friends, you dare, you slave, to mention your son, when you have a duty to follow me—you and everybody else in your household including your wife! You are going to learn that men's passions are in their ears—when someone hears fair words, his body fills with pleasure, but when he hears the opposite, he swells with rage. You were saying other kinds of things when you were a useful servant, and you couldn't boast that you were able to surpass a king in generosity. Now that you've disgraced yourself, you won't get what you deserve—you'll get less, because your hospitality will protect you and your four sons. Your fine will be the life of that one son, the one you love so much." No sooner had he given this answer than Xerxes called his executioners and commanded them to find the oldest son of Pythias, cut him down the middle, and set up one half of his body on the right-hand side of the road and the other half on the left so that the army would march between them as it set out.

They obeyed the order, and the army went forth. The provisioners and pack animals led the way, followed by the multinational army marching haphazardly together without formation. They made up more than half the army, and when they had passed there was a space: they did not mingle with the king. He was preceded by one thousand choice cavalrymen, selected from all over Persia, and after them came a thousand spearmen, also an elite group, who kept their spears turned down toward the ground. Next came ten sacred "Nisaean" horses wearing their finest ornamentation. (This is why they call the horses "Nisaean": there is a vast plain in Media called Nisaea, and this plain is the source of these large horses.) Positioned behind these ten horses was the sacred chariot of Zeus, drawn by eight white horses, with their charioteer holding the reins and following them on foot because no mortal may mount to that seat. Right behind this came Xerxes himself, on a chariot drawn by Nisaean horses. Alongside him rode the charioteer, whose name was Patiramphes, son of a Persian named Otanes.

That was how Xerxes rode out of Sardis, although he would switch from the chariot to a covered wagon whenever he felt like it. Behind him came one thousand of the noblest and bravest of Persia's spearmen, who carried their spears in the usual way, and then another thousand picked Persian horsemen followed by ten thousand foot soldiers selected from all the remaining men of Persia. A thousand of these men carried gold pomegranates instead of spikes on the butt ends of their spears and surrounded the other nine thousand, who carried silver pomegranates. The spearmen who turned their spears toward the ground also had gold pomegranates, while the noblemen right behind Xerxes carried spears with apples. Positioned behind the ten thousand foot soldiers was a Persian cavalry ten thousand strong. Behind this cavalry was a space of a quarter of a mile, and then came the rest of the army, a horde of soldiers marching without formation.

The army took the road out of Lydia to the Caicus River in the Mysian region. Then they struck out from Caicus, keeping Mount Cane on the left, and traveled through Atarneus to Carene. From there they made their way through the plain of Thebe, passing by Adramyttium and Pelasgian Antandrus. Xerxes occupied Ida, and then, bearing left, he entered the land described in the *Iliad*. First, though, while they were spending the night at the base of Mount Ida, they were hit by thunder, lightning, and violent rainstorms which killed a sizable number of the army.

When the army reached the Scamander, it was the first river they had come to since setting out on the road from Sardis which ran dry and couldn't satisfy the thirst of the animals and men. After Xerxes arrived at the river, he had a desire to see the acropolis of Troy, so he climbed up to it. After he saw it and learned of everything that had happened there, he sacrificed one thousand cattle to Athena of Ilium while his Magi poured out drink offerings to the heroes. After they had done this, and night fell, panic gripped the camp. They left Troy at daybreak, keeping the Gergithian Teucrians on the right, and on the left skirting Rhoeteum, Ophryneum, and Dardanus, which borders on Abydos.

After they arrived in Abydos, Xerxes wanted to look at his whole army. Xerxes had already commanded the people of Abydos to build a throne of white marble fit for a king atop a nearby hill, and as he sat on the throne and looked down at the shore, beholding his army and navy, he had a sudden desire to see his ships race each other. After it was over and the Sidonian Phoenicians had won, he was delighted with both the race and his legions.

When he saw the whole Hellespont covered with his ships, and all its coast and the whole plain of Abydos swarming with men, Xerxes congratulated himself on his own happiness and then, in a while, began to weep.

When his uncle Artabanus noticed him—the one who had freely and publicly given the opinion that Xerxes should not make war on Greece— when Artabanus saw him and realized that Xerxes was crying, he said, "How differently you behave now from the way you did just a little while ago, Your Majesty. First you congratulate yourself, and then you cry!"

And Xerxes said, "As I was computing the size of my army, I thought how sad it was that human life should be so short, since out of so very many men not a single one will be around in a hundred years."

And Artabanus said, "There are even sadder things about our existence, because in this short life, no one—not these men and not anyone else—will ever be so happy that he won't want, not once but many times, to be dead rather than alive. Troubles assail us, and sicknesses dizzy us, and though our life is short, they make it seem all too long. And thus in the hardships of life we pine for the refuge of death, and we taste the resentment of god so much more than his sweetness."

Xerxes answered, "Human life is such as you describe it, Artabanus, but let's stop talking about that or thinking about the bad when there are so many good things at hand. Tell me this. If that dream had not clearly appeared to you, would you still hold your original opinion—not wanting me to make war on Greece—or would you have changed your mind? Come on now. Tell me the truth."

Artabanus said, "We both wish, Your Majesty, that the dream that appeared to us comes true. For my part, though, I am full of fear about this expedition—hardly able to control myself, in fact. I've thought about it in great detail, and I see two circumstances in particular which seem to me to be the most hostile of all."

Xerxes answered, "I can't figure you out! What are these two circumstances you say are so hostile to me? Do you find fault with the size of the infantry? Does it look as if the Greek army is going to be much larger than ours? Or does our navy fall short of theirs? Or is it a combination of both? Because if you think our expedition is lacking in any way, we could gather another army immediately."

And Artabanus answered, "No, Your Majesty, nobody with any sense would find fault with the size of either your army or your navy. And besides, if you muster more men, the two circumstances I'm referring to will become even more hostile. These two things are the land and the sea. As far as I can tell, there isn't a harbor anywhere in the sea large enough to hold your navy—one you could count on to save your ships if a storm blows up. Besides, there shouldn't be just one harbor; they should be all along the coast you are following. There are no harbors to receive you, though, and you ought to know that men can't control chance. Chance controls men. I've told you about one of the two things; now let me tell you about the other one. This is how land is your enemy. Even if absolutely no one opposes you, the land will become that much more your enemy the farther you advance. And you'll always want to steal a little more of what's ahead, because a man can never get enough of success. What I'm trying to tell you is that even if nobody stands up to you, the land will grow more and more vast as more and more time goes by until finally it will yield—starvation. The best man is the one who makes plans timidly, anticipating every possible disaster, and only then moves confidently into action."

Xerxes answered, "You've thought things through very plausibly, Artabanus, but you shouldn't be so afraid of everything or give everything equal weight, you know, because if you really did take every conceivable accident into account, why then you would never do anything! It's better to go ahead in full confidence and experience half of the dire consequences than to fear every little thing in advance and never experience anything at all. Anyway, if you challenge every argument, yet have no sure answers yourself, you're as likely to go wrong as the one who is arguing the other side. It all comes out even. How on earth can a human being know anything for sure? I don't think he can. The advantage usually goes to those who are willing to act, not to those who hesitate and think everything over. Just look at how powerful Persia has become. If the kings who came before me had thought like you or had advisers like you, you would never have seen our empire advance so far, but they rolled the dice and ran their risks and led it to where it is today. Great things can be achieved only by running great risks. We will show ourselves to be the equals of our predecessors by marching in the finest season of the year, conquering all of Europe, and returning home again without meeting up with hunger anywhere or suffering any harm of any kind. In the first place, we're taking along plenty of food, and in the second place, we will have the grain of whatever people and land we invade—we're making war on farmers, after all, not nomads."

After this Artabanus said, "Since you won't let me worry about anything, Your Majesty, please do take this advice, because it really is necessary to discuss all kinds of things at great length. Cyrus, son of Cambyses, subjected all Ionians except the Athenians to the payment of tribute. Now, I advise you under no circumstances to lead the Ionians against the Athenian motherland. We'll be able to get the upper hand over our enemies even without the Ionians, but if they join us, either they will have to become criminals by enslaving their mother city or they will have to do the right thing and help to liberate it. They won't be much use to us as criminals, and if they become righteous, they will be capable of doing some serious damage to your campaign. Take this advice to heart, Your Majesty, and there is something to be said for my earlier words, too, that the end is not apparent from the beginning."

"Artabanus," answered Xerxes, "that's an idea you are especially mistaken about. Fearing that the Ionians will change sides! I have the highest opinion of them, and you yourself and everybody else who marched with Darius against the Scythians will be my witnesses that when it was up to the Ionians whether to destroy or save the whole Persian army, they proved to be trustworthy, just, and not ill willed at all. Besides, you can't suppose that they are going to revolt when they are leaving their women, children, and possessions in our power. So don't worry about that, either—just protect my palace and my throne with a stout heart, because I'm going to entrust my scepter to you and you alone."

After saying this, Xerxes dispatched Artabanus to Susa and summoned the most prominent Persians for the second time. This is what he said to them after they arrived: "Men of Persia! I have brought you together to call on you to be men of valor and not to disgrace the great and glorious Persian deeds of old. Let us, one and all, act zealously to promote this boon for the common good. I tell you that you must see this war through to the end because although I have heard that we are going to fight with brave men, there is no other army on earth that will oppose us if we defeat them. Now, before we cross the bridge, let us pray to those gods who hold the land of Persia in their hands."

They spent that day preparing for the crossing. The next day, as they waited to see the sunrise, they burned all kinds of incense on the bridges and spread their path with myrtle branches. When the sun had fully risen, Xerxes poured a libation into the sea from a golden cup and, facing the sun, prayed that no accident happen to prevent him from conquering Europe—or before he reached the utmost limits of the continent. After his prayer, he threw the cup into the Hellespont along with a golden bowl and what they call an "acinaces," or Persian sword. I can't decide for sure whether he threw these things into the sea as an offering to the sun, or whether he regretted his scourging of the Hellespont and gave them to the sea in recompense.

When all this had been done, the whole army and cavalry crossed the Pontic bridge and the pack animals and servants crossed the bridge that was on the Aegean side. The ten thousand Persians, all crowned with wreaths, led the way, followed by the unranked multinational army. These groups crossed on that day, and on the next the cavalry went first, followed by the troops who pointed their spears downward. They also wore wreaths. After them came the sacred horses and the sacred chariot, then Xerxes himself and the spear carriers and the thousand cavalrymen, and finally the rest of the army. Meanwhile, the fleet set out for the other side. (I have also heard, by the way, that the king crossed last of all.)

After he had gone over into Europe, Xerxes gazed at his army as it crossed under the lash. Although it wasted no time, the army took seven days and seven nights to make the crossing. They say that after Xerxes had already crossed the Hellespont, a man from those parts exclaimed, "O Zeus, why do you take the shape of a Persian man, change your name from Zeus to Xerxes, and lead forth all mankind if you want to devastate Greece? After all, you could have done it without them!"

An important omen appeared to them after they had all crossed over and set off on the road to Greece. Xerxes paid it no mind, although it was easy enough to figure out. A mare foaled a rabbit. Now, it obviously meant that Xerxes was about to lead a proud and stately army against Greece, but that he would run for his life back to his own land. There had been another omen when he was in Sardis. A mule had given birth to another mule with two sets of genitals, male and female, the male genitals being on top. Xerxes paid no attention to either omen, and kept on marching forward.

*　*　*

Chapters 89–105

There were twelve hundred and seven triremes, and this is who supplied them. The Phoenicians and the Palestinian Syrians gave three hundred. Their crews were equipped with helmets closely resembling the Greek helment in design. They wore linen corselets and carried rimless shields and javelins. According to the Phoenicians themselves, they used to live on the Red Sea in antiquity, but they migrated from there to the Syrian coast. This part of Syria and the region as far as Egypt is all called Palestine.

The Egyptians supplied two hundred ships. Their crews wore chain mail helmets on their heads and carried boat hooks, large battle-axes, and concave shields with wide rims. Most of them wore breastplates and carried large daggers. That, then, is how they were armed.

The Cyprians gave one hundred and fifty ships, and this is how they were equipped: their princes wrapped turbans around their heads, while everyone else wore pointed felt hats. In other respects, they were outfitted like the Greeks. The Cyprians themselves say that some of their people came from Salamis and Athens, some from Arcadia, some from Cythnus, some from Phoenicia, and some from Ethiopia.

The Cilicians supplied a hundred ships. They wore native helmets on their heads, carried shields of hairy oxhide rather than metal, and were dressed in woolen chitons. Each crewman carried two javelins and a sword which closely resembled the Egyptian dagger. In antiquity, the Cilicians used to be called the Hypachaeans, but they took their present name from a Phoenician—Cilix, son of Agenor.

The Pamphylians, who were outfitted with Greek armor, gave thirty ships. These Pamphylians are descended from followers of Amphilochus and Calchas, who were scattered after the Trojan War.

The Lycians supplied fifty ships. They were outfitted in breastplates and shin guards, and were armed with cherrywood bows, unfledged cane arrows, and javelins. They wore goatskins hanging from their shoulders, felt caps rimmed with feathers on their heads, and they carried short swords and scimitars. The Lycians were also called the Termilae and originated in Crete. They got their name from Lycus, son of an Athenian named Pandion.

The Asian Dorians supplied thirty ships. They wore Greek armor and were descended from the Peloponnesians.

The Carians gave seventy ships and were armed with scimitars and short swords, although in other respects they were outfitted like the Greeks. I have already discussed what their original name was in the first part of my narrative.[5]

The Ionians, who were outfitted like Greeks, supplied one hundred ships. They came to be called Ionians after Ion, son of Xuthus. The Greeks say that before Danaus and Xuthus came to the Peloponnese, the Ionians were known as the Coastal Pelasgians while they lived in the present-day Peloponnesian Achaea.

The islanders, who wore Greek armor, contributed seventeen ships. They were also a Pelasgian people, but they came to be known as Ionians in the same way as did the twelve Ionian cities founded by Athenians.

The Aeolians, who also wore Greek armor, supplied sixty ships. According to Greek tradition, the Aeolians also used to be known as Pelasgians.

Except for the people of Abydos, who had been detailed by the king to stay in their territory and guard the bridges, the other inhabitants of the Hellespont and Pontus who went on the campaign supplied a hundred ships. They were originally Ionian and Dorian colonists, and they were outfitted like Greeks.

Persians, Medes, and Sacae served as marines on all the ships. The very best ships were Phoenician, and the best of the Phoenician ships came from Sidon.

All these sailors and infantrymen were commanded by their own native officers, but I won't give their names, since they aren't needed in this record of my research. The native officers don't deserve to be mentioned

5. In book 1, chapter 171.

anyway, and each nation had as many officers as it had towns. Besides, these officers went not as leaders but as slaves along with everybody else except for the generals, who ruled over all the nations and had complete power and whose names—the Persian ones anyway—I have already mentioned.

These are the names of the admirals: Ariabignes, son of Darius; Prexaspes, son of Aspathines; Megabazus, son of Megabates; and Achaemenes, son of Darius. Ariabignes, the son of Darius and of the daughter of Gobryas, commanded the forces of Ionia and Caria. Xerxes' full brother Achaemenes commanded the Egyptians, and the remaining two admirals commanded the rest of the navy. Counting triconters[6] and penteconters along with light cruisers and small horse transports, there were three thousand ships in the fleet.

These are the most noteworthy commanders who served under the admirals: from Sidon, Tetramnestus, son of Anysus; from Tyre, Matten, son of Siromus; from Aradus, Merbalus, son of Agbalus; from Cilicia, Syennesis, son of Oromedon; from Lycia, Cyberniscus, son of Sicas; from Cyprus, Gorgus, son of Chersis, and Timonax, son of Timagoras; from Caria, Histiaeus, son of Tymnes, Pigres, son of Hysseldomus, and Damasithymus, son of Candaules.

There is no need for me to give the names of the other squadron commanders—except for Artemisia, a woman I admire for going to war against Greece. She took power after her husband died, and although she had an adult son and was not forced to go, she went on the campaign out of sheer will and courage. Again, her name was Artemisia—the daughter of Lygdamis. On her father's side, her forebears were from Halicarnassus; on her mother's side, from Crete. She commanded the forces of Halicarnassus, Cos, Nisyrus, and Calydna, and supplied five ships. After the Sidonian ships, they had the best reputation in the whole fleet, and out of all his allies, Artemisia gave Xerxes the best advice. I've listed the cities whose forces she commanded, and I ought to say that their people were all Dorian. The Halicarnassians were originally from Troezen, while the others were from Epidaurus.

So much, then, for the fleet.

After the army had been counted and put in battle order, Xerxes wanted to ride past his troops and review them, which he did. He rode past the forces of each nation in his chariot, asking questions while his scribes wrote down the answers until he had gone from one end of the army to the other and reviewed both infantry and cavalry. After he had done this, the ships were dragged down into the sea and Xerxes transferred from his chariot to a Sidonian ship. He sat under a golden awning and sailed along the prows of the ships, asking questions and having answers written down just as he had done with the army. The captains had taken

---

6. A thirty-oared ship.

their ships back about four hundred feet from shore, lined them up with
their prows facing land, and dropped anchor after posting the marines at
their battle stations in full gear. Xerxes conducted his naval review while
sailing between the ships' prows and the shore.

When he had sailed past his fleet and disembarked from his ship,
Xerxes summoned Demaratus, son of Ariston, who was accompanying
him on the campaign against Greece. As Demaratus approached, Xerxes
called out to him and said, "Demaratus, there's something it would give
me great pleasure to ask you about right now. You are a Greek, and as
far as I can tell from you and the other Greeks who have had conversations with me, your city is by no means the smallest or the weakest. Tell
me this, now, are the Greeks going to take up arms and resist? Because
I believe that neither all the Greeks nor all the other people who live to
the west put together are going to be able to resist my assault—unless
they are united, that is. Still, I want to hear from you what you have to
say about it."

When Xerxes had finished, Demaratus answered, "Should I tell you
the truth, Your Majesty, or just something pleasing?" And Xerxes commanded him to tell the truth—he wouldn't like him any less than before.

When he heard this, Demaratus said, "Since you demand that I tell
the truth by all means, Your Majesty, and not something you will later
find to be a lie, why then, poverty is congenital to Greece, but bravery
is an import, bought with skill and strict rules, and Greece uses bravery
to fend off both poverty and despotism. Now, while I praise all Greeks
who live in Dorian lands, I'm not really talking about all of them, but
solely about the Lacedaemonians. First: there is no way they will ever
accept any terms of slavery you bring to Greece. Second: they will oppose
you in battle even if all the other Greeks come around to your way of
thinking. Don't bother finding out whether there will be enough of them
to do it. If there are a thousand, they will fight you, and they will fight
you if there are fewer and fight you if there are more."

After Xerxes heard this, he said through his laughter, "What nonsense
you talk, Demaratus! A thousand men fighting with an army like this!
But come, now, tell me. You say that you yourself used to be king over
these people. How would you like to fight with ten men right now? But
really, if your citizens are all such as you describe them, then under
your laws it would be fitting for you, as their king, to fight with twice
that number. If each of them is worth ten men from my army, then I
look for you to be worth twenty. That way you can make good on what
you've said. Because if they are all like you and the other Greeks who
come to talk to me—like you, that is, in size and shape—and you all
brag in this way, then see to it that your boast isn't made in vain. Come
now, look at it reasonably. How could a thousand, or ten thousand, or
fifty thousand men who are all equally free and not ruled by one man
stand up to an army this size? Because if there are five thousand of them
we will outnumber them by more than a thousand to one! If, like us,
they were ruled by one man, they would either surpass themselves through

fear of him or they would, under the lash, go up against forces that outnumbered them. But if they are left to their own devices, they won't do either. Anyway, I think that even if the numbers were the same, it would be hard for the Greeks to fight with just the Persians. We, too, have this quality you speak of. There isn't much of it—it's rare, but there are some of my Persian bodyguard who want to take on three Greeks at a time. You've never come up against them, and that's why you can talk so much drivel."

Demaratus answered, "I knew from the beginning, Your Majesty, that if I told you the truth, you wouldn't like what I had to say. But since you forced me to tell you the whole truth, I told you what the Spartans are like. You, though, more than anyone, know how much I love them now—they who stripped me of my rank and my privileges, who drove me from the city of my fathers and made me an exile while your father welcomed me and gave me an income and a home. A rational man is much more likely to appreciate goodwill than to reject it. As for me, I don't claim to be able to fight with ten men or with two. I wouldn't even willingly fight with one. But if I had to, or if a great cause spurred me on, then I would gladly fight—especially with one of those men who say they're a match for three Greeks. In the same way, when the Lacedae-monians fight one at a time, they are no worse than any other men, but when they fight together, they are the best in the world. Because though they're free, they aren't totally free. Custom is the despot who stands over them, and they secretly fear it more than your people fear you. They do whatever it commands, and its command is always the same: not to run away from any force, however large, but to stay in formation and either prevail or die. If I seem to be talking drivel to you, then I'll keep quiet from now on. I spoke just now only because you made me, but let it be as you think best, Your Majesty."

Although Demaratus answered him in this way, Xerxes didn't get at all angry. Instead, he turned it into a joke and genially sent Demaratus away.

*   *   *

Chapters 138–152

While Xerxes' campaign was ostensibly aimed at Athens, he had really set out against all of Greece. The Greeks came to know this before long, but they didn't all take it in the same way. Some of them rendered land and water to Persia and felt confident that they would not suffer any harm from the barbarians. Others, who had refused to yield, lived in terror because there weren't enough battle-worthy ships in Greece to resist the attack, and because most people preferred collaborating with Persia to becoming actively involved in war.

At this point, I feel that I must express an opinion which will be very unpopular with most people, but I believe it to be true and I will not hold it back. If the Athenians had abandoned their land in dread of the

coming danger, or even if they had remained and given themselves up
to Xerxes, then there would have been no one to oppose the king at sea.
And if no one had opposed Xerxes at sea, this is what would have happened on the mainland: even if a network of walls had been thrown up
across the Peloponnesian Isthmus, Sparta's allies would have betrayed
her, not because they wanted to, but because they would have been
conquered, one by one, by the barbarian armada. Then the Spartans
would have been isolated, and even if they had performed great acts of
heroism, they would have perished, nobly and alone. Either that would
have happened, or they would long before have seen the other Greeks
capitulating to Persia and they would have come to terms with Xerxes.
In either case, Greece would have fallen to Persia. For I just cannot see
what good it would have done to build fortifications across the Isthmus
if the king had controlled the sea.

Thus, if someone were to say that the Athenians were the saviors of
Greece, he would not fall short of the truth, because the Athenians
would have tipped the scales toward whatever side they inclined to. They
chose that Greece should live free, though. They were the ones who
mobilized all the Greek states which had not capitulated and, with the
help of the gods, repelled the king. Even a frightening oracle from Delphi which threw them into a panic didn't persuade them to abandon
Greece; they remained, and summoned the strength to resist the attack
against their land.

You see, the Athenians were eager to consult the oracle, and so they
sent ambassadors to Delphi. The ambassadors had performed the customary rites and had just entered the inner sanctum and sat down when
Aristonice, the Pythian priestess, uttered these verses:

> Good for nothings! Why sit still? Flee to the ends of the earth!
> Leave your homes and the high-topped hill of your city with its
>   wall like a hoop!
> For the head stays not, nor the body, nor the extremities of
>   hands and feet.
> Nothing in between remains. It is gone, unseen.
> For fire and sharp-tipped Ares bring low the city and the Syrian-
>   built chariot
> Gives it chase. Many another tower and not just yours he brings
>   to ruin.
> With many a temple of the immortal gods will he feed the
>   eager flame.
> Now your statues are standing and pouring sweat. They shiver
>   with dread.
> The black blood drips from the highest rooftops. They have
>   seen the necessity of evil.
> Get out, get out of my sanctum and drown your spirits in woe!

When the Athenian ambassadors heard this, they were overwhelmed
by despair; but after they had completely given themselves over to grief

because of the prophecy of doom, Timon, son of Androbulus, a man second to none in Delphi, advised them to take up the olive branches of supplication and to go to consult the oracle again—this time as supplicants. The Athenians accepted this advice, went to the temple, and said, "Lord, grant us a better oracle about our fatherland. Respect these olive branches we bear. Otherwise we will not leave your sanctum but will remain right here until we die." After they said this, the prophetess uttered this second oracle:

> Even Pallas of Athens cannot placate Olympian Zeus,
> Though entreating with many arguments and dense reasons.
> Yet I will tell you again in words unbreakably hard:
> When all is taken within the bounds of Cecrops
> And the vale of sacred Cithaeron,
> Then wide-viewing Zeus will grant Tritonis-born Athena
> A wall of wood to be alone uncaptured, a boon to you
> And to your children. Await not in quiet the coming horses,
> The marching feet, the armed host upon the land.
> Slip away. Turn your back. You will meet in battle anyway.
> O holy Salamis, you will be the death of many a woman's son
> Between the seedtime and the harvest of the grain!

These words seemed to be—and actually were—milder than the first. The ambassadors wrote them down and returned to Athens. When they got back, the ambassadors gave a report to the people, and, though many opinions were expressed as they sought the meaning of the oracle, the following two were most in opposition. Some of the older people said that they thought the god was prophesying that the Acropolis would survive because long ago it had been fenced around with thorn bushes. They took this to be the meaning of the "wall of wood." Others, though, said that the god meant ships, and they urged the people to build ships and forget about everything else. The last two verses of the prophecy, however, were a problem for those who said that ships were the "wall of wood." They were baffled by

> O holy Salamis, you will be the death of many a woman's son
> Between the seedtime and the harvest of the grain

because the official oracle interpreters took these last words of the priestess to mean that if the Athenians prepared for a naval battle, they would be defeated at Salamis.

Now, there was a man from Athens who had recently become prominent. His name was Themistocles, and he was the son of Neocles. This man denied that the official interpreters were entirely correct about the oracle. He argued that he didn't think the verses would have been so mild if they had really been meant for the Athenians. They would have been "O cruel Salamis," instead of "O holy Salamis," if the people who lived near Salamis were the ones who in fact were going to die. Rightly interpreted, the god meant those words not for the Athenians but for their enemies. Themistocles advised them, therefore, to prepare for a naval battle: *that* was what was meant by the "wall of wood." The Athenians realized that Themistocles' opinion was far preferable to that of the official interpreters who would not allow them to prepare for a naval battle—who would not, to put it simply, allow them to so much as raise their hands to resist but wanted them to abandon Attica and go and live somewhere else.

Even before this, Themistocles had given another outstanding and timely opinion. The Athenians once had a huge surplus of wealth in the public treasury which they had accumulated from the mines in Laurium, and they were about to distribute ten drachmas to each male citizen.[7] At that time, Themistocles persuaded the Athenians to halt this distribution of wealth and to use the money to make two hundred ships for the war—the war with the Aeginetans, I mean. The war that was raging then really saved all of Greece because it forced Athens to become a sea power. The ships that were built then were not used in that war, but they were there when Greece really needed them. Those ships, therefore, were already built and available to the Athenians, but they had to build even more, because they decided in the deliberations that took place after the oracle to resist the coming barbarian attack on Greece at sea and in full strength, trusting in god and in any other Greeks who would go along with them.

Those, then, were the oracles given to the Athenians.

Those Greeks who had the best interests of Greece at heart then met in council to make plans and exchange allegiances. The council decided that the very first thing they had to do was to reconcile their differences and to end all warring among themselves. A number of them were mixed up in hostilities with each other, but the biggest conflict was between Athens and Aegina. When the council learned that Xerxes and his army were in Sardis, they decided to send spies into Asia to gather information about the king's activities. Then they sent some ambassadors to Argos to forge an alliance against Persia, others to Gelon, son of Deinomenes, in Sicily, and still others to Corcyra,[8] calling on them to come to the aid of Greece. They also sent ambassadors to Crete in an attempt somehow to combine Greek forces and to induce them all to act in unison on the grounds that a great danger threatened every Greek alike. Besides, Gelon was said to have immense power—greater than that of any other Greek.

The first thing they did after reaching these decisions and patching up their feuds was to send three spies into Asia. These men reached Sardis and obtained intelligence about the king's army, but they were discovered, interrogated under torture by the commanding officers of the infantry, and then led away to their deaths. When Xerxes learned that

---

7. These were mines at Laurium, near Cape Sunium, which were owned by Athens and which yielded large quantities of silver and lead.
8. Corcyra is the modern Corfu.

the spies had been given a death sentence, he rebuked the officers and dispatched some of his bodyguard with orders to bring the spies back to him if they were still alive. The bodyguards caught up with them and brought them back alive into the presence of the king. Then, as soon as he found out what their mission was, Xerxes ordered the bodyguards to take them on a guided tour of his whole infantry and cavalry and, when they had had their fill of sightseeing, to send them off unharmed to wherever they wanted to go.

Xerxes gave the following explanation for this order: if they had killed the spies, they wouldn't have done their enemies much harm by killing three men, and the Greeks would have had no advance notice that his strength was beyond anything they had imagined. If the spies returned, though, and the Greeks heard about his army, Xerxes believed that they would give up this freedom of theirs and that he would achieve his objective without having to mount a campaign against them.

He had another insight which was just like this one. When he was in Abydos, Xerxes saw ships transporting grain out of the Pontus and through the Hellespont on their way to Aegina and the Peloponnese. When his advisers noticed that they were enemy ships, they were eager to capture them, and they kept looking over at the king for a command. Xerxes asked where the ships were sailing to, and they said:

"They are bringing food to your enemies, Master . . ."

But he interrupted them and said, "Well, aren't we sailing to the same place they are, and bringing grain—along with a lot of other things? What harm are they doing us by transporting our food?"

Thus, after the spies made their observations, they were sent away and returned to Europe. After their return, the Greek allies against Persia sent ambassadors to Argos. Now, the Argives say that this was their situation: they had known from the very beginning that the barbarian mobilization was aimed at Greece. They also realized that the Greeks would try to enlist them against Persia, so they sent ambassadors to Delphi to ask the god what was the best thing for them to do. You see, six thousand Argives had just been killed by the Lacedaemonians under Cleomenes, son of Anaxandrides, and that was why they sent for an opinion. This is how the Pythian priestess answered their question:

> Hated by your neighbors, loved by the deathless gods,
> Keep your spear indoors and sit on guard.
> Protect your head, and your head will save your body.

This was the prophecy the priestess had given before the ambassadors of the allies arrived in Argos and went to the council chamber to give their message. For their part, the Argives answered that they were ready to join on condition that they conclude a thirty-year peace treaty with the Lacedaemonians and that they have joint command, with Sparta, over the whole alliance. By rights, they said, they should have full command, but they would, nevertheless, be satisfied with half.

The Argives say that their council gave this reply even though the oracle had forbidden them to form an alliance with the Greeks. Even though they dreaded the oracle, they were eager for a thirty-year treaty so that their sons could reach full manhood during those years. They feared that if they suffered another disaster at the hands of the Persians on top of the one that had already taken place, they would, without a treaty, be subject to the Spartans forever. In reply to the council's statement, the Spartan contingent of ambassadors said that they would submit the matter of a truce to the people of Sparta. They were, however, empowered to respond on the question of command, and they told the Argives that the Spartans had two kings, while the Argives had one. Now, although it was impossible for either Spartan king to relinquish command, there was nothing to prevent the Argive king from having one vote to their two. The Argives say that it would have been intolerable to be outvoted by the Spartans; they would rather be ruled by the barbarians than give in to the Lacedaemonians. So they told the ambassadors to get out of Argive territory by sundown or be treated as enemies.

That is the Argive version of those events. There is, though, another story prevalent throughout Greece, and it is that Xerxes sent an envoy to Argos even before he set out on his campaign. The story goes that when the herald arrived, he said, "Men of Argos! This is what King Xerxes has to say to you. We believe that we are descended from Perses, whose father was Perseus, son of Danae, and whose mother was Andromeda, daughter of Cepheus. This would make us your descendants. Thus, since it would not be proper for us to make war on you, our forebears, or for you to go to the aid of anyone else and become our enemies, the best thing is for you to stay home and remain neutral. If things go according to my plan, there is no one I will regard more highly than you."

It is said that the Argives were deeply honored when they heard this, and that at first they neither made any demands nor offered to join the alliance; but then, to have a pretext for remaining neutral, they demanded to share power when the Greeks tried to enlist them, knowing full well that the Lacedaemonians would never go along with it.

Some Greeks tell the story of an event that took place many years later and that jibes with this version. An Athenian delegation made up of Callias, son of Hipponicus, and others happened to be in Memnon's city of Susa on other business, when, at the very same time, a group of Argive ambassadors arrived to ask Artaxerxes, son of Xerxes, whether the close friendship Xerxes had formed with Argos was still good or whether he now considered the Argives to be his enemies. King Artaxerxes said that it was as good as ever and that no city was a better friend to him than Argos.

Now, I can't say for sure whether Xerxes sent that herald and that message to Argos or whether Argive ambassadors went up to Susa to ask Artaxerxes questions about friendship. Nor do I profess any opinion about those stories other than that of the Argives themselves. I do know this, though: if all the people in this world brought their dirty deeds out into the open with the idea of exchanging them for those of their neighbors, everybody would gladly go back home with what he'd brought after getting a peek at what his neighbors had to offer. The Argives didn't do the worst things that were done. I have an obligation to report what is said, but I have no obligation to believe all of it—and that goes for this whole work. Why, people even say that it was the Argives who invited Persia to invade Greece in the first place, because they were so afflicted by the Spartan spear that they would prefer anything to what they were suffering at that time.

So much for the Argives.

*   *   *

Chapters 172–239

Thessalian displeasure with the plots of the Aleuadae made it clear that they had been forced, at first, to collaborate with Persia.[9] Also, as soon as the Thessalians learned that the Persians were about to cross over into Europe, they sent ambassadors to the Isthmus, where there was an assembly of the elected delegates from the cities involved in developing the best strategy for Greece. When they came before this group, the Thessalian ambassadors said, "Men of Greece! The pass at Mount Olympus must be defended to save Thessaly and all of Greece from war. We are now ready to share in its defense, but you, too, must send a large force, because you should know that, if you don't we will come to terms with Persia. We are not, after all—lying as we do so far to the east of Greece—going to go to our deaths for her alone. If you decide not to give us help, you will never be able to force us to fight. Force is never more powerful than inability. We'll try to figure out some way to save ourselves."

The Greeks responded to the Thessalian statement by voting to send a force of infantry by sea to defend the pass. When this force was assembled, it sailed through the Euripus to Achaean Alus. They disembarked there and, leaving their ships behind, made their way to Thessaly. At Tempe they reached the pass which bears from lower Macedonia into Thessaly along the Peneus River, between Mount Olympus and Mount Ossa. The combined force of ten thousand Greek hoplites[1] camped there and was joined by the Thessalian cavalry. The Lacedaemonian commander was Euaenetus, son of Carenus. He had been chosen from among the division commanders, but was not from the royal family. The Athenian commander was Themistocles, son of Neocles. They remained

---

9. The Aleuadae were one of many aristocratic families in Thessaly.

1. A hoplite was a heavily armed Greek soldier.

there only a few days because messengers from Alexander, son of Amyn-
tas the Macedonian, arrived, told them the numbers of Persian men and
ships, and advised them to withdraw and not stay in the pass, where they
would be trampled underfoot by the coming army. It seemed like good
advice, and the Macedonian was obviously well intentioned, so the
commanders decided to follow it. In my opinion, though, it was fear
that persuaded them, because they found out that there was another pass
into Thessaly via upper Macedonia through Perrhaebia at the city of
Gonnus—and that in fact is where the army of Xerxes penetrated Greece.
So the Greeks went back down to their ships and returned to the Isthmus.

Those were the activities of the Greek army in Thessaly while the
king was in Abydos on the point of crossing into Europe from Asia. The
Thessalians, bereft of allies, now collaborated with the Persians eagerly
and without reservation, and they proved to be extremely useful to Xerxes
in later events.

In view of Alexander's message, when the Greeks got back to the Isthmus, they deliberated about where and in what kind of terrain they should
take their stand. The prevailing opinion was to defend the pass at Thermopylae. It seemed to be narrower than the one in Thessaly; it was
closer to central Greece, and it was the only way in. (The Greeks didn't
know of the existence of the mountain trail the Persians later used to
capture the defenders at Thermopylae until they reached the region and
found out about it from the Trachinians.) This, then, was the pass they
decided to defend in order to keep the barbarians from entering central
Greece; meanwhile, the fleet was to sail up the Histiaean coast to Artemisium. Thermopylae and Artemisium are close enough to each other
for there to be communication between the land and naval forces.

This is the geography of the two places. First, Artemisium. There is a
point where the expanse of the Sea of Thrace contracts into the narrows
between the island of Sciathus and the Magnesian mainland. Artemisium is on the Euboean coastline you follow once you clear that strait. It
has a temple dedicated to Artemis. As to the pass through Trachis into
Greece at Thermopylae, it is fifty feet wide at its narrowest point. This
spot, however, is not the narrowest in the whole region. Above Thermopylae at the Phoenix River near the town of Anthela, and below it at
Alpeni, it is wide enough for only one wagon to pass through at a time.
To the west of Thermopylae there is a high, steep, impassable mountain
stretching up to Mount Oeta, while to the east of the road the terrain
runs into a shallow, marshy sea. There are hot springs in the pass. The
locals call them "the Kettles," and an altar to Heracles has been erected
over them. There used to be a wall across this pass, and in antiquity
there was a gate in the wall. Fearful Phocians built the wall when the
Thessalians migrated out of Thesprotia to live in the Aeolian territory
they still inhabit. The Thessalians tried to conquer them, so the Phocians protected themselves by building the wall and by flooding the pass
with the hot spring water so that the terrain would be broken into ravines—

anything to keep the Thessalians from invading their land. Most of the wall that was built in antiquity had collapsed over time, but the Greek forces rebuilt it, thinking it would block the passage of the barbarians into Greece. Also, there is a village called Alpeni right near the road, and the Greeks counted on getting food there.

These seemed the best places for the Greeks to take their stand, for after taking everything into consideration, they decided to meet the attack on Greece in places where they thought the barbarians would get the least advantage out of their cavalry or their numerical superiority.

When they learned that the Persian was in Pieria, they broke camp at the Isthmus and went to war—some on foot to Thermopylae, others by sea to Artemisium.

At the same time as the troops were moving out on the double to take up their positions, the Delphians consulted the god, dreading for themselves and for the rest of Greece. The oracle told them to pray to the winds because they would be great allies of Greece. The first thing the Delphians did after they received the oracle was to announce it to all the Greeks who wanted to be free. They, too, were terrified of the barbarians, and by telling them the oracle, the Delphians won their undying gratitude. Next the Delphians dedicated an altar to the winds in Thyia. The sacred precinct of Cephisus' daughter Thyia is located there and gives the place its name. There the Delphians conciliated the winds with sacrifices, and in fact they propitiate the winds to this day on account of that oracle.

Xerxes' fleet set out from Therma after sending ten of its best ships straight to Sciathus, where three Greek ships—one from Troezen, one from Aegina, and one from Attica—were standing watch. When they saw the barbarian ships coming, they ran for it. The barbarians pursued and quickly captured the Troezenian ship, which was under the command of Prexinus. Then they led the handsomest sailor to the prow of the ship and cut his throat to make a good-luck sacrifice of the first handsome Greek they had captured. The name of the man whose throat was cut was Lion, and maybe he owed his fate to his name.

The Aeginetan trireme, under the command of Asonides, gave the barbarians quite a struggle, thanks mainly to Pytheas, son of Ischenous—a marine who was the bravest man of the day. After the ship was grappled, Pytheas held out for so long that he came to look as if he had been hacked by a butcher. There was still life in him when he fell, and the Persian marines did everything they could to keep him alive because of his bravery. They treated his wounds with myrrh and wrapped them in linen bandages, and when they brought him back to their base, they admiringly showed him off to the whole army and took very good care of him. As to the others they captured on that ship—they treated them like slaves.

Two of the triremes were taken in this way, but the third, under Phormus the Athenian, ran aground at the mouth of the Peneus River while trying to get away. The barbarians captured the hull but not the men, because as soon as the Athenians beached the ship, they jumped off, made their way through Thessaly, and returned to Athens.

The Greeks camped at Artemisium learned of these events by signal fires from Sciathus. They were so alarmed at the news that they left lookouts in the Euboean bluffs and changed anchorage from Artemisium to Chalcis in order to guard the Euripus. Three of the ten barbarian ships ran aground on the reef—known as the Ant—between Sciathus and Magnesia. After that, the barbarians brought out a pillar and set it up on the reef. Then, once the obstacle was clearly marked, the whole fleet which had set out from Therma could sail on—eleven days after the king had left the town with his army. (It was Pammon the Scyrian who showed them just where the reef was in the passage.) The barbarians sailed all day long, arriving at Sepias, in the Magnesian territory, at the beach between Cape Sepias and the town of Casthanaea.

Since Xerxes' forces had suffered no losses as far as Sepias and Thermopylae, these are their numbers at that time, as far as I can compute them. There were one thousand two hundred and seven Asian ships with their original complement from different nations of two hundred forty-one thousand four hundred men, reckoning on the basis of two hundred men per ship. Not counting local marines, there were thirty Persian, Median, or Secan marines on every ship. This other force came to thirty-six thousand two hundred and ten men. To these numbers, I add the crews of the penteconters—putting them at more or less eighty men apiece. As I said earlier, there were three thousand of these ships in all. This would come, then, to two hundred and forty thousand men. All together, therefore, there were five hundred seventeen thousand six hundred and ten men in the Asian fleet. Meanwhile, there were one million seven hundred thousand foot soldiers and eighty thousand cavalrymen in the army. I add to these the number of Arabian camel drivers and Libyan charioteers—twenty thousand men in all. Therefore, the combined land and sea forces came to two million three hundred seventeen thousand six hundred and ten men. So much for the force that was led out of Asia itself, not counting servants and the crews of ships carrying provisions.

One must, however, add to this computation the numbers of men who were enlisted in Europe—and here one can only guess. Greeks from Thrace and from the islands off the Thracian coast supplied one hundred and twenty ships with twenty-four thousand men aboard them. I believe that the Thracians, Paeonians, Eordians, Bottiaeans, assorted Chalcidians, Brygians, Pierians, Macedonians, Perrhaebians, Enianians, Dolopians, Magnesians, Achaeans, and inhabitants of the Thracian coast—that all these nations contributed three hundred thousand foot soldiers. Now, if all these myriads are added to the tens on tens of thousands of fighting men who came out of Asia, the number of combatants comes to two million six hundred forty-one thousand six hundred and ten.

That was the number of fighting men; but the servants, the crews of the small food transports as well as of the other ships accompanying the army—I believe that there were not fewer but more of these men than there were soldiers. Nevertheless, I won't make their number greater or smaller, but the same, so this number must be added to an equal number of fighting men. Thus Xerxes, son of Darius, led five million two hundred eighty-three thousand two hundred and twenty men to Sepias and Thermopylae.

That, then, is the total number of the army of Xerxes, although no one can give an accurate number for the female cooks, concubines, and eunuchs; and as to pack animals and other beasts of burden and the Indian dogs that followed the army, there were so many that no one could give a number for them, either. Therefore, it doesn't amaze me at all that the rivers sometimes gave out. What amazes me instead is how there was ever enough food for so many myriads of people, because when I calculate that even if each man consumed a quart of grain each day, and no more, then the daily ration for the army would have come to one hundred seventy thousand bushels—and I'm not including women, eunuchs, beasts of burden, and dogs.[2]

Yet out of so many millions of men, no one but Xerxes had the countenance or the stature to deserve such power!

Again, after the fleet set out, it sailed to the Magnesian coast and harbored at the beach between the town of Casthanaea and Cape Sepias. The first row of ships was moored to the land, while the rest rode at anchor behind them, and because it was not a large beach, they were anchored in rows eight ships deep, with their prows facing seaward. They lay there that night under a clear and windless sky, but just before dawn the sea began to churn and they were hit with a violent storm accompanied by gusting northeasterly winds, what the local people call a Hellespontic. The skippers who saw the wind rising and who were conveniently anchored to do so got the jump on the storm and dragged their ships up onto the beach, thus saving their ships and their lives as well. Ships that were caught in the high sea were either carried out to the so-called Ovens at Mount Pelion or dashed onto the beach. Some wrecks washed up at Sepias itself, others at the city of Meliboea, while others were thrown ashore at Casthanaea. The force of the storm was absolutely irresistible.

There is a story that the Athenians appealed to the north wind, Boreas, on the advice of another oracle they received telling them to call on their in-law for help. The story goes that Boreas has a wife from Attica, Orithyia, daughter of Erechtheus. According to the tale, the Athenians figured that they were related to Boreas because of Orithyia's relationship

---

2. Herodotus's numbers are grossly exaggerated throughout. Xerxes had perhaps one-tenth the fighting men enumerated here. The figures for camp followers are impossible to verify and are probably worthless.

to Attica. Now, when the Athenian fleet stationed at Chalcis, in Euboea, saw the storm gathering—or maybe even before then—they sacrificed to Boreas and Orithyia and appealed to them to come to their aid and destroy the barbarian ships, just as they had done, years before, at Athos. I can't say whether that's the reason Boreas stormed the barbarians as they lay at anchor, but the Athenians insist that Boreas had come to their rescue once before and that he brought about what happened this time, so when they returned home, they built a temple to Boreas along the Ilissus River.

They say that at least four hundred ships were destroyed in this disaster, along with countless men and untold wealth—so much wealth that the shipwrecks were a tremendous boon for Ameinocles, son of Cretines, a Magnesian landowner near Sepias. Over time, he gathered numerous gold and silver drinking cups, found Persian treasure chests, and took possession of vast amounts of wealth. But even though all this flotsam made him very rich, he was unlucky in other ways because he experienced the cruel grief of accidentally killing his own son.

The number of food transports and other craft destroyed over and above the warships isn't even known. During a storm that lasted three whole days, the naval commanders became afraid that the Thessalians would hit them when they were down, so they threw a high barricade made of ship's wreckage around their position. Finally, on the fourth day, the Magi calmed the wind after propitiating it with incantations and offerings and after performing sacrifices, as well, to Thetis and the other Nereids—either that, or the wind just died down by itself. They sacrificed to Thetis because they heard the story from the Ionians that Thetis had been abducted from that region by Peleus, and that all of Cape Sepias belonged to her and to the other Nereids.

The storm, then, abated on the fourth day. Meanwhile, two days after the storm began, the lookouts on the Euboean bluffs had rushed off to the Greeks and given a full report of the shipwreck. As soon as they heard it, they said prayers and poured drink offerings to their savior, Poseidon, and then hurried back to Artemisium in the belief that they would now be opposed by just a few ships. For the second time, then, the fleet went to its battle station at Artemisium, and from that day to this, the Greeks have called Poseidon "the Savior."

As soon as the wind died down and the waves lay smooth before them, the Persians dragged their ships back down into the water and, after hugging the shore and rounding the Magnesian cape, sailed straight into the gulf which leads to Pagasae. There is a place in this Magnesian gulf where they say that Jason and his companions abandoned Heracles after sending him off the Argo in search of water at the start of their voyage to Aea to retrieve the Golden Fleece. That was where they had intended to lay in supplies of water before casting off for the open sea, and that is how the place came to be called the Launch.

Xerxes' ships anchored in that gulf, but a squadron of fifteen ships which had set out much later than the rest somehow spotted the Greek fleet at Artemisium. The barbarians actually thought they were their own ships, so they sailed up to them and landed right smack in the middle of their enemies! The barbarian ships were commanded by Sandoces, son of Thamasius, and governor of Aeolian Cyme. Before this, Sandoces had been one of the royal judges, and King Darius had arrested him and nailed him to a stake for taking a bribe to render an unjust decision. While Sandoces was hanging there, though, Darius reflected that Sandoces' crimes were outnumbered by the many services he had rendered the royal household. Darius realized that he had acted with more haste than judgment, and released Sandoces. But though Sandoces may have escaped death at the hands of Darius, he wasn't about to escape a second time when he sailed into the Greek fleet. As soon as the Greeks saw him approaching and realized his mistake, they set out after his ships and easily captured them.

Aridolis, the tyrant of Alabanda, in Caria, was captured on one of the ships, and on another, the Paphian general, Penthylus, son of Demonous. He had led twelve ships out of Paphos, but lost eleven of them in the storm off Sepias and was captured in his one remaining ship as he sailed into Artemisium. The Greeks interrogated these men concerning details they wanted to know about Xerxes' army and then sent them to the Isthmus of Corinth in chains.

Aside from these fifteen ships, which were, as I have said, commanded by Sandoces, the remainder of the barbarian fleet arrived at the Launch. Three days later, Xerxes and the army reached Malia, after having made their way through Thessaly and Achaea.

In Thessaly, Xerxes had held a race to test his mares against the mares of Thessaly, which he had heard were the best in Greece. That time, anyway, the Greek mares were left far behind. The Onochonus was the only river in Thessaly that didn't have enough water to satisfy the thirst of the army; but even the biggest river in Achaea, the Apidanus, could only just barely hold out.

When Xerxes had reached Alus, in Achaea, his guides (who wanted to explain everything to him) told him the local legend about the temple of the Laphystian Zeus. Ino, they said, along with Athamas, son of Aeolus, had plotted and brought about the death of Phrixus. Later, though, an oracle commanded the Achaeans to impose the following ordeal on the descendants of Phrixus: the Achaeans were to station guards to prevent the oldest male member of the line from entering the Hall of the People—which is what the Achaeans call their town hall. If he does go in, he can't go out again except to be sacrificed. Many of those who were liable to be sacrificed fled in terror to other lands. Over time, they returned, but if any one of them is captured in the town hall he is still led out in solemn procession, covered with garlands, as if to the sacrifice. The descendants of Phrixus' son Cytissorus have to go through this because just as the Achaeans, at the command of an oracle, were about to sacrifice Athamas, son of Aeolus, in order to cleanse the land of guilt, this Cytissorus came out of Aea, in Colchis, and rescued him. Because of this, the wrath of god fell on all the descendants of Cytissorus. Xerxes was near the temple when he heard this story, but he stayed out of it and made it off-limits to his whole army. He also respected the house and grounds of the descendants of Athamas.

So much for what happened in Thessaly and Achaea. From there, Xerxes went to Malis, following a bay which fills and drains with the daily tide. The land is flat around this bay—broad in some places though quite narrow in others. The route is surrounded by the high, impassable mountains which lock in the whole Malian territory and which are called the Cliffs of Trachis. Anticyra is the first town you come across on this bay after leaving Achaea. The Spercheius River, which comes down from the Enianian territory, flows past the town and into the sea. There is another river about two and a half miles beyond this, called the Dyras, and the story goes that it first welled up to help the burning Heracles. Two and a half miles past the Dyras, there is another river, called the Melas.

The town of Trachis is about half a mile from the river Melas. Trachis was built where the stretch between the mountains and the sea is widest, on a plain with an area of some five thousand acres. There is a gorge in the southern part of the ring of mountains around this region, and the Asopus River flows through it into the foot of the mountains. South of the Asopus is the little Phoenix River, which streams out of the mountains and into the Asopus. The country is narrowest at the Phoenix River, and the road there is wide enough for only one wagon. It is two miles from the Phoenix to Thermopylae. A village called Anthele lies between the Phoenix and Thermopylae; the Asopus flows beside it and into the sea. There are wide tracts of land around Anthele, with a temple to Demeter of the Amphictyons, as well as a temple to Amphictyon himself and seats for members of the Amphictyonic League.[3]

King Xerxes, then, was bivouacked on the Trachinian side of Malis, and the Greeks were in the pass. Most Greeks call this place Thermopylae—the Hot Gates—while the locals and their neighbors call it just Pylae—or the Gates. Xerxes controlled everything from Trachis to the north wind, while the Greeks guarded the south and the continent of Europe.

These were the Greeks who awaited the Persian in that place. There were three hundred Spartan hoplites, and one thousand Tegeans and Mantineans—five hundred apiece. From Orchomenus, in Arcadia, there

---

3. The Amphictyonic League, or Council, was a league of clans at first organized around the temple of Demeter near Thermopylae and later asso-   ciated with the Delphic oracle. Its purpose was religious and political, and it also conducted the Pythian Games.

came one hundred twenty men, and from the rest of Arcadia a thousand. To this number of Arcadians were added four hundred Corinthians, two hundred Phlians, and eighty Mycenaeans. This was the Peloponnesian contingent, but seven hundred Thespians and four hundred Thebans came from Boeotia.

In addition to these, the Opuntian Locrians came in full strength, and the Phocians sent one thousand men. They had been called in by the Greeks at Thermopylae themselves. They had sent out messengers to say that they had come in advance of the rest of the army and that they expected the other allies any day. The sea, they said, was being guarded by the Athenians, the Aeginetans, and the other forces of the fleet, so the Phocians and Locrians had nothing to fear. After all, Greece was not being attacked by a god but by a man, and there never was and never would be a mortal who wasn't wedded to trouble from the day he was born—and the greater the man, the greater the trouble. Since he who was driving down on them now was a mortal, he was bound to be riding for a fall from glory. The Phocians and Locrians heard this message and marched out to Trachis.

Now, there were different commanders from the various cities, but the most admired was the Spartan commander in chief of the whole army. Leonidas, son of Anaxandrides, son of Leon, son of Eurycratidas, son of Anaxander, son of Eurycrates, son of Polydorus, son of Alcamenes, son of Telecles, son of Archelaus, son of Hegesilaus, son of Doryssus, son of Labotas, son of Echestratus, son of Agis, son of Eurysthenes, son of Aristodemus, son of Aristomachus, son of Cleodaeus, son of Hyllus, son of Heracles.

He had never expected to gain the throne of Sparta. Because he had two older brothers, Cleomenes and Dorieus, the monarchy was the furthest thing from his mind. Cleomenes, though, died without male issue, and Dorieus was no longer living—having died in Sicily—so the kingship devolved on Leonidas because he was older than Cleombrotus, the youngest son of Anaxandrides, but especially because he was married to the daughter of Cleomenes. Before setting off for Thermopylae, Leonidas selected the king's usual contingent of three hundred men—making sure that they all had sons. Along the way, he picked up the Thebans I included in my list. They were commanded by Leontiades, son of Eurymachus. Leonidas made a point of going to get them because they had been seriously accused of collaborating with the Persians; he personally called them to battle because he wanted to see whether they would send troops or openly refuse an alliance with the Greeks. They sent the men, but their hearts weren't in it.

The Spartans sent Leonidas with an advance guard so that the other allies would go to war after seeing them do so and not use any delay on Sparta's part as an excuse for also collaborating with the Persians. Later, after celebrating the Carneian festival, which prevented them from going to battle immediately, they would station a guard in Sparta and march out on the double in full strength. Their allies had the same idea. The Olympic Games were taking place at the same time as these events, so the allies, too, sent their advance guards, never thinking that the battle of Thermopylae would be decided so quickly.

These, then, were their intentions. Meanwhile, when the Greeks at Thermopylae saw the Persians approaching the pass, they panicked and talked about retreat. In general, the Peloponnesians thought they should return to the Peloponnese and guard the Isthmus, but when the Phocians and Locrians became extremely agitated over this idea, Leonidas voted to stay where they were and to dispatch messengers calling on the allies to come to the rescue since they were too few to hold off the Persian army.

While the Greek commanders were discussing their plans, Xerxes sent out a mounted spy to see how many Greeks there were and what they were doing. He had already heard while still in Thessaly that a small army had gathered at Thermopylae, and that it was led by Lacedaemonians under the command of Leonidas, a descendant of Heracles. The horseman could not observe or even see the whole camp as he rode toward it, because some of the men were posted out of sight inside the wall, which they had rebuilt and were guarding. He did see the men outside the wall, though, and their weapons lying nearby. During that watch, the Spartans happened to be stationed outside. He saw some of the men exercising, others combing their long hair. He was amazed at what he saw. He noted their numbers and, after carefully observing everything he could, trotted back unmolested. Nobody pursued him; nobody paid any attention to him at all. When he returned, he told Xerxes everything he had seen.

Xerxes heard it, but he couldn't understand that what they were doing was getting ready to kill or be killed. They seemed to him to be acting so absurdly that he sent for Demaratus, son of Ariston, who was in the camp. When he arrived, Xerxes asked him about everything in detail; he was eager to find out just what the Lacedaemonians were doing. Demaratus said, "I already told you about these men as we were setting out against Greece. You laughed at me for seeing that things would turn out just as they have. I keep trying to tell you the truth, Your Majesty, but it's a struggle. Listen to me now. Those men came here to fight with us for this pass, and that's what they are getting ready to do. It's their way. They comb their hair whenever they are about to risk their lives. But know this: if you defeat these men and the force that remains in Sparta, there are no other people on earth who will take up arms against you, because you are about to face the noblest king and the bravest men in all of Greece."

What he said seemed to Xerxes to be absolutely incredible, and Xerxes asked him for the second time how so few men could do battle with his army. Demaratus said, "Consider me a liar, Your Majesty, if things don't turn out as I say."

That's what he said, but Xerxes didn't believe him.

He let four days go by, expecting the Greeks to run away at any moment. When they had not only not left on the fifth day but seemed to be staying out of sheer reckless effrontery, Xerxes became furious and sent the Medes and Cissians out to attack them, with orders to bring them back into his presence alive. Waves of Medians rushed the Greeks. Many men fell, and others followed in their wake, but none retreated from the overwhelming disaster. The Medes made it clear to everyone and not least to the king himself that he had many troops but few real men. Nevertheless, the battle lasted all day long.

The Medes finally retreated after being thoroughly manhandled. The Persians were the next to attack—the men Xerxes called his Immortals. They were under the command of Hydarnes, and indeed they thought that they would easily prevail, but it was no different for them when they mixed it up with the Greeks from what it had been for the Medes. It was just the same because they were fighting at very close quarters, using spears shorter than the Greeks', and were unable to take advantage of their numerical superiority. The Lacedaemonians fought a battle to remember! Among these men who knew nothing of warfare, they showed in all sorts of ways that they really knew how to fight—like when they turned their backs and pretended to run away, the barbarians would see them running and would chase after them shouting and making noise, and then the Greeks would wheel around and face the barbarians just as they were about to be overtaken and slaughter countless numbers of them.

A few of the Spartans fell there, too.

The Persians couldn't take the pass after attacking it company by company and in every other way, and they finally retreated.

They say that the king, who was observing these assaults, jumped up from his throne three times in fear for his army. That, then, is how the battle went on that day; and the barbarians fought with no more success the next day, either. They attacked in the belief that the small number of Greeks must have suffered so many casualties that they wouldn't even be able to raise their arms to resist. The Greeks, however, stood in formations of tribes and regiments and took turns in the fighting—all except the Phocians, who had been posted on the mountain to guard the trail. The Persians retreated when they didn't see anything different from what they had found the day before.

Xerxes was at a loss as to how to deal with this situation when a Malian, Ephialtes, son of Eurydemus, came to talk to the king in the hope of receiving a large gift.[4] He told Xerxes about the trail leading through the mountains to Thermopylae and thereby doomed the Greek defenders at the pass. Ephialtes later fled to Thessaly in fear of the Lacedaemonians,

---

4. Ephialtes is also called a Trachinian in the next paragraph. Malia (or Trachis) along with the rest of Thessaly reluctantly collaborated with Persia.

but at a meeting at Pylae, the Amphyctionic delegates—the Pylagorae—
offered a reward for the fugitive. When he returned to Anticyra some
time later, he was killed by Athenades, a man from Trachis. Now, Athenades killed Ephialtes for a different reason (which I will talk about in
a later narrative),[5] but the Lacedaemonians honored him for it nonetheless.

Ephialtes, then, died after these events. They tell another version of
the story—although I don't believe it in the least—which is that a Ca-
rystian man, Onetes, son of Phanagoras, and Corydallus of Anticyra
were the ones who spoke to the king about the trail and guided the
Persians over the mountains. In the first place, you have to base your
decision on the fact that the Pylagorae offered a reward for Ephialtes the
Trachinian and not for Onetes and Corydallus, and that they must have
done so on the surest evidence. In the second place, we know that
Ephialtes was a fugitive from this charge. Now, provided that Onetes
was very familiar with the country, it *is* possible that he could have
known about this trail even though he was not a Malian; but no, Ephialtes
was the one who led the way over the mountains by the trail, and I
hereby record that he was the traitor.

Xerxes was delighted with what Ephialtes had offered to do, and soon
became positively overjoyed. He immediately dispatched Hydarnes and
his Immortals, who left camp at dusk, at around the time the lamps are
lit.

Malian locals discovered this trail and then guided the Thessalians
over it to attack the Phocians after the Phocians had walled up the pass
to hold off an invasion. That's how long the Malians have known about
this deadly trail! The trail begins where the Asopus issues through the
gorge, and its name is the same as the mountain's—the Anopaea. The
Anopaea trail runs along the mountain ridge and leaves off at Alpeni,
the first town on the Malian side of Locris, at a place called Black Ass
Rock and the Cercopian Butts.[6] This is the narrowest part of the pass.

The Persians crossed the Asopus and made their way over the trail
through the night, keeping the Oeta Mountains on the right and the
mountains of Trachis on the left. They reached the top of the mountain
with the glimmering of dawn. As I have already said, a thousand heavily
armed Phocians were stationed there to guard the trail and defend their
own homeland. The Phocians had voluntarily given their oath to Leonidas to guard that mountain trail, and we know very well who was guarding the pass below.

The Persians could go up the mountain unnoticed because it was
covered with oak trees, so the Phocians only found out that the Persians

5. Herodotus does not keep his promise to write
this narrative.
6. Legend had it that two dwarfs stole Heracles'
weapons while he slept near these rocks. He caught
the dwarfs and hung them upside down from a
pole he carried on his shoulders. The dwarfs made
jokes about his backside, and the amused Heracles
released them. The legend was perhaps invented
to explain the shape and color of the rocks.

had already gotten up there when, on that perfectly still day, they heard the loud noise of fallen leaves crackling under the tramp of feet. The Phocians sprang up and were putting on their battle gear as the barbarians came in sight. The Persians were astonished to see men putting on their armor. They had thought they would meet with no opposition, and yet here was an army! Hydarnes dreaded that the Phocians might be Spartans, so he asked Ephialtes where they were from. When he was sure of their nationality, he arrayed his Persians for battle. After being showered with arrows thick and fast, the Phocians thought the attack was aimed at them, and they ran up to the very top of the mountain ready to fight to the death; but they were mistaken, because the Persians under Ephialtes and Hydarnes paid no further attention to them and hurried down the mountain.

Meanwhile, Megistias the seer had examined the sacrificial animals and told the Greeks at Thermopylae that they would die at dawn. Also, deserters had told them during the night that the Persians were circling around behind them. Finally, their lookouts ran down from the mountaintops with the news at the dawn's early light. The Greeks then held a meeting, and their opinions were divided between those who would not leave their positions and those who took the opposite view. The two sides parted company: some retreated and scattered into their respective cities; others prepared to take their stand there with Leonidas.

It is said that Leonidas himself sent the others away, concerned lest they be destroyed—while as for him and the Spartans who were with him, they couldn't rightly abandon the post they had come to guard in the first place. I myself am inclined to the view that when Leonidas saw that his allies were balking, unwilling to stay with him and risk their lives, he must have ordered them to retreat, though he himself couldn't go home honorably. He would stay to leave eternal fame behind him, and see to it that Sparta's prosperity was not snuffed out. You see, the Spartans had consulted the Delphic oracle as soon as the war broke out, and the Pythian priestess had prophesied that either the Lacedaemonian people would be uprooted by the barbarians or their king would die. She uttered the prophecy in the following hexameter verses:

> But for you, O dwellers in Sparta's wide land,
> Either your glorious city shall be sacked by the men of Persia
> Or, if not, she will mourn the action of Heracles,
> The dead ruler over all the land of Lacedaemon.
> The strength of bulls and lions cannot resist the foe,
> For he has the strength of Zeus. No, he will not leave off,
> I say, until he tears city or king limb from limb.

Leonidas dismissed the allies with this prophecy in mind, and because he wanted to be the only Spartan to win such fame; they did not go home in disarray over a difference of opinion.

For me, not the least evidence for this view is the well-known fact that Leonidas also tried to dismiss the army seer I mentioned—Megistias the Acarnanian, who they say was descended from Melampus, and who foretold the future from his sacrificial animals. But although he had been dismissed to keep him from being killed with everyone else, he didn't leave; instead, he sent home his only son, who had gone to war with him.

The allies who had been dismissed obeyed Leonidas and left. Only the Thespians and the Thebans stayed with the Lacedaemonians. The Thebans remained without wanting to because Leonidas, regarding them as hostages, held them against their will. The Thespians, on the other hand, were very willing to stay. Refusing to abandon Leonidas or desert his men, they stayed behind and died along with them. The Thespian commander was Demophilus, son of Diadromes.

Xerxes poured out drink offerings at sunrise. He waited until about midmorning and then began the attack. This plan had been arranged in advance with Ephialtes, because the descent from the mountain would be much quicker, with much less ground to cover, than the march around and the climb up had been. The barbarians under Xerxes moved forward while the Greeks under Leonidas advanced like men who are going out to their deaths; and this time they went much farther out into the wider part of the pass than they had at first. In the first days of battle, concerned with protecting the defending wall, they would only make forays into the narrowest part and fight there. This time, as the two sides grappled with each other beyond the narrow neck of the pass, very many barbarians fell while their company commanders whipped each and every man, driving them constantly forward. Many of them fell into the sea and drowned; many others trampled each other alive; no one cared about the dying. And because they knew that death was coming from the troops who had circled the mountain, the Greeks fought the barbarians with all the strength they had, fought recklessly out of their minds.

Most of their spears were broken by now, so they slaughtered Persians with their swords. That brave man Leonidas fell in the struggle, and other renowned Spartans along with him. I have learned the names of these noble men, as I have learned the names of all the three hundred Spartans who perished. And, indeed, many brave Persians died there, too, two sons of Darius among them—Abrocomes and Hyperanthes, Darius' children by Phratagune, daughter of Artanes. This Artanes was the brother of King Darius, and the son of Hystaspes, son of Arsames. When he married his daughter to Darius, Artanes gave up his whole estate along with her since she was his only child.

Thus two brothers of Xerxes died in the battle.

There was a tremendous crush of Persians and Lacedaemonians around the body of Leonidas, until by sheer courage the Greeks dragged him away after beating back the enemy four times. The fight continued until Ephialtes arrived. The nature of the battle changed as soon as the Greeks realized that he was there. They fell back to the narrow part of the pass and, after ducking behind the wall, massed together on the hillock behind it and dug in—all except the Thebans. This mound is in the pass where the stone lion now stands in honor of Leonidas. The men defended themselves on this hillock with daggers, if they still had them, or with their hands and teeth, while some of the Persians came at them head-on after pulling down and demolishing the wall and others surrounded them and stood there burying them under arrows, spears, and stones.

They say that Dieneces the Spartan stood out even in this company of Lacedaemonians and Thespians. Just before the battle with the Persians, he heard some Trachinian say that when the barbarians shot their arrows the sky was so full of them that the sun was blotted out—that's how many Persians there were. Dieneces wasn't fazed at all. He pooh-poohed the Persian numbers, and is reported to have said that his Trachinian friend had brought good news, because if the Persians blotted out the sun they could have their battle in the shade rather than in the sunlight. They say Dieneces the Spartan left this and other witticisms to be remembered by. After him, they say, two Lacedaemonian brothers, Alpheus and Maron, sons of Orsiphantus, distinguished themselves. The most outstanding Thespian was named Dithyrambus, son of Harmatides.

The men were buried where they fell, along with those who had died before the departure of the men Leonidas had dismissed. There is an epitaph over the mass grave which says:

> IN THIS PLACE FOUR THOUSAND PELOPONNESIANS
> FOUGHT FOUR MILLION MEN

That epitaph was for all the men. These words commemorate the Spartans alone:

> STRANGER GO TELL THE LACEDAEMONIANS
> THAT WE WHO LIE HERE OBEYED THEIR ORDERS

That was for the Lacedaemonians. This was for the seer:

> IN MEMORY OF MEGISTIAS WHOM PERSIANS
> CROSSED SPERCHEIUS STREAM TO KILL
> A SEER WHO COULD GAZE AT THE ADVANCE OF DOOM
> HE DID NOT DARE DESERT HIS SPARTAN CHIEF

The Amphictyons are the ones who honored the dead with pillars and inscriptions—except for the one to Megistias, which was dedicated by Simonides, son of Leoprepes, in token of friendship.

A story has it that Leonidas had sent two of the three hundred, Eurytus and Aristodemus, out of camp to Alpeni because both were suffering from extreme cases of inflammation of the eyes. Thus it was possible for them to decide to save themselves and return to Sparta or, if they didn't want to return, to die along with the others. They could do one or the other, but they couldn't agree on which and quarreled instead. When Eurytus found out about the Persian flanking attack, he asked for his war gear, put it on, and commanded his helot servant to lead him to the battle. The helot took him and then immediately ran away; Eurytus joined the throng and was killed; Aristodemus lost heart and stayed behind. Now, if Aristodemus had been the only one to be sick and to return to Sparta, or if both of them had made it back together, the Spartans would not, I believe, have been at all angry with them; but when one of them had given up his life although he had the same excuse for living as the one who had refused to die, the Spartans had no choice but to take out their anger on Aristodemus.

(That, by the way, is the excuse some people say Aristodemus used to get back to Sparta safely. Others say that he had been sent out of the camp as a messenger, and that although it was possible for him to return to the battle in time, he didn't want to, while his fellow messenger joined the battle and died.)

Aristodemus suffered shame and disgrace after his return to Sparta. This is the kind of disgrace he had to put up with: no Spartan would give him a light for his fire or talk to him; meanwhile, he was shamed by being called Runaway Aristodemus. Nevertheless, at the Battle of Plataea, Aristodemus made up for all the shame that had been heaped on him.

They say that yet another man of the three hundred had been sent as a messenger to Thessaly and survived. His name was Pantites, and after he returned to Sparta he hanged himself in disgrace.

While they were with the Greeks, the Thebans under Leontiades were forced to fight Xerxes' army, but when they saw the Persians getting the upper hand and the Greeks falling back on the mound with the corpse of Leonidas, they split off from the others, stretched out their hands, and approached the barbarians, saying what was all too true, that they had collaborated with Persia and were among the first to send earth and water, that they had come to Thermopylae only because they had to, and that they were not responsible for any harm the king might have suffered. They spoke these words (which they called on the Thessalians to corroborate), and they lived. Not everything turned out well for them, though. The barbarians killed some of them as they approached, but most were taken prisoner and, at Xerxes' command, were branded in the forehead with the king's mark as slaves—beginning with their commander, Leontiades, whose son Eurymachus was later killed by the Plataeans after he captured their capital city at the head of four hundred Thebans.

That, then, is how the Greeks fought at Thermopylae.

Later, Xerxes sent for Demaratus and began by saying, "You are a good man, Demaratus—I can tell from your truthfulness. Everything has happened just as you said it would." Then Xerxes asked, "But tell me now, how many more Lacedaemonians are there, and how many of them fight like this? Or is it all of them?"

"There are many Lacedaemonians, Your Majesty," he said, "and they live in many towns! But I will tell you what you really want to know. There is a city in Lacedaemon—Sparta—with eight thousand men in it, all of whom are just like the men who fought here. The neighboring Lacedaemonians are not exactly like these, though they *are* brave."

Then Xerxes said, "How, Demaratus, can I subdue these people with the least amount of trouble? Come, tell me. You used to be their king; you know all the twists and turns of their thinking."

"Your Majesty," said Demaratus, "since you are so eager for my advice, it is only right for me to give you the best I have. Let's say you sent three hundred of your ships to Laconia. There is an island off the coast called Cythera, and Chilon, the wisest man we ever had, said that it would be much better for the Spartans if it were under the sea rather than above it, because he constantly expected that the kind of thing I'm now going to tell you about would come from there. Not that he foresaw *your* expedition, but he feared an army there all the same. If you make sorties from this island, you will strike terror into the Lacedaemonians. If they have their own war close to home, you needn't fear that they will come to the rescue of the rest of Greece as you conquer it with your infantry; and once the rest of Greece is enslaved, Laconia will be left isolated and weak. If you don't do this, here is what you can expect: there is a narrow isthmus in the Peloponnese; there, with every inhabitant of the Peloponnese bound by the most solemn oaths to resist you, you will meet with far fiercer battles than you have had so far. If you do as I advise, though, that isthmus and the towns of the Peloponnese will surrender without a fight."

Achaemenes, who was Xerxes' brother and the admiral of the fleet, happened to be present during this speech, and, fearing that Xerxes might be persuaded to do as Demaratus advised, he said "I see, Your Majesty, that you are receptive to the arguments of a man who either begrudges your success or aims to sabotage your whole enterprise. That's the way these Greeks are—they envy success and hate superior strength. If, in a situation in which we have just lost four hundred ships, you detach another three hundred from the fleet to go sailing around the Peloponnese, why then your adversaries will become a match for you. If the fleet is kept together, though, it will be very hard for them to handle. The Greeks will be no match for you from the very beginning, and the fleet will be able to support the army while the army will move in conjunction with the fleet. If you divide the fleet, though, you won't be any use to it or it to you. Have a strategy which serves your own best interests and don't bother about the affairs of your enemies—where they'll fight, what they'll do, how many of them there are. They can take care of themselves, and the same goes for us! If the Lacedaemonians go up against the Persians in battle, they'll never heal the wound they've just been given."

Xerxes said, "I think you've given me good advice, and I'll do as you say. Demaratus said what he believed was best for me, though your opinion won out over his. Judging by what he said before, though, I will not accept the idea that he doesn't wish my campaign well, even though the reality is that one citizen does resent the success of another and either shows his hostility through silence or fails to give the best advice when his neighbor asks for it—unless, that is, he has achieved a very high degree of integrity, and such people are rare. But allies always have the most favorable view of each other's success, and one will always give the other the best possible advice. I hereby command everyone to refrain from denigrating my ally and my guest, Demaratus, from now on."

After saying this, Xerxes inspected the dead. When he came on the corpse of Leonidas and heard that he had been the king and the commander in chief of the Lacedaemonians, Xerxes commanded that his head be cut off and stuck on a pole. This is not the least of many proofs which make it very clear to me that King Xerxes had hated Leonidas more than any other living man. Otherwise he would never have violated the corpse in this way, since the Persians, more than any people I know, honor men who are brave in battle. A special detail carried out Xerxes' order.

I want to go back to a part of the story that I left out earlier. The Lacedaemonians were the first to find out that the king was going to campaign against Greece, and that's why they sent ambassadors to the Delphic oracle, where they were given the prophecy I mentioned a little while ago. But the way they found out is very interesting. You see, in my view—and probability is on my side in this—Demaratus, son of Ariston, wasn't very well inclined toward the Lacedaemonians when he fled to Persia. Still, it's anybody's guess whether what he then did was well intentioned or whether he did it to exult—because Demaratus was in Susa when Xerxes decided to invade Greece, and when he found out about it, he wanted to report it to the Lacedaemonians. But he didn't have a way to get the message out, because there was great danger that he might be caught. This is what he came up with: he took a folding writing tablet, scraped off its wax cover, and wrote down the king's plan on the wood underneath. Then he melted the wax back over the writing so that the tablet would not arouse the suspicions of the border guards. When the tablet reached Sparta, the Spartans didn't know what to do with it until, as I have learned, Gorgo, wife of Leonidas and daughter of Cleomenes, figured it out and suggested that if they scraped off the wax they would find some writing on the wood. They took her advice, found and read the writing, and then sent it around to the other Greeks. Anyway, that's how they say it happened.

Book 8

The focal point of book 8 is the Battle of Salamis, which took place after the Persian army seized and burned an abandoned Attica. Herodotus' account of the battle turns on the character of Xerxes and Themistocles, underlining the importance of individuals in the unfolding of history. Both men faced difficulties in obtaining accurate information and evaluating evidence in order to frame the best strategy, and Themistocles did the better job. Herodotus ascribes the Greek victory in large part to Themistocles' intellect and enterprise. Understanding the necessity to force a battle despite the divisions and anxieties in the Greek camp, and knowing the temperament of Xerxes, Themistocles—with a cunning worthy of an earlier rogue, Odysseus—decided to deceive Xerxes by sending him the message that the Greek navy was on the verge of disintegrating. Posing as a friend, Themistocles advised Xerxes that a prompt battle would be in the king's interest. Themistocles' ruse succeeded, and the Greek victory at Salamis led to the eventual expulsion of the Persian force from Greece. This in turn was the source for tensions that eventually, toward the end of Herodotus' lifetime, drew Athens and Sparta into the long and deadly Peloponnesian War.

Themistocles' stratagem was made necessary by the diffidence of the Greeks, who were prevented by both fear and shortsightedness from evaluating their situation at Salamis correctly. Themistocles, however, was able to see the situation clearly, a factor to which Herodotus attributes a great deal of the success or failure of human enterprise. It was the absence of this skill that would account for Xerxes' downfall, just as it had caused that of Croesus and countless others.

The moral is present, too, in Herodotus' account of the conduct of Artemisia, queen of the historian's native Halicarnassus. She wisely advises Xerxes not to fight the Greeks and to wait for their coalition to disperse, but Xerxes, convinced that his presence would inspire the Persian soldiers to victory, rejects the advice. Herodotus' message is clear: it is not, in the end, loyalty to an individual monarch that makes good fighters but rather love of land and law.

As so often, Xerxes is out of touch, but he is not entirely without perceptiveness. Artemisia's friends, Herodotus maintains, worried that she would be punished for her rash advice, and her enemies exulted in the prospect of her destruction. But Xerxes, although rejecting the strategy she proposed, continued to admire Artemisia. Herodotus recounts that when the battle was finally joined, this daughter of Halicarnassus eluded capture by ramming another Persian ship, thus persuading the pursuing Greeks that she was one of their own. Seeing Artemisia in action, and believing that the ship she had sunk was Greek, Xerxes exclaimed that his men were turned into women

and his women into men. His observation is fraught with Herodotean iro-
nies. Xerxes has been deceived by careless observation, a fatal flaw: Artemisia had actually caused the deaths of an entire shipload of men fighting on
the Persian side. Xerxes, although in many ways reflective, does not think
carefully enough, and hence loses the war. Herodotus constantly reminds
us that people all too easily imagine they are in control of the facts when
they are not.

Chapters 1–125

These are the Greeks who were assigned to the fleet. The Athenians
supplied one hundred and twenty-seven battleships;[1] and Plataeans,
though inexperienced sailors, manned the ships along with the Athenians out of eagerness and bravery. The Corinthians furnished forty ships
and the Megarians twenty. The Chalcidians manned twenty ships which
the Athenians had given them. The Aeginetans supplied eighteen ships,
the Sicyonians twelve, the Lacedaemonians ten, the Epidaurians eight,
the Eretrians seven, the Troezenians five, the Styrians two, and the Ceans
two triremes and two penteconters. The Opuntian Locrians helped out
with seven penteconters.

These states, then, listed according to the number of ships they supplied, were the ones that went to war at Artemisium. Not counting the
penteconters, there were two hundred and seventy-one ships at Artemisium. The Spartans sent the commander in chief, Eurybiades, son of
Eurycleides, because the allies refused to follow Athenian leadership
and would have disbanded the projected fleet if it had not been commanded by a Spartan. From the beginning, even before Sicily was
approached about an alliance, the argument was made that the fleet had
to be entrusted to Athens. When the allies objected, though, the Athenians yielded, because their great objective was the survival of Greece,
and because they knew that Greece was lost if they wrangled over leadership. And they were right, because civil war is worse than united war
to the same degree that war is worse than peace. Because they understood this fact the Athenians did not hold out for command; they gave
in, but only for so long as they desperately needed Sparta—as they later
made clear. After the Persians had been pushed back and the war was
being fought on Persian soil, the Athenians used the issue of the arrogance of Pausanias and wrested command from the Lacedaemonians.

But that happened later. At this stage, when the Greeks at Artemisium
saw the many ships anchoring at the Launch and the huge numbers of
Persian troops everywhere, they realized that the barbarian campaign
was going very differently from what they had expected. They panicked,
and began talking about making a run for it from Artemisium to Greece's

1. By "battleships," Herodotus means triremes.

sheltered waters. The Euboeans knew they were discussing this and implored Eurybiades to remain long enough for them to get their children and the rest of their households to safety. When he would not agree, they approached the Athenian commander, Themistocles, with a bribe of nearly a ton of silver on condition that the Greeks stay where they were and have the naval battle in defense of Euboea.

This is how Themistocles induced the Greeks to stay. He took three hundred pounds of this silver and gave it to Eurybiades as if it were actually coming from himself. After Eurybiades was bribed, the only remaining commander who resisted was the Corinthian, Adeimantus, son of Ocytus, who said that he wouldn't stay but would leave Artemisium with his ships. Themistocles spoke to him and made him this promise: "You aren't going to abandon us, because I'm going to give you a bigger present than the king of Persia himself would give you for deserting your allies." No sooner had he said this than he sent one hundred and seventy-five pounds of silver to Adeimantus' ship. Overwhelmed by these bribes, the commanders obliged the Euboeans, while Themistocles profited by keeping the rest of the money for himself—unbeknownst to the others, who thought that their share of the money had come from Athens expressly for this purpose.

That, then, is why they stayed and had a naval battle at Euboea. Here is how the battle developed. The barbarians arrived at the Launch in the early afternoon. When they saw for themselves what they had already heard, that a small fleet of Greek ships was stationed at Artemisium, they were very eager to attack and, perhaps, capture it. They decided not to sail directly across, because the Greeks might see them coming and take flight. Then, under cover of night, they would certainly escape—and the Persians were determined (in their own words) that "not so much as a single torchbearer would get away alive."

This is the strategy they devised. They detached two hundred ships from the rest to be sent back out around Sciathus and to sail around Euboea and into the Euripus via Caphareus and Geraestus without being seen by the enemy. In this way, they would surround the Greeks by coming at them from behind and cutting off their retreat while the main force attacked them head-on. After forming this plan, they dispatched the designated ships, and since they had no intention of attacking the Greeks that day, or until they saw a signal that the squadron had arrived, they took an inventory of the ships that remained at the Launch.

In the time it took for them to carry out this muster of the ships . . . Let me put it this way. Scyllias the Scionian, the best diver of his day, was with the Persian fleet and had salvaged many valuables for the Persians after the shipwrecks off Pelion. He had also accumulated much of it for himself. This Scyllias had for some time had a mind to desert to the Greeks, but he had never gotten the chance until now. I can't say for certain just how he reached the Greek ships, though I would be astonished if what they say is true, because they say that he dove into

the sea at the Launch and didn't get out again until he arrived at Artemisium after swimming a distance of about ten miles. All kinds of similar
stories are told about the man, some of them false and some of them
true, but as to this story, it is my opinion that he came to Artemisium
by boat. When he arrived, he immediately told the commanders all
about the shipwrecks and about the squadron that had been sent around
Euboea.

The Greeks held a meeting after they heard this news. There was a
long discussion, but the prevailing view was that they should spend the
day and the evening where they were; then, after midnight, they would
set out to attack the ships sailing around Euboea. Later, though, when
they saw that no one was sailing out to attack them, they decided to sail
over to the enemy with the idea of testing the fighting and maneuvering
skills of the barbarians.

When Xerxes' commanders and their men saw the Greeks coming at
them with so few ships, they thought the Greeks were completely out of
their minds and got under way themselves, expecting to capture them
easily—a very reasonable expectation when they compared the small
numbers of Greek ships with their own, huge, swift fleet. Holding the
Greeks in contempt, the Persians began to draw around them in a circle.
Ionians who were sympathetic to the Greeks and who had gone to war
against them unwillingly were very distressed to see them being surrounded, because they thought that not a single one of them would get
away—that is how weak the Greek attack seemed to be. Those who
enjoyed what was happening had a contest to see who would be the first
to capture an Athenian ship and get a reward from the king, for the
Athenians had the greatest reputation throughout the Persian navy.

When the signal was given, the Greeks brought their sterns together,
turning their prows outward toward the barbarian ships. At a second
signal, even though they were hemmed into a small space and face-to-
face with the enemy, they set to work and captured thirty ships along
with one of the foremost men in the Persian navy, Philaon, the son of
Chersis and the brother of Gorgus, king of Salamis. An Athenian—
Lycomedes, son of Aeschraeus—was the first Greek to capture an enemy
ship, and he was the one who won the prize for valor. Night fell though,
and brought an indecisive sea fight to an end. The Greeks sailed back to
Artemisium, and the barbarians returned to the Launch after a battle
that had gone very differently from how they had expected. Antidorus of
Lemnos was the only Greek with the king who deserted to the Greeks
during this battle, and the Athenians gave him a plot of land in Salamis
because of it.

Even though it was the middle of summer, pouring rain and shattering thunder from the direction of Pelion began as soon as it was dark
and kept up all night long. Dead bodies and wreckage were carried over
to the Launch; they clustered around the prows of the Persian ships and
knocked against their oar blades. The crews were thrown into a panic on

hearing all this noise and thought they had embarked on a disaster that would utterly destroy them, because even before they had a chance to catch their breaths after the storm and shipwreck off Pelion, they had to fight an arduous battle which was now followed by savage rainstorms, torrential streams pouring into the sea, and oppressive claps of thunder.

That's what the night was like for the men at the Launch; for the men who had been ordered to sail around Euboea, the very same night was much more savage and ended much more disastrously because the storm fell on them in the open sea. The wind and water overwhelmed them as they were sailing past the Euboean Hollows, and, without knowing where the wind was blowing them, they were thrown against the rocks and wrecked. All of this was done by god so that the Persian fleet would equal the Greek fleet and not so vastly outnumber it.

Those barbarians died, then, off the Euboean Hollows; the ones at the Launch were grateful to see the dawning of a new day. They left their ships where they were, content, after their rough treatment, to lie low for the time being.

Meanwhile, the Greeks were reinforced by fifty-three ships from Attica. The arrival of these ships raised their spirits, as did the message that all of the barbarians sailing around Euboea had been destroyed in the storm. Then, after once again waiting for late afternoon, they sailed out to attack some Cilician ships. They destroyed them and sailed back to Artemisium at nightfall.

On the third day, the barbarian commanders, furious over being so battered by so few ships, and dreading Xerxes' reaction, didn't wait for the Greeks to begin the battle but set sail at midday after putting their ships in order. It happened that these naval engagements and the battles at Thermopylae took place on the very same days. At sea, the whole struggle was over control of the Euripus, while for Leonidas and his men it was about defending the pass. One side had orders to keep the barbarians from entering Greece, and the other side had orders to destroy the Greek forces and control the strait.

The Greeks held steady at Artemisium while Xerxes' fleet started to attack in formation. The barbarians fanned out into a crescent, aiming to encircle and trap the enemy ships. At that point, the Greeks put out to sea and engaged the Persians. In this battle, the two sides were about equal in strength. Because of its size and numbers, Xerxes' fleet kept getting in its own way, its ships bumping into and damaging each other. Still, they held firm and did not yield, dreading to be put to flight by such a small force. Yet, though many Greek ships and many Greek men were lost, the barbarians lost many more ships and many more men. After fighting in this way, the two sides disengaged.[2]

2. Herodotus seems to mean in this unclear passage that the Greeks and the Persians were equal in fighting strength, although the Persians outnumbered the Greeks. The Greeks made up in ability for what they lacked in ships.

The Egyptians stood out more than any of Xerxes' other forces in this sea battle; they performed many acts of great courage and captured five Greek ships along with their crews. Among the Greeks, the Athenians distinguished themselves most on this day, and among the Athenians the most distinguished was Clinias, son of Alcibiades, who had gone to war at his own expense, supplying his own ship and a crew of two hundred men.

After they disengaged, both sides hurried gladly back to their moorings. The Greeks did succeed in holding on to the wreckage and the dead after they had broken away from the battle, but they had, nevertheless, been in a very rough fight—not least the Athenians, half of whose ships were damaged, and who had decided to retreat to Greece's more sheltered waters.

Meanwhile, just as Themistocles was thinking that if he could only split the Ionian and Carian forces off from the barbarians it would be possible for the Greeks to get the upper hand over the remaining ships, the Euboeans happened to drive their flocks down to the sea. Themistocles assembled the commanders at the place and told them that he thought he had found a trick whereby he hoped to induce the king's best allies to rebel. That was all he disclosed for the time being, except to tell them that under the circumstances they ought to slaughter as many of the Euboean flocks as they liked since it was better for them than for the enemy to have them. He also advised every commander to order his men to light fires. Meanwhile, he would make it his business to find the right time for their departure, so that they could return to Greece unharmed. They agreed to do all this, and as soon as the men had lit fires for themselves, they went after the flocks.

You see, the Euboeans had ignored the prophecy of Bacis as nonsensical, and because they had neither evacuated their possessions nor stored up food for the coming war, they brought their own misfortunes on themselves. Here is what the prophecy said about these matters:

> Make sure to get your ever-bleating goats out of Euboea
> When a foreign babbler casts a yoke of papyrus on the sea.

They ignored these words at a time of actual and expected trouble, and they came to experience trouble so great that it could not be ignored.

While the Greeks were slaughtering the Euboean flocks, the lookout from Trachis arrived. You see, there was an Anticyran lookout at Artemisium named Polyas, who had an oared boat and orders to let the troops in Thermopylae know if the fleet ran into any trouble. Likewise, an Athenian—Abronichus, son of Lysicles—was with Leonidas and was ready to carry a message in a thirty-oared boat to the fleet at Artemisium if the army met with any mischief. This Abronichus arrived to tell them the news about Leonidas and his army. They didn't delay their withdrawal for a moment after hearing it, but immediately fell into formation and got under way, the Corinthians first and the Athenians last.

Themistocles picked out the fastest ships and made the rounds of the freshwater springs, carving messages on the rocks which the Ionians read when they got to Artemisium the next day. The messages said, "Men of Ionia, it is not right for you to make war on your fathers and to try to enslave Greece. The best thing would be for you to come over to our side. If you can't do that, you could still take a position of neutrality and ask the Carians to do the same. If you can't do either of these things, but are under a yoke of necessity so powerful that you can't break away from it, then intentionally fight badly when we have a battle, remembering that you are descended from us and that this feud with the barbarians began because of you in the first place." In my opinion, Themistocles had a couple of things in mind when he wrote these words: either the king wouldn't notice them and they would make the Ionians change sides and come over to the Greeks, or they would be reported to Xerxes as an accusation against the Ionians and make them so suspect that he would keep them out of any naval battles.

After Themistocles wrote these messages, a Histiaean man immediately went over to the barbarians by boat with the news of the Greek escape from Artemisium. In disbelief, the Persians put the messenger under guard and sent out some fast ships to reconnoiter. After these ships returned with a report that the news was true, the whole fleet sailed off to Artemisium together at the crack of dawn. They stayed there until noon and then set off for Histiaea. When they arrived, they took the city and overran all the Histiaean coastal villages known as the district of Ellopia.

While this was taking place, Xerxes sent a herald to the fleet after getting his display of corpses ready. This is what he had done: he held back about a thousand of his army's twenty thousand dead at Thermopylae and buried the rest in trenches. He filled the trenches with earth and covered them with leaves so that they could not be seen by the sailors. After the herald got to Histiaea, he assembled all the men and said, "Allies! King Xerxes grants any of you who so wishes the chance to leave your posts and go to see how he fights those foolish people who thought to overcome the king's might."

After this message was delivered, nothing was harder to find than a boat—that's how many wanted to go and see the battlefield! After the men got across, they walked among the bodies and saw it all for themselves. Everyone thought that the Greeks lying there were all Lacedaemonians and Thespians, although they were also looking at helot servants. But the men who went through didn't fail to notice what Xerxes had done with his own dead. It was ridiculous, really. A thousand dead, lying here and there, while all the others—four thousand of them—lay heaped together in the same place! So the sailors spent that day sightseeing, and the next day they returned to their ships in Histiaea while the men under Xerxes got back on the road.

A few deserters came to them from Arcadia in need of work and ready to do anything. They were led into the presence of the king, and the

Persians, through an interpreter, asked them questions about what the Greeks were doing. They said the Greeks were holding the Olympic Games, where they were watching gymnastic and equestrian competitions. The next question was what prize they competed for, and the Arcadians answered that it was for a crown of olive branches. At that point, Tritantaechmes, son of Artabanus, made a highly aristocratic remark that only succeeded in making the king think of him as base, because as soon as he understood that the prize was not money but an olive wreath, he couldn't hold his peace and said for all to hear, "Don't tell us, Mardonius, that you're leading us to battle against the kind of men who don't compete for money but for glory!"

Meanwhile, immediately after the Greek defeat at Thermopylae, the Thessalians sent a herald to the Phocians, toward whom they had an ongoing grudge—especially after the last bruising the Phocians had given them. Not many years before the king's campaign, the Thessalians and their allies had invaded Phocis in full strength and had been handed a very rough defeat. Although the Phocians had been forced up Mount Parnassus, they had a seer, Tellias the Elean, who came up with a wily plan. He covered both the bodies and the armor of six hundred of the bravest Phocians with chalk and sent them out against the Thessalians after dark with orders to kill anyone they saw who wasn't all white. The Thessalian sentries, who saw them first, thought they were some kind of supernatural beings and felt a terror which spread throughout the army as the Phocians killed four thousand of them and carried away their bodies and their shields. They dedicated half the shields to the oracle at Abae and the other half to the oracle at Delphi, while a tithe of all the loot from this battle went for the large statues standing around the tripod in front of the temple in Delphi and for similar statues at Abae.

That is just what the Phocians did to the Thessalian foot soldiers who were besieging them; they also did irremediable damage to the Thessalian cavalry as it was invading their territory. They dug a long trench at the pass at Hyampolis and filled it with empty earthen pots. Then they threw the earth back over the pots, landscaped the area to make it conform to the rest of the terrain, and waited for the Thessalians to attack. The cavalry charged the Phocians, thinking to take them by storm, but the horses fell into the pots and broke their legs.

The Thessalians still held a grudge on account of these two events when they sent a herald to Phocis with this announcement: "Men of Phocis! It is time you acknowledged that you are not our equals. Even in the past, when we were content to be among the Greeks, we always carried more weight than you did; but now that we are with the barbarians, we have so much power that we can strip you of your land and enslave you to boot. Still, even though we could do with you as we pleased, we bear you no grudge. Instead, you will give us three thousand pounds of silver in exchange for our promise to avert the evils that threaten your land." That was the Thessalian offer.

You see, the Phocians were the only people in this region who did not collaborate with the Persians—for no other reason, as far as I can tell, than their hatred for the Thessalians. In my opinion, the Phocians would have gone over to Persia if Thessaly had stayed with Greece. Anyway, in the face of this Thessalian proposition, the Phocians refused to give any money. They said that, like Thessaly, they could have collaborated with Persia if they'd had a mind to, but they would never willingly become betrayers of Greece.

When this answer was brought back, the Thessalians became so furious with the Phocians that they showed the barbarians the way there themselves. The army marched from Trachis into Doris and through a narrow neck of land about three and a half miles wide that runs through Doris between Malis and Phocis. In antiquity, this region was known as Dryopis, and it is the mother country of the Dorians in the Peloponnese. The barbarians did not lay Doris waste after they invaded; the Dorians collaborated with them, for one thing, and besides, the Thessalians prevented it.

The barbarians did not capture the Phocians after they crossed into Phocis from Doris. Carrying their possessions, some of the Phocians had gone up to the heights of Mount Parnassus—to Tithorea, the solitary summit, which is above the town of Neon and which is big enough to accommodate a large number of people. Most of them, though, had sought refuge among the Locrians of Ozolae, in the city of Amphissa, above the Crisaean plain. With the Thessalians in the lead, the barbarians ran riot over all of Phocis, burning and leveling everything they touched, torching town and temple alike.

They made their way along the Cephisus River and destroyed everything. They burned the city of Drymus to the ground, along with the towns of Charadra, Erochus, Tethronium, Amphicaea, Neon, Pedies, Trites, Elateia, Hyampolis, Parapotamii, and Abae, where there was a rich temple of Apollo, endowed with treasure-houses and many offerings. There was then and still is an oracle there, but the barbarians looted the temple and burned it to the ground. They also tracked down and caught some Phocians in the mountains, and gang-raped some of the women to death.

The barbarians passed by Parapotamii and arrived in Panopes. At that point, the army was divided into two parts. The larger and more powerful part, headed by Xerxes himself, entered the Orchomenian region of Boeotia en route to Athens. All the people of Boeotia collaborated with the Persians, and Macedonians had been appointed and sent off by Alexander to administer her cities. This was done in order to make it perfectly clear to Xerxes that Boeotia would be of one mind with Persia.

While these barbarians turned toward Athens, the other group followed its guides and headed for the temple at Delhi, skirting Mount Parnassus on its right. They, too, ravaged every part of Phocis they passed through, burning down Panopes, Daulis, and Aeolidae. This contingent had been split off from the rest of the army to go to Delphi, strip its temple, and deliver its riches to King Xerxes. I have heard that because of the constant talk about them, Xerxes knew more about all the famous treasures of Delphi than about what he had left behind in his own palace—and especially the offerings of Croesus, son of Alyattes.

When the Delphians learned of this force, they were thrown into utter panic. Terrified, they consulted the oracle about the sacred treasures—should they bury them, or should they carry them away to some other region? The god wouldn't allow the Delphians to move the treasures, saying that he was able to defend his own possessions. After the Delphians heard this, they began to think about themselves. They sent their wives and children over to Achaea, and then most of the men went up to the heights of Mount Parnassus after storing their goods in the Corycian cave, while the others slipped away to Amphissa, in Locris. Except for sixty men and the oracle interpreter, all the Delphians abandoned the city.

When the barbarians had come near enough to see the temple from a distance, the oracle interpreter, whose name was Aceratus, saw some armor lying in front of the temple—armor which had been carried out from the great inner hall, and which it was a desecration for any mortal to so much as touch. He ran to the remaining Delphians to tell them about this miracle, but after the barbarians had moved rapidly forward to the temple of Athena Pronaia, there occurred an even greater miracle than the previous one. It was enough of a marvel for weapons of war to move outside the temple on their own and lie in front of it, but the second event is one of the most astonishing phenomena of all time, because, suddenly, as the barbarians were approaching the temple of Athena Pronaia, lightning fell on them from the sky, while two boulders broke off from Parnassus and came roaring down on top of them, killing many of them. At the same time, a war cry came bellowing out of the temple of Athena.

The barbarians were panic-stricken by this conjunction of events. The Delphians fell on the barbarians after they saw them running away and killed a large number of them. The survivors ran straight to Boeotia. I have learned that these returning barbarians said that they saw yet another divine portent: two heavily armed warriors, much larger than humans, were chasing them and trying to kill them.

The Delphians say that these two were local heroes, Phylacus and Autonous, who have sacred precincts near the temple—Phylacus' along the road above the temple of Athena Pronaia, and Autonous' near the Castalian spring, under the Hyampeian cliff. The boulders that fell from Parnassus are still there, lying where they fell on the barbarians in the precinct of Athena Pronaia. That, then, is how those men were routed at the temple.

At the request of Athens, the Greek fleet had put in at Salamis after it left Artemisium. The Athenians had made this request so that they could evacuate their wives and children from Attica and so that they could deliberate about what to do next. Under the circumstances, a council had to be called because they had been mistaken in their opinion: they had thought that the Peloponnesians would be in Boeotia, awaiting the barbarians in full strength, but none of them were to be found there. On the contrary, the Athenians had learned that they had put the defense of the Peloponnese first and were fortifying the Isthmus—everything else was expendable. This information led them to ask the fleet to put in at Salamis.

It was the other Greeks who went to Salamis—the Athenians returned to their own harbors. After their arrival, the cry went out that every Athenian should get his children and his household to safety wherever he could. Most sent their families to Troezen, others to Aegina or Salamis. They hurried to evacuate the city because they wanted to comply with the oracle, but not least for the following reason: the Athenians say that a huge serpent lives in the temple and guards the Acropolis. This is not just a legend—they serve it a monthly offering as if it were really alive. They give it a honey cake every new moon. In the past the honey cake had always been eaten, but this month it was left untouched. When the priestess made this known, the Athenians were that much more anxious to abandon the city because it meant that the goddess had abandoned the Acropolis. When the men had gotten everyone and everything to safety, they sailed to the base at Salamis.

Meanwhile, after the other ships from Artemisium had put in at Salamis, the rest of the Greek fleet had found out what had happened and streamed in from Troezen. You see, they had been given orders to rendezvous at the Troezenian harbor of Pogon. When they were all together at Salamis, they amounted to many more ships from more cities than had fought at Artemisium. The same admiral was in command as at Artemisium—Eurybiades, son of Eurycleides, who was a Spartan, although not of the royal line. Nevertheless, Athens supplied by far the largest number of ships and the best crews.

These are the forces that took part in the battle. From the Peloponnese, the Lacedaemonians supplied sixteen ships and the Corinthians the same number as they had sent to Artemisium. The Sicyonians furnished fifteen ships, the Epidaurians ten, the Troezenians five, and the Hermionians three. Except for the Hermionians, all these people are of Dorian and Macedonian ethnicity, and had last emigrated from Erineus, Pindus, and Dryopis. The Hermionians are Dryopians who were uprooted by Heracles and the Malians from the territory now known as Doris.

Those were the Peloponnesian forces. As to the mainland states outside the Peloponnese, Athens supplied one hundred and eighty ships, more than any other state. They manned them all by themselves, because the Plataeans did not fight side by side with them at Salamis. The reason is that when the Greeks reached Chalcis after leaving Artemisium, the

Plataeans disembarked on the opposite shore, in Boeotia, to evacuate their households. In order to save their families, though, they had to be left behind.

When the Pelasgians occupied what is now called Greece, the Athenians, who were a Pelasgian people, were known as the Cranaeans. During the reign of King Cecrops, they came to be called Cecropians. When Erechtheus inherited the throne, they changed their name to Athenians, and then when Ion, son of Xuthus, became their war chief, they were called Ionians after him.

The Megarians sent the same number as they had to Artemisium, and the Ambraciots helped out with the seven ships they had. The Leucadians, who are a Dorian people from Corinth, sent three.

Of the islanders, the Aeginetans supplied thirty ships. They had other fully equipped ships, but they used these to guard their own waters and sent their thirty fastest ships to the battle at Salamis. The Aeginetans are Dorians from Epidaurus, and their island used to be called Oenone. After the Aeginetans, the Chalcidians sent the twenty and the Eretrians the seven ships they had sent to Artemisium. These two peoples are Ionians. The Ceans also supplied the same number. They are of Ionian ethnicity from Athens. The Naxians gave four ships. Like the crews of the other islands, they had been dispatched by their fellow citizens to the Persians, but they disregarded their orders and joined the Greeks at the insistence of Democritus, a leading citizen who was at that time the commander of a trireme. The Naxians are Ionians of Athenian descent. The Styreans sent the same number of ships as they had to Artemisium, and the Cythnians sent one battleship and a penteconter. Both of these people are Dryopians. Seriphians, Siphnians, and Melians participated in the battle: these were the only islanders who did not give earth and water to the barbarian.

All these people live between this side of the Acheron River and Thesprotia. The Thesprotians border on the Ambraciots and the Leucadians, who came from farthest away to fight in the battle. The Crotoniats were the only people living beyond these who helped an endangered Greece. They sent one ship, commanded by Phayllus, a three-time winner at the Pythian Games. The Crotoniats are of Achaean stock. Everyone sent triremes to this battle except the Melians, the Siphnians and the Seriphians, who sent penteconters. The Melians, who are of Lacedaemonian stock, sent two, and the Siphnians and Seriphians, who are Ionians from Athens, one apiece. Not counting the penteconters, the number of all the ships was three hundred and seventy-eight.

When the commanders from the cities I have mentioned met at Salamis, Eurybiades proposed that anyone who wanted to should give his opinion about which place under their control would give them the greatest advantage in a naval battle. He meant any place but Attica, which had already been abandoned. Most of the speakers were inclined to sail to the Isthmus and fight to defend the Peloponnese, reasoning that if they should be defeated in a battle at Salamis, they would then be trapped on an island, where no help whatever could reach them, whereas they would be able to go ashore at the Isthmus and return to their own cities.

This view was being argued by the Peloponnesian commanders when an Athenian arrived with the message that the barbarian was in Attica and that he was setting it on fire. Xerxes and the army that marched through Boeotia had burned the cities of Thespia and Plataea to the ground after their inhabitants had abandoned them for the Peloponnese. He had just entered Athens and was destroying everything there. He had burned Thespia and Plataea after the Thebans told him that those people would not collaborate.

After crossing the Hellespont, where the barbarians had begun their campaign, and where they had wasted a month just getting over to Europe, it took them another three months to reach Attica, which they did when Calliades was the chief magistrate at Athens. They captured a deserted city, although they learned that there were a few Athenians in the temple—temple wardens and some poor people who had barricaded the Acropolis with wooden doors and logs to keep off the invaders. It was mostly poverty that had kept them from evacuating to Salamis, but it was also their belief that they understood the prophecy the Pythian priestess had given them: the "wall of wood" would be impregnable. According to the prophecy, the barricade would surely be their refuge and not the ships.

The Persians took up a position opposite the Acropolis, on a hill the Athenians call the Areopagus, and besieged the Acropolis by setting fire to pieces of rope tied around their arrows and then shooting the arrows at the wooden barricade. The besieged Athenians nevertheless continued to hold out even though they had been driven to despair after being betrayed by their barricade. They would not accept Pisistratid terms for a truce, and continued to improvise defenses—for example, rolling boulders down on the barbarians as they approached the gates—so that Xerxes was at a standstill for quite some time, stymied by his inability to capture them.

Eventually, the barbarians found a way out of this impasse: after all, according to the oracle, the whole Attic mainland was destined to fall to Persia. In front of the Acropolis, but behind the gates and the way up to the top, there was a place which no one guarded and which no one imagined that any human being could climb. Still, even though the place was a sheer cliff, some men did manage to get up by way of the temple of Aglaurus, the daughter of Cecrops. As soon as the Athenians saw that these men had gotten to the top of the Acropolis, some of them committed suicide by throwing themselves off the wall, and others ran into the temple. The Persian climbers turned to the temple gates, opened them, and slaughtered the people who had taken refuge there. With the bodies lying at their feet, the barbarians looted the temple and set the Acropolis on fire.

When he had Athens completely under his control, Xerxes sent a mounted messenger to Susa to give Artabanus the news of his success. The day after sending the messenger, either because he had had some dream vision telling him to do so or because he felt some remorse over burning down the temple, Xerxes summoned the Athenian exiles who were accompanying him and ordered them to go up to the Acropolis and offer sacrifices in keeping with customary Athenian ritual. The Athenian exiles did as they were told.

Let me explain why I mention this. There is a temple on the Acropolis dedicated to Erechtheus, who is said to have emerged, at birth, from the soil. A saltwater well and an olive tree are on the temple grounds, and Athenian legend has it that they bear witness to a struggle between Poseidon and Athena for this land. Now, it happened that the tree was burned down by the barbarians along with the temple, and yet the day after the fire the Athenians who had been commanded to go up to the temple to offer sacrifice saw a young branch well over a foot long shooting up from the stump of the olive tree. That, anyway, is what they said.

When the Greeks at Salamis got the news of what had happened to the Athenian Acropolis, they were thrown into such a commotion that some of the commanders didn't even stay to vote on a course of action. They just rushed aboard their ships, hoisted their sails, and prepared to make a run for it while the officers who remained voted to give battle at the Isthmus. When night fell, they adjourned their meeting and boarded their ships.

After Themistocles boarded his ship that night, Mnesiphilus the Athenian asked him what plans they had been discussing. When Mnesiphilus heard that they had decided to take the ships up to the Isthmus and defend the Peloponnese, he said, "No! I tell you that if you move these ships from Salamis, you won't have a country to fight for. Everyone will head for his own city. Neither Eurybiades nor anyone else will be able to prevent them from scattering the fleet, and Greece will be lost through sheer heedlessness! If there's any way, go and try to dissolve this decision and see whether you can get Eurybiades to change his mind and stay here."

Themistocles liked this suggestion very much, and without saying another word he rowed over to Eurybiades' ship. When he got there, he said that he wanted to talk to him about a matter that affected them all. Eurybiades told him he could come aboard and talk, if he liked. When Themistocles was sitting beside him, he told Eurybiades everything he had heard from Mnesiphilus (though he pretended that it was his own), and added a great many other arguments until his sheer persistence persuaded Eurybiades to leave the ship and call the commanders to a meeting.

As soon as the commanders were assembled, and even before Eury-biades had a chance to explain why he had reconvened them, an urgent Themistocles broke into torrents of speech. While he was talking, the Corinthian commander Adeimantus, son of Ocytus, said, "Runners who start too soon at races are whipped, Themistocles." Themistocles said by way of excuse, "Yes, but the ones who are left behind don't win any prizes."

He gave the Corinthian this mild answer for the moment and, turning to Eurybiades, made a speech in which he used none of the arguments he had given before, for example, that the ships would go off in different directions once they left Salamis—after all, it would have been unseemly for him to denounce the allies in their own presence. Instead, he used a different argument and said, addressing Eurybiades, "It is now in your power to save Greece if you will only take my advice and stay here to fight our battle and not heed the arguments of these men by shifting our base from here to the Isthmus. Listen, and compare the arguments. If you give battle at the Isthmus, you will be fighting in open water, which offers us the least advantage since we have heavier and fewer ships. Also, you will lose Salamis, Megara, and Aegina—even if you are lucky at the Isthmus. Furthermore, their army will follow their fleet, and by going to the Isthmus you yourself will lead them to the Peloponnese and put all of Greece at risk.

"On the other hand, if you do as I recommend, these are the advan-tages you will have. First, you will be fighting at close quarters with few ships against many, and if things turn out as they have before in this war, we will win a great victory. At close quarters a naval battle favors us; in the open sea, it favors them. Next, Salamis is saved—and that is where we have evacuated our children and our wives. And there is this further advantage—the one you care about most: you will be fighting for the Peloponnese just as much here as at the Isthmus, and, if you think about it sensibly, you will not be leading the enemy into the Pelo-ponnese.

"If it turns out as I hope, and our ships are victorious, the barbarians won't advance on you at the Isthmus or indeed go any farther than Attica. They will retreat in disarray, and we will benefit from having held on to Megara, Aegina, and Salamis, where the oracle says that we are destined to have the upper hand. In general, things go well when people make sound plans; when their plans are flawed, even god has no use for their mere mortal opinions."

At these words, Adeimantus the Corinthian objected and demanded that the man without a country be silent and that Eurybiades not allow a stateless person to call for a vote. He demanded that Themistocles produce a city to represent before contributing his opinions to the coun-cil. He made this objection because Athens had been captured and occupied. That was when Themistocles profusely insulted Adeimantus and the Corinthians and made it very plain that for so long as the Athenians had two hundred fully manned ships, it was *they*, the Athenians, who would have a greater city and a greater countryside than the Corinthians, because no Greek state would ever be able to repel their attack.

Then he redirected his words to Eurybiades, and said with real passion, "If you stay here, and, having stayed, act like a brave man—it will be as the gods wish; if not, you will be the downfall of Greece. The whole war depends on our ships. Do as I advise, then, because if you do not, we will put our families aboard our ships and go, just as we are, to Siris, in Italy. It has been ours since antiquity, and the oracles say that it is destined to be colonized by us. Then, when you have been forsaken by allies like us, you will, all of you, remember my words."

This speech of Themistocles made Eurybiades think better of the plan. It seems to me that he especially dreaded that the Athenians would leave if he took the fleet up to the Isthmus, because if the Athenians left, those who remained would be no match for the Persians. He took Themistocles' advice and stayed to fight it out to the end where they were.

After the verbal sparring, and after Eurybiades made his decision, the commanders at Salamis prepared their ships for battle. The next day at the crack of dawn an earthquake rocked both land and sea. The Greeks decided to pray to the gods and to invoke the aid of the Aeacidae, which they immediately did. They offered their prayers to the gods; they invoked Ajax and Telamon right there at Salamis; and they dispatched a ship to fetch the statues of Aeacus and the other Aeacidae at Aegina.

Dicaeus, son of Theocydes, an Athenian who was in exile at the time, and who had become well known among the Persians, said that he happened to be with Demaratus the Lacedaemonian on the Thriasian plain while Xerxes' army was leveling the countryside after the Athenians had abandoned Attica, and that he saw a dust cloud coming up from Eleusis big enough to have been raised by thirty thousand men. He and Demaratus were wondering who could have raised the cloud when they suddenly heard the sound of voices, voices that seemed to him to be singing the mystical song of Bacchus—'Iacchus! O Iacchus!" Now, Demaratus was ignorant of the sacred rites of Eleusis, so he asked what the sound was. As Dicaeus tells it, he said, "Demaratus, there is no way the king's army can avoid a great disaster. Since Attica is a wasteland, it is obvious that this is the voice of a god, wafting from Eleusis to aid the Athenians and their allies. If it drifts down to the Peloponnese, the king himself and the army on the mainland will be in danger, but if it makes its way to the ships at Salamis, the king risks losing his fleet. This sound you hear is the hymn the Athenians chant to Bacchus during a festival they celebrate every year to honor the Mother and the Virgin, and any Athenian or any Greek who so desires can be initiated into its mysteries."[3]

---

3. The Mother and the Virgin, that is, Demeter and Persephone.

"Keep quiet about this," said Demaratus, "and don't tell it to anyone else. If what you've said should reach the king, it will mean your head, and neither I nor any other man on earth will be able to save you. Just keep still and let the gods worry about the army."

As Demaratus was giving this advice, a mist arose from the song-filled cloud of dust; it was borne through the air toward the Greek base at Salamis, and the two men knew that Xerxes' fleet was doomed.

That is the story Dicaeus, son of Theocydes, used to tell, and he called on Demaratus and others to be his witnesses.

After the men assigned to Xerxes' fleet had seen the blow inflicted on the Spartans at Trachis, they crossed back over to Histiaea. They waited there for three days before sailing through the Euripus, and in another three days they were in the Athenian harbor at Phalerum. In my opinion, no fewer men invaded Athens by land and sea than had come to Sepias and Thermopylae. I make up for the men lost in the storm and at the battles of Thermopylae and Artemisium with men who later joined the king: Malians, Dorians, and Locrians; Boeotians, who, except for the Thespians and Plataeans, joined the king in full strength; and also Carystians, Andrians, Tenians, and men from all the other islands except for the five I mentioned earlier. For the farther into Greece the Persian advanced, the more peoples joined him.

When all the land forces had arrived at Athens (all, that is, except the Parians, who had stayed at Cythnus, waiting to see how the war would turn out), and all the naval forces had arrived at Phalerum, Xerxes himself went down to the fleet to mingle with the sailors and hear their opinions. When he arrived, he sat on his throne of state, and the lords of the nations and the admirals of the fleet came when he beckoned and took their places according to the rank he had conferred upon them: first, the satrap of Sidon, next, the satrap of Tyre, and then the others in their turn. When they were seated in their order of precedence, Xerxes sent Mardonius to test them by asking each one whether he favored a naval battle or not.

Beginning with the satrap of Sidon, Mardonius made the rounds with his question, and all of them expressed the same opinion: they called on Xerxes to fight at sea. All of them, that is, but one. Artemisia said, "Tell the king from me, Mardonius, that this is what I say—I, who was neither the last to fight in the battle at Euboea nor the least in what I had to show for it. Tell him: That gives me the right, Master, to reveal my true opinion—what I think is best for the success of your campaign. My advice is, hold back your ships; do not give battle. At sea, these men are stronger than yours by as much as men are stronger than women. Why do you need to risk anything on a naval battle? Don't you have Athens, which is why you went to war in the first place? Don't you have all the rest of Greece? No one stands in your way, and those who did got what they deserved.

"Let me tell you what I think will come of the opposition. If you show that you are in no hurry for a naval battle, but keep your ships here, near shore, and then either stay where you are or advance on the Peloponnese, it will be easy for you, Master, to gain everything you came here for. The Greeks aren't able to hold out for a long time; you will force them to disperse and seek refuge in their cities. I have learned that they have no food on that island, and it isn't likely, if you march on the Peloponnese with your army, that contingents from those parts will sit still here. *They* aren't interested in fighting a naval battle for the Athenians!

"But if you hurry into a sea fight now, I'm really worried that if your fleet comes off badly, your army will suffer as well. Furthermore—and take this to heart, Your Majesty—good men tend to have bad slaves, and bad men good ones. You are the greatest man on earth, and yet you have awful slaves. They are the Egyptians, the Cyprians, the Cilicians, the Pamphylians. They are called your allies, but they are useless to you."

After she said this to Mardonius, her friends were very concerned lest she suffer some retribution from the king for a speech urging him not to fight. Others, who envied her and begrudged her position as the most honored of the allies, delighted in the thought that this difference of opinion would mean the end of her. After the opinions had been brought to Xerxes, he was especially pleased with Artemisia's, and though he had thought highly of her before, he thought even more highly of her now. He nevertheless commanded that they go along with the majority, suspecting that the morale of his troops has been low at Euboea because he had not been there, whereas this time he had made preparations to observe the battle in person.

The order was given for the fleet to put out to sea, and when they reached Salamis, the ships took up their battle positions in a leisurely way. Since night was coming on and there wasn't enough daylight left for a battle, they prepared to attack the next day. Fear and dread gripped the Greeks, and especially the Peloponnesians, because here they were in Salamis about to do battle for Athenian soil, where, if they were defeated, they would be trapped and besieged on an island after having left their own homeland unguarded. Meanwhile, that very night, the barbarian army was advancing on the Peloponnese.

Every possible measure had been taken to keep the barbarians from invading the Peloponnese by land. As soon as the Peloponnesians learned that Leonidas and his men had been wiped out at Thermopylae, they rushed out of their cities and joined forces to take up positions at the Isthmus. Leonidas' brother Cleombrotus, son of Anaxandrides, was in command. They blockaded the Scironian road, and later decided in council to build a wall across the Isthmus. There were many tens of thousands of them, and since every man worked on it, they were able to finish the work. Rocks, bricks, wood, and baskets full of sand were brought in, and the men worked day and night without rest.

These are the Greeks who came in full strength to defend the Isthmus: the Lacedaemonians and all the Arcadians, along with Eleans, Corinthians, Sicyonians, Epidaurians, Phliasians, Troezenians, and Hermionians. All these people came to help because they dreaded the danger to Greece. The other Peloponnesians didn't care about it, even though the Olympic and Carneian festivals and games were already over.

Seven peoples inhabit the Peloponnese. Two of them, the Arcadians and the Cynurians, are indigenous and are still settled on the same land they occupied in antiquity. One people, the Achaeans, did not migrate from the Peloponnese, although they did move to another part of it from their original territory. The remaining four of the seven are immigrants—the Dorians, Aetolians, Dryopians, and Lemnians. There are many important Dorian cities, while there is only one Aetolian city, Elis. The Dryopians have Hermione and Asine, near Cardamyle, in Laconia, while all the Paroreatae are Lemnians. The Cynurians seem to be the only indigenous Ionians in the Peloponnese, although in the course of time they have become thoroughly Dorianized under Argive rule. They live in Orneae and its environs. Aside from the ones I have mentioned, all the cities of these seven peoples remained neutral in the war, and, if I may be permitted to speak freely, by remaining neutral they collaborated with Persia.

All those people at the Isthmus, then, were struggling to finish the wall. After all, the race they were running was for their lives, and they never expected to win any battles with their ships. Their men at Salamis knew what they were doing and were frightened not for themselves but for the Peloponnese. Men stood together, talking in whispers, amazed at Eurybiades' bad judgment, and in the end the talk broke out into the open. A meeting was held, and the same subject kept coming up—one side arguing that they had to sail away to the Peloponnese and risk their lives for her, not stay and fight for a country that had already been conquered, while the Athenians, Aeginetans, and Megarians insisted that they stay where they were and fight.

When Themistocles saw that his plan was about to be defeated by the Peloponnesians, he slipped away from the meeting unnoticed and sent a man in a boat to the Persian base with instructions on what to say. The man's name was Sicinnus, and he was the slave who took care of Themistocles' sons. Later, after all these events were over, Themistocles made the man a Thespian citizen (since the Thespians were naturalizing new citizens) and gave him enough money to make him rich. When Sicinnus reached the base in his boat, this is what he said to the Persian commanders: "The Athenian admiral has sent me here unbeknownst to the other Greeks because he is on the king's side and wants you, and not the Greeks, to win this war. He has sent me to tell you that the Greeks are frightened and planning to escape, and that if you don't just stand by and watch them escape you will have the chance to win your greatest victory. They can't agree with one another about anything, and they won't resist you. Instead, you'll see them fighting a naval battle among themselves, between those who support you and those who don't."

After delivering this message, he left them and got away. The Persians found the message credible, so they began to land large numbers of men on the islet of Psyttaleia, between Salamis and the mainland. Then, at midnight, they shifted the west wing of the fleet around toward Salamis and brought up the ships off Ceos and Cynosura, thereby blockading the whole passage as far as Munychia with their ships. The reason the Persians brought up the ships was so that the Greeks would not be able to escape; instead, trapped at Salamis, they would pay for the battles off Artemisium! This islet off Psyttaleia lay in the path of the coming naval battle, and the Persians landed the troops there so that they could save their own men and kill the Greeks when men and wreckage were washed ashore after the battle began. All these movements were made in silence and in secret to keep the enemy from learning of them, but all the preparations meant that the Persians got no sleep that night.

When it comes to oracles, I can't argue that they aren't true. I certainly wouldn't try to discredit them when they speak clearly—not when I look at something like this:

> When those who are mad with hope to ravage shining Athens
> Make a bridge of ships from watery Cynosura
> To the sacred shore of Artemis of the golden sword,
> Then shall radiant Justice squelch mighty Excess,
> That terrible, raging son of Insolence
> Who thinks he can devour everything.
> Bronze will strike on bronze
> And Ares will redden the sea with blood,
> But lady Victory and the far-seeing son of Kronos
> Will bring the day of freedom to Greece.

In the face of such a clear statement from Bacis, I myself would not dare to impugn oracles, and I do not approve when others do it.

Meanwhile, there was an immense verbal wrangle going on among the commanders at Salamis. The Greeks didn't yet know that the barbarians had completely surrounded them with their ships, and thought that their enemies were still where they had been during the day.

Aristides, son of Lysimachus, had made the crossing from Aegina while the commanders were arguing. He was an Athenian, and although he had been ostracized by the people, I have come to know his character and have concluded that he was the noblest and the justest Athenian who has ever lived. This man stood at the door of the council chamber and asked Themistocles to come out of the room. Now, not only was Themistocles not his friend; he was his worst enemy. Nevertheless, Aristides overlooked their past differences because of the immensity of the present danger and called Themistocles out to talk. He had heard that the Lacedaemonians were eager to withdraw their ships to the Isthmus, and when Themistocles came out of the room, Aristides said, "We ought to always quarrel, and especially now, about which of us will do more good for our country. I want to tell you that it doesn't make any difference how much or how little the Peloponnesians say about sailing away from here. I've seen it with my own eyes, so I can tell you that the Corinthians and even Eurybiades himself can't sail away no matter how much they want to, because we are completely surrounded by the enemy. Go back in and tell them that."

Themistocles said, "You give very good advice, and you bring good news, because you have seen for yourself what I wanted to happen. You should know that the Persians did this because of me. Since the Greeks didn't want to stay and fight willingly, I had to make them do it unwillingly. But since you are the one with the good news, you go in and tell it to them. If I say it, they'll think that I'm making it up. I'll never persuade them that this is what the barbarians have done. You go in and tell them how it is. If they believe you after you tell them, that will be fine. If they don't, it will be all the same to us, because if, as you say, we're completely surrounded, they won't run very far."

Aristides did go in and tell them. He said that he had just come from Aegina and that he had barely slipped through the blockading ships unnoticed. The whole Greek base was surrounded by Xerxes' fleet, so he advised them to get ready to defend themselves. He left after making his statement, and another debate immediately began—most of the commanders didn't believe the message.

While they were in doubt, a trireme full of Tenian deserters arrived at the base. She was commanded by Panaetius, son of Sosimenes, who brought the true facts. Because of this service, the Tenians are inscribed on the tripod at Delphi among those who defeated the barbarians. This ship which deserted to Salamis and the Lemnian ship which had earlier deserted at Artemisium brought the size of the Greek fleet up to a full three hundred and eighty ships. It had fallen two short of that number before then

The Greeks *did* believe what the Tenians said, and they got ready for battle. They assembled the marines at daybreak, and various speeches were made, but the finest speech of all was given by Themistocles. It was about how the best in the nature and character of man is pitted against the worst, and, as he came to the end of his speech, he called on them always to choose the best. Then he ordered them aboard their ships, and, as they started to board, the trireme that had gone to Aigina to fetch the statues of the Aeacidae arrived. Just as the Greeks set sail with all their ships, the barbarians began their attack.

Most of the Greeks then backed water and were about to beach their craft when Ameinias, an Athenian from the ward of Pallene, drove his ship forward and rammed an enemy vessel. After they had become entangled and could not separate, the others came to Ameinias' rescue, and the battle began. That is, the Athenians say the battle began in this way; the Aeginetans say that it was begun by the ship carrying the statues of the Aeacidae from Aegina. It is also said that the ghost of a woman appeared to the men and that she urged them on after first upbraiding them in a voice so loud the whole fleet could hear it: "Are you crazy? How far do you think you can retreat?"

Lined up against the Athenians were the Phoenicians, who held the western wing of the Persian fleet toward Eleusis; to the east, toward Piraeus, were the Ionians, who opposed the Lacedaemonians. Some of the Ionians obeyed Themistocles and slacked off in battle, but most did not. I could list the names of many captains who captured Greek ships, but I won't name any except for Theomestor, son of Androdamas, and Phylacus, son of Histiaeus, both Samians. I mention only these two because Theomestor was installed as the tyrant of Samos as a reward for his service, while Phylacus was enrolled as a benefactor to the king and rewarded with a large tract of land. Royal benefactors are called orosangae in Persian.

So much for those two. Apart from them, though, most of the Persian ships were demolished at Salamis. Some were wrecked by the Athenians, others by the Aeginetans. It was bound to turn out for the barbarians as it did because the Greeks went to battle in orderly formations while the barbarians fought out of formation and with no idea of what they were doing. Still, they proved themselves to be far better on that day than they had been at Euboea. Every one of them fought with more energy for fear of Xerxes, since each man thought the king was watching him.

I don't know the details about how each of the Greek and barbarian commanders fared in the battle, but this did happen to Artemisia, and it made the king admire her more than ever. Artemisia's ship was being chased by an Athenian vessel just after the king's attack had fallen into disarray. She was close to the enemy, and there were other friendly ships in front of her, so she had nowhere to run. She decided on a maneuver which turned out to her advantage, because with the Athenian trireme in pursuit, she sailed full speed ahead and rammed a friendly Calyndian ship that had Damasithymus, the king of Calynda, himself on board. Now, I can't say whether she had premeditated what she did because of some quarrel with him while they were still at the Hellespont, or whether the Calyndian ship just happened to be where it was at the time, but after she rammed and sank the ship, she was lucky enough to gain two advantages from doing so. When the captain of the Athenian trireme saw her ramming an enemy ship, he put about and headed for another ship after concluding that Artemisia was either a Greek woman or that she had deserted from the barbarians and was now fighting with the Greeks.

So the first thing she gained was to escape the battle with her life. The second is that even though she had behaved ignobly, her action made the king think even more highly of her. They say that while the king was watching what happened, one of his attendants said, "Your Majesty, did you see how well Artemisia fought to sink that enemy ship?" The king asked whether it really was Artemisia who did it, and they said yes, they knew the insignia of her ship very well. Meanwhile, they were sure the ship that was sunk belonged to the enemy. Her luck held out even further, they say, because none of its crew survived to accuse her. The story goes that this is what Xerxes said about the news: "My men have become women on me, and my women, men!" Anyway, that's the story they tell.

The son of Darius—Xerxes' brother, admiral Ariabignes—died in this struggle, along with many other famous Medes, Persians, and allies. Only a few Greeks died, though. Because they knew how to swim, those who had not been killed in the hand-to-hand fighting were able to swim to Salamis when their ships were disabled. Not knowing how to swim, most of the barbarians drowned in the sea. Most of the Persian ships were destroyed when those in the front ranks turned and fled. You see, the ships in the rear kept trying to make their way forward to show the king what *they* could do and ran afoul of their own escaping ships.

The following event took place in the confusion: some of the Phoenicians whose boats had been sunk came before the king to denounce the Ionians. The ships were lost because of them! They were traitors! It turned out, though, that the Ionian commanders were not executed and that their Phoenician accusers earned the following reward. While the Phoenicians were still talking, a Samothracian ship rammed an Athenian trireme. While the Athenian ship was sinking, an Aeginetan ship bore down on the Samothracian ship and sank *her*. But the Samothracians are javelin throwers. They hurled their weapons at the Aeginetan marines, knocked them off the ship, and then boarded and took her. This act saved the Ionians, because when Xerxes saw them performing such a brave deed, he turned to the Phoenicians (he was so furious anyway that he was ready to blame anybody) and ordered that their heads be cut off so that they, who were cowards, would never slander men who were their betters. (You see, Xerxes was seated at the base of a mountain called Aegaleos, opposite Salamis, and whenever he saw any of his captains making a good show of it in the battle, Xerxes found out the man's name and his scribes wrote it down along with his father's name and the city he came from.) Ariaramnes the Persian, who was present and who was friendly to the Ionians, also contributed to the fate of the Phoenicians.

Xerxes' men, then, turned their attention to the Phoenicians. Meanwhile, the barbarian sailors were turning *their* attention to fleeing from the battle, but Aeginetans were waiting in ambush in the strait and engaged in some really memorable actions when the barbarians tried to sail out in the direction of Phalerum. The Athenians, who were in the thick of things, were destroying both the ships that opposed them and the ones that were running away, while the Aeginetans sank the ships that were trying to sail through the strait. Whatever managed to get away from the Athenians sailed full speed ahead only to fall in with the Aeginetans.

At one point, Themistocles' ship, which was in hot pursuit of an enemy vessel, happened to meet up with the ship of Polycritus, son of Crius, an Aeginetan, just as it was ramming a Sidonian craft. It was the very one, in fact, which had captured the Aeginetan ship that was on the look out at Sciathus with Pytheas, son of Ischenous, aboard—the man the Persians admired so much because of his bravery while he was being practically butchered that they took him along with them on their ship. Well, the Sidonian vessel and its Persian crew were captured with him on board, and that's how Pytheas got back to Aegina alive. When Polycritus saw the Athenian trireme and recognized the insignia of the admiral's flagship, he shouted insults at Themistocles for having once accused the Aeginetans of collaborating with Persia—and he did it while ramming a Persian ship!

Meanwhile, the barbarian ships that survived escaped to the protection of the army at Phalerum.

The bravest Greeks in this naval battle are said to have been the Aeginetans and, after them, the Athenians. The bravest men were Polycritus the Aeginetan and the Athenians Eumenes of Anagyrus and Ameinias of Pallene, the one who had given chase to Artemisia. If Ameinias had only known that Artemisia was aboard that ship, he would never have stopped until he had captured her or been captured himself, because orders had been given about her to the captains of the Athenian triremes and there was, in addition, a ten thousand–drachma reward for whoever took her alive. It infuriated them that a woman should make war on Athens. As I said earlier, though, she escaped. Others—those whose ships managed to survive the battle—were in Phalerum.

The Athenians say that as soon as the battle began, Adeimantus, the Corinthian admiral, hoisted his sails in panic terror and began to run away, and that when the other Corinthians saw the flagship running away, they ran too. A fast ship met them when they were off Salamis at the temple of Athena Sciras. No one appears to have sent the ship, and the Corinthians knew nothing about what was happening at the battle when they met it. The Athenians guess that it was sent by the gods— that it was a divine event—because when they were near the Corinthian ships, the men aboard the cutter said, "You put your ships about, Adeimantus, you run away and betray the Greeks while they are winning the battle and overpowering their enemies, just as they prayed they would!" Adeimantus didn't believe what the men said, but they immediately told him that they would be willing to be held as hostages and killed if it turned out that the Greeks were not winning the battle. Adeimantus and the others turned their ships around and arrived back at the base after the battle was over. That, anyway, is the rumor that was spread by the

Athenians. The Corinthians, of course, do not agree. They maintain that they were in the front ranks of the battle, and all the other Greeks bear them out in this.

The Athenian, Aristides, son of Lysimachus—whom I mentioned a little earlier as a brave man—well, this is what he did in the midst of the tumult at Salamis. With the help of large numbers of the Athenian hoplites who had been stationed along the coast of Salamis, he landed on the islet of Psyttaleia and slaughtered all of the Persians who were lying there in ambush.

After the battle had wound down, the Greeks hauled over to Salamis whatever wrecks happened to remain afloat and prepared for another battle, since they fully expected that the king would still use the ships he had left. The west wind blew many of the wrecks over to the Attic beach called Colias. Thus every single prophecy about this battle ever uttered by Bacis and Musaeus was fulfilled, along with one about shipwrecks drifting over to this beach that had been uttered many years before by Lysistratus the Athenian oracle collector—a prophecy whose meaning the Greeks had completely failed to understand:

The women of Colias will do their roasting with oars.

This would have had to happen after the king's retreat.

When Xerxes fully understood the disaster that had occurred, he began to plan his escape. He dreaded that some Ionian would advise the Greeks to sail to the Hellespont and break up the bridges, or else that they would think of it themselves. If this happened, he would be trapped in Europe and would run the risk of annihilation. Not wanting his intentions to become known either to the Greeks or to his own forces, he began to build a jetty out to Salamis and started tying Phoenician merchant ships together to serve as both a pontoon and a breakwater, while at the same time he prepared for combat as though he would force another naval battle. When they all saw Xerxes engaging in these operations, they naturally thought that he was staying on and getting ready to continue the war with all his might, but Mardonius, who was most familiar with Xerxes' way of thinking, was not deceived by any of these maneuvers.

While Xerxes was doing all this, he sent a messenger to Persia with news of his situation. No mortal thing is faster than these couriers, and they say that this is the system the Persians have devised. There are as many horses and men along the way as there are days for the journey, one horse and one rider for each day's travel, and neither snow, nor rain, nor heat, nor dark of night can stay these couriers from the swift completion of their appointed rounds. The first rider passes on his message to the second, and the second to the third, and so on in relays from one to the next just like the torch race the Greeks hold at the festival of Hephaestus. The Persians call this kind of pony express an "angareion."

The first message to arrive in Susa was that Xerxes had captured Athens, and the Persians who had been left behind were so happy that they spread all the streets with myrtle, lit incense everywhere, and kept up constant sacrifices and celebrations. When the second message arrived, though, they became so distraught that they all tore their garments, moaning and shrieking endlessly and blaming it all on Mardonius. Yet the Persians didn't do this so much in grief over the ships as out of fear for the safety of Xerxes.

The Persians remained in this state from then on, until Xerxes returned and put an end to it.

Mardonius could see that Xerxes was deeply depressed over the naval battle and suspected that he was planning his escape from Athens. Mardonius also secretly realized that he would have to pay the price for having persuaded the king to make war on Greece, and that it would be better for him to gamble on either conquering Greece or bravely ending his life while playing for high stakes—though he naturally preferred to conquer Greece! With these thoughts in mind, he made this proposal to the king: "Master, don't put yourself through any pain and suffering at all on account of what has happened. Our lives don't depend on battles with planks of wood but on men and horses. Not a single one of these people who think they have accomplished so much would leave his ship or come out of the hinterland to try to oppose us, and those who did oppose us got what they deserved. So if you think we should, let's immediately attack the Peloponnese; if you think we should wait, we can do that, too; but whatever you do, don't lose heart. There is no way out for Greece except to pay for what they, your slaves, have done now and in the past. Attack or wait—either is the best thing for you to do. But if you really have decided to march back with the army, I have an alternative plan. Your Majesty, you must not allow the Persians to become a laughingstock to the Greeks, because, after all, no Persian ruined your operation and you will never be able to say that we were cowards. If the Phoenicians and Egyptians and Cyprians and Cilicians were cowards, their defeat does not concern Persia. So then, since the Persians are not responsible, trust me. If you have decided not to stay here, return home and take most of the army with you. I will take three hundred thousand men, and it will be up to me to deliver Greece to you in chains."

When Xerxes heard this, he became as pleased and cheerful as he could be in the midst of his troubles. He told Mardonius that he would hold a council to decide which course to follow. While he was deliberating with his Persian advisers, though, he decided to summon Artemisia to the council because she had once been the only person who knew what ought to be done. After she arrived, Xerxes dismissed the others, both his advisers and his bodyguards, and said, "Mardonius urges me to stay here and attack the Peloponnese. He says that the Persians and the army aren't responsible for the defeat and that they want the chance to show what they can do. That is, he either urges me to do that, or let him take three hundred thousand men and deliver Greece to me in chains while I return home with the rest of the army. Tell me now— after all, you gave me good advice when you told me not to have that naval battle—which advice will give me the best results?"

She said, "It's hard for me, Your Majesty, to find the best advice to give you, but under the circumstances I think that you should march back while Mardonius stays behind—if that is what he wants, and if that is what he has promised to do. On the one hand, if he achieves what he says he wants and things go as he intends, the accomplishment, Your Majesty, will really be yours because your slaves will have achieved it. On the other hand, if it turns out otherwise than as Mardonius plans, it won't be a great disaster, because you and your whole government will survive. If you and your palace survive, these Greeks will still run many a race for their lives, and if anything happens to Mardonius, it won't matter. The Greeks won't win anything by their victory, because they will have killed your slave. You, meanwhile, will have withdrawn after setting Athens on fire, and that is why you formed this expedition to begin with."

Xerxes was delighted with this advice: she happened to say just what he had been thinking himself. In my opinion, he would not have stayed even if every man and woman in his entourage had advised him to do so—that's how frightened he was. He praised Artemisia and sent her ahead to Ephesus with his sons. You see, some of his illegitimate sons were accompanying him. To protect the boys, he sent along Hermotimus, a Pedasian who was second to none among the king's eunuchs.

This man inflicted the greatest revenge I know of for a wrong that had been done him. After an invading army had captured him and sold him into slavery, he was bought by Panionius, a man from Chios who made his living at an obscene trade. Whenever Panionius acquired some handsome boys, he would castrate them and take them to Sardis and Ephesus, where he would sell them for large sums of money. Eunuchs are extremely expensive among the barbarians because they are considered much more trustworthy in every way than anyone with testicles. So Panionius castrated a great many boys, including Hermotimus. After all, that was how he made his living. Nevertheless, Hermotimus wasn't unlucky in every way. He came to the king's household from Sardis as one of many gifts, and in the course of time he became Xerxes' most highly respected eunuch.

When the king was in Sardis preparing to lead the Persian army out against Athens, Hermotimus went on some business or other to a town called Atarneus, in the Mysian territory. The town is administered by Chios, and when he was there, he bumped into Panionius, whom he immediately recognized. Hermotimus said all kinds of friendly things to him, and listed all the advantages he had had, thanks to him. Hermotimus promised to do as much for Panionius in return if only he would move his family to Hermotimus' household in Sardis. Panionius gladly accepted this offer and moved his wife and children to Sardis. But when Hermotimus had Panionius and his whole family in his power, he said, "You, who made your living from the filthiest trade in the world, what harm did I or any of my people ever do you or any of yours that you should have turned me from a man into a nothing? You thought the

gods didn't notice what you were doing then, but as you went about
your obscene business they have led you down the paths of justice and
delivered you into *my* hands, just so you won't have any reason to complain about the punishment I give you." After Hermotimus upbraided
him, his four sons were brought in, and Panionius was forced to cut off
the genitals of his own boys; and do it he did, though under torture.
When he was finished, his sons were forced to castrate him. Thus vengeance—and Hermotimus—came around to Panionius.

After Xerxes turned over his sons to Artemisia so that she could take
them to Ephesus, he summoned Mardonius and ordered him to choose
the regiments he wanted from the army and to try to match his deeds to
his words. The whole day was taken up with these matters, and that
night, on orders from the king, his naval commanders set out with the
fleet from Phalerum to the Hellespont as fast as they could to secure the
bridges for the king's crossing. When the barbarians were sailing near
Zoster, though, where some small rocky promontories stretch out into
the sea, they thought the rocks were enemy ships and ran as far away
from them as they could. The barbarians eventually realized that they
weren't ships but rocks and continued on their way after regrouping.

At daybreak the Greeks saw that the Persian land army was still in
place and supposed that the fleet was still at Phalerum. In the belief that
there would be another naval battle, they prepared for their defense, but
when they found out that the Persian ships had gone, they immediately
decided to pursue them. The Greeks gave chase as far as Andros, but
Xerxes' fleet was nowhere to be seen. They had a conference at Andros,
and Themistocles expressed the view that they should continue the chase
clear through the islands, sail straight for the Hellespont, and destroy
the bridges. Eurybiades, though, advanced just the opposite opinion,
saying that breaking up the bridges would be the worst possible thing
they could do to Greece. The reason, he argued, was that if the Persians
were trapped and forced to remain in Europe they wouldn't just quietly
stay there. They would be in a situation in which they could neither
retreat nor successfully carry out their invasion, and they would die of
starvation. If they kept up their attack, though, and stayed in action, it
was possible that all of Europe would eventually surrender to them because
city after city and people after people would either be conquered or forced
to come to terms. Meanwhile, Greece's annual crops would always supply them with food. As it was, the Persians had been defeated in the
naval battle and had decided not to remain in Europe. They ought to
be allowed to flee as far as their own country, Eurybiades insisted, where
the Greeks could continue the fight on enemy territory. The other Peloponnesian commanders also held this view.

When Themistocles realized that he wasn't going to persuade the
majority to sail to the Hellespont, he turned to the Athenians, who were
furious over the escape of the Persians and who would have gone to the

Hellespont on their own even if the others refused, and he said, "I've been at many places—and heard about many more—where desperate, defeated men, forced to return to battle, have made up for earlier disasters. We somehow found a way to drive this cloud of men away from ourselves and from the rest of Greece, but let's not pursue them now that they are running away. After all, it wasn't really we who did this; it was our gods and our heroes, who resented the idea that one impious and presumptuous man should rule over Asia and Europe, a man for whom the sacred and the profane were one and the same thing, a man who smashed and burned the statues of the gods, and who scourged and sank fetters into the sea. We're all right, for now, so let's stay in Greece and look after ourselves and our families. Let every man rebuild his house and see that his crops are planted, now that he has driven the barbarian clean away! In the spring, we'll sail to Ionia and the Hellespont." He said this because he wanted to store up some favors from the king so that he would have somewhere to turn just in case he ever had any trouble with the Athenians, as, in fact, he later did.

The Athenians were persuaded by this misleading speech of Themistocles because whereas he had merely seemed to be wise before, he was now thought to be truly wise, especially in counsel, and they were ready to believe anything he said. As soon as the Athenians were won over, though, Themistocles sent off some men in a boat, men he trusted to keep their mouths shut no matter what the torture, until they delivered a message he had given them for the king. One of the men was, again, his slave Sicinnus. When they reached Attica, the others stayed with the boat while Sicinnus went up to Xerxes and said, "The Athenian commander Themistocles, son of Neocles, and the noblest and wisest of all the allies, has sent me to tell you that he, Themistocles, wishing to do you a good turn, has kept the Greeks from pursuing your ships and destroying your bridges across the Hellespont as they intended. Take your time in going home." The men sailed back after delivering this message.

Since the Greeks had chosen not to pursue the king's ships any farther or sail to the Hellespont and destroy his crossings, they decided to blockade and capture Andros. You see, the Andrians were the first island people to refuse a demand by Themistocles for money. He had made a little speech about how the Athenians had come there with two mighty gods, Persuasion and Force, to whom the Andrians would have to contribute large sums of money. The Andrians answered that it was understandable that the Athenians were so great and prosperous—they would naturally be well off with such profitable gods. But since the Andrians were desperately poor in land and since they were in thrall to two useless gods, Poverty and Inertia, who loved their island and would never leave it, the Andrians would give nothing. Besides, Athenian power could never be greater than Andrian inability to pay. They were then laid under siege as much because of this answer as because they would not pay.

Meanwhile, Themistocles—the man's greed was insatiable!—sent threatening demands to the other islands via the same messengers he had sent to the king, saying that if they did not give Themistocles what he wanted, he would attack them with the Greek fleet, blockade them, and wipe them out. This threat enabled him to collect large sums of money from the Carystians and the Parians. They sent the money out of fear because they knew that Andros was being blockaded for collaborating with the Persians and that Themistocles was the most dreaded of the commanders. I can't say whether any of the other islanders made payments, though I suppose that these were not the only ones and that others did too. Nevertheless, the Carystians weren't able to buy off the day of reckoning, although the Parians were, in fact, able to escape the ravages of the fleet by propitiating Themistocles with money. Thus, using Andros as a base of operations, Themistocles was able to acquire a lot of money without the other commanders' knowing about it.

Xerxes' forces waited a few days after the naval battle and then marched back to Boeotia by the same way they had come. Mardonius decided to escort the king part of the way: since it was now a bad time of year for fighting, it would be better for him and his troops to spend the winter in Thessaly and attack the Peloponnese in the spring. When the army arrived in Thessaly, Mardonius selected all the so-called Persian "Immortals" for his army—all except for General Hydarnes, who refused to leave the king. Next, he chose the Persian troops equipped with breastplates as well as the thousand Persian cavalry. He also took both the cavalry and the infantry of the Medes, Sacae, Bactrians, and Indians. He chose all these nations in their entirety, but he made more sparing selections from the other allies, basing his choice on the bearing of the soldiers and on whether he knew them to have performed some useful service. The single largest group selected was the Persians—men who wear necklaces and bracelets!—and, after them, the Medes, who were no fewer in number than the Persians though much weaker in fighting strength. Counting the cavalry, Mardonius' army numbered three hundred thousand men.

During this time, while Xerxes was still in Thessaly and Mardonius was choosing his army, the Lacedaemonians received an oracle from Delphi telling them to go to Xerxes, demand compensation for the death of Leonidas, and accept whatever Xerxes offered them. The Spartans immediately sent off a herald, and, finding the whole army still in Thessaly, he came into the presence of the king and said, "King of Persia, the Lacedaemonians and the Spartan Heraclids demand compensation for the death you inflicted on their king while he was defending Greece." Xerxes laughed and then fell silent for quite some time. Then he pointed to Mardonius, who happened to be standing by, and said, "Well, now!

Mardonius here will give them just the kind of compensation they deserve!"

The herald accepted this statement and left.

Xerxes left Mardonius behind in Thessaly and made his way on the double to the Hellespont. He reached the bridges in forty-five days, bringing back very little of his army to speak of. His men had seized and eaten the harvests of whatever people they had been among, but if they found no harvest, they ate the grass growing in the earth and the bark and leaves they stripped and plucked from trees, whether wild or cultivated. They refused nothing; they were driven by starvation. Plague and dysentery also beset the army and devastated them along the way. Xerxes left the sick behind, assigning them to be nursed and fed by the cities he happened to be passing through—in Thessaly, at Siris in Paeonia, in Macedon. Xerxes had left the chariot sacred to Zeus at Siris on the march into Greece, but he didn't get it back on his retreat. When he asked for it, the Paeonians said that they had given it to the Thracians and that the chariot's horses had been stolen from their pastures by the upland Thracians who live near the sources of the Strymon River.

In this region, also, the Thracian king of the Bisaltians and of Crestonia committed a monstrous act. After declaring that he would never willingly enslave himself to Xerxes, the king withdrew to Mount Rhodope. He also forbade his sons to go to war against Greece, but they ignored him and joined Xerxes' campaign, more because they just wanted to see the war than for any other reason. When they came home safely— all six of them—their father gouged out the eyes which had disobeyed him to see the war. That, then, was their combat pay.

After leaving Thrace, the Persians reached the Hellespont, where they rushed into their boats and crossed over to Abydos. As it turned out, they found that the pontoons were not still linked and that the bridges had been broken up by a storm. At Abydos they could get much more food than had been available on the road, and the combination of stuffing themselves with food and changing their drinking water caused the death of many of the survivors of the campaign. The remnant went to Sardis with Xerxes.

There is another version of the story which says that when Xerxes reached Eion-on-Strymon after his retreat from Athens, he no longer made his way home by land. Instead, he entrusted the army to Hydarnes to take it the rest of the way to the Hellespont, while he himself returned to Asia aboard a Phoenician vessel. After he had set sail, the story goes, a strong wind surging off the Strymon billowed the waves under his ship. The increasingly furious storm so wracked a ship already heavily laden with the many Persians on deck who were accompanying Xerxes home that the king panicked and shouted a question to the pilot about whether there was any way out of this alive. The pilot said, "No way at all, Your Majesty, unless we can get rid of some of these passengers."

When Xerxes heard this, the story goes, he said, "Men of Persia, you now have the chance to show how much you care for your king, because it looks like my safety is up to you." After he said this, they prostrated themselves before him, got up, and jumped into the sea—and the lightened ship made its way safely to Asia. As soon as Xerxes was on solid land, this is what he did: for saving the king's life, he gave the pilot a golden crown; but for causing the deaths of so many Persians, he had the man's head cut off.

I certainly do not believe this version of the story of Xerxes' return—for all sorts of reasons, but especially because of the part about the Persians. If the pilot had really said those words to Xerxes, I can't think of one person in ten thousand who would disagree that the king would have ordered the Persians (and the chief Persians at that) off the deck and sent them below into the ship's hold and that he would then have thrown an equal number of Phoenician rowers overboard.

As I have already said, though, Xerxes and his army returned to Asia by land, and here is yet another proof of that fact. Xerxes is known to have stopped at Abdera on his return and to have made a friendship pact with them which was sealed by the gift of a golden sword and a turban made of golden gauze. I don't believe it, but the Abderites say that this was the first time since his flight from Athens that Xerxes felt safe enough to loosen his belt. In any case, Abdera is closer to the Hellespont than is Eion or the Strymon, where they say he boarded that ship for Asia.

When the Greeks proved unable to capture Andros, they made their way to Carystus, where they devastated the countryside, and finally returned to Salamis. The first thing they did there was to make a varied selection of the firstfruits of victory as an offering to the gods. This included three Phoenician triremes: one for Poseidon at the Isthmus, which was still there in my time; one for Poseidon at Sunium; and one for Ajax at Salamis. They divided the booty among themselves and then sent the first fruits to Delphi. They were used to make the statue of a man holding the prow of a ship in his hands. The statue is eighteen feet high and stands near the golden statue of Alexander of Macedon.

After the Greeks sent the firstfruits to Delphi, they jointly asked the god whether he found the offering complete and satisfactory. He said that he did, from all the Greeks except the Aeginetans, and he demanded from them the best booty they had taken at the battle of Salamis. When the Aeginetans learned this, they dedicated the three gold stars mounted on a bronze mast, which stands in the corner nearest Croesus' bowl.

After the division of the spoils, the Greeks sailed to the Isthmus to award the prize for valor to the man who, of all the Greeks, had been most valuable during the war. After the commanders arrived, they voted at the altar of Poseidon for the first- and second-place winners. Each one voted for himself for first place, since each considered himself to be the best, but most voted for Themistocles for second place. No one, therefore, got more than one vote for first, but Themistocles was the overwhelming choice for second.

Envy kept the Greeks from confirming the vote, though, and they all sailed home without reaching a decision. Nevertheless, the name of Themistocles was cried up everywhere, and he was considered to be by far the shrewdest man in all of Greece. But because the men who had fought at Salamis wouldn't honor him in spite of his victory, Themistocles immediately went to Lacedaemon to be honored there; and, indeed, the Lacedaemonians received him very handsomely and conferred the highest honors on him. They gave the prize for valor—a crown of olive branches—to Eurybiades, but Themistocles received another olive wreath as his prize for strategy and skill. In addition, they gave him the most beautiful chariot in Sparta. After he was acclaimed with kudos, three hundred handpicked Spartans called the Knights formally escorted him in a procession to the border at Tegea. He is the only man I know of whom the Spartans ever honored with such a procession.

When Themistocles arrived in Athens from Sparta, one of his enemies, an otherwise undistinguished man named Timodemus, from the Athenian township of Aphidnae, went crazy with envy and taunted Themistocles over the procession from Lacedaemon on the grounds that the honor really belonged to the Athenian people and not to him. Since Timodemus never wearied of this accusation, Themistocles finally said, "It's like this. Maybe I wouldn't have been so honored by the Spartans if I'd been from Belbina, but they would never have honored you, my friend, even though you *are* from Athens."[4]

* * *

---

4. Belbina is a tiny coastal island of no importance and is the equivalent in this sentence of the American "Podunk."

Book 9

Herodotus did not finish book 9, but he got far enough to recount the Greeks' final victories over the Persians. After the flight of Xerxes, Mardonius remained in Greece, where he continued the war. Following some setbacks, the Greeks gave battle at Plataea. In 479 Mardonius was killed and his army narrowly defeated in this closely fought battle near the border of Attica and Boeotia. On the same day (or so the tale went) the Persians lost a decisive naval battle off Mycale, in Ionia. Thus ended the Persian Wars. Shortly after Herodotus has narrated the Greek victory at Mycale and the mutilation of Xerxes' sister-in-law by his jealous wife, the narrative breaks off.

* * *

Chapters 51–64

The Greek generals had a meeting and decided that they would retreat to 'the Island' if the Persians put off the battle that day. This island is in front of the town of Plataea, one and a quarter miles from where they were then camped at the Asopus and the Gargaphian spring. It is a kind of island on land. A river flowing out of Mount Cithaeron divides above the plain and then flows down into it in two streams, separated by as much as a half mile, before reuniting into one river again. The river's name is the Oeroe, and the natives say that it is the daughter of the Asopus. The generals decided to retreat to the part of the plain between the streams so that their men could have unlimited access to water and so that they would not be decimated by the enemy cavalry as they had been when they were out in front of them. The generals decided to retreat during the second watch that night so that the Persians would not see them moving out and harass them with their cavalry. They decided that when they reached the point at which the river divides after it flows out of Mount Cithaeron, they would send half the army to Cithaeron to relieve the provisioners who had gone off in search of food and who were now trapped on Mount Cithaeron.

After the generals reached this decision, the army endured relentless punishment from cavalry assaults all day long, but the day and the cavalry charges came to an end, night fell, and the time they had agreed on for their departure came. Most of the men broke camp and left, although they had no intention of going to the place the generals had decided on. As soon as they began to move, they fled in the direction of the town of Plataea, and went as far as the temple of Hera, glad to escape the cavalry.

They took up a position in front of the temple, which is outside the town and two and a half miles from the Gargaphian spring.

Meanwhile, when Pausanias saw these troops leaving camp, he thought that they were going to the Island, as ordered, and he sent word to the Lacedaemonians to take up their weapons and follow the men in front of them. All of Pausanias' officers were ready to obey him except for Amompharetus, son of Poliades and commander of the regiment from Pitane. He refused, he said, to run away from the foreigners or to willingly bring disgrace on Sparta. (The maneuver bewildered him because he had not been present at the generals' meeting.) Pausanias and Euryanax thought it was terrible that he didn't obey their order, but they thought it would be even more terrible, in view of his refusal to move, to abandon the regiment from Pitane, because if they did abandon it to keep their rendezvous with the other Greeks, Amompharetus and everyone with him would be stranded and destroyed. With this thought in mind, they kept the Spartan camp where it was while they tried to persuade Amompharetus that he was wrong.

While the Spartans were urging on the recalcitrant Amompharetus, the Athenians were doing as follows: they remained where they had been stationed because they knew that the Peloponnesians had a habit of saying one thing and thinking another. Therefore, when the army got on the move, the Athenians sent a rider to see whether the Spartans had also gotten under way and to ask Pausanias what they should do if it turned out that the Spartans in fact had no intention of moving.

When the man arrived at the Lacedaemonian camp, he saw the troops still in place and saw their leaders quarrelling among themselves. You see, Pausanias and Euryanax had been so long and so unsuccessfully pleading with Amompharetus not to endanger his men by staying behind that they had fallen to quarreling, and when the Athenian herald arrived in their midst, an angry Amompharetus was picking up a rock with both hands, dropping it at the feet of Pausanias, and saying that this was the ballot he cast for never running away from the strangers, by whom he meant the barbarians. Pausanias was calling him "crazy," "out of his mind," and when the rider delivered his message Pausanias ordered the man to describe the situation to the Athenians and to tell them to bring their troops close to his and to follow Sparta's lead in making their retreat.

The rider returned to the Athenian camp, and the Spartans kept arguing with each other until the dawn put an end to it. Pausanias had not moved his men during all that time, but he finally decided that Amompharetus would not want to be left behind while the other Lacedaemonians marched away—and that's just what happened. Pausanias gave the order and began to lead his remaining men through the hills of Cithaeron, with the Tegeans following. The Athenians fell in next to the Lacedaemonians, as ordered. Thus, for fear of the Persian cavalry, the Lacedaemonians hugged the foothills and ranges of Cithaeron, while the Athenians took the low road through the plain.

At first, Amompharetus never dreamed that Pausanias would dare to abandon him and kept insisting that they stay there and not leave their post; but when Pausanias' troops began to draw ahead, he realized that they really were leaving him outright, so he ordered his regiment to take up their weapons and slowly led them toward the main force. Pausanias advanced about half a mile and then waited for Amompharetus' regiment, halting on the Moloeis River at a place called Argiopium, where there is a temple to the Demeter of Eleusis. They waited so that they could go back to the rescue if Amompharetus and his regiment really didn't leave their position and stayed where they were. Amompharetus and his men did join them, though, whereupon the whole barbarian cavalry immediately began to harry the army: when the cavalry saw that the terrain the Greeks had occupied on the previous day was now deserted, they resumed their usual tactics of charging forward and attacking as soon as they caught up with the enemy.

When Mardonius learned that the Greeks had slipped away by night * * * he believed the Greeks were running away, and led his Persians out on the double, following their trail across the Asopus. He was actually going after only the Lacedaemonians and the Tegeans because he couldn't see the Athenians who had turned in to the plain below the hills. When the commanders of the remaining barbarian regiments saw the Persians going off in pursuit of the Greeks, they all raised their standards and, out of formation and without order or discipline, a shouting mob of soldiers joined the chase as fast as their feet could carry them, expecting to fall on the Greeks and take them by storm.

After the cavalry had attacked Pausanias, he sent a rider to the Athenians saying, "Men of Athens! The great battle is at hand over whether Greece will be enslaved or free, and we, the Lacedaemonians and the Athenians, have been betrayed by our allies, who ran away last night. The best thing for us to do now is to defend ourselves and support each other as best we can. If the cavalry had begun by attacking you, it would have been necessary for us and for the Tegeans who are with us not to betray Greece and to come to your rescue. As it is, the whole cavalry has advanced on us, and it is only right for you to rush to the defense of the most hard-pressed detachment of the army. If it turns out, though, that you cannot help, at least do us the favor of sending us your archers. We know, though, that you have been the most zealous fighters in this war and that you will comply with our request."

When the Athenians heard this, they started off, eager to give the Spartans as much help and support as they could; but as soon as they were on the march, they were frontally attacked by Greeks fighting for the king, and it was no longer possible to relieve the Spartans, because of the pressure on themselves. As a result, the Lacedaemonians and Tegeans were on their own. Counting lightly armed troops, the Lacedaemonians had fifty thousand men, and the Tegeans (who would never under any circumstances abandon the Lacedaemonians) had three thousand. They started to sacrifice animals in preparation for the battle with Mardonius and his army, but the sacrifices were unfavorable and many men died and many more were wounded while they waited. The Persians, protected by wicker shields, let fly such an all-out barrage of arrows that, what with the suffering of the Spartans and the unfavorable omens, Pausanias looked away to the temple of Hera and, calling on the goddess, begged her to stop cheating them of their hopes.

While Pausanias was still praying, the Tegeans rushed forward and attacked the barbarians. Then, immediately after Pausanias finished his prayer, the sacrifices became favorable for the Lacedaemonians, and they, too, finally attacked the Persians, who had set aside their bows and arrows and were also beginning to advance. The battle began at the wicker shields. When these fell, the fierce fight continued for a long time at the temple of Demeter. Then, after the barbarians took hold of the Spartan spears and broke them, the two sides came to hand-to-hand combat. The Persians were not inferior to the Greeks in courage and strength, but they had no shields or armor and were, besides, ignorant men unequal to their opponents in military tactics. Darting forward by ones and tens, in groups large and small, they rushed at the Spartans and were destroyed.

Mardonius fought on a white horse surrounded by a select group of the thousand best Persian troops, and the Greeks were most hard-pressed wherever he happened to be. As long as Mardonius was alive, the Persians held out in their own defense and killed many of the Lacedaemonians, but when Mardonius was killed and his detachment—the strongest part of the army—fell, why then all the others turned and fled before the Lacedaemonians. What hurt the Persians most was their outfits, which were lacking in any sort of armor: they were lightly armed soldiers doing battle with armored men.

That was when the oracle was fulfilled, and Mardonius gave retribution to the Spartans for the killing of Leonidas. Meanwhile, the finest victory we know of was won by Pausanias, son of Cleombrotus, son of Anaxandrides.

*   *   *

BACKGROUNDS

AESCHYLUS

Aeschylus, who lived from 525/4 to 456 B.C., is believed to have fought at Marathon and Salamis. He wrote tragic dramas with religious and patriotic themes, and was particularly concerned with power and its responsible use. *The Persians*, which was performed in Athens in 472 B.C., is the only surviving Greek tragedy on a contemporary historical event. The following lines, spoken by a Persian messenger to Atossa, the mother of Xerxes, describe the disaster at Salamis and the subsequent Persian retreat. Aeschylus' account is clearer and more straightforward than Herodotus'. Its power and fervor make it one of the greatest passages in all of Greek literature.

The Persians†

ATOSSA: . . . What number was there of Hellenic ships
That dared give battle to the Persian host
In naval combat?

MESS.: As you know, the Persian fleet
Was strong enough by far to win. The Greeks
In all had ten times thirty ships
Plus ten of special excellence.
Xerxes commanded ships that numbered to
A thousand—I saw them all myself—
Not counting two hundred sixty more
Of blazing speed. That was the count.
Does that seem inferior to you?
But some divine spirit destroyed
Our host, weighing down the scale
With balance-tilting luck.
The gods protect the city of godly Pallas.

AT.: The city, then, of Athens goes unsacked?

MESS.: While she has men, her fortress is secure.

AT.: Tell me. How did the clash of ships begin?
Who began the battle?
Was it the Greeks or my son, exulting
In the numbers of his ships?

MESS.: It seems, my lady, that some avenging god
Or evil spirit is the cause of all this woe.
A Greek, you see, from the Athenian camp
Came to your son Xerxes and said

† Lines 334–514, translated by Walter Blanco.

That when the dark of the black night
Fell, the Greeks would not remain,
But spring aboard their ships' decks
And go in secret flight their several ways
To save their lives.
When Xerxes heard this, not suspecting
The Greek's deceit or the jealousy of the gods,
He called this order to all his ships' commanders:
"When the sun stops scorching earth with flashing
Points of light, and darkness fills
The temple of the sky, array your ships
In rows of three. Encircle Ajax Island.
Guard the channels and the sea-beat access ways.
If the Greeks should flee their evil fate,
You will all be stripped of your commands."
He spoke with vigor, confident of heart:
He knew not what the gods would bring.
In good order and with obedient hearts,
They took their supper. Sailors fitted
The oars yarely to their tholepins.
When the sun's flame died away
And night came on, the elite oarsmen
And crack fighters made their way
Down to the ships. Orders were shouted
Throughout the long warships and each one
Sailed where it was told. All night long
The captains stationed the host of ships.
Night waned, but the Greek force
Made no attempt to steal away.
When day rode in on her white steeds
And the whole earth gleamed to see,
The first loud shout of joyful song
Rang echoing from the island rocks,
And fear crept over barbarians
Whose hope had come to naught.
The Greeks, you see,
Sang not their stately hymn in flight,
But as they sped to battle with cheerful strength.
Their trumpet flamed through all that place.
Their oars dipped and struck as one
The briny splashing water from the deep.
Soon enough we saw them all.
The right wing led in tight array,
But then the whole fleet charged
With everywhere the shout:
"Row, you sons of Greece, row on,
To free your fatherland, to free
Your sons, your wives, the sacred seats

Of your ancestral gods, and your forefathers' tombs.
This fight is to the death!"
From our side, a rush of Persian
Answered back. The wait was over.
Straightway their bronze-sheathed ramrods
Struck our ships; a Greek ship led the charge.
Shattering the flared Phoenician sterns
Timber aimed at timber and the long line
Of the Persian fleet withstood the charge.
Since most of our ships were packed into the narrows,
Though, we could not give each other aid.
Again and again they struck with bronze-toothed rams
While all our oar blades shivered in the crush.
Not without skill, the Greek ships raced around us
In a circle. You could not see the sea
So full it was of upturned hulls, of jetsam
And of human gore.
Corpses covered the headlands and the hog-backed reefs,
And every ship in the barbarian fleet
Rushed away in routed flight.
They beat us with their splintered oars
And with the wreckage of the ships.
They cut us to pieces like tunas in a net.
Shrieking and wailing filled the sea
Till night's dark eyes closed on the slaughter.
I could not tell you all, no,
Not if I told the tale for ten straight days.
Know this, though: never in one day
Has such a number of men perished.

AT.:   Oh woe! What evils the sea has broken
         Over the Persians, over the whole barbarian race!

MESS.:   Yet you should know that evils have no measure.
         Such sorrowful calamity came on them
         As weighed twice as heavily in the scales as these.

AT.:   And what worse luck could come than this?
         Speak. What calamity came to the army
         Weighing more heavily in the scales of woe?

MESS.:   Those Persians who had reached the peak of nature
         Standing out in breeding and nobility of soul,
         Most loyal always to the person of the king,
         Have suffered the ignoblest fate in death.

AT.:   Oh how I suffer, dear friends, through this calamity.
         Tell me in what way these men have perished.

MESS.:   There is an island fronting Salamis,
           Small, and with no anchorage for ships.
           Dance-loving Pan haunts the sea-girt
           Promontories of the place. The king
           Sent these men there, so that when the enemy,
           Bereft of ships, should seek their safety on this isle,
           Their slaughter would come easily to our hands,
           While we might rescue friends from the watery ways.
           He read the future badly.
           On the very day the god
           Gave the battle's glory to the Greeks,
           They clad themselves in armor of well-tempered bronze
           And leaped ashore there from their ships.
           Their boats surrounded the whole island:
           There was nowhere to turn.
           Many were battered by hand-flung stones
           While arrows flew from bowstrings bringing death
           Until in the end the Greeks rushed forward with a shout,
           Chopping the wretched limbs to messes
           And utterly destroying them, every one.
           Xerxes groaned to see the depth of evil.
           He had a seat in sight of his whole army
           High on a hill near the sea.
           He wailed and tore his clothes and after
           Signaling his infantry prepared for hasty flight.
           This is all the more woe for you to add
           To that which went before.

AT.:   Oh hateful spirit! How you have cheated
           The Persians of their wits! A bitter vengeance
           My son has taken on the famed Athenians,
           As if the barbarians who fell at Marathon
           Were not enough for you! Thinking to exact
           Requital for them, my son has drawn
           Instead this multitude of woe!
           But tell me. Where did you last see the ships
           That fled their doom? Can you say for sure?

MESS.:   The captains of the remaining ships took
           Their hasty flight without formation
           To anywhere the wind would bear them.
           The remnant of the army perished, some in Boeotia,
           Around her gentle springs, faint with thirst
           Or gasping emptily for breath;
           Some as we made our way through
           Phocis, Doris, and the Malian Gulf
           Where Spercheius waters the plain with its kindly flow.
           From there, the plain of Achaea and the cities
           Of Thessaly took us in as we starved for food.

Many died there of hunger and thirst,
For, yes, we had enough of both.
We came to Magnesia and the plain of Macedon,
To the river Axius' ford.
We came to the marshy reeds of Bolbe,
To Mount Pangaeus and to Edones land.
On that night, god sent a snowstorm
Out of season and froze the stream
Of holy Strymon. We prayed to gods
We had ere thought as nothing,
Propitiating earth and sky.
When the army had done
With calling on the gods,
It tried to cross the frozen ford.
He who set off before god scattered
The beams of the sun was saved,
For when the shining circle of the sun
Shot the flaming rays of burning heat
Through the ford, the men collapsed
Into one another. The lucky ones were those
Who quickly snapped the breath of life.
Those who made it safe across
Barely made their way through Thrace
With many hardships, and came—not many—
To the land of hearth and home,
So that the capital of Persia might lament
The loss of its soil's beloved youth.
All this is true, though I have left off telling
Much of the evil god rained on the Persians.

BACCHYLIDES

The fifth-century lyric poet Bacchylides uses Croesus as an example of generosity and piety in one of his odes. In Bacchylides, Croesus is saved and wafted away to the land of the Hyperboreans; in Herodotus, he becomes a friendly adviser to Cyrus. Also, in Bacchylides, Croesus himself builds the pyre as a way of committing suicide; in Herodotus, Cyrus does it. Bacchylides' account suggests that Croesus is justified in blaming the gods for his downfall.

Third Epinician Ode†

Ah, three-times happy man
Who, winning Zeus's lottery

† Book 11, lines 10–62, translated by Walter Blanco.

Of wide privilege among the Greeks,
Knows better than to hide his towering wealth
In black-blanketing darkness!

No, his sacrificial feasts teem with cattle
And his streets are filled with welcome;
His gold lights the way with gleaming
Where the crafted three-legged caldrons
Stand before the temple,
There where the Delphians tend
The great demesne of Phoibos
Near Castalia's springs.
The noblest happiness is glorifying god.
Take that time the chief
Of the horse-mastering Lydians,
Croesus of the golden sword,
Was rescued by Apollo
On the day Sardis fell to Persia's host,
The day Zeus enacted the appointed fate.

After racing to that unexpected day,
Croesus did not mean to stay in bitter slavery long.
He had a pyre heaped up
Before the bronze-walled courtyard,
And mounted there, with wedded wife
And long-haired daughters inconsolably wailing,
And raised his hands to the high heavens
Shouting, "Great spirit,
Where is the gratitude of god?
Where is the lord, the son of Leto?
Gone are the palaces of Alyattes
Bursting with their million riches.
The golden whirlpools of Pactolus
Swirl red with blood,
And our women are shamelessly
Dragged from their well-built homes.
What once was hateful is now held dear,
And the sweetest thing is just to die."
So he spoke, and called a slave to light
The cruel scaffolding of wood.
The virgins wept,
Flinging their dear hands toward their mother.
The death we can see coming is the worst.
But when the strength of the awful fire
Leaped up and shone,
Zeus brought over a black cloud
Of dark rain to extinguish the auburn flame.
Nothing incredible is framed by god's solicitude,

For then Delos-born Apollo
Wafted the old man and his slender-ankled girls
To the land of the Hyperboreans
And settled them there,
A reward for piety, for offering
More than any other mortal to sacred Pytho.

THUCYDIDES

The large role played by Themistocles and the Athenian navy in turning back the Persian invasion combined with later events to create a dramatic shift in the balance of power among the Greek city-states. Before the Persian Wars, the primacy of Sparta in power and prestige had been unquestioned. The reputation of the Athenians, however, was greatly enhanced by the leadership they had shown in the war and by the prominent part they had played in the victory at Salamis. Soon after the final Greek victories at Plataea and Mycale, the Spartan commander in Byzantium, Pausanias, thoroughly alienated the Ionian allies by his arrogant and overbearing conduct. Offended by Pausanias and impressed by the Athenians' newfound naval prowess, the Greek cities nearest to Persia decided to form a new maritime alliance under the leadership of Athens.

The Spartans were divided about the acceptability of this development, but after a certain amount of debate they acquiesced in the new order. The Athenian statesman Aristides assessed the amount of tribute each member of the league would pay, and a treasury was established on the island of Delos. The good feeling that attended the founding of the so-called Delian League, however, was soon replaced by ambivalence among Athens' allies. While the league was fulfilling its avowed purposes of affording protection against potential attacks from Persia and making retaliatory raids on Persian territory, many saw it as a tool of self-interested expansion and aggression on the part of the Athenians. When the Athenians began compelling reluctant cities to join and forbidding dissatisfied allies to withdraw, and as the danger of a new Persian invasion grew increasingly remote, disaffection within the league worsened, prompting the Athenians to move the treasury from Delos to Athens (454 B.C.). Traditionally this is the date at which classicists begin referring to the Delian League as the Athenian empire.

Historians are deeply divided about just how unpopular Athens' leadership was with the allies, but all agree that the existence of the alliance strained relations with Sparta, which had for many generations headed its own loose organization, the Peloponnesian League. One of the most powerful members of this league was Corinth, whose commercial ambitions made it Athens' natural rival. During the half century that divided the war with Persia from the long, devastating Peloponnesian War between Sparta and Athens, tensions between Athens' allies and those of Sparta rose and fell. The "First Peloponnesian War," an undeclared war that lasted from 461 to 446, seemed for a while to have resolved some of these tensions, and for about a decade the chances for peace seemed promising. Late in the 430s, however, under their forceful leader Pericles, the Athenians took a number of steps that called forth the anger of several Peloponnesian allies, particularly Corinth. Athens' actions probably did not constitute a violation of the peace treaty that had ended the First Peloponnesian War, but they were still questionable; it was provocative, for example, for Athens to make an alliance with the neutral island of Corcyra—just when Corcyra was about to go to war with Corinth. In 432 the Spartans voted to go to war with Athens. The Peloponnesian War began the following year and lasted, with some interruptions, until 404. It was attended with tremendous loss of life, and when it was finally over, much of the strength of Greece had been sapped.

Thucydides, the son of Olorus, was an Athenian aristocrat probably related to the family of Miltiades. In the course of writing his history, which he started when the war first broke out, Thucydides sought to define his work in relation to the existing traditions of Greek narrative—Homeric epic and Herodotean researches. His familiarity with Herodotus' writings and with the thinking of doctors like Hippocrates encouraged him to think carefully about how history developed, how it should be understood and written about, and how evidence was to be evaluated and analyzed. Thucydides was an eager student of politics and diplomacy, but he devoted no space to social or intellectual history. We would never guess from his work that some of the most brilliant drama in world history was produced during the war, or that the structure of the Spartan family was changed by the absence and death of so many men in the field. He also had a number of highly visible axes to grind. Although a great admirer of Pericles, for example, he did not like Athenian democracy; he consistently portrayed its other leaders as either hapless victims of an irrational populace or as demagogues who exploited the fickleness of the people. While Thucydides' narrative is far more linear than Herodotus' and more to the taste of moderns who favor the elusive "scientific" history, many readers could wish that Thucydides had produced the kind of rich cultural description in which Herodotus' work abounds. Herodotus' interest in religion, custom, geography, geology, and folklore precludes the tight narrative structures of Thucydides, but it also satisfies in both the specialist and the general reader a curiosity that is sometimes frustrated by the austere historian of the Peloponnesian War.

Thucydides' pained ambivalence toward his native Athens lends additional drama to a gripping story of war. Like Herodotus, he was interested in human nature above all, and he believed that it was people—not gods, fate, chance, or market forces—who determined the course of events. His accounts of the way people reacted to the stress of the plague that swept Athens at the beginning of the war or to the civil strife in Corcyra were meant to stand as general observations about the way humans respond in critical situations, and they have been cited by scholars throughout modern times as monuments of historical writing. His fascination with what he viewed as the irresistible human drive to power and its consequences accounted in large part for his ambivalence toward Athens—a city laid low, he believed, because of a will to expand inherent in human creatures. Thucydides believed he was watching his fellow citizens destroy themselves in obedience to the inexorable laws of their own nature. This tragic theme lends added force to Thucydides' narrative of the long, sad war that drained so much life from the vital civilization of classical Greece.

The Peloponnesian War†

I, Thucydides of Athens, wrote the history of the war that was fought between the Peloponnesians and the Athenians. I began the history as soon as the war broke out, in the belief that it would be the most important, most interesting war of any that had gone before, and I reached this conclusion because both sides were at the highest state of readiness for it in every way, and because I saw the whole Greek world joining one side or the other, some immediately, some planning to do so eventually. This was the greatest movement ever to sweep the Greeks and many of the barbarians—in other words, the majority of the human race. Because of the amount of time that has gone by, I have been unable to obtain accurate information about the period that preceded this war or about epochs in the still more distant past, but on the basis of the most reliable evidence I could find after the most painstaking examination, I do not consider those times to have been very important as far as either war or anything else is concerned. The reason is that what is now called Hellas does not seem to have been stably settled in the past; rather, migrations kept occurring and people learned to abandon their land easily after constantly being forced out by larger groups. There were no markets, and people could not traffic safely with each other by either land or sea. They occupied only as much territory as they needed to live on, and they neither cultivated the soil nor accumulated excess wealth, because they never knew when someone would attack their unwalled settlements and take away their land. Because they believed that they could satisfy their basic daily needs anywhere, they were able to pull up stakes and move away without difficulty, and as a result they never gained power through the strength of their cities or through their military might. The settlers always migrated through the best land: what is now called Thessaly, Boeotia, most of the Peloponnese except Arcadia, the most secure regions of other places. Communities were torn apart by civil strife because some men had grown more powerful than others through ownership of the best land, while at the same time foreigners plotted ways to take such land for themselves. Thus Attica enjoyed civil peace because of her thin topsoil and has kept her indigenous population from the beginning. This fact really proves my theory that the rest of Greece grew unevenly because of migrations: wealthy people uprooted from other parts of Hellas by war or civil strife moved to Athens for its security. They started becoming citizens from antiquity on and kept increasing the population of the city—so much so that the Athenians later sent colonists to Ionia because Attica was no longer big enough for its population.

---

†Book 1, chapters 1–23 and 89–118, and book 3, chapter 104, translated by Walter Blanco.

The weakness of the ancients is plain to me not least because Hellas does not appear to have accomplished anything through a concerted effort before the Trojan War. Indeed, it seems to me that the whole country was not even called by the name of Hellas. The appellation did not even exist before Hellen, son of Deucalion. Instead, each tribe gave its territory its own eponymous designation, with "Pelasgian" predominating. When Hellen and his sons came to power in Phthiotis and other cities called on him for help, they each came to be called Hellenic by association, though it took a long time for the name to win out over all of them. The best witness is Homer, because although he lived many years after the Trojan War, he nowhere calls all the Greeks "Hellenes"—only those who came from Phthiotis with Achilles, since they were the first Hellenes. He calls the others Danaans, Argives, and Achaeans in his epics. In my opinion, Homer did not even refer to "barbarians," because the Hellenes had not yet been differentiated from them under one name. Thus cities that spoke the same language, and that came, one by one, to be all later called Hellenic, accomplished nothing jointly before the Trojan War, because of weakness and lack of communication among themselves. Indeed, they were able to set out on this campaign together only because they had by now gained enough experience at sea.

We know through oral tradition that Minos was the earliest man to build a navy, that he controlled most of what is now the Greek Sea, and that he ruled over the Cyclades Islands and became the first colonizer of most of them after driving out the Carians and setting up his own sons in power.[1] It is likely that he rid the sea of piracy to the extent that he could in order to safeguard his maritime revenues. In the past the Greeks and the barbarians who either lived along the mainland coast or occupied islands turned to piracy as soon as they started crossing back and forth to one another in ships. These pirate ships were commanded by the most powerful men, as much for their own gain as to provide a livelihood for their poor. They would attack and plunder unwalled clusters of villages, and, for the most part, they made their livings in this way. This sort of work did not entail the slightest shame; on the contrary, it brought great renown, as is made clear by some mainlanders for whom piracy remains an honorable activity to this very day. Furthermore, when the ancient poets asked mariners sailing far and wide whether they were pirates, the men they asked would never disown their work, while those who did the asking would never reproach it.

They also raided each other on land, and even now this ancient system prevails over much of Greece around Ozolian Locris, Aetolia, Acarnania, and the rest of the mainland in that region.[2] Because of those

---

1. According to Greek tradition King Minos ruled at Cnossus, in Crete, during the distant past. It was this Minos who was reputed to have kept the half-human, half-bull Minotaur in the middle of a labyrinth.

2. Thucydides is referring here to regions in northwest Greece, north of the Peloponnese.

ancient raids, it has remained the practice of these mainlanders to carry weapons. Indeed, all Hellenes used to go armed because of their unfenced homesteads and the unsafe roads between them, and they made it their habit to live with their armor on, just like barbarians. The fact that people still carry weapons in that part of Greece is an indication that it used to be the practice everywhere.

The Athenians were the first to lay down their arms and to switch to a more relaxed and gracious way of life, and it has not been long since their wealthy old homosexuals stopped wearing linen underwear or doing up their hair in buns and fastening it with gold, cricket-shaped barrettes. Because of Ionia's kinship with Athens, even the older Ionians wore this outfit for a long time. The more moderate fashion of the present day was first adopted by the Lacedaemonians, and their rich people also adopted a way of life in other ways as much like that of the masses as possible. Their athletes were the first to work out naked, to undress openly and to rub their bodies with oil after exercise. In antiquity, athletes used to compete with supporters around their genitals even at the Olympic Games, and it has not been many years since they stopped doing so. Even now, there are some barbarians—especially Asians—who wear supporters during their boxing and wrestling matches. Indeed, there are many other ways in which one could show that the ancient Greeks led a life similar to that of the modern barbarians.

With increasing safety of navigation, new cities could be built right on the coast, using their growing surplus wealth to construct protective walls. Isthmuses were occupied, too, both for the sake of trade and as strong points against neighbors. Because of piracy, the old cities on both the islands and the mainland were built away from the sea since pirate states plundered not only one another but also low-lying nonmaritime towns. These inland cities remain inhabited to this day.

The islanders were no less piratical than the others. After all, they were Carians and Phoenicians, for those were the people who had settled the islands. (A proof of this is that when Delos was purified by the Athenians during the present war, and all the corpses on the island were taken out of their graves, over half of them were obviously Carians.[3] They could be recognized by the design of the armor that was buried along with them, and by the method of burial, which they still use.) The rise of Minos' navy, however, made navigation safer because he forced the criminal element out of most of the islands when he colonized them. Also, the people who lived on the coast lived more safely as they acquired more wealth, and some even used their evergrowing riches to throw walls up around themselves. In their desire for gain, the weaker cities put up with being subject to the stronger, while the stronger

3. On the purification of Delos see Herodotus 1. 64 and the selection from book 3 of Thucydides included below.

cities with surplus wealth won the weaker cities over to servitude. This was the state of Greek society when they later made war on Troy.

In my opinion, Agamemnon was able to raise that army not so much because the suitors of Helen were bound by their oath to Tyndareus as because he was the most powerful man of his time.[4] The Peloponnesians who remember the best traditions they received from their forebears say that Pelops, with his vast wealth, first came among their poverty-stricken people from Asia, and that after acquiring power he gave his name to the country even though he was an immigrant. Later his descendants became even more powerful when Eurystheus, because of their kinship, entrusted his maternal uncle Atreus with the government of Mycenae before going to war against Attica, where he was killed by the sons of Heracles. (It happened that Atreus had run away from his father because of the death of Chrysippus.) When Eurystheus never returned, the Mycenaeans came to dread the sons of Heracles, and Atreus, who was thought to be powerful and who had courted the Mycenaean masses, took over the kingship and the domains of the Mycenaeans with their consent, thus making the sons of Pelops more powerful than the sons of Perseus. Agamemnon inherited this kingdom, and commanded, as well, a more powerful navy than did other states; therefore, the army he gathered was, in my opinion, based less on goodwill than on fear. It is obvious that Agamemnon reached Troy with the greatest number of ships and that he outfitted the Arcadian ships as well. Homer makes this clear— if, that is, Homer is sufficient evidence. Also, in the scene in which Agamemnon receives the scepter, Homer says that he is "the lord of many islands and of all Argos." Now, as a mainlander, Agamemnon could not have controlled any but neighboring islands (and there are not many), unless he also had a substantial navy. We can also infer from Agamemnon's armada what those which preceded it must have been like.

The fact that Mycenae was small, or that none of the cities of that time is worth noticing by present-day standards, is not sure enough evidence to doubt that the expedition was as large as the poets say or as popular opinion maintains. If, for example, Sparta were to be deserted and only the temples and the foundations of the buildings remained, I imagine that people in the distant future would seriously doubt that Sparta's power ever approached its fame. Its power would appear to have been less because although the Spartans occupy two-fifths of the Peloponnese, and have hegemony over all of it as well as over many foreign allies, they never developed one metropolitan area or built lavish temples and buildings but rather live in scattered settlements in the old-fashioned Greek way. If the same thing were to happen to Athens, its power would

4. Tradition told that the competition to marry Helen was so intense that her suitors promised her father, Tyndareus, to come to her aid if anyone snatched her from the man who succeeded in becoming her husband.

be put at double what it is because of the visual impression it makes. It is not fair, therefore, to have doubts based on a study of the appearance of cities instead of on their power. If we can trust the poetry of Homer—which, considering that he was a poet, was probably exaggerated—we must conclude that the expedition against Troy was the greatest of any that had gone before it, though it does seem to have fallen short of those of the present day. Homer puts the number of ships at twelve hundred. The Boeotian ships have crews of one hundred and twenty men, and Philoctetes' ships have crews of fifty, thus marking, in my opinion, the largest and smallest contingents. At any rate, no other numbers are mentioned in the Catalog of Ships. Homer makes it clear through the description of Philoctetes' ships that all the crews served as both rowers and soldiers because he says that all of Philoctetes' rowers were also archers. It is unlikely that there were any passengers on board aside from the kings and their highest officers, especially in view of the fact that they were crossing the open sea with military equipment in ships without decks and outfitted like ancient pirate vessels. Taking the average of the largest and the smallest ships, therefore, and considering that it was a joint venture sent from all of Greece, it does not appear that many men went.

The reason was not so much lack of men as lack of money. Because of a shortage of supplies, the Greeks took a small army—one they hoped would be able to fight and live off the land. After they arrived and won some battles (as they clearly did; otherwise, they would not have been able to build a wall around their beachhead), they do not seem even then to have used all their forces. For want of food, some men were diverted to farming the Chersonese or to pillaging. This scattering of the Greek forces enabled the Trojans to withstand ten years of war because they were always a match for the men who were left behind. The Greeks would easily have taken Troy by force if they had arrived with surpluses of food and had continuously fought the war in full strength without having to resort to farming and pillaging. As it was, they held on with a fraction of their full force. They would, therefore, have captured Troy with less trouble and in less time if they had dug in and besieged the city in strength. Previous campaigns had been weak before this one for want of funds, and so, too, was this, even though it was the most famous of all. It is clear, though, that its deeds did not come up to its fame or to the now prevalent tradition about it which the poets have created.

Even after the Trojan War, Hellas continued to undergo migration and colonization, and thus lacked the tranquillity necessary for growth. The withdrawal of the Hellenes from Troy took a long time and resulted in political changes. In general, there were insurrections in the cities, thus creating exiles who founded yet other cities. The present-day Boeotians, for example, were forced out of Arne by the Thessalians sixty years after the fall of Troy and founded what is now Boeotia in the former Cadmeian territory. (There had already been a Boeotian subgroup in this territory, and some of them had gone off to fight in the Trojan War.) Furthermore, the Dorians, along with the Heraclids, captured the Peloponnese eighty years after the war. After a long time, and with great difficulty, Hellas achieved a secure peace and sent forth, not forced migrants any longer, but colonists. The Athenians settled Ionia and many of the islands while the Peloponnesians settled most of Italy and Sicily and places here and there in Hellas. All of these colonies were founded after the Trojan War.

As Hellas became more powerful and accumulated ever increasing quantities of wealth, tyrannies came to be established in most of the cities. (Formerly, there had been patrilineal kingships with specified prerogatives.) As revenues increased, Hellas began to outfit navies and to take increasingly to the sea. They say that the Corinthians came closest to conducting naval operations in the modern way, and it was in Corinth that the first Hellenic triremes were built. It seems that the Corinthian shipbuilder Ameinocles built four ships for the Samians, and Ameinocles went to Samos about three hundred years before the end of the present war. The oldest naval battle we know of was carried out against the Corcyraeans by the Corinthians, and this happened about two hundred and sixty years before the same date.

The Corinthians have had a commercial center from the time that they built their city in the Isthmus. In antiquity more business was conducted by land than by sea, and most Hellenes, both inside and outside the Peloponnese, had to travel through Corinthian territory to trade with one another. They became powerful through their wealth, as the ancient poets make clear: after all, their epithet for the place was "rich." As the Hellenes took more and more to the sea, the Corinthians built ships and rid the seas of piracy, and their markets brought economic power to the city through both maritime and overland revenue.

Later the Ionians also became an important naval power in the reign of Cyrus, first king of the Persians, and of his son Cambyses; and during their war with Cyrus, the Ionians gained control over their own territorial waters for a time. Polycrates, who was the tyrant in Samos in the time of Cambyses, used his fleet to conquer other islands and make them subject to him. He also captured Rhenea and dedicated it to the Delian Apollo. The Phocians also defeated the Carthaginians in a naval battle while founding Marseilles.

These, then, were the most powerful navies, and it seems that they were using few triremes many generations after the Troyan War, continuing to outfit penteconters and long boats just as in that conflict. Shortly before the Persian War and the death of Darius, who ruled Persia after Cambyses, triremes were used in strength by the tyrants in Sicily and by the Corcyraeans. These were the last fleets in Greece worth mentioning before the expedition of Xerxes. Aegina, Athens, and perhaps a few other states had paltry navies, made up mostly of penteconters. Later, when

Athens was at war with Aegina and in expectation of the barbarian invasion, Themistocles persuaded the Athenians to build the ships with which
they fought the Persians—and even these ships were not yet fully equipped
with decks.

That, then, is what the Greek navies were like, both those of antiquity
and those which developed later. Nevertheless, the states which turned
their energies to the sea were assured of power in the form of revenue
and of hegemony over others. Naval powers, and especially those which
did not have enough land for their own needs, would attack the islands
by sea and conquer them. As to land wars, there were none—none, that
is, which resulted in the acquisition of any power. Such wars as there
were were all against neighboring states: the Greeks did not send armies
very far from their own borders on wars of conquest. States did not grav-
itate toward greater powers as subjects, nor did they make equal contributions toward the creation of allied armies. Instead, neighboring cities
just made war on each other. It was only in the ancient war between the
Chalcidians and the Eretrians that the rest of Greece formed alliances
and took sides.

Different states met different obstacles to their growth. Thus, when
the affairs of Ionia were meeting with great success, Cyrus and the Persian empire overthrew Croesus, invaded the territory on this side of the
Halys River as far as the sea, and enslaved the cities on the mainland.
Later, with the help of the Phoenician navy, Darius even gained control
over the islands.

What tyrants there were in the Greek cities looked out only for themselves—for their own safety and for the growth of their personal households—and governed their cities to guarantee their own security as much
as possible. Nothing that was done by them is worth mentioning, except
for whatever they may have done for their neighbors. (The Sicilian tyrants
did, however, very greatly advance their power.) Thus a situation long
prevailed throughout Hellas in which they accomplished nothing
remarkable in common and in which individual cities were even more
timid.

The tyrannies which had long prevailed in Athens and even longer in
the rest of Greece were finally put down by the Spartans—all but those
in Sicily. (After it was occupied by the Dorians who now inhabit it,
Sparta experienced the longest period of turmoil we know of. Nevertheless, it has been both well governed and continuously without a tyrant
since antiquity. Reckoning from the end of the recent war, Sparta has
had the same form of government for somewhat more than four hundred
years, and this has given it the strength to put the affairs of other states
in order.) Not many years after the dissolution of the tyrannies in Greece,
the battle between the Greeks and the Persians at Marathon took place.
Ten years later the barbarian returned at the head of a large army with
the aim of enslaving Greece. With the gravest danger hanging over Greece,

the Spartans, as the foremost power, led the Greek alliance. Faced with a Persian attack, the Athenians decided to abandon their city. They packed off their possessions, boarded their ships, and became a naval power. They jointly repelled the barbarian, but not much later both the allies and the Greeks who revolted from the Persian king gravitated toward either the Athenians or the Spartans. These had proved themselves to be the most powerful states, the one on land and the other at sea. The alliance between the two lasted but a short time, whereupon the Athenians and the Spartans quarreled and, with their respective allies, made war on each other. Meanwhile, any Greek states which were at variance with one another took sides with either the Athenians or the Spartans. Thus, from the end of the Persian War to the beginning of this one, by always either making treaties or fighting with each other or with their own rebellious allies, they prepared their war machines and became more experienced as they conducted their military exercises in a climate of actual danger.

The Spartans led their allies without subjecting them to taxation. Instead, they set up puppet oligarchies so that the states would be governed in the interests of Sparta. Over time, the Athenians had taken over the navies of their allies (except those of Chios and Lesbos) and required all the city-states to pay taxes. Thus Athens and Sparta were individually at greater strength for this war than they had been at their peak as one undivided allied force during the Persian War.

This, then, is what I have been able to find out about the more remote past given the difficulty of trusting every bit of evidence. People, you see, unquestioningly accept the legends handed down by their forebears even when those legends relate to their own native history. Why, most Athenians even believe that Hipparchus was the dictator of Athens when he was assassinated by Harmodius and Aristogeiton. They do not know that Hippias, as the oldest, was the leader of the sons of Pisistratus (his brothers, Hipparchus and Thessalus) and that on the very day set for the assassination, Harmodius and Aristogeiton decided, on the spur of the moment, to refrain from killing Hippias because they suspected that they had been betrayed by their co-conspirators and that Hippias had advance knowledge of the plot. Nevertheless, Harmodius and Aristogeiton were determined to do something bold before they were captured, so they killed Hipparchus when they accidentally met him forming up the procession for the Panathenaic festival at what is known as the temple of the Daughters of Leos.

Other Greeks, indeed, even have inaccurate opinions about many contemporary facts, facts not lost in the passage of time, such as that the kings of Sparta cast two votes apiece instead of one apiece or that they command the "Pitanate Battalion," when there never was such a thing. Thus most people expend very little effort on the search for truth, and prefer to turn to ready-made answers.

Nevertheless, one will not go wrong if he believes that the facts were such as I have related them, based on the evidence, and not as they are sung by the poets—who embellish and exaggerate them—or as they are strung together by popular historians with a view to making them not more truthful but more attractive to their audiences; and considering that we are dealing with ancient history, whose unverified events have, over the course of time, made their way into the incredible realms of mythology, one will find that these conclusions, derived as they are from the best known evidence, are accurate enough. Even though people always think that the war they are fighting is the greatest there ever was, and then return to marveling at ancient wars once theirs have ended, it will be clear, after we examine the events themselves, that this war actually was the greatest there has ever been.

As to the statements the participants made, either when they were about to enter the war or after they were already in it, it has been difficult for me and for those who reported to me to remember exactly what was said. I have, therefore, written what I thought the speakers must have said given the situations they were in, while keeping as close as possible to the consensus about what was actually said. As to the events of the war, I have not written them down as I heard them from just anybody, nor as I thought they must have occurred, but have consistently described what I myself saw or have been able to learn from others after going over each event in as much detail as possible. I have found this task to be extremely difficult, since those who were present at these actions gave varying reports on the same event, depending on their sympathies and their memories.

My narrative, perhaps, will seem less pleasing to some listeners because it lacks an element of fiction. Those, however, who want to see things clearly as they were, and, given human nature, as they will one day be again, more or less, may find this book a useful basis for judgment. My work was composed not as a prizewinning exercise in elocution but as a possession for all time.

The Persian War was the greatest event of the past. Nevertheless, it was quickly decided by two battles on land and two at sea. In contrast, the recent war was of great duration and brought such suffering to Greece as had never before been seen in an equal amount of time. Never before had so many cities been abandoned to be captured either by the barbarians or by other hostile Greeks, and, in some cases, to be resettled by new inhabitants. Never before had there been so many refugees and so much killing, some brought about by the war itself and some by civil strife. Ancient events which were better established in legend than in experience now seemed less incredible, such as violent earthquakes spread through most of the world, eclipses of the sun, which now occurred much more frequently than ever before in memory, terrible regional droughts and the famines they caused, and, last but not least, plagues, which caused great harm and great loss of life. All of these things were associated with this war.

The Athenians and the Peloponnesians began the war after breaking the thirty-year truce they had made after the capture of Euboea. I have begun by describing the differences between the two sides and their pretexts for breaking the truce so that no one will have to look very far to understand why a war of this magnitude broke out among the Greeks. I believe, however, that the truest explanation for the war is that Sparta was forced into it because of her apprehensions over the growing power of Athens—although this explanation is least obvious from the statements that were made. The following, however, are the openly avowed reasons why they broke the truce and entered into a state of war.

* * *

This is how the Athenians achieved the conditions which made their growth possible. The Persians had withdrawn from Europe, their infantry and their navy defeated by the Greeks, and the escaping remnant of their fleet destroyed at Mycale. Leotychides, the king of Sparta and the man who had led the Greeks at Mycale, returned home with his Peloponnesian allies. Meanwhile, the Athenians and their allies from Ionia and the Hellespont who had rebelled against the Persian king stayed behind to besiege Sestos, which was still in Persian hands. They maintained the siege through the winter, captured the city after the barbarians abandoned it, and then sailed away from the Hellespont to their respective cities. Once the barbarians had left their land, the men of Athens immediately brought their wives, children, and remaining possessions back from their hiding places and prepared to rebuild their city and its wall. Only short stretches of wall were still standing, and most of the houses had collapsed; the few that survived were those in which the Persian commanders had been quartered.

When the Spartans learned of what was happening, they sent a delegation to Athens, as much because they would have been most pleased to see neither the Athenians nor anyone else with a walled city as because they had been egged on by allies frightened over the size of the Athenian navy, which had not existed in the past, and over the audacity the Athenians had shown in the Persian War. The Spartans advised the Athenians not to build the wall and to join them in demolishing whatever walls there were in other cities. They did not disclose the thinking or the suspicions behind this option to the Athenians, but rather said that if the barbarians should come again they would not have a stronghold from which to operate, as they had just had in Thebes. The Spartans said, in addition, that the whole Peloponnese was military base and shelter enough. On the advice of Themistocles, the Athenians dismissed the Spartans who delivered this message right after responding that they would dispatch ambassadors to Sparta to discuss the matter. Themistocles then urged the Athenians to send him off to Sparta and then to select other ambassadors besides himself whom they should not send immediately but should hold back until the wall was just high enough to fight from. Meanwhile, the whole population of the city—men, women, and children—should work on the wall, sparing neither private nor public buildings which might be of use. Everything should be torn down for the project. After leaving these instructions and explaining that he would take care of things in Sparta, Themistocles set off. When he reached Sparta, he did not go directly to the magistrates but found excuses for delay; and whenever one of the authorities asked him why he did not go before the assembly, he said that he was waiting for his fellow ambassadors, who had been left behind on important business. He was expecting them to arrive any minute, however, and was astonished that they were not yet there.

At first, the Spartans believed Themistocles out of their high regard for him, but it became impossible for them to doubt others who came with detailed allegations that the wall was being built and that it was already quite high. When Themistocles became aware of this, he urged the Spartans not to be influenced by hearsay but to send some reliable men of their own to study the situation and return with a trustworthy report. The Spartans dispatched such men, but Themistocles sent a secret message ordering the Athenians to detain them discreetly and not to release them until he and the others returned. (You see, his fellow ambassadors, Abronichus, son of Lysicles, and Aristides, son of Lysimachus, had arrived by now.) They had brought the message that the wall was high enough, and Themistocles feared that the Spartans would not let them go once they heard the news. As ordered, the Athenians detained the envoys, and Themistocles went before the Spartans and openly declared that his city had been walled sufficiently to protect its inhabitants. If the Spartans or their allies wanted to consult with them, he said, it would be, from now on, with people who would know how to distinguish their own interests from those of the alliance. The Athenians had known what to do without their allies when the time had come for them boldly to abandon their city and take to their ships, and when, later, they had deliberated with those allies, their opinion proved to be second to none. In their view, then, it was now best for their city to be fortified with a wall: it would be an advantage for the individual citizens of Athens as well as for all of the allies, since it was not possible for Athens to participate in joint deliberations on any other than the same footing as everyone else. He said that either everyone in the alliance should have an unfortified city or acknowledge that the situation in Athens was fair.

When the Spartans heard this, they showed no open anger toward the Athenians—after all, they said, they had sent their ambassadors to the Athenian assembly merely to express an opinion, not to keep the wall from going up; and besides, they felt an especial friendship toward Athens because of her zeal in fighting the Persian foe. Nevertheless, the

Spartans were secretly vexed over the failure of their policy. The envoys from both sides returned home without formal charges being made against them.

In this way, the Athenians built a wall around their city in a very short time. And even now it is quite clear that the wall was hastily built. The foundation is made of different kinds of stones, unsquared here and there and laid down as they came to hand. Many gravestones and bits of sculpture were also built into the wall. The circumference of the wall everywhere exceeded the size of the city, so they put everything they could move to use. Themistocles also persuaded them to build up the rest of the Piraeus, something he had already begun during his year as chief magistrate of Athens. He thought that the location was suitable, with its three natural harbors, and that if they became a maritime nation the harbor would contribute greatly to the growth of their power. He had been, after all, the first man bold enough to say that the Athenians must take to the sea, and with the construction of the Piraeus he prepared the way for the Athenian empire.

The thickness of the wall was made according to his plan, and is visible to this day around the Piraeus. Two wagons abreast carried stones atop it. It was held together by neither mortar nor mud; instead huge hewn stones were fitted together and secured on the outside by iron and lead clamps. The height of the wall was only half what Themistocles had intended. He had wanted the sheer height and width of the wall to deter the battle plans of Athens' enemies, and he believed that a few of the least combat-worthy men would be enough to guard the wall while the rest would man the ships. In my opinion, he inclined so much toward naval power because he saw that the Persian king's attack force could make its approach more easily by sea than by land. He also believed the Piraeus to be more valuable than the upper city, and he frequently urged the Athenians to go down to it if they were ever attacked by land and to take on all comers in their ships.

In this way, then, the Athenians built themselves a wall and made other preparations immediately after the retreat of the Persians.

Soon afterward, Pausanias, son of Cleombrotus, was dispatched from Sparta with twenty ships in command of the Greek forces. The Athenians accompanied him with thirty ships of their own and with a large number of ships from the other allies. They attacked Cyprus and conquered most of it. Later, still under the command of Pausanias, they attacked and besieged Byzantium, which was held by the Persians.

Pausanias had already grown excessively authoritarian. The Greeks were irked by him, especially the Ionians and others who had recently liberated themselves from the king. They approached the Athenians with the view that Athens should become their leader on the basis of their kinship, and that they should not allow Pausanias to hold on to command by force. The Athenians accepted their arguments. The Athenians took the position that they would no longer overlook the high-handedness of Pausanias, and they arranged things in a way which seemed best suited to their own interests. Under the circumstances, the Spartans recalled Pausanias for questioning about the news they had been hearing. He had been accused of all sorts of wrongdoing by Greeks who had come to Sparta, and he seemed to be imitating the ways of a tyrant more than those of a general. Furthermore, at the same time as his recall, the allies, with the exception of the Peloponnesian soldiers, went over to the Athenians out of hatred for him. When Pausanias arrived in Sparta, he was held accountable for any private wrongdoing he had committed toward individuals but was acquitted of the most serious charges, not least of which was the accusation of collaborating with the Persians, for which there seemed to be a clear-cut case. It was, however, no longer he who was sent out as a commander but Dorcis and others with a small force, although the allies no longer acknowledged their supremacy. They left when they found that this was so, and the Spartans did not dispatch any other forces later, for fear that they would become as corrupt as they had seen Pausanias to be. Sparta withdrew, instead, from the war with Persia in the belief that the Athenians were capable of leading the fight and that they were, at that time, loyal to Sparta.

After the Athenians had taken over the command in this way, and with the consent of allies who had hated Pausanias, they determined which cities should contribute money and which should contribute ships to fight the barbarians. The Athenian plan was to make up for what they had suffered by plundering the king's territory. Athens also appointed Greek treasurers for the first time. They were the ones who received the "revenue," which was the name given to the tribute. The allies were at first required to yield revenues of four hundred and sixty talents. Delos served as the Greek treasury, and the treasurers met in the temple.

At first, the Athenians led independent allies who engaged in joint deliberations. What follows is what they accomplished in the administration of their alliance and in warfare between the Persian War and the present war with respect to the barbarians, to their own rebellious allies, and to Peloponnesians, who were constantly involved in each and every situation. I have recorded these events and included this digression because this subject has been omitted in all previous histories, which narrated either the events that occurred before the Persian War or the events of the Persian War itself—although Hellanicus does touch on the subject in his history of Attica, albeit sketchily and with inaccurate dates. He also includes a discussion of how the Athenian empire was established.

First, with Cimon, son of Miltiades, in command, the Athenians besieged, captured, and enslaved Eion-on-Strymon, which was in the hands of the Persians. Then they enslaved and colonized the Aegean island of Scyros, which was inhabited by Dolopians. In addition, a war broke out between the Athenians and the Carystians, though not with the other Euboeans, which was eventually resolved through negotiations. Next, they made war on the rebellious Naxians and set up a siege. This was the first allied city to be enslaved in violation of the terms of the alliance. It later happened to the other cities, for one reason or another.

The main causes of rebellion included shortfalls in tribute and ship production, and, in some cases, refusal to serve in the army. The Athenians were strict taskmasters and dealt harshly with those who did not wish or did not intend to put up with them as they pressed their demands. For various reasons, then, Athenian leadership was no longer as agreeable as it had once been, but since they did not campaign with equal numbers of allies it was easy for them to reduce rebel cities to subjection. The allies themselves were to blame for this. Because most of them did not want to be away from home, they were reluctant to serve in the armed forces; so instead of supplying ships and crews, they supplied enough money to defray the cost of the ships. The money they contributed thus went to increase the Athenian navy, while they rendered themselves inexperienced and unprepared for warfare in the event of rebellion.

Next, there was a land and sea battle at the Eurymedon River in Pamphylia between the Athenians and their allies and the Persians. The Athenians, with Cimon, son of Miltiades, in command, won both battles on the same day, capturing or destroying up to two hundred Phoenician triremes. Later the Thasians rebelled against them, disagreeing about the markets on the opposite shore in Thrace and about the mine they owned. The Athenians brought a fleet against the Thasians, defeated them in a naval battle, and went ashore. At about the same time, the Athenians sent ten thousand of their own and their allies' colonists to the Strymon River to colonize what was then known as the Nine Roads, although it is now called Amphipolis. They gained control of the Nine Roads, which had been held by the Edonians, and then, after advancing into the interior of Thrace, they were destroyed at Edonian Drabescus by a combined force of Thracians who considered the colonization of the territory to be an act of war.

Defeated in battle and under siege, the Thasians called on the Spartans to help by invading Attica. Unbeknownst to the Athenians, the Spartans agreed and were about to invade when they were deterred by an earthquake, after which the Helots and the neighboring Thuriatae and Aethaeae rebelled and took Ithome. Most of the Helots were the descendants of the ancient Messenians, who had been enslaved. For this reason, they were all called Messenians. Because the Spartans were preoccupied with the war against the rebels in Ithome, the Thasians came to terms with the Athenians in the third year of the siege. They agreed to tear down their wall and surrender their ships. They raised the money they owed and paid it immediately, and agreed to pay their share in the future. They also gave up their claim to the mainland and to the mine.

Because the war at Ithome dragged on, the Lacedaemonians called on their allies, including the Athenians, for help. The Athenians came, with a not inconsiderable force, under the command of Cimon. The Athenians were called in because they were thought to be especially skilled at siege warfare, and the Lacedaemonians had clearly shown their inability to conduct long sieges. Otherwise, they would have taken the place by storm. This campaign led to the first open breach between the Spartans and the Athenians. When the place could not be taken by storm, the Spartans grew afraid that the bold, revolutionary character of the Athenians would lead them, if they remained, to fall under the influence of the rebels in Ithome and to promote reforms. The Spartans also looked upon the Athenians as outsiders. They therefore dismissed the Athenians, and only the Athenians, though without disclosing their suspicions. The Spartans said, instead, that they did not need their help any longer. The Athenians knew this was not the real reason they were being dismissed—that it was because of some distrust or other—and took great offense, feeling that they did not deserve to suffer this indignity at the hands of the Lacedaemonians. As soon as they returned to Athens, they broke their existing alliance with Sparta against Persia and made an alliance with Sparta's enemies, the Argives. At the same time, the Athenians and Argives became bound by the same oaths of alliance to the Thessalians.

In the tenth year, the rebels in Ithome were unable to hold out any longer, so they came to an agreement with the Spartans by which they would leave the Peloponnese under a truce and never return to it again. If anyone was captured doing so, he would become the slave of his captor. (The Spartans had, incidentally, received an oracle from Delphi before the agreement commanding them to release "the suppliant of Ithomian Zeus.") The rebels left with their women and children, and the Athenians accepted them out of what was by now their hostility toward the Spartans. They sent them to colonize Naupactus, which they had recently captured from the Ozolian Locrians. The Megarians also approached the Athenians about an alliance after revolting from the Spartans because the Corinthians were making war against them over a border dispute. The Athenians accepted Megara and Pegae in alliance and built the Megarians a long wall, which they themselves garrisoned, from the city to Nisaea. This was the beginning of the intense hatred of the Corinthians toward the Athenians.

Inaros, son of Psammetichus, a Libyan and king of the Libyans who bordered on Egypt, set out from the town of Marea, south of the city of Pharos, and incited most of Egypt to rebel against King Artaxerxes. After taking power, he asked the Athenians for help. They and their allies happened to be campaigning in Cyprus with two hundred ships. They abandoned Cyprus and, sailing up the Nile from the sea, gained control of the river as well as of two-thirds of the province of Memphis. They attacked the last third, the so-called White Wall, where Persians and Medes had taken refuge along with Egyptians who had not gone along with the rebellion.

The Athenians launched an amphibious assault on the Corinthians and Epidaurians at Halieis. The Corinthians won the battle. Later the Athenians engaged in a sea battle with Peloponnesian ships off Cecryphalia, which the Athenians won. After war broke out between the Athenians and the Aeginetans, there was a large naval battle between the two sides off Aegina, in which the allies of both sides took part. The Athenians won the battle, capturing sixty ships, and then, under the command of Leocrates, son of Stroebus, went ashore to besiege the city. The Peloponnesians, wanting to assist the Aeginetans, landed on Aegina with three hundred hoplites who had previously been serving with the Corinthians and Epidaurians. The Corinthians took the heights at Geraneia and then descended into the Megarid with their allies in the belief that the Athenians would be unable to help the Megarians while so much of their army was away in Aegina and Egypt; if they did help, they would have to withdraw from Aegina. The Athenians did not, however, move the army attacking Aegina. Instead, their oldest and youngest men, who had been left behind in the city, went to Megara under the command of Myronides. They fought the Corinthians to a standstill before the two sides separated from each other, and both sides felt that they did not have the least of the fight. The Athenians, who had in fact had the better of it, set up a trophy after the Corinthians had left. About twelve days later, after suffering insults from the elders of the city, the Corinthians made their preparations and went forth to set up a victory trophy of their own. The Athenians then forayed out from Megara, killed the men who were setting up the trophy, and defeated their companions in battle. The beaten Corinthians retreated, and a large contingent of them, harassed by the enemy, lost their way and wandered into some private property which was surrounded by a large ditch and from which there was no escape. When the Athenians realized this, they blocked off the front of the area with their hoplites and then, stationing lightly armed troops around the ditch, stoned to death all the Corinthians who had fallen into it. The Corinthians suffered a terrible loss, but most of their army made its way back home.

At about this time, the Athenians began to build their long walls down to the sea—one to Phalerum and one to Piraeus. The Phocians also attacked Doris, the homeland of the Spartans. It contained the towns of Boeum, Citinium, and Erineum, and after the Phocians had captured one of them the Spartans came to the assistance of the Dorians with fifteen hundred of their own hoplites and ten thousand belonging to their allies. Nicomedes, son of Cleombrotus, was in command because King Pleistoanax, son of Pausanias, was still a minor. After forcing the Phocians to agree to return the city, the Spartans began to withdraw. Athenian ships, however, patrolled the Crisaean Gulf and would stop them should they try to cross the sea. Meanwhile, it did not seem safe to pass through Geraneia, since the Athenians held Megara and Pegae. The road through Geraneia was rough, in any case, and constantly guarded by the Athenians, and the Spartans had learned that the Athenians intended to stop them from taking it this time. They decided, therefore, to stay in Boeotia and to consider the best way to return home. Some Athenians, meanwhile, had been secretly urging them to adopt this course in hopes of tearing down both the Athenian democracy and the long walls. The Athenians then attacked the Spartans in full strength along with one thousand Argives and contingents from their other allies. There were fourteen thousand men in all. They attacked then, both because they believed the Spartans had no way out and because they suspected the plot to undo the Athenian democracy. In keeping with the terms of the alliance, a troop of Thessalian cavalry came with the Athenians, but they deserted to the Spartans in the heat of battle.

The battle took place in Tanagra, in Boeotia. The Spartans and their allies won, with great carnage on both sides. The Spartans next went into Megara, destroyed its crops, and returned home via Geraneia and the Isthmus. Sixty-two days after the battle, the Athenians, with Myronides in command, marched into Boeotia. In a battle at Oenophytas, they defeated the Boeotians and gained control of Boeotia and Phocis. They tore down the fortifications at Tanagra and took hostage one hundred of the richest Opuntian Locrians. Later the Athenians finished building their own long walls. After this the Aeginetans made a treaty with the Athenians whereby they would tear down their walls, surrender their ships, and pay tribute in the future. Also, under the command of Tolmides, son of Tolmaeus, the Athenians sailed around the Peloponnese, burned the Spartan shipyard, captured the Corinthian town of Chalcis, and defeated the Sicyonians after an amphibious assault.

The Athenians and their allies remained in Egypt and saw many kinds of warfare. At first the Athenians controlled Egypt, and the king sent Megabazus the Persian to Sparta with money in hopes of bribing them to invade Attica so as to draw Athenian troops out of Egypt. Since the plan met with no success, and since the money was being spent to no purpose, Megabazus made his way back to Asia with what was left of the money and the king sent another Persian, Megabuzus, son of Zopyrus, to Egypt with a large army. He traveled overland, defeated the Egyptians and their allies in battle, drove the Greeks out of Memphis, and ended up by isolating them on Prosopitis Island, where he besieged them for eighteen months. During that time, Megabuzus diverted the water from the channels around the island and dried them up. After turning the island into mainland for the most part and causing the Greek ships to rest on dry land, he crossed the channel and took the island on foot.

Thus the Greek expedition to Egypt was undone after six years of fighting. A few of the many men who took part in it made their way through Libya to Cyrene and were saved; but most were killed. Egypt reverted to the king of Persia, except for the marsh country, which was ruled by King Amyrtaeus. It was not possible to capture him, because of the extent of the marshes, and besides, the marsh dwellers are the most combative of the Egyptians. Inarus, king of Libya, who was responsible for everything that had happened in Egypt, was impaled on a stake after being betrayed and abandoned. Meanwhile, fifty Athenian and other allied triremes sailed into Egypt in squadrons through the Mendesian mouth of the Nile without knowing anything about what had happened.

They were attacked by land-based troops and by a Phoenician fleet sailing up from the sea, and most of the ships were destroyed, though a few were able to escape. This, then, was how the great expedition of Athens and her allies against Egypt came to an end.

After fleeing Thessaly, Orestes, son of King Echecrates of Thessaly, persuaded the Athenians to put him on the throne. The Athenians enlisted the help of their Boeotian and Phocian allies and attacked Pharsalus, in Thessaly. Though they were able to control the countryside, the Thessalian cavalry prevented them from venturing very far from their camp. They were not, however, able to capture the city or to achieve any of the objectives for which they had launched the expedition. They returned, unsuccessful, with Orestes. Not much later, one thousand Athenians took ship in Pegae (which they now controlled) and sailed along the coast to Sicyon under the command of Pericles, son of Xanthippus. After landing, they defeated the defending Sicyonians in battle. They then immediately picked up the Achaeans and sailed across to Acarnania, where they attacked and besieged Oeniadae. They did not capture it, however, and returned home.

After an interval of three years, the Peloponnesians and the Athenians agreed to a five-year truce. The Athenians, barred from a Hellenic war, attacked Cyprus with two hundred of their own and their allies' ships under the command of Cimon. At the request of Amyrtaeus, king of the marsh country, sixty of the ships sailed to Egypt. The rest besieged Citium. After Cimon died and they ran out of food, the fleet withdrew from Citium, and, as they were sailing off Cyprian Salamis they fought battles on land and sea against Phoenicians, Cyprians, and Cilicians. After winning both battles, the Athenians returned home along with the ships which had come back from Egypt. After this, the Spartans fought the so-called holy war. They gained control of the temple at Delphi and turned it over to the Delphians. Immediately after their withdrawal, however, the Athenians attacked and captured the temple and turned it back over to the Phocians.

Some time after this, with Boeotian exiles holding Orchomenus, Chaeronea, and other areas of Boeotia, the Athenians, under the command of Tolmides, son of Tolmaeus, attacked the enemy territory with one thousand of their own hoplites and with some of the allied forces. They captured Chaeronea, enslaved the population, and withdrew after leaving a detachment to guard the place. Then, as they were passing through Coronea, they were attacked by the Boeotian exiles from Orchomenus along with exiles from Euboea, with Locrians, and with anyone else who shared their ideology. These forces defeated the Athenians in battle, killing many and taking many others alive. After making a treaty whereby they got their men back, the Athenians abandoned the whole of Boeotia. The exiled Boeotians returned to power, and all the other states regained their independence.

Not much later, Euboea revolted from Athens. Then Pericles, who had already gone to Euboea with an army, received a message from Athens saying that Megara had also rebelled, that the Peloponnesians were about to invade Attica, and that, except for those who had been able to escape to Nisaea, the Athenian garrisons had been wiped out by the Megarians. In carrying out their rebellion, the Megarians had enlisted the aid of the Corinthians, Sicyonians, and Epidaurians. Pericles withdrew his army from Euboea on the double. After this, the Peloponnesians attacked and plundered Attica up to Eleusis and Thria under the command of the Spartan king Pleistoanax, son of Pausanias. They returned home without penetrating farther. Then the Athenians again crossed over to Euboea under the command of Pericles and subdued all of it. The Athenians settled matters with the Euboeans by treaty, except for driving the Hestiaeans out of their homeland and occupying it themselves.

Not long after they withdrew from Euboea, they made a thirty-year truce with the Lacedaemonians and their allies, by which they returned Nisaea, Pegae, Troezen, and Achaea, all of which they had captured from the Peloponnesians.

In the sixth year of the truce, war broke out between the Samians and Milesians over Priene. When the Milesians were defeated in the war, they went to Athens to denounce the Samians. They were joined along the way by some private citizens from Samos itself who wanted to reform their constitution. The Athenians then sent forty ships to Samos and set up a democracy. They also took hostage fifty Samian boys and an equal number of men and deposited them on Lemnos. They stationed a garrison on Samos and left. There were some Samians, however, who would not abide by the democracy and who fled to the mainland. They had formed an alliance with some of the most powerful people on Samos, as well as with Pissuthnes, son of Hystaspes, who held Sardis at that time. The exiles assembled seven hundred mercenaries and crossed over to Samos by night. They first attacked the democrats, detained most of them, and rescued the hostages from Lemnos. They then gave the Athenian guards and their officers to Pissuthnes and immediately prepared to attack Miletus. The Byzantians, incidentally, revolted along with the Samians from Athens.

When the Athenians learned of this, they sent sixty ships to Samos. They did not actually use sixteen of the ships, some of which had gone to Caria to reconnoiter the Phoenician fleet, while some had gone to Chios and Lesbos to call on them for help; but with the forty-four remaining ships, and with Pericles in command and at the head of nine other officers, they engaged seventy Samian ships returning from Miletus, of which twenty were troop ships, and defeated them in battle off the island of Tragia. They were later reinforced by forty ships from Athens and by twenty-five from Chios and Lesbos. They then landed their troops on Samos, where they defeated the infantry and built three walls with which to besiege the city, while at the same time the ships blockaded the island by sea.

Pericles then detached sixty ships from their moorings and hurriedly sailed to Caunus and Caria after receiving news that a Phoenician fleet was about to attack them. What had happened was that Stesagoras and others had left Samos with five ships to call in the Phoenicians.

Under the circumstances, the Samians quickly sailed out to the attack. They fell on the undefended beachhead, destroyed the sentry ships, defeated any vessels that opposed them in battle, and controlled their own waters for over fourteen days, going and coming at will. When Pericles returned, he again blockaded them with his ships. His fleet was also later reinforced from Athens by forty ships commanded by Thucydides, Hagnon, and Phormio, as well as by twenty under the command of Tlepolemus and Anticles, and another thirty from Chios and Lesbos. The Samians put up a brief struggle at sea, but they were unable to hold out against the siege and surrendered nine months later on terms dictated by Athens. They agreed to tear down their city wall, give hostages, surrender their fleet, and pay war reparations to Athens over the course of time. The Byzantians also agreed to return to their former subject status.

Not many years after the foregoing, the events in Corcyra and Potidaea provided the immediate causes for the present war. All the above-mentioned actions which the Greeks took against each other and the barbarians occurred in the fifty years between the retreat of Xerxes and the beginning of the present war. During this time, the Athenians increasingly strengthened their empire and greatly enlarged their power. The Spartans realized this, but made only sporadic efforts to hinder them. They held their peace for most of those years since even before this time they had not been quick to go to war unless they were forced to; and besides, they were prevented from intervening by local wars. But now the power of Athens had risen to an unmistakable height and had begun to impinge on Sparta's allies. The strength of Athens then became unendurable to them, and having decided that they must try to suppress it, if they could, with all their might, they started this war.

*   *   *

In the following selection—book 3, chapter 104—Thucydides shows that for him, as for Herodotus, Homer is a source to be taken seriously even though neither historian accepts the testimony of Homer without question.

That same winter the Athenians also purified Delos because of some oracle or other. Even the tyrant Pisistratus had earlier purified the island—not all of it, but as much of it as could be seen from the temple. This time, though, the whole island was purified in the following way: the Athenians carried away all of the tombs of the dead in Delos and proclaimed that, from now on, people could neither die nor be born on the island but must be taken over to Rhenea. (Rhenea is so close to Delos that when Polycrates, the tyrant of Samos, had a temporary naval superiority and ruled over the other islands, he captured Rhenea and dedicated it to the Delian Apollo by attaching it to Delos with a chain.) After the purification, the Athenians held the first Delian festival, thereafter to be held every five years. At some time in the past, there was a great deal of travel to Delos by the Ionians and the neighboring islanders. They went to see the spectacle with their wives and children, just as the Ionians do now at the festival of Ephesus. Both gymnastic and musical competitions were held, and the city-states organized choruses. Homer makes it clear that this was so in these verses from the Hymn to Apollo:

> But when your heart was most delighted, Apollo, in Delos,
> There where the long-robed Ionians gathered
> With their wives and children on your streets,
> There, commemorating you with boxing, dance, and song,
> They gave you delight whenever they set up their games.

In the same hymn, Homer also makes it clear that contestants frequented the musical competitions, for, after celebrating the Delian women's dance, he ends his panegyric with these verses, in which he also mentions himself:

> So then, girls, farewell to you all, and Apollo be gracious,
> And Artemis, too. Think of me, though, from time to time,
> Whenever some other long-suffering mortal
> Arrives hereabouts and asks,
> "Girls, which of the singers who frequents these parts
> Is sweetest to you, the one you delighted in the most?"
> Let every one of you then answer politely,
> "A blind man, but he lives in rocky Chios."

In this way, Homer bears witness that there was a large gathering and festival in Delos. Later the islanders and the Athenians sent choruses along with animal offerings, although in all likelihood most of the pageantry surrounding the competitions was abandoned because of changing fortunes before the Athenians ever set up their games, including horse races, which there had not been before.

*   *   *

ARISTOTLE

A pupil at Plato's Academy for nearly twenty years, Aristotle (384–322) was born in northern Greece and lived much of his adult life at Athens. His philosophical works have established him as powerful influence in Western thought. In addition to many volumes on biology, metaphysics, and rhetoric, he also produced a tremendously influential work in political theory, the *Politics*. He probably gleaned much of his information about Greek tyranny from his reading of Herodotus, who wrote about many of the tyrants Aristotle mentions, and whose style Aristotle discusses in his *Rhetoric*. Herodotus' discussion of the best kind of state in book 3 is a prototype which Aristotle develops with greater sophistication in the *Politics*.

Politics †

Tyrannies preserve themselves in two opposing ways. The most time-honored method is the one by which most tyrants have consolidated their rule. It is said that most of its techniques were developed by Periander of Corinth, although many could have been learned from the administration of the Persian empire. First, there is the method I have already referred to for preserving tyrannies (insofar as this is possible), and that is to discourage anyone from distinguishing himself in any way and to destroy all independence of spirit. There must be no mess halls, clubs, classes, or anything else of that kind. The tyrant must, instead, be on guard against whatever promotes two things: independent thinking and trust. He must allow his people neither free time nor any of the associations that free time makes possible. He must do everything he can to create a situation in which everyone is unknown to everyone else, because, more than anything, familiarity creates trust between people.

Those who live in his city must always be out in the open, passing their time near his gates, because in this way their actions will least escape detection and they will get into the habit of constantly being slaves to petty concerns. These and other Persian and barbarian practices are tyrannical and all lead to the same end. The tyrant must try to be aware of whatever any of his subjects is saying or doing. There must be spies wherever people gather and talk to one another, like the so-called "busybodies" of Syracuse or the "eavesdroppers" that Hieron used to send out. People speak less freely for fear of such spies, and if they do speak freely, they are less likely to escape detection. The tyrant encourages people to inform on one another and pits friend against friend, the common people against the elite, the rich against each other.

One practice is to put the people to work so as to support the tyrant's personal army and to make sure that no one has any free time in which to form conspiracies. Examples of this sort of thing are the Egyptian pyramids, the sacred offerings of the Cypselid family, the construction of the temple of Olympian Zeus by the Pisistratid family, and Polycrates' public works projects in Samos. (All of these things lead to the same result, which is to keep the people busy and poor.) Then there are taxes,

---

†Column 1313a, line 34, to column 1314a, line 14, translated by Walter Blanco.

like those in Syracuse, where, under Dionysius, the value of all the wealth in the city was collected within five years.

The tyrant is also a warmonger, both to keep his people occupied and to make sure that they are always in need of a leader. Furthermore, while a king keeps himself on the throne with the help of his friends, the tyrant trusts his friends least of all since they all have ambitions and are more able than others to achieve them.

What is true of radical democracies is also true of tyrannies. Women are given the run of their houses so that they can inform against the men, and the laws governing slaves are relaxed for the same reason. Neither women nor slaves tend to plot against tyrants, and they will be well inclined toward both tyranny and democracy for so long as they are kept happy. After all, the people also want to be the supreme ruler. The flatterer is appreciated in both kinds of society. In democracies he is a demagogue, for the demagogue is the flatterer of the people, and in tyrannies, it is those who practice self-abasing familiarity, which is the function of flattery. As a result, tyrants love contemptible people: they enjoy being flattered, and no one with an independent mind would do it. Able people prefer other things to engaging in flattery, while contemptible people are good for contemptible things. "Birds of a feather," as the saying goes. The tyrant never appreciates anything dignified or free, because he thinks that he himself is the only one who is fit for these things. Whoever has a dignity and freedom of his own deprives tyrants of their despotic pride, and they hate him as they would hate a threat to their government. The tyrant prefers to dine and keep company with foreigners, because the citizens are hostile while the foreigners pose no threat.

These and others like them are the practices and means of preserving tyrannies, and they are wicked in every way.

PLUTARCH

Plutarch, who lived from ca. A.D. 50 to ca. A.D. 120, spent most of his life in his native Chaeronea, in northern Boeotia. He traveled to Athens, Egypt, and Rome and spent the last thirty years of his life as a priest at Delphi. He is best known for his lives of famous Greeks and Romans and for his "moral essays," which profoundly influenced many European writers, most notably Montaigne, Shakespeare, and Rousseau. In this essay, Plutarch raises the question, discussed on and off throughout the history of commentary on Herodotus, whether Herodotus was the father of history or the father of lies. As a Boeotian, Plutarch was particularly aggrieved at Herodotus for his disparaging view of Boeotia's relationship with Persia, but Plutarch's touchiness about his native region is only a part of his indictment of what he considers to be Herodotus' prettily written collection of prejudices, distortions, and lies. One irony is that the well-traveled, cosmopolitan Plutarch criticized Herodotus for his sympathy toward foreigners, denouncing him as a "philobarbaros," or a "barbarian-lover." Plutarch's views are more Eurocentric and Herodotus' more global.

On the Malice of Herodotus †

The simple and easy style of Herodotus, moving, as it does, so effortlessly from one subject to another, has deceived many people, but even more have been deceived as to his character. Plato says that the ultimate injustice is to seem to be just when you are not, but it is also the ultimate malice to go undetected in the pretense of good-natured simplicity. This is especially true of Herodotus, who fawns on some with outrageous flattery while traducing and denigrating others. So far, no one has dared to expose his lies, especially the ones he tells about the Boeotians and the Corinthians, though no one is spared. I think, then, that it falls to me to uphold both the truth and the reputation of my ancestors in those sections of his narrative.[1] It would take many scrolls of papyrus for someone to go through all his other lies and distortions. "Persuasion has a scary face," as Sophocles says, especially when the power and charm of its arguments enable a writer to conceal his character and the absurdity of what he has to say. Philip used to say to the Greeks who revolted from him and gave their allegiance to Titus that they were merely changing one collar for another that was softer but more long-lasting.[2] The malice of Herodotus is surely smoother and softer than that of Theopompus,[3] but it is tighter and really hurts more, just as hidden drafts that seep through cracks are more harmful than the open air.

I think, though, that it would be better for me to list the general headings under which we can find the signs and tokens of what is sound and sincere as opposed to what is malicious in a narrative. We can then place each and every passage we examine wherever it fits.

First, there is the historian who uses the harshest words and phrases in his narrative when more moderate ones are available. For example, instead of saying that Nicias[4] had an excessive propensity toward superstition, he would call him "a religious fanatic," and instead of saying that Cleon spoke without thinking, he would call him a "hothead" and a "lunatic." This is not fair play, just the historian's pleasure in hearing himself tell his story.[5]

---

† Translated by Walter Blanco.

1. Plutarch, who was from Boeotia (of which Thebes was the principal city) thought that Herodotus was unfair to Boeotia in his history.
2. The Greek states were freed from Philip V of Macedon by the Roman army of Titus Quinctius Flaminius in 197 B.C.
3. Theopompus of Chios, born ca. 378 B.C., con-

tinued the history of Thucydides from 411 B.C. onward.
4. Nicias (ca. 470–413 B.C.) was a deeply religious, moderate Athenian politician and general.
5. Cleon, who died in 422 B.C., was a popular Athenian politician attacked by Thucydides and Aristophanes as a demagogue.

Second, it is obvious that a historian enjoys slander when he latches onto people's faults and unnecessarily inserts them into his history even though they do not belong there, protracting the narrative and digressing from it so as to include their bad luck or their pointless and foolish actions. For this reason, Thucydides never gave a detailed account of even Cleon's crimes, though there were many, and dismissed Hyperbolus the demagogue by calling him a "rascal."[6] In addition, Philistus left out all the crimes of Dionysius against the barbarians which could not be woven into the history of events in Greece. The digressions and meanderings in Philistus' history are mostly devoted to myths and legends, or to praising his characters.[7] The historian who writes parentheses of abuse and censure would seem liable to the tragic curse on those who "recount the miseries of mortal men."

The opposite of this, clearly, is the omission of what is good and noble. It would seem that this practice cannot be criticized, but it is in fact malicious if what is left out has a proper place in the history. It is not kinder to give fainthearted praise than to enjoy finding fault: it may even be worse than unkind.

I suggest that the fourth indication of a historian's bias is his adoption of the worst version of events when two or more versions of the same story are available. Professors may at times make an exercise of taking up the lesser of two arguments and prettifying it. They are not, however, attempting to create any firm belief in the argument, and they would usually admit that they are trying to give an unexpected twist to dubious ideas. The real historian, however, says what he knows to be true and, when the facts are unknown, says that the better version appears to be true and not the worse one. Many historians leave out the worse version altogether. * * *

* * *

One could list even more such characteristics, but these are enough to give an idea of Herodotus' aims and methods.

He begins his narrative at his own doorstep, with Io, the daughter of Inachus. All Greeks consider her to have been elevated to the status of a goddess by the barbarians and to have given her name to many seas and straits because of her fame.[8] She is also thought to have been the source and spring of the most illustrious of the royal families. And yet our worthy Herodotus says that she gave herself up to some Phoenician merchantmen because she had been willingly seduced by their captain

---

6. Hyperbolus was a demagogic Athenian politician who died in 411 B.C.
7. Philistus of Syracuse lived from ca. 430 to 356 B.C. and wrote the history of Sicily in thirteen books. Plutarch probably refers to Dionysius I, who was a powerful, active tyrant of Syracuse and who lived from ca. 430 to 367 B.C.

8. The Ionian Sea and the Bosporus were thought to have been named for Io, a young girl beloved by Zeus and later turned into a heifer. Io was identified with the cow goddess Isis; hence Plutarch's comment on her status as a goddess among the barbarians. See Aeschylus, *Prometheus*, lines 640–87.

and was afraid her pregnancy would be detected! Furthermore, he falsely accuses the Phoenicians of telling this story about her. Then, after asserting that Persian scholars corroborate the story that Io and some other women were carried off by the Phoenicians, he goes on to disclose his opinion that the Trojan War, the greatest and noblest feat of Hellas, was an act of folly undertaken for a worthless woman, "because it is obvious," he says, "that women could not be raped if they did not want to be."[9] He would have to say, then, that the gods are foolish when they are furious with the Spartans after the rape of the daughters of Leuctra, or when they punish Ajax for the rape of Cassandra, because it is obvious, as Herodotus says, that those women would not have been raped if they had not wanted to be.[1] And yet he himself says that Aristomenes was carried off alive by the Spartans.[2] Later the same thing happened to the Achaean general Philopoemen, and the Carthaginians captured Regulus, the Roman consul. It would be a hard job to find braver soldiers than those men.[3] There is nothing surprising about this, since people even capture live leopards and tigers, and yet Herodotus censures these violated women and makes excuses for their abductors.

Herodotus is also so pro-barbarian that he acquits Busiris of his alleged human sacrifice and murder of strangers, and in bearing witness to the piety and justice of all Egyptians he turns the charges of this filthy slaughter back on the Greeks.[4] He says in his second book that Menelaus reclaimed Helen from Proteus and that he became the vilest and most unjust of men after having been honored with the greatest gifts. When Menelaus was prevented from sailing by adverse winds, "he came up with an unholy solution. He seized two native children and cut them up as sacrificial victims. He became hated for this and fled to Libya in his ships, with the Egyptians in pursuit." I do not know what Egyptian told Herodotus this story, but it is contradicted by the many honors still paid by the Egyptians to Helen and Menelaus.[5]

Our historian persists in this sort of thing when he says that the Persians learned from the Greeks to have sex with boys.[6] Yet how could the Persians have taken lessons from the Greeks in this kind of debauchery when almost everybody agrees that the Persians castrated boys long before they ever saw the Greek sea? Herodotus says that the Greeks learned about parades and festivals from the Egyptians and that they also learned

9. Plutarch misunderstands this passage. Herodotus makes a point of giving this as the opinion of the Persians, not as his own. See book 1, chapter 4.
1. This refers to the story of some girls from Leuctra (a town in Boeotia) who committed suicide after being raped by a group of Spartans. Ajax the Lesser (not the more famous Ajax, son of Telamon) raped Cassandra at the altar during the sack of Troy.
2. Herodotus does not mention Aristomenes, who led the Messenians in their war with Sparta.

3. Philopoemen was in Achaean soldier and statesman who lived from ca. 253 to 182 B.C. Marcus Atilius Regulus was captured by the Carthaginians during the First Punic War.
4. Herodotus, without mentioning Busiris, relates this story in book 2, chapter 45.
5. Herodotus discussed this episode in book 2, chapters 119ff. There is no evidence that the Egyptians honored Helen and Menelaus.
6. See book 1, chapter 135.

to worship the twelve gods from them. He says that Melampus learned the name of Dionysus from the Egyptians and then taught it to the Greeks, and that the mystery rites of Demeter were brought out of Egypt by the daughters of Danaus. He tells us that the Egyptians beat themselves in grief, but refuses to name the god they mourn for, because he wants to keep silent about religious matters. Yet he never shows this kind of restraint when he discloses that the Egyptians worship Heracles and Dionysus as ancient gods while the Greeks worshiped them as men who could sink into their dotage. He goes on to say that the Egyptian Heracles belongs to the second generation of gods and Dionysus to the third, so that they were not eternal but had a beginning to their existence. Nevertheless, he does claim that they are gods, while he believes that we should make offerings to the Greek Heracles and Dionysus as mortals and heroes and not sacrifice to them as gods. He says the same kinds of things about Pan, thus overturning the most solemn and sacred beliefs of Greek religion with Egyptian fairy tales and nonsense.[7]

And this is not the worst of it. . . . Herodotus uses Solon to mask his own abuse of the gods when he makes him say, "Croesus, when you ask me about the affairs of men you are asking someone who knows how utterly jealous and disruptive the gods are." By attributing his own views of the gods to Solon, Herodotus adds blasphemy to his malice.

* * *

* * * As to the four battles that were fought with the barbarians at that time, Herodotus says that the Greeks ran away at Artemisium and that the Spartans stayed at home to celebrate the Olympic and Carneian festivals, indifferent to the fact that its army and its king were in jeopardy at Thermopylae.[8] In his account of Salamis, he writes at greater length about Artemisia than about the whole naval battle.[9] Finally, he says that the Greeks sat idle at Plataea, knowing nothing about the battle until it ended. . . . As to the Spartans, he says that their courage was no greater than that of the barbarians, who lost because they were lightly armed and fought without shields. Thus when Xerxes himself was present at a battle, the Persian soldiers could barely be made to attack the Greeks by being driven forward with whips. At Plataea, on the other hand, it seems that they had a change of heart, for they "were not inferior to the Greeks in courage and strength," though "what hurt them most was their outfits, which were lacking in any sort of armor: they were lightly armed troops doing battle with armored men."[1]

Is there any greatness or glory left for the Greeks in these battles, if the Spartans fought with unprotected soldiers, and if their allies did not even know that a battle was going on nearby?

7. These are all references to book 2 of Herodotus.
8. See book 7, chapter 206.

9. See book 8, chapters 68–104.
1. See book 8, chapters 62 and 63.

* * * What do we make of all this then? The man is an artist. The story is a pleasure to read. There is charm, vigor, and beauty in his narrative, but he "tells his tale like a poet," not with understanding, in this case, but mellifluously and with a honeyed tongue.[2] His book attracts and beguiles everyone, but like the beetle in the rose, blasphemy and slander lie beneath his smooth, delicate surface, and we must beware of unconsciously accepting his false and absurd ideas about the greatest and noblest cities and men of Greece.

2. Plutarch quotes from Homer, *Odyssey*, 11.368.

COMMENTARIES

Early Modern Criticism

DAVID HUME

In this selection, the Scottish philosopher and historian David Hume (1711–1776) discusses the kinds of difficulties oral historians face in evaluating the testimony of their informants when it seems to conflict with common sense and with what is known about the laws of nature and probability. Although Herodotus is not mentioned here, this passage is a reasoned exposition of the principles Herodotus intuited in the presentation of testimony he did not believe. To Herodotus, however, what Hume says was not explicit and self-evident, and Herodotus did not necessarily make Hume's assumption about human nature. Still, Herodotus did accelerate the process of dislodging fact from fable and thus helped to establish precisely the rationalist approach to testimony by which he himself was, paradoxically, later judged and found wanting.

The world was more miraculous to Herodotus than to Hume, but Herodotus did not unquestioningly accept the stories about all the wonders he was told. He reported them, as he tells us, but he did not believe them all. We include this passage from Hume because most modern readers will probably approach Herodotus from Hume's standpoint. The reader would do well to bear in mind that Herodotus' history is one of the first texts in a tradition to which Hume belonged.

Of Miracles †

* * *

* * * We may observe, that there is no species of reasoning more common, more useful, and even necessary to human life, than that which is derived from the testimony of men, and the reports of eye-witnesses and spectators. This species of reasoning, perhaps, one may deny to be founded on the relation of cause and effect. I shall not dispute about a word. It will be sufficient to observe that our assurance in any argument of this kind is derived from no other principle than our observation of the veracity of human testimony, and of the usual conformity of facts to the reports of witnesses. It being a general maxim, that no objects have

†From An Enquiry Concerning Human Understanding (1748), sec. 10, pt. 1, cited from The Philosophical Works of David Hume, vol. 4 (Boston and Edinburgh, 1854), pp. 126–32.

any discoverable connexion together, and that all the inferences, which we can draw from one to another, are founded merely on our experience of their constant and regular conjunction; it is evident, that we ought not to make an exception to this maxim in favour of human testimony, whose connexion with any event seems, in itself, as little necessary as any other. Were not the memory tenacious to a certain degree, had not men commonly an inclination to truth and a principle of probity; were they not sensible to shame, when detected in a falsehood: Were not these, I say, discovered by *experience* to be qualities, inherent in human nature, we should never repose the least confidence in human testimony. A man delirious, or noted for falsehood and villainy, has no manner of authority with us.

And as the evidence, derived from witnesses and human testimony, is founded on past experience, so it varies with the experience, and is regarded either as a *proof* or a *probability*, according as the conjunction between any particular kind of report and any kind of object has been found to be constant or variable. There are a number of circumstances to be taken into consideration in all judgements of this kind; and the ultimate standard, by which we determine all disputes, that may arise concerning them, is always derived from experience and observation. Where this experience is not entirely uniform on any side, it is attended with an unavoidable contrariety in our judgments, and with the same opposition and mutual destruction of argument as in every other kind of evidence. We frequently hesitate concerning the reports of others. We balance the opposite circumstances, which cause any doubt or uncertainty; and when we discover a superiority on any side, we incline to it; but still with a diminution of assurance, in proportion to the force of its antagonist.

This contrariety of evidence, in the present case, may be derived from several different causes; from the opposition of contrary testimony; from the character or number of the witnesses; from the manner of their delivering their testimony; or from the union of all these circumstances. We entertain a suspicion concerning any matter of fact, when the witnesses contradict each other; when they are but few, or of a doubtful character; when they have an interest in what they affirm; when they deliver their testimony with hesitation, or on the contrary, with too violent asseverations. There are many other particulars of the same kind, which may diminish or destroy the force of any argument, derived from human testimony.

Suppose, for instance, that the fact, which the testimony endeavours to establish, partakes of the extraordinary and the marvelous; in that case, the evidence, resulting from the testimony, admits of a diminution, greater or less, in proportion as the fact is more or less unusual. The reason why we place any credit in witnesses and historians, is not derived from any *connexion*, which we perceive *a priori*, between testimony and reality, but because we are accustomed to find a conformity between them. But when the fact attested is such a one as has seldom fallen under our observation, here is a contest of two opposite experiences; of which the one destroys the other, as far as its force goes, and the superior can only operate on the mind by the force, which remains. The very same principle of experience, which gives us a certain degree of assurance in the testimony of witnesses, gives us also, in this case, another degree of assurance against the fact, which they endeavour to establish; from which contradiction there necessarily arises a counter-poize, and mutual destruction of belief and authority.

I should not believe such a story were it told me by Cato, was a proverbial saying in Rome, even during the lifetime of that philosophical patriot.[1] The incredibility of a fact, it was allowed, might invalidate so great an authority.

The Indian prince, who refused to believe the first relations concerning the effects of frost, reasoned justly; and it naturally required very strong testimony to engage his assent to facts, that arose from a state of nature, with which he was unacquainted, and which bore so little analogy to those events, of which he had had constant and uniform experience. Though they were not contrary to his experience, they were not conformable to it.

But in order to encrease the probability against the testimony of witnesses, let us suppose, that the fact, which they affirm, instead of being only marvellous, is really miraculous; and suppose also, that the testimony considered apart and in itself, amounts to an entire proof; in that case, there is proof against proof, of which the strongest must prevail, but still with a diminution of its force, in proportion to that of its antagonist.

A miracle is a violation of the laws of nature; and as a firm and unalterable experience has established these laws, the proof against a miracle, from the very nature of the fact, is as entire as any argument from experience can possibly be imagined. Why is it more than probable, that all men must die; that lead cannot, of itself, remain suspended in the air; that fire consumes wood, and is extinguished by water; unless it be, that these events are found agreeable to the laws of nature, and there is required a violation of these laws, or in other words, a miracle to prevent them? Nothing is esteemed a miracle, if it ever happen in the common course of nature. It is no miracle that a man seemingly in good health, should die on a sudden: because such a kind of death, though more unusual than any other, has yet been frequently observed to happen. But it is a miracle, that a dead man should come to life; because that has never been observed in any age or country. There must, therefore, be a uniform experience against every miraculous event, otherwise the

---

1. Probably Marcus Porcius Cato, sometimes referred to as Cato the Censor, and Cato the Elder, lived from 234 to 149 B.C. He was a stern moralist who upheld Roman ideals of courage and honor and hated what he regarded as modern licentiousness.

event would not merit that appellation. And as a uniform experience amounts to a proof, there is here a direct and full *proof*, from the nature of the fact, against the existence of any miracle; nor can such a proof be destroyed, or the miracle rendered credible, but by an opposite proof, which is superior.

The plain consequence is (and it is a general maxim worthy of our attention), "That no testimony is sufficient to establish a miracle, unless the testimony be of such a kind, that its falsehood would be more miraculous, than the fact, which it endeavours to establish; and even in that case there is a mutual destruction of arguments, and the superior only gives us an assurance suitable to that degree of force, which remains, after deducting the inferior." When anyone tells me, that he saw a dead man restored to life, I immediately consider with myself, whether it be more probable, that this person should either deceive or be deceived, or that the fact, which he relates, should really have happened. I weigh the one miracle against the other; and according to the superiority, which I discover, I pronounce my decision, and always reject the greater miracle. If the falsehood of his testimony would be more miraculous, than the event which he relates; then, and not till then, can he pretend to command my belief or opinion.

Because of the cultural achievements of the Greeks and their contributions to the history of republican institutions, Western thinkers have frequently speculated how different history might have been had the Greeks failed to turn back the Persian invasions. The British utilitarian philosopher and man of letters John Stuart Mill (1806–1873) offers a secular interpretation of the impact of the Greek victory in his review of George Grote's pro-democratic *History of Greece*. Mill's contemporary Isaac Taylor (1787–1865) provides a religious one in the introduction to his translation of Herodotus.

ISAAC TAYLOR

[The Consequences of the Greek Victory for Western Civilization: A Christian View]†

* * *

More than once within the limits of authentic history, and once even in our own times, there has stood in opposition on the field of war, on the one side the enslaved myriads of a brutal despotism, and on the other, the champions of intelligence and liberty: and the chance of battle— rather should we say the disposing hand of Him who rules among the

† From the preface to *Herodotus*, translated by Isaac Taylor (London, 1829), p. xiv.

nations, has in an hour determined the fate of mankind for many succeeding ages. On these memorable occasions, if lawless ambition had
triumphed, the spark of mind must have been extinguished, and the
germ of improvement destroyed. Such a crisis for the human family was
brought to its issue in the fields of Plataea and in the straits of Salamis.
There the light of knowledge, the splendors of art, and the substantial
benefits of freedom, were preserved from threatening destruction for the
advantage of all succeeding times. It may even be added that, although
the divine wisdom might doubtless have found other means of accomplishing its designs, yet was it in fact by the preservation of the independence of Greece, when almost crushed beneath the Asiatic hordes, that
the western world was held in preparation for the diffusion of Christianity.

*   *   *

JOHN STUART MILL

[The Consequences of the Greek Victory for Western Civilization: A Secular View]†

The interest of Grecian history is unexhausted and inexhaustible. As a
mere story, hardly any other portion of authentic history can compete
with it. Its characters, its situations, the very march of its incidents, are
epic. It is an heroic poem, of which the personages are peoples. It is
also, of all histories of which we know so much, the most abounding in
consequences to us who now live. The true ancestors of the European
nations (it has been well said) are not those from whose blood they are
sprung, but those from whom they derive the richest portion of their
inheritance. The battle of Marathon, even as an event in English history, is more important than the battle of Hastings. If the issue of that
day had been different, the Britons and the Saxons might still have been
wandering in the woods.

The Greeks are also the most remarkable people who have yet existed.
Not, indeed, if by this be meant those who have approached nearest (if
such an expression may be used where all are at so immeasurable a
distance) to the perfection of social arrangements, or of human character. Their institutions, their way of life, even that which is their greatest
distinction, the cast of their sentiments and development of their faculties, were radically inferior to the best (we wish it could be said to the
collective) products of modern civilization. It is not the results achieved,
but the powers and efforts required to make the achievement, that measure their greatness as a people. They were the beginners of nearly every-

† From a review of the first volume of George   84 (Oct. 1846): 343.
Grote's *History of Greece*, in the *Edinburgh Review*

thing, Christianity excepted, of which the modern world makes its boast. If in several things they were but few removes from barbarism, they alone among nations, so far as is known to us, emerged from barbarism by their own efforts, not following in the track of any more advanced people. If with them, as in all antiquity, slavery existed as an institution, they were not the less the originators of political freedom, and the grand exemplars and sources of it to modern Europe.

THOMAS BABINGTON MACAULAY

Commentary on Herodotus comprises a spectrum of opinion in which he appears at one end a charming but simpleminded teller of delightful tales and at the other an astute observer of individuals and societies, the first writer to attempt a synthesis of the multifold facts and events of his world. Thomas Babington Macaulay (1800–1859) inclines more to the former than to the latter opinion, but the modern historian who saw the history of England as a series of stages on the way to the triumph of liberal principles can appreciate the ancient historian who saw the Persian Wars as a triumph of republican institutions over Persian autocracy. The two historians also implicitly or explicitly accept the idea that the best history presents not only the facts but a worldview with which to interpret them.

[The Purpose and Method of History] †

To write History respectably—that is, to abbreviate dispatches, and make extracts from speeches, to intersperse in due proportion epithets of praise and abhorrence, to draw up antithetical characters of great men, setting forth how many contradictory virtues and vices they united, and abounding in *withs* and *withouts*; all this is very easy. But to be a really great historian is perhaps the rarest of intellectual distinctions. Many Scientific works are, in their kind, absolutely perfect. There are Poems which we should be inclined to designate as faultless, or as disfigured only by blemishes which pass unnoticed in the general blaze of excellence. There are Speeches, some speeches of Demosthenes particularly, in which it would be impossible to alter a word without altering it for the worse. But we are acquainted with no History which approaches to our notion of what a history ought to be—with no history which does not widely depart, either on the right hand or on the left, from the exact line.

The cause may easily be assigned. This province of literature is a debateable land. It lies on the confines of two distinct territories. It is under the jurisdiction of two hostile powers; and, like other districts similarly situated, it is ill-defined, ill cultivated, and ill regulated. Instead of being equally shared between its two rulers, the Reason and the Imagi-

† Excerpted from the *Edinburgh Review* 32 (1828): 331–40.

nation, it falls alternately under the sole and absolute dominion of each. It is sometimes fiction. It is sometimes theory.

History, it has been said, is philosophy teaching by examples. Unhappily what the philosophy gains in soundness and depth, the examples generally lose in vividness. A perfect historian must possess an imagination sufficiently powerful to make his narrative affecting and picturesque. Yet he must control it so absolutely as to content himself with the materials which he finds, and to refrain from supplying deficiencies by additions of his own. He must be a profound and ingenious reasoner. Yet he must possess sufficient self-command to abstain from casting his facts in the mould of his hypothesis. Those who can justly estimate these almost insuperable difficulties will not think it strange that every writer should have failed, either in the narrative or in the speculative department of history.

It may be laid down as a general rule, though subject to considerable qualifications and exceptions, that history begins in Novel and ends in Essay. Of the romantic historians Herodotus is the earliest and the best. His animation, his simple-hearted tenderness, his wonderful talent for description and dialogue, and the pure sweet flow of his language, place him at the head of narrators. He reminds us of a delightful child. There is a grace beyond the reach of affectation in his awkwardness, a malice in his innocence, an intelligence in his nonsense, an insinuating eloquence in his lisp. We know of no writer who makes such interest for himself and his book in the heart of the reader. * * * He has written an incomparable book. He has written something better perhaps than the best history; but he has not written a good history; he is, from the first to the last chapter, an inventor. We do not here refer merely to those gross fictions with which he has been reproached by the critics of later times. We speak of that colouring which is equally diffused over his whole narrative, and which perpetually leaves the most sagacious reader in doubt what to reject and what to receive. The most authentic parts of his works bear the same relation to his wildest legends, which Henry the Fifth bears to the Tempest. * * * Shakspeare gives us enumerations of armies, and returns of killed and wounded; which are not, we suspect, much less accurate than those of Herodotus. There are passages in Herodotus nearly as long as acts of Shakespeare, in which everything is told dramatically, and in which the narrative serves only the purpose of stage-directions. It is possible, no doubt, that the substance of some real conversations may have been reported to the historian. But events which, if they ever happened, happened in ages and nations so remote that the particulars could never have been known to him, are related with the greatest minuteness of detail. We have all that Candaules said to Gyges, and all that passed between Astyages and Harpagus. We are, therefore, unable to judge whether, in the account which he gives of transactions respecting which he might possibly have been well informed, we can trust to anything beyond the naked outline; whether, for example, the * * * expressions which passed between Aristides and Themistocles at their famous interview, have been correctly transmitted to us. The great events are, no doubt, faithfully related. So, probably, are many of the slighter circumstances; but which of them it is impossible to ascertain. The fictions are so much like the facts, and the facts so much like the fictions, that, with respect to many most interesting particulars, our belief is neither given nor withheld, but remains in an uneasy and interminable state of abeyance. We know that there is truth, but we cannot exactly decide where it lies.

The faults of Herodotus are the faults of a simple and imaginative mind. Children and servants are remarkably Herodotean in their style of narration. They tell everything dramatically, Their *says hes* and *says shes* are proverbial. Every person who has had to settle their disputes knows that, even when they have no intention to deceive, their reports of conversation always require to be carefully sifted. If an educated man were giving an account of the late change of administration, he would say—"Lord Goderich resigned; and the King, in consequence, sent for the Duke of Wellington." A porter tells the story as if he had been hid behind the curtains of the royal bed at Windsor: "So Lord Goderich says, 'I cannot manage this business; I must go out.' "So the King says,—says he, 'Well, then, I must send for the Duke of Wellington—that's all.' " This is in the very manner of the father of history.

Herodotus wrote as it was natural that he should write. He wrote for a nation susceptible, curious, lively, insatiably desirous of novelty and excitement; for a nation in which the fine arts had attained their highest excellence, but in which philosophy was still in its infancy. His countrymen had but recently begun to cultivate prose composition. Public transactions had generally been recorded in verse. The first historians might, therefore, indulge without fear of censure, in the license allowed to their predecessors the bards. Books were few. The events of former times were learned from tradition and from popular ballads; the manners of foreign countries from the reports of travellers. It is well known that the mystery which overhangs what is distant, either in space or time, frequently prevents us from censuring as unnatural what we perceive to be impossible. We stare at a dragoon, who has killed three French cuirassiers, as a prodigy; yet we read, without the least disgust, how Godfrey slew his thousands, and Rinaldo his ten thousands.[1] Within the last hundred years, stories about China and Bantam, which ought not to have imposed on an old nurse, were gravely laid down as foundations of political theories by eminent philosophers. What the time of the Crusades is to us, the generation of Crœsus and Solon was to the Greeks of the time of Herodotus: Babylon was to them what Pekin was to the French academicians of the last century.

1. Godfrey of Bouillon (ca. 1058–1100) was a Crusader who became ruler of Jerusalem in 1099. His exploits were memorialized in medieval epics. Rinaldo was a chivalric hero who appears in the epics of Ariosto, Tasso, and others.

* * *

Between the time at which Herodotus is said to have composed his history, and the close of the Peloponnesian war, about forty years elapsed,—forty years, crowded with great military and political events. The circumstances of that period produced a great effect on the Grecian character; and nowhere was this effect so remarkable as in the illustrious democracy of Athens. An Athenian, indeed, even in the time of Herodotus, would scarcely have written a book so romantic and garrulous as that of Herodotus. As civilization advanced, the citizens of that famous republic became still less visionary, and still less simple-hearted. They aspired to know, where their ancestors had been content to doubt; they began to doubt, where their ancestors had thought it their duty to believe. Aristophanes is fond of alluding to this change in the temper of his countrymen. The father and son, in the Clouds, are evidently representatives of the generations to which they respectively belonged. Nothing more clearly illustrates the nature of this moral revolution, than the change which passed upon tragedy. The wild sublimity of Æschylus became the scoff of every young Phidippides.[2] Lectures on abstruse points of philosophy, the fine distinctions of casuistry, and the dazzling fence of rhetoric, were substituted for poetry. The language lost something of that infantine sweetness which had characterised it. It became less like the ancient Tuscan, and more like the modern French.

The fashionable logic of the Greeks was, indeed, far from strict. Logic never can be strict where books are scarce, and where information is conveyed orally. We are all aware how frequently fallacies, which, when set down on paper, are at once detected, pass for unanswerable arguments when dexterously and volubly urged in Parliament, at the bar, or in private conversation. The reason is evident. We cannot inspect them closely enough to perceive their inaccuracy. We cannot readily compare them with each other. We lose sight of one part of the subject, before another, which ought to be received in connexion with it, comes before us; and as there is no immutable record of what has been admitted, and of what has been denied, direct contradictions pass muster with little difficulty. Almost all the education of a Greek consisted in talking and listening. His opinions on government were picked up in the debates of the assembly. If he wished to study metaphysics, instead of shutting himself up with a book, he walked down to the marketplace to look for a sophist. So completely were men formed to these habits, that even writing acquired a conversational air. The philosophers adopted the form of dialogue, as the most natural mode of communicating knowledge. Their reasonings have the merits and the defects which belong to that species of composition; and are characterised rather by quickness and subtilty,

---

2. Phidippides is a young wastrel in Aristophanes' *Clouds*, produced in 423 B.C.

than by depth and precision. Truth is exhibited in parts, and by glimpses. Innumerable clever hints are given; but no sound and durable system is erected. The *argumentum ad hominem*, a kind of argument most efficacious in debate, but utterly useless for the investigation of general principles, is among their favourite resources. Hence, though nothing can be more admirable than the skill which Socrates displays in the conversations which Plato has reported or invented, his victories, for the most part, seem to us unprofitable. A trophy is set up; but no new province is added to the dominions of the human mind.

Still, where thousands of keen and ready intellects were constantly employed in speculating on the qualities of actions, and on the principles of government, it was impossible that history should retain its old character. It became less gossiping and less picturesque; but much more accurate, and somewhat more scientific.

The history of Thucydides differs from that of Herodotus as a portrait differs from the representation of an imaginary scene; * * * In the former case, the archetype is given: in the latter, it is created. The faculties which are required for the latter purpose are of a higher and rarer order than those which suffice for the former, and indeed necessarily comprise them. He who is able to paint what he sees with the eye of the mind, will surely be able to paint what he sees with the eye of the body. He who can invent a story, and tell it well, will also be able to tell, in an interesting manner, a story which he has not invented. If in practice, some of the best writers of fiction have been among the worst writers of history, it has been because one of their talents had merged in another so completely, that it could not be severed; because, having long been habituated to invent and narrate at the same time, they found it impossible to narrate without inventing.

Some capricious and discontented artists have affected to consider portrait-painting as unworthy of a man of genius. Some critics have spoken in the same contemptuous manner of history. Johnson puts the case thus: The historian tells either what is false or what is true. In the former case he is no historian. In the latter, he has no opportunity for displaying his abilities. For truth is one: and all who tell the truth must tell it alike.

It is not difficult to elude both the horns of this dilemma. We will recur to the analogous art of portrait-painting. Any man with eyes and hands may be taught to take a likeness. The process, up to a certain point, is merely mechanical. If this were all, a man of talents might justly despise the occupation. But we could mention portraits which are resemblances,—but not mere resemblances; faithful,—but much more than faithful; portraits which condense into one point of time, and exhibit, at a single glance, the whole history of turbid and eventful lives—in which the eye seems to scrutinize us, and the mouth to command us—in which the brow menaces, and the lip almost quivers with scorn—in which every wrinkle is a comment on some important transaction. The account which Thucydides has given of the retreat from Syracuse, is, among narratives, what Vandyk's Lord Strafford is among paintings.[3]

Diversity, it is said, implies error: truth is one, and admits of no degrees. We answer, that this principle holds good only in abstract reasonings. When we talk of the truth of imitation in the fine arts, we mean an imperfect and a graduated truth. No picture is exactly like the original: nor is a picture good in proportion as it is like the original. * * * The same may be said of history. Perfectly and absolutely true it cannot be: for to be perfectly and absolutely true, it ought to record *all* the slightest particulars of the slightest transactions—all the things done, and all the words uttered, during the time of which it treats. The omission of any circumstance, however insignificant, would be a defect. If history were written thus, the Bodleian library would not contain the occurrences of a week. What is told in the fullest and most accurate annals bears an infinitely small proportion to what is suppressed. The difference between the copious work of Clarendon, and the account of the civil wars in the abridgement of Goldsmith, vanishes, when compared with the immense mass of facts, respecting which both are equally silent.[4]

No picture, then, and no history, can present us with the whole truth: but those are the best pictures and the best historians which exhibit such parts of the truth as most nearly produce the effect of the whole. He who is deficient in the art of selection may, by showing nothing but the truth, produce all the effect of the grossest falsehood. It perpetually happens that one writer tells less truth than another, merely because he tells more truths. In the imitative arts we constantly see this. There are lines in the human face, and objects in landscape, which stand in such relations to each other, that they ought either to be all introduced into a painting together, or all omitted together. A sketch into which none of them enters, may be excellent; but if some are given and others left out, though there are more points of likeness, there is less likeness. An outline scrawled with a pen, which seizes the marked features of a countenance, will give a much stronger idea of it than a bad painting in oils. Yet the worst painting in oils that ever hung at Somerset House resembles the original in many more particulars. A burst of white marble may give an excellent idea of a blooming face. Colour the lips and cheeks of the bust, leaving the hair and eyes unaltered, and the similarity, instead of being more striking, will be less so.

History has its foreground and its background: and it is principally in the management of its perspective, that one artist differs from another.

---

3. Thomas Wentworth, first earl of Strafford (b. 1593), an English statesman and soldier, was a ruthless and despotic lord deputy of Ireland from 1623 to 1640 and was beheaded in 1641. Sir Anthony Van Dyck (1599–1641) was a Flemish painter best known for his portraits of aristocrats.

4. Edward Hyde, first earl of Clarendon (1609–1674), an English statesman and historian, was author of the *History of the Rebellion*, a history of the English civil war. Oliver Goldsmith (1730–1774) was an Anglo-Irish writer, author of *She Stoops to Conquer* and *The Vicar of Wakefield*.

Some events must be represented on a large scale, others diminished; the great majority will be lost in the dimness of the horizon; and a general idea of their joint effect will be given by a few slight touches.

In this respect, no writer has ever equalled Thucydides. He was a perfect master of the art of gradual diminution. His history is sometimes as concise as a chronological chart; yet it is always perspicuous. * * *

Thucydides borrowed from Herodotus the practice of putting speeches of his own into the mouths of his characters. In Herodotus this usage is scarcely censurable. It is of a piece with his whole manner. But it is altogether incongruous in the work of his successor, and violates, not only the accuracy of history, but the decencies of fiction. When once we enter into the spirit of Herodotus, we find no inconsistency. The conventional probability of his drama is preserved from the beginning to the end. The deliberate orations, and the familiar dialogues, are in strict keeping with each other. But the speeches of Thucydides are neither preceded nor followed by anything with which they harmonize. They give to the whole book something of the grotesque character of those Chinese pleasuregrounds, in which perpendicular rocks of granite start up in the midst of a soft green plain. Invention is shocking, where truth is in such close juxta-position with it.

Thucydides honestly tells us that some of these discourses are purely fictitious. He may have reported the substance of others correctly. But it is clear from the internal evidence that he has preserved no more than the substance. His own peculiar habits of thought and expression are everywhere discernible. Individual and national peculiarities are seldom to be traced in the sentiments, and never in the diction. The oratory of the Corinthians and Thebans is not less attic, either in matter or in manner, than that of the Athenians. The style of Cleon is as pure, as austere, as terse, and as significant, as that of Pericles.

In spite of this great fault, it must be allowed that Thucydides has surpassed all his rivals in the art of historical narration, in the art of producing an effect on the imagination, by skillful selection and disposition, without indulging in the license of invention. But narration, though an important part of the business of a historian, is not the whole. To append a moral to a work of fiction, is either useless or superfluous. A fiction may give a more impressive effect to what is already known, but it can teach nothing new. If it presents to us characters and trains of events to which our experience furnishes us with nothing similar, instead of deriving instruction from it, we pronounce it unnatural. We do not form our opinions from it; but we try it by our preconceived opinions. Fiction, therefore, is essentially imitative. Its merit consists in its resemblance to a model with which we are already familiar, or to which at least we can instantly refer. Hence it is that the anecdotes which interest us most strongly in authentic narrative, are offensive when introduced into novels; that what is called the romantic part of history, is in fact the least romantic. It is delightful as history, because it contradicts our previous notions of human nature, and of the connexion of causes and effects. It is, on that very account, shocking and incongruous in fiction. In fiction, the principles are given to find the facts: In history, the facts are given to find the principles; and the writer who does not explain the phenomena as well as state them, performs only one-half of his office. Facts are the mere dross of history. It is from the abstract truth which interpenetrates them, and lies latent among them, like gold in the ore, that the mass derives its whole value: And the precious particles are generally combined with the baser in such a manner that the separation is a task of the utmost difficulty.

Twentieth-Century Criticism

I. BACKGROUND
R. G. COLLINGWOOD

R. G. Collingwood (1889–1943) was one of the most important twentieth-century students of the philosophy of history. He was professor of metaphysical philosophy at Oxford and the author of many books, including *Roman Britain* (1923) and *The Philosophy of History* (1930). Collingwood's well-known book *The Idea of History*, from which the following selection is taken, gives an excellent general view of the goals and methods of historians.

History's Nature, Object, Method, and Value †

What history is, what it is about, how it proceeds, and what it is for, are questions which to some extent different people would answer in different ways. But in spite of differences there is a large measure of agreement between the answers. And this agreement becomes closer if the answers are subjected to scrutiny with a view to discarding those which proceed from unqualified witnesses. History, like theology or natural science, is a special form of thought. If that is so, questions about the nature, object, method, and value of this form of thought must be answered by persons having two qualifications.

First, they must have experience of that form of thought. They must be historians. In a sense we are all historians nowadays. All educated persons have gone through a process of education which has included a certain amount of historical thinking. But this does not qualify them to give an opinion about the nature, object, method, and value of historical thinking. For in the first place, the experience of historical thinking which they have thus acquired is probably very superficial; and the opinions based on it are therefore no better grounded than a man's opinion of the French people based on a single week-end visit to Paris. In the second place, experience of anything whatever gained through the ordinary educational channels, as well as being superficial, is invariably out

† Excerpted by permission of Oxford University Press
from R. G. Collingwood, *The Idea of History*
(Oxford, 1946), pp. 7–10.

of date. Experience of historical thinking, so gained, is modelled on text-books, and text-books always describe not what is now being thought by real live historians, but what was thought by real live historians at some time in the past when the raw material was being created out of which the text-book has been put together. And it is not only the results of historical thought which are out of date by the time they get into the text-book. It is also the principles of historical thought: that is, the ideas as to the nature, object, method, and value of historical thinking. In the third place, and connected with this, there is a peculiar illusion incidental to all knowledge acquired in the way of education: the illusion of finality. [A student] has to believe that things are settled because the text-books and his teachers regard them as settled. When he emerges from that state and goes on studying the subject for himself he finds that nothing is settled. The dogmatism which is an invariable mark of immaturity drops away from him. He looks at so-called facts with a new eye. He says to himself: "My teacher and text-books told me that such and such was true; but is it true? What reasons had they for thinking it true, and were these reasons adequate?" On the other hand, if he emerges from the status of pupil without continuing to pursue the subject he never rids himself of this dogmatic attitude. And this makes him a person peculiarly unfitted to answer the questions I have mentioned. * * *

The second qualification for answering these questions is that a man should not only have experience of historical thinking but should also have reflected upon that experience. He must be not only an historian but a philosopher; and in particular his philosophical thought must have included special attention to the problems of historical thought. Now it is possible to be a quite good historian (though not an historian of the highest order) without thus reflecting upon one's own historical thinking. It is even easier to be a quite good teacher of history (though not the very best kind of teacher) without such reflection. At the same time, it is important to remember that experience comes first, and reflection on that experience second. Even the least reflective historian has the first qualification. He possesses the experience on which to reflect; and when he is asked to reflect on it his reflections have a good chance of being to the point. An historian who has never worked much at philosophy will probably answer our four questions in a more intelligent and valuable way than a philosopher who has never worked much at history.

I shall therefore propound answers to my four questions such as I think any present-day historian would accept. Here they will be rough and ready answers, but they will serve for a provisional definition of our subject-matter and they will be defended and elaborated as the argument proceeds.

(a) *The definition of history*. Every historian would agree, I think, that history is a kind of research or inquiry. What kind of inquiry it is I do not yet ask. The point is that generically it belongs to what we call the sciences: that is the forms of thought whereby we ask questions and try to answer them. Science in general, it is important to realize, does not consist in collecting what we already know and arranging it in this or that kind of pattern. It consists in fastening upon something we do not know, and trying to discover it. Playing patience with things we already know may be a useful means towards this end, but it is not the end itself. It is at best only the means. It is scientifically valuable only in so far as the new arrangement gives us the answer to a question we have already decided to ask. That is why all science begins from the knowledge of our own ignorance: not our ignorance of everything but our ignorance of some definite thing—the origin of parliament, the cause of cancer, the chemical composition of the sun, the way to make a pump work without muscular exertion on the part of a man or a horse or some other docile animal. Science is finding things out: and in that sense history is a science.

(b) *The object of history.* One science differs from another in that it finds out things of a different kind. What kind of things does history find out? I answer, *res gestae*[1]—actions of human beings that have been done in the past. Although this answer raises all kinds of further questions many of which are controversial, still, however they may be answered, the answers do not discredit the proposition that history is the science of *res gestae*, the attempt to answer questions about human actions done in the past.

(c) *How does history proceed?* History proceeds by the interpretation of evidence: where evidence is a collective name for things which singly are called documents, and a document is a thing existing here and now, of such a kind that the historian, by thinking about it, can get answers to the questions he asks about past events. Here again there are plenty of difficult questions to ask as to what the characteristics of evidence are and how it is interpreted. But there is no need for us to raise them at this stage. However they are answered, historians will agree that historical procedure, or method, consists essentially of interpreting evidence.

(d) Lastly, *what is history for?* This is perhaps a harder question than the others; a man who answers it will have to reflect rather more widely than a man who answers the three we have answered already. He must reflect not only on historical thinking but on other things as well, because to say that something is "for" something implies a distinction between A and B, where A is good for something and B is that for which something is good. But I will suggest an answer, and express the opinion that no historian would reject it, although the further questions to which it gives rise are numerous and difficult.

My answer is that history is "for" human self-knowledge. It is generally thought to be of importance to man that he should know himself:

1. *Res gestae* has been a common Latin expression (dating from ancient Rome) for accounts of precisely what Collingwood describes: "actions of human beings that have been done in the past "

where knowing himself means knowing not his merely personal peculiarities, the things that distinguish him from other men, but his nature
as man. Knowing yourself means knowing, first, what it is to be a man;
secondly, knowing what it is to be the kind of man you are; and thirdly,
knowing what it is to be the man *you* are and nobody else is. Knowing
yourself means knowing what you can do; and since nobody knows what
he can do until he tries, the only clue to what man can do is what man
has done. The value of history, then, is that it teaches us what man has
done and thus what man is.

CHRISTIAN MEIER

Professor of ancient history at the University of Munich, Christian Meier is
well known for his work on both Greek and Roman history. His book *The
Greek Discovery of Politics* (cited below in note 5) has just been translated
into English (Cambridge, Mass., 1990); his *Caesar* was published in Berlin
in 1982. In this essay Meier stresses the role Herodotus played in the development of an art which gave "historical answers to historical questions"
rather than falling back on a priori generalizations about the way things are
and always will be.

The Origins of History in Ancient Greece †

In my opinion Herodotus' discovery of history should be characterized
as follows: He examines the genesis of certain events, namely the Persian
War and the Greek victory. His answer is determined by the fact that he
traces a political and military process through two or three generations
as a sequence of events, i.e., as caused by many different subjects which
met as chance would have it. Thus, he wrote a multi-subjective, contin-
gency-oriented account. He did this using empirical data and writing in
as comprehensive a form as possible. That is the new and unprecedented
element of his work, at least in the cultures of the Near East and the
Mediterranean. It may even have been absolutely new, although I am
not qualified enough in Chinese historiography to say. Now I would like
to explain this characterization.

First, by asking questions, Herodotus sets himself apart from all those
whose primary aim was to inform and preserve, such as the oriental
kings, their courtiers, priests or scribes. Herodotus also wants to inform
and preserve—and to a much greater extent, going far beyond the deeds

† Excerpted by permission of the author and of the
editors of *Arethusa* from Christian Meier, "Historical Answers to Historical Questions: The Origins
of History in Ancient Greece," *Arethusa* 20 (1987):
44–57. Most footnotes have been omitted.

of the kings—but at the same time he is inspired by the question of how the war and the victory of the Greeks came about. This determines the whole of his work and gives it its coherence. It is historical causality which he has in mind.

Second, the empirical principles of Herodotus' research stem from Ionian history. He has a relatively strict principle, which is that he must report eyewitness accounts, although not of course always believe them, and that he should limit himself to what he knows from these sources. For this reason, except for the *logos* on Egypt and a few other histories, he begins with Croesus, King of Lydia, since that is as far back as his information reaches. As far as I know, it is also entirely novel to publish a research report *in historicis*, as an individual, a private person with specific interests, and not speaking with a special authority, for instance one borrowed from a king. On the other hand, Herodotus' approach differs in principle from all the constructs of historical connections which were customary for the Greeks of his period when dealing with earlier epochs, for example in the case of the fifth-century theories of the origin of culture.

The third characteristic, the multi-subjectivity arising from Herodotus' orientation toward sequences of events, originates from his conviction that the essence of the long-term political and military events seen as a whole lies in the fact that various subjects, whether they be individuals or groups, armies, cities, peoples or empires, meet in a contingent manner in constantly new situations. Any references to divine intervention can be disregarded in this case. They are mostly a part of the eyewitness accounts which Herodotus is documenting, and do of course offer an interpretation of actions and their results, but whether the gods exert an effective influence or not must remain unrevealed. It goes beyond the bounds of empirical research.

I suggest that it would be practical to distinguish two ideal types of history and accordingly of historiographical approaches. On the one hand, there would be the history of actions and events, to which corresponds a contingent history *(ereignisgeschichtliche Betrachtungsweise / histoire événementielle)*. On the other hand, there would be a history of processes, to which corresponds a processual history *(prozessuale Betrachtungsweise/ histoire processuale)*. Both types are theoretical constructs in the sense of Max Weber's ideal types.[1] In reality they scarcely occur in pure form. They do not exclude each other and by applying both approaches we may consider the same happenings in different ways. But it is nevertheless true that there are some essential differences between such forms, not only of historical approach but of history itself. Whereas for Herodotus everything that happened was the action of a limited number of subjects and the events in which they met under contingent circum-

---

1. Max Weber (1864–1920) was a German economist and sociologist.

stances, other historians may perceive primarily historical processes in a narrow sense of the word, which were basically independent of individual human actions and events. Consciously or unconsciously the processual approach assumes that either a certain process is initiated by a divine power (as in the ancient cultures of the Middle East), or that for some reason or other an infinite number of effects and side effects of human actions finally cumulate in a particular direction. In any case, it is not the events that are of interest here, but the process of change. Of course the sequence of events can also be called a process, but that is not the meaning of the word which designates it in contrast to *histoire événementielle*. If we make this differentiation, it also becomes clear that although the approach through single historical events must of course deal with more than one force, it can in fact take into account only a limited number of individual or group subjects. Unless for example you want to describe a battle as a chaos or as a large process, you cannot avoid describing the many people who are participating in it as being organized into a few units, even if it is their dissolution which may have to be described.

There is, of course, nothing unusual in the multi-subjective approach. Hardly any battle, hardly any diplomatic mission or intrigue, no complicated decision-making process (in the wider sense of the word) can be understood otherwise. Therefore we have to assume that the Egyptians and Assyrians, for example, were perfectly capable of applying this approach. Otherwise they would not have been able to judge the success or failure of such events. Thus this sort of story was not only reconstructed in the cabinet room but also told round the campfire and in other places. In the Old Testament, for example, we can find the story of David's successors constructed along similar lines. In general, however, affairs of state will hardly have appeared to the public as contingent.

Nevertheless, in all these stories the plurality of the subjects and their necessarily contingent interaction belongs within the framework of short limited events, such as a battle, a military campaign, or a diplomatic mission. Herodotus' innovation is that he composes longer pieces of history, as we would call it, covering several generations, in this multi-subjective way: he sees them as long sequences of human actions and events, caused not merely by human beings but by very different human beings and political or military units. I know of no other examples of this. Perhaps there were some in China and perhaps also in the lost Book of the Chronicles of the Kings of Israel (1 Kings 15.23), but certainly not in the form in which the history of the Israelites is found in the Old Testament.

I call Herodotus' method "giving historical answers to historical questions." Historical questions are those that look for long-term changes to explain an outcome. Of course one could explain the origins of the Persian War in other ways, such as by a mythical connection between histories, which caused East and West repeatedly to wrong and to punish each other. This has been done, as Herodotus shows, perhaps not without irony, at the beginning of his work. Or it could be explained as the result of a mood or dream of the Persian king, or as the expression of the momentum of his dynasty or empire pushing for expansion, or as a reaction to the Ionian rebellion. All these explanations are documented by Herodotus. The mythical and political questions also stretch into time in various ways, but do not aim at longer sequences of events seen multi-subjectively.

There were also various non-historical answers to questions about the Greek victory over the Persians, such as the religious answer that Zeus did not want one person to rule over East and West. If this explanation is accepted, the way in which the Persian purpose failed is no longer so important. There was also the politico-ethical answer, which introduced the question of the qualitative superiority of the Greeks, their freedom and virtues, as opposed to the quantitative superiority of the Persians. There is also the geographical answer, which maintained that the large Eastern power was unable to work to its full potential in the small space of the Aegean.

Herodotus reports all these answers in a way that does not necessarily mean that he was indifferent to them. But they were certainly insufficient for him. He wanted to know how everything had really happened, what had followed what, and what had influenced what. So he showed how the Persian Empire grew up, how Sparta and Athens became powerful, and how it was various chance motives, some of them highly personal, of individual leaders which in a very complicated interaction caused the Ionian conflict with the Persians. He told how Athens let herself be persuaded to support the rebellion, how this again was connected with the fact that the city was organized on principles close to democracy and had just become one of the most powerful cities in Greece, and how the Persian attacks on the Greek mother country followed the Ionian rebellion. He traced the developments which, thanks largely to chance, led to the battle and victory at Marathon, then to Xerxes' decision to go to war, his preparations for it, the treaty between the Greek cities and the equipping of the fleet in Athens. And finally he provides a long list of military events.

However important the other explanations might have been for Herodotus, he left them as it were melted down, or let us say "dissolved" into his history. He could not verify them—at least not as the causes of all that happened, which appeared to him to be much more complex—and if they were going to prove to be true, then they would have to do so within the framework of actions and events. In this Herodotus was on the one hand following a principle of Ionian *historia* in its sense of "research," since he tried to keep as close as possible to the empirical facts, i.e., to reports on specific individual events. The novelty in his work was merely that he applied this method to historical processes.

Other motives apart, the result of this was that he had to write down his results, whereas in the case of all the other explanations of the Persian War and the Greek victory he would have been able to limit himself to oral statements.

On the other hand, however, in this long-term historical reconstruction, another experience may have found its expression, one of which the Greeks of Herodotus' time were especially conscious. Those who were living in a democracy or in some pre-stage of it were in a very strange political position, since they were able to participate in politics and join in making decisions, but were at the same time often observers of it. For a broad spectrum of the population, particularly in Athens, was so involved in politics, without necessarily being able to specialize in it, that they had a great deal of political knowledge. Even if these people did not influence Herodotus' perspective directly, in Athens the idea of politics must have been influenced by the fact that many political interrelationships had to be explained in detail in the assemblies and also in many discussions in the squares and streets. These discussions had to be different from deliberations among experts. And in general, democracies made it impossible for politics to appear as the work or isolated decision of individuals, or for a battle to be seen only in terms of a king's victory. Everyone knew how many different forces were working contingently on each other. However, even if it were possible to experience politics in this way in Herodotus' period in the middle of the fifth century, we can still assume that it was an exceptional step for him to apply the same model to the interpretation of a long-term sequence of events.

Here, as whenever we are considering what is new or specific to the Greeks, we must draw on other cultures for comparison. This is done all too rarely and leads to our statements often being irresponsibly amateurish. I, too, am able to offer only limited competence, on which I would like to base a hypothesis to illuminate one field at least from the aspect of classical antiquity, while other disciplines must contribute to its more detailed study.

As far as I am able to tell, the pre-classical high cultures had on the one hand formulas and explanations for longer processes, which amounted to longer stretches of time being divided up into periods according to certain characteristics or in some cases to a numerical pattern. Their conception of this was extremely imprecise. The interrelationships of events played no part at all; it was a question of differentiating between different periods to discover a meaning which was attributed specifically to the relevant empire or people, possibly from without, but if so, from the gods, with foreign powers acting only as agents of their will.

Thus for example in the story of Joseph, the seven fat years are followed by seven lean years. There can be a regular cycle of good and bad times alternating with each other. The Chinese "mandate theory" sees a regular sequence in the rise and fall of dynasties. Or, again in China, an inevitable succession of old/new/old/new is constructed, seen as different states but morally of the same value. In Egypt a cycle is recognized between chaos and the re-establishment of order, in small matters as well as in larger ones.

Besides this division into periods, we have on the other hand the recognition of far-reaching events resulting usually from cultic transgressions of kings or peoples. We find this for example in Mesopotamia. But the Israelites are also capable of explaining important events solely within the framework of their own history: they have done wrong and are punished; in this interpretation the history of the great Assyrian Empire with which they became involved is quite functionally related to their own small race. Here would be an opportunity to adopt the idea of contingency in the approach to history, but in the end its place is taken by the idea of the will of God.

These interpretations all have in common that historical processes are understood wholly within the framework of their own political unit—as if the multi-subjectivity of history meant nothing, as if one only had to suffer because of one's sins or because it was an inevitable part of that particular period of history! The meaning of events is assigned to the relevant empire or kingdom alone. The people understand it as if everything revolved around them, they relate everything to themselves. It is my theory that the members of these cultures were only capable of a multi-subjective approach in the case of small units of experience, and that they were not able to translate events as they experienced them into greater temporal dimensions or into the context of a long-term history of events. Moreover, when considering the larger dimensions, for them any idea of contingency gets lost in the wholesale assumption that there is some coherence of meaning. And I believe that this is an anthropological principle which is seldom disregarded (and then for special reasons), to such an extent that any divergence from this "ethnocentric" or "imperiocentric" approach becomes an exception. This is the case, for example, in Greece and in the modern age. The Greeks in particular could endure the perception of contingency as far as it was necessary to understand history—when it was necessary.

Norbert Elias maintains that in the modern age, the ability to understand that natural events are ruled by autonomous laws was preceded by a new level of "self-distancing," and "increased control of the spontaneous feelings" of people, that everything they experience, and in particular everything that concerns them, is also shaped for them and is the expression of a purpose, an aim, something predetermined, which they relate to themselves, i.e., to the people who are experiencing and involved.[2] This is the reason why it was not at all easy to accept the truth of the heliocentric system.

2. Norbert Elias, *Über den Prozess der Civilisation* (Bern and Munich, 1969), pp. lviiif. [*Author*].

The early Greeks were also familiar with this idea of relating anything that happened to themselves. For Hesiod, for example, the whole fate of a city depends on the way in which the judges interpret the law—not only the political fate of the city but also the wealth of its inhabitants, and even the question of whether the oak trees on the hills bear acorns or the sheep give any wool.[3] But this way of looking at things was difficult to uphold in the smallness of the Greek world. Aeschylus uses the history of the Persians and their king to explain why they were conquered by the Greeks: he explains it as a consequence of a lapse of the time limit allotted to their empire and as a result of the hybris of Xerxes. In the case of Herodotus we find the old attitude, which presumably was still prevalent outside Greece, side by side with the new attitude. In the *logos* on Egypt he tells us how the Greeks of Cyrene defeated King Apries and "since he was destined to be met by misfortune this did in fact happen and for reasons which I . . . will explain in more detail later" (2.161.4). On the other hand, further on he says in connection with the history of Cyrene, "since the Egyptians had never measured themselves against the Greeks before and had underestimated them, they were totally defeated" (4.159.6). Thus in one case it was a battle between two armies, and in the other the fulfillment of fate, whose source is unknown. It is impossible to trace precisely the stages through which the Greeks went to reach their more exact understanding—and their conspicuously high tolerance for contingency. But it is at least clear that even in the age of Solon, as far as domestic affairs were concerned, they had gained such a high understanding of the natural laws of politics that the only reason to see them as divine punishment was to find religious corroboration for political knowledge. Political events were thus completely disconnected from natural events; hence in the long run it was only superstition which brought them together (for example when an army related an eclipse of the sun to itself).

Only when considering these examples does it become clear how seminal and important an achievement it was to recount long-term history objectively, focusing only on events. Nevertheless, there were still numerous older attitudes influencing Herodotus (for example, the idea that no power was fated to become too great, that a rise was always succeeded by a fall), which determine his understanding of many histories and particularly of the defeat of the Persians. They did not, however, make his history unnecessary for him, because they were only presumptions—presumptions as to the meaning of events—and because he still remained bound to empirical research.

Fourth, by expressing the results of his research in written form, Herodotus was indeed following a certain tradition, but one which had hitherto dealt with different things. Moreover, it was essential if he wanted

---

3. Hesiod was an epic poet roughly contemporary with Homer (perhaps around 700 B.C.) intensely concerned with social issues and the well-being of the community.

to order the enormous amount of material that covered not only a long period of time but also a large area. However, experience must also have shown him how quickly stories and deeds from the past are forgotten. Besides the historical aspect it was clearly also his aim to preserve what he had discovered by writing it down. It was obviously important to him in its own right; several of his digressions can hardly be otherwise explained.

Although the Greeks' interest in writing down and preserving past works and events had previously been conspicuously limited, it increased notably later. It is difficult to say how far what was handed down was changed by being recorded in written form. The variety of attitudes and interpretations which we find in Herodotus' *logoi* would suggest that he recorded them more or less as they were told to him. On the other hand the sequence in which he wrote them in the work as a whole gave them a new implication.

Two final questions remain to be asked:

(1) how did Herodotus come to write his *History*, and
(2) to what extent did his perception of sequences of events coincide with the quality of ancient history (in the sense of *Geschehen*, i.e., the combination of events seen as a whole)? Or, in broader terms, why did historiography in classical antiquity confine itself largely to the history of events? How far developed was the awareness of processes? And—what is by no means the same thing—what was the attitude of the Greeks toward the history of structures?

First, it is not very satisfactory to assume that the general advance of Ionian research would necessarily have led to the discovery of history, even if we do see all the scientific abilities of the Greeks concentrated here. Of course it played its part, but why was it Herodotus who discovered history around 450, and not somebody else in 500 B.C.? That is why it is often assumed that the Persian War prompted his question. There may be a reasonable amount of truth in this, whatever other explanations there were. And it is not difficult to accept that the special understanding of political processes which developed within the Attic democracy (and its observation by outsiders) was a further decisive factor. There would have been sufficient opportunities to arouse Herodotus' interest and channel it in certain directions.

It is my opinion that there was a further factor, which was that Herodotus felt that his idea of predetermined laws of nature in the world and of the limits of mankind were being called into question by all kinds of new and almost modern attitudes in contemporary Athens. For there it was thought that as far as knowledge, ability and the development of power were concerned, numerous barriers had been broken down or could be broken down, which had previously always been valid and had been either respected or disregarded to one's own cost. And for quite a long time this worked amazingly well. A whole city, the most powerful city in Greece, appeared to have burst its bounds. Then the questions were asked: was it still valid to say that no one could become too powerful, that every rise was followed by a fall? But Herodotus' answer was precisely that this was still the case. It had been demonstrated at least to a large extent in the greatest event that was known, the Persian War. This far-reaching event that caused so much change still adhered to the old predetermined patterns. Was it not particularly this question that led Herodotus to write history?

Second, Greek historiography was also in the following centuries determined by the fact that sequences of political and military events were constructed on the basis of source material, which was however sometimes used only indirectly and could be padded out with rhetorical embellishments. It was to this that the type of narration called history referred; this was its content. Many other things which influenced events could be included, such as the development of weapons, techniques of communication and reports on foreign peoples, but these were not given in the form of a history of culture but rather of a description of a state of affairs. Information was also given on economic factors when relevant. But the focus remained on the political aspects.

Structural history on the other hand is usually understood as a part of the history of events. As far as it is recognized at all, it consists almost entirely of actions, such as legislation or the reform of constitutions, and much less of processes. However, those things that we include in it on the basis of our modern conception of history, such as economic history, the history of science and certain gradual changes in constitutional history, were at that time usually to be found outside historiography, for example as the history of philosophy in Aristotle's first book of the *Metaphysics* or in his sketches of constitutional history, in Plato's works and those of many representatives of the individual sciences, such as medicine, who were concerned with their predecessors. Relatively few connections were set up between the various histories: Plato relates constitution and music, Aristotle relates constitution and demography or military affairs and also philosophy and economics. But these histories were never synchronized to comprise a whole. I maintain that this would not have been possible, because the Greeks were scarcely able to perceive this type of historical connection; or in other words, it was not a part of historiography or only marginally such, since historiography did not comprise all that we understand as history today. It is not without reason that it was not until the modern age that this type of historical connection was included in the concept of history (when it became "singularized" according to social aspects).

Seeing history as a series of politico-military events corresponded closely to the way classical antiquity perceived, caused and experienced events and changes within the framework of time. This was particularly true for the fifth century. At that time the citizens of Athens developed a political identity unprecedented in world politics: they were primarily citizens, conscious of themselves as such, and behaved accordingly. Developments in the field of politics were of prime importance to them and to anyone who had dealings with them.

The world of small city-states in which this took place possessed an extraordinary "commensurability" between the individuals and the events, a close correlation between the dimensions of the scope of the individual and of his world, which was largely synonymous with his city, and the dimensions of the events which he could perceive. He had a say in what decisions were taken, including those on the battlefield; things took place visibly among all the people and between the cities. Here, political actions and events stood in the foreground of attention for everyone. The relationship between an individual and all that happened in his surroundings was enormously favorable to human pride. Here, relatively speaking, it was possible to achieve a high level of human greatness and people were necessarily strongly disinclined to see themselves or others as the function of a process, which for particular reasons is possible and imperative in modern times. Changes of any note in the economic situation or in other respects were usually a function of politics and warfare and therefore of interest in relation to these.

Generally speaking, we can say that the gravitations of perceptions in Greece were directed toward continuity and not toward change. This is true in spite of the great changes which took place in the field of politics and advances made in the scientific field, as well as in the skill and use of methodology in so many areas in the fifth century. On the whole these remained within the bound of "increase of human ability."[4] The variety of observations consolidated and developed toward a "consciousness of human ability," but never reached the state where progress was perceived as a process of comprehensive change.[5] Therefore it restricted its focus to individual participants or a small circle and its object was limited to factual ability and knowledge, not including those changes which can result from a multiplication of such an ability and knowledge.

Therefore I would most strongly urge that we consider the relevance of historical anthropology in this context, and in doing so take into account among other things the difference between a conception of history which is oriented toward actions and events and one which centers on processes. We have to consider the difference between various types of people, and their relationships with the events and changes they produce and with which they are confronted—but also the different ways in which a person relates to what he can experience as the past and to the world as a whole by identifying with larger units.

I would like to add one last thought in respect to classical antiquity. The Greek tolerance for contingency was obviously connected with the

4. For details see Edelstein, 1967 [Author]. Meier refers to L. Edelstein, The Idea of Progress in Classical Antiquity (Baltimore, 1967).

5. Cf. Meier 1980, 435ff. [Author]. Meier is referring to his book Die Entstehung des Politischen bei den Griechen (Frankfurt, 1980).

fact that, as Vernant has shown, the Greeks could conceive of the cosmos and nature as unrelated to any single human or godly force that was particularly responsible for them.[6] On the contrary, cosmos and nature were determined by laws which stretched beyond any single force. It is true that the order of the polis could be understood in analogy with that of the cosmos, but since Solon the fate of the political unit was no longer interrelated with that of the cosmos and of nature, as it had been in the Orient. It depended rather on the decision of the citizens. Moreover, the totality of the cosmos corresponded to the variety of political units in it, so the individual units could not interpret the meaning of what happened to them only with reference to themselves. There was no room for interpretations based on differentiating between periods, such as a regular cycle of good and bad times alternating with each other. Accordingly, a completely new attitude toward the enemy developed: instead of being despised, he was regarded as an equal.

In addition, parallel to the cosmos, the justice and stability of the political order had to be considered as interrelated. The difficulties which this could cause were countered by historical constructions among other things: Aeschylus, for example, appears to have invented especially for Zeus a long story whose beginnings were most unsavory, so that continuity could be guaranteed for the future: to make his reign eternal and just, Zeus first had to learn moderation. Solon had already discovered that the characteristic of good order lay in the fact that within it no processes progressed toward a bad end. This opinion, which focused on the heart of the polis, corresponded outwardly with that of Herodotus. He thought that justice finally won through in the numerous units which formed the stage of history, because every rise was balanced by a fall, as a reparation for the harm that had been caused. Combined, they both showed that the law of justice is unchanging: the world as a whole remains untouched by any contingency, whereas on the smaller scale, it is all too full of it, since it is a world of limited actions. So the preconditions of the Greeks' ability to understand history as a history of events were apparently related to many other peculiarities of their thinking.

Since all this belongs to that history which itself led to democracy and therefore to far-reaching changes touching even the question of identity, it is a part of one of the most important steps made in the progress of mankind. And should we try to deny that *histoire événementielle* was also such a step when, on the political level which originated at that time in the cities, there evolved the possibility of applying empirical, scientific methods to the study of long-term histories of events?

6. Vernant, 1962 [Author]. Meier refers to J.-P. Vernant, Les origines de la pensée grecque (Paris, 1962).

OSWYN MURRAY

A fellow of Balliol College, Oxford, Oswyn Murray is the author of *Early Greece* (Stanford, 1980). He provided much of the historical work for the *Oxford History of the Classical World*, of which he is coauthor with the archaeologist John Boardman and the philologist Jasper Griffin. This selection is an introduction to the special contribution Greek historians made to the techniques of historiography and to the ways in which Greek historians differed in their approaches to history.

Greek Historians †

Many societies possess professional remembrancers, priests or officials, whose duty it is to record those traditions thought necessary for the continuity of social values; many societies also possess priestly or official records, designed to help regulate and placate the worlds of gods and men, but capable of being converted by modern scholars into history. Yet the actual writing of history as a distinct cultural activity seems in origin independent of these natural social attitudes, and is a rare phenomenon: it has in fact developed independently only in three very different societies: Judaea, Greece, and China. The characteristics of history in each case are distinct: history is not a science, but an art form serving the needs of society and therefore conditioned by its origin.

The Greek tradition of history writing is our tradition, and we can best see its peculiarities by comparing it with that other tradition which has so strongly influenced us, the Jewish historical writings preserved in the Old Testament. Greeks and Jews came to history independently, but at roughly the same time and in response to the same pressures, the need to establish and sustain a national identity in the face of the vast empires of the Middle East: just as the struggles with Assyria, the exile in Babylon, and the return to the promised land created Jewish historical writing, so the sense of national identity resulting from the defeat of Persia created Greek historical writing. But the presuppositions and the materials with which the two historical traditions worked are very different. For the Jews history was the record of God's covenant with His chosen people, its successes and disasters conditioned by their willingness to obey His commands. History was therefore a single story, belonging to God: the different elements and individual authors are moulded (not always successfully) into a continuous account. Greek history, while it could recognize a moral pattern in human affairs, regarded these affairs as in the control of man: history was the record, not of the mercy or wrath of God, but of the great deeds of men. Among those deeds was

† Excerpted by permission of Oxford University Press and the author from J. Boardman, J. Griffin, and   O. Murray, eds., *The Oxford History of the Classical World* (New York, 1986), pp. 186–97.

the writing of history itself: so a Greek historian is an individual who "signs" his work in its first sentence—"Herodotus of Halicarnassus, his researches . . . ," "Thucydides of Athens wrote the history of the war . . ." The great exception to this rule serves to confirm it: those who, like Xenophon, sought to continue the unfinished work of Thucydides, chose not to reveal their identity: Xenophon begins his work, "Some days later . . . ," and nowhere mentions his own name, although he is far freer than Thucydides with opinions delivered in the first person.[1] We do not even know the name of the author of another (and better) continuation of Thucydides, partly preserved on papyrus, the "Oxyrhynchus historian" (so called from the village in Egypt where the copy of his text was found). Later Christian generations in fact tried to transform this individualistic group of historical writings into a tradition of the Old Testament type, and succeeded through instinct or economy of effort in selecting a "chain of histories," so that only one historical account now survives for each period, and these accounts give a relatively continuous narrative history of the ancient world. A proper history of Greek history writing must take due notice of what has been lost as well as of what survives.

A second difference between Jewish and Greek historical writing is in their sources and attitudes to the sources. The Jewish historical account is built on a multiplicity of evidences which would do credit to a modern historian, and are of three basic types—acts (customs, taboos, rituals, and their explanations), the spoken tradition (hymns, poetry, prophecy, myths, folk-tales), and the written tradition (laws, official documents, royal and priestly chronicles, biographies); it is prone to quote proofs and evidence such as documents. The source material used by Greek historians is initially far simpler and more rudimentary, and the Greeks were always more concerned with the literary, rather than the evidential, aspects of history; they therefore seldom quote documents. Paradoxically the Greek tradition remains superior to the Jewish in its ability to distinguish fact from fiction: God can falsify history far more effectively than the individual historian with his mere mortal bias. The Greeks indeed taught the West how to create and write history without God.

Both peoples learned the alphabet from the same source, the Phoenicians who invented it; writing came to Greece in the eighth-century B.C., yet Greece long remained an oral culture in which men spoke in prose, but composed in verse. The distinction between poetry and prose was later a mark of the difference between myth and history, but the earliest known prose literary work was philosophical rather than historical, and related to the need to formulate and convey thoughts in a precise and accurate form; about 550 B.C. the philosopher Anaximander of

---

1. Murray refers here to Xenophon's *Hellenica*, a seven-book work which continued Thucydides' history down to 362. On Xenophon, see the Glossary.

Miletus wrote a book *On Nature,* which discussed both the basic structure of the physical world and its visible forms: it contained the first maps
and descriptions of both earth and the heavens. Some fifty years later
Hecataeus of Miletus similarly wrote a *Description of the Earth* accompanied by a map: it was divided into two books, one for Europe and one
for Asia, and recorded the information he had gathered from his own
and others' travels. Geography and ethnography are important compo-
nents in the Greek view of history.

Another work of Hecataeus called *Genealogies* has often been thought
to be the first to exhibit that spirit of critical enquiry which is characteristic of western history writing, for it began: "Hecataeus the Milesian
speaks thus: I write these things as they seem true to me; for the stories
told by the Greeks are various and in my opinion absurd." * * * The
book actually seems to have been a collection of heroic myths and
genealogies of heroes, designed to reduce them into a pseudo-historical
account by rationalizing them; it is a curious false start to history, on the
one hand recognizing the need to understand the past in rational terms,
but on the other hand using the fundamentally unsuitable material of
myth. It shows both a desire to liberate history from myth, and an inability to distinguish between the two.

Herodotus

From time to time critics have tried to discover lost historians in the
generation after Hecataeus to help explain the next development in the
writing of history; but such theories are based on shaky evidence and a
mistaken belief that local history or the monograph must come before
general history with a grand theme. Herodotus of Halicarnassus in fact
deserves his ancient title of "father of history." His work is the earliest
Greek book in prose to have survived intact; it is some 600 pages or nine
"books" long. Its theme is presented in the first sentence: "This is the
account of the investigation of Herodotus of Halicarnassus, undertaken
so that the achievements of men should not be obliterated by time and
the great and marvellous works of both Greeks and barbarians should
not be without fame, and not least the reason why they fought one
another."

The ultimate justification of the work is the account of the conflict
between Greece and Persia, culminating in the Great Expedition of Xerxes
to Greece in 480 BC described in the last three books: it is the story of
how an army of (allegedly) one and three-quarter million men and a
navy of 1,200 ships was defeated by the fragmented forces of the Greeks,
who in no battle could muster more than 40,000 men and 378 ships; we
may doubt the Persian numbers, but the strategy shows that we cannot
doubt the fact that the Greeks were heavily outnumbered on each occasion. * * * A fleet from Herodotus' city had fought on the Persian side,
and one of his earliest memories was perhaps of the setting out and
return of that fateful expedition; he grew up in an Ionia suffering the

joys and pains of its liberation and then subjection by the victorious Athenian navy. * * * For the generation of Herodotus the epic achievements of their fathers had created the world in which they lived, as the return of the exiles from Babylon had created the world of Ezra. In his last books Herodotus sought to raise a fitting monument to the new race of heroes, using all the literary skills at his command, "so that the achievements of men should not be obliterated by time."

The central theme of his conflict requires Herodotus to go back to its origins: "who was the first in actual fact to harm the Greeks." So the work begins with the earlier struggles between the Ionian Greeks and the kingdom of Lydia, before passing on to the origins of Persian power and the story of Cyrus the Great, and then the further conquests of the Persians, in Egypt and north Africa, and around the Black Sea, until we see that the conflict was inevitable.

But this central theme is merely one aspect of the work; there is another, at least as important—"the account of the investigation" or "researches" of Herodotus (this is in fact the original meaning and the first recorded use of the word *historiē*). Like Hecataeus, Herodotus was a traveller: in the first four books and often thereafter the theme of the conflict is subordinate, a thread on which to hang a series of accounts or stories gathered from different places. These range from individual stories about famous figures (the mythical poet Arion or the Persian court doctor Democedes of Croton, for instance) to substantial histories of the rise and fall of cities (Athens, Sparta, Naucratis in Egypt) and finally to full-scale geographical and ethnographic accounts of civilizations, the most extended of which, on Egypt, occupies the whole of Book 2.

The result is far more than an account of the causes and events of a mere conflict. It is rather a total picture of the known world, in which the geography, customs, beliefs, and monuments of each people are at least as important as their often tenuous relationship to the war. It is this which gives added depth to Herodotus' account, and makes it both a great work of art and a convincing history of a conflict not just between two peoples but between two types of society, the Mediterranean egalitarian city-state and the oriental despotisms of the Middle East. It also makes Herodotus more modern than any other ancient historian in his approach to the ideal of total history.

Herodotus' openness to other cultures indeed caused him to be called a "barbarophile." It reflects in part an older Ionian view from an age of exploration, reinforced perhaps by the traditions of Herodotus' own community of Halicarnassus, which was a mixed Greek and Carian city. But these attitudes have been systematized under the influence of the new sophistic interest in the relationship between culture and nature, *nomos* and *physis*; "For if anyone, no matter who, were given the opportunity of choosing from amongst all the nations of the world the set of beliefs which he thought best, he would inevitably, after careful consideration of their relative merits, choose those of his own country." Herodotus illustrates the point with a story of the confrontation between

Greeks and Indians arranged by King Darius; the Indians were disgusted to hear that the Greeks burned the corpses of their dead parents, the Greeks appalled that the Indians ate theirs: "One can see from this what custom can do, and Pindar, in my opinion, was right when he called it 'king of all' " (3.38).

The two aspects of the work in one sense reflect the two main literary influences on it, Homer and the world of war and conflict, Hecataeus and the world of peace and understanding. They also probably reflect a chronological progression in the development of Herodotus' book. He seems to have begun as an expert on foreign cultures, a travelling sophist who lectured on the marvels of the world; only later did he arrange his researches around a unifying theme. Despite much modern controversy, that still seems the most satisfactory account of the various peculiarities in the book.

How did Herodotus acquire his information? Some information may have come from previous literary works; but Hecataeus is the only such author Herodotus mentions, and no convincing traces of the use of earlier written narratives have been detected. Herodotus can quote poetry and oracles, and occasionally gives information ultimately based on eastern documentary sources; but it is clear that he did not regard written documents as an important source of information, indeed that he knew no language but Greek. Herodotus' own characterization of his sources is always the same, and is consistent with the types of information he gives. He claims to practise that most modern of historical disciplines, oral history, the collection and interpretation of the living spoken tradition of a people: his sources are "sight and hearing," what he has seen and what he has been told; the two of course interrelate, since monuments and natural phenomena preserve and call forth verbal explanations. His travels included Egypt and Cyrene in north Africa, Tyre in Phoenicia, Mesopotamia as far as Babylon, the Black Sea and the Crimea, and the north Aegean, apart from the main cities of Asia Minor and Greece, and ultimately (though this has left little if any trace in the *Histories*) south Italy where he settled. In each place he seems to have sought out "men with traditions," particular groups, interpreters, priests, or leading citizens, and to have recorded a single version of the oral tradition available, a version which may of course often have been partial, biased or merely frivolous; he compares different versions only if they come from different places. The difficulties of writing oral history are well recognized today; yet on the main cultures such as Egypt and Persia, where Herodotus can be checked he is revealed to be remarkably well informed for someone working from such oral sources.

It is in his Greek history that Herodotus reveals the most important aspect of his artistic personality. For mainland Greece his information seems to come from the leading political groups in the cities. For Sparta he gives an official line, for Athens a version based at least in part on particular aristocratic traditions; the narrative is concerned with events and wars, rational in tone, without moral or religious colouring, and designed to enhance or justify the status of particular groups. At Delphi a different type of tradition was available, a series of stories told by the priests and related to the monuments and offerings at the shrine. These stories contain many folk-tale motifs and have a strong moral tone: the hero moves from prosperity to misfortune as a victim of divine envy— the ethical teaching is not aristocratic, but belongs to the shrine of a god whose temple carried the mottoes, "Know yourself," and "Nothing too much." The same types of story pattern are dominant in Ionia: Herodotus' history of his home area is far less "historical" and far less political than his account of mainland Greece. He is, for instance, often thought to have had particularly good sources for the history of Samos, where he spent much of his youth, yet his account of the tyrant Polycrates only two generations earlier has already turned into a folk-tale.

This characteristic of his Ionian sources suggests a popular, non-aristocratic tradition of story-telling which is directly related to Herodotus' achievement. For the overall shape of his history shows the same moral patterning as his Ionian and Delphic stories: the story of the Persian Wars is a story of how "the god strikes with his thunderbolt the tall, and will not allow them to display themselves, while small beings do not vex him; you see how the lightning throws down always the greatest buildings and the finest trees" (7.10). The message is created through a series of devices derived from the art of the folk-tale: the warning dream, the figure of the wise counsellor disregarded, the recurrent story pattern. Just as behind Homer there lies a long tradition of oral poetry sung by professional bards, so behind Herodotus there lies an Ionian tradition of story-telling of which he himself was the last and greatest master.

Thus Herodotus' collecting of information was not guided by any spirit of systematic enquiry, neither was it the product of random curiosity. It was informed from the start with the principle of the *logos*. Herodotus uses the word *logos* to refer to the whole of his work, to its major sections (the Egyptian or the Lydian *logos*), and to the individual stories within it: he surely regarded himself as a *logos*-maker in the same way as he regarded both Hecataeus the mythographer and Aesop the creator of animal fables; Thucydides indeed dismisses him as a "*logos*-writer." The word *logos* in this context may very often seem to mean little more than the English "story," as long as we remember that a story has a shape, a purpose: it is not an isolated fact preserved for its own sake; it may be true, but it must be interesting. The achievement of Herodotus was to harness the skills of the *logos*-maker to the description of human societies in peace and war.

From the evidence for his friendship with the poet Sophocles, Herodotus was already active as a lecturer in the late forties of the fifth century; the final version of his history was published shortly before 425 BC, when Aristophanes parodied his account of the causes of the Persian Wars in his comedy, *The Acharnians*. Already Herodotus seemed old-fashioned, for the wider Ionian responsiveness to the interplay of civilizations had been replaced by a narrower concern with the Greek city-state and its interests; history became the history of the *polis*, and took new directions.

Local History and Chronography

The first of these consisted in a fragmentation of the synoptic view of Herodotus into the systematic exploitation of local traditions, and more importantly local archives. These local or ethnic histories satisfied the interests of a local audience for the history of their particular city, and continued to be written throughout antiquity as long as the *polis* survived; all are now lost, but the Augustan critic Dionysius of Halicarnassus describes their general characteristics:

> These men made similar choices about the selection of their subjects, and their powers were not so very different from one another, some of them writing histories about the Greeks and some about the barbarians, and not linking all these to one another, but dividing them according to peoples and cities, and writing about them separately, all keeping to one and the same aim: whatever oral traditions were preserved locally among peoples or cities, and whatever documents were stored in holy places or archives, to bring these to the common notice of everyone just as they were received, neither adding to them nor subtracting from them. (*On Thucydides 5*)

This movement for the first time in Greece set the written archive alongside oral tradition as a source for history; two figures from its earliest stages will illustrate its character. About the end of the fifth century Hippias of Elis, travelling sophist and lecturer on antiquities of cities, published the victor list of the Olympic Games, which took chronology back in a four-year cycle to 776 BC; this became the basis for Greek time-reckoning, just as the Romans counted from the foundation of their city, the early Christians from the birth of Abraham, and ourselves from the birth of Christ. Chronology, the dating and ordering of human events, is the basic grammar of history: Hippias began a tradition which continued through the Hellenistic period, to produce in late antiquity the surviving chronological tables of sacred and profane history compiled by the Christian writers Eusebius and Saint Jerome.

Hellanicus of Lesbos in the last third of the fifth century similarly published a whole series of local histories and chronographies (at least twenty-eight), based at least in part on archival research. Among these was the first history of Athens; and the discovery in Egypt of a papyrus of Aristotle's lost work on the *Constitution of Athens* (written in the late fourth century) enables us to reconstruct the development of one city history in some detail. The *Atthis* (or history of Athens) began with

Hellanicus, a non-Athenian working in a wider tradition; later authors were mainly Athenian, often from priestly families (Cleidemus) or politicians (Androtion, the author on whom Aristotle largely relied) or both (Philochorus). Their works were characterized from the start on the one hand by a strong interest in local myth, on the other by the possession of a firm chronology: events were arranged (perhaps somewhat arbitrarily) in accordance with the Athenian list of their annual chief magistrate or *archon*. Fragments of such a list inscribed on stone and dating from the 420s BC have in fact been found in the Athenian *agora*: the public record is almost certainly evidence of state interest in the discoveries of Hellanicus, which stimulated the Athenians to set their archives in order. This is a good illustration of the interplay between civic pride and the writing of history; not surprisingly such a tradition is dominated by the interests of the *polis*, its local cults and its politics. Thucydides too is a product of the world of the developed city-state, and belongs to roughly the same generation as the first local historians; but he proclaims himself a conscious rival of Herodotus in his first sentence:

> Thucydides of Athens wrote the history of the war between the Peloponnesians and the Athenians, beginning it as soon as war broke out and believing that it would be a great war and more worthy of record than any preceding one, on the evidence that both sides went into it at the height of preparedness, and seeing the rest of the Greek world taking one side or the other, either immediately or after consideration.

The main themes emerge at once: the explicit rivalry with Herodotus in the description of a great war, the claim to contemporaneous recording, the emphasis on proving his views, the self-conscious assertion of being a writer not a performer in an oral tradition, all expressed in a prose of extraordinary density and sophistication. The war that Thucydides describes is the Great Peloponnesian War between Athens and Sparta, which lasted for a whole generation from 431 to 404 BC with only a short interlude of official, but broken, peace from 421 to 416, and ended with the defeat of Athens and the collapse of her empire. Thucydides did not live to complete his work; Book 8 breaks off in mid sentence in 411; and whereas Books 6 and 7 on the Athenian expedition to Sicily seem to be a polished work of art, there are signs of lack of finish in Books 5 and 8. Thucydides' own activities in the war are best described by himself:

> I lived through the whole of the war, being of an age to comprehend events, and giving my attention to them in order to know the exact truth about them. It was also my fate to be an exile from my country for twenty years after my command at Amphipolis [in 424 he had failed to save the city from a surprise attack]; and being present with both parties, and more especially with the Peloponnesians by reason of my exile, I had considerable leisure to observe affairs. (5.26)

Thucydides is first of all a historian's historian: he is obsessed with methodology. He sets out to prove the greatness of his war by a long excursus on earlier history designed to show the comparative insignificance of earlier wars and the poverty of earlier generations; and at the same time he offers a devastating critique of the standards of evidence employed by Herodotus. He establishes with precision the starting-point and the end of his war, and argues carefully that the so-called period of peace was really part of a single war. Like his contemporaries he is fascinated by chronology, but he rejects their lists of magistrates as unsuitable for military history; instead he dates by campaigning seasons, "by summers and winters." He attacks the lack of care others take in ascertaining facts, and asserts that he was not satisfied with any one eyewitness account, but took great pains to correlate and judge between the often differing accounts of different participants. Even for the speeches in his work, he claims in a famous problematical passage to give "whatever seemed most appropriate to me for each speaker to say in the particular circumstances, keeping as closely as possible to the general sense of what was actually said." These principles he recognizes will detract from the literary charm of his work: no matter, for its aim is scientific, to be "a possession for all time, not a display piece for instant listening" (I.22). In such attitudes we recognize the first critical historian, the founder of the western tradition. It is perhaps curious that we do so, for Thucydides is not of course a historian at all. He claimed that it was impossible to write accurately about the past; his methods and his standards of proof are applicable only to the present. He is a social scientist, a student of the contemporary world, not a historian. It was not until the nineteenth century that the discovery of archives and the invention of the techniques of source criticism allowed historians of the past to believe that they could meet the standards demanded by Thucydides. And it was not until this century that these standards could even begin to be applied to the study of Greek history, with the publication by F. Jacoby of the fragments of the lost Greek historians.[2]

One area illustrates well Thucydides' advance on Herodotus: his account of the causes of the war. Contemporaries found Herodotus' frivolous mythology of rape and counter-rape, from Io to Helen of Troy, hilarious,[3] and failed to note the problem that a clash of cultures ultimately leads to a war whose causes are incapable of being isolated, inherent in the nature of the societies in question. In the case of Greek city-states, however, there were established rules of international relations: an act of aggression or the refusal of a just request were causes of war which had an overt political nature. It is to Thucydides' credit that he does not remain on this level of claim and counter-claim. Instead he argues in detail for two episodes as the generally accepted grievances which led to

---

2. The publication of F. Jacoby's *Fragmente der griechischen Historiker* was begun in 1923.

3. See Aristophanes' *Acharnians*, lines 513–39.

war, and for a "truest cause seldom mentioned explicitly." The two episodes were military adventures involving a clash of interests and of military forces between Athens and Sparta's leading ally, Corinth. The nature
of "the truest cause" is harder to define, and it is indeed described as a
personal opinion—"the Athenians becoming great and provoking fear in
the Spartans compelled them to fight" (I.23). Is this a statement about
social psychology, or an assertion of inevitability? How unmentioned
was it, and where does it leave responsibility for the war? These questions have been endlessly debated; here we need only note the sophistication of a view which goes behind the diplomacy, and asserts two types
of forces at work, two levels indeed of causation. It is this abandonment
of the obvious, and of the idea of a single cause or type of cause, which
is the decisive step in our understanding of the idea of causation in
human affairs.

Where did Thucydides learn his method? The theory of politics and
society was still in its infancy, and there is nothing of comparable depth
in any contemporary sophist. The medical writers operated with ideas of
underlying disposition to illness, and active cause for it, not unlike those
of Thucydides, and they had developed a science combining theory with
practical insight which was analogous to his. But we have only to read
Thucydides' account of the Great Plague at Athens in Book 2 to see his
superiority even in describing a medical phenomenon: no contemporary
medical writer has his clear description of the two central medical con-
cepts in disease of contagion and immunity. In fact we may say with
confidence that Thucydides' conception of social and historical method
is his own creation. The problem of Thucydides is essentially his isola-
tion.

This conclusion is reinforced by consideration of Thucydides' literary
style. It derives ultimately from the antithetic periods of contemporary
sophistic orators; but these have been twisted to present a succession of
broken opposites and ill-matched pairs, where no one word is the obvious
word and each phrase is unexpected. Its vice is that the simple becomes
tortuous, the complex incomprehensible; its virtue is not in its precision
(for the precision is a false one), but in the way that it forces the reader—
even the contemporary Greek reader—to consider the exact significance
and placing of every word. No other Greek ever wrote or thought like
Thucydides.

The result is, of course, that he has his limitations. The silences of
Colonel Thucydides are impenetrable for us; we have no means of knowing
why he does not mention what he does not mention, or how much he
does not mention. We cannot construct history from him, we can only
accept or reject his conclusions. This would not matter if he were as
perfect a historian as some have believed. But there is good reason to
suspect that he was sometimes swayed by personal bias: his account of
Pericles is surely too favourable, his account of Cleon omits a number
of vital facts. Again what ultimately do the speeches represent, if no one

ever spoke like that, and word and thought are so closely connected? Where does this leave his account of decision-making? Moreover the very power of Thucydides' illumination throws into prominence the darkness around it: he systematically ignores the significance of Persia—the war is a war of Greek states. Would he ever have faced the fact that ultimately it was Persian gold which defeated the Athenians?

Many of these limitations reflect the aims of his work: "it will be enough if it is considered useful by those who wish to judge clearly both what has happened and what will come about again in the future, in the same or similar fashion, given the nature of man" (I.22). Thucydides here asserts no crude theory of repetition, but merely the usefulness of the study of human society in action. But what sort of society? Obviously not Persian, yet equally perhaps not merely Greek—rather the self-conscious political society in which decisions are taken by rational and open discussion and in accordance with rational principles. That is why political scientists from Machiavelli onwards have taken Thucydides as their ideal historian: Thomas Hobbes called him "the most politick historiographer that ever writ."[4]

The influence of the sophists on Thucydides' theory of politics is clear. Thucydides seems to accept as a general fact about human society that "might is right"—societies are in fact organized in terms of self-interest, and states act in accordance with self-interest: appeals to sentiment are seldom made in his work, and when made are unsuccessful. Athens holds her empire as a tyranny "which it may have been wrong to acquire, but is dangerous to surrender" (speech of Pericles, 2.63). The philosophical expression of such views is given most clearly by the sophist Thrasymachus in the first book of Plato's *Republic*. So in terms of social morality no one is ever in the right or the wrong: once Sparta's fear of Athens has been isolated, it is clear that the war is "in accordance with nature." We know that this view of society was not a universal view in the fifth century, and very probably not a majority view; nevertheless it was clearly an influential one, and Thucydides cannot be accused of solipsism or completely falsifying the nature of political debates. That he has not given a full account of the decision-making procedure is already obvious from the way that the speeches are offered as antithetical pairs, not as part of a general debate. Many of the speeches in fact serve more as a vehicle for exploring the consequences of the Thucydidean view of politics than as an accurate account of what was actually said. On the two occasions when Thucydides himself offers sustained political analysis he is less successful: the account of the development of political leadership at Athens after the death of Pericles (2.65) and the discussion of the nature of political revolution during the war in relation to the example of Corcyra (3.82–4) are both unsatisfactory in their attempt to impose a linear progression on complex phenomena.

4. Thomas Hobbes (1588–1679) the English political philosopher and author of *Leviathan*, whose translation of Thucydides was published in 1628.

Despite his acceptance of this type of social theory, Thucydides is deeply concerned with its consequences, and especially with the resulting problems of morality; he seems particularly interested in the effects of such theories on internal politics. The famous funeral oration of Pericles over the Athenian dead in Book 2 portrays a society without conflict or tension, united in pursuit of an ideal, in contrast to the pathological state of a city like Corcyra, torn apart by civil strife. In general he highlights the occasions which raise such questions in their most crucial form. In Book 3, for instance, there are three great set episodes, the question of how Athens should punish the Mytileneans for their revolt, the question of how Sparta should deal with the captured Plataeans, and the story of the revolution at Corcyra. In the first, the new morality of empire leads to the conclusion that it is more advantageous to rule by kindness than by terror. In the second, the representatives of the old morality reject an appeal to sentiment, and destroy the sacred city of the Persian Wars: they decide to liberate the Greeks through terror. In the third, Thucydides explores the breakdown of trust and social order when a society is entirely ruled by the new morality, and the only madness is to be a moderate.

Book 3 is the centre of the original history of Thucydides, which described the first part of the war and ended at 5.24. Already he has shown himself ambivalent about the desirability of the world he portrays as reality. In the second half of his work this unease, this sense of an "anti-Thucydides in Thucydides," is magnified. The reason lies in the logic of events: if the laws of politics which Thucydides has accepted are laws of nature, then their full horror will be brought home in the greatest tragedy of all, the destruction of Thucydides' own city of Athens; and the pessimism of the historian concerning human nature will be finally justified in that fall. There are strong signs that Thucydides began to articulate the second half of his history around the conception of a tragedy. In Book 5 the Athenians make an unprovoked attack on the small island of Melos, and the Melians challenge the morality of their action in a passage cast in dialogue form: the Athenians respond with the arrogance of a tyrannical city. The episode in Thucydides is deeply influenced by the literary forms of Greek tragedy, and it also embodies that deed of pride on the part of Athens which will lead to calamity in the Great Sicilian Expedition of Books 6 and 7; the story of that expedition itself is told with a passion and an artistry which show Thucydides' belief that it is the turning-point of the war: his own involvement in the telling of it is all the more effective for being disguised. We do not know how Thucydides would have ended his story; in particular we do not know how he would have explained why Sparta did not destroy Athens completely, as she should surely have done on his theory: the problem for the historian is that history is not capable of being an artistic unity, it is always being falsified by events. Thucydides' history demonstrates on the one hand the moral development of an author experiencing the events he describes as a contemporary, and on the other hand the impossibility of scientific history.

Thucydides' view of history was dominant in antiquity, as it is today. Each society gets the sort of history it deserves. Machiavellism or *Realpolitik* is still seen as the only rational response in politics, even when it leads to self-destruction.[5] That is natural once Thucydides' characterization of history is accepted, as being the realm of politics and war. The lesson is already there in Thucydides himself, that society which lives solely by such criteria will inevitably destroy itself.

II. HERODOTUS
AUBREY DE SELINCOURT

An accomplished translator, the Englishman Aubrey de Sélincourt taught for many years and translated several texts for the Penguin Classics series, including not only Herodotus' *Histories* (1954) but also Arrian's *Life of Alexander* and Livy's history of Rome.

[The Life of Herodotus] †

Little is known of Herodotus' life. His birth-place was Halicarnassus, the modern Bodrum, originally a Carian town on the south-west coast of Asia Minor; it was later occupied by Dorian emigrants from Troezene, and became in time, like the other Greek settlements on the eastern coast of the Aegean, subject first to the Kings of Lydia and then, after the conquest of the Lydian Kingdom by Cyrus the Great in 546 B.C., to the Persian Empire. It was governed in Herodotus' time by a woman, Artemisia, who was responsible to the local Persian satrap for tribute in money and for the supply of troops on demand.

The date of Herodotus' birth was round about 480 B.C. or perhaps a few years earlier, between, that is, the two Persian attempts at the subjugation of Greece. The best, though not very precise, evidence for this is an anecdote which Herodotus recounts of a dinner-party given by a wealthy Theban called Attaginus to fifty Persian grandees and fifty of his fellow-countrymen on the eve of the battle of Plataea. Amongst the Greek guests was one Thersander, a native of Orchomenus, and he was surprised and much moved when a Persian, his neighbour at table, suddenly said to him: "You see these countrymen of mine eating and drinking

5. The Italian political theorist Niccolò Machiavelli (1469–1527) shocked his contemporaries by divorcing politics from morality in his treatise *The Prince*. The later German policy of *Realpolitik* also involved a politics of self-interest.

† Reprinted by permission of Little, Brown from chapter 2, "Biographical," in *The World of Herodotus* (Berkeley, 1962), pp. 28–33.

here—and the great army we have left in camp along by the river? In a day or two from now, few of them will be left alive."

"I heard this story," Herodotus adds, "from Thersander himself." Thus Herodotus was old enough at any rate to have spoken with men who took an active part in the war, though too young to have been himself involved either in the fighting of 490 B.C., the year of Marathon, or in the campaigns of the second Persian invasion, ten years later, under Xerxes.

He came of a good Halicarnassian family. Suidas,[1] an only moderately trustworthy information-monger, tells us that he was related to a certain Panyasis, now forgotten, but apparently in his day a man of letters not without repute, writing epic poetry and—which was perhaps more important for the young Herodotus—attempting rational explanations of dreams, portents and other phenomena which popular belief attributed to gods. Not that Herodotus was ever to become a rationalist; but the atmosphere of free inquiry was a natural and necessary element for his growing mind. Of far greater weight for his future development than his kinsman Panyasis, was the general intellectual climate of that portion of the Asiatic coast, especially of Miletus, a town some forty miles to the northward, founded long before by Ionian settlers from Attica. Asiatic Ionia was the true cradle of what was to prove most vital and permanent in the development of Greek and consequently of European civilisation; a man's right, namely, to inquire into, and to speculate upon, the enveloping mystery of his situation. Once reason, acting upon the data of the senses, is recognised as being one of the avenues towards truth and not in itself a forbidden or impious activity, a necessary consequence is the recognition of the individual as a person instead of a unit. Every thinker stands upon the shoulders of his predecessors, and though Anaximander, Anaximenes, Thales and the rest may have nothing directly to tell us today, with their guesses at water, or air, or "the unlimited" as the first principle of the physical universe, yet they are the men who started Europe on its march away from the static and ant-like civilisations of the East. Their belief in the human intellect, a belief which in their own age was a revolutionary one, led to what we now know, for better or worse, as Western Man. Athens always felt a strong bond, not only of blood but also of the spirit, with Miletus; Herodotus relates that after its capture by the Persians in 494 B.C., the playwright Phrynichus produced at the Great Dionysia a tragedy on the theme of its fall.[2] The Athenian spectators are said during the performance to have burst into tears. The play was banned, and Phrynichus fined a thousand drachmas for reminding his fellow-citizens of *their own* sorrows.

---

1. For Suidas (= the Suda), see the Glossary.
2. Tragic and comic dramas were presented at the religious festivals celebrated in honor of Dionysus, god of vegetation and wine. The festival of the Great Dionysia or the City Dionysia was held at Athens in the spring.

There is no means of knowing if the education of boys in grammar, gymnastics and music, which was generally accepted in Greece a few years later, had any equivalent in Halicarnassus during Herodotus' boyhood; but it is obvious from his History that he had a wide and deep knowledge of all available literature, both ancient and contemporary. He quotes or familiarly refers to in the course of his work such names as Hesiod, Sappho, Aeschylus and Pindar, with many others of less note, while his knowledge of the Iliad and Odyssey was evidently so much a part of his mind as to be almost unconscious.[3] Such details, however, though dear to scholars, may perhaps be taken for granted, as it is not likely in any age that a man of letters will be ignorant of literature. Herodotus' real education—that part of it which differed from the education of his contemporaries—consisted in his travels, during which he saw, like Odysseus, "many cities of men" and came to know their ways. To judge by the extent of these travels and the fact that they were over by the time he was forty, he must have begun them at an early age. The precise limits of the regions he visited have been disputed, but it is certain that he went to Babylon, penetrated deep into Upper Egypt, knew Thrace and parts of Scythia (southern Russia) as far East as the Crimea, and visited Cyrene on the north African coast. He was familiar with most of the Greek mainland, with southern Italy, the other countries of Asia Minor in addition to his native Caria, and all the more important islands of the Aegean, including, probably, Crete. So wide a first-hand knowledge of the world was a rare thing in Herodotus' day; indeed, I suppose it was unprecedented, except in the travels of Scylax, who left a book, now lost, in which he told, amongst other odd things, of certain Indian peoples whose ears were so big that they wrapped themselves up in them to sleep, and of others who, finding the heat of the sun inconvenient, used their large flat feet as parasols. Herodotus himself enjoyed a tall story; but he apparently drew the line at Scylax, for he made no use of his book.

About the year 447 B.C., when Herodotus was in his late thirties, he left Halicarnassus for good and went to live in Athens, then the intellectual centre of the Greek world. Halicarnassus had recently gone through one of the political revolutions which were endemic to Greek life, and had joined the Athenian confederacy, having got rid of her "tyrants," as they were called, or irresponsible rulers, as Artemisia and her grandson Lygdamis had been. It was thus easier for Herodotus to find a welcome—though Athens always tended to be hospitable to strangers, especially to strangers who had something to give her. He had already written much of his *History*, and we are told that he gave public readings of it

---

3. Hesiod, Sappho, Aeschylus, and Pindar were Greek poets of different stamps. On Hesiod, see above, p. 301; Sappho (ca. 612–?) and Pindar (518–438) were lyric poets—Sappho was unusual in being a female poet—and excerpts from the tragic dramatist Aeschylus appear in this volume, pp. 241–45.

in Athens, and probably in other towns as well. Athens, under the leadership of Pericles, though her actual power, after the defeat at Coronea, had declined, was at the height of her glory and influence. Herodotus identified himself with what she stood for—political and intellectual liberty. He seems to have been admitted into the group of distinguished men of whom Pericles was the recognised leader, and he became a friend of Sophocles who (if we may believe Plutarch) wrote a poem in his honour. In all likelihood it was while he was in Athens that the final form of his *History* became clear in his mind; he had begun it as separate accounts of the manners, geography, monuments and antiquities of the various countries—Lydia, Egypt, Scythia and the rest—which he had visited, a work similar in kind to that of the Ionian logographers though larger in scope, and enriched by far more first-hand observation and direct inquiry; but now, caught up as he was by admiration of the Athenian spirit and of Athenian institutions, he determined so far as he could to make his wide and various researches subserve a master plan. This plan was to tell the story of the Persian wars, and in the course of the story to celebrate the decisive contribution of Athens to their successful outcome. Inevitably this left large portions of his work as merely episodical and digressive; but, happily for us, Herodotus was a superb digressor: the digressions are in themselves nearly always of fascinating interest, and he had the knack of beguiling his reader into a belief that some sort of thread, however slender, does, after all, connect them with the leading theme.

After four years in Athens he left for Italy, to return to Athens only once during the remainder of his life. Guesses have been made at the reasons for this removal: perhaps his funds were running low and he no longer felt able to maintain himself in the sort of Athenian society to which he had become accustomed; possibly he was irked at his political position—or rather *no* position, for it was not the Athenian custom to grant full citizenship to strangers. In any case, it so happened that just at this time Athens was determined to found under the auspices of Pericles a new settlement at Thurii on the gulf of Taranto in southern Italy, close to the site of the ancient town of Sybaris which half a century previously had been destroyed by its neighbours and rivals in Crotona. Herodotus went with the settlers and made Thurii his home. Readers of Plato's dialogue the *Republic* will like to remember that amongst the settlers were the two sons of Cephalus, the old man so delightfully described in that book as reversing the common Greek attitude to old age by the declaration that to him, at any rate, as to the poet Sophocles, it was a sweet and welcome refuge from the savage tyranny of physical desires.

In Thurii Herodotus lived for the next fifteen years or so, travelling a little in Sicily and Italy, visiting Cyrene in North Africa, polishing his *History* and bringing it as near as he could to completion. Some time between 430 and 425 B.C. he died. The exact year cannot be determined, but that it was after 430 is proved by the mention in his book of certain events in the Peloponnesian war which occurred at or after that date, notably the betrayal of the Spartan and Corinthian ambassadors into the hands of the Athenians. Some commentators have tried to give him a much longer life; but it is hardly conceivable that, had he lived even to as late as 415, the year of the Athenian expedition to Sicily, he would have made no mention at all in his work of that irretrievable disaster to his beloved Athens. His tomb in Thurii had the inscription: "This dust hides the body of Herodotus, son of Lyxes, and prince of old Ionian history. He sprang from a land of Dorian men, but fleeing from their scorn made Thurii his home." It is a puzzling epitaph—but there are many puzzles, or rather blanks, in the life of Herodotus for us, who know so little. Why did the Dorian men of Halicarnassus scorn Herodotus? The word I have translated as "scorn" might mean merely "blame," and there was, to be sure, a story once current that Herodotus got into trouble with Lygdamis, the town's political boss, under the Persians, and was forced to take refuge in the island of Samos, before he finally went westward to the Greek mainland and Italy. The story goes on to say that he subsequently led an expedition back to his native town and expelled the despot, Lygdamis. What, then, of the "scorn" or "ridicule"? Rawlinson, one of the best nineteenth-century commentators on Herodotus, suggested that the whole Lygdamis tale was a myth to account for the dislike of despotic government which is everywhere apparent in Herodotus' book, and that the "ridicule" of the epitaph was aroused, if it was aroused at all, by certain religious credulities revealed in the *History*: such credulities would not have been to the taste of the rising generation of free-thinkers in that part of the world.

With this meagre collection of biographical facts, and of even less satisfying bits of guess-work, we must be content. None the less, I suppose we are not content, requiring, as we have learnt to do of late, a kind of biography of famous men and women which would have made the ancients stare. The ancients did not feel—nor perhaps did the moderns before Rousseau wrote his *Confessions*—that there could be any permanent or public interest in the minutiae of personal life. [4] A man's work, or his large acts on the world's stage, were all they thought worth remembering; and, if they wanted more, they were apt to invent a myth which would satisfy their fancy or their sense of fitness, like the story of Herodotus reading his *History* at the Olympic Games and of the boy Thucydides, as he listened, bursting into tears of admiration.

Let us admit, then, that we know less of Herodotus, in the way of biographical detail, even than we know of Shakespeare. Perhaps it does not matter; for, like Shakespeare, Herodotus might well say to any one of us,

---

4. Rousseau began work on this intimate and compelling autobiography in 1766.

My spirit is thine, the better part of me;

for that spirit looks out from and greets us familiarly in every page of his book.

JAMES ROMM

James Romm received his Ph.D. from Princeton in 1988 and is currently teaching classics at Bard College. His book, *The Edges of the Earth in Ancient Thought*, a study of geography and travel literature in antiquity, will be published by Princeton University Press in 1992. The following discussion of Herodotus' view of the physical world was written especially for this volume.

The Shape of Herodotus' World

Herodotus is known primarily as a historical writer, but his work attests to the fact that political history, as practiced in fifth-century Greece, could scarcely be separated from geography, ethnography, and anthropology. The *Histories*, in fact, represents our only complete record of how the Greeks of this era perceived the lands and peoples around them, and the structure of the earth as a whole. It is a fascinating record, moreover, in that it affords a glimpse of an empirically minded researcher taking his first, tentative steps toward a truly scientific depiction of the world, that is, one based on firsthand evidence rather than on speculation. Modern readers may be tempted to sneer at the credulity of Herodotus' geographical excursuses, as indeed some of his successors did in later eras of antiquity, when the world stood revealed in much sharper outlines. However, if we read Herodotus in the light of the archaic geographical schemes which preceded him, rather than of those which followed, he emerges as a geographer of the first importance, who attempted, albeit with limited success, to revise completely the prevailing conception of the earth.

The geographical excursuses of the *Histories*, which are largely concentrated in the first four books, present a virtually complete tour of the *oikoumené*, the "inhabited world" known to the Greeks at the time. This *oikoumené* consisted of three continents: Asia, including the Arabian peninsula and part of Egypt, to the east; Africa (or Libya, as the Greeks termed it) to the south, and Europe, of which the northern and western extremes were as yet unknown. Herodotus discusses each of these areas in turn. Thus in the first book we learn about the peoples of the East—the Babylonians, Assyrians, Lycians, Carians, and, most important, the Persians, who become the central focus of the historical narrative. The second book deals exclusively with Egypt, a land so rich in wonders that

Herodotus feels it merits such an unusually full discussion. The third book takes us to other southern climes, Arabia and Ethiopia, and also includes a general discussion of the lands which lie farthest off from Greece, in all directions; the fourth book begins with an account of northern Europe, proceeds to the Scythians of western and central Asia, and ends up in Libya (northwestern Africa); and the fifth book opens with a tour of Thrace and the regions immediately north of it. Taken collectively, this first half of the *Histories* contains a reckoning of virtually every foreign land and tribe known to the Greeks of the day, as if Herodotus had been compiling a kind of universal Guidebook. At the same time, there is very little in *Histories* concerning the geography of the Greek world, either because Herodotus assumed that his readers were already sufficiently familiar with these regions, or simply because he found the subject less interesting than barbarian exotica.

In creating this world atlas in prose, Herodotus was essentially following in the train of his Ionian predecessors in geography and ethnography, but with an important difference. Earlier writers in this field, of whom Hecataeus of Miletus was the most famous, had similarly attempted comprehensive tours of the *oikoumené*, as implied by the titles of their works: *periplous, periodos, periegesis,* all implying "journey around" the circumference of a circular landmass. These early works have largely perished, but even the scanty fragments which survive indicate that they were based largely on the old Homeric model of a circular earth, completely surrounded by the river Ocean. Herodotus, however, is not willing to follow this myth-based tradition, as we shall see in more detail below. His was the first work of geography which could not also be considered a *periplous* or *periodos*; that is, since Herodotus' earth no longer has any clearly defined perimeter, it cannot be explored by means of a circular "journey around."

Let us go back for a moment to the roots of this Ionian image of the world. The conception of the earth as a perfect circle, bounded by water, had been firmly fixed in the Greek imagination at least since the time of Homer. It can be illustrated in both of the great shield descriptions of archaic poetry, the Shield of Achilles in book 18 of the *Iliad* and the Shield of Heracles in the Hesiodic poem *Scutum.* In the sixth and early fifth centuries B.C., it formed the basis for the first maps of the world, those constructed by Anaximander, Hecataeus, Hellanicus, and Damastes, and continued to dominate the literature and folklore surrounding the distant spaces of the earth. We can easily understand how such a scheme arose, with no empirical evidence about the border of the *oikoumené*, the early Greeks adopted a theoretical construct which seemed inherently plausible and which, moreover, satisfied their intuitive sense of the symmetry of the cosmos. In addition, the few vague reports which trickled into the Greek world from parts unknown must have confirmed the notion that there was water at the edge of the earth in any direction, and hence seemed to bear out the validity of the circular model.

Given the strong conceptual foundation of this circular earth, then, it is remarkable that Herodotus had the courage to reject it so vehemently, after finding no evidence to support it. In an oft-quoted passage of book 4 (chapter 36), Herodotus casts scorn on the "*periodos*-authors" (here perhaps equivalent to "mapmakers") of the past, among whom Hecataeus was surely a prominent target, for pretending that the world map could be drawn with a compass, containing three continents of equal size, and bounded by the river Ocean running around the perimeter. In other words, he tosses the archaic scheme, with all its geometric elegance, right out the window, and with it an entire era of geography based on theory rather than empirical evidence. In reading this passage, we should bear in mind that, by the end of the fifth century, the Greeks had begun to penetrate the hinterlands of northern Europe for the first time, and in addition their contact with the Persian empire had made them aware of vast new territories to the east. Herodotus, following up on these advances, tries everywhere to base his accounts of distant lands on eyewitness reports or, when possible, on his own, firsthand observations; where these are lacking, he generally refuses to indulge in mere speculation, or else tiptoes with great caution around semimythical reports obtained from second- or third-hand sources. And, since there is no confirmation from any reliable source for the river Ocean, and hence for the circular world it defined, Herodotus junks both constructs, thereby invalidating at least four centuries of cosmologic thought.

The debunking of Ocean is therefore one of the more spectacular moves in Herodotus' treatment of the archaic geographers in general and of Hecataeus in particular. A similar attack is mounted in book 2 (chapters 19ff.), where Herodotus examines a series of theories explaining the yearly floodings of the Nile. Those who claim that the Nile has its source in Ocean, Herodotus asserts, have removed the debate into *aphanes*, literally "the invisible realm," where no tests of veracity can be brought to bear. Later he adds that, since no one claims to have actually seen the river Ocean, the entire legend must be a fable invented by the early poets. In both these arguments a new standard of evidence, hitherto unknown in the field of geography, is taking shape: information about the distant world is to be treated as false, unless proven true. No longer will Herodotus allow the poets to hide their inventions in the *aphanes*, the region beyond direct investigation, a realm which the Hellenistic scientist Eratosthenes[1] was to call *eukatapseusta*, "easy to lie about." The creative license which extreme distance had conferred on Homer, Hesiod, Pindar, and Aeschylus, and on the geographers who had followed their lead, has for the first time been revoked.

1. Eratosthenes of Cyrene (ca. 275–194 B.C.), head of the library at Alexandria, was a scholar, critic, geographer, and poet.

Thus Herodotus was disturbed both by the unverifiability of Ocean and by its perfectly geometric structure, which seemed too neat for the earth as he knew it. Indeed, the world picture which Herodotus goes on to construct, after abandoning that of his predecessors (4.37ff), is that of a rough-edged and irregular mass of land, with continents of unequal size, and oddlyshaped peninsulas jutting out from its shores. Above all, it is an open-ended world, at least in three of its four quadrants. For, although Herodotus tentatively accepts the report of a Phoenician circumnavigation of Africa, proving that the southern *oikoumené* is indeed bounded by water, he asserts on several occasions that "no one knows whether Europe is surrounded by sea to the north and west" (4.42) and that Asia most certainly stretches out into undelimited distance. Instead of water, Herodotus' researches have discovered only *erémos* at the edges of the earth, "desert" or "wasteland," about which no one has any certain knowledge. Into this shadowy realm Herodotus may peer from time to time, but always with an awareness that the boundary must remain beyond the reach of empirical investigation. Thus he ultimately leaves the edge of the world map an open question, surrounded now with a dotted line rather than a solid one.

Given his commitment to empiricism with regard to Ocean, however, we are startled to come across a handful of passages dealing with other aspects of the *aphanes*, the unseen world, in which this "new geography" is completely abandoned, and the old geometric model of the earth reinvoked. In two noteworthy examples, Herodotus makes Europe symmetrical to Africa, across an imaginary east–west axis: he deduces the length and position of the Danube from those of the Nile, by assuming that the two rivers must parallel one another on opposite sides of the Mediterranean (2.34), and invents a hypothetical tribe in the far south called the Hyperaustralians ("those beyond the south wind") to balance the Hyperboreans ("those beyond the north wind") in the north (4.36). Elsewhere, he speaks of the *eschatiai*, or "most distant lands," as a kind of continuous belt which frames and encloses the *oikoumené*, almost as if creating his own, terrestrial version of the river Ocean. All these passages show that Herodotus was far from having fully escaped the geometric model he derides in book 4. Indeed, it seems that his geography was so nonschematized that he remained blithely unaware of these inconsistencies; or, alternatively, he may have followed two different approaches at different stages of composition, and simply neglected to reconcile them. At any rate, the traditional schemes of Anaximander and Hecataeus are still far more alive in the *Histories* than Herodotus was willing to admit. The same might be said of Homer: although Herodotus rejects the epic poets' account of Ocean as a fiction, he nevertheless cites Homer as a reliable witness for a different aspect of the unreachable world, the existence of horned rams in Libya.

Thus Herodotus' geography, like his history, is not an exact science, nor perhaps a science at all, by modern standards. In order to apply this rubric we must wait until the third century B.C., when the Alexandrians, and in particular Eratosthenes of Cyrene, began using mathematics and astronomy to formulate a more precise picture of the *oikoumené*, and of the globe on which it was situated. Nevertheless, Herodotus' *Histories* represents an important break with the Ionian tradition, which was heavily dominated by mythical constructs and by the geometry of the circle. In fact, the standard of evidence created by this work was seldom matched by succeeding ages, which tended to reimport the myth of Ocean whenever hard information about the distant world was lacking. Thus, whereas Herodotus (and later Aristotle) had correctly identified the Caspian as a landlocked sea, with an indeterminate mass of land on its farther side, other geographers almost inevitably assumed it to be an inlet of Ocean; in this way they created a convenient eastern boundary to the earth, where Herodotus had seen only *erémos*, uninvestigable waste. When Alexander's expedition reached the river Hyphasis, in central India, they therefore supposed, on the basis of prevailing theory, that they were only a few days' travel from the edge of the world.

CHARLES W. FORNARA

A specialist in Greek political history, Charles Fornara is professor of classics at Brown University. This selection from his book on Herodotus focuses on the way Herodotus' treatment of Themistocles reflects his awareness of the perspective his Greek audience would have brought to his *Histories*. Students may also wish to consult Professor Fornara's book *The Nature of History in Ancient Greece and Rome* (Berkely, 1983).

Herodotus' Perspective †

No person is depicted by Herodotus with more care and more skill than Themistocles. It is therefore illustrative of the manner in which Herodotus has been studied, of the presuppositions which we bring to our reading of his work, that his portrait of Themistocles has been held up as an example of Herodotus' malignity and incomprehension. * * * That opinion is misconceived. Far from lacking a conception of Themistocles' personality, Herodotus is responsible for having created it. He presents us with a person whose distinguishing characteristics are cleverness and foresight on the one hand and greed and unscrupulousness on the other. The problem has not been that Herodotus lacks a self-consistent idea of Themistocles but that we evidently would prefer a different conception. And that preference has facilitated the view that

† Excerpted by permission of Oxford University Press and the author from Charles W. Fornara, *Herodotus: An Interpretive Essay* (Oxford, 1971), pp. 66–74. The footnotes have been omitted.

Herodotus was either unaccountably malicious or that he mechanically reproduced "hostile traditions" without clearly knowing what he was doing. It is ironic that an author who is supposed to have written an encomium of Athens is suspected of malignancy towards that state's greatest hero and is regarded as incapable of distinguishing a "hostile" tradition from a favourable one.

Herodotus' "intent" deserves clearer analysis than it has received. * * * Herodotus assuredly did not write his history in order to present Themistocles as if he were the hero of a nineteenth-century novel. The important consideration for judging Herodotus' historical perception is that he recognized Themistocles' genius and resource and, more important, that the picture he paints of Themistocles is one which permits *us* to recognize his greatness. For Themistocles is the dominant figure in his account of Xerxes' War.

Again, I suggest, the cardinal assumption has been that Herodotus was writing "scientific" history—that he intended his sketch of Themistocles to be a straight-forward "historical" portrayal like that of Thucydides. Thucydides, from his perspective, wanted future generations to realize that the intelligence and the foresight of Themistocles were crucial factors in the development of the Athenian state. His moral character and even the question of whether he became treasonable are irrelevant to that concern—not, by any means, that his own opinion of Themistocles' character is noticeably different form Herodotus'. Thucydides' emphasis is different. Herodotus, though he provides us with the material permitting us to form a proper estimate of Themistocles' intellectual capacity, was concerned to present a dramatic portrait of this figure which would be credible to his contemporaries. He was dealing with the expectations of his audience. Merely consider, for instance, that oft-discussed and unappreciated first mention of Themistocles made by Herodotus in VII. 143. "Now there was a certain Athenian man who recently had stepped up to the forefront whose name was Themistocles and who was called the son of Neocles" * * * .

Most commentators consider this introduction a slap. Would his audience have thought so on hearing it? Herodotus has just finished describing very dramatically the plight of Athens, the fact that "authority" was against any attempt to fight a sea-battle at Salamis (which the audience well knew was crucial). Dark was the moment; "but there was a certain Athenian man who had recently stepped to the forefront." The first two words, [now there was], are enough to show a rift in the clouds. And then, deliberately, the name is withheld until the sentence runs to its end. Expectation, suspense and understatement: Herodotus has given Themistocles a drumroll. The formula is an excellent one with which to start an important episode. Homer used it to introduce Dolon (*Iliad* X. 314). The tone of such an introduction is nicely indicated by Xenophon in *Anabasis* III. 1. 4. At a critical moment, when the Greek mercenaries faced crisis, Xenophon introduced the hero with these words:

"Now there was a certain man in the army, Xenophon the Athenian." * * * We seem to expect that Herodotus should have provided us with some reference to Themistocles' earlier career (assuming he had knowledge of it) or have made some weighty historical judgment when actually his own concern was dramatic.

Let us therefore consider Herodotus' Themistocles from the point of view of his audience. The artistic and dramatic problems which the expectations of his audience would have created for him, if his account was to be successful, were considerable. Whatever his contemporaries may have known of Themistocles' contributions in 480–79 B.C. and however they viewed his epochal work in making Athens a sea-power, we may assume that he was chiefly pre-eminent as the personification of wiliness. The popular conception of this great man undoubtedly centred on his suppleness and craft. He had been condemned to death for treason and after a sensational flight to Persia had gained an extraordinary reception from the Great King. Themistocles' life was the kind to make people marvel; the final chapter of it would have been as notable and even more inciteful of speculation about the man and anecdotes about his nature than the earlier ones. His greatness may have been proved by his leadership in 480–79 B.C.; but to a later generation removed from that era the amazing dexterity and capacity to look after himself signalled by his final Asiatic venture will have been the most remarkable and most notorious of all. That final chapter must, for Herodotus, have been the starting point in his attempt to fathom the character of that remarkable man. The challenge to his skill was to create a believable character who was capable of being at once the saviour of the Greeks in Xerxes' War and the presumed traitor of not very long after. Herodotus married the known unscrupulous but invariably successful figure who died in Persia with the man who in 479 B.C. was proclaimed "the wisest man in Greece" (VIII, 124.1).

As in the case of Pausanias, Herodotus expected his audience to superimpose its knowledge of the sensational downfall of Themistocles on to his description of that character. Where we are apt to make him an abstraction, Herodotus gave him verisimilitude. An admirable instance of his technique is provided by his narration in VIII. 108ff. of Themistocles' famous message to Xerxes after the battle of Salamis. The Greeks, having reached Andros in pursuit of Xerxes, halted for a council of war (VIII. 108). Themistocles as usual hit upon the most effective means to wound the enemy and advanced the proposal that the Greeks race to the Hellespont and dismantle the bridges. We are reminded of former occasions when the others are hostile to his bold and successful measures. However, though Herodotus could attribute the resolve to Themistocles, the nature of the case forbade him from presenting us here with the successful operation of his powers or his craft. The plan was not attempted. Yet Themistocles' defeat is but temporary, for he is able to capitalize even on that. "When he understood that he would not persuade the many, at any rate, he changed course with the Athenians. For they were especially grieved at the thought of the Persians escaping, and were eager to sail to the Hellespont even if the others did not want to and even if they must act alone." Themistocles then dissuades them with an effective speech and Herodotus resumes (VIII. 109. 5): "This he said intending to lay up store with the Persian in order that he might have some place of refuge if by some chance a disaster should come upon him from the Athenians. And this was the very thing that happened. Themistocles deceived them in his speech and the Athenians were persuaded" to give up the venture. Sicinnus was thereupon sent by Themistocles to tell Xerxes that "Themistocles, desiring to do Xerxes a service, *stopped the Greeks* when they wished to pursue his ships and break down the bridges at the Hellespont" (VIII. 110.3).

*   *   *

Surely [scholars who have seen this passage as hostile to Themistocles] have studied it with the wrong lens. Herodotus' intent was to show Themistocles' great capacity for the clever ruse. Deceit, to be sure, is part of the nature Herodotus, like Thucydides, supposed him to possess. That, after all was the key to his strategic genius. But the purpose of the anecdote is not to show some treasonable intent on Themistocles' part. Herodotus went to considerable length to make that clear; one half of the episode should not be separated from the other. Themistocles was forestalled by his colleagues from inflicting the crushing blow that he had himself conceived of. If Herodotus had intended to make Themistocles a *traitor*, he would have presented the story differently. Themistocles did not deceive the Greeks; he fooled Xerxes. His allegation that he had stopped the Greeks form racing to the Hellespont was the reverse of the truth. But Xerxes did not know it and so Themistocles laid up store of credit with the King.

What is worthy of especial note in Herodotus' narrative is the care he has taken *not* to suggest that Themistocles was already marching down the path of treason. Herodotus has attributed to Themistocles a remarkable instance of his famous foresight. But he put Themistocles' prevision in the most general terms—"If possibly * * * some evil fall upon him from the Athenians." His Themistocles viewed the possibility of a dangerous turn in his career very hypothetically. Herodotus has separated the actual treason everyone thinks of from Themistocles' own prognostication. It is a splendid example of Herodotus having it both ways, and intentionally so.

What we, in an overprotective way, have taken to be an anecdote derogatory of Themistocles would to his audience have appeared to be the ultimate example of Themistocles' capacity to look after himself. Herodotus did not intend to suggest that Themistocles was a traitor to the Greek cause. But he very definitely permitted that conception of Themistocles to illuminate his account. His purpose is artistic. He was attempting neither to blacken Themistocles' reputation nor to whitewash it. He was recreating Themistocles' character for the sake of his story, not for the "historical record." If we do not like this fifth-century Odysseus, it is perhaps because we are apt to glorify our heroes in more conventional terms and because we are unaccustomed to finding this kind of dramatization in a history. That was not the opinion of Cicero or, one suspects, of Thucydides. The Greeks were not so prim in their younger days. They could admire cleverness and dexterity for their own sake. We have only to think of Themistocles' predecessor and his protector's attitude to *him:*

> Athena began to smile;
> She caressed him, her form now that of a woman,
> Beautiful, tall, skilled at weaving fine things.
> She spoke to him in winged words:
> "Cunning and thievish the man who could beat you
> In all your tricks, even if some god were to try it.
> You devil! You schemer! Fraud! You never cease,
> Not even at home, from the cheats
> And lying words that are your nature.
> But we'll say no more: we're both
> Alike."[1]

Herodotus' treatment of Themistocles * * * is directed to contemporaries well aware of what he leaves unsaid. The impact derives from his reliance on the response of his audience, from what he knows his hearers will conclude. His procedure is not substantially different from that of the tragedians. The basics were known, the end result predictable. What mattered was the presentation of the detail in such a way as to keep the audience involved and make the pattern explicable. This is the essence of Herodotus' art and the key to his technique. The instances already discussed provide what are perhaps the most remarkable examples of this technique because of Herodotus' subtlety and because his imaginative recreation was so daring. But it is the same with Xerxes. No Greek was unaware that this splendid figure would fall heavily and Herodotus, in presenting Xerxes to his audience, made him the more splendid so that the fall would be more dramatic. In this case, to be sure, our own presuppositions coincide with those of Herodotus' contemporaries. What I have tried to suggest, however, is that this is not inevitably so, as the usual interpretation of his treatment of * * * Themistocles should show. When our expectations do not jibe with contemporary expectations, it is easy to misconstrue Herodotus' intentions as being * * * to "vilify" Themistocles. We expect him to "tell the truth" where he expected his contemporaries to use "the truth" as the touchstone of his account. How different might our interpretation of Herodotus' [portrait of] Themistocles have been if we realized that * * * Herodotus expected his

1. *Odyssey*, 13.287–97.

audience to be thinking primarily of the fall of [Themistocles]. Instead we * * * dissociate that final chapter [of Themistocles' career] from the earlier and virtually condemn Herodotus for remembering it. The difference between Herodotus and Thucydides, between the *Histories* and "history," is at once subtle and profound.

We must therefore think away the predisposition to approach Herodotus as if he were speaking to us directly, and understand him, as best we can, as his contemporaries would have done. There are fundamental but unspoken connections he relied on his audience to make. In this respect, also, we must abandon that general willingness to judge events from a perspective favourable to Athens, to assume that everyone shared it. The projection of that attitude into Herodotus has made his sympathies seem a chaos of inconsistency. Herodotus did not write his history for the partisans of the Athenian democracy. He directed his work to the Greek world in general and more particularly to a class which he, like Thucydides (II. 8.4) considered hostile to the state of Athens. Finally, since it is Herodotus' technique to mesh his narrative with the predictable thoughts of his contemporaries, we must remind ourselves constantly that the people for whom he was writing were living during the outbreak of the Archidamian War. [2]

STANLEY ROSEN

Stanley Rosen was educated at the University of Chicago, where he received both his B.A. and his Ph.D. Since 1956 he has taught philosophy at Penn State University. He has published widely on both Greek and modern philosophy, with special interests in Plato and in Hegel. The following essay is an important modern effort to take Herodotus seriously as a thinker and historian, to place him firmly in the best intellectual company of his time, and to demonstrate his significance to what Professor Rosen clearly regards as a viable Western tradition.

Herodotus Reconsidered †

1. It is an expression of the difference between classical and modern thought that, in the last three hundred years, the relationship between philosophy (as distinguished from theology) and history has become a problem of fundamental importance. This problem has its origins in a gradual but decisive redefinition of the terms "philosophy" and "history"

2. The first ten years (431–21) of the Peloponnesian War (431–404) between Athens and Sparta, named after King Archidamus of Sparta.

† Reprinted by permission of the author and of the editors of the *Giornale di Metafisica* 18 (1963): 194–218. Most notes have been omitted.

themselves. One could almost say that this process of redefinition has alienated contemporary man from his classical origins. For example, the careful study of classical philosophers, to whom "history" in the modern sense was not a serious affair, has for the most part devolved upon those who call themselves (and are called) "historians" of philosophy. Without impugning the seriousness or excellence of their work, we may observe the following paradoxical situation: especially in the Anglo-Saxon world, despite the concern with and commitment to history—the temporal, contingent, particular—and the subsequent insistence upon the historical nature of truth, academic philosophers have tended to distinguish between philosophy as a living enterprise and the history of philosophy as an antiquarian, even unnecessary or useless interest. This is substantiated rather than contradicted by the fact that classical scholarship has become a meticulous *historical* science, for the canons of such a science are derived from schools of thought which are alien to or alienated from the classical authors themselves. Similarly, the way in which we read the classical historians is inevitably conditioned by the modern conception of the nature of history. We are faced by a problem of historical understanding, to say nothing of philosophical comprehension. Why does our conception of history lead us on the one hand to identify history and philosophy, and on the other to distinguish them sharply? Has this conception of history prevented us from understanding the classical elements in modern thought? Have we failed to understand ourselves because we have failed to understand the classics? Is it not a contradiction of our own historical sense to believe that we are intelligible independently of our antecedents?

Perhaps the relationship between history and philosophy is only to be understood by a reconsideration, *in its own terms*, of the classical separation of philosophy from history, of the step by which the dialectic between history and philosophy was initiated. In this paper, I should like to take one step in such a reconsideration by discussing the thought of Herodotus. When we speak of Herodotus as "the father of history," we use the word "father" in a scientific sense: the simple initiator of what has become sophisticated only in the passage of time, through much trial and error, and after having learned the correct methodology. In order to understand Herodotus, however, we must put aside this condescension and remind ourselves that the word *historia* means "inquiry" or "investigation." Herodotus' excellence as a historian in the modern sense is independent of his excellence as an inquirer or investigator in the original sense. Indeed, his status or function as a historian in the modern sense is secondary to, or derivative from, his inquiry into the nature of human and divine things.

The denigration of Herodotus begins with Thucydides. And yet, to appreciate the sense in which Thucydides criticises him, we must treat Herodotus with the same seriousness. The criticism of Plato begins with Aristotle; but, without Plato, there would have been no Aristotle, and

Aristotle's respect for Plato is indicated by his criticism. We would do well to recall the anecdote that, as a boy, Thucydides wept upon hearing Herodotus read his work aloud. The tears of the young Thucydides, whether "historical" or not, are symbolic of a relationship or influence which can be supported from the texts of both men. This influence is positive as well as negative. To give a negative example, Thucydides criticises Herodotus by implication when he dismisses the importance of the Persian War. But it is necessary for him to depreciate the importance of the Persian (and especially the Trojan) war in order to establish the crucial significance of the Peloponnesian war. The implied criticism of Herodotus (and especially of Homer) is an essential part of Thucydides' claim that his book gives to man the understanding of war and peace as a possession for all time. Herodotus is important enough to be alluded to; he and Homer are the thinkers whom Thucydides considers as his rivals. With respect to the philosophers of Greece, and even of the Athens which is one of the two poles of his book, Thucydides is absolutely silent.

If philosophy is a deeper rival of Thucydides than are Homer and Herodotus, if his silence is more profound and even more eloquent than are his allusions, he nevertheless may be understood to call our attention to the question of the worth of Homer and Herodotus as prior to the question of the worth of philosophy. One must pass through the surface in order to plunge the depths. One must try to understand Thucydides' enterprise as he himself understood it and wished it to be understood. The surface of the enterprise is the starting point, and, on the surface, we find Homer and Herodotus. But fidelity to the surface is in no way compatible with superficiality. Thus, it would be superficial to say that Thucydides dismisses Homer and Herodotus because they are not "critical" or "scientific" historians. This is to judge the issue entirely in modern terms. Thucydides complains about those writers who do not trouble sufficiently to verify their facts, but that Thucydides is concerned with something more than "facts" is shown by his speeches, which he himself tells us are not literally factual. The emphasis upon Thucydides' similarity to modern historians leads us to overlook or to criticise the respects in which he is totally dissimilar to modern historians. The question is precisely to understand what Thucydides meant by history. And we wish to know the way in which history, in his view, differs from, and is related to, *philosophy*. This problem takes its decisive form in the work of Herodotus. Not only is the study of Herodotus the prelude to the study of Thucydides; it is the study of the theoretical origin of what we now call "history." For, although Herodotus is by no means a "historian" in the modern sense, it is nevertheless appropriate to call him the father of history. We must be concerned with the theoretical reasons for which he engages in an inquiry that gives birth to, although it is not itself identical with, history.

We need to take Herodotus seriously, but this does not require us to lose our sense of humor. Thucydides casts some light on how to take Herodotus seriously by tacitly linking him to Homer. From the sober viewpoint of Thucydides, Homer and Herodotus are too playful: they adorn their works with *mythōdes* and write for the sake of prizes. A *mythos* is a fable or legend, which means in this context that it is untrue: Homer and Herodotus deal in part, and perhaps in the crucial parts, with *lies*. Furthermore, they do not write for eternity, but for the decision of the moment. Prizes are awarded by public opinion: Homer and Herodotus are more concerned with public opinion than is Thucydides. The public desires, not truth, but *pleasure*; for the sake of pleasure, it will tolerate lies. Thucydides is austere; apparently he neither lies nor seeks to please, except insofar as we may be pleased by the truth. Homer and Herodotus tell pleasant lies. The austerity of Thucydides and his unadorned presentation of the truth about human behavior gives to his book an almost unbearable grandeur. The pleasure which is derived from Thucydides is not just a possession for eternity; the eternal things are hard and pleasing to relatively few, whereas the pleasure of the moment, the public pleasure, is accessible to almost everyone. And one may wonder whether even the relatively few are faithful to the almost unbearable grandeur of Thucydides' book. Do we not avoid its harshness by reflecting upon his factual accuracy, his freedom from personal bias, his artistic skill, and so on? In any event, the explicit repudiation of pleasantness and lies is paralleled by the austerity with which Thucydides reveals the bestiality of man. Thucydides does not spare the public; he does not ask for their applause.

To expand this notion of public applause: Thucydidean truth is akin to the truth of tragedy, whereas the pleasing lies of Herodotus remind us of comedy. We are reminded of the fact that Homer, with whom Thucydides associates Herodotus, wrote two books, the *Iliad* and the *Odyssey*, which could provisionally be classified as a tragedy and a comedy. The heroes of tragedy are the exceptional few; the heroes of comedy are the multitude. The hero of the *Odyssey*, however, is not the hero of Athenian comedy, but the wily Odysseus, who pleases by his lies. The comedy of the *Odyssey* is higher than the comedy of the Athenian stage with respect to its hero, but it is linked to that comedy by the pleasing lies which its hero tells. Similarly, Herodotean comedy is Odyssean. Odysseus makes the journey to many lands to see the *nomoi* (customs) of many people; he spurns eternal life in order to return to his home, his family, his city. He chooses his own *nomoi*, thereby obeying the adage of Pindar which Herodotus cites affirmatively: *nomos* is the king of all men. The analogy between Odysseus and Herodotus seems to be quite appropriate. The Herodotean inquiry is an Odyssean comedy spoken for the pleasure of the many. The hero of the *Iliad*, however, is Achilles, war-lord of the Myrmidons, the greatest Greek warrior, a man

of simple passion and directness, semi-divine, literally a *hero*. But Thucydides' simplicity is only the surface of an incredible complexity, his
passions are controlled, he is not a great warrior but in fact a failure as a
general. Homer teaches us about war through the instrumentality of
Achilles and men of his nature; Thucydides is the antithesis of Achilles
and he repudiates the teaching of Homer. The Thucydidean inquiry is
an anti-Homeric or anti-Achillean tragedy spoken for the pleasure of the
few.

Both Homer and Herodotus tell pleasant lies (whereas the unpleasant
truths of Thucydides are pleasant in an entirely different sense). The
purpose of these lies is to win the public applause. Socrates also speaks
of the relationship between pleasant lies and the public. The pleasantness of the Socratic lie differs from that of the Homeric-Herodotean lie
in that it adheres to the noble *(gennaion)*: the Socratic lie has received
more than a tincture of Thucydidean austerity. Nevertheless, the noble
lie is designed to guarantee the acceptance by the public of the city that
just men wish for, the city which has its being in speech. Since it does
not in fact exist, the city in speech is at least partly *fabulous*; it corresponds to the legendary city of Atlantis which Socrates boldly makes the
wished-for city in deed. The noble lie and the *mythos* serve a political
function: they subordinate the many to the few, or the unjust to the just.
Philosophy has a political setting; just as the Homeric-Herodotean ana-
logue of philosophy, the correct teaching about man and the gods, is
fundamentally a political teaching. It is clear that the Socratic conception of the wished-for city would be pleasant to a very few, perhaps to
none at all. The modern judgment of this city is that it is *utopian*, by
which we mean impossible. The impossibility of the Socratic city, one
may conjecture, is a direct consequence of the replacement by Socrates
of *noble* for pleasant *lies*. In this sense, Homer and Herodotus are closer
to the modern taste; the pleasant lie is appropriate to the desire for public
consensus. The journeys of Odysseus, which are in themselves pleasant
lies, are his preparation for the return to his throne, to rule over his city.
He replaces the eternal (immortality) by the temporal (his *nomoi*). The
journeys of Herodotus are the preparation of his readers, by the use of
pleasant lies, for the task of living in their own cities. For some, this
preparation will extend to the understanding, and consequently to the
ruling, of their cities. The journeys of Odysseus and Herodotus are such
that they may be made at the same time in different ways, both by the
many and by the few. They reconcile the many and the few to the public
nomoi, albeit in different ways.

Homer and Herodotus present us with a journey to already existing
cities; Socrates replaces this journey with the founding of a radically new
city. Thus, Homer and Herodotus are more "pious" than Socrates. By
not replacing the existing cities with a radically new city, they indicate
their respect for tradition, for the ancestral ways. But the ancestral ways

are many, in principle as many as there are cities. All men have ancestors and ways inherited from them. All these ways are to be respected: *nomos* is the king of all men. The teaching of Homer and Herodotus is compatible with the retention by each city of its ancestral ways; it is a teaching which is pleasant to the public. Homer and Herodotus will be awarded prizes; they will not be put to death like Socrates. The pleasant lie is more serviceable or practical than the noble lie. It makes possible the public teaching of a teaching about the public which is very far from pleasant. Behind the pleasantness of Homer and Herodotus, there is a bitterness; to those who are familiar with irony, there is a sting behind their smiles. In a real sense, Socrates is much franker than Homer and Herodotus: with all due qualifications, he nevertheless tells his lies openly, in public. But the pleasant lies of Homer and Herodotus mask by their pleasantness the bitter necessity of conforming to the public taste. The correct teaching about human affairs not merely conforms publicly to the public taste, but teaches that it is correct to do so. The correct teaching about human affairs is in a fundamental sense equivalent to the public taste: *nomos* is the king of all men. The piety of Homer and Herodotus veils a reserve which goes beyond the reserve of Thucydides or Socrates.

For Homer and Herodotus, there is something in the nature of things which forbids the public transcendence of the ancestral. At this point the public and private teaching correspond. What looks to many contemporary readers like naiveté is rather a profound sophistication. It is no exaggeration to say that Homer and Herodotus are "men of the world," that is, of *this* world; and, as is often the case, the sophistication of men of this world may be criticised for being *too* sophisticated. Such a sophistication dismisses as naive the public possibilities of philosophy or serious theoretical reflection. By committing itself to *nomos*, it seeks to prevent the public appearance of such reflection. But this commitment, in Herodotus' case, is itself based upon theoretical reflection of the most serious kind. The absence, or allusive presence, of philosophy on the surface of Herodotus' writings is thus a prelude to Thucydides' silence about philosophy. The inquiries of Herodotus and Thucydides are a preparation for modern "history" insofar as both men are antagonists to philosophy in the Socratic sense. To put this antagonism briefly, and therefore in a necessarily over-simplified way: Herodotus denies the eternal, whereas Thucydides regards it as impotent if noble. Both are related to Heracleitus, and consequently to each other, in the following way. [1] Herodotus' teaching is in essence the teaching of Homer, and Homer, as Socrates points out, makes all things subservient to motion. One could not say the same about Thucydides, but his main theme is also *kinesis*: the motion

1. The philosopher Heraclitus (ca. 500 B.C.) stressed the primacy of motion and of the laws which govern it. He is most famous for his statement *"panta rhei"*: everything is in flux.

of political bodies in decay. War is the biggest motion, and war is the key to the understanding of man. With the massive exception of Parmenides, [2] the pre-Socratics (or anti-Socratics), like the thinkers of modernity, are obsessed with *kinesis*, and *kinesis* is the father of history.

2. We need not call Herodotus a philosopher in order to say that he attempts to know the truth about man and the gods. The greatest obstacle to any reconsideration of Herodotus as a profound thinker lies in his opposition to the public appearance of serious theoretical reflection. This opposition is expressed in and reinforced by an extraordinarily rich and subtle style. An introductory inspection of Herodotus must be faithful to his meticulous use of concrete detail, while at the same time illustrating the general principles of his thought. For these reasons, I have almost entirely narrowed my analysis to the first three books. A complete study of Herodotus, it goes without saying, would have to deal with his entire work. Nevertheless, in my opinion, the principles of the work as a whole may be extracted from those very books which, according to a number of modern scholars, are peripheral to Herodotus' end.

We must first be certain that we understand Herodotus' end. We do not assume that we are wiser than he, nor that we understand his intentions more adequately than he. Herodotus himself tells us in his initial sentence that these intentions are much broader than simply to give an account of the Persian war. He identifies his publication as a *historia*: an inquiry or the knowledge obtained by an inquiry. A *historia* is distinguished from two other kinds of writing: poetry (especially the *epopoiie* of Homer) and the chronicles or tales *(logoi)* of the Persians and Egyptians. The poet (Homer) represses information if it is not compatible with the purpose of the epic; Herodotus, on the other hand, will write *on principle* the stories or traditions he has heard. At first this seems to mean that Herodotus is franker than Homer, but a moment's reflection upon our passage shows that this does not follow. For, at II. 123, Herodotus says that those who find the Egyptian stories persuasive may accept them; his own function is to record them all. Herodotus both casts doubt on the *logoi* (some of which he explicitly repudiates) and suggests that it is up to the reader to decide in each case which are reputable, and why it is compatible with the purpose of the *historia* to record each tale. This does not mean that Herodotus shares the modern historian's desire to record everything about the past, to have all "the facts." Herodotus' inquiry is not restricted to the past; it is equally dedicated to the present. But more specifically, the indiscriminate or exhaustive gathering of facts is not the function of the *historiai*, but rather of the *logioi*. The Egyptians who dwell in the corncountry are by far the

2. The work of the philosopher Parmenides of Elea (ca. 480 B.C.) survives only in fragments and concerns the nature of being.

best *logioi* whom Herodotus has tested by conversation because they are the greatest cultivators of the memory.

Herodotus again indicates that he has not indulged in an indiscriminate recording of tales when he discusses his trip to Phoenicia to investigate stories told to him by the Egyptians about Heracles. He then says: "The Greeks say many other things without having looked upon them *(anepiskeptōs)*." And: "The Greeks seem to me . . . to be altogether ignorant of the nature and customs of the Egyptians." Herodotus, no less than Thucydides, expends great efforts to certify the evidence of his inquiry. His efforts differ from those of Thucydides insofar as his inquiry is also different. Herodotus sheds light on this inquiry by using the word *anepiskeptōs* in criticism of the Greeks: they speak without having directly seen what they describe. I believe that this is related to the interesting omission, in the first sentence of the *historia*, of reference to a subsequent concern for speeches; he emphasizes his interest in great and marvelous deeds, and especially war. (Of course he records many speeches, and often discusses his method, but never in as explicit and preliminary a form and as Thucydides.) Herodotus, unlike Socrates, for example, makes an Odyssean journey to many cities in order to look upon the objects of his discourse. As he says in discussing the source of the Nile, he judges the unknown or unperceived by the *visible*. The failure of the Greeks to do so leads them to err concerning the *physis* and *nomos* of the Egyptians, a crucial distinction.[3]

Let us notice one more qualification about the recording of tales. In a previously cited passage (II. 123), Herodotus implies that he will record whatever he has been told. But this is not his intention; Herodotus continuously refuses to mention certain details which are well known to him, the most important of these pertaining to religion. The principle by which Herodotus decides what may be said about religion and what he must suppress is not self-evident, but he explicitly states that he is not acting from caprice. He refuses, for example, to tell us why the Egyptians consecrate animals to the gods, for this would lead him into speech about "divine things, which I especially flee from mentioning," unless constrained by necessity. One may make the following suggestion. In an interesting passage, Herodotus tells us that he restricts his discussion of religion because he believes that all men know the same about the gods; what he tells us will be by the necessity of his narrative. The very next chapter begins with the phrase "As for human affairs, . . ." and proceeds with copious details. Herodotus does not flee from speaking about human affairs, even though he may do so in a cryptic manner. He distinguishes between the human and the divine things or affairs. The human things are not divine; man is independent of the gods, and Herodotus' subject is the affairs of man as so independent. If all men know the same about

---

3. On *physis* and *nomos*, see the Glossary s.v. *nomos*.

the gods, and this knowledge takes the form of *nomos*, then the *nomos* of one city is exchangeable for that of another. To say that *nomos* is the king of all men is to say that they do not know of this equivalence: they do not know about the gods.

The second book of Herodotus' *historia*, the story of the Egyptians, has furnished us with some clues concerning his conception of writing. Book II has often been regarded as "superfluous" to Herodotus' main theme, but this opinion rests upon a disregard of Herodotus' own statement of that theme. He does not say that his intention is to describe the war between Greek and Persian. He says rather that he wishes to preserve the record of the great and marvelous deeds of Greek and barbarian, and to publish the *cause* of their war. At the most, a description of the war can be only a part of this enterprise. Furthermore, the emphasis of the history is on human deeds as such. In his preface, Herodotus is totally silent about the *gods*. In order to make clear the greatness, the marvelousness of human deeds, one must show them to belong to men, and not to gods. The independence of man from the gods accentuates the marvelousness of human deeds. It is a mark of the greatest subtlety and irony that Herodotus makes the distinction between human and divine things in his account of the Egyptians, who, he tells us, are *extraordinarily pious*; they fear god more than do all other men. Men of extreme piety will never observe the independence in question; they will not observe that Herodotus is not himself extremely pious, despite his statement that all men know the same about the gods. For, as we have seen, this means that that greek religion is *no better than* the barbarian faiths. Parallel to this, Herodotus drops the distinction between Greek and barbarian; he wishes to preserve the great deeds of both. Whatever the difference between Greek and barbarian, the deepest distinction in Herodotus' thought is between men and gods.

For example, the Egyptians, the most religious of men, whose knowledge of the gods is essentially the same as that of the Greeks, pay no divine honors to heroes. For they deny that men could be descended from the gods. Thus, the people who are on the surface most religious, in fact themselves make the human things independent of the gods. Herodotus directs us to look more deeply than the surface of piety. This distinction between the appearance and the "reality" of piety corresponds to the distinction, also made in contrasting the Greeks and Egyptians, between *physis* and *nomos*.

* * *

Man is by nature independent of the gods because nature is *in motion*. There cannot then be an eternal and hierarchical relationship between man and the gods. It is precisely *nomos*, and not the gods, that rules all men. *Nomos* rules, not because of the absence of *physis*, but because *physis* is *kinesis*. Herodotus has reversed the Parmenidean distinction between the appearance of motion and the reality of rest. The identification of *physis* as *kinesis*, which prepares the way for "history" in the modern sense, is also made in Book II; and this is appropriate to its importance for religion. *Physis* includes the gods, men, and the world. Herodotus indicates that each of these three has come into being; he denies the eternal. As for the gods, the Greeks knew nothing until "the other day" concerning their origin and forms. Hesiod and Homer, no more than four hundred years earlier, made the Greek theogony, and gave to the gods their names, honors, and duties, while pointing out their forms. And both Homer and Hesiod say that the gods came into being from Ocean and Tethys, or from some prior source.[4] The confusing plurality of gods and genealogies in Hesiod reminds us of the Egyptians. On the surface we have the present rule of the Olympians (not without inner strife), but the origins are literally *chaotic*. The origins are in motion, and Socrates, in discussing Heracleitus and the contention that everything moves, in fact attributes this doctrine to Homer and the ancients, who he says concealed their meaning from the multitude in poetry. Socrates opposes this doctrine because it renders the Whole unintelligible and undermines a belief in the gods and the immortal soul, upon which a healthy society depends. We shall see that Herodotus, although he accepts the identification of *physis* and *kinesis*, agrees that such a view is better concealed. With respect to man, Herodotus, in discussing the age of the Egyptians and their land, says that not only they, but the whole race of man came into being *(egeneto)*. And the earth, too, has come into being.

Such is the bitter medicine which lies beneath the surface of Herodotus' tranquility and simplicity. The phrase "bitter medicine" is apt; according to Herodotus, the Egyptians, next to the Libyans, are the healthiest people, thanks to their unchanging climate; for diseases come especially when men are subject to change. If the Egyptians are free from the sicknesses appropriate to the motion of their cosmology, it is because they have not thought through the consequences of their piety. They dwell in a surface of calm, imitative of their climate, where *nomos* veils over the ultimate Heracleitean unrest. It is the Greeks who are in danger of succumbing prematurely to the underlying motion, because they are inclined to theoretical reflection. Paradoxically, this reflectiveness is due to their surface stillness, i.e., their civilised or *citified* nature. Ultimately, of course, the motion below cannot be avoided; man's very existence is characterised by disease because the nature of things is motion. The Scythians and Herodotus himself represent the two extreme ways of postponing the disease of existence, but for the majority of mankind, the best solution lies between the two extremes: in moderation.

4. Tethys, the consort of Ocean, was the daughter of Earth and Heaven.

Moderation means acceptance of the ancestral ways, the *nomoi*. It means that, with highly infrequent exceptions, the private teaching about human things becomes identical with the public teaching. The Greeks are then wiser than the Egyptians insofar as they worship the heroes and trace through them their descent from the gods. This divine descent is the fundamental premise of the public teaching or moderation, which guarantees health for the majority for as long as possible. Doom can only be postponed; but at least wise (moderate) men may elude it and die *happily*. The most we may hope for is to get safely through life: death is the last disease and escape from the danger of disease. Thus Herodotus conceals his denial of the major premise upon which rests the happiness of the majority, but he is not simply concerned with them. He knows that, for some men, true happiness arises, not from public applause, but from private reflection upon the reasons for acquiescing in this applause. For the sake of these men, Herodotus only partly conceals his knowledge of private truths. He imitates Homer, who reveals that he is familiar with certain tales, although his purposes require that others be used, and also Odysseus, who speaks differently to the few and the many.[5] By preserving the memory of great and marvellous deeds, Herodotus' book stands in place of the eternal for the few, while it preserves the eternal for the many. When the distinction between the few and the many comes to be dropped, history is transformed into the replacement of the human for the eternal.

We turn now to the discussion of the outrages committed by the Persian king Cambyses, where Herodotus says that Cambyses was clearly mad, for otherwise he would not have mocked the holy rites and customs. The madness of such tampering with rites and customs is due not to their being truly sacred, but to the fact that men believe them to be sacred. Man's preference for his own *nomoi* is his best safeguard against the corruption of change. For Herodotus, it is "natural" that *nomos* rule over all; it is not accident or stupidity, but an instinctive recognition of the healthy. Moderation is expressed by a reverence for the ancestral. In political terms, moderate men are *conservatives* (and this is compatible with Herodotus' high regard for democratic Athens, when that regard is properly understood). Freedom and conservatism are by no means mutually exclusive, unless conservatism degenerates into a form of madness. Since the origins are chaotic, there is no natural or divine justification for custom *except* in terms of compatibility with stillness. Customs are criticised on the basis of their deviation from regularity. An example of this is Herodotus' distaste for the Babylonian custom which requires every native woman to have sexual intercourse with a stranger once in her life. When community of women is the regular custom, as among the Massagetae and Agathyrsi, Herodotus raises no objection. The single irregularity, in face of otherwise uniform chastity, is too dangerous to be

5. *Iliad*, 2.188ff.

uncensured, for it gives experience in vice to everyone. By reinforcing his condemnation of Cambyses with a story about the relativity of burial rites, Herodotus virtually reveals his opinion of religion, although he partially disguises it by attributing the experiment to Darius. Among the ancients, the manner of burial was an extremely important, direct expression of their religion. But Herodotus is scrupulous in recording the heterogeneity of burial customs, nor does he ever express shock or disapproval at any of these ways. Nothing could be less pious. The equivalence of burial rites is a fundamental refutation of Greek religion.

3. We have spoken of the relation between moderation and conservatism. Herodotus' political views are subtly presented in his recording of a conspiracy, a revolution, and the first political dialogue, one which, unlike those of Socrates, actually culminates in the founding of government. I shall consider this section at some length, both for its intrinsic interest and to provide a model of interpretation for those passages which cannot be discussed here. The section in question is the account of the Persian rebellion against the Magi [in book 3]. It falls naturally into three parts: (i) the conspiracy (68–79); (ii) the dialogue about the new regime (80–84); (iii) the decision about the new ruler (85–87). The "theoretical" section (the dialogue) is surrounded by sections dealing with violence and deceit. The section on conspiracy is longer than the other two sections combined; furthermore, it, too, falls naturally into three parts: (i) Otanes' discovery and his convocation of the conspirators (68–76); (ii) the dialogue about the conspiracy, with a description of the counterconspiracy of the Magi (71–74); (iii) the failure of the Magian and the success of the Persian conspiracy (75–79).

As a prelude to the entire section, we may notice chapter 65, in which Cambyses, whose madness had permitted the Magi to take power, summarizes his own folly and the revolt itself, in a period of recaptured lucidity. He states one of Herodotus' favorite themes: "Man's nature does not permit his turning aside the future." Again nature and chaos are linked together. Cambyses demands that the Persians recover the throne, either by deceit or by might, depending upon which was responsible for their losing it. He does not mention the third possibility that the two occurred together; although this was indeed the case. Smerdis the Magian had been substituted for Smerdis the son of Cyrus, whom Prexaspes had killed at Cambyses' instruction. This instruction was due to a dream which, in the event, Cambyses misinterpreted. The regularity with which men in high places are deceived by ambiguous dreams or oracles is too striking to be accidental: the gods are the presumed authors of dreams and oracles. Men try to fashion their conduct on the basis of these presumed messages, but there is no real harmony between the divine and the human mind. At the very least, if the gods speak to man, they are unable to speak clearly, because they are subordinate to higher forces, whose will is veiled from man.

Acting upon information received from his daughter, Otanes, who will speak for democracy, organizes the conspiracy. His motives are freedom (from the Medes) and justice (against the impostor). The seven conspirators engage in a dialogue of six speeches: three by Darius, two by Otanes, and one by Gobryas, who is entirely subordinate to Darius. Otanes and Darius are the central figures, but Darius is twice as forceful. The dialogue falls into two groups of three speeches each. Darius begins the first group by recommending immediate action; he emphasizes the haste with which he has come to arrange for the death of Smerdis, and in this brief speech reveals his eagerness to seize the throne. Otanes replies that Darius is the son of a good father and seems no less good; but he should not act without counsel but rather more moderately; additional allies are required. Otanes emphasizes our initial impression of Darius' rashness together with his own moderation. He implies modestly that it is his own counsel which Darius needs, and he shows his disinterestedness in power by wishing to bring others into the scheme. Otanes prefers the many to the few. Darius responds more than immoderately: he rejects Otanes' advice as mortally dangerous, and indicates that he distrusts the other conspirators already. If they delay, he warns, someone will betray them to the Magi for gain. Therefore, unless they act at once, he will protect himself by going directly to the Magus and informing him of the plot.

At this point, it seems to be well established that Darius is ambitious, rash, suspicious, and even unprincipled. But this means that Otanes, the moderate and presumably prudent man, has failed to judge Darius correctly. His attempt to restrain Darius, whom he had called *agathos*, succeeds only in moving him to an extreme position. Even if Otanes recognizes Darius as a rash and ruthless man, his patronizing effort at restraint is still more ineptly made. We are in doubt as to our original estimate of the speakers (70–71). Darius' threat is decisive; in the second set of speeches, we see that Otanes has been outmaneuvered at one stroke (72). He indicates his surrender, and also that the dialogue is in a second phase, by asking how it will be possible for the conspirators to gain entrance into the palace. Darius' response is extremely curious. Hitherto he has spoken directly to the point, as befits an unprincipled, headstrong and ambitious man. Suddenly he reverses his tactics, and makes a rather elaborate introduction to an answer that should be obvious to conspirators against the throne: "There are many things impossible to reveal in speech but possible in deed. Some things can be spoken, but no noble *(lampron)* deed is engendered." Why this reticence in face of Darius' prior fluency and precision, and his freedom from moral scruple? His answer to Otanes, when it does come, is both clear and bold: "Where it is necessary to lie, one must do so." Men lie or tell the truth for the same reason: gain, either immediate or eventual.

Two reasons may be given for Darius' caution, one from his viewpoint and one from Herodotus'. In Book I, Herodotus says of the Persians that they hold it unlawful to speak of what it is forbidden to do, and "they believe that the most shameful thing of all is to tell a lie . . ." (138). Despite his own accommodating nature, Darius must be cautious in proposing that Persian gentlemen must lie. Besides, as we learn from I. 135, the Persians are more than all other men susceptible to foreign customs. Persian virtue is one of *nomos* rather than *physis*; the former, as we learned from Socrates, is easily corruptible. Darius is about to set what must be for his suspicious nature an especially dangerous precedent. If he finally obtains the throne, his present companions may well conspire against him; having lied once, it is easier to lie a second time. The very fact of the conspiracy is sufficiently dangerous in this respect. The rule of the false Smerdis may be unjust and foreign. But it is quite compatible with the behaviour of aristocracies they they adhere to a code of personal honor even while engaged in war: to tell a lie is from the viewpoint of honor a greater sin than to murder a tyrant and impostor. And Herodotus himself, by making Darius argue that justice and freedom depend upon lies and murder, anticipates Machiavelli by maintaining that good states depend upon a foundation of violence.

Peace originates in war, rest in motion. The origins are chaotic, but in order to safeguard man's "health," this bitter truth must be veiled by a surface of stillness and piety, just as Darius attempts to place his praise of lying within a context that emphasizes the unusualness of the situation. He attempts to veil the boldness of this praise by putting it within the brackets of revolution, an extra-legal situation. And this veiling harmonizes with the secrecies which such conspiracies require. But despite all the dangers, Darius cannot keep still: it is *necessary* to lie. Herodotus phrases his speech so as to distinguish between purity and necessity; the latter takes precedence. Purity or nobility is derivative from lying and murder; it is possible only when men have established order in accord with necessity. In face of chaos, or the denial of an eternal framework, of a link between gods and man, the establishment of order depends upon the satisfaction of self-interest. Herodotus makes this connection by having Darius emphasize that men tell the truth and lie for the same end: gain. Gain is the link between the chaotic origin and the piety which conceals the chaotic origin. Gain replaces the gods. Similarly, Darius' form of moderation (boldness and lying veiled by caution) replaces that of Otanes. Moderation is a mean between two extremes. Otanes' version of moderation is the middle of the first set of three speeches, whereas Darius' version is the middle of the second and more decisive set. Given the nature of political origins, Darius is more prudent than Otanes. Gain is the basis of nobility.

Thus Herodotus indicates that men of Otanes' nature have not thought through the foundations of political activity. Still, there is a sense in which Otanes is right, although it is not Darius, but the nature of things, which is to blame. Darius is forced to reveal the ugly underside of human affairs in order to move his collaborators to the necessary action. Their naiveté, together with the pressure of events, leads Darius to a slight overstatement of his case. Herodotus subtly corrects him in the chapters about the Magian attempt to use Prexaspes in silencing Persian suspicion (74–75). Prexaspes agrees to assist them in deceiving the Persians; the Magi trust him because Cambyses, while mad, had killed his son. But Prexaspes betrays the Magi; as soon as the Persians are assembled he tells them the truth about the false Smerdis, exhorts the Persians to recapture their throne, and kills himself by leaping from the tower on which he had been standing. Prexaspes has lied twice, but the result is splendid or noble. Herodotus' language emphasizes the interplay of visibility and invisibility, of appearance and reality. Prexaspes "made manifest the truth, saying that he had before hidden it." He speaks now from *necessity*, just as he kept silent when the truth would not have been *safe*. This seems to agree with Darius' earlier statement, but there is a crucial difference. Prexaspes is not governed by self-interest; he has already lost his son, he loses the power granted by the Magi, and he loses his life. The "gain" which determines his behavior is not his own but that of the Persian people. Herodotus tells us that Prexaspes was a trustworthy or esteemed gentleman. The same code of honor which requires Darius to be cautious leads, in altered circumstances, to the splendid action that Darius said could not follow from lies. A full comprehension of political affairs requires us to combine the behavior of Darius with that of Prexaspes. The understanding of Darius is prior to the nobility of Prexaspes, but both are necessary for a healthy polity.

The Persian conspirators, unaware of the Prexaspes episode, offer prayers (the veil of piety) and then proceed to the palace (76). They learn of the events just described as they are "at mid-point," i.e. they are balanced between the fact of their conspiracy and the possibility of concluding it. Again the group dissolves into two factions, led by Darius and Otanes. Otanes and his men urge postponement; the attack should not be made when affairs are in a ferment. Those with Darius insist upon continuing straightway. Herodotus shows the superstition of the Persians (which will again be useful to Darius) by attributing the adoption of the extremist position to an omen: seven hawks appear in pursuit of two vultures and tear them to pieces. This is the first of three strokes of luck, by all of which Darius is benefitted. When the conspirators arrive at the palace, it is unnecessary for them to lie, although they had been prepared to do so: the guards suspect nothing and let them in without asking any questions. "They seemed to be under god's care" (77). Then the eunuchs' questions are terminated, not by lies, but the more honorable expedient of force. Finally, when the Persians are a step away from victory, Gobryas, Darius' chief supporter, is locked in a struggle with one of the Magi. The room is dark, and Darius hesitates to strike a blow for fear that he will kill Gobryas. Gobryas insists that Darius act; chance directs the dagger so that the Magus is killed and Gobryas unharmed. Previously Darius hesitated to speak; now he hesitates to act. Both cases are compatible with Darian moderation. Gobryas is a valuable piece of property and should not be lost. As Herodotus later reports, the Persians now speak of Darius as a "huckster" because "he tried to profit in everything" (89). Cambyses and Cyrus are regarded as a "despot" and "father" respectively. The art of politics requires all three.

In a transitional chapter (79), the Persians, led by the seven conspirators, slaughter the Magi; before the new government can be founded, one's opponents, as Machiavelli teaches, must be destroyed. [6] And in this way the independence of man from the gods is emphasized; political origins are not derivative from religion. The sense in which the political replaces the religious is indicated by the fact that the Persians have made the day upon which the Magi were slaughtered into a great festival. We turn now to the political dialogue which takes place five days after the slaughter of the Magi, "when the tumult subsided." The atmosphere is calmer than during the conspiratorial dialogue. Seven distinct speeches or topics are mentioned: the defenses of democracy, aristocracy, monarchy, Otanes' withdrawal from the election of the king, the privileges of Otanes, the privileges of the group, the procedure for choosing the king. The regimes are defended in order of the diminishing number of rulers; thus the aristocracy holds the central position, the position of *moderation*. The pivotal speech of this section is Otanes' rejection of the throne, and the last three topics are parallel to the first three (Otanes' privileges bear upon the democracy, those of the group upon the aristocracy, and the method of selection upon the monarchy). Herodotus insists that the speeches really took place, although "some" Greeks do not believe it. The status of these speeches may be compared to those which Thucydides says he wrote "as speak. . . ." [7] They represent what Herodotus regards as essential to the three regimes, but we must also allow for the nature of the speakers, and for the author, as well.

Otanes begins by recommending that "affairs" should be invested in "the Persians" as a whole. His moderation and indecision lead him to support the *plēthos*. Otanes seems almost to be "thinking out loud" and in some confusion. He says first that he does not think "one of us" should be monarch, rather than that there should be no monarch at all. In a moment, we shall have more evidence that he has been considering, if only as an extreme hypothesis or *day-dream*, the possibility of himself as absolute ruler. The reason which he gives for opposing a monarch is that "it is neither pleasant nor good." [8] The good for Otanes is linked with the pleasant, a notion which is especially characteristic of

6. On Machiavelli, see above, p. 318.
7. Thucydides, The Peloponnesian War, 1.22.
8. Cf. Iliad, II. 169–206, where Odysseus takes almost the reverse position: "the rule of many is not good." Compare Aristotle, Politics 1292 a 13. I suggest that Herodotus is indicating his disapproval of extreme democracy in this way. Such disapproval is not contradicted by his subsequent praise of Athenian freedom and isēgoria for at least two reasons: (i) Athens during the Persian war was a conservative democracy (Plato, Laws, 698 b ff.); (ii) the dialogue contains Herodotus' political "ideal," to which historical Athens may well have been the closest approximation. [Author]

the *plēthos*. A monarch, warns Otanes, can do as he *wishes* (i.e., his *day-dreams* come true), and this gives rise to *hybris*. Then Otanes implies that his fear of monarchy is in part a recognition of his own susceptibility to its temptations: "even the best of all men, holding such power, would be moved beyond the traditional customs." Otanes correctly regards himself as a good man, but his excessive caution or false moderation drives him into a dangerous extreme. He wishes to protect the Persians from the rule of *any* individual and so he advocates the rule of the people. As the last sentence of his speech ("everything is in the many") indicates, he does not see that he is advocating the creation of a single ruler in his very effort to avoid one.

Otanes continues: the tyrant is a prey to *hybris* and envy, and so possesses every wickedness. Otanes begins by speaking of a *monarchy*, which can take the form either of a *kingdom* or a *tyranny*. It is true that "tyrant" may be used in the sense of "king," but Otanes' failure to distinguish them is underlined by the fact that Darius never mentions the *tyrannos*; he speaks continually of the neutral *monarchia*. For Otanes, *tyrannos* is interchangeable with *king (basileus)*, not because he holds the position of Hobbes or contemporary political science, but because he regards all forms of monarchy as equally base. The "disharmony" of the tyrant makes it impossible for his subjects to behave moderately *(metriōs)* toward him. Then Otanes introduces the one point which the speeches of the three advocates have in common: he attributes *motion* and *violence* to the regime against which he is arguing; the worst features of the tyrant are: "he changes *(kineei)* the laws of the land, rapes women, and kills men without a trial." In praise of the rule of the multitude, which has the most beautiful name of *isonomia*, he says that offices are distributed by lot, the magistrate is held responsible for his acts, and all proposals are carried out in common. This counter-description is not parallel to the statement of the defects of a monarchy; nothing is said about freedom from rape and untried executions. The violence of the monarch cannot be eliminated merely by the institution of the lot and universal franchise: the multitude has its own violence, corresponding to their distribution of offices by chance.

Megabyzus is quick to point out that Otanes, in his timidity, has fallen into a greater danger than the one from which he runs. (Otanes never mentions the aristocracy or oligarchy, a sign of his haste and *immoderateness*: he moves from one extreme to the other.) Otanes' critique of tyranny is entirely acceptable, but, in asking that power be given to the people, he has erred in his judgment of *the best*. Megabyzus' choice of words makes clear that he favors an intellectual aristocracy; he is the only speaker to mention knowledge or intelligence. Thus, in criticizing the "useless rabble," he not only accuses them of being *more full of hybris*, but also of being *more unintelligent*: the latter is the cause of the former. There follows the crucial sentence of his speech: "When the tyrant acts, he does so knowingly, but the mob acts in ignorance. For how could it understand when it was neither taught nor can see for itself the noble and fitting, but flings itself into the midst of affairs without *nous*, like a torrential river." The intensity of Megabyzus' concern for intelligence is matched by the degree of violent stupidity which he attributes to the mob. Here again we have the repudiation of motion: the rabble is the political equivalent of the chaotic beginnings, the flowing river of Homer, Hesiod, and Heracleitus. And the beginnings, precisely because of their destructive motion, which is identical with the end (the *break-up* of things), are without *nous* or mind: the gods are not present in the first and last things. Megabyzus concludes by wishing a democracy onto those whom the Persians think ill of; he votes for an aristocracy (which will *include* the conspirators, i.e. and others as well: Megabyzus is less restricted than Otanes at all steps of his argument), for the mob should be in the hands of the best. Finally, we note that Megabyzus does not speak against a monarchy.

This leads to Darius' speech. Megabyzus is right about the mob, but wrong about the oligarchy. Just as Darius never uses the word *tyrannos*, so he does not speak of the *best (hoi aristoi)* but rather of *oligarchy* or "rule of the the few." When he says "*ho aristos,*" he means the king, i.e., himself. Thus he softens Otanes' criticism by tacitly restoring the neutral term. Darius attempts first to prove the superiority of a monarchy by pushing Megabyzus' argument to its "apparent" conclusion: "it would appear that no one is better than the one best man" (82). It is easy to see that this is a flimsy deduction. Even if we assume that Darius is *the* best Persian, how can we guarantee that his successors will be? If the throne is hereditary, the odds against this are massive; consider the recent example of Cambyses. If, on the other hand, an elective monarchy is established, the argument which Darius applies against an oligarchy (turmoil from the struggle for power) will cut as sharply against his own position. There follows a curious conjunction of reasons for preferring a monarch. As the best man, his counsels are best, so the mob will never blame him; and his measures against evil-doers are kept as secret as possible. Why does Darius not say that the *aristoi* or *oligoi* will not blame him? Can it be that he has already identified them in his mind as the evil-doers to be punished? Will the hucksteringe nature of Darius seek the property of the few while deriving his support from the many: i.e., is this a criticism which Herodotus tacitly levels against the monarchic form? There is also in Darius' words a subtle allusion to the recent conspiracy and the need for secrecy which was imposed upon it. He goes on to argue that the faults of the two other regimes necessarily culminate in the establishment of monarchy. The oligarchs struggle for power; from the resultant bloodshed and stasis, monarchy emerges. The democracy is necessarily characterized by malpractice, which again produced faction; the evil continues until one of the *demos* comes forward to eradicate it. As a result of the admiration which he wins, the people make him a monarch. Therefore, a monarchy should be established from the beginning.

Thus, *motion* and *violence* find their cessation in the stillness of a monarchy. And Darius' two examples substantiate our suspicion that the oligarchs or the few office-holders are the "evil-doers" to be punished; in both cases it is they who commit the crimes in their pursuit of power and wealth. Darius plans to restrain the few and be supported by the many. This is emphasized by the fact that he criticizes the oligarchic regime, but is silent about the democracy, except for the virtually oligarchic element in it. Once again, Herodotus seems to anticipate Machiavelli, this time in his criticism of the aristocracy. The monarch replaces the gods as the source of order. Darius' final argument emphasizes the unhealthy character of change by appealing to tradition and the conservatism of the aristocracy. As the Persians were freed by one man, so should they now institute a monarchy; and besides, "it is not right to change the customs of our forefathers, for there are none better." Darius' explicit allusion is of course to Cyrus, but implicitly he is reminding the interlocutors that their present freedom is due to his boldness. To go one step deeper: Herodotus indicates in this way that Persian freedom was also *lost* by a king, the mad Cambyses. The interlocutors are in an interregnum; the *nomoi* of the previous Persian regime have been suspended by the rule of the Magi, and the revolutionists are in effect the seven founding fathers of a new regime and new *nomoi*.

Otanes' second speech, after the vote has been carried by the promonarchists, reminds his comrades that they are revolutionaries by beginning with the words "fellow partisans" (literally, "gentlemen revolutionaries") (83). He states explicitly what was before only alluded to: it is clear to him that one of those present will become the king, regardless of the method of selection. But he himself wishes to withdraw from the competition: "I wish neither to rule nor to be ruled." In this way he personifies the classical criticism of the extreme democracy: where everyone rules, there is no ruler, and it is not truly a *political* association, in which each man rules and is ruled. The democracy relies upon the lot: it emphasizes the absence of a ruling principle by submitting to chance. This is reinforced by the nature of Otanes' freedom: he and his descendents will be subject, not to the will of the king, but to the Persian *nomoi*. Custom is the determination by chance of the popular will. The last chapter of the dialogue shows the specious nature of Darius' appeal to the unchanging *nomoi*; new customs, designating the privileges of the conspirators, are established. Finally, they decide upon a method for choosing the new king: they will ride out to the suburbs at dawn; he whose horse first neighs when the sun is up shall be king.

In the final part of our section, the naïveté of the Persians is sharply contrasted with the shrewdness of Darius. He consorts with his groom Oebares, and urges him to devise a scheme which will guarantee that his horse neighs first. Darius has not only counseled the necessity of lies; he again shows that he is under no fear of the gods by making a mockery of what is intended to be a solicitation of divine opinion. The mockery is in fact an *obscenity:* Darius' horse is persuaded to neigh by the scent of its favorite mare. The passion of a horse replaces the decision of the gods, just as men are ruled by their own passions rather than by those of the gods. The kingdom of Darius is established by the destruction of the link between gods and men, and by the violation of the most sacred *nomoi:* by lies, boldness, violence, greed, deceit.

4. I have tried to show how Herodotus' conservative formulation of political freedom is linked to his acceptance of the pre-Socratic (or pre-Parmenidean) teaching about nature or the origins. Man is free just because of his independence from the gods, because of the chaotic origins. This motion is man's nature as well; it leads to the political expansion and rise of civilization which culminates in the Persian war. For example, in his opening account of the troubles between Europe and Asia, two fundamental points emerge. The link between Asia and Europe is the Phoenician journey westward in search of economic profit. It is absolutely wrong to credit Thucydides with beginning the "realistic" economic tradition of historical analysis. Despite the radical difference in style, Herodotus' introductory statement is the precursor of Thucydides' introductory analysis of the reasons for the Trojan war. Greed together with motion are the origins of progress, and so too of stability. And the Greeks, although the Phoenicians instigate the conflict, are guilty of perpetuating it: they commit *two* retaliatory acts of injustice, and are also the first to send troops into the enemies' continent, thereby universalizing the disturbance. This is re-emphasized by an important discussion of the two most prominent Greek cities. The Athenians, who brought the love of power, art, and philosophy to its peak, were great *wanderers,* while the Spartans, anti-intellectual and ultra-conservative, never traveled abroad. This motionlessness is lost by them when they begin to prosper: "they were no longer willing to be quiet."

As we noted with respect to Herodotus' ironical praise of the Scythians, there is a connection between motion and knowledge. Herodotus himself, as did Odysseus, acquires his understanding of human things (and so of divine things) by *wandering,* like the Athenians (and Phoenicians). He comes to an understanding of nature by imitating its restlessness. But this wandering is dangerous; and so, too, is the understanding which it yields. Herodotus' agreement with Pindar that men are ruled by *nomos* must be modified as follows: so long as men obey their *nomos,* their chances for security are highest. It is when men change their *nomos* that danger becomes manifest. Extreme behavior, whether intellectual or physical, constitutes a violation of the protective traditional conservatism. Therefore, Herodotus never ceases to warn against those who would overstep the middle or secure way, and these warnings must be taken into account when we evaluate his praise of the Athenians. At the same time, we have accounted for Herodotus' decision always to phrase this advice in the most pious terms. The deeper sense of Pindar's dictum is that, just as nations differ in *nomoi*, so too do individuals. There are some individuals, like Herodotus, whose *nomos* is to free themselves from the *nomos* of the city; to become *apolis* or a traveler, to obey the higher *nomos* of those who love to see things as they are. But such men are few, and their understanding is dangerous for the many.

For noble as well as for practical reasons, Herodotus, like the responsible aristocrat, recognizes his duty both to the few *and* to the many (his praise of Athens, for example, is based ultimately upon the highest excellence of seeing things as they are). Ultimately, it is impossible to restrain the force of motion; as Yeats put it, "things fall apart; the center cannot hold." [9] But Herodotus will do his best to hold things together; his teaching for the few is consequently inlaid within, and veiled over by, his teaching for the many. His caution may be most easily understood as a consequence of his praise of moderation. The "moving center" of things leads to the consequence that what we value most turns into its opposite almost as soon as we have acquired it. Wealth leads to corruption, power to defeat by greater powers, piety to destruction by false or misinterpreted dreams and oracles. Wisdom, too, when it is made public, brings public disaster because it moves the people to break the restraints of ancestral tradition. The deeper wisdom of a Herodotus must therefore be concealed by a public wisdom. Herodotean wisdom has both a public and private form. This is indicated by his never praising anyone for wisdom except those whose public speech is compatible with public understanding.

What the academician would regard as "philosophy" is entirely absent from the surface of Herodotus' writings; by an act of nobility, he dooms himself, in less sophisticated times, to a reputation for naïveté. The danger of publicity and the importance of the ancestral are beautifully illustrated in the story of Gyges and Candaules. Candaules is destroyed by a deviation from custom. Because of excessive pride, he makes the private beauty of his queen publicly visible. Candaules revels in the glory which he derives from the possession of so beautiful a wife; so, too, does Croesus revel in the glory of his wealth, and so does the love of glory lead to self-destruction. But Gyges' words have a doubly symbolic meaning: "men have long since discovered righteousness, from which discoveries one ought to learn; among them is this one: let each one look at his own possessions." If we violate the old ways,the changes which follow will contradict our original intention. If we see the queen's beauty unadorned, we see also the character of political life in naked terms. We see the harsh demand which passion and glory make on us: *kill the king.* But there is an alternative: having seen the naked queen, we may, unlike Gyges, choose death, i.e., privacy and silence, rather than pursue her charms. We may pursue in private the deeper understanding of human

---

9. The Irish poet William Butler Yeats lived from 1865 to 1939. The line "Things fall apart; the cen-   ter cannot hold" is from his poem "The Second Coming."

affairs, and in this deeper sense, we see the queen as she really is. But "let each man look at his own possessions."[1] The correct vision of the queen is restricted for those whose eyes can really see. Justice demands that each of us see those things which are healthy for our natures. And *eudaimonia*, which all men seek as the end of existence, is dependent upon health in its various senses.

To conclude this essay, I should like to give a necessarily brief analysis of the encounter between Solon and Croesus, because it brings together Herodotus' main themes in a discussion between a wise man and a king about happiness. Solon is the great Athenian law-giver (*nomothetēs*). In the sense that *nomos* is the king of all men, we may say that Solon is the king of the Athenians. He is responsible for the order which will make possible their great speeches and deeds. But Solon's kingship is of the mind; he does not desire political power. In compliance with the advice of Gyges, and like Herodotus, he will see his own sights; he sets out "in order to see." As the etymology suggests (*theorein*), his seeing is indeed *theoretical*; as a theoretical man who gives the laws, he is himself in the highest sense (unlike Otanes) *above* the law. There is then a link between Solon and Herodotus. Both are travellers and both are law-givers; but the laws which Herodotus gives are not restricted to the Athenians: they are the *nomoi* of *all* men. Solon is a *sophistēs*; Herodotus, one may say, as the law-giver to all men, is the king of the *sophistai*. There are two kinds of law; the *nomos* of subjects, as given to them by their *nomothetēs* (kings are subjects in this sense), and the *nomos* of the *nomothetai* or true kings themselves. The relation between the *nomos* of true king and the *nomos* of true subjects is similar in at least one respect to the relation between *physis* and *nomos* in the technical Socratic vocabulary. Knowledge of the *nomos* of true kings is the Herodotean equivalent to the Socratic knowledge of *physis*.

Croesus praises Solon for his *philosopheōn* and *sophia*; and thereby underlines Solon's status. Indeed, all of the sages had made the pilgrimage to Sardis, according to Herodotus. Thus Croesus may be assumed, within the story, to have acquired a certain familiarity with the ways of the wise, if only from an external position. His amazement at Solon's response to his question about the happiest man indicates that the other sages may have flattered his vanity; it is necessary that Solon be less cooperative in order for Herodotus to make his points. But it does not follow from this that Solon speaks with full frankness. As a mark of Herodotus' subtlety, we note that the word introduced by Croesus for "happiness" in his question, and regularly used by Solon and Croesus, thereafter, is *olbios*. Herodotus avoids the term which he had previously used, and which, especially among the philosophers, comes to have a

---

1. Just as the Persian belief that lying and owing money are the greatest injustices is reminiscent of the businessman Cephalus' definition of justice in the *Republic*, so is Gyges' formulation of the ancestral code similar to the Socratic definition of justice: *ta heautou prattein* [Author].

more theoretical or spiritual usage: *eudaimonia*. The word *olbios* has the connotation of material prosperity, and it is fitting that it should be used by Croesus. But one should be asked as to what answer Solon would give to another *sophistēs*.

In answer to Croesus' question, Solon replies that Tellus was the happiest of all men (30). This answer contains a number of elements. To begin with, Tellus was an Athenian (just as Cleobis and Bito, from Argos, were also Greeks), whereas Croesus is a barbarian. Second, Tellus lived at a time when Athens was flourishing *(eu hēkousas)*; there was consequently much opportunity for glory. But, in accepting Croesus' standards, Solon corrects them; there is a difference between Greek and barbarian glory. And behind Solon, we may detect Herodotus, who corrects the contemporary (to him) Athenian concept of prosperity by praising the era of Tellus. Third, Tellus has a good family of sons and grandsons; he complied with the religious and social *nomoi*. Fourth, he lived in comfort (as distinguished from the excess of Croesus), and his death was splendid, publicly visible *(lamprotaton)*; he dies publicly in defense of the public good. Thus Herodotus indicates the public nature of Solon's teaching. The career of Tellus is that of a man who exemplifies the *nomos* of his city and in no way questions it. His relation to the *nomoi*, even in the act of dying for them, is *passive*; they define his beliefs and tastes, and he is able to satisfy both. In giving Tellus as his public answer to the question about the *olbiotatos bios*, Solon also gives his public answer to the unasked question about the *olbiotatos polis*; he practices his function as law-giver and constructs an idealized picture of ancient Athens. He is covering over the past with a veil of peace and piety. He is not speaking to a true king, but to a "nomic" king in the secondary sense. He teaches Croesus a lesson in discipline by praising a man who had only moderate wealth.[2] Solon's praise of Tellus, Cleobis and Bito is public praise, just as Herodotus, in picturing the impractical admonition by a wise man of a corrupt king to live like virtuous private citizens, is not speaking to the kings but to the public.

To pursue this point in just one way: Tellus, Cleobis and Bito are all citizens, whereas Croesus is a king. As a king (and so apart from his personal identity), he has an ambiguous relation to the *nomos*. He is subject to it in the sense that it defines his beliefs and tastes, just as was true for Tellus, Cleobis and Bito. But in another sense, Croesus is similar to Solon rather than to the three citizens: he is also *above* the *nomos*. As absolute ruler, Croesus could change the *nomos* if he so desired. There is almost no desire (as Otanes said) of his which could not be fulfilled; he *is* the *nomos*. But this means that it is not possible for him to respect the *nomoi* in the same way as the virtuous citizens. He knows

---

2. So too Socrates in the *Republic*, where he also constructs an ideal picture of the most just city in answer to the question about justice, and similarly "disciplines" young men by depriving them of luxury in his best city [Author].

too well that the *nomoi* are subordinate to his wishes. As the source of power in an empire, he is in a position to "see the queen naked", to see far more clearly than his subjects the disjunction between public morality and the basis of that morality. He is by virtue of that position standing with one foot outside the *nomos*, yet he is not a *sophistēs*: he cannot adhere to the *true nomos*. Even when freed from the lower *nomos*, he must still be subject to it. And, insofar as he satisfies his desires for wealth and glory, the chances increase, because of the intrinsic nature of political existence, that he will be destroyed.

For obvious reasons, Solon cannot speak frankly to Croesus; but the similarity between them makes it possible for them to converse. It is clear that Solon is admonishing Croesus, *urging him on (proetrepsato)*. The king is high enough, relative to the *nomos*, that it is in principle possible for him to hear private undertones in the public teaching. But he is not high enough; Croesus understands Solon's meaning only at the point of death, when he is no longer king. At the point of death, Croesus becomes similar to an old man, and respect for the old is a traditional aspect of Greek conservatism. To be on the point of death is to have one foot beyond the *nomos*, but in a different sense from the king. The king's vision is obscured by the ease with which his desires are satisfied. The man who is on the point of death has no such obstacles: he has lost his appetites, as Croesus has lost his wealth. He sees clearly the nature of the appetites to which during his life he had been enslaved, like Darius' horse. In this whole episode, then, the significance of death is related to clarity of vision. It is impossible not to be reminded of another old man, Socrates, who, on the verge of death, tells us (in the *Phaedo*) that philosophy is a preparation for dying. Death not only terminates life, but it also completes it. By completing one's life, death also makes the form of that life more clearly visible. But the problem, of course, is to see clearly the form of one's life without dying. We need to be rescued from death in the way that Croesus was rescued, thanks to his new-found wisdom, by Cyrus.

Herodotus becomes the Cyrus who rescues us from death if we understand his wisdom: he teaches us the form of human and divine things. It is in this context that we must understand Solon's words: "in these things god showed forth how much better it were for man to die than to live." Neither Herodotus nor Solon seek literal death. The praise of death is the praise of privacy, which comes only through freedom in the highest sense, from the public *nomoi*; upon this freedom, happiness rests. The superiority of private happiness is proved by the defect of public happiness: as Herodotus ironically emphasizes, no man can be counted happy until he dies. The more we have of public happiness, the more we are in danger of losing it; in seeking it so zealously, we entail great risks, and so are in effect pursuing death. But death is what we most fear. Herodotus asks us in our public *personae* to be consistent: death prevents the deterioration of happiness into grief. Put ironically: public happiness can be secured only by losing it.

But the profound loss of public happiness is the gain of private happiness. We free ourselves from *to theion pan* who is jealous and malicious, when we understand god correctly. Solon gives us Herodotus' clue to this understanding a few lines after his characterization of god: *man is all chance.* Chance replaces the jealous god. When we think through this substitution, we shall have earned the right to be called, not *eutuxea*, but *olbion* in the deepest and richest sense (32). Man's true freedom lies in the mastery of chance *(symphorē, tuchē)* by thinking it through. But true freedom depends upon the theoretically lower but practically indispensable public freedom. Since the public cannot think through its freedom without in effect losing it, Herodotus composes his *historia* in such a way that no one will be harmed, neither the many, nor, as Stendhal put it, "the happy few."

ARNALDO MOMIGLIANO

Arnaldo Momigliano was one of the greatest ancient historians of our time. Of his hundreds of publications, perhaps the most important are *Studies in Historiography* (1966), *Alien Wisdom: The Limits of Hellenization* (1975), *Essays in Ancient and Modern Historiography* (1977), and *On Pagans, Jews and Christians* (1987). He occupied the chair of ancient history at University College, London, from 1951 until his retirement in 1975. The essay included here is an overview of Herodotus' reputation as a historian from antiquity to modern times.

The Place of Herodotus in the History of Historiography †

I have often felt rather sorry for Dionysius of Halicarnassus.[1] How embarrassing it must have been for a budding historian to have the father of history as his own fellow-citizen. No wonder that Dionysius left Halicarnassus and emigrated to Rome where the name of Herodotus, if adroitly used, could even become an asset. In Rome Dionysius was wholeheartedly devoted to the memory of his formidable predecessor. Dionysius is in fact the only ancient writer who never said anything unpleasant about Herodotus. Yet even he never dared to defend Herodotus from the most serious accusation of his enemies, the accusation of being a liar. To us it may perhaps seem odd that the ancients saw nothing incongruous in being at one and the same time the father of history

† Reprinted with permission from the Historical Association and from Weidenfeld and Nicolson from *History* 43 (1958): 1–13.
1. Dionysius of Halicarnassus was a late first-century B.C. Greek historian and rhetorician who lived and taught in Rome and who is best remembered for his literary criticism.

and a liar. But, as far as I know, Francesco Petrarca was the first to notice the implicit contradiction between these two terms and to object to it. [2]

Petrarch had never seen a manuscript of Herodotus, nor would it have made a great difference to him if he had: he never got beyond the most rudimentary knowledge of Greek. But he read most carefully what his Romans told him about the Greeks and was struck by what Cicero said about Herodotus. In the same sentence * * * Cicero refers to Herodotus as "the father of history" and brackets him with Theopompus as another notorious liar: ["although in the writings of both Herodotus the father of history and Theopompus there is a lot of nonsense."] [3] This indeed, as Petrarch noticed, was not the only occasion on which Cicero treated Herodotus as a liar. * * * [Cicero also] expressed the suspicion that Herodotus himself had fabricated and attributed to Delphi the ambiguous oracle about the results of the war between Croesus and Cyrus. [4] In the same way, Cicero added, Ennius must have fabricated the story of the ambiguous Delphic oracle that encouraged Pyrrhus to march against the Romans. [5] Petrarch was shocked by the suggestion that the father of history could be the author of a forgery. There was no harm in attributing an oracle to the imagination of Ennius. A poet, Petrarch knew, had a right to invent—not so the father of history [: "Consequently it is perfectly believable that Ennius would have made this up on his own, but I would not be so prone to believe that Herodotus, whom Cicero himself calls the father of history, invented an oracle and attributed it to an earlier time."] [6]

This passage * * * is typical of Petarch's shrewd, yet naïve, understanding of the classical world. If he had been able to read Greek, he would have seen that Cicero was simply conforming to a traditional opinion about Herodotus. Herodotus was not denied the place of "first discover" of history, but at the same time was distrusted to the point of being considered a liar.

Admittedly, the Greeks and Romans were not apt to kneel in silent adoration before their own classical writers. Historians were especially open to accusations of dishonesty. But no other writer was so severely criticized as Herodotus. His bad reputation in the ancient world is something exceptional that requires explanation. It does so the more because the ancient opinion had a considerable influence on Herodotus' reputation among the students of ancient history from the fifteenth century to our own times. The story of Herodotus' posthumous struggle against

---

2. Francesco Petrarca (Petrarch) (1304–1374), one of the great figures in world literature, played an important part in the revival of learning in Italy and was a passionate student of Latin literature.

3. De legibus (On the Laws), 1.1.5.

4. De divinatione (On divination), 2.116.

5. Quintus Ennius (239–169 b.c.) was an early Roman poet and historian. Pyrrhus (319–272 b.c.) was the king of Epirus, in northwestern Greece. He fought several battles against the Romans, in one of which, at Asculum in 279, his victory was so costly that it was tantamount to a defeat. The phrase "Pyrrhic victory" derives from this event.

6. Petrarch, The Book of Things to Be Remembered, 4.25–26.

his detractors is an important chapter in the history of historical thought: it is also, in my opinion, an important clue to the understanding of Herodotus himself.

Herodotus combined two types of historical research. He enquired about the Persian war—an event of one generation earlier—and he travelled in the East to collect information about present conditions and past events in those countries. The combination of two such tasks would be difficult for any man at any time. It was particularly difficult for a historian who had to work in Greece during the fifty century B.C. When Herodotus worked on Greek history, he had very few written documents to rely upon: Greek history was as yet mainly transmitted by oral tradition. When he travelled to the East, he found any amount of written evidence, but he had not been trained to read it.

Let us say immediately that Herodotus was successful in his enterprise. We have now collected enough evidence to be able to say that he can be trusted. Curiously enough we are in a better position to judge him as a historian of the East than as historian of the Persian Wars. In the last century Orientalists have scrutinized Herodotus with the help of archaeology and with the knowledge of languages that he could not understand. They have ascertained that he described truthfully what he saw and reported honestly what he heard. Where he went wrong, either his informants misled him or he had misunderstood in good faith what he was told. We are not so well placed for the history of the Persian Wars because Herodotus himself remains our main source. Wherever we happen to be able to check him with the help of inscriptions or of simple topography, we have no reason to be dissatisfied with him. This, however, does not mean that we are in a position to say how Herodotus wrote his history. We do not yet know exactly how he proceeded in his enquiry, compared different versions, wrote down his notes, gave them their present literary form. Above all we cannot say how much he owed to earlier writers. But we know enough about Herodotus' alleged predecessors—Cadmus of Miletus, Hecataeus, Dionysius of Miletus, Charon of Lampsacus, Xanthus of Sardes—to state confidently that they did not do the work for him. There was no Herodotus before Herodotus.

The almost total loss of the geographical and ethnographical literature that preceded and accompanied Herodotus' work makes it impossible for us to assess exactly how much he owed to earlier and contemporary writers. But any careful reader of his work will agree that his main research must have been done not on written, but on oral tradition. After all, Herodotus himself tells us that he used *opsis*, *gnome* and *historia*: his eyes, his judgement and his talent for enquiry. This can be confirmed by an analysis of the main episodes of the Persian wars. It is easy to see that what he knows about Thermopylae chiefly comes from Sparta, whereas Athenian traditions are behind his accounts of Marathon, Salamis and Plataea.

In other words Herodotus managed to produce a very respectable history mainly on the basis of sightseeing and oral tradition. He succeeded in putting together a trustworthy account of events he was too young to have witnessed and of countries whose languages he did not understand. We know that his history is respectable because we are now able to check it against independent evidence. But we must admit that if we had to give an *a priori* estimate of the chances of success in writing history by Herodotus' method, we should probably shake our heads in sheer despondency. Herodotus' success in touring the world and handling oral traditions is something exceptional by any standard—something that we are not yet in a position to explain fully. The secrets of his workshop are not yet all out. Therefore we cannot be surprised if the ancients found it difficult to trust an author who had worked on such a basis as Herodotus.

It is only too obvious that Thucydides ultimately determined the verdict of antiquity on his predecessor. He carefully read (or listened to) his Herodotus and decided that the Herodotean approach to history was unsafe. To write serious history, one had to be a contemporary of the events under discussion and one had to be able to understand what people were saying. Serious history—according to Thucydides—was not concerned with the past, but with the present; it could not be concerned with distant countries, but only with those places in which you lived and with those people whose thoughts you could put into your own words without difficulty. Thucydides did not believe that there was a future in Herodotus' attempt to describe events he had not witnessed and to tell the story of men whose language he could not understand. We now know that Thucydides was insensitive to Herodotus' bold attempt to open up the gates of the past and of foreign countries to historical research. But we must recognize that he knew what he was doing in criticizing Herodotus. He was setting up stricter standards of historical reliability, even at the risk of confining history to a narrow patch of contemporary events. Thucydides claimed that a historian must personally vouch for what he tells. He allowed only a limited amount of inferences from present facts to events of the past. He also implied that it is easier to understand political actions than any other type of action. With Thucydides history became primarily political history and was confined to contemporary events.

Now Thucydides certainly did not succeed in imposing his strict standard of historical reliability on other historians, but he succeeded in discouraging the idea that one could do real research about the past. Greek and Roman historians in fact, after Herodotus, did very little research into the past and relatively seldom undertook to collect firsthand evidence about foreign countries. They concentrated on contemporary history or summarized and reinterpreted the work of former historians. Search for unknown facts about the past was left to antiquarians,

and the work of the antiquarians hardly influenced the historians. * * *
Indeed, the very existence of the antiquarians was conditioned by the
fact that historians interested themselves only in a small sector of what
nowadays we should call history. Every generalization of this kind is
bound to do violence to a certain number of facts. But on the whole it
is apparent that the great historians of antiquity left their mark either on
first-hand accounts of contemporary events or on the reinterpretation of
facts already collected by previous historians. * * * The surviving books
of Tacitus' *Annals* are the most conspicuous example of a great work of
history written with a minimum amount of independent research. [7] And
Tacitus himself is an example of what can happen to a historian who
relies on interpretation rather than on research: if he is not wrong in his
facts, he is liable to be arbitrary in his explanations.

Ancient historiography never overcame the limitations imposed by
what we can call the paramouncy of contemporary history. The more
remote the past, the less likely historians were to contribute anything
new to the knowledge of it. Ephorus and Livy were honest men. [8] They
were by no means deprived of critical sense. Ephorus decided that it was
no use trying to tell the story of the Greeks before the Dorian invasion.
Livy was acutely aware of the legendary character of the traditions he
was bound to follow about the early history of Rome. But neither of
them knew how to go beyond the literary sources for an independent
enquiry about the past.

Thus Thucydides imposed the idea that contemporary political history was the only serious history; and Herodotus was cut off from the
stream of ancient historiography. He was neither a contemporary nor a
political historian. His tales, however attractive, looked oddly unprofes-
sional. Even those who liked him as a patriotic and pleasant writer could
hardly defend him as a reliable historian. Herodotus invited awkward
questions: how could he tell so much about events he had never seen
and about people whose language he did not know and whose countries
he had only visited for a short time, if at all? *Either* he had concealed
his sources, and was a plagiarist, *or* he had invented his facts and was a
liar. The dilemma dominated ancient criticism of Herodotus. There was
not a very great choice of predecessors, as we know, from whom he
could have stolen his facts, but some could be found. A few were authentic
enough: the geographer Hecataeus, the mythographer Acusilaus, the
genealogist Pherekydes of Athens, perhaps also Xanthus the historian of
Lydia, and Dionysius of Miletus the historian of Persia. Others were late
forgers, but were accepted as authentic archaic writers by the majority

7. The Roman historian Tacitus was born around
A.D. 55 and wrote his *Annals* about the period from
the death of Augustus in A.D. 14 through the reign
of Nero. The manuscript broke off in A.D. 66.
8. Ephorus of Cyme (ca. 405 to 330 B.C.) wrote a
history of the world down to 341 B.C. Livy, or Titus
Livius (59 B.C. to A.D. 17, wrote an annalistic history of Rome from its founding in 753 B.C. to his
own day.

of ancient critics: for instance the alleged first historian Cadmus of Miletus. Furthermore there were genuine historians whom Hellenistic scholarship placed before Herodotus, whereas some at least of the most authoritative modern scholars incline to take them for his younger contemporaries. * * * All these historians counted in the eyes of ancient scholars as potential sources of Herodotus and were made to contribute to the case for Herodotus' plagiarism. But even with the help of writers who were later than Herodotus and therefore may have used him, rather than having been used by him, the case for plagiarism can never have been a very impressive one. Many of Herodotus' enemies seem to have preferred the alternative line of attack which was to present him as a liar. It was obviously easier to dismiss his evidence than to trace his sources. After all, he could not have been considered the father of history if it had been so evident that he had copied from his predecessors. Though we shall see that there were books on Herodotus as a plagiarist, the final impression left by the ancient criticisms of Herodotus is that he was a story-teller—a liar. Here again we can measure the impact of Thucydides' verdict on his predecessor.

Herodotus had hardly ceased writing his history when Thucydides began to reflect on the mistakes and shortcomings of his predecessor. A few decades after Thucydides, Ctesias launched another attack against Herodotus by questioning his competence both as a student of Greek history and as an historian of the East.[9] Ctesias had all the external qualifications for checking Herodotus' results. He had lived several years at the Persian court and must have understood Persian. He had opportunities of access to Persian records certainly denied to Herodotus. The impact of Ctesias' attack was somewhat reduced by its very violence and extravagance. A historian who puts the battle of Plataea before Salamis in order to impress on his readers his independence from the despised predecessor is likely to get himself into trouble. People were not slow to realize that Ctesias was no less open to suspicions than Herodotus. But, as we know, conflicting suspicions do not cancel each other out. Herodotus' reputation remained tarnished. Paradoxically, he was often associated with Ctesias as an unreliable historian. Even Aristotle went out of his way to denounce Herodotus' mistakes over small details of natural history; and he formulated his criticism in such terms as to involve the reliability of the whole of Herodotus' history. He calls Herodotus a "story-teller."

The expedition of Alexander the Great, by opening up the East, certainly revealed lacunae in Herodotus' information. Strabo in his *Geography* repeatedly echoes and makes his own the criticisms of Alexandrian scholarship.[1] Meanwhile, the Orientals themselves were being Hellenized. They learnt to read what the Greeks had written about them in

9. Ctesias, a late-fifth-century B.C. historian who lived in Persia for many years, wrote a history of Persia.

1. Strabo was a Stoic historian and geographer who lived from 64 B.C. to circa A.D. 21.

former centuries and, not unnaturally, found it unsatisfactory. Manetho, the Egyptian priest who tried to present the history of his people to the Greeks, also wrote a pamphlet against Herodotus. The Greeks themselves became increasingly impatient with Herodotus for patriotic reasons. What may seem to us the wonderful serenity and sense of humour of Herodotus in judging the issues between Greeks and Barbarians was for them evidence that the historian had been "a friend of the barbarians." Even the local patriotism of Hellenistic Greeks operated against his reputation. Local historians and antiquarians were glad to show him up: he had not said enough about the glories of their own cities. All the anti-Herodotean literature of the Hellenistic age is unfortunately lost, but Plutarch's [essay *On the Malice of Herodotus*] can give us some idea of the complaints that were lodged against the father of history. Plutarch puts together a series of criticisms against Herodotus: excessive sympathy for the barbarians, partiality for Athens, gross unfairness towards the other Greek cities, lack of truthfulness where facts are concerned and lack of balance where judgments are involved. History was a form of encomium to Plutarch, and evidently Herodotus did not fit into the pattern. It is a pity that nobody has yet produced a competent commentary on Plutarch's pamphlet against Herodotus, both because it is typical of the way in which late Greeks looked at their past and because it influenced the judgment about Herodotus of many classical scholars from the fifteenth to the nineteenth century. Plutarch does not seem to have said the worst about Herodotus. To guess from the titles of lost works, even worse was in store for the father of history. Titles such as *On Herodotus' thefts* by Valerius Pollio or *On Herodotus' lies* by Aelius Harpocration—not to speak of the book by Libanius *Against Herodotus*—seem to imply that there was no dishonesty of which he was not capable.

With all that, Herodotus remained a classic. The immaculate grace of his style defied criticism. His information about Oriental countries was more easily criticized than replaced. * * * His epic tale of the Persian wars was a unique document of the Greek past. The accusation of lack of patriotism could hardly pass unchallenged. We can easily draw up a list of admirers of Herodotus. Theopompus summarized him in two books. [2] No less a critic than Aristarchus wrote a commentary on him. [3] The discovery of a fragment of this commentary has been enough to dispose of the legend that Herodotus was almost forgotten in the Hellenistic age. From the first century BC to the late second century AD Herodotus was in special favour as a model of style. Archaism operated in his favour. Dionysius of Halicarnassus, Arrian and Lucian were his champions. [4] Dionysius says, "If we take up his book, we are filled with

2. Theopompus was a Greek historian writing in the fourth century B.C.
3. Aristarchus was a prominent scholar who became head of the Alexandrian Library in Egypt ca. 150 B.C.
4. Arrian, governor of Cappadocia under the emperor Hadrian during the second century A.D., wrote histories of Parthia and India and the *Anabasis*, a history of Alexander. The critic and satirist Lucian of Samosata lived around the middle of the second century A.D. and was a contemporary of Arrian.

admiration till the last syllable and always seek for more." What more splendid compliment could Herodotus desire? Lucian is no less enthusiastic: "If only we could imitate Herodotus—not all his good qualities because this is beyond hope—but at least one of them."

Yet there are very disturbing features in these apologies for Herodotus. Dionysius does not argue that Herodotus is a reliable historian: he compares him with Thucydides and gives reasons for the superiority of Herodotus that can persuade only those who do not care for reliability in a history. According to Dionysius, Herodotus chose a better subject than Thucydides, because he told the glories and not the misfortunes of the Greeks. He gave his history a better beginning and a better end. He wrote up his subject in a more interesting way and he arranged his materials better. In points of style he can at least compete with Thucydides. If Thucydides is more concise, Herodotus is more vivid; if Thucydides is more robust, Herodotus is more graceful. Herodotus' beauty is "radiant," where Thucydides' is awe-inspiring. All is in favour of Herodotus—except truth.

In the same way Lucian admires him without ever implying that he is a reliable historian. Indeed Lucian positively denies that Herodotus is trustworthy. At least twice he couples him with Ctesias as one of the historians who are notorious liars. In the pamphlet of "How to write history" * * * Lucian definitely presents Thucydides as the model of the fearless, incorruptible, free, sincere and truthful historian. He emphasizes the fact that Thucydides developed his rules for the historian after having observed what Herodotus had done. Those who speak about Dionysius and Lucian as the great champions of Herodotus in antiquity too often forget to add that Dionysius implicitly and Lucian explicitly deny his truthfulness.

It is my submission that all this resulted from the fact that Herodotus had dared to write a kind of history of which Thucydides disapproved and which later historians found remote and uncongenial. The legend of Herodotus the liar is the result of the authentic achievements of Herodotus the historian. But it will have been observed that if Thucydides disapproved of writing on the past, he did not challenge Herodotus' assumption that history can be written from oral tradition. In the circumstances of the fifth century it was hardly possible to think otherwise. At least in Greece there were not enough written documents to make a sufficiently broad basis for history. Thucydides was far from being blind to the possibilities offered by the exploitation of written documents. Indeed he was one of the very few ancient historians to use written diplomatic records. But it could never occur to him that written records were the primary source for history: if he had thought so, he would never have written the history of the Peloponnesian War. More remarkable is the fact that later historians never tried to modify an approach that had originally been dictated by the conditions of fifth-century Greece. In Hellenistic Egypt there would have been an embarrassing wealth of written records to exploit; and written records were certainly not scarce in Rome during the late Republic and the Empire. But the study of written records remained to the end an exceptional occupation for the Greek and Roman historians. If Thucydides dictated the paramouncy of contemporary history, Herodotus determined the paramouncy of oral evidence. This explains why, though discredited, he remained the father of history.

The pre-eminence of personal observation and oral evidence lasted until historians decided to go to the record office. Familiarity with the record office, as we all know, is a recently acquired habit for the historian, hardly older than a century. It is true that the Roman and Greek antiquarians knew something about the use of documents and that the antiquarians of the Renaissance perfected this approach to the past. But this method became really effective and universally accepted only a hundred years ago. The antiquarians began to study systematically the records of the past in the fifteenth century, but only in the eighteenth century did the barriers between antiquarianism and history break down, and only in the nineteenth did it become established practice for the historian to look for new evidence before writing new books of history. * * *

* * * We may indulge in the illusion that if Thucydides were to come back to life he would not reject our methods with the contempt with which he rejected the method of Herodotus. The labours of the antiquarians between the fifteenth and the nineteenth centuries prepared the way for an approach to the past that effectively undermined the paramouncy of contemporary history. By excavating sites, searching the files of the record office, comparing coins, reading inscriptions and papyri, we have gone into the past with the same confidence with which Thucydides and his informants went about the assembly places of contemporary Sparta and Athens. We can collect reliable facts without being eye-witnesses in the Thucydidean sense. In unguarded moments of pride we may even be tempted to tell Thucydides that we know more about Athenian tribute lists than he ever did.

It would however be a great mistake of historical perspective to believe that the documentary approach to history has been the only way in which modern historiography has overcome the limitations imposed by Thucydides on ancient historiography. Before the study of documentary and archaeological evidence became a generalized practice, there was a revival of the Herodotean attempt to get into the past by way of enquiries founded on travels and the study of oral tradition. Defeated in antiquity, Herodotus triumphed in the sixteenth century. The revival of the Herodotean approach to the past, which happened then, is the first contribution of modern historiography to an independent study of the past.

In the sixteenth century historians travelled once more in foreign countries, questioned local people, went back from the present to the past by collecting oral traditions. In some cases they acted as ambassadors, in others they were missionaries and explorers: they were seldom professional historians. But they wrote history—a history extraordinarily reminiscent of Herodotus both in style and in method. The new diplomacy required careful examination of the traditions of foreign countries; religious propaganda made urgent the production of objective accounts of the peoples to be converted. Above all, there was the discovery of America with all that it implied. There is no need to assume that the Italian diplomats and Spanish missionaries who worked on their *"relazioni"* or *"relaciones"* were under the influence of Herodotus. * * * As the historical approach is approximately the same in all of them, it is evident that classical models counted far less than direct experience and contemporary needs. The influence of Herodotus and other classical scholars may colour some details, but the *"relazioni"* as a whole are certainly independent of classical models. What matters to us is that they vindicated Herodotus, because they showed that one could travel abroad, tell strange stories, enquire into past events, without necessarily being a liar. One of the standard objections against Herodotus had been that his tales were incredible. But now the study of foreign countries and the discovery of America revealed customs even more extraordinary than those described by Herodotus.

Classical scholars soon became aware of the implications of these discoveries. They were delighted to find the New World a witness in favour of the classical authors. As I recently wrote in another context, one of the consequences of the discovery of the New World was to confirm classical scholars in their belief that the perfect ancient world had been perfectly described by perfect ancient authors. If Herodotus did not inspire the students of America, students of America and other foreign countries inspired the defenders of Herodotus. He regained his reputation during the sixteenth century.

My theory that Herodotus recovered from Thucydides' attack only after two thousand years in the sixteenth century can be proved both positively and negatively. I shall show that in the fifteenth century the old suspicions about him revived, but that in the sixteenth century his reputation improved considerably as a result of the new interest in ethnography.

I must admit that in order to dramatize the role of America I have so far underrated the part of Turkey in this development. The emergence of the Turks is another factor that must be taken into account in the story of the fortunes and misfortunes of Herodotus. What happened to Herodotus in Byzantine civilization is beyond my competence. But in the last century of the Byzantine empire the story of the old struggle between the Greeks and the Persians acquired a new poignancy. The Turks had replaced the Persians. Herodotus contained a tale of glory that could be a consolation in the present mortal predicament; but he seems to have been appreciated especially because in his quiet way he had understood the Persians, and through him the Turks could be seen more objectively. An understanding of the approaching rulers was perhaps more needed in that situation than celebration of past victories.

The last great historian of Byzantium, Laonicus Chalcocondyles, was a student and imitator of Herodotus. It is impressive to see how he described the contemporary world from London to Baghdad in Herodotean terms. He was either the brother or the cousin of one of the Byzantine masters of the Italian humanists, Demetrius Chalcocondyles, and there can be no doubt that he was one of those who directly or indirectly transmitted interest and admiration for Herodotus to the Italian scholars of the first half of the fifteenth century.

The first reaction of the West to the rediscovery of Herodotus was indeed one of sheer delight, as it well ought to have been. Guarino, who translated the first seventy-one chapters of Herodotus about 1416, repeatedly expressed his joy in reading him. About 1452 Lorenzo Valla translated him entirely; though his translation was not printed until 1474, it made an impression even when it was only in manuscript. Not much later, about 1460, Mattia Palmieri Pisano produced another complete translation into Latin which was never printed. It can be read in an elegant manuscript of the university library of Turin and contains a most significant eulogy of Herodotus. The father of history is appreciated not only for his style, but also for his method of working, for his journeys, for his free and independent mind.

But the Italian humanists, while learning to read Herodotus, were also learning to know his ancient critics. They realized that Thucydides had attacked him, knew of course Cicero's dubious compliments by heart, got to know what Aristotle, Strabo and Diodorus had said: above all they were impressed by Plutarch's systematic and ruthless attack. [5] On top of all that, religious and scholarly controversies troubled the relations between the Italian humanists and their unfortunate Byzantine colleagues. The Greek name became disreputable again in many humanistic minds; and the psychological resistance to the belief that Herodotus had been a liar decreased correspondingly. The change in the situation is already clear about 1460. Giovanni Pontano was asked to write a preface for an edition of Valla's translation of Herodotus that did not materialize. We have this preface. We can see how prudent and reserved Pontano has become. He defends Herodotus, but he knows only too well that there is an old and impressive case against him. Ultimately he admits that in judging Herodotus one must keep in mind that when he wrote the standards of truth were not so strict as in modern times. A generation later, Ludovicus Vives has no difficulty in saying plainly that Herodotus deserved the title of father of lies rather than that of father of history. * * * The very fact that each translator and editor of Herodotus felt it necessary to defend him against Thucydides and Plutarch shows that at the beginning of the sixteenth century his reputation was, generally speaking, bad.

---

5. Diodorus Siculus was a first-century B.C. historian whose history of the world in forty books was primarily a compilation and abridgment of the work of preceding historians. For Plutarch's attack, see this volume, pp. 271–76.

We can begin to notice a change of attitude in the preface of
I. Camerarius to his edition of Herodotus of 1541. The change becomes
complete, the defence of Herodotus against traditional accusations
becomes confident and aggressive in the [Apologia for Herodotus] by
Henricus Stephanus, first published in 1566. It is an interesting coincidence that the Apologia by Stephanus appeared in the year in which
Bodin published his [Method for the Easy Comprehension of History]. [6]
Both Stephanus and Bodin were fighting for a wider historical outlook
and had perhaps more points in common than they would have liked to
admit. But Bodin could not yet get over the fact that Thucydides, Diodorus and Plutarch had criticized Herodotus so severely. Stephanus, for
once the more independent of the two, definitely rejected the judgement
of the ancients. Stephanus' main argument is that a comparative study
of national customs shows Herodotus to be trustworthy. Here the impact
of the modern relazioni from distant countries is obvious. What we might
call the comparative method of ethnography vindicates Herodotus. This
is not the only argument produced by Stephanus. He remarked, for
instance, that Herodotus could not be a liar, because he had a religious
soul. But the strength of the Apologia [for Herodotus]—a work of decisive importance in the history of European historiography—lies in its
comparison between Herodotus' descriptions and modern customs. As
is well known, a few years later Henricus Stephanus used this comparison for satirical purposes in the Apologie pour Hérodote, which is no
longer a study of Herodotus, but a satire on modern life. We can see the
immediate effects of Stephanus' Apologia * * * in a book by Loys Le
Roy, [On the Vicissitude or Variety of Things in the Universe], which
appeared in 1576. * * * [Le Roy] deals at length with Mesopotamia,
Egypt, Persia, and Greece, and has an almost unlimited faith in Herodotus. Indeed he puts Herodotus and Thucydides together as the best
two historians.

If the new ethnographic research was the main factor in the revalua-
tion of Herodotus, the Reformation added a second motive. Interest in
biblical history was revived, independent enquiries were encouraged up
to a point. Herodotus proved to be a useful complement to the Bible. As
David Chytraeus put it in 1564, it was providential that Herodotus should
begin ["where prophetic history leaves off"]. In the second part of the
sixteenth century a new interest in Greek and Oriental history developed; it encouraged the study of Herodotus and was in its turn encouraged by a greater trust in his honesty. By the end of the century he had
been recognized as the indispensable complement to the Bible in the
study of Oriental history. This is not to say that the discussion of Herodotus' credibility did not go on well beyond the sixteenth century. There

6. Henricus Stephanus or Henri Estienne (1531?–
1598) and Jean Bodin were French political philosophers.

were still fierce controversies on this subject in the eighteenth century. Indeed the discussion is still going on as far as particular sections of his work are concerned. But after Henricus Stephanus there was no longer any question of relegating Herodotus among the story-tellers. He was the master of and the guide to archaic Greek History and Oriental History. As the greatest of the sixteenth-century scholars, Joseph Scaliger, [7] said, Herodotus is ["a storehouse of Greek and non-Greek antiquities, an author never to be put aside by the learned, and never to fall into the hands of the pseudo-learned, pedagogues, or other dumb apes"]. Scaliger himself made Herodotus one of the corner-stones of ancient chronology. One century later Sir Isaac Newton drew up chronological tables to "make chronology suit with the course of nature, with astronomy, with sacred history and with Herodotus the father of history." The course of nature, astronomy, sacred history—Herodotus was now moving in very respectable circles. About the same time, in 1724, the French Jesuit Lafitau discovered with the help of Herodotus a matriarchal society in America. His *Moeurs des sauvages Amériquains* [Customs of the American savages] revealed to the world the simple truth that also the Greeks had once been savages.

The stupendous developments of the study of Greek and Oriental history in the last three centuries would never have happened without Herodotus. Trust in Herodotus has been the first condition for the fruitful exploration of our remote past. The people who went to excavate Egypt and Mesopotamia had primarily Herodotus as their guide. But there is something more to Herodotus than this. It is true that professional historians now mainly work on written evidence. But anthropologists, sociologists and students of folklore are doing on oral evidence what to all intents and purposes is historical work. The modern accounts of explorers, anthropologists and sociologists about primitive populations are ultimately an independent development of Herodotus' *historia*. Thus Herodotus is still with us with the full force of his method of studying not only the present, but also the past, on oral evidence. It is a strange truth that Herodotus has really become the father of history only in modern times.

J. A. S. EVANS

J. A. S. Evans has taught in both the United States and Canada and is currently professor of classics at the University of British Columbia. His interests range from Herodotus to the sixth-century A.D. Greek historian Procopius of Caeserea to Father J.-F. Lafitau, who modeled himself on Herodotus in his research into Iroquois customs in the eighteenth century

---

7. Joseph Scaliger (1540–1609) was a French classical scholar.

and who is mentioned in this context by Momigliano in the preceding selection. Professor Evans is the author of *Herodotus, Explorer of the Past: Three Essays* (Princeton, 1991). In the following essay, he seeks out the reasons for Herodotus' reputation as "the father of lies."

Father of History or Father of Lies: The Reputation of Herodotus †

In choosing my title, Herodotus, father of history *or* father of lies, I have betrayed a modernist standpoint. In the ancient world, the occasional falsehood did not vitiate a writer's claim to be called an historian. It is true that we can cite many protestations which might lead us to believe otherwise: Timaeus of Tauromenium is supposed to have stated that lack of truth was the greatest fault of history, and he exhorted those of his predecessors whom he had convicted of falsehoods to find some label other than "history" for their product; while Lucian anticipates von Ranke by announcing that it was the historian's duty to "tell the story as it happened."[1] In actual fact, the relation between history and accuracy was always equivocal. This seems to have been tacitly acknowledged by Cicero, who gave Herodotus the title "Father of History." In the opening scene of Cicero's *Laws* (1.5), Cicero, his brother Quintus and Atticus were discussing the merits of Cicero's poem on Marius, and Atticus raised the question of accuracy. Cicero demurred; accuracy, he suggested, was the business of the historian, not the poet.

"I understand, brother," said Quintus, "that you think one set of rules should be observed in history and another in poetry."

"Yes," agreed Cicero, "for in history everything is meant to lead to the truth, but in poetry a great deal is intended for pleasure—although in Herodotus, the father of history, and in Theopompus, there are a countless number of legends."

So history was not intended to make pleasureable reading, but it was to tell the truth, and in time this became a rhetorical commonplace, repeated by historians as late as Ammianus Marcellinus and Procopius of Caesarea.[2] But Herodotus, whose reputation as a liar was well established within a couple of generations of his death, was still recognized as the "father of history." When Cicero wrote his [essay on divination] *De Divinatione*, he accused Herodotus of one outright invention (2.56.116). Herodotus (1.53) relates how Croesus of Lydia consulted oracles of Amphiaraus and of Apollo at Delphi before making war on

---

† Reprinted with permission from the *Classical Journal* 64 (1968): 11–17. The footnotes have been omitted.

1. The Sicilian Timaeus of Tauromenium lived ca. 300 B.C. and wrote a *History* concerned primarily with Sicily but dealing also with Italy, Libya, and Greece. The German Leopold von Ranke (1795–1886) is regarded as the father of the modern objective historical school.

2. Ammianus Marcellinus lived during the fourth century A.D.; Procopius, during the sixth.

Persia, and the oracles replied that if he fought Cyrus, a great empire
would fall. The oracles were of course, quite right; the empire of Croesus fell. Cicero suggested that the whole story was a fabrication, and in
spite of his view that historians should adhere to the truth, it does not
seem to have occurred to him, or to anyone else in the ancient world,
that a fabricator of history might not deserve to be called its father.

To my knowledge, it was not until the Renaissance that anyone pointed
out the contradiction in Herodotus' reputation. Francesco Petrarca referred
to Cicero's charge that Herodotus had fabricated the oracle to Croesus
and declined to believe it. He pointed out that Cicero himself had called
Herodotus the "father of history," and the father of history could not be
guilty of fabrication. [3]

This was a shrewd judgment, and it highlighted the ambiguity of Herodotus' reputation rather more sharply than had been done up to that
time. The historical tradition of the west started with him. Moreover, as
an artist and a master of style, his reputation if anything increased
throughout antiquity, and the Renaissance rediscovered him with delight.
But at the same time, he was treated as a story-teller who disregarded
the truth and aimed rather to give his reader pleasure, and he was accused
sometimes of ignorance, sometimes of deliberate deceit and malice. His
histories apodexis [the setting forth of his research], published ca. 426
B.C., probably after his death, was a new invention and was recognized
as such. The *Periodos* of Hecataeus of Miletus, though earlier, was
something quite different, and Hellanicus' works appeared too late to
influence him. Herodotus was the father of history and yet, soon after
his history was published, he began to enjoy an ambivalent reputation
which is not easy to explain.

Back in 1842, Thomas de Quincey took up cudgels on Herodotus'
behalf, and wrote an essay titled "The Philosophy of Herodotus," which
attempted to explain his reputation. [4] He produced the theory that it had
arisen from the fact that no one had really understood what Herodotus
was trying to do. "But whence arose the other mistake about Herodotus—the fancy that his great work was exclusively (or even chiefly) a
history? It arose simply from a mistranslation, which subsists everywhere
to this day." *Historia* in Herodotus, de Quincey pointed out quite rightly,
meant "inquiries" or "investigation," not "history." But this will not do.
Historia does mean "researches" in Herodotus rather than history in our
sense, but the word soon picked up the connotation of history, and for
this Herodotus was largely responsible. For the fact is that Herodotus did
write history, no matter what he called it, and I know of no one in the
ancient world who thought otherwise. I cite de Quincey simply as an

3. On Petrarch and Herodotus, see the Momigliano essay included in this volume, pp. 356–68.
4. Thomas De Quincey (1785–1859) was an

English essayist and author of *Confessions of an
English Opium Eater* (1822).

example of the host of scholars since the Renaissance who have believed that Herodotus needed to be defended, and the desperate tactics for defense they sometimes used.

The reputation of Herodotus has a curious history. After him came Hellanicus and Thucydides. [5] What Hellanicus thought of Herodotus, we do not know, but he was a research scholar of a different type. For Hellanicus, research meant dates. Thucydides never mentions Herodotus by name, but we can be certain of his disapproval. He contradicts Herodotus on a number of points, and his statement that his history was not a prize essay but a "possession of lasting value" sounds like a shaft aimed at Herodotus; at least later writers thought so. But more important for Herodotus' reputation is the fact that Thucydides, in the famous chapters in his first book (20–22) where he sets forth an historian's credo, turns his back on the type of history which Herodotus wrote. For Thucydides saw no future in Herodotus' attempt to describe events he had not witnessed or to tell the story of men whose language he could not speak. The historian had another and more serious purpose. He was to put down an accurate record of human experience, in Thucydides' case, the Peloponnesian War, and since human experience was a manifestation of human nature which was constant, then the historian's account would be of educational value to men of discernment. Thucydides' actual words (1.22.4) sound like a massive reproof of the Herodotean product:

"The absence of an element of romance in my account of what happened, may well make it less attractive to listen to, but all who wish to attain a clear view of the past, and also of the same or similar events which, human nature being what it is, will recur in the future—if these people consider my work useful, I shall be content. It is written to be a possession of lasting value, not a work competing for an immediate hearing."

Both Hellanicus and Thucydides left marks on the traditions of ancient historiography. * * * Who were Herodotus' spiritual descendants?

He did have one of some importance: Ctesias of Cnidos, the Greek physician of the Persian king Artaxerxes II, who is best known for his attacks on Herodotus' veracity. But in the matter of style, Ctesias was almost completely dependent on Herodotus. Herodotus belonged to the intellectual milieu of Ionia, and his style owed most to Homer. Ctesias is the final flowering of the same school, untouched by the teachings of Gorgias or the example of Thucydides. But the school was degenerate. It had no serious moral purpose, and it lent itself to propaganda and fraud.

For two points should be made about Ctesias. First, we have the testimony of Diodorus (2.32) that he claimed to have used sources which

---

5. Hellanicus of Lesbos, a Greek historian and contemporary of Herodotus, is cited by Thucyd- ides in *The Peloponnesian War*, 1.97. See p. 261 in this volume.

sound like official Persian documents: royal records written on leather. Exactly what he meant is an open question, but it is clear that Ctesias was what we would call an "inside dopester," who attacked Herodotus under the pretense that he really knew what he was talking about. After Alexander the Great opened up the Near East to the Greeks, a great many more of these "inside dopesters" appeared, and although their knowledge of the east increased, their propensity for telling the truth did not. No doubt Ctesias' claims were fraudulent, but there was some truth mixed with the fiction, and he created an impression which lasted. Even when Ctesias' pretensions were exposed, faith in Herodotus was not restored. In fact, Ctesias and Herodotus were often coupled as unreliable historians. The reason was, it appears, that both were entertaining.

Second: Ctesias may have had a motive. His *Persika* appeared after Sparta had taken over the Athenian empire, and there was a general scramble among the states in Ionia to accommodate their traditions to the new order. Herodotus' verdict on the Persian Wars was that it would not be excessive to say that Athens had saved Greece (7.139). Ctesias was *philolakōn*,[6] Plutarch says (*Artaxerxes*, 13), and his version tended to favour Sparta. He transposed the battles of Plataea and Salamis in his chronology, and although this may have been motivated in part by a desire for originality, it also served to make Sparta's claim to be the saviour of Greece more convincing. Just who defeated the Persians was still a sore point in international mythology in the early fourth century, and as Herodotus himself realized would happen, his praise of Athens did not win plaudits everywhere.

In the long run, it was not Ctesias' attack on Herodotus' veracity which was so damaging. It became a *topos* among ancient historians to attack their predecessors, and Ctesias did not start the custom. Herodotus himself wastes no praise on Hecataeus of Miletus, and Thucydides mentioned Hellanicus, whom he probably used, only to find fault with him. But more damaging to Herodotus was the development of a kind of Ctesias-school of history, to which the rhetoricians were to make their contribution with not altogether happy results. The historians of this ilk were the type attacked by Polybius and satirized in Lucian's *Verae Historiae*.[7] They were really historical novelists, but unfortunately they were called historians, and Herodotus, like Socrates, suffered from the reputation of his pupils. He ceased to be taken seriously.

We must, however, recognize that from the early Hellenistic period on, Herodotus did not suffer merely from being coupled with Ctesias as an entertaining liar. He was attacked by a whole series of essays designed to expose his naïveté, his plagiarisms and falsehoods, and the flow of this anti-Herodotean literature continued pretty well down to the late Roman

---

6. *Philolakōn* means "biased in favor of Sparta."   7. On Lucian, see above p. 369.

Empire. "Herodotus," wrote Josephus[8] (*Contra Apion.* 1.3), "is attacked by everyone without exception." All but one of these pamphlets is lost but we have some of the titles. There was *Against Herodotus* by Manetho, *On Herodotus' thefts*, by Valerius Pollio, *On Herodotus lies*, by Aelius Harpocration, *Against Herodotus* by Libanius and of course, Plutarch's *On the malignity of Herodotus*, which has survived. Of these, I suspect that Manetho's attack had considerable influence, although the only fragment of it still extant contains the surprising information that lions never sleep. Since I gather that lions do sleep at every opportunity, this does not say much for Manetho's powers of observation. But Manetho was Egyptian high priest at Heliopolis under the first two Ptolemies, and he was in a good position to expose Herodotus, for he was accepted as an authority on Egypt. He was also an "inside dopester" of sorts, and although as far as we know, he treated Herodotus without rancour, his contribution to Herodotus' reputation was considerable. A number of authors who impugn him later can be shown to have read Manetho.

The only example of this anti-Herodotean literature which we have is Plutarch's *De malignitate Herodoti*, and from this we can guess what part of the trouble with Herodotus was. As the Persians Wars receded into the past, they became a great patriotic crusade, where Greeks united heroically to fend off hosts of barbarians. Wars of this sort should belong to mythographers. They are too important to be left to mere historians, not, at least, historians like Herodotus who had so serious moral purpose. Plutarch had personal reasons for his attack, for he was a patriotic Boeotian, and there is perhaps some justice to his claim that Herodotus had been overly severe with Thebes and Corinth.[9] Also it is probable that Plutarch reflected in part the feelings of his social stratum: the wealthy upper class in Greece on whom Rome leaned for support. They accommodated themselves comfortably to the Roman Empire, but they looked back on the classical age of Greece with pride, and the regret of men who knew that their greatness would not return. They did not like to be reminded that not all the Greeks who fended off the Persian invaders were heroes. The Roman historians who wrote of the early years of the Republic were better aware of their duties as mythographers.

But what roused Plutarch's animus against Herodotus was his view of what history was all about. For Plutarch, history had a serious educational purpose. Thucydides' views on the usefulness of history had been filtered down through Polybius, and had finally emerged as the exemplar theory of historiography. History's purpose was to teach by providing examples for future generations. Of course an historian was to tell the truth, but he need not tell the whole truth, and Plutarch's view was that

8. Flavius Josephus was a first-century A.D. Jewish Pharisee. He wrote *The Jewish War*, the story of the Jewish resistance to the Roman occupation of Palestine, and the *Antiquities of the Jews*, the his- tory of the Jews from the Creation to the struggle with Rome.
9. Thebes was the leading city in the territory of Boeotia, north of Attica (see the Glossary).

if a writer could not say something nice about a great man, he might better say nothing at all. He accused Herodotus of bias in favour of the barbarians, and deliberate malice; moreover, his malice was masked behind a show of good humour and frankness, which, for Plutarch, was the height of injustice. Not only did Herodotus diminish the glory of the Greek victory by telling falsehoods with malicious intent, but he wrote so well that people read him.

For the simple fact is that Herodotus was read. His reputation as a stylist if anything increased as time went on. Perhaps it was local pride which led Dionysius of Halicarnassus to praise Herodotus, for both men came from the same city. The famous passage in his *Letter to Pompey* (3) which compares Herodotus to Thucydides and gives Herodotus most of the prizes, has been characterized by one scholar as "Dionysius at his worst and weakest," but the admiration for Herodotus' prose was general among rhetoricians. We should note, however, that nowhere does Dionysius suggest that Herodotus was accurate. Lucian of Samosata praises Herodotus for the beauty and careful arrangement of his diction, the aptness of his Greek and his intellect, but, in his essay *How to write history* (39–42), he couples him with Ctesias as a storyteller, and his models of just historians are Thucydides and Xenophon. [1] *Quid enim aut Herodoto dulcius?* wrote Cicero (Frag. 2.49), and Quintilian (10.1.13) echoes the praise: *dulcis et candidus et fusus Herodotus, remissis adfectibus melior, sermonibus, voluptate.* [2] As well as Lucian, Dio Chrysostom, Arrian, Aelian and Philostratus fell under his influence. [3] The admiration continued down into the Byzantine period. Procopius of Caesarea made both Herodotus and Thucydides his models. Photius called Herodotus the greatest master of Greek prose. But no one held him up as a model of reliability.

The Renaissance inherited Herodotus' ambivalent reputation. He was fairly popular; there are 44 editions and translations in Europe between 1450 and 1700 compared with 41 of Thucydides, but the strictures of the ancients on his reliability were duly noted. Professor Momigliano has dated the beginning of Herodotus' rehabilitation to 1566, when Henri Estienne brought out an edition of Lorenzo Valla's Latin translation of Herodotus in Paris, and prefaced it with his own *Apologia pro Herodoto.* [4] The *Apologia* was reprinted three times in later editions, the last of which dates to 1763. But it should be noted that Estienne's edition, which had his *Apologia* as a preface, contained the fragments of Ctesias

1. Lucian (ca. A.D. 120–185) wrote satirical dialogues in Greek.
2. "Who is sweeter than Herodotus?" and 'Sweet, clear, and flowing Herodotus. Delightful and colloquial, he gently improves one's mood."
3. Dio Chrysostom, a philosopher and orator of the first century A.D. Arrian (Flavius Arrianus), a second-century A.D. soldier and historian, wrote a

history, *The Anabasis*, of Alexander the Great. Aelian (Claudius Aelianus) (ca. A.D. 200) was a prolific historian who wrote in Greek. Philostratus "the Athenian" (ca. A.D. 200) was the author of a life of Apollonius of Tyana.
4. Lorenzo Valla (ca. 1407–1547) was an Italian humanist who translated Herodotus and Thucydides into Latin.

as an appendix, so that both sides of the question received fair treatment. Herodotus' reputation was still an open question in the eighteenth century, and I suspect that Napoleon's expedition to Egypt did as much for it as the battles among scholars. We have come a long way when we reach James Rennell's *The geographical system of Herodotus examined and explained by a comparison with other ancient authors and with modern geography*, in 1800. "We may add," wrote Rennell, "that superstition made him credulous in *believing* many improbable stories, but love of truth prevented him from asserting falsehoods." Herodotus was honest, but naive. At this watershed the nineteenth century left the verdict on Herodotus' reputation, and scholars turned their attention to uncovering Herodotus' sources, thereby developing a new mythology of their own. Only in the present day has Herodotus gained the reputation not only for honesty but for a modicum of shrewdness as well.

One may ask why an historian, recognized as the father of history and greatly admired, nevertheless enjoyed such a reputation for falsehood. It is not an easy question to answer. According to Momigliano whose essay, "The place of Herodotus in the history of historiography" deals with this problem, it was Thucydides who was ultimately responsible for the verdict of antiquity on Herodotus.[5] He decided that the Herodotean method of doing research into the past was unsafe, and turned his back on it, and by so doing, he left Herodotus at the head of the western historical tradition but at the same time isolated from it. In part, Momigliano is right. But there are, I believe, two other related reasons for Herodotus' ambivalent reputation.

Both Herodotus and Thucydides wrote of war; war became the stuff of ancient history. Thucydides' aim in writing, as he states himself, was to provide a useful record of the war between Athens and Sparta which would serve to enlighten men in the future, and what he meant by this is less important for our purpose than what later writers thought he meant. Historians after Thucydides usually failed to copy his standards of accuracy, but they still wrote to enlighten and to educate. In this serious atmosphere Herodotus was suspect, and probably the very excellence of his style told against him. We are all familiar with the type of criticism which begins: "Professor X writes well; however if we measure him as an historian, we must express reservations etc." The sentiment is not purely modern.

Herodotus, as we know, does state a purpose for his history. He wrote so that the great deeds of men might not be forgotten and to show what was the *aitia* of the war, that is, who was to blame for it.[6] The first motive was borrowed from the epic, and later generations interpreted it as using history for entertainment. That did not do at all. Granted that there were more rhetorical historians in the ancient world than severe

---

5. Reprinted in this volume, pp. 356–68.   6. *Aitia* in Greek means "cause."

devotees of accuracy as far as mere numbers were concerned; but after Thucydides, poetry and history went their separate ways and history was expected to be useful. Herodotus' second motive, his concern for the *aitia* of the war, was simply misunderstood, for it was already becoming archaic in the fifth century B.C. In Homer, the word *histor* is used twice, and both times it means not an historian but an arbitrator, who determined who was to blame for a quarrel by examining the customs and laws of a tribe and inquiring into the facts. His stance was studiously fair. So the attitude of Herodotus to the barbarians was *sine ira et studio*; it was a world apart from that of Isocrates and Aristotle in the fourth century. [7] For Herodotus, the Persians are no less brave than the Greeks, but their inferior weaponry put them at a disadvantage. What Herodotus' successors thought of this attitude we can learn from Plutarch, who accused him of being *philobarbaros*. [8] Historians after Herodotus no longer approached the problem of war as arbiters, concerned to discover the *aitia* responsible for it.

The reason for this was, I believe, that Thucydides, perhaps without intending it, introduced a new concept of war. For him, imperialism and expansionism were natural to man, for the stronger naturally tried to dominate the weaker. Therefore war was a natural phenomenon and should be studied like any other. There was no point asking for the *aitia* of the war; the real causes, the only ones worth attention, were to be discovered in the realm of politics. War was a matter of politics, and up until this century, that is what it remained in the minds of historians. The Herodotean view was very different. For Herodotus, war could be explained in terms of customs and usages, vengeance and counter-vengeance. When Xerxes announces his intention of invading Greece to the Persian satraps and nobles (Hdt. 7.8) he presents it as a Persian custom never to keep the peace. The expansionism of the Persian empire, which is the *leit-motif* of his *History* is apparently to be grouped among Persian *nomoi*, and it was proper for the historian to treat it as such.

As for war itself, Herodotus refused to glorify it. "No one," said Croesus to Cyrus, "is so foolish as to prefer war to peace. In peace, children bury their fathers; in time of war, fathers their children." (Hdt. 1.87) Speaking of the earthquake which shook Delos when Datis passed by, Herodotus says (6.98) that it was a portent of evils to come, for during the reigns of Darius, Xerxes and Artaxerxes, more evils befell the Greeks than under the twenty generations preceding Darius. So much for the imperialism of Periclean Athens. And finally, there is the phrase reminiscent of Homer (*Il.* 5.63) which Herodotus applies to the ships sent

---

7. Isocrates (436–338 B.C.), an Athenian orator and sophist, was a disciple of Socrates in his youth. *Sine ira et studio*: "without enmity or partisanship" (Tacitus, *Annals*, 1.1).

8. *Philobarbaros* means "prejudiced in favor of the barbarians."

from Athens to help the Ionians in their revolt: "the beginning of evils. . . ." So also the Trojan ships which carried Paris to Sparta and Helen. Neither Herodotus' treatment of the causes of war nor his attitude to war itself had a future. After Thucydides, serious historians did not look for anthropological or sociological causes for war. The reasons for war were political, and war itself was judged as a political act. It was not evil *per se;* it could even be glorious and provide examples for the education of future generations. But Herodotus continued to be admired as the master of a good story, and this was the portion of the tradition which Ctesias took over, with the results which we have seen.

The Thucydidean view of war as a political act became the view of the ancient world, and until this century, the view of the modern one. There are still historians who would defend it, but essentially our present attitudes are changing. In the light of such books as Konrad Lorenz's *On aggression* and Robert Ardrey's *The territorial imperative,* anthropological causes of war have reappeared to challenge the established view, and Herodotus is probably less isolated from the historical tradition now than he ever was in the past. Perhaps one reason for the high regard which this generation of scholars has for Herodotus is that it is only the twentieth century which has been able to regard him as a serious student of warfare.

III. THE PERSIAN WARS
A. T. OLMSTEAD

Albert T. Olmstead was professor of Oriental history at the Oriental Institute of the University of Chicago. His *History of the Persian Empire* was published shortly after his death in 1945. Olmstead's essay is a refreshing attempt to view the war between Persia and Greece from a Persian perspective.

Persia and the Greek Frontier Problem†

"Greece and the Persian Wars" is a threadbare subject; "Persia and the Greek Frontier Problem" has at least the virtue of novelty. Such novelty must be found in the point of view, that of a Persian, rather than in any particular access of new source material. It is true that we have today literally thousands of contemporary documents in the various oriental languages, Persian, Elamite, Babylonian, Aramaic, Phoenician,

†Reprinted by permission from *Classical Philology* 34 (1939): 305–22. The notes have been omitted.

Hebrew, Egyptian, Lycian, Lydian, and that some of these are narratives; their value for the culture history of the Persian Empire and as a
background against which we project the events now to be related cannot
possibly be over-exaggerated, but an extremely small portion throws direct
light on the political relations of Persia with Greece. This absence of
reference is in itself highly significant. While Persia was undoubtedly
the controlling factor of contemporary Greece, the Greeks on the western frontier were for long of small interest to Persian great kings.

Our chief narrative source remains Herodotus, the story eked out by
scraps from other Greek writers like Ctesias. But we tend to forget that
Herodotus was born a Persian subject, that his wide travels were possible
only through the Persian peace, that after his retirement to Continental
Greece he was still in contact with Persian friends, and that he employed
Persian sources, written or unwritten. Nor does he show himself violently anti-Persian if naturally he rejoices in Greek successes which had
already become legendary. He presents honestly the facts to the best of
his ability, and if he has not always detected partisan distortions, his facts
generally permit us to correct the interpretation. Our main task is to
confront the conventional treatment by present-day writers with his own
stated facts.

When in 558 B.C., Cyrus marched west against Croesus of Lydia,
Persia was in no sense the mighty power it was soon to become. By the
conquest of Media, he had secured only the western half of the Iranian
Plateau, by this very expedition he was to add Assyria, western Mesopotamia, Cilicia, Cappadocia, and finally Lydia (557), which was formed
into the satrapy of Saparda or Sardis.

Before the final battle with the Lydians, Cyrus had offered terms to
the Greek coastal cities, which for long years had been subject to Lydia;
the majority refused, but Miletus accepted, and the Persians had learned
their first lesson in handling the Greeks—divide and conquer. By right
of conquest, title to the former Lydian vassals passed to Cyrus, and the
refusal of the Greeks to submit made them automatically rebels. Their
position was not improved by their demand that they enjoy the same
favored position as under Croesus, and when this demand was naturally
refused as coming too late, the fortifying of their cities meant war. The
Greeks appealed to Sparta, known to Cyrus as a summoned ally of Croesus which had made no appearance, and to his amazement the great
king received an embassy which forbade him to injure any Greek city!
Miletus at least was loyal, and when Pactyas, native treasurer of the
satrapy, revolted with aid from Greek mercenaries, Apollo of Milesian
Branchidae ordered his surrender. Henceforth Apollo was to remain a
consistent friend of Persia.

Then came the turn of the rebel Greeks, who fought bravely but without unity and were taken one by one; when Cnidus attempted to insure
safety by cutting through the isthmus, Apollo of Delphi followed Apollo
of Branchidae and forbade the project. Carians, Lycians, and Caunians

fought with equal bravery and equal lack of union, others surrendered, and in short order the seacoast was organized as Yauna, Ionia; it was not, however, a regular satrapy but was controlled by the satrap at Sardis. Hellespontine Greeks, on the contrary, were under a satrap, who from Dascylium administered Tyaiy Drayahya, "Those of the Sea."

This brief episode taught the Persians much. They learned that as individuals the Greeks were excellent fighters, worthy incorporation in Persian armies, also that the city-states were incapable of united action and that they would always have friends among them. Best of all friends was Apollo, god of oracles. But the most important discovery was that of the class divisions within the city-states themselves.

Most of the Greek states had long since abandoned kingship for a hereditary nobility of landholders. New economic forces had brought into prominence a new aristocracy of trade-bought wealth, which through the tyrant often supplanted this older aristocracy of birth. While the patriotism of the older nobility was inevitably narrow, men of trade could appreciate opportunities offered by inclusion in a great empire; obviously it was to Persian advantage that Greek cities should be intrusted to tyrants.

Under their tyrants the Greeks remained quiet while Cyrus rapidly expanded his empire. Conquest of eastern Iran gave Cyrus an enormous addition of first-class fighting men and determined the conquest of Babylon, Syria was occupied, the Phoenicians submitted. Henceforth the empire possessed another war fleet, equal at least in numbers and skill to the Greeks should they ever combine in revolt, the Greek traders within the empire now faced the keenest competition from merchant-princes who ruled city-states much like their own. Cambyses rounded out the huge empire by subjugation of Egypt, the Greek "factory" at Naucratis was in his possession, the lucrative Greek trade with the Nile was at his mercy. When Greeks of Cyrene sent in their submission, a good half of the Greek states, certainly the wealthier and more advanced half, was under Persian control.

Suddenly the empire was convulsed by the usurpation of Darius I (521), and the more important of the states recently conquered declared their independence. Aryandes, satrap of Egypt, announced himself ruler, Oroetes of Sardis killed the satrap of neighboring Dascylium, but the Greeks of these satrapies were held loyal to Persia by their tyrants, who took no action even when the most powerful of them all, Polycrates of Samos, was treacherously killed by Oroetes.

The revolts put down and the gold of northwest India added to the imperial resources, Darius was prepared to continue extension of the empire. With the more important half of the Greek states already his, incorporation of the remainder must have appeared inevitable. A court physician, Democedes of Italian Croton, was dispatched from Sidon to make a preliminary survey of the western coasts. Ariaramnes, satrap of Cappadocia, crossed the Black Sea for a reconnaisance of the north shore in preparation for a Scythian expedition. By this expedition, led by the king in person, the Scythians were warned off, Thrace and Macedonia submitted, the European conquests were formed into the satrapy of Skudra, named from the Macedonian town Scydra it has been suggested. Artaphernes, the king's brother, arrived as satrap of Sardis, Otanes captured Byzantium with its command of the straits, Lemnos and Imbros were secured with ships loaned by friendly Lesbos.

The path to Continental Greece was being cleared when in 507 Artaphernes received an embassy which offered direct access to the heart of the desired area. Athens under Cleisthenes was experimenting with a mild democracy which as a matter of course was threatened by ultra-conservative Sparta; Sparta was the declared enemy of Persia, Persian alliance was therefore indicated. Artaphernes received the embassy and demanded the usual tokens of submission, earth and water. The envoys complied and the first contact of Greek democracy and Persian imperialism was made memorable by the promise of the rising democracy to accept Persian vassalage! During the interval public sentiment had changed, the envoy's action was disavowed and Cleisthenes was banished. Two years later, their opponents sent another embassy which begged the satrap not to aid the expelled tyrant Hippias; as might have been expected, they were ordered to restore him under pain of death.

Large numbers of Ionian Greeks had been brought together by the Scythian expedition. Conscious at last of their strength if united but quite failing to realize that they had lost their chance; now that the troubles incident to the accession had been composed, they decided to revolt. Opposition to the tyrants imposed by the Persians had grown, the commercial classes fostered by the tyrants were losing trade to the Phoenicians and to the European Greeks, and the nationalistic land-holding aristocracy took advantage of the shift in sentiment. Their leader was Aristagoras, himself tyrant of Miletus, who requested one hundred ships to restore certain Naxian exiles and thus extend Persian rule in the islands. Thus far Miletus had been the most loyal of Greek vassals, but Artaphernes had his suspicions and sent instead two hundred commanded by the king's nephew Megabates and manned largely by non-Greeks; as might have been expected, the Naxians were warned and the project failed.

Aristagoras next summoned the leaders to revive the Ionic League. Only Hecataeus opposed the revolt. When preparing his "World Tour" he had learned at first hand the empire's strength and he listed in order all the nations subject to the great king. His protest went unheeded and it was voted to abolish tyranny; Aristagoras resigned, the other tyrants were killed, imprisoned, or expelled.

Despite her brave words, Sparta held back once Aristagoras had incautiously displayed his bronze map of the world and had let slip it was three months' journey from the coast to Susa. Argos inquired of Delphian Apollo, and received the expected reply, a threat that for its wickedness Miletus would be destroyed. Athens, conservative once more, met the appeal that Miletus was a daughter-city by voting twenty ships, Eretria five. The small European contingent took part in the capture of Sardis, then retreated from the burning city, and was recalled to meet the war with Aegina; Persian diplomacy had done its work. The naval war was transferred to Cyprus, the first of many struggles between Phoenician vassal city-states and their Greek rivals on the island. Persia quickly recovered Cyprus, city after city in western Asia Minor was captured or submitted, when Lade was fought (494) half the Ionian states had already made their peace. Lade was a complete rout, all the former subject states were regained, Chios, Lesbos, and Tenedos were new acquisitions.

Hecataeus had been justified, the historian was the one man to make peace with the satrap. Artaphernes professed himself quite willing to forget the wrongs he had suffered in the rebellion; he would restore to the rebel states their laws, but at a price to be set at a meeting of the Ionian deputies. Hitherto they had been allowed a considerable degree of autonomy, now they were brought more effectively into the satrapial organization. Private war between the states must be abandoned, they must submit to arbitration. Persia had followed Assyria in taking a census for purposes of taxation; now such a census was imposed on Yauna Tyaiy Ushkahya, "Ionia of the Dry Land," as opposed to "Ionia of the Sea." The satrapy was measured in parasangs, the "double-hour march" of the Assyrians; the tribute was fixed at approximately the pre-war level, though punishment of the revolting states by loss of considerable tracts of land increased the pressure on those which were left. A lion weight of a Euboeic talent, inscribed in Aramaic "exact according to the satrapy of the king," has been found at Abydos to witness the new tax administration.

Mardonius, son of Gobryas, and just become son-in-law of the king, superseded the officers at the seat of war. He announced a new policy. Darius had observed the tendency in some of the Greek states of Asia to experiment with a primitive democracy. Adherents of Cleisthenes had promised earth and water, their opponents had aided Ionian rebels. When that aid had brought threats of Persian revenge, the enemies of the present conservative government, the friends of the expelled tyrant Hippias and the members of the young democracy, had shown their teeth by fining the poet Phrynichus for staging a tragedy on the fall of Miletus. Darius therefore instructed Mardonius to reorganize the recovered Greek states as democracies. For the first time in history democracy had conquered a large and important section of the Greek world and the sturdy infant nestled under the protecting aegis of a "barbarian" monarchy.

The hint was not lost on European Greece, where in a goodly number of states democratic factions were rising into prominence and might be expected to welcome the liberator from the hated conservatives. Furthermore, Greek cities in Asia would remain quiet only if freed from the constant temptation offered by independent kinsmen across the seas, who were ready to sympathize with, if not always prepared to assist, conservative anti-Persian reaction. Once and for all to destroy hope of outside aid, the "hot trail" of the invaders must be followed back.

Mardonius continued the plan of slow penetration from the north under protection of the fleet. Thasos fell to the navy, Macedonia again recognized Persian overlordship, but these successes were counterbalanced by loss of half the ships off Mount Athos and by a serious defeat at the hands of the Bryges, and Mardonius was recalled (492). Hitherto Persian strategy and diplomacy had been virtually without flaw, now began that series of blunders which was to bring ultimate disaster.

The first mistake was to abandon, for a purely temporary setback, the policy of slow penetration from the north. Instead, it was decided to send a fleet directly across the Aegean and to punish the chief offenders in the Ionic revolt, Athens and Eretria. At first there was no indication that a blunder had been committed. The heralds sent out to the Greek mainland with the usual demand for earth and water met with conspicuous success. To be sure, at Sparta and Athens the heralds were killed, but almost without exception the other states furnished the usual symbols of bondage. Darius added to his lists another satrapy, Yauna Takabara, "Ionians who bear shields on their heads" as the Akkadian version translates; perhaps the broad petasos hat is meant. Among these accessions was Aegina, which once before had done Persia good service by starting the war which recalled Athenian ships from Asia; Athens complained to Sparta whose king Cleomenes demanded intervention; when his colleague Demaratus protested, he was deposed and like Hippias took refuge with Darius.

The expedition began auspiciously. Commanded by Datis the Mede and the king's nephew, the younger Artaphernes, the fleet occupied and burned Naxos. The Delians fled to Tenos but the Persians begged them to return and offered frankincense and a gold collar to their good friend Apollo. After six days' investment Eretria was betrayed by a friendly citizen.

Datis might well hope that Athens would likewise be handed over by friends, either the partisans of the former tyrant Hippias, now with the army, or by the democratic leaders, the Alcmaeonidae. These well-grounded hopes were dashed by a second stupid blunder, the destruction of Eretria and the "netting" of the inhabitants; neither democrat nor man of trade could behold unmoved the burning of the beloved city. When therefore Datis landed on the Marathon plain, whose inhabitants were supposed to be friendly, he found the whole Athenian levy drawn up to meet him. After a delay which spoke only too eloquently of still divided counsels, Miltiades attacked and won the battle. Datis yet hoped that Athens would surrender if the fleet arrived while the army was absent, and the Alcmaeonidae actually did signal by shield from Cape Sunium, but the army hurried back in time. Once convinced there was no longer a chance of betrayal by their partisans, the disappointed Persians sailed home. The Eretrians were deported to Ardericca in Cissia, the land of the earlier Kashshites, and there in the first century of our era Apollonius of Tyana found them still holding in remembrance their earlier home and speaking their ancestral language.[1]

To Darius, Marathon was only a temporary setback in a policy of steady frontier advance. A larger army was all that was needed to crush opposition and to incorporate the remaining Greeks into the empire. Preparation for a renewal of this troublesome frontier war was begun and of course this demanded fresh taxes. In June, 486, Nabu-ittanu discovered from Shatamaksu and Nubagaza, the major domo, that he must pay a new toll on the barley, wheat, and mustard he was bringing through the storehouse on a Babylonian canal. They told him: "It was determined, before the judge it was recorded." "According to the king's law," the same Persian word is used as in the Artaxerxes decree in Ezra, "the toll for the king's house he shall give."

Fresh additions to an already increased tax burden led Egypt to revolt in this same year, 486. A Persian law decreed that a successor must be chosen before the king departed for war. Ariobarzanes was eldest of three sons by a daughter of Gobryas; he may be the "king's son of Elam," forced labor for whom is commuted by a money payment in 507 and for whom a palace was constructed at Babylon in 498. Partisans of Xerxes, eldest of four sons by Atossa, daughter of Cyrus, contested his claim, and a bitter palace quarrel ensued. As purple born and as descendant of the empire's founder, Xerxes was naturally chosen. New evidence has been found in new inscriptions of Xerxes, further evidence may be seen in the many reliefs at Persepolis, the best those recently excavated by the Oriental Institute, where Xerxes stands dutifully behind his father seated on the throne.

Before Darius could put down the Egyptian rebellion, he died, about October 15, 484. Xerxes succeeded, and the rebellion was put down in his second year, 483. He was more interested in completing the magnificent structures begun by his father on the Persepolis terrace than in testing by European adventures the formidable army machine his father had built up; he was urged on by his cousin Mardonius, ambitious to be made satrap of newly won territories, and by exiled Athenians who even hired an oracle-monger. The kings of Thessaly invited his appearance. Reluctantly Xerxes prepared to continue his father's policy of expansion on the western frontier.

Direct attack across the Aegean had failed and Xerxes wisely returned to the former policy of gradual advance by land, the army supported by the fleet. To avoid another shipwreck at Athos, a canal was dug through the isthmus. The entire navy was to be utilized and half the regular troops, three of the six army corps, each about sixty thousand strong.

1. The sage and purported healer Apollonius of Tyana lived a wandering life, and his adventures were recounted by his biographer Philostratus ca. A.D. 200.

While the expeditionary force wintered at Sardis, the threatened Greeks vainly endeavored to form an effective alliance. As might have been expected, appeal to the Delphic Oracle brought only discouragement. Apollo bade the Athenians escape to earth's end. A second oracle predicted occupation of all Attica and promised safety only in the wooden walls of the ships. Argos, suspected of inviting Persian intervention after defeat by Sparta, was ordered by Apollo to sit still. Corcyra's ships were "detained" by contrary winds. Gelo of Syracuse promised much and sent three small boats to watch the outcome. Theognis of Megara was typical of many when he urged revelry without fear of a war with the Medes.[2] Awake at last to his danger, he could only appeal to the god—Apollo of all divinities!—for protection against the wanton host of the Medes; he was afraid when he saw the lack of sense and the folk-destroying internal struggles of the Greeks.

Still more affrighting was the action of Xerxes when the allied spies were caught at Sardis; full of confidence, he ordered them shown the whole vast array and then released them to report home. At the first sign of spring, 480, he marched to the Troad and climbed the citadel of Priam to sacrifice to the local Athena while Magi poured libations to the spirits of those who had died in defense of Troy. Thus Xerxes announced himself protagonist of the Orient in the new Trojan War.

Assembled at the Corinthian Isthmus, which the Peloponnesian members of the alliance had already decided was the only tenable line of defense, the allies received a Thessalian request for aid in guarding the Olympus Pass. Ten thousand heavy-armed infantry, supported by a naval force, occupied the Vale of Tempe and were reinforced by Thessalian cavalry, representatives of the conservatives, the commons were as naturally pro-Persian. Alexander of Macedonia did good service for his Persian master by urging the allies not to remain and be trampled by the king's host and soon they hurried home to the Isthmus.

The Hellespont was crossed by bridges constructed by a Greek, and the combined land and naval forces marched south without opposition. On the way Xerxes was met by heralds bringing earth and water from abandoned Thessaly, Locri, and all Boeotia except Plataea and Thespiae, for it was already plain that the allies from the Peloponnese had no intention of offering serious opposition north of the Isthmus.

Victory appeared certain to the Persians. Not only did they control all the Greeks of Asia and Africa whose ships were included in their navy, already half the European Greeks had submitted and there remained to be subdued only a few recalcitrant states in the Peloponnese since it was now clear that all north of the Isthmus was to be abandoned. Apollo of Delphi was their loyal friend. Athens, ruled by the democracy under Themistocles, would certainly go over to democracy's patron once the

2. Theognis of Megara was a Greek elegiac poet of the late sixth century B.C.

Peloponnesians retired behind the Isthmus. With the Athenian fleet safely Persian, the Isthmus wall could be turned, Argos would declare itself openly, a wedge would be driven between Sparta and Corinth, each would be defeated when fighting alone.

Nor was the picture changed as the march southward was resumed. Loss of Thessaly did bring Leonidas north as far as Thermopylae with three hundred Spartans and a few allied contingents, but the small number loudly proclaimed that only rear-guard skirmishes were intended to delay, not to stop the advance until the Isthmus wall was complete. The fleet took its position near Artemisium but retired to the narrower Euripus once the Persian navy was sighted. Even the loss of many Persian ships in a sudden gale did not encourage Leonidas, who was prepared for immediate retirement; only the indignant protests of the Locrians and Phocians compelled him to remain to meet a hero's death and to win posthumous fame. The opening of Thermopylae more than canceled any advantage won by the first allied attack on the divided Persian fleet, in the second battle at Artemisium the tide had already turned, the Egyptians had taken five ships, half the Athenian ships had been disabled when news of Thermopylae arrived and the whole naval force retreated from a position become untenable.

Phocis was ravaged, the army entered Boeotia, held safely for them by Alexander of Macedon. A flying column took the road to Delphi, to reward Apollo for his pro-Persian oracles and to support his further efforts, we should have supposed, to loot the treasures his priests later explained with some plausibility. As he had promised, the god protected his own, he thundered and hurled down cliffs on the barbarians who fled with great slaughter; such at least was the Delphic version—after the defeat of Persia.

At Theban urging, Xerxes burned Thespiae and Plataea and entered Attica which he found deserted, for the allied fleet had paused at Salamis only to evacuate the civilian population. A few zealots barred the Acropolis, trusting to Apollo's ambiguous oracle; once the terms offered by the followers of Hippias were refused, the Acropolis was taken and burned and the failure at Marathon was redeemed. The Persian fleet anchored off Phalerum and panic seized the allies. Salamis was a veritable trap and all but the interested Athenians, Aeginetans, and Megarians were rightly anxious to escape before the trap was sprung. Only the threat of Themistocles to sail off with his whole fleet and the knowledge that the democratic leader was quite capable of carrying out his threat drove the Spartan admiral Eurybiades to command preparation for battle.

At the Persian council, only the lady tyrant of Halicarnassus, Artemisia, opposed immediate attack. Victory seemed to be within their grasp. Sparta had abandoned one ally after another, and the alacrity with which each had made terms proclaimed loudly the strong pro-Persian sentiment hitherto repressed. Athenian ships were manned by the commons and captained by the leader of the democratic faction; flouted at every turn by the Peloponnesians, he should now be prepared to return to the normal policy of his party, since it was amply clear that the Peloponnesians had determined to leave the Athenians in the lurch.

The awaited message was quickly received. Themistocles declared himself the king's friend who desired his success. The Greeks were frightened and ready to flee, lest the king prevent their escape; dissensions had broken out and soon the pro-Persians would fall upon the king's enemies. There was no reason for Xerxes to doubt these protestations of loyalty.

Yet both letter and decision of immediate attack were mistakes. Had Xerxes taken no action at all, the few remaining allies would have retired to the Isthmus. The Athenians, Megarians, and Aeginetans would have been compelled to accept terms. With their aid the Isthmus wall would have been outflanked and there would have remained only the mopping up. Quite as effective was the actual procedure of Xerxes. The eastern exits were blocked by a triple line of ships, the Egyptians, "marsh dwellers, skillful rowers of galleys" with two hundred ships sailed to block the western. Now the whole allied naval force was bottled up and could be left for exhaustion of supplies and for mutual recriminations to do their work, either to compel surrender or the attempt to break the encirclement with the consequent opportunity to pick off the ships as they emerged. On the basis of the actual situation, the Persians were entirely justified in dispatching that very night their infantry and cavalry to fight the decisive battle at the Isthmus.

Unfortunately for Persia, Xerxes was not content to leave well enough alone; he must win a spectacular victory, and he therefore ordered a direct attack on men sullen because they had been allowed to be entrapped and now fighting desperately for escape. At first the assault was a success, the Ionian Greeks badly worsted the Spartans, but later the Aeginetans and then the Athenians broke through and attacked in their turn. Against an allied loss of forty ships, the Persians lost two hundred, a third of their naval strength.

Taken by itself, Salamis was a check to the Persian frontier advance and nothing more. None of the recently acquired territory was lost, the army was intact, the fleet was still powerful and needed only reorganization. The allies, to be sure, had been encouraged by an unexpected victory, but they were reduced in numbers and the next year should see them conquered. What made Salamis important was not the victory itself but its effect on the mind of Xerxes. Although he and no one else was responsible for the defeat by ordering an offensive when a simple blockade would have been effective, he completely lost his head and executed the Phoenician captains for alleged cowardice; incensed by their maltreatment, the Phoenicians returned home and were followed by the Egyptians. It was this justified desertion and not the defeat at Salamis which left the Aegean wide open to the allied fleet and permitted the truly decisive operations of the next year.

In a very real sense Salamis was actually a Persian blessing. Discouraged by his fiasco, Xerxes hurried off to Sardis, where he spent the next year keeping watch over Ionia. Direct conduct of the European campaign was transferred to the seasoned campaigner Mardonius, who retained for himself only one army division, composed of Immortals, Persians, Medes, Sacae, Bactrians, and Indians, a force almost exclusively Iranian and so of the best fighting material. Even thus reduced, it was superior in numbers to the allies, and it was supported by half the troops of Continental Greece. A second army under Artabazus, son of Pharnaces, guarded the long seaboard route by which alone supplies could be forwarded, a third under Tigranes held Ionia quiet.

Potidaea revolted; Olynthus threatened to follow its example, but Artabazus took the city and handed over the ruins to the Chalcidians. Friends of Persia led a detachment under the walls of Potidaea at ebb tide, but the tide turned too soon and those who were not drowned were slaughtered from boats.

From his winter camp in Thessaly, Mardonius sent the Athenian proxenos, Alexander of Macedon, to offer complete forgiveness, rebuilding of the temples, restoration of territory with any lands additional which they might desire, and equal alliance as a free city. Such generous terms must have appealed strongly to the poorer classes, for whom new invasion could only mean new miseries and the loss of their few remaining possessions. But the democracy had lost control. Themistocles had admittedly written a letter to the great king urging him to attack at Salamis; though now he maintained that he had done it in subtlety, he was not believed. After his exile he once more claimed that he had acted as Persia's friend; this time he *was* believed and was richly rewarded by Artaxerxes, Xerxes' son! The reaction had given power to the conservatives who replied that Athens would make no peace.

Mardonius was advised by the Thebans to remain in Boeotia and win over the recalcitrant Greeks through bribes to their leaders. It was sound advice, based on intimate knowledge of their own ethnic character, and Mardonius' refusal to accept it was another in the chain of Persian blunders. Ten months after the first inroad, Athens fell again into his hands and once more failure of the Peloponnesians to give adequate support drove the citizens to take refuge on Salamis or on their ships. Mardonius repeated his proposals in hope that his presence with an army might enable his friends to force compliance, but the man who merely urged consideration was stoned. Yet there was still hope for Mardonius. As usual, the Spartans were "celebrating a feast"; the Isthmus wall was complete and could be held, they fatuously imagined, even against the Athenian fleet. Even after the victory of Salamis, it appeared, the inability of Sparta to understand the most elementary factors of the situation would drive Athens, despite the conservatives, into the Persian alliance. Finally the disillusioned Athenian ambassadors told Sparta this was exactly what they were compelled to do. To their amazement the envoys learned that

at last a Tegean had convinced the Spartans of their utter folly and that
troops were already on the way. At the very last second, fortune had
again snatched victory from the Persians.

Friendly Argives relayed the information to Mardonius, who had
hitherto refrained from plundering Athens in the well-grounded hope
that Spartan procrastination, if not actual disloyalty to an ally, would
force Athens to come to terms. Once more disappointed, he again burned
Athens and withdrew to Boeotia, where, with Thebes as a base, he could
secure adequate supplies. Trees were cut down to construct a stockade
over a mile square and Mardonius awaited the allied moves.

The allied forces advanced through Attica and timidly encamped on
the north slopes of Cithaeron, opposite the Persians on the Aesopus.
Immediately squadron after squadron of cavalry charged the Megarians
on the low ground which constituted the weakest part of the line in hope
of breaking through to the pass and cutting off supplies. Athenian reinforcements came up and the attack was beaten off. Encouraged, the
allies then descended to the lower slopes where encampment was easier
and where there was water, the Persians moved up to meet them.

Again Mardonius was advised, this time by Artabazus, to retire and
employ bribery, again the general mistakenly refused the advice. The
position of the allies was already desperate. They suffered incessant cavalry raids, one of which closed the passes and the road home to the
Peloponnese and captured a much-needed provision train. Food was
scant, the fountain of Gargapha was choked, the men suffered from
thirst. The generals decided to retire at nightfall. Their retirement was
made in disorder. The main body lost their way, a stubborn captain
delayed the Spartans, who at dawn were drawn up in a thoroughly
untenable position. Had the allies been permitted to withdraw unmolested, the coalition would undoubtedly have broken up, the Athenians
would have made terms, the Peloponnesians would have retreated to the
Isthmus, and the individual states would have been subjugated in detail.

Once more the end of the war was in sight. Once more a Persian
commander underestimated the fighting ability of the individual Greek,
backed against a mountain wall. Once more the general was lured by
hope of an immediate and spectacular victory and threw away the certain advantages of a dilatory policy. At that, the battle was fiercely contested. From their line of wicker shields the Persian archers poured showers
of arrows on the Spartans who were compelled to ask aid from the
Athenians; when the Athenians started to the rescue, they were stopped
by the Medizing Greeks. Even when the Tegeans, followed by the Spartans, broke down the wicker wall, the Persians fought on, snapping off
the spears with their bare hands. Then Mardonius made his last and
fatal mistake, he entered the battle in person and was slain. Deprived of
their leader, it was only a matter of hours before the stockaded camp was
taken and the Persians slaughtered without mercy. Pausanias was a national

hero; no one dreamed that before another year was passed he would be plotting to betray his fellow-Greeks for the empty honor of a son-in-law to the Persian king.

Like the earlier battles, Plataea by itself was not decisive. But one of the Persian armies had entered the battle, a second army of equal size was close by. Yet instead of throwing fresh troops upon the battle-weary allies and sweeping them rapidly to the southernmost tip of the Peloponnese, Artabazus retired and the war in Europe was ended. The reason was that Artabazus had heard news from Asia.

In the spring of 479 a new allied fleet had been made ready. The Athenian contingent was under Xanthippus, for his fame as the victor of Salamis had not saved Themistocles from the suspicion of planned betrayal which had aided the conservative reaction. At first the allied captains feared to sail beyond Delos, even when offered the opportunity of deposing the Samian tyrant. Half the Persian fleet was still available, though in large part Ionian and shaken in its loyalty by Salamis. Under Mardontes, son of Bagaeus, Artayntes, son of Artachaeus, and his nephew Ithamitres, it ventured from its winter quarters at Cyme as far as Samos. The allies plucked up courage to visit the island and the Persians withdrew; the still dissatisfied Phoenicians were permitted to return home, the others beached their ships on Cape Mycale, where they formed a stockade of stones and tree trunks surrounded by a deep trench and under the protection of the third army commanded by Tigranes.

A herald from the allies summoned the Ionians to revolt and the suspicious Persians disarmed the Samians. The Milesians, deeply incensed by the disclosure of the treasures of Didymaean Apollo to their Persian masters, were sent off on pretense of guarding the trails. Then the allies attacked; after a desperate resistance, the Athenians broke the wicker wall and followed their fleeing opponents into the stockade. While their other subjects fled and the Ionians turned against them, the Iranians died almost to the last man and with them Mardontes and Tigranes. Stockade and ships were burned. By their own request the Milesians who had betrayed Didymaean Apollo were settled in Sogdiana, where they built a new Branchidae, and the oracle of Apollo became silent.

Although the allies did not at once realize it, Mycale and not Plataea was the decisive battle. Two of the six Persian armies had been destroyed, a third must abandon Europe to guard disaffected western Asia. Truly the allies might say that the gods had fought for them; the war had been lost by repeated military and diplomatic blunders on the part of the Persians, it had not been won by timid, incompetent, or disloyal allied commanders. But victory it was and a new phase of Perso-Greek relations was initiated.

ARTHER FERRILL

A specialist in the military history of the ancient world, Arther Ferrill is
professor of history at the University of Washington, where he has taught
since 1964. He recently published *The Origins of War: From the Stone Age
to Alexander the Great* (New York, 1985) and *The Fall of the Roman Empire:
The Military Explanation* (London, 1986). In this essay, he argues that Herodotus' grasp of military strategy was greater than many historians have
believed.

Herodotus and the Strategy and Tactics
of the Invasion of Xerxes†

*   *   *

To most scholars Herodotus is a good source for the study of the Persian
Wars because he tried diligently to arrive at the truth. They feel that it
is possible for the modern military historian to read his history, make
allowances for his ignorance of strategy and tactics, and find the clues to
the proper reconstruction of the military aspects of the war that Herodotus himself had missed. Throughout there is an underlying assumption
that the Greek and Persian generals of the early fifth century B.C. understood the strategic and tactical problems confronting them, and that
Herodotus was the one who was confused. By applying sound military
analysis they have arrived at innumerable, conflicting reconstructions of
battles, and few of them can agree even on the strategy followed by the
Greeks in the course of the war.

Herodotus himself, however, was far from ignorant of strategy and
tactics despite the naïveté that he shows in assigning a huge force to the
Persians. * * * Herodotus used the large numbers because they were
part of the tradition about the war from a very early period and because
they suited the grandeur of his theme. The greater the Persian force, the
greater was Xerxes' *hubris*. Herodotus' final figure—5,283,220—is nothing short of ridiculous (8.186).

It is important to note, however, that the large figure given by Herodotus does not reflect in any way on his understanding of strategy and
tactics. To the modern military historian, who can actually and correctly
conceive of an army as large as 5,000,000, a host of problems immediately appear, but it is unlikely that Herodotus or his contemporaries had
any true conception of the magnitude of such a force. Some later military historians with relatively good knowledge of strategy and tactics and

†Reprinted with permission from the author from   Footnotes have been omitted.
the *American Historical Review* 72 (1966):104–8.

with personal military experience, Arrian for example, were prone to flirt with abnormally high figures. It should be emphasized that Herodotus understood perfectly the basic point, that the Persian force was much larger than the Greek force and that this fact had major strategic and tactical repercussions (7.177).

Many passages in Herodotus' narrative indicate that he had an active and conscious understanding of strategy and tactics, and there are several cases where he applied this knowledge to reject or revise conceptions about the Persian War that were current in his day. He knew that tactical factors forced the Greeks to consider topography quite closely in their planning. On the whole an excellent topographer, Herodotus combined his knowledge of topography and his understanding of strategy and tactics to good advantage. Rather than accept the story that the Greeks withdrew from Tempe because Alexander of Macedon warned them that the Persians were coming with superior numbers, he said:

> In my opinion what chiefly wrought on them was the fear that the Persians might enter by another pass whereof they now heard, which led from Upper Macedonia into Thessaly through the territory of the Perrhaebi, and by the town of Gonnus, the pass by which soon after the army of Xerxes actually made its entrance (7.173).

In addition, Herodotus pointed out that the Greeks chose their position at Thermopylae because there the Persians "could make no use of their vast numbers, nor of their cavalry . . ." (7.177).

In the speeches of Xerxes, Mardonius, and Artabanus (7.8–10) Herodotus gives a respectable analysis of the strategic problems that the Persians had to face during their invasion. Artabanus noted that it was necessary for the Greeks to defeat the Persians only on land or sea, not both, and that in any event it would be difficult for the Persians to solve their logistical problems (7.10; see also 7.49, 118–20).

Herodotus fully realized the interdependence of the Persian army and fleet. That can be inferred from the passages cited in the above paragraph, but lest anyone claim that these prove only an unconscious awareness of this fact by Herodotus, I refer to the debate on strategy between Demaratus and Achaemenes after the Persian victory at Thermopylae. In this passage Achaemenes, the winner of the debate, said:

> But let us keep our whole fleet in one body, and it will be dangerous for them to venture on an attack, as they will certainly be no match for us then. Besides, while our sea and land forces advance together, the fleet and army can each help the other; but if they be parted, no aid will come either from you to the fleet, or from the fleet to you (7.236).

If it is true that Herodotus wrote the speeches in his work solely to convey his own observations about the events he described, and this is generally agreed, then the speech of Achaemenes reflects Herodotus' own awareness of the interdependence of the Persian army and fleet.

Again, by the use of a speech, Herodotus pointed out that the Persians adhered too rigorously to the principle of interdependence of army and fleet. Demaratus suggested that Xerxes detach some ships from his fleet to attack the Peloponnesus: "If once they have a war of their own close to their doors, fear not their giving any help to the rest of the Greeks while your land-force is engaged in conquering them. In this way may all Greece be subdued; and then Sparta, left to herself, will be powerless" (7.235).

Herodotus was also aware of the tactical problems that affected Greek strategy. He knew, as we can tell from a speech of Mardonius, that the Greek phalanx was designed for fighting another phalanx in an open plain (7.9). He also knew that the Persians could defeat the Greeks in a plain because of their superior numbers and cavalry and their use of the bow (7.177). He therefore realized that the Greeks had to modify their way of fighting on land by defending passes such as Thermopylae where the Persian advantages would be minimized and in fact nullified. At close quarters and under proper conditions the Greeks were superior because they were better armed and better disciplined (7.211; 962–63).

Herodotus' analysis of Greek strategy at Salamis, which is presented in the form of a speech by Themistocles at the council there, is quite accurate:

With you it rests, Eurybiades, to save Greece, if you will only listen to me, and give the enemy battle here, rather than yield to the advice of those among us, who would have the fleet withdrawn to the Isthmus. Hear now, I beseech you, and judge between the two courses. At the Isthmus you will fight in an open sea, which is greatly to our disadvantage, since our ships are heavier and fewer in number than the enemy's. . . . The land and sea force of the Persians will advance together; and your retreat will but draw them towards the Peloponnese, and so bring all Greece into peril. If, on the other hand, you do as I advise, these are the advantages which you will secure; in the first place, as we shall fight in a narrow sea with few ships against many, if the war follows the common course, we shall gain a great victory: for to fight in a narrow space is favourable to us—in an open sea, to them. . . . Nay, that very point by which you set most store, is secured as much by this course as by the other; for whether we fight here or at the Isthmus, we shall equally give battle in defense of the Peloponnese. Assuredly you will not do wisely to draw the Persians upon that region. For if things turn out as I anticipate, and we beat them by sea, then we shall have kept your Isthmus free from the barbarians, and they will have advanced no further than Attica, but from thence have fled back in disorder . . . (8.60).

This speech shows a fine understanding of strategy and tactics, especially for a historian who is considered to know nothing about such matters.

Herodotus understood the basic strategic and tactical factors of the Greek decision to fight at Salamis, but he did not believe that those factors were the chief cause of the decision. He thought that fear and local and political jealousies were more important (8.56–57). In fact he committed himself to the view that it was not the strategic and tactical soundness of the speech made by Themistocles that persuaded Eurybiades to defend Salamis, but rather Eurybiades' conviction that the Athenians would not sail to the isthmus to fight the Persians (8.63). In view of Spartan policy throughout the war, this certainly seems reasonable.

Herodotus appreciated two basic tactical factors of Salamis. He knew that the Greek navy was inferior to the Persian navy on the open sea and needed a narrow battle area to be effective (8.60). He also knew that the Greeks backed water at the beginning of the battle to draw the Persians into a narrow and crowded position (8.84–85) and that they fought in better order and with less confusion (8.86).

What has been said up to now should establish that Herodotus was not ignorant of the principles of strategy. His analysis of Salamis is simply too sound to have been written by one as uninformed on strategy as most modern historians paint him.

* * *

IV. ASPECTS OF HERODOTUS' WORK
A. W. GOMME

A. W. Gomme lived from 1886 to 1959. Prominent among his many contributions to the study of Greek history was his multivolume *Historical Commentary on Thucydides*, begun in 1945 and completed after his death by K. J. Dover and A. Andrewes. In the following selection, Gomme compares the ways in which Aeschylus and Herodotus give meaning to the struggle between the Greeks and the Persians and argues that the very act of seeking such meanings was a hallmark of their culture.

Herodotos and Aeschylus†

* * * As day broke, the Persians—you will remember, of course, that the whole of the play is presented from the Persian side and that there are no Greek characters in it—heard a great cry from the Greek camp,

†Excerpted from A. W. Gomme, *The Greek Attitude to Poetry and History* (Berkeley and Los Angeles, 1954), pp. 95–110.

and it was not a cry of despair, as they had been led by the false message
to expect, but of courage, and the signal for attack was given and the
Greek ships advanced in good order. With that another call was heard:
* * * "Come, sons of Greece: free our country, free our wives and children, the temples of our gods and the tombs of our fathers; now is the
moment which will decide all"; but, if we are thinking of the story of
the Persian Wars, of what does it remind us? Surely of the speech of
Miltiades to Kallimachos in Herodotos before battle was engaged at Marathon (vi 109.3). * * * The Athenians are in their strong defensive position at Marathon, while the Persians, greatly outnumbering them (as
Herodotos sees it, at least), face them near the shore. For days neither
side moves and the Athenian generals are divided over whether to engage
the enemy or no; Miltiades was urgent for battle:

> It lies with you now, Kallimachos, either to bring Athens to slavery
> or, by making her free, to win a memory for all time such as not
> even Harmodios and Aristogeiton won. Athens has never been in
> such danger. If we yield to the Persian, we know the fate decreed
> for us, but if we gain the battle, she will be the first city in Greece.
> We generals are divided, but I am convinced that if we do not
> engage in battle, a serious strife of opinion will shake our resolve
> and make us take the Persian side; but if we engage, before rot sets
> in among certain groups in Athens, then, if the gods grant equal
> chances, we shall win. All this has now come to you, depends on
> you; if you take my side, our country will be free and our city the
> first in Greece; if you take the other, the very opposite of all this
> will befall us.

Kallimachos chooses right; he joins Miltiades, and Athens and Greece,
with all that they stood for, were saved. With this great speech Herodotos
achieves two aims: first (which does not concern us here), he makes clear
why Miltiades and not Kallimachos was always regarded as the moral
author of the victory in spite of the latter's position as polemarch, and
his vote the decisive one, and his brave death in the battle; secondly,
and this is what is important for us, he makes clear in a dramatic way
the historic importance of the campaign and the Athenian victory—the
tension of the moment, the hard-won adhesion of Kallimachos, who is
persuaded only by such moving eloquence, and the subsequent battle.
So does Aeschylus bring before us so well the tension of the moment at
Salamis; νῦν ὑπὲρ πάντων ἀγών.[1]

[Miltiades'] speech is central in that by its means Herodotos makes
clear the importance, that is, the historic and not simply the dramatic

---

1. Gomme translates this as "now is the moment
which will decide all." On p. 243, the line is rendered "this fight is to the death."

importance, of the campaign and of the Athenian victory. The victory foreshadowed that of 480–479, and subsequent events. It foreshadowed, first, the rise of Athens herself to be "the foremost city of Greece" and a formidable power, supreme at sea, in all the eastern Mediterranean, though Miltiades, in the speech, restricts himself to "the first city of Greece"; second, the victory of the Greeks generally over the Persians. Herodotos says that the Athenians were the first Greeks to face the Persians bravely in battle; before them the Greeks had been frightened at the very sight of a Persian army—a great exaggeration, as we know from his own history. But an understanding one, for not only was Marathon the first victory in set battle, but the subsequent victory was against all the odds, a well-nigh impossible victory of a small, poor, and hopelessly divided people over a powerful and well-organized empire, still in full tide of recent expansion and victory, so that the Greeks may well have been frightened. Professor Kitto in his recent short study of the Greeks, in the Penguin series, has well brought out the fortunate circumstances in which the Greek states, as we know them, came into being in the Aegean world, from the ninth to the seventh century, fortunate because there was then no strong power in Asia or Egypt, or in Europe, in Macedonia or Thrace, either to oppose their settlements around the Aegean and later in South Italy and Sicily, or to interfere with them in their early years; no aggressive empire, and no state in Asia ready even to claim the whole of the continental area as its own. They were left free to expand, and then to establish themselves with, in the East, the Aegean rather than peninsular Greece as their center. It was, when you think of it, to the last degree improbable that a people of one blood, one speech, one religion, as they did not cease to remind themselves, should divide into hundreds of little states with populations of thirty or forty thousand each, jealous of their political independence, each ready to defend itself in arms against its neighbor; that they should, jointly, take over a system of writing from the Phoenicians and make the first true alphabet, but each keep to its own way of writing it; should borrow another fruitful invention, a coinage, but each state issue its own, with its own device and differing standards; that all should be tenacious of that common religion, but that each should devise a separate calendar for its festivals— doing, that is, things, new things, in common as a single people, but also doing them separately. As it happened, with such happy results for the Greeks and so for the world, there was none to interfere with them in the early centuries; they were left free to quarrel among themselves, to develop agriculture, manufacture, and trade, to try political experiments, to devote long hours to philosophy, art, and letters; and thus to reach their unalterable conviction that this was the life for them. What was to be expected, happened: a power did arise to threaten them. The Medes and Persians took over the old Mesopotamian empires, and spread their rule. With hardly more than a shrug of the shoulders they absorbed the flourishing, active Greek states in Asia Minor, and, being a tolerant people, left them to live as they would, so they kept the peace and paid some taxes. This Persian empire was well organized; the wise Darius is one of the great figures of history. Its further expansion began soon afterward; after a failure in Scythia, they moved westward against Europe; the Thracian tribes, Macedonia, and the Greeks of that seaboard, all succumbed. How could peninsular Greece hold out? Xerxes laughed the idea to scorn, and indeed it *was* absurd. Even if all the states there had been of one mind for resistance, even if all quarreling had been laid aside and a superhuman good-will had sprung up among them, yet an army composed of many small, separately trained units could hardly hold its own against a more numerous and, apparently at least, a better trained and organized force. And they were very far from unanimity; some states kept aloof, nursing old grudges; others hesitated, fearful of destruction; some went over to the enemy, eager for power. There were the expected jealousies and recriminations among the individual commanders. But the miracle happened and they won decisively.

Neither in the moment of danger when the invading army was approaching, nor afterward in the light of the risk that had been run, did the Greeks think of changing their political system, that of the numerous separate states; they did not attempt a federal government, a single state, and imagine that they would be at once by so much the more efficient. Had the idea occurred to them, their answer would have been: "We do not want that kind of political life and we are fighting to defend the life we prefer, whatever our weaknesses; that is what the war is about." And, from another point of view: "We shall fight all the better if we fight in our own way in which we have been trained, not in another hastily learned."

There was another thing the Greeks were fighting for: within each state the rule of law, constitutional government as we should call it; whether oligarchic or democratic did not matter so long as law prevailed and not the will of an individual or a clique. They pictured the Eastern monarch as ruling by his own will, not constrained by a law which bound all, whether he was generous and kind like Croesus, wise like Darius, or was the mad Kambyses or the foolish Xerxes. They had had autocrats of their own in many states, and some of them had been wise and competent rulers, but they had got rid of them all and preferred the rule of law.

All this Herodotos understood very well. He did not know much about the management of public affairs, any more than he did about the movement of armies in battle, or before battle, and most of his accounts of politics and war are naïve, but he understood the essential truth, what was at stake, what the war was about. He does not minimize or conceal the weaknesses on the Greek side; on the contrary, all that we know and more than what we know of their jealous quarrels and incompetences comes from him. He could expressly praise Persia when she recovered the Greek cities of Asia after their revolt for the way she established peace among them, stopped their constant internecine warfare, and ruled them well. (True, they were Ionians, and he could think it good for them to be cared for like children.) But he was a Greek all right, like the others as glad as he was astonished that the war was won and the invader sent home; glad that by these unexpected victories their peculiar institutions had been saved, and that on the political side the small state, in which each citizen could take a direct part in government, and the rule of law would continue. It might be objected that it is Herodotos, Aeschylus, and other Greeks on whom we rely for this interpretation of the Persian Wars; that they have imposed their view on posterity, and that if we had the full Persian story we might think differently. The answer is that no such history on the Persian side was written. Official records, yes, and if we possessed them we might know the true numbers of Xerxes' army. Brief chronicles, yes, but exactly not the kind of history which the Greeks wrote. This is no accident. The Persians did not write like Herodotos and Aeschylus; they had not that aptitude and inclination to put themselves on record consciously and intellectually, and so with an understanding of what the difference between Persia and Greece was. Thus the interpretation of Aeschylus and Herodotos *is* right; one thing that the Greek victory decided was whether men would continue to think as Aeschylus and Herodotos thought, and act as Tellos or Themistokles or Leonidas, or Aeschylus himself and his brother, acted.

There is, further, something in Herodotos, an essential part of him, which it is difficult to define, yet should not be ignored. It is not an inconsistency, for that would interfere with our enjoyment of his work, and I suppose there is no book, not even Boswell, of which we can be more sure that at whatever place we begin reading, it will give us pleasure; not therefore an unevenness in his art, but a difficulty which in reading him we might not notice, but would think about it afterward— gaps like chasms on a hill journey which, perhaps, we pass by and only remember when we are home. His military understanding is really very defective; he does seem to think that an army of a million and a half men, with an equal number of camp followers, just starts from one place at the signal given, marches for so many days, and arrives at another, and that too in a mountainous and nearly roadless country, and that these hundreds of thousands actually fought with the few thousands of Leonidas at Thermopylai. Yet in two passages he shows that he understood the main strategical problems, the first (vii 47–49) on the Persian side, when Artabanos warns Xerxes, himself excited only by the great size of his army, of the difficulties of supply, sure to increase the further they went into Greece (so Aeschylus too, *Persai* 790–794); the second from the Greek side, where he gives his judgment about the war, "a judgment which will not be popular" (vii 139). Athens, he says, by providing the largest number of ships and the best naval commanders and by the inspiring courage and endurance of all her citizens in the Salamis campaign, was chiefly responsible for the victory at sea, and it was this

which made the over-all victory possible. It is not that he does not, here
as elsewhere, give due praise to the Spartan hoplite who fought the bravest at Thermopylai and made the victory at Plataia (as Aeschylus again,
"the victory of the *Dorian* spear," 817), and Persia was primarily a land
power; but without Salamis, he says, Leonidas' death would have been
in vain, for there would have been no Plataia. There might have been a
second Thermopylai, but no victory. Most men, Herodotos implies, simply
praise Sparta; but Athens, had she so chosen, *and she was sorely tempted,*
could have spoiled everything. So that, in spite of all, he did understand
the strategy of the war.

* * * Herodotos had a profound understanding of what the war was
about; what it was that made the difference between Greece and Persia,
and what the Greek victory meant: the one disunited and fragmentary,
the states numerous and small, exclusive, governed by amateurs, the
citizens free, subject only to their own laws; Persia enormous by comparison, comprehensive and multifarious, tolerant, ruled by a governing
class which had been trained in the art. * * *

That is what the victory meant for Greece and so for all western Europe.
But humanity is wider than Greece, and Aeschylus, who was a patriotic
Greek like Herodotos and saw what the victory meant, politically, for
Greece, and says so in his play (vv. 213–214, 241–245), saw also that it
had a wider significance for all men; the Persians were defeated because
power corrupts, because great dominion breeds a desire for yet greater,
and because success and prosperity are dangerous except for the wisest
heads (as perhaps for Darius) and lead not only to an unthinking opti-
mism, such as Croesus had, but to braggart boasting and insolent action
that *must,* sooner or later (have we not seen it time and again?), bring
disaster. This will happen to all men, quite independent of Greek or
Persian. Herodotos understood that too, as Aeschylus did, and this philosophy pervades his *History*; but here again there is, it seems to me, in
some way a contradiction. I do not mean by this that Herodotos often
speaks of fate as though men's actions were impersonally determined so
that they were not responsible and could not be *guilty* of *hubris*—in the
story of Croesus, for example, when, after the fall of his country, he
upbraids the god of Delphi for the false oracles he had given to one who
had been so generous with his gifts, and Apollo replies that not even a
god can avoid fate, and it was fated that in the fifth generation after
Gyges, who had killed his king Kandaules and usurped his throne, his
successor should pay the penalty. To emphasize this by the exception
that proves the rule, Apollo adds that in gratitude to Croesus he had
tried to get the fates to postpone the fall of Lydia till after Croesus' death,
and had got them to postpone it for three years but could do no more.
Yet in no story does Herodotos make it more clear that a man is responsible for his own actions; that Croesus, because he was prosperous, was
unthinkingly optimistic, was sure he would win, and lightheartedly
undertook the war with Persia, and for that reason did not take the trouble to inquire further what the oracle meant; for Croesus admits that that

was just the mistake that he made—he learned Solon's wisdom too late. Or take the earlier event, the tale of Gyges, the first in the book. Kandaules' wife says to him: "Gyges, I offer you the choice between two ways; take what you will" (i II.2); here free-will is clearly implied * * * , and that too though *necessity* is mentioned immediately after (i II.4), which does not mean that Gyges had not power to choose. * * * There is, in fact, no possible story ("poetic" story) about human beings which does not imply free-will. A dramatist or novelist, or any other storyteller, may believe in determinism or fatalism in the abstract, but he must give his characters free-will, or they will be without interest; they must have a choice, as Herodotus knew by instinct even if he muddled his philosophy, and as Aristotle explained so clearly.

But if there is a confusion here when Croesus' fate is both ordained five generations back and brought about by his own thoughtlessness, that will be, I think, a case of what Professor Dodds had called in his recent Sather lectures "double determination," which is so frequently found in Homer (Achilles was "fated to die young," but that does not mean that he was not responsible for his actions);[2] at most it means that Herodotos was a historian, not an analytical philosopher. The sort of contradiction, however, which I had in mind lies rather in his skeptical and humorous attitude toward human affairs, in this so unlike Aeschylus, as though he were not really serious about either fate or human will. He tells, at the very beginning of the whole book, the story of Kandaules (another who, in but a few words, is depicted as the prince *delighted*, like Croesus and Xerxes, with his good fortune: he has the most beautiful of women as his wife), but he tells it as a *lighthearted* story. (If the newly found fragment of a play with this plot is, as it seems to be, from a tragedy, it must have been written in a very different spirit from that seen in Herodotos.) * * * He has other stories that are tragic or grim, and his account of the folly of Xerxes is as eloquent (though so much more varied) as that of Aeschylus. Why in fact did Aristotle, when he was contrasting the austerity and the greater concentration of tragedy with the much greater length and variety of epic (26, 62bI ff.; ch. 23, 59a30), not think also of comparing Aeschylus with Herodotos? He might have added something of value to what he says about history. Herodotos has every kind of story in his book, from the grimmest to the most gay. He was indeed a man of varied genius with an unceasing interest in the ways of mankind.

M. E. WHITE

Mary White was a founder of *Phoenix*, the journal of the Classical Association of Canada, which she served as general editor between 1946 and 1964. In this selection, she discusses the problems Herodotus confronted and overcame in conducting his research and in selecting the story of Croesus as the proper place at which to begin his histories.

2. *The Greeks and the Irrational*, Sather Lectures 25 (1951): 31–34 [*Author*].

Herodotus' Starting Point†

The limitations imposed by the nature of the source material available to Herodotus and other early historians have been recognized, as also the difficulty Herodotus faced in attempting an enquiry far-ranging in both time and space when there was no universally accepted era date by which the separate chronologies of oriental monarchies or Greek city-states could be interrelated. Herodotus drew mainly upon *akoē*, oral tradition, and *opsis*, visual testimony, that is what he himself saw or could learn from other eyewitnesses. He spent his life travelling, questioning, observing; he listened to men of all walks of life: the political leaders of the Greek cities where he resided or visited, learned men like the priests in Egypt and the custodians of famous oracles, scientists, philosophers and poets; the gossip of the market-place and harbour, travellers' tales, and the reminiscences of old soldiers—in a word everything he could collect. This is the method of the modern anthropologist and sociologist and it was also the only method for the historian before the days of copious written records. Oriental chronicles and documents existed but he could not read them and had to accept what his informants told him they contained. There were some Greek records and he does mention especially dedications fairly frequently. But for the other kinds of documents which a historian might be expected to use, lists of magistrates, decrees, treaties, and the like, very few inscribed copies of such documents from the centuries before the fifth are extant, and the existence of significant numbers of them on permanent or perishable materials available for a researcher like Herodotus to consult is doubtful. Even Thucydides writing about a period for which much more "documentary" evidence was available makes what seems to us surprisingly little use of it; he like Herodotus accepted oral tradition and visual testimony as the primary stuff of history, but with this difference, that for his main subject he confined himself to contemporary military and political history where he could apply much stricter standards to his evidence and where the chronological problem was much simpler. When he deals with earlier events his method is similar to that of Herodotus. For example, he refers to the archonship of the younger Peisistratos and mentions his two dedications, the altar of the Twelve Gods, and the later of the Pythian Apollo quoting its inscription, but he uses the archonship not as a date, but as an illustration of Peisistratid policy. Both historians assumed that their readers knew when such important events occurred.

The retentiveness and reliability of oral memory has been underestimated by some modern historians who have doubted that the substantial accuracy of the chronological knowledge in Herodotus and Thucydides about, e.g., the time of colonial foundations or the intervals between

†Excerpted with permission from *Phoenix* 23 (1969): 40–47. Most footnotes have been omitted.

events was possible without contemporary *written* records. They have assumed chronological records—lists of magistrates, kings, victors, or priests—kept by Greek states from as early as the eighth century. The further assumption is made that "Herodotus and Thucydides had at their disposal a far greater number of dated events than they included in their histories." These "pre-literary" Greek chronological records, as Jacoby describes them, are unprovable assumptions since no remains exist, and they are unlikely for many reasons. The few early documents we know (either from inscriptions or literary reference)—treaties, decrees, law codes, dedications—bear no internal date by an eponymous magistrate or the like, but the date has to be deduced from the content, contemporary circumstances, letter forms, or other datable archeological material found with them. Even Attic decrees do not regularly include the name of the archon until the last quarter of the fifth century. However the strongest reason for doubting the existence, or at any rate the availability, of such systematic lists is the chronological structure of Herodotus' *Histories* which we shall be examining. Thucydides' practice also in the Archaeology and Pentekontaëtia would be surprising if the use of an Athenian archon list had become common by the time he was writing.[1]

Approximately the first half of the *Histories* * * * is concerned with the rise and extension of the Persian Empire from the time of Kyros' defeat of Kroisos to the beginning of the Persian expeditions against Greece, and with the Greek states who were involved from time to time in this process of expansion. In these books Herodotus had collected, ordered, and recorded the vast amount of material he amassed in his research (*historiē*) into the history, customs, geography, and antiquities of barbarian and Greek states. The chronological framework is the successive reigns of the Persian kings from Kyros to Dareios, the lengths of which he gives at the death of each one: Kyros 29 years (1.214.2), Kambyses 7 years and 5 months (3.66.2), the pretender Smerdis 7 months (3.67.2), and Dareios 36 years (7.4). The first book, to which we shall return, is the most complex because in it he must launch the subject, introduce the chief participants, and start the sequence of the Persian kings by explaining how Kyros came to the throne of Media-Persia, defeated the Lydians, and thereafter made the Greek cities, which had been subjects of Lydia, his subjects. These books are not annalistic in the sense that Herodotus could fix events to the years of a reign. Events follow in order with pauses for geographic and ethnological description, and, more important, with episodes often fairly sizeable from the history of the Greek states. It is Herotodus' custom to insert these sections at points of synchronism, starting back in each excursus as far as he can with relevant earlier history and tracing it to the moment from which he began, then continuing with the main narrative. He is able thus to maintain the chronological structure, while at the same time interrelating events

---

1. See the selections from Thucydides on pp. 249–269 of this volume.

in the Greek world with each other and with the external world of the non-Greek Aegean powers. Whenever possible he gives time intervals in terms of generations or numbers of years; more often, however, the synchronism and interrelations are the significant clues for chronological reconstruction. Because the scope in time and space is so broad, so many strands have to be interwoven, and so much of the Greek material is episodic and disconnected, these books at first reading may seem diffuse. As Professor Immerwahr has remarked: "Both in antiquity and in modern times readers have thought of it as a fascinating conglomeration of disparate stories, judgments and insights, based on the excitement of marvel *(thôma)*, and on a love of detail for its own sake."[2] It is only Herodotus' skill that makes it seem so effortless: in fact the whole structure is highly organized, although it did not and could not have the precise chronology which a universally accepted calendar with an era date would permit, and modern readers expect.

In the second half, from the beginning of the revolt of Naxos (5.28) to the end, the structure tightens, the focus of action shifts to Greece itself, and the narrative is concentrated on the final stages of the conflict between Persia and Greece and moves forward rapidly, with fewer pauses and insertions, through the campaigns of the Ionian Revolt, Marathon, and the two years of Xerxes' great expedition. It is generally agreed that the year of Salamis (480 B.C.) is the base date used by Herodotus, that he worked back from this in his preliminary research to the attack on Naxos (500/499 B.C.) in the year before the outbreak of the Ionian Revolt, and then as he wrote worked forward marking all the intervals carefully and precisely in what is a year-by-year account of events from 500/499 to 479/8 B.C. The more detailed chronology of this later half of the *Histories* is related to the earlier half at Book 7.4 by the mention of the death of Dareios after thirty-six years of rule. Dareios' death was in 486/5 (the year after the revolt of Egypt, which occurred in the fourth year after Marathon in 7.1.3, i.e., by the usual Greek inclusive reckoning in 487/6). From this synchronism Herodotus could work back through the regnal years of the Persian kings to Kyros (1.214.3) and beyond that to the Median kings as far back as Deiokes (1.102.1).

The structure of Book 1 demonstrates Herodotus' skill in working back and forth from his central focus. After introducing Kroisos he immediately goes back to the beginnings of his dynasty and relates the story of how the first of his family Gyges seized the Lydian kingship from the last king of the previous Heraklid dynasty, Kandaules or Myrsilos, and slew him. Kroisos' untimely end is hinted at in Chapter 13 by the Pythia's warning that in the fifth generation from Gyges vengeance will come for the murder, and there is also a hint of the *hybris* that will contribute to that end in Gyges' contemptuous disregard of the prophecy. The reigns

2. Henry R. Immerwahr, *Form and Thought in Herodotus*, American Philological Association   Monograph Number XXIII (Cleveland, 1966), p. 325 [Author].

of Gyges, Ardys, Sadyattes, and Alyattes are briefly sketched, emphasizing their relations with the Greek cities, and for each the length of the reign is stated. By Chapter 26 we have returned to Kroisos who mounted the throne when he was thirty-five years old, and whose conquest of the Greek cities is described. When he was at the height of his prosperity Solon visited him to warn him that no man should call himself happy until his life was over (1.29–33), and a second dreadful warning was given him when his beloved son Atys was killed accidentally by Adrastos, a man polluted by blood guilt to whom he had given refuge (34–44). At this point Kroisos receives the news that Kyros the Persian has seized the throne of Media-Persia from his brother-in-law Astyages, and he must decide whether he should attack Kyros to check his growing power. The testing of the oracles follows, the sending of gifts, and the consultations of Delphi (46–55). On Delphi's advice that he ally himself with the strongest of the Greeks, he sent the embassies to Athens (59–64) and to Sparta (65–68). At this synchronism Herodotus inserts his accounts of Peisistratos' first attempts at tyranny and final success at Pallene, and the excursus on Spartan history to explain Sparta's present favourable position.[3] In Chapter 69 we return to the main action: Kroisos makes his alliance with Sparta and launches his attack on Kyros by an invasion of Cappadocia. After the first year of indecisive fighting, Kroisos dismisses his army with orders to reassemble in the spring, Kyros attacks unexpectedly in the late autumn, the Spartans fail to appear because of their war with Argos which is decided by the Battle of the Champions, Sardis falls, and Kroisos is captured. His miraculous escape from the funeral pyre, and Delphi's defence of its oracles against his complaint that he had been misled, conclude the Kroisos-*logos* at Chapter 92.

There is then a pause in the narrative which emphasizes that the fall of Kroisos is a turning point in Greek fortunes, and that now they will be face to face with a more relentless foe, the new conqueror Kyros. Chapters 93–140 deal with Lydian monuments and customs, the rise of Media under Deiokes and his successors down to Astyages whom Kyros deposed, Kyros' birth and the attempts to destroy him, his successful revolt and seizure of the throne of Media-Persia, and an excursus on Persian customs. This section provides the transition from Lydia to Persia and from Kroisos to Kyros, the man with whom the Greeks will hereafter have to deal. Using what we have come to see is his usual technique, Herodotus has inserted the earlier history of the new power at the relevant point, the moment when Kyros emerges as victor. By Chapter 141 we have come full circle to that moment, when Kyros' next task will be to bring Kroisos' Greek subjects on the Asia Minor seaboard under his control. Again Herodotus goes back to describe the origins of

3. It is worth noting that Herodotus' continuous narrative of Athenian history begins with this excursus. His references to Solon suggest the sage and traveller rather than the political reformer, and from the pre-Solonian period he knows only isolated incidents such as the Kylonian conspiracy and the early Aiginetan wars. It seems that oral memory could not supply a continuous narrative further back than three generations. [Author]

these Greek cities—the early migrations of the Greeks and the foundation of the three groups, the Panionion of twelve cities, the Aeolian
eleven, and the Dorian Pentapolis (142–151). Kyros had invited the
Greeks to join him against Kroisos but they had refused. Now they tried
to avoid forcible conquest by a voluntary submission but received Kyros'
ominous answer of the fable of the piper and the fishes: "Cease your
dancing now, as you did not choose to come and dance when I piped to
you." On this reply they sent for help to Sparta, who dispatched one
penteconter with the message that Kyros was not to molest any city of
Greece since they would not allow it. Kyros' reply was: "Who are the
Spartans? . . . If I live, they will have troubles enough of their own to
talk of without concerning themselves about the Ionians." This anecdote
is a deliberate forewarning of the dangers from Persia threatening not
only the Asiatic cities but Greece itself.

Kyros left the conquest of the Greek cities to his generals, returning
to Ecbatana to prepare his assault upon Babylon. Chapters 154–176
describe its implacable execution by Harpagos, in the face of spirited
Greek resistance. The remainder of the book (177–216) is taken up with
the conquest of Babylon, which includes a vivid description of the walls
and city, the defences and bridges along the Euphrates built by Queen
Nitocris, and an account of Babylonian customs, and it concludes with
Kyros' death during his mysterious last campaign which Herodotus says
was against the Massagetae north of the Caspian Sea.

This is the way Herodotus began his *Histories*. The Kroisos story is
the focus—a tragic drama of human greatness and fall and an event of
crucial historical importance, the approximate time of which his readers
knew by oral memory without need of demonstration. At appropriate
stages of the action are inserted sections of the earlier history of the
participants; the descriptive sections provide pauses at transitions in the
narrative; the primarily Hellenic interest of the whole is made clear by
the constant interaction between Greek and barbarian and the preservation of a nice balance between the amounts of material on each and
through it all, in parable or anecdote or narrative, Herodotus comments
on the nature of the human situation and the historical process. If one
asks where else he could have launched his subject, how else his chronological sequence could be made intelligible to his readers, it is not
easy to find an answer.

ROSARIA VIGNOLO MUNSON†

A translator as well as a classicist, Rosaria Munson taught for several years
at the University of Pennsylvania and is now a member of the Department

† The original version of this essay appeared in   here by permission of Aureal Publications.
Ramus 15 (1986): 93–104, and it is reproduced

of Classics at Swarthmore College. Her translation of Giovanni Comotti's *Music in Greek and Roman Culture* was published in 1990. In the following selection, she discusses how Herodotus reinforces the narration of wondrous historical events with more anecdotal stories about the wonders which befall individuals.

The Celebratory Purpose of Herodotus: The Story of Arion in the *Histories* 1.23–24

The first sentence of the *Histories*, which identifies and justifies the work as a whole, reveals the author's double aim of celebration and explanation:

> This is the exposition of the research of Herodotus of Halicarnassus
> 1) lest the events of men become faded with time, and the great and wonderful deeds performed by both Greeks and Barbarians be deprived of glory,
> 2) [the exposition of] among other things how they came to war with one another.

Both explanation and celebration account for Herodotus' inclusiveness. On the one hand, anything great and wonderful should be saved from oblivion, and is therefore appropriate subject for the exposition. On the other hand, the research of the causes of an event leads the historian beyond the simple narrative of the event itself into its remote antecedents and any stance which may have possibly affected it. Thus the specific focus of the inquiry—the war between Greeks and Barbarians—is doubly broadened even before it is announced.

If the two purposes implied in the Proem are achieved through a necessarily inclusive account, they seem however to dictate opposite criteria of inclusiveness, thereby pulling Herodotus' narrative in different directions and creating a tension that lasts throughout the work. The explanation of causes requires suitable factual connections from one historical stage to the next, all leading ultimately to the main event; but the history of the East-West conflict, as extensive as it promises to be on the basis of this criterion alone, is in Herodotus' introduction inserted in a yet broader and more generalized context. * * *

* * *

* * * In its present formulation, Herodotus' celebratory purpose not only does not imply the requirement that an event be part of the chain of cause and effect in order to be reported, but it even completely frees the author from any such restriction imposed upon him by his other task of explaining a specific occurrence.

Are celebration and explanation, then, conflicting or mutually cooperative goals in Herodotus? The relationship that the report of wonderful deeds of Greeks and Barbarians will bear to the account of their conflict is not clearly expressed here, but a special passage inserted early in the narrative, the story of Arion and the dolphin (1.23–24), and the nature of the transition to it, clarify this relationship, and show what use Herodotus makes of that freedom of composition which he has claimed for himself in the first sentence.

The Arion episode represents in fact the limiting case of celebratory and non-explanatory narratives in Herodotus. The beginning of the historical account of the origin of the war between East and West from Croesus (1.5.3–6.3) leads the historian to explore Croesus' political antecedents. During a survey of Croesus' predecessors he describes how the Lydian king Alyattes repeatedly attacked the Greek city of Miletus, but failed to conquer it because of fortuitous circumstances and thanks to the cunning of the Milesian tyrant Thrasybulus (1.17–22). In his dealings with Alyattes, Thrasybulus had apparently received from his friend Periander of Corinth helpful information (20) which enabled him to trick the Lydians and gain a peace treaty. At the end of the narrative of the Lydo-Milesian war, Herodotus reports the "great wonder" of Arion and the dolphin, which happened during Periander's lifetime and in which Periander was indirectly involved.

Arion of Methymna was a poet who lived at the court of Periander. Once he spent some time in Italy and Sicily, where he accumulated great wealth. During his voyage back to Corinth on a Corinthian ship, the sailors plotted to do away with him and steal his gold, and although Arion begged them to take his possessions and spare his life, they ordered him to kill himself or jump overboard. In this strait Arion begged them, and obtained his request, to sing one last song standing on the deck and dressed in his singing robes. This done, he leapt into the sea. The ship went on to Corinth, but in the meantime a dolphin rescued Arion and carried him to Peloponnesian Taenarum, so that Arion was then able to return to Corinth by land and inform Periander of the sailors' crime. When the ship arrived, Periander asked the sailors about Arion and they alleged that he had remained in Italy. At that point Arion appeared and their lie was detected (24). After this episode Herodotus resumes the previous narrative and reports the death of Alyattes and the story of Croesus (25ff.).

The practice of interrupting a chronological narrative with insertions, narrative or descriptive, that mark a change of time, setting, or subject matter, is of course common for Herodotus. However, what makes the Arion story unusual is that the other insertions in the work have at least an initial explanatory impulse: they relate actions or features of characters in the history, and are therefore presented as background reports. * * * The Arion passage is the only purely episodic insertion in the *Histories*. By contents, it has nothing to do with Lydians or Milesians, protagonists of the narrative from which it originates; it does not define in any way Periander, to whose mention it is attached, but whose role it keeps to a minimum.

The introduction to the Arion episode does not merely stress its factual autonomy; it places it on a different level with respect to the surrounding history. While the change of focus from Periander *tyrannos* to Arion *kitharōidos*[1] separates the passage that follows from the previous account of rulers and wars, Herodotus here also starts mixing the real with the "unreal," and prepares a transition from the one to the other. Periander is a historical figure, and Arion really lived in his time. We know at least that he did those things which no one in the world, "as far as we know," did before him. But with the conspicuous mention of the sources for the central event of Arion riding the dolphin (". . . the Corinthians say, the Lesbians agree . . ."), Herodotus exonerates himself from taking responsibility for the veracity of the report.

For Herodotus hearsay and tradition are part of the evidence, and often the only evidence that *historiē* can provide (see e.g. 1.95). This explains partially why the historian feels bound to record what people tell him, even though he may not believe it (7.152.3). The inclusion in the *Histories* of things explicitly qualified as *ta legomena*[2] concerning events in the historical development, or their origin and results, or the background of their protagonists, serves the search for truth and factual explanation. Herodotus may report uncertain information so as to let his readers decide for themselves. Often he includes stories which he rejects as false precisely in order to reject them, to set the record straight, correcting popular opinion, much as Thucydides does. Yet, Herodotus' careful reporting of *ta legomena*, especially of the most unreliable sort, in certain cases reveals how for him tradition, regardless of how much it contributes positively or negatively to our knowledge of how things really happened, may have another compelling function, that of suggesting, be it even through fiction, a valid interpretation of historical facts.

☆   ☆   ☆

For Herodotus, the factual explanation of "the reason why they came to war" and the recording of wonderful things constitute two means, superimposed on one another, to achieve that goal: the one requiring carefully ascertained causal connections among historical facts, and the other based on conceptual analogies and on the author's freedom to seek them within *and* beyond the boundaries of his well-defined topic.

JOHN HART

John Hart, who teaches in Great Britain, assesses Herodotus' treatment of the character of Themistocles and finds the origin of its main traits in the epic hero Odysseus.

---

1. Greek words for "tyrant" and "lyre player."   2. The Greek means "what is said."

Themistocles in History†

What did Herodotus think of Themistocles? It seems to me that he fully recognised the man's greatness and regarded him as the architect of victory in 480, if any one man was entitled to be so called. In three separate fields he is shown as making a decisive contribution: policy (ship-building), morale (the oracle) and strategy (Salamis). Even those ideas of his which did not come off or were not adopted show his flair and imagination, and in war, which can so easily become a matter of routine or of automatic response, the leader who can generate ideas is invaluable. Far more credit is directly given by Herodotus to Themistocles than to any other individual leader of the two years—Leonidas, Eurybiadas, Pausanias (of whom, more later), Leotychidas, Xanthippus or Aristeides. The last-named in fact gets the barest mention as commander of the Athenian hoplites at Plataea. Read Plutarch's "Life of Aristeides" and you will see that roughly one-third of it is taken up with a narrative of that battle; and much of *that* reads like a simple reworking of Herodotus' narrative, only with "Aristeides" substituted for "the Athenians." It may very well be that later tradition sought to put Aristeides on a pedestal as high as Themistocles'; Herodotus knew better.

Too much has been heard about the hostile portrait of Themistocles that Herodotus has allegedly painted, under the influence of his friends in the Athenian aristocracy. We have already examined two supposed instances of hostility and found that in them at least it is imaginary. The charge of avarice that he levels against Themistocles, however, deserves to be taken a bit more seriously. Like just about every active politician in ancient Greece and Rome, * * * Themistocles was keenly alive to the importance of money and the power of patronage that it brought with it. Such anecdotes in Plutarch as touch on his finances certainly suggest that he was a free spender, with, it seems, ulterior political motives, rather than a miserly hoarder. No doubt, too (again in common with many others), he quit public life a good deal better off than when he entered it. Themistocles' immense services to Athens and to Greece were as a statesman and strategist, and Herodotus feels himself under no obligation to idealise his personal qualities. His greed and unscrupulousness form the reverse side of his foresight and cleverness.

As it happens this charge goes back to a very ancient source, though not perhaps an untainted one. In 478/7 Timocreon of Ialysos (in Rhodes), a rather disreputable exile, wrote a vitriolic short poem in the form of a drinking song. It takes as its pretext Aristeides' founding of the Delian League. Themistocles was excluded from all participation in this process, a thing that Timocreon recognised, correctly, as an enduring polit-

† Excerpted by permission of St. Martin's Press from John Hart's *Herodotus and Greek History* (London, Canberra, and New York, 1982), pp. 150–52. Footnotes have been omitted.

ical defeat for him. "You may praise Pausanias, you, Xanthippus, and you, Leotychidas; but as for me, I praise Aristeides, the finest man to come out of holy Athens, since Lato[1] conceived a hatred for Themistocles . . ." He goes on to accuse Themistocles of corruption and other dishonesty; Themistocles had promised to arrange the restoration of his "friend" Timocreon to his native town, but broke his word in consideration of a bribe of three talents, and so on. How much truth underlies this (if any does) is impossible to say. It would be altogether too flattering to Timocreon's importance to suggest that his little song has shaped the whole hostile tradition about Themistocles, but it was probably seized on by Themistocles' political enemies and given wide circulation. This would explain why the piece survived at all, for as a man of letters Timocreon ranked low.

The other thing that ought to be examined seriously is Themistocles' second message to Xerxes, after the decision not to destroy the Hellespont bridge. The first point to note is that Herodotus nowhere accuses Themistocles of treachery, actual or intended. The worst he does is to deceive the Athenians as to his future intentions *after* the decision has been definitely taken not to sail to the Hellespont. His conduct does not damage the allied cause in the smallest degree: if anything, he bluffs Xerxes out of Europe all the more quickly. The whole story seems to be pretty improbable, flying (as it does) in the face of the axiom, once bitten, twice shy. Why *should* Xerxes have been expected to treat such a message seriously? And yet Thucydides, writing a a generation later than Herodotus, seems to entertain no doubts as to the truth of the story.

That question, however, need not detain us. What matters is the dramatic purpose of Herodotus' story. In it Themistocles' resourcefulness and dexterity is shown in the highest degree: he has been overruled in his plan to cut off Xerxes in Europe, but even that setback he turns to advantage. His need for a refuge, should he fall foul of his fellow citizens, is presented as only a remote contingency. And yet every Athenian reader in Herodotus' own day would know that Themistocles did so come to grief and did find not just a refuge but a splendid position with King Artaxerxes. They would experience a pleasurable "frisson" on reading or hearing Herodotus' narrative—a fine example of what Thucydides called "a composition designed to catch the ears of an immediate public."

It is sometimes thought that Thucydides' account of Themistocles is intended, in part at least, as a correction of the picture wrought by Herodotus. A careful reading of his text, however, will show this to be false. The excellent story of the refortification of Athens in 479/8 shows Themistocles at his best: he displays, in combination, all the guile, boldness and devotion to Athenian interests that Herodotus credits him with. His exile and flight is made the vehicle of some strongly "Herodotean" episodes, of which his preventing the sea captain from giving him away

1. Doric for the goddess Leto, guarantor of oaths.

must take the palm. This is Themistocles the unscrupulous at work again. The entire narrative speaks of the man's inventiveness, adaptability and capacity for survival.

Near the end of his digression, Thucydides treats Themistocles to a generalised obituary, praising in fine terms his intellectual gifts—his power of rapid decision, his ability to expound a case, but above all his foresight. As far as Thucydides is concerned, the foresight (in the context) clearly consisted of his having foreseen the enmity that would necessarily arise between Athens and Sparta, and having advocated measures to meet it. But each of these qualities is found in ample measure in Herodotus also, the foresight above all—not least in the last example we considered, his second message to Xerxes. No Athenian politician, recalling the fate of Miltiades and the crop of ostracisms in the 480s, could count on absolute security of tenure; but actually to hit on the form of insurance policy adopted by Themistocles argues foresight of a singular kind.

The developments in Themistocles' political position in the 470s, his policy of opposition to Sparta and the reasons for his ostracism make an exceptionally interesting study, but do not fall within the range of this work. Themistocles was a great man by any standards, a towering figure around whose complex personality anecdotes were destined to gather in abundance: compare Plutarch's "Lives" of Themistocles and Aristeides, and the difference is readily apparent. Themistocles, as portrayed by Herodotus, stands firmly in a literary and historical tradition of characters who were determined, resourceful and cunning. In history his predecessor is Peisistratus; in legend, Odysseus—survivors all!

VIRGINIA HUNTER

Virginia Hunter is professor of history and humanities at York University in Ontario. A historian of Greece, she has published *Thucydides: The Artful Reporter* (Toronto, 1973), as well as articles on Greek and Roman women and on the interplay between anthropology and classics. The following selection discusses Herodotus' use of his Greek and Egyptian sources in his critique of the story of Helen of Troy.

[Homer, Herodotus, and the Egyptian *Logos*]†

In chapters 116–120 [of book 2] Herodotus relies on two sources, Homer and Egyptian tradition, the latter referred to as a *logos*. Expressions of personal judgment recur sufficiently throughout the chapters to indicate by the end of chapter 120 which of the two sources Herodotus

† Reprinted by permission of Princeton University Press from Virginia Hunter, *Past and Process in*   *Herodotus and Thucydides* (Princeton, 1982), pp. 52–61.

considers the more reliable. From this passage, and the several chapters preceding it, it is also clear that one of the tasks Herodotus undertook during his stay in Egypt was to enquire about the "facts" of early Greek history transmitted by the epic poems; here, specifically, the story of Helen as recorded by Homer. He begins his account of Helen in chapter 112. There, in offering certain conjectures about a temple in Memphis dedicated to Aphrodite *xeine*,[1] he mentions the *logos* he had heard that Helen spent some time at the court of Proteus. The *logos* itself he proceeds to relate in the next three chapters, first indicating that it was in response to his own enquiries (113.1) that the priests told him the particulars about Helen. These particulars will not interest us *per se*, but rather their central feature, a real discrepancy between Homer's account and that of the priests. For, according to the latter, Helen and Paris not only visited Egypt, but Paris aroused such indignation and ire in Proteus that he ordered him out of Egypt, pledging to keep Helen at his court until Menelaos should reclaim her. Having related the details of the *logos*, Herodotus states again at the beginning of chapter 116 that it was the priests who told him the story. Realizing that the *logos* is quite in opposition to Homer's account, he offers an explanation of the discrepancy that is tantamount to a judgment on the poet.

Let us consider Herodotus' attitude to Homer in chapter 116. He expresses it first as an opinion: "I believe that Homer was also aware of this story." He was aware of it, but considered it unsuited to his needs as an epic poet and so chose another version, the one extant in his poems. Herodotus is sufficiently interested in the fact of Homer's knowledge of the Egyptian *logos* that he attempts to prove it by an appeal to the internal evidence of the *Iliad* itself. He reasons thus: Homer inserted in the *Iliad* an account of the wanderings of Paris and Helen that brought them on their return to Troy to Sidon in Phoenicia. His evidence is *Iliad* 6.289–292, a passage referring specifically to Sidon as the source of the many-colored robes acquired on the journey to Troy. Syria, Herodotus points out, borders on Egypt, and the Phoenicians, to whom Sidon belongs, dwell in Syria. It follows then that in the lines cited Homer makes it evident (116.6) that he knew of Paris' wanderings to Egypt. Two additional points are significant here. Herodotus emphasizes that Homer is consistent about Paris' travels on his return to Troy. So insistent is he about this fact—or so important is it to his overall thesis—that he rejects Homer's authorship of the *Kypria*. Why? Because in that poem Paris reached Troy three days after leaving Sparta. Since this contradicts the *Iliad* and its author, Homer, whom Herodotus has already judged consistent, the *Kypria* must be the work of someone else. Secondly, Herodotus pictures Homer as working rather like himself, gaining knowledge through enquiry (116.1) and at times choosing among variant versions. As a poet, however, Homer used a selective principle

---

1. The foreign Aphrodite.

rather different from that of Herodotus, the suitability of a particular version for epic poetry. Thus, by the end of chapter 117 Herodotus has succeeded in proving to his own satisfaction the following: Whatever Homer chose to relate in his poems about Helen, he did know of another version of the story. That version gains in stature when its rejection by Homer is stated to be due to the requirements of epic poetry and not some more reliable principle.

If one looks at chapters 116–120 as a whole, it is possible to make a number of additional observations about Herodotus' attitude to Homer. First, like Thucydides he never doubts the factual basis of Homer's poems; the occurrence, for example, of the Trojan War, or the existence of Paris, Helen, Priam—any of the characters depicted in the poems. In fact, he has enough respect for the poet of the *Iliad* to note his consistency in the matter of Paris' travels. Secondly, again like Thucydides he indicates that the poems must be used with caution, at least in so far as some of the minute details of the story are concerned. This would seem to be the import of the qualification at 120.3 ("if it is possible to say anything on the basis of the epic poets"), where he uses the many losses of Priam recorded by Homer as part of his own argument in support of Egyptian tradition. Thirdly, he locates the unreliability of Homer in poetic license: in the face of variant versions his principle of selection led him, as a poet, to a bad (or at least an incorrect) choice. Herodotus himself then challenges Homer's version of Helen's presence at Troy with another version, which Homer himself knew but rejected, but which Herodotus affirms is the correct one: the *logos* he derived from the Egyptian priests.

It is now possible to consider the Egyptian *logos* itself, which extends beyond the story of Helen to details of the Trojan War, elicited by Herodotus' additional enquiry of the priests as to the validity of the Greek account of events at Troy (118.1), though presumably he still has Helen in mind. The priests reply with their own version of how the Greeks came to Troy and ultimately discovered the truth of what the Trojans had continued to assert, that Helen was not there. In addition to these facts, presented in chapter 118, in the next chapter the priests describe Menelaos' visit to Egypt, his stay at the court of Proteus, and some of the indignities he perpetrated in their country. Again the particulars of the *logos* will not concern us, but rather the way in which Herodotus indicates the reliability of the priests' testimony and, implicitly, his reasons for accepting their *logos* as the true version in preference to Homer's account. The priests have two means of justifying their assertions, on which basis they are able to say they have genuine knowledge. About events at Troy they have Menelaos' own testimony, the account of an eyewitness, for enquiries were directed to him while he was in Egypt. Their opening statement of certainty they repeat at the end of the *logos*, where they assure their listener that part of their account they know from enquiry (119.3, 118.1). The rest they know because it happened in their own country. It is, in other words, part of their indigenous tradition, the certainty of which they strongly emphasize. Chapter 120 makes it clear that Herodotus found the priests' account, and in turn their sources, unassailable, for in 120 he proceeds to offer an argument of his own in support of it. In fact, at one point he specifically declares Helen's absence from Troy to be the truth (120.5).

To sum up, then, according to the priests, genuine knowledge derives from two sources, the testimony of an eyewitness and indigenous tradition. Furthermore, since Herodotus makes it clear in this passage that he accepts the priests' account, he thereby indicates his own trust in the reliability of such sources. Naturally, many questions arise in the mind of the modern reader. Even if Menelaos was an eyewitness, why should one believe in his veracity? Can an eyewitness not lie, distort, or display partiality or prejudice? Why in fact should one believe the account of the Egyptian priests, when hundreds of years had elapsed since the Trojan War and the visits of Helen and Menelaos? Herodotus does not at this point acknowledge such problems, nor does he feel called upon to justify his trust in Egyptian tradition. It is possible, however, to turn to a statement made earlier in the same book, which provides at least a partial explanation of this trust. At chapter 77.1 Herodotus describes the Egyptians who live in the arable part of the country (that is, Upper Egypt, which includes places like Memphis and Heliopolis) as by far the "most learned" men he has met anywhere. In what sense they are learned he makes clear by specifying that they, more than any other people in the world, devote themselves to "memory" or here "records." In other words, Herodotus was impressed by the Egyptians' concern for records and their preeminence in preserving them. Thus, he could rest assured on one count, that Egyptian memory easily stretched back to Menelaos' time and that, given their skills, the priests retained an accurate record, written or otherwise, both of his visit and of Helen's stay. If, then, Herodotus adopted a rather special attitude to indigenous tradition in general, he must have felt even more regard for Egyptian tradition, which, as a kind of living entity, was not just a floating substance but the concern of a skilled caste, conscious of its reponsibility.

In the passage under scrutiny, 116–120, the last chapter represents a new departure for Herodotus. Up to this point, in relating the Egyptian *logos*, he has *ostensibly* not veered from the account of his informants but has been repeating a story, albeit a variant version. Now, in defense of that version, which he accepts, he appends some reasoning of his own, in which he reconstructs the situation at Troy, using the data supplied by both Homer and the Egyptians. It is his own interpretation of the evidence and, like Thucydides' interpretation of similar data in the Archaeology, is a lengthy argument from probability. Underlying his argumentation are some vague generalizations about human behavior. Briefly, he argues as follows: If Helen had been at Troy, the Trojans would have given her up. And even if Priam and his kin had not acted initially to preserve themselves and their city from danger, surely they would have done so after experiencing many serious losses at the hands of the Greeks. Nor could their failure to do so have been due to Paris' influence, since not he, but Hektor, was heir, and Hektor no more than his father Priam would have allowed such calamities to befall the Trojans. This appeal to probability on a number of levels proves that the Egyptians' *logos* is the truth: the Trojans could not give Helen back because she was not there.

There is finally an additional argument presented as Herodotus' own judgment *(gnome)*. It is worth noting at this point, because it is a form of explanation that recurs throughout the *Histories*. Having presented a fairly cogent argument from probability, Herodotus is not satisfied to leave the matter in the realm of mere human behavior. To allay any skepticism in the listener's mind as to the Greeks' inability to discover over a period of ten years, and come to believe, that Helen was not present at Troy, he resorts to a religious explanation. The great calamities visited on Troy—its utter destruction—were in fact part of a divine plan to make it evident to mankind that massive wrongdoings bring massive punishments from the gods. Like his arguments from probability and his "Homeric criticism" this final judgment serves to reinforce the Egyptian *logos*. Indeed, the whole of chapters 116–120 would seem to have as its purpose the verification of that *logos*.

On the basis of the above discussion it is now possible to offer a tentative answer to the questions posed at the outset. In specifically human terms Herodotus justifies his assertions in two ways: first, by inference or arguments from probability and, secondly, by an appeal to a reliable source. The latter alone he designates as knowledge or truth. Seen from the perspective of truth, chapters 116–120 are a coherent entity and not an example of variant versions. A conflict of versions is clearly implicit in the passage, and it may well have been distrust of the epic poets' "early history of Greece" that led Herodotus to make enquiries of the priests in Memphis. At one point, in other words, he faced variants. But the way in which he narrates and justifies the Egyptian *logos* reveals that there is no conflict in his mind about its truth. Thus, he does not introduce Homer as a variant but as a poet who made certain choices *qua* poet, but who left traces in his poetry of another version, the true version, the Egyptian *logos*, which he knew and rejected. The entire passage then, including the historian's so-called Homeric criticism with its inferences, and his reconstruction of events, argued on the basis of probability, serves to verify the Egyptian *logos*. In human terms Herodotus has established the truth about a commonly accepted fact of Greek history derived from the epic poets. He is able to do so because he trusts the reliability of a source that in its antiquity and care takes precedence over Homer. In turn, the reliability of that source is due to the levels of personal observation or autopsy on which the priests base their knowledge. What produces knowledge is a combination of antiquity, care in the preservation and transmission of records or tradition, and finally that tradition itself, an indigenous one, which is rooted in personal observation or autopsy and which, in this instance, stretches back to information gleaned by enquiry from an eyewitness. All these elements together produce a true *logos*.

DONALD LATEINER

Donald Lateiner is professor of humanities and classics at Ohio Wesleyan University, where he has taught since 1979. He has published not only on Herodotus, Thucydides, and Ovid but on religious entrepreneurs and non-verbal behavior. The present selection makes the argument that Herodotus generally posits rational explanations for human events.

Five Systems of Explanation†

Herodotus uses at least five often overlapping, sometimes inconsistent systems for the explanation of historical events. The most studied, although least frequently encountered, is an *immoral and divine jealousy*. Solon, Amasis, Artabanus, and Themistocles, four individuals who are credited with perspicacity, endorse some such concept, and therefore it is unlikely that Herodotus rejects it, yet there are no other references to it in the *Histories* whereas there are hundreds of other "explanations." It does not provide Herodotus' preferred variety of historical cause. Divine envy represents "more piety than theology, more curiosty than determined faith." Its early and privileged first appearance in the Solon episode establishes an important precedent, but every time that it is explicitly applied, there also appear human motives and causes sufficient for the action.

A determined destiny, *Fate*, sometimes appears as a second form of Herodotean causality. Delphi declared that neither Apollo nor the other gods could alter this fate, called μοῖρα. Croesus, Polycrates, Cambyses, and Arcesilaus meet their destined end. Such destiny is often amoral and incomprehensible to man, and when Herodotus invokes it, he is trying to account for an unexpected occurrence, a terrifying reversal of expectations. From it there is no escape; this much wise men can know. A chastened Cambyses near death says: "It was not possible for a human being to turn aside what was going to happen." What must happen to Candaules, to Apries, to Scyles, or to Miltiades can only be known when it has happened, and therefore later generations can say "it had to happen; look, it did happen," without requiring any theology. Such a limited determinism will be divine, if a man believes in divinity, as Herodotus

† Excerpted by permission of the author and of the Toronto University Press from Donald Lateiner, *The Historical Method of Herodotus* (Toronto,   1989), pp. 196–205. Notes and many textual references have been omitted.

did. It is neither predictive nor even an historical theory since it offers no explanation. It is invoked rarely, only when natural expectation has been confounded. Herodotus certainly did believe in moral choices, not in external determinism or fatalism. When someone topples, the reader is told that he had to, not because he was fated to fall because of the stars or divine malice, but because being who he was, when and where he was, he had to err as he did. There is an internal logic to political events.

Herodotus' alleged determinism seems supported by a few references to irrepressible cyclical movements in history. The "cycle of history," κύκλος, implies a circular or pendulum-like view, a history without progress or regress. It is not a history without moral values, because this cycle reduces or destroys the great men and powers which seek aggrandizement. Morality based on Presocratic metaphors of statics ties in nicely with other metaphoric systems such as retribution and "boundary transgression." Asia and Europe are in counterpoise; they are separate but not unrelated, and no one should attempt to alter nature's arrangements. The kyklos represents the active principle of equipoise, to ison, functioning through time, which will appear again in the fourth type of explanation.

References to divinity form the third group, a parallel but different set of explanations. They require extended comment to defend the historian from being dismissed as a cracker-barrel apologist for popular religion. Herodotus does not produce a theological explanation of the Persian Wars. He believes that supernatural powers exist, that they sometimes know events are about to occur, and that humans obtain oracles and dreams that may be announcements from the gods (although these are very often comprehensible only after the event). Unlike Thucydides who generally suppresses the supernatural, except insofar as men's beliefs cause them to act in certain ways, Herodotus sprinkles his pages with tales of the supernatural, most of them reported as local or national tradition, and very few are recognized as due to divine causation. Croesus was a victim of god's *nemesis*, Troy was destroyed by the gods to show men that great crimes are punished, Pheretime died from a dreadful disease because her inhuman personal revenge was abominated by the gods.[1] Other supposed cases, where, for instance, *tisis* is mentioned or oracles and dreams are cited or characters attribute events to divine interference, do not carry with them or establish the historian's belief. Herodotean *tisis* does not require gods; furthermore, oracles and dreams—as humans experience them—can be right without a god's say-so (as Thucydides notes, 5.26.3–4); finally, we know that Herodotus reports many state-

1. See book 4, chapters 162–205. Pheretime was an exiled North African queen who returns to take a cruel revenge on her persecutors and who is, according to Herodotus, in turn punished by the gods with a horrible death as a punishment for her excess.

ments that he does not endorse. Miracles are eschewed, not on the level of incidental events but as sufficient and necessary explanations. If we consider a difficult but unrepresentative passage in which the supernatural is extremely prominent, such as the passage from the priests at Delphi's temple (8.36–9: oracle, weapons moving themselves, thunderbolts, rocks breaking off, giant hero warriors), we find Herodotus to be very wary and he repeatedly distances himself from what he reports ("the Delphians say," "so I have been told," "the prophet reported the marvel to the Delphians who were present"). As so often, the bias of his sources appears to derail his rationalism but really calls forth his reserve. Herodotus believed in the divine, yet he gives non-divine explanations for all historical events. Aside from rumours of divine interference, he informs us that Croesus was an imperialist, that the Trojans could not make the demanded reparations, and that Pheretime contracted a fatal case of worms. Herodotus more often reports battles and the actual campaigns without recourse to any divine causality.

References to gods personalize nature and the tendency to balance and stability. The Delos earthquake was a τέρας, a portent of extraordinary disaster. The oracle, divinity's mouthpiece, stated: "I shall move Delos though it be unmoved and unmoveable." The god acts similarly to (and foreshadows) the Persian king: he shakes the order of the world. Herodotus avers: "Somehow a sign is wont to appear beforehand, whenever great disaster approaches city or people." In this passage only two of one hundred Chiote boys in a chorus sent to Delphi escape plague, and one of 120 Chiote schoolchildren survives the collapse of a school's roof just before the island suffers severe losses at Lade and subsequent conquest. The god gave advance notice of this catastrophe; indeed, the gods (θεοί) are those who arrange (θέντες) the universe, ordering all affairs in all their detail, sometimes in a helpful way. Their will is done: "Stranger-friend," a Persian says at an Orchomenian banquet, "whatever by the god's will must happen, there is no way for man to turn it aside." In a mere one hundred years the unprecedented might of the Persian empire developed, reached its greatest extent, and then was stopped and reduced on its western fringe. Cyrus created it, Darius led it to its height of power, Xerxes mismanaged it more seriously than they had and caused the deaths of thousands. The period of expansion approaches term through divine will. Solon's words to Croesus on the fickleness of prosperity are of the highest generality, yet their dogmatic philosophy does not supplant the novel and difficult business of explaining the recent past.

Herodotus prefers to limit his explanations of phenomena to subjects, times, and places that allow direct observation and opportunities for verification. When observation is not possible, he still prefers to limit his narrative to what could once have been observed and to events that his various informants as a group would vouch for, even if they disagreed on details, motives, and interpretation.

Herodotus generally suppresses the fantastic, as in his account of Gyges[2] (no ring as in later versions) and Croesus' salvation (no Apolline journey) or disbelieves the absurd, such as the impossible accounts of Scyllias' ten-mile underwater swim and of Sophanes' having held his hoplite's position by means of a real anchor at Plataea. On occasion his loyalty to *opsis* prevents him from passing over the incredible, as in his report of Arion's miraculous rescue, where his personal observation of the statue (supposedly) of Arion on a dolphin leads him to report the tradition of the miraculous rescue. Even here the narrative abounds in prudential *caveats* (such as the distancing words λέγουσι [they say], τῶν ἡμεῖς ἴδμεν [of the examples we know], and the use of *oratio obliqua*) that permit various gradations of credence and allow him to preserve the fact (the existence of the man Arion), discount the probably fictitious tale (a dolphin saves him), and nevertheless present themes (bravery, disciplined skill, adherence to *nomos*) that are fundamental to the entire work. Human agency and human actions keep their centrality; supposed incidents with specific divinities or supernatural events are more often "explained," doubted, or denied than admitted. For example, consider the talking birds of Zeus at Dodona and Poseidon's handiwork at Tempe.

Herodotus sometimes (although rarely and reluctantly) includes descriptions of gods, but hedges most statements about particular divinities by reporting them only on others' testimony. He recognizes only belief (δόξα), not knowledge, in these matters. He detects a pattern of divine action, but he suggests that it is distinct from historical causation, his particular concern. He doubts direct divine intervention, and he scoffs at Homer's and Hesiod's manufacture of Greek religion and at Egyptian doctrines of metempsychosis. He prefers to speak vaguely of "some god" or "the divine."

"Coincidences" are sometimes understood to suggest Herodotus' endorsement of divine interference in history. That is, the specified events somehow appear more than accidentally synchronic. * * * The phrase "divine fortune" suggests that Herodotus' speakers see a certain few occurrences as manifestations of some non-human force, but it appears either in the speeches of others or in accounts of legends. No theology becomes evident or necessary. As with all the examples of coincidence noted earlier in this paragraph where the verb ουμπίπτειν, "to coincide," occurs, the phrase θείη τύχη[3] seems to mark something humanly remarkable rather than the divine and miraculous. Compare the current use of the word "incredible." Synchronisms are curious, but explain nothing. They are noted not to exhibit any world-view, but to display the effect of religious belief on men and policy.

David Hume remarked in his essay "Of Miracles" that men enjoy surprises, reputed miracles, and violations of the laws of nature.[4] He

2. In one version of this story, not used by Herodotus, Gyges made himself invisible with the help of a magic ring.

3. The Greek *theie tyche* means "divine fortune."
4. See Hume's "Of Miracles" on pp. 279–82 of this edition.

denies however that these laws are violated and he avers that "Experience only . . . gives authority to human testimony." "No species of reasoning is more common, more useful, and even necessary to human life, than that . . . derived from the testimony of man." Degrees of assurance, he remarks, vary as interest, distance, time, and type of event separate an informant from the act reported. Herodotus' method, however, leads him to include even suspicious traditions that have only minimally historical origins or minuscule contemporary repercussions. External and internal criteria for testing or verifying data were by later standards rather elementary, and Herodotus would rather preserve a traditional error than discard a potential fact. Further, group belief as well as factuality was a criterion for inclusion in his search for why people had acted as they did. The historian of the unexpected victory had to be suspicious and cautious with information but also open to accounts that contradicted normal expectations or common opinions. Otherwise he would fall into the trap of Hecatacan hyper-criticism and hyper-rationalism. Right or wrong, the method is empirical. When he includes stories of miracles and divine interference, he searches for visible proof or at least some evidence. The mute boulders that broke off Mount Parnassus at Delphi and which Herodotus was taken to see, were an inadequate proof, of course, that gods were meddling in human affairs, and Herodotus does not here endorse that interpretation. The unlikely victory of the Greeks over powerful invaders requires acknowledgment of the possibility of extra-terrestrial aid, but Herodotus' search for explanation went much further.

Herodotus considers oracles of the gods to be unlikely sources for human knowledge of earthly phenomena. Even when they were "right," they were generally misunderstood and too obscure to be useful. According to an oracle, for instance, the land of Attica had to fall to the Persians, but for Herodotus the oracle is only something that men spoke of, not the historical cause. It was a fifth-century game for intellectuals (including Herodotus) to show that oracles were sometimes right. Yet even if prophecies were a source of real knowledge, they never explain events or supply the most important causes. Herodotus works on explanations in human terms of the Greeks' military victory. He analyses the military and political issues: what would have happened to Greece had the Athenians joined the enemy Persians. The analysis of chapter 139 concentrates on the Athenians' freedom of political choice and praises them for their dangerous choice of freedom. The intrusions of the gods are brief because they are known only by inference and hearsay, not by investigation. The realm of the divine is clearly demarcated and largely dismissed.

An inventory of the passages where divine interference might have been expected would be less helpful than the observation that even in the mythic past, Herodotus prefers to rationalize and humanize divine tales rather than theologize earthly events. In the *Histories*, whether we count examples or examine the emphasis of the author, man is largely free to decide his own actions. Foolish or deliberate human choice, not external, divine compulsion, accounts for the "rapes" which open his work, for the rape of Helen, and for Gyges' decision. The women choose to elope with their lovers and Gyges chooses to survive. Gods are conspicuous by their absence. Homer's version of Helen's whereabouts is not fully disproved, but Herodotus dismisses it from rational historical discussion.

Herodotus, like the author of the Hipocratic treatise *On the Sacred Disease* will not assert that divinity cannot be found in nature * * *. Herodotus and the medical writers desire to describe events accurately, explain adequately, and record without recourse to the supernatural. Nevertheless a scientific, empirical approach need not rule out belief in divinity and divine activity on earth, if that belief does no violence to observable phenomena. * * *

Miracles, marvels, and divine interference are not accepted so frequently as the believers in a naive Herodotus suggest. Exceptions to the laws of nature are often denied, doubted, rationalized, offered on the authority of others, or distanced by indirect discourse or by wholly historical alternative theories.

*   *   *

The fourth kind of explanation briefly acknowledges the gods, but this causality discovers a natural, dynamic equilibrium in historical events, not daily interference by supra-terrestrial beings. *Tisis* will be examined now as a type of explanation rather than as the structuring narrative principle of chapter six.

This explanation offers a cosmic ecology, the equalizing code of *tisis* in action, act for act, retribution for offence. Divinity reduces those with "excessive" power or fortune, through *nemesis*, or *tisis*, the principal expression of *dike*, justice. Divinity is thus posited as the guardian, but often the balance manages to restore itself. Occasionally a merely "poetic justice" appears, as when Gyges sets out to slay Candaules "from the same spot," even "at the same door" at which he has been posted by Candaules to view the naked queen. Similarly Croesus dismisses his visitor Solon, thinking him a fool, specifically for giving him the very advice that eventually saves his own life. When humans seek *tisis* by executing their own vengeance (τιμωρίη), they risk offending the gods, even if the justice of the wish is justified. * * * The nature of things— whether called "the divine" or inner necessity—encourages the restoration of balance and ensures penalties matching the crime. Violating acknowledged laws of all mankind engenders some communal calamity for Athens. Europa was taken as compensation for Io, ἴσα πρὸς ἴσα [tit for tat, like for like], nature maintains a balance of species. Solon and Artabanus aver that misfortune balances good fortune.

Explanations based on "divine vengeance" have symbolic value for any god-fearing audience, but they always allow and often coexist with other, non-theological causes. When Cleomenes went mad and committed suicide, Herodotus comments that most Greeks explained it as punishment for corrupting Apollo's Pythian priestess, but the Athenians explained it as revenge for devastating the fields of the gods at Eleusis, and the Argives as revenge for the sacrilegious slaughter of Argive suppliants and the burning of the holy grove (6.75). Each people chooses the offence nearest and dearest to its heart and gives it the name of a god. The Spartans, however, explicitly deny any divine agency and ascribe his madness to a mundane cause, excessive drinking. Herodotus positions himself somewhere in between, endorsing the concept that Cleomenes "got what he deserved" for abusing Demaratus, but not endorsing the hypothesis of divine interference.

Anaximander had said: "[Every thing] pays a penalty (δίκη) and retribution (τίσις) to each other for injustice (ἀδικία) as time assesses it." Here the physical universe is expressed in moral or judicial terms by an Ionian "scientist"; history is conceived similarly by the Ionian historian. *Tisis* can effect its purposes without recourse to any *deus ex machina*. Herodotus rejects the Hellenic search for simple and single—mythical or theological—root causes.

Herodotus' main concern is not religion and the supernatural, but the phenomena of terrestrial experience. His analysis of historical action requires a fifth form of explanation: historicist, down-to-earth, political analysis, the sort of explanation expected from a modern historian. For this he has no one term, but it is his invention, and often a first-person verb or pronoun indicates the presence of a novel, rational, and entirely human explanation. He is not the theoretician of this type of analysis, but no previous extant author had ever employed it. Human action reveals character, and individual and ethnic character appeared decisive to him for comprehending the historical process. From book 7 on, historical means of explication predominate, and the importance of vengeance and the other modes of explanation decline. Xerxes' expedition, for instance, is *both* voluntary and necessary, but the necessity grew out of the *nomoi*—habits, laws, and customs—of the Persians, Xerxes' own insecurity and need to prove himself, and his megalomania. Xerxes' Grand Council and the Dream represent two versions of the "causes" of Xerxes' decision, either of which might have sufficed. If, however, Xerxes had been no more than the gods' joke, a victim, would Herodotus have written his history at all? A secular and a theological version of Xerxes' decision to attack the Hellenes may be juxtaposed in 7.1–19, but Herodotus did not suspend judgment. The text presents a perfectly adequate set of human motives, both psychological and strategic analysis; it distances itself from the report of the dream. The ghoulish antics of the dream are entirely absent from Xerxes' sober reflections at 7.44–52, where he takes full responsibility as man and king for his expedition. This secular interpretation represents Herodotus' own and final judgment. Rational analysis is harder to remember in the *Histories*, because it does not lend itself to dramatic scenes; it never becomes a structural motif or acquires a set of striking images, and it is not clearly expounded as a theory of explanation. Nevertheless it is embedded in the text of each *logos* with historical content.

Xerxes' failure may indicate to the faithful that the gods smash the over-weening and to the philosophical that vast power will corrupt a mere human, because the *Histories* provide different meanings on several levels. For the historically minded, it is enough to read of the acts of Xerxes' predecessors to see Xerxes as their successor following their policies, and to discover the immediate causes and the more systemic differences between Hellas and Persia. Xerxes' infamous but unique "dream" inspired by Homer appears between two presentations of prosaic and historical motives (7.12–18). Its inclusion further dramatizes the *Histories'* most fully realized narrative. Nevertheless, it is redundant as explanation for an event destined to happen (7.17.2) for other, more verifiable, historical reasons. Herodotus' world is as ruthless and harsh as Thucydides' in its aggression and imperialism. * * *

The student of Herodotus' thinking, faced with these disparate causes (really different levels of explanation) notes that it is futile "to assess the relative importance of each of these motivations [of Xerxes' invasion] . . . after we have realized that Herodotus resorts even to different styles for motives that have no common denominator." * * * Divine vengeance or annoyance sometimes supplement but they never prevent human motives and political causes from appearing (eg, the story of Croesus). * * * Herodotus' interpretation of events on individual, political, and metaphysical levels permits the audience to see events in more dimensions than most historical writers allow. The other inherited systems of explanation should not detract from Herodotus' accomplishment, the first extant presentation of recent events with their ascertainable causes, the invention of historical thinking. The αἰτίη or explanation of the war promised by the proem comprises all the kinds of αἴτια (causes) which Herodotus can assemble. His work constitutes a comprehensive and patient clarification of the elements that contributed to that fateful nexus, the Persian Wars. Perhaps Herodotus began his *Histories* to answer a limited question such as "Why did the Greeks win the battle of Salamis?" Yet the work grew into a study and explanation of the clash of polities and their cultures.

Glossary

For geographical information, the reader is urged to consult the map on p. xxi. Of the many place names that Herodotus mentions, only those of particular significance are listed below. Words beginning with either *c* or *k* will be found here under *c*. As elsewhere in this volume, all dates are B.C. unless otherwise specified.

Adeimantus Corinthian commander at the Battle of Salamis.

Adrastus grandson of Midas who inadvertently killed the son of Croesus.

Agamemnon commander in chief of the Greek expedition against Troy.

Aegina powerful island state, near Athens and rival to it.

Alcmaeonidae Athenian family prominent in politics. Cleisthenes the democratic reformer (ca. 505) was a prominent Alcmaeonid, and Pericles had an Alcmaeonid mother. The Alcmaeonidae were suspected of treacherous dealings with the Persians during the Persian Wars.

Alexander alternative name for Paris, the Trojan prince who abducted Helen of Sparta (later Helen of Troy).

Anaxagoras of Clazomenae teacher and friend of Pericles, born ca. 500, the first philosopher to live at Athens. An innovative and scientific thinker, he was indicted for impiety by Pericles' enemies but managed to escape Athens and founded a school in Asia Minor.

Anaximander born 610, philosopher and astronomer who wrote the first Greek prose treatise. Anaximander was apparently the first Greek to conceive of the entire universe as subject to a single law.

Amasis Egyptian pharaoh ca. 569–524. Amasis allowed the Greeks to settle the city of Naucratis, in Egypt, which became a flourishing port. His long reign was peaceful and prosperous.

Amphiaraus Greek hero or demigod who had an important oracular shrine at Oropus, on the border between Boeotia and Attica.

Amphictyonic League a Greek league organized around the temple of the grain goddess Demeter near Thermopylae and later around the oracle of Apollo at Delphi. The functions of the league were principally religious and social; although the league council sometimes issued mandates in the field of politics, its orders were frequently disregarded.

Aphrodite Greek goddess of love and sex, parallel to the Roman goddess Venus.

Apollo strong-willed and often capricious Greek god of arts, sciences, intellect. The Delphic oracle was sacred to Apollo.

Apries Egyptian pharaoh overthrown ca. 569 by an uprising of his mercenaries which put Amasis on the throne.

Archilochus of Paros irreverent Greek lyric poet, ca. 700.

Argos powerful Greek state in the Peloponnesus.

Aristagoras of Miletus one of the organizers of the Ionian rebellion.

Aristides ca. 520–467, Athenian statesman and general, rival of Themistocles. He was ostracised in 482.

Aristogeiton see **Harmodius.**

Artabanus uncle and counselor of Xerxes.

Artabazus Persian commander under Xerxes.

Artaphernes (1) Persian commander, half brother of Darius.

Artaphernes (2) son of the above, also Persian commander.

Artemis Greek virgin goddess associated with childbirth and hunting, parallel to the Roman Diana.

Artemisia of Halicarnassus ruler under Persian suzerainty over several cities in Caria, and trusted adviser to Xerxes.

Artemisum promontory north of Attica, site of naval battle between Greeks and Persians in 480.

Asia Minor Roman term used by modern scholars to mean the territory occupied today by Turkey.

Astyages the Mede grandfather of Cyrus. Astyages tried to have Cyrus put to death as a baby because of an oracle.

Atossa wife of Darius and mother of Xerxes.

Attica the territory governed by Athens. All citizens of Attica were also citizens of Athens.

Atys son of Croesus slain by Adrastus.

Bacchiadae oligarchic clan who exercised a monopoly of power in Corinth until they were overthrown by Cypselus ca. 655.

Battus founder of Cyrene, in North Africa.

Callimachus Athenian polemarch and commander in chief in the Marathon campaign. Callimachus was killed in the battle.

Cambyses son of Cyrus the Great, king of Persia 529–521, known for his madness and for his conquest of Egypt in 525.

Candaules king of Lydia overthrown by Gyges ca. 680.

Carnea a Dorian festival celebrated in late summer, originally sacred to an old god Carnus or Carneius but later sacred to Apollo.

Chios large island city-state in Ionia, active in Ionian rebellion, later an important ally of Athens.

Cleomenes Spartan king who assisted the Athenians in expelling the tyrant Hippias in 510.

Croesus wealthy ruler of Lydia (ca. 560–546), last king of the dynasty of the Mermnadae. He was overthrown by Cyrus.

Cylon an Athenian who tried unsuccessfully to become tyrant in Athens ca. 630. The government official to whom Cylon and his supporters surrendered, Megacles, violated his promise to spare their lives. This story explains in part the curse that was believed to lie upon Megacles' family, the Alcmaeonidae.

Cypselus son of a lame Bacchiad mother and a Corinthian commoner. He overthrew the Bacchiad oligarchy and became tyrant of Corinth ca. 655.

Cyrene North African port city founded ca. 630.

Cyrus the Great founder of the Persian empire, 559–529. He was regarded by many Greeks as a model ruler.

Darius I king of Persia 521–486, who led the first Persian invasion of Greece.

Deioces 690–656, a private lawgiver and arbitrator who was so esteemed by the Medes that he was made their first king.

Delian League a confederacy organized by the Athenians in 478 to continue vigilance against Persia and to make retaliatory raids on Persian territory. Its membership included over a hundred states. The Athenian Aristides assessed the tribute owed to the league treasury by each state. In time Athens began to suppress attempts to secede from the league and moved the treasury from the island of Delos to Athens. The conversion of the league into an Athenian empire was a major source of friction between Athens and Sparta.

Delphi oracular shrine of Apollo, site of the most politically influential oracle in Greece, the Delphic oracle, located on the southwest spur of Mount Parnassus.

Demaratus exiled Spartan king who fled to Persia and accompanied Xerxes in his invasion of Greece. Herodotus portrays him warning Xerxes constantly of the ferocious resistance he would encounter from the Spartans.

Demeter Greek goddess of agriculture, parallel to the Roman Ceres.

Democedes Greek physician at the court of Darius.

Dionysus also known as Bacchus, Greek popular god associated with wine, revelry, highly emotional religion, and the theater. The famed Athenian dramas were performed at the festival of Dionysus.

Dorians race of Greeks. The Dorians invaded from the north around 1100 and settled primarily in the Peloponnese. The most powerful city ruled by Dorians was Sparta. Dorians prided themselves on austerity and on physical and moral rigor.

Elephantine (Elephant City) Egyptian city on an island below the first cataract of the Nile.

Ephialtes Greek who betrayed the Thermopylae pass to the Persians. He is not to be confused with the later democratic reformer and associate of Pericles.

Ephors five influential Spartans selected to serve as advisers to the kings, a cabinet of sorts.

Ephorus of Cyme ca. 405–330, Greek historian whose works are preserved largely in the later works of Diodorus of Sicily, books 11–16.

Erechtheus legendary king of Athens, considered to be the son of Earth. His worship was eventually superseded by that of Athena and Poseidon, but he continued to reside on the Acropolis in the form of a sacred snake.

Eretria Greek city which along with Athens furnished assistance to the Ionians in their rebellion against Darius.

Eurybiades Spartan admiral who served as commander in chief of the Greek allied fleet against Xerxes.

Gerousia the Spartan council of elders.

Halicarnassus Carian town on the coast of modern Turkey, birthplace of Herodotus.

Harmodius Athenian youth who with his friend Aristogeiton hatched a conspiracy to murder the sons of Pisistratus in 514. There was a slipup, and only Hipparchus was killed, leaving a disgruntled and justifiably paranoid Hippias in charge.

Harpagus kinsman of Astyages ordered to dispose of the infant Cyrus. He was cruelly punished for disobeying Astyages' orders by being served the flesh of his own child.

Hecataeus Ionian historian of unorthodox and rationalist views who sought to correct false accounts of history. He was involved in the Ionian rebellion and had considerable influence on Herodotus.

Helen of Sparta later of Troy, wife of King Menelaus of Sparta who was abducted by Paris, the son of the Trojan king. Her abduction sparked the Trojan War.

Hellenistic age the period in Greece following the death of Alexander in 323.

Hellespont known today as the Dardanelles, the narrow strait dividing Europe from Asia where the Black Sea meets the Mediterranean.

Hera wife of Zeus, parallel to the Roman Juno.

Heracles Greek demigod and hero, son of Zeus and the mortal Alcmena, parallel to the Roman Hercules.

Hesiod poet from mainland Greece (ca. 700) who wrote about the origins of the universe and the genealogy of the gods.

Hestia Greek goddess of the hearth, similar to the Roman Vesta. Unlike other Greek deities, Hestia was not commonly personified, though she was considered to have chosen perpetual virginity, but was usually represented as the flame at the hearth.

Hipparchus son of Pisistratus who ruled Athens along with his brother Hippias until a conspiracy was formed against the brothers in 514. Although Hippias escaped, Hipparchus was killed.

Hippias son of Pisistratus, who along with his brother Hipparchus ruled Athens after their father's death. He was exiled from Athens in 510. He accompanied the expedition Darius sent under Datis and Artaphernes and pointed out the plain of Marathon to them as the most suitable place to land.

Hippocrates of Cos 469–399, founder of scientific method. The Hippocratic oath still taken by doctors today is named for him.

Histiaeus of Miletus one of the instigators of the Ionian rebellion against Darius.

Hoplite heavily armed Greek infantryman.

Hubris or Hybris an important concept in Greek thought, and a challenge for a translator: it can be rendered as pride (in the negative sense), insolence, arrogance, or perhaps chutzpah. Greek tragic heroes have sometimes been viewed as outstanding individuals who nonetheless suffered the "tragic flaw" of hybris and thus came to bad ends. Both Herodotus and Aeschylus attribute the failure of Xerxes' invasion of Greece in part to the king's hybris, a flaw frequently attributed by Greeks to autocratic rulers.

Hydarnes Persian commander, in charge of the Immortals.

Hystaspes father of Darius.

Immortals elite Persian troops, the bodyguard of Xerxes.

Ionia central area of the west coast of Asia Minor (Turkey), settled by Greeks traditionally thought to be from Athens. Ionia was the home of much early Greek philosophy and science. The Ionians were associated with elegance, refinement, and intellectual inquiry, and Ionian Greeks (including the Athenians) were frequently contrasted with Dorians. Among other things, the Peloponnesian War of 431–404 pitted Dorians against Ionians.

Ionian rebellion unsuccessful revolution of the Greek cities of Ionia. The cities sought freedom from Persian rule. The Persian victory at the Battle of Lade in 494 brought the rebellion to an end. Assistance to the rebels from mainland Greece was one factor in provoking the invasion of Darius.

Lacedaemon alternative name for Sparta.

Lade site of decisive defeat of rebellious Ionian Greeks in 494.

Leonidas heroic Spartan king killed while in command at Thermopylae in 480.

Leotychides see **Mycale.**

Logographers early Greek chroniclers who produced some of the first Greek prose literature. Their work survives today only in fragments. The best-known were Hecataeus and Hellanicus. Hecataeus preceded Herodotus, and Hellanicus wrote at the same time as Herodotus or perhaps a little before.

logos an important Greek concept, wide-ranging in meaning and difficult to translate. A logos is frequently, but not always, a tale with a moral or an underlying structure of deep significance. It is variously rendered as system, story, reason, meaning, logic, history, tradition, method, moral, theme.

Lycurgus legendary selfless Spartan lawgiver, who spurned an opportunity to become king and instead overhauled Spartan government and society and established the rigorous system that continued into classical times. Solon and Lycurgus have often been linked as glorious founders.

Lygdamis tyrant of Caria at Halicarnassus in whose overthrow Herodotus was instrumental.

Magi the priestly caste in Persia, revered in antiquity as wise men. It was the power the Magi were believed to have over demons that gave rise to the word "magic."

Mandane mother of Cyrus.

Marathon city in northern Attica. The Athenians defeated the Persians on the plain of Marathon in August 490.

Mardonius nephew and son-in-law of Darius, adviser and general. Xerxes left Mardonius behind in Greece after the Greek victory at Salamis in 480. Mardonius was in command at the Persian defeat at Plataea the following spring (479).

Masistes Persian commander and brother of Xerxes. Herodotus tells a brutal story of Xerxes' passion for Masistes' wife and daughter which ends with the death of Masistes and the horrible mutilation of his wife.

Massagetae warlike people of Central Asia.

Memphis one of the most powerful cities in Egypt, early capital of Upper (southern) Egypt.

Menelaus king of Sparta, husband of Helen, brother of Agamemnon.

Midas king of Phrygia whose wealth was legendary, hence the story that everything he touched turned to gold.

Miletus powerful Ionian city, home of the philosopher Thales.

Miltiades Athenian of the aristocratic Philaid family, in command at the Greek victory at Marathon in 490. He was exiled the following year after an unsuccessful expedition against the island of Paros.

Muses the nine daughters of Mnemosyne, Greek goddesses of literature and the arts. Nine was a lucky number in Greece. The muses were Calliope (epic poetry), Clio (history), Euterpe (flute playing), Melpomene (tragedy), Terpsichore (dancing), Erato (the lyre), Polyhymnia (sacred song), Urania (astronomy), and Thalia (comedy).

Mycale site on the coast of Asia Minor where Leotychides, the king of Sparta, who had fomented the rebellion from the Persians of Chios and Samos, defeated the Persians in a land and sea battle. Legend placed the battle on the same day as the Battle of Plataea.

Naucratis Greek trading community in the Nile Delta, settled in the sixth century.

Nitocris (1) enterprising early-sixth-century queen of Babylon, probably the wife of Nebuchadnezzar, who cleverly diverted the course of the Euphrates River.

Nitrocris (2) queen of Egypt who deviously drowned all those involved in her brother's murder.

Olympia flat plain in the northwest Peloponnesus, site of the principal sanctuary of Zeus and also of the Olympic Games, first held in 776. Greeks dated events in terms of Olympiads, that is, periods of four years, starting with 776.

Olympus tall mountain (nearly ten thousand feet) in northern Greece believed by the Greeks to be the home of the gods.

Ostracism a bizarre inverse-popularity contest known at Athens (and, under the name "petalism," in Syracuse in Sicily). The first known case is dated to 487. By this procedure Athenians would each spring have the option of sending one of their citizens into banishment for ten years, at the end of which he was free to return and resume his property and his civic rights. Ostracism was evidently intended as a safety valve (to prevent factional disputes from consuming the citizens' energy by banishing one of two rival leaders) or to discourage tyranny. Both Aristides and Pericles' father, Xanthippus, were ostracized in the 480s, and Themistocles was ostracized at some point after the war.

Otanes Persian nobleman involved in the coup that placed Darius on the throne in 521. In the debate on government recounted by Herodotus, Otanes favored democracy.

Pan frolicsome Greek woodland god with human torso and goat's feet. Pan was honored in Athens after the Persian Wars because of the story that he struck terror ("pan-ic") into the Persians that caused them to flee at Marathon.

parasang a Persian measure of distance equaling perhaps a little under four miles. Greeks sometimes counted a parasang as thirty stadia.

Parnassus sacred mountaian about eight thousand feet tall associated with Apollo and with the Muses.

Pausanias Spartan commander whose overbearing conduct in Byzantium following the end of the Persian Wars alienated the Ionian Greeks and led them to seek protection from Athens instead. The unpopularity of Pausanias led indirectly to the foundation of the Athenian empire.

Peisistratus see **Pisistratus.**

Peloponnesian War a devastating war between Athens and Sparta (and their respective allies) that broke out in 431 and continued, with some interruption, until Athens was defeated in 404.

Peloponnesus or **Peloponnese** large peninsula on the southwest of the Greek mainland, dominated politically in classical times by Sparta.

Periander tyrant of Corinth, succeeded his father, Cypselus.

Pericles the most prominent statesman of classical Athens. Pericles was elected repeatedly to Athens' board of ten generals and was the most influential man in Athens during the years preceding the Peloponnesian War. Pericles' friends included controversial philosophers such as Anaxagoras. The funeral oration for the war dead that Thucydides ascribed to Pericles is a dramatic portrayal of the open society and a defense of democracy against its oligarchic critics. Pericles was instrumental in the outbreak of the Peloponnesian War in 431 but died within two years. His death created a serious political vacuum in Athens.

Phalerum early harbor of Athens.

Pheidippides or **Philippides** the Athenian courier who was said to have covered 150 miles in two days in order to announce the Persian landing at Marathon to the Spartans. He is said to have seen a vision of Pan along the way. Several modern thinkers have wondered whether this vision may be connected with the "runner's high" some people claim to experience while running or jogging.

Pheretima wife of Battus III, king of Cyrene. Pheretima inflicted cruel punishment on those involved in the murder of her son. She later died of a loathsome disease in Egypt.

Pisistratus or **Peisistratus** three times tyrant of Athens from 560 to 527. Despite two expulsions, Pisistratus returned with determination to Athens and finally consolidated his hold on the city, which he then ruled until his death. His reign was generally regarded as a beneficial era for the Athenian economy; drama and the arts seem to have flourished, and during this period the citizens had day-to-day practice in the democratic machinery set up earlier by Solon. There was strain, however, between Pisistratus' family and that of the other powerful families such as the Alcmaeonidae and the Philaids, and some resented the very idea of tyranny. Pisistratus was succeeded by his sons, and the family tyranny was eventually overthrown with Spartan assistance in 510.

Plataea Greek town between Athens and Thebes, the site of the Greek victory over Mardonius and the Persians in 479.

polemarch military commander in early Athens. Of the nine judicial officials (archons), the polemarch (war archon) was originally head of the armed forces, but the position lost its importance to the ten generals after the archons began to be selected by lot in 487. The most famous Athenian polemarch was Callimachus, who was in command at the Battle of Marathon.

Polycrates ruler of the island state of Samos, ca. 540–522.

Poseidon powerful Greek god of sea and earthquakes, parallel to the Roman Neptune.

proxenos a citizen charged with maintaining good relations between his state and another state where he was highly regarded.

Psammetichus powerful Egyptian potentate who became sole ruler in 652, partial to Greeks and the first king of Egypt who opened the country up to strangers.

Rhampsinitus Egyptian pharaoh, possibly Ramses III (twelfth century), who was instrumental in fighting off the invaders of uncertain origin called the Sea Peoples.

Salamis island west of Attica, site of a decisive Greek naval victory in 480.

Samos powerful island city-state off western Asia Minor (Turkey).

Sardis capital of Lydia.

Satrap a Persian provincial governor, similar to a vassal king, owing allegiance to the king of Persia.

satrapy a Persian province.

Sesostris Egyptian pharaoh and conqueror, perhaps to be equated with Ramses II, who ruled for sixty-seven years during the thirteenth century.

Solon Athenian political, social, and economic reformer. In the 590s he was appointed sole legislator to overhaul the Athenian government and put an end to civil strife. He was considered a hero by the Athenians and became legendary throughout Greece for his wisdom. The story Herodotus tells of his encounter with Croesus is difficult to credit, for although Solon traveled extensively after his legislation, he was back in Athens long before his death around 558, and Croesus did not become king of Lydia until around 560.

stadion Greek measure of distance amounting to about six hundred feet. Parasangs are sometimes measured as thirty stadia.

Suidas reference work about classical antiquity compiled ca. A.D. 1000.

Susa winter residence of Persian kings.

talent a large Athenian measure of wealth, worth several thousand American dollars.

Thebes (1) powerful Greek city-state north of Athens. Thebes often dominated the surrounding area, Boeotia, but it lost this power in the Boeotian League for some years because of its support of the Persians during the invasion of Xerxes.

Thebes (2) capital of Upper Egypt, supplanting Memphis at the time of the twelfth dynasty (ca. 2000).

Themistocles audacious Athenian general and politician of humble origins generally credited with the naval buildup at Athens after the invasion of Darius and with the victory at Salamis in 480. He was subsequently exiled and, ironically, spent his last years at the Persian court.

Theopompus of Chios fourth-century Greek historian.

Thermopylae (the "Hot Gates") an important mountainous defense line in Greece, the site of the Persian victory in summer 480.

Thurii colony founded under Athenian auspices in 443. Herodotus is said to have been one of the colonists.

trireme Greek warship, roughly 20 feet by 120 feet.

tyrant a ruler who came (or whose family had come) to power outside the constitution, that is, not by election, appointment, or inheritance but by a coup d'état. The word (Greek *tyrannos*) at first meant simply a ruler who had come to power in this irregular way, and many early Greek tyrants (e.g., Pisistratus and Cypselus) were popular, even beloved, rulers, but in time many Greeks came to associate tyranny with autocratic and selfish government, and the word acquired the negative associations it has today. Greek tyrannies rarely lasted past the third generation or past the year 500, with the exception of western Greece, where tyranny remained the standard form of government in Sicily.

Xerxes son of Darius and Atossa, succeeded Darius as king of Persia in 485. He led the unsuccessful invasion of Greece that ended at the battles of Salamis and Plataea.

Zeus son of Cronus, head of the pantheon of Greek gods who lived on Mount Olympus, ruler of gods and mortals, parallel to the Roman Jupiter.

Bibliography

Texts of Herodotus

The text of Herodotus is available in several classical series that include all major Greek and Roman authors. Students of ancient civilization are well served by these collections. They include the Oxford Classical Texts and the Bibliotheca Teubneriana (in the original languages), the Loeb Classical Library (Greek or Latin text with facing English), and the Bibliothèque Guillaume Budé (Greek or Latin with facing French). The Loeb Classical Library will probably be most useful to American readers; its volumes are easily recognizable by their green (Greek) or red (Latin) covers. Herodotus appears in these valuable series as follows: [Oxford:] *Herodoti Historiae*, ed. Carolus Hude (Oxford, 1908); [Loeb:] *Herodotus*, ed. A. D. Godley, 4 vols. (London and New York, 1920–24); [Teubner:] *Herodotus, Historiarum libri ix*, ed. H. R. Dietsch and H. Kallenberg (Leipzig, 1894); and [Budé:] *Hérodote*, ed. Ph.-E. Legrand, 4 vols. (Paris, 1908). In addition, readers may want to refer to commentaries on Herodotus available in English, such as R. W. Macan, *Herodotus, the Fourth, Fifth and Sixth Books*, with introduction, notes, appendixes, indices, maps (London and New York, 1895); W. W. How and J. Wells, A *Commentary on Herodotus*, with introduction, appendixes, maps, index (Oxford, 1912, reprinted with corrections, 1928); and O. Kimball Armayor, A *Historical Commentary on Herodotus, Book VII* (Oak Park, Ill., 1988). Several English translations of the complete *Histories* are also available: *The History of Herodotus of Halicarnassus*, trans. George Rawlinson (originally 1889), revised and annotated by A. W. Lawrence, with engraved illustrations and maps and a life of Herodotus (London, 1935); *Herodotus, The Histories*, trans. Aubrey de Sélincourt (originally 1954), revised with introduction and notes by A. R. Burn (Harmondsworth, England, and Baltimore, 1972); and *Herodotus, The History*, trans. David Grene (Chicago, 1987).

Modern Scholarship

A great deal of the best scholarship on Herodotus is written in English, and we have cited works in English or in English translation wherever possible. Where reference works in foreign languages appeared to us to be particularly useful to students of Herodotus, we have included them also, but we have tried to keep citation of works not available in English to a minimum. Most of the books and journals cited here are to be found in college, university, and public libraries.

A number of the most helpful standard reference works in classical studies are not in English, such as C. Daremberg and E. Saglio, eds., *Dictionnaire des antiquités grecques et romaines* (Paris, 1877–1919; reprint, Graz, 1962–63); A. Pauly, G. Wissowa, and W. Kroll, eds., *Realencyclopädie der classischen Altertumswissenschaft* (Stuttgart, 1894–); and W. Schmidt and O. Staehlin, *Geschichte der griechischen Literatur* (Munich, 1934). Standard reference works in English include N. Hammond and H. Scullard, eds., *The Oxford Classical Dictionary* (Oxford, 1949; 2d ed., 1970), and D. Bowder, *Who Was Who in the Greek World* (Ithaca, 1982).

Standard histories of Greece during the periods Herodotus discusses (the archaic period and the fifth century) include the pertinent volumes of the *Cambridge Ancient History* (new edition, 1970–). There are also several standard one-volume works, such as V. Ehrenberg, *From Solon to Socrates: Greek History and Civilisation during the Sixth and Fifth Centuries B.C.* (London, 1968); J. B. Bury, A *History of Greece*, 3d. ed., rev. by Russell Meiggs (London and New York, 1967); G. W. Botsford and C. A. Robinson, A *Hellenic History*, 5th ed., rev. by D. Kagan (London, 1969); R. Sealey, A *History of the Greek City-States, 700–338 B.C.* (Berkeley, 1977); P. Green, *Ancient Greece: An Illustrated History* (London and New York, 1979); and J. V. A. Fine, *The Ancient Greeks: A Critical History* (Cambridge, Mass., and London, 1983).

In addition to the works excerpted in this volume, readers may want to consult general works on Herodotus, such as T. R. Glover, *Herodotus* (Berkeley, 1924); J. Myres, *Herodotus, Father of History* (Oxford, 1953); H. Immerwahr, *Form and Thought in Herodotus* (Cleveland, 1966); S. Benardete, *Herodotean Inquiries* (The Hague, 1969); J. A. S. Evans, *Herodotus* (Boston, 1982); S. Stambler, "Herodotus," in T. J. Luce, ed., *Ancient Writers: Greece and Rome*, vol. 1 (New York, 1982), 209–32; and S. Flory, *The Archaic Smile of Herodotus* (Detroit, 1987). The best multivolume, detailed history of Greece in English remains G. Grote, *History of Greece*, 12 vols. (London, 1846–56, and subsequent editions).

Several books deal with Herodotus, Persia, and the conflict of East and West, such as A. R. Burn, *Persia and the Greeks: The Defense of the West, 546–478 B.C.* (New York, 1962); P. Green, *Xerxes at Salamis* (New York, 1970); C. Hignett, *Xerxes' Invasion of Greece* (Oxford, 1963); R. Drews, *The Greek Accounts of Eastern History* (Washington, D.C., 1973); W. Donlan and J. Thompson, "The Charge at Marathon," *Classical Journal* 71 (1976): 339–43; and J. M. Cook, *The Persian Empire* (New York, 1983).

Herodotus' methods and sources are discussed in B. Baldwin, "How Credulous Was Herodotus?" *Greece and Rome* 11 (1964): 166–77; D. Fehling, *Herodotus and His Sources* (Liverpool, 1989); J. Cobet, *Herodots Exkurse und die Frage der Einheit seines Werkes*, Historia Einzelschriften, no. 17 (Wiesbaden, 1971), 1–22; J. W. Neville, "Herodotus on the Trojan War," *Greece and Rome* 24 (1977): 3–12; D. Konstan, "The Stories in Herodotus' Histories, Book 1," *Helios* 9 (1983): 3–12; and M. Lang, "Herodotus: Oral History with a Difference," *Proceedings of the American Philosophical Society* 128 (1984): 93–103. On Herodotus' debt to Homer, readers are referred to T. G. Rosenmeyer, "History or Poetry? The Example of Herodotus," *Clio* 11 (1982): 239–59. The influence of Greek tragic drama on Herodotus is discussed in F. Walbank, "History and Tragedy," *Historia* 9 (1960): 216–34, and C. Chiasson, "Tragic Diction in Herodotus: Some Possibilities," *Phoenix* 36 (1982): 156–61.

On Herodotus' place in Greek historiography, readers may consult M. Pohlenz, *Herodot, der erste Geschichtschreiber des Abendlandes* (Leipzig, 1937; reprint, Stuttgart, 1961); T. S. Brown, "Herodotus and His Profession," *American Historical Review* 59 (1954): 829–43; A. Cook, "Herodotus: The Act of Inquiry as a Liberation from Myth," *Helios* 3 (1976): 23–66; S. Flory, "Who Read Herodotus' *Histories?*" *American Journal of Philology* 101 (1980): 12–28; and M. Lang, *Herodotean Narrative and Discourse* (Cambridge, Mass., 1984).

Collections of essays on Herodotus appear in W. Marg, ed., *Herodot: Eine Auswahl aus der neueren Forschung*, 3d ed. (Darmstadt, 1982), and in D. Boedeker and J. Peradotto, eds., *Herodotus and the Invention of History*, published as vol. 20, nos. 1–2 (1987) of the journal *Arethusa*.

The theme of Herodotus and Greek politics is explored in K. Waters, *Herodotus on Tyrants and Despots: A Study in Objectivity* (Wiesbaden, 1971); A. Ferrill, "Herodotus on Tyranny," *Historia* 27 (1978): 385–98. The following recent studies of Themistocles may be of interest: R. J. Lenardon, *The Saga of Themistocles* (London, 1978); A. Podlecki, *The Life of Themistocles: A Critical Survey of the Literary and Archaeological Evidence* (Montreal and London, 1975); and F. J. Frost, *Plutarch's Themistocles* (Princeton, 1980).

On the subject of Herodotus and social history, readers are directed to S. Pembroke, "Women in Charge," *Journal of the Warburg and Courtauld Institute* 30 (1967): 1–35; D. S. Wiesen, "Herodotus and the Modern Debate over Race and Slavery," *Ancient World* 3 (1980): 3–16; and C. Dewald, "Women and Culture in Herodotus' *Histories*," in H. Foley, ed., *Reflections of Women in Antiquity* (New York, London, and Paris, 1981).

Further Bibliographies

Bibliographical essays of work on Herodotus appear in G. T. Griffith, "The Greek Historians," in M. Platnauer, ed., *Fifty Years (and Twelve) of Classical Scholarship* (Oxford, 1968), 182–241, and also in three successive essays by P. MacKendrick in the periodical *Classical World*: "Herodotus: The Making of a World Historian, *CW* 47 (1954): 145–52; "Herodotus, 1954–1963," *CW* 56 (1963): 269–75; and "Herodotus, 1963–1969," *CW* 63 (1969): 37–44. More recent work appears in the bibliography to K. Waters, *Herodotus the Historian: His Problems, Methods and Originality* (Norman, Okla., 1985), 177–89; and D. Boedeker and J. Peradotto, eds., *Herodotus and the Invention of History* (cited above), 263–83.